*Diagnosis and Psychopharmacology of
Childhood and Adolescent Disorders*

Diagnosis and Psychopharmacology of Childhood and Adolescent Disorders

Second Edition

Edited by
JERRY M. WIENER

JOHN WILEY & SONS, INC.

New York • Chichester • Brisbane • Toronto • Singapore

Tables in Chapter 6 were used with permission from the
Diagnostic and Statistical Manual of Mental Disorders.

This text is printed on acid-free paper.

Copyright © 1996 by John Wiley & Sons, Inc.

All rights reserved. Published simultaneously in Canada.

This publication is designed to provide accurate and authoritative
information in regard to the subject matter covered. It is sold
with the understanding that the publisher is not engaged in
rendering professional services. If legal, accounting, medical,
psychological, or any other expert assistance is required, the
services of a competent professional person should be sought.

Library of Congress Cataloging-in-Publication Data:

Diagnosis and psychopharmacology of childhood and adolescent disorders
   / edited by Jerry M. Wiener. — 2nd ed.
      p.   cm.
   Includes bibliographical references and index.
   ISBN 0-471-04262-5 (cloth : alk. paper)
   1. Pediatric psychopharmacology. 2. Child psychopathology.
  3. Adolescent psychopathology.   I. Wiener, Jerry M., 1933–
   (DNLM: 1. Mental Disorders—in infancy & childhood. 2. Mental
Disorders—in adolescence. 3. Psychopharmacology—in infancy &
childhood. 4. Psychopharmacology—in adolescence.   WS 350 D536
1996)
RJ504.7.D53   1996
618.92' 89—dc20
DNLM/DLC
for Library of Congress   95-24343

Printed in the United States of America

10 9 8 7 6 5 4 3 2 1

To Matthew, Ethan, Ross, and Aaron

Contributors

Jorge L. Armenteros, M.D., Research Fellow in Child Psychiatry, New York State Psychiatric Institute/College of Physicians and Surgeons, Columbia University, New York, New York

Claudia K. Berenson, M.D., Associate Professor of Psychiatry and Pediatrics, University of New Mexico Health Sciences Center, Albuquerque, New Mexico

Magda Campbell, M.D., Professor of Psychiatry, New York University Medical Center, New York, New York

F. Xavier Castellanos, M.D., Senior Staff Fellow, Child Psychiatry Branch, National Institute of Mental Health, Bethesda, Maryland

Donald J. Cohen, M.D., Irving B. Harris Professor of Child Psychiatry, Pediatrics and Psychology, Director, Yale Child Study Center, Yale University School of Medicine, New Haven, Connecticut

C. Keith Conners, Ph.D., Professor of Medical Psychology, Department of Psychiatry, Duke University Medical Center, Durham, North Carolina

Jeanette E. Cueva, M.D., Assistant Professor of Psychiatry, New York Medical College, Valhalla, New York, and Medical Director, Children's Psychiatric Inpatient Service, Department of Psychiatry, St. Vincent's Hospital and Medical Center, New York, New York

Drew Erhardt, Ph.D., Assistant Clinical Professor of Medical Psychology, Department of Psychiatry, Duke University Medical Center, Durham, North Carolina

Gustavo A. Goldstein, M.D., Senior Resident in Child Psychiatry, Children's Hospital National Medical Center, Washington, DC

Peter C. Gherardi, M.D., Assistant Attending in Psychiatry, McLean Hospital, Belmont, Massachusetts, and Instructor in Psychiatry, Boston University School of Medicine, Boston, Massachusetts

Alejandra Hallin, M.D., Resident in Psychiatry, New York University Medical Center, New York, New York

Robert L. Hendren, D.O., Professor of Psychiatry/Associate Professor of Pediatrics, Director, Division of Child and Adolescent Psychiatry, University of New Mexico, Health Sciences Center, Albuquerque, New Mexico

Steven L. Jaffe, M.D., Associate Clinical Professor, Department of Psychiatry, Emory University, Clinical Professor of Psychiatry, Morehouse School of Medicine, Atlanta, Georgia

Ledro R. Justice, M.D., Senior Resident in Psychiatry, Children's Hospital National Medical Center, Washington, DC

Javad H. Kashani, M.D., Professor of Psychiatry, Psychology and Pediatrics, University of Missouri-Columbia, and Director, Child and Adolescent Services, Mid-Missouri Mental Health Center, Columbia, Missouri

Markus J. P. Kruesi, M.D., Professor of Psychiatry, Director, Institute for Juvenile Research, and Chief, Child and Adolescent Psychiatry, University of Illinois-Chicago, Chicago, Illinois

David F. Lelio, M.D., Assistant Medical Director, Chicago Metro Child and Adolescent Services, Assistant Professor, Department of Psychiatry, University of Illinois-Chicago, Chicago, Illinois

Jyotsna Nair, M.D., Senior Child Psychiatry Fellow, Department of Psychiatry and Neurology, Division of Child and Adolescent Psychiatry, University of Missouri-Columbia, Columbia, Missouri

Charles W. Popper, M.D., Editor, Journal of Child and Adolescent Psychopharmacology, Harvard Medical School, Belmont, Massachusetts

Judith L. Rapoport, M.D., Chief, Child Psychiatry Branch, National Institute of Mental Health, Bethesda, Maryland, and Clinical Professor of Psychiatry, George Washington University School of Medicine, Washington, DC

David Shaffer, M.D., Irving Phillips Professor of Child Psychiatry, Professor of Pediatrics, Director, Division of Child and Adolescent Psychiatry, College of Physicians and Surgeons, Columbia University, New York, New York

Theodore Shapiro, M.D., Professor of Psychiatry and Professor of Psychiatry in Pediatrics, Cornell University Medical College, and Director of Child and Adolescent Psychiatry, Payne Whitney Clinic, New York Hospital, New York, New York

Kenneth E. Towbin, M.D., Director of Residency Training in Psychiatry, Children's National Medical Center, and Associate Professor of Psychiatry and Behavioral Sciences and Pediatrics, George Washington University School of Medicine, Washington, DC

Bruce D. Waslick, M.D., Research Fellow in Child Psychiatry, College of Physicians and Surgeons, Columbia University, New York, New York.

Jerry M. Wiener, M.D., Leon Yochelson Professor and Chairman, Department of Psychiatry and Behavioral Sciences, Professor of Pediatrics, George Washington University School of Medicine, Washington, DC, President, American Psychiatric Association (1994–1995)

Preface

This is formally the second edition of this book, but actually it is the third version; the precursor appeared first in 1977 when the field was very young and new, before the publication of DSM-III in 1980 revolutionized the diagnosis, epidemiology, and treatment of psychiatric disorders. The first edition of this book in 1985 added diagnostic criteria and epidemiology to the earlier version, incorporating DSM-III and III-R.

This edition follows shortly upon the publication of DSM-IV™ and reflects the changes in classification and criteria in childhood and adolescent disorders, most notably in the anxiety and eating disorders categories. These, and all the other reorganizations in classification, are detailed and discussed in Chapter 2. As before, methodological, assessment, and developmental considerations are updated and again comprehensively discussed by experts. Clinical usage is organized by diagnostic disorders—this is the way clinicians think about treatment—so that a discussion of antidepressant medication, for example, appears in several different chapters and clinical usage is discussed in the context of specific disorders or syndromes. Each clinical chapter is authored by a recognized authority and each chapter is similarly organized: diagnostic criteria and considerations, epidemiology, psychopharmacology (pro and con) and side effects, clinical usage, efficacy studies, and pertinent research issues. The state of the science and the art of the psychopharmacology of childhood disorders is embodied in the context of a biopsychosocial model.

I want to offer my appreciation to all the authors for their contributions to this book, to Herb Reich of John Wiley & Sons who has shepherded into print all three of its versions, and especially to Laurie Young in my office for her superb administrative and secretarial support.

JERRY M. WIENER, M.D.

Washington, DC

Contents

6. Schizophrenia and Other Psychotic Disorders   193

Magda Campbell, M.D.
Jorge L. Armenteros, M.D.

7.   Affective/Mood Disorders   229

Javad H. Kashani, M.D.
Jyotsna Nair, M.D.

8.   Attention-Deficit/Hyperactivity Disorder   265

Judith L. Rapoport, M.D.
F. Xavier Castellanos, M.D.

9. Anxiety Disorders

Charles W. Popper, M.D.
Peter C. Gherardi, M.D.

10. Tic Disorders   **349**

Kenneth E. Towbin, M.D.
Donald J. Cohen, M.D.

11. Obsessive Compulsive Disorder

Kenneth E. Towbin, M.D.

12. **Disorders of Conduct and Behavior**   **401**

Markus J. P. Kruesi, M.D.
David F. Lelio, M.D.

13.   Eating Disorders   **449**

Robert L. Hendren, D.O.
Claudia K. Berenson, M.D.

David Shaffer, M.D.
Bruce D. Waslick, M.D.

Basic Issues

Historical Overview of Childhood and Adolescent Psychopharmacology

JERRY M. WIENER, M.D., STEVEN L. JAFFE, M.D., GUSTAVO A. GOLDSTEIN, M.D., and LEDRO R. JUSTICE, M.D.

Parts of this chapter, reviewing the period up to 1970, have appeared previously in J. Wiener (Ed.), *Psychopharmacology in Childhood and Adolescence,* published in 1977 by Basic Books.

1970 TO 1980

The Stimulants

During the past several years, psychopharmacological research on the stimulants has further supported by better methodological studies the positive effects of dextroamphetamine and methylphenidate for treatment of the symptoms of Attention Deficit Disorder (ADD). *The Diagnostic and Statistical Manual of Mental Disorders* (DSM-III; American Psychiatric Association [APA], 1980) replaced the diagnosis of Hyperkinetic Reaction with Attention Deficit Disorder because the attention-span problems were felt to be central to the disorder, and hyperactivity may or may not be present.

Improved placebo-controlled studies on dextroamphetamine have been done. Huestis, Arnold, and Smeltzer (1975) in a placebo crossover study obtained significant improvement for the drug by teachers' and parents' ratings for hyperactivity and distractibility. Gordon, Forehand, and Picklesimer (1978) in a placebo-controlled crossover study found improved attention and increased task-related behavior for 15 hyperactive children when on dextroamphetamine.

In a similar manner, more sophisticated studies on methylphenidate (MPH) continue to demonstrate significant improvement for the symptoms of ADD with hyperactivity. Schain and Reynard (1975) reported a double-blind placebo-controlled study of 98 hyperactive children in which the code was broken if maximum dose did not produce improvement. MPH was markedly superior to placebo. Gittelman-Klein, Klein, Katz, Saraf, and Pollack (1976) demonstrated, with teacher ratings, significant superiority for MPH over placebo for conduct problems, inattentiveness, hyperactivity, and sociability in the classroom. Numerous studies (Firestone, Davey, Goodman, & Peters, 1978; Conners & Taylor, 1980) showed significant drug effect, and Barkley's review (1977) of over 110 studies demonstrated an improvement rate of approximately 75%.

Since Conners' (1972) study on magnesium pemoline, which demonstrated positive effects for ADD symptoms only after 6 weeks, a few further studies have been done. A study by Page, Janicki, Bernstein, Curran, and Michelli (1974) demonstrated a significant drug effect beginning at 3 weeks, whereas the study by Conners and Taylor (1980) showed a weak but significant effect after 8 weeks.

Along with the studies demonstrating significant effect of the stimulants on the symptoms of ADD with hyperactivity, many laboratory studies with hyperactive children have demonstrated that stimulants positively affect laboratory measures of learning. Cohen, Douglas, Weiss, and Minde (1971) showed that MPH produces faster and more consistent reaction time in hyperactive children. MPH improves sustained attention on the Continuous Performance Test (Sykes, Doyles, Weiss, & Minde, 1971) and

4

lowers error scores on the matching Familiar Figures test measuring impulsivity (Brown & Sleator, 1979). Swanson, Kinsbourne, Roberts, and Zucker (1978) demonstrated that 70% of hyperactive children show significant improvement with MPH on a paired association test.

Because of the demonstration that stimulants improve behavior and the cognitive processes of attention and short-term memory for ADD children, it was expected that stimulants would enhance academic achievement. Barkley and Cunningham (1978) reviewed 120 studies and concluded that there was little support for the view that stimulants improve academic performance. This became a major conceptual and therapeutic issue in the 1980s, with the interpretation by some that the ADD child is not "really" helped by medication but only "slowed down." Aman's review (1980) of seven different follow-up studies similarly indicates no long-term educational gains resulting from stimulant medication treatment. There have been a number of possible explanations for this discrepancy. Some relate to research methodological problems such as lack of clearly defined diagnostic criteria for group studied or lack of a good control group (Swanson et al., 1978). Of most importance is the issue of the effect on specific learning disabilities in the "hyperactive" population studies. Lerer, Lerer, and Artner (1977) demonstrated that MPH improved handwriting.

During the 1970s, the side effects of the stimulants have been further studied and a clear contraindication for use of stimulants has been described. Although studies in the early 1970s raised the issue of growth inhibition (Safer, Allen, & Barr, 1972), other studies did not substantiate this finding (Gross, 1976).

A number of studies related stimulant dosage level to clinical effects. Halliday, Gnanck, Rosenthal, McKibben, and Callaway (1980) studied 15 hyperactive children at three dosage levels. Teacher ratings showed that the group did better at the higher dosage administered, but a few had better results at the lower level. Sprague and Sleator (1977) compared placebo with MPH at dosage of 0.3 mg/kg and 1.0 mg/kg. The effect on a visual memory task was optimal at the lower dosage, but the clinical effect using teacher ratings was best for the higher dosage. Swanson et al. (1978) used a paired association learning task to show that higher than optimal dosage may yield decreased task performance.

There is one study on the effects of stimulants on normal children. Rapoport et al. (1978) in a double-blind placebo-controlled study of normal prepubertal boys demonstrated that amphetamine had similar effects on normal children as on ADD children. Motor activity and reaction time were decreased, and performance on cognitive tests was increased. Although this study is at variance with the view that stimulants have a "paradoxical effect" on ADD children, Rapoport states that "lack of specificity of a treatment is no argument against its use."

A few studies comparing stimulant treatment with other treatment modalities for ADD-hyperactive children have been done, but further research in this area is sorely needed to further define what treatment methods are best for which children. Gittelman-Klein et al. (1980) compared methylphenidate alone, placebo plus behavior modification, and methylphenidate plus behavior modification for an 8-week treatment period. Results demonstrated significant improvement on parent and teacher ratings for all three, but MPH plus behavior modification was the most effective. MPH alone was next and was better than behavior modification. Firestone, Kelly, Goodman, and Davey (1980) compared parent training in behavior modification plus placebo, MPH alone, and MPH and parent training over a 3-month period. All groups showed improved home and school behavior, but only with MPH were there gains in measures of attention and impulse control. There was no evidence of significant benefit from the addition of parent training to the administration of MPH. These studies are only preliminary in an area that needs much more extensive research.

After a backlash against medication use in children in the late 1960s, a more considered approach was adopted in the late 1970s. With diminished popularity of the Feingold diet as well as the increased recognition of severe side effects with major tranquilizers (tardive dyskinesia), the use and acceptance of stimulants increased through the 1980s. Future directions included studies on more defined diagnostic groupings, neurochemical studies (Hunt, Cohen, Shaywitz, & Shaywitz, 1982), combinations with and comparisons to other treatment modalities.

The Antipsychotics

Studies during this period of the indications for use and comparative efficacy of antipsychotics reflect the period before and after the introduction of DSM-III (APA, 1980). Studies before DSM-III are difficult to evaluate and compare because of diagnostic variability and heterogeneity both within and among the study populations. After DSM-III, the diagnostic criteria used to define study groups became more standardized into the categories of schizophrenic disorders, autism, and childhood-onset pervasive developmental disorders.

Campbell, Fish, Shapiro, and Floyd (1970) compared thiothixene (Navane) to the results obtained in a previous study with trifluperiodol (Fish, Campbell, Shapiro, & Floyd, 1969). In a well-matched population of 10 preschool autistic-schizophrenic children, the two drugs were not significantly different in effectiveness, but thiothixene had a much greater margin of safety with no side effects observed at therapeutic levels.

Waizer, Polizos, Hoffman, Engelhardt, and Margolis (1972) supported this positive impression of thiothixene efficacy on an outpatient population of 18 school-age children diagnosed by the Creak criteria as childhood schizophrenics. This group of children was considered highly homogeneous for severe to moderate illness. Ratings were by a single blind observer, with a preceding period of placebo. They reported thiothixene to be highly effective and very safe at a mean daily dose of 17 mg/day. Significant improvement over placebo occurred in motor activity, stereotyped behavior, coordination, and affect, with little improvement in language function in short-term administration.

In a study measuring both clinical change and neurophysiological correlates, Saletu, Simeon, Saletu, Itil, and DaSilva (1974) compared thiothixene with placebo in hospitalized boys aged 5 to 15 (mean age 10), diagnosed as psychotic with long-standing illness and severe functional impairment. Compared with placebo, thiothixene produced a significant and persistent improvement, beginning in the second week, in areas of motor activity, speech, social relationships, affect, and behavior disturbance. In addition, the drug treatment period was correlated with a trend toward normalization of the visual evoked potential recorded by the EEG, compared with normal controls.

Three further studies of haloperidol compared its effects with those of thioridazine (Claghorn, 1972) and with fluphenazine (Faretra, Dooher, & Dowling, 1970; Engelhardt, Polizos, Waizer, & Hoffman, 1973). Methodological problems make the results reported by Claghorn difficult to evaluate. The other two studies found haloperidol and fluphenazine to be significantly and about equally effective in producing improvement in the target symptoms of children diagnosed as schizophrenic. Haloperidol tended to be quicker acting and effective at a mean daily dose of 10.4 mg/day (Engelhardt et al., 1973).

By way of some contrast to the preceding results comparing a butyrophenone with a piperazine phenothiazine, Campbell, Fish, Shapiro, and Floyd (1972) reported a comparison study of trifluperiodol ("prototype of a stimulating neuroleptic") with chlorpromazine (a sedating aliphatic phenothiazine), and placebo. Following the methodology previously established by this research group, 15 preschool severely disturbed children were studied. Trifluperiodol was consistently statistically significantly better then chlorpromazine or placebo in producing improvement in functioning and target symptoms. They found consistent sedative effect and worsening of hyperactivity with chlorpromazine.

Infantile Autism. Campbell (1975) has provided a comprehensive review and commentary on pharmacotherapy in "early infantile autism" up to that time.

Campbell, Anderson, et al. (1978) reported that haloperidol in doses of 0.5 to 4.0 mg/day was significantly superior to placebo in improving withdrawal and stereotypy in young (2.6–7.2 years) autistic children (but not in those below 4 years of age), and that the combination of haloperidol with behavior therapy was more effective than either alone in facilitating the acquisition of imitative speech. The beneficial effects of haloperidol on stereotypy and attention in autistic children was replicated by this same group of workers (Cohen, Campbell, et al., 1980).

The question of antipsychotic medication dosage, plasma level, and response relationships in children was as yet little studied. One report on haloperidol found a 15-fold variability between dose and plasma level, with younger patients having lower plasma levels than older patients at equivalent doses, and a plasma level to response relationship in Tourette's syndrome but not in psychosis (Morselli et al., 1979).

Pervasive Developmental Disorders, Schizophrenic and Conduct Disorders, and Tourette's Syndrome.   Pervasive development disorders are defined in DSM-III as onset after 30 months, but are different from schizophrenia in the absence of hallucinations, delusions, and overt thought disorder. There was remarkably little in the literature that specifically defines this disorder as a subject for drug studies.

The same can be said for children with the diagnosis of schizophrenic disorder made by DSM-III criteria, which are the same for children as for adults. Although many children with this diagnosis probably are included in earlier studies of childhood "psychosis," most of these are older children with earlier onset autism. The presumption of DSM-III is that schizophrenic disorder as seen in adults may and does begin in childhood, and such children should respond similarly to antipsychotic medication. No study was reported of medication efficacy in carefully diagnosed prepubertal onset schizophrenic disorder.

Conduct disorders (aggressive/nonaggressive and socialized/unsocialized subtypes) represent another DSM-III category extensively treated with antipsychotics, based on many reports of their antiaggressive properties (for a review, see Campbell, Cohen, & Small, 1982).

The other major use of haloperidol has been in the treatment of Gilles de la Tourette's syndrome. The first report of such use was by Seignot (1961). Shapiro, Shapiro, and Wayne (1973) cited an additional 10 studies between 1962 and 1970 reporting haloperidol as the most effective treatment for the syndrome. These authors summarized their experience with haloperidol in the treatment of 34 cases of Tourette's syndrome with a mean age of onset of 7 plus years. They reported strikingly successful results in 21 of 34 cases on whom there was adequate follow-up. These patients required a median daily dose of 4 mg, with a daily maintenance dose ranging from 1.5 to 44 mg.

Side Effects.   The study and better understanding of the adverse effect of antipsychotic medication usage in children is a feature primarily of the last five or six years of this decade (1970–1980).

Engelhardt and Polizos (1978) reported that symptoms involving the skin (rash and photosensitivity), bone marrow depression, liver function, and the autonomic system are either rare and/or clinically insignificant. However, many authors observed weight gain and sedation as common and potentially serious (Engelhardt & Polizos, 1978). Most attention focused on the extrapyramidal adverse effects: dystonic, Parkinsonlike, akathesic, and dyskinetic reactions.

McAndrew, Case, and Treffert (1972) and Polizos, Engelhardt, Hoffman, and Waizer (1973) reported dyskinetic and akathesic symptoms in children after withdrawal from relatively long-term administration of chlorpromazine and haloperidol, respectively. This syndrome was described as reversible, usually spontaneously remitting, and was termed the "withdrawal emergent syndrome" (WES) by Engelhardt and Polizos (1978). The relationship of this syndrome to tardive dyskinesia in children remained unsettled.

Antidepressant Medication

Important research during this period reported on indications and efficacy of the tricyclic antidepressants (TCAs) in separation anxiety disorders (school phobia), affective disorders, anorexia nervosa, hyperactivity, and enuresis. From the mid-1970s onward, studies on the diagnosis and treatment of depression in childhood were the dominant theme around which research was organized.

Separation Anxiety Disorders. Gittelman-Klein and Klein (1970) reported on the efficacy of imipramine at doses of 100 to 200 mg/day in the treatment of children with the school phobia syndrome, considered an expression of separation anxiety. In this controlled study, children treated with imipramine and psychotherapy returned to school significantly sooner than children treated with psychotherapy and placebo.

Hyperactivity. Attention Deficit Disorder with Hyperactivity (ADDH) and without hyperactivity (ADD) are defined as diagnostic categories in DSM-III (1980), replacing the diagnosis of minimal brain dysfunction/disorder and the hyperactive child syndrome. Earlier studies used hyperactivity per se as the major identifying and target symptom for medication efficacy.

Rapoport, Quinn, Bradbard, Riddle, and Brooks (1974) studied imipramine in doses up to 80 mg/day in 76 outpatient hyperactive, middle-class grade-school boys. Comparing imipramine with methylphenidate in a double-blind placebo-controlled study, both drugs were superior to placebo, but all ratings favored methylphenidate, with a higher incidence of imipramine discontinuance on follow-up (Quinn &

Rapoport, 1975). Both drugs were associated with a decreased rate of weight gain, but with no effect on height. Winsberg, Beater, Kupietz, and Tobias (1972) also compared imipramine (150 mg/day × 1 week), and dextroamphetamine (15–30 mg/day × 1 week) in a double-blind placebo-controlled study of 32 children with hyperactivity and aggressiveness (the latter not necessarily a symptom of ADDH). Both drugs decreased target symptoms, but only imipramine affected attention span. Comparing imipramine in doses of 100 to 200 mg/day with placebo, Waizer, Hoffman, Polizos, and Engelhardt (1974) report significant advantage for imipramine in reducing hyperactivity and defiance, and increasing attention span and sociability. Additional studies (Greenberg, Yellin, Spring, & Metcalf, 1975; Yepes, Balka, Winsberg, & Bialer, 1977) support the efficacy of imipramine in treating hyperactivity, but see it overall as less useful and with more side effects than the stimulants.

Anorexia Nervosa. Initial open trials and single case studies reported successful treatment with tricyclic antidepressants (Mills, 1976; Needleman & Waber, 1977; White & Schnaulty, 1977).

Enuresis. Clinical efficacy for tricyclics in treating enuresis is well established (see Chapter 14). The major clarifying studies regarding phenomenology, relationship to sleep architecture, associated psychopathology, response to tricyclics, and correlation of response to plasma level appeared in two reports from Rapoport and her colleagues at the NIMH (Mikkelson et al., 1980; Rapoport et al., 1980). They reported on 40 severely enuretic boys treated with imipramine (75 mg/day), desipramine (75 mg/day), methscopolamine bromide, and placebo in a carefully controlled double-blind study. Both tricyclics were equally effective and significantly superior to placebo and methscopolamine. Neither enuresis itself or treatment response is related to sleep stage, nor is response related to associated psychopathology or to peripheral anticholinergic or psychotropic effect. There is a weak but significant correlation with plasma level. Both true nonresponders and patients who develop tolerance are identified.

Depression. Since the 1972 publication and application to children of the Research Diagnostic Criteria (RDC), a large number of studies (see this review and Chapter 7) report on the reliability and validity of adult criteria for the diagnosis of depressive disorder and assessment instruments for use in childhood, on the psychobiological correlates and biological continuity of childhood depressive disorder with the adult condition, and on the efficacy of antidepressant medication. Since its 1980 publication, DSM-III criteria are generally accepted for the diagnosis of affective disorders in childhood as well as in adults, although many research studies continue to use the somewhat more stringent RDC criteria.

Weinberg, Rutman, and Sullivan (1973), and many others since then, accepted and applied the reliability and validity of the RDC and the later DSM-III criteria, eliminating from common use the previously held concepts of "masked depression" and "depressive equivalents" (Cytryn, McKnew, & Bunney, 1980; Puig-Antich, Blau, Marx, Greenhill, & Chambers, 1978; Gittelman-Klein, 1977; Carlson & Cantwell, 1979, 1980). Several authors suggest specific features related to age and developmental level (Malmquist, 1971; Poznanski, Carroll, & Banegas, et al., 1982), with Poznanski, for example, describing a different sleep pattern in children and less diurnal variation in mood.

Clinical efficacy for tricyclic antidepressants is reported in a number of open or otherwise methodologically limited clinical trials (Kuhn & Kuhn, 1972; Weinberg et al., 1973; Puig-Antich et al., 1978; Frommer, 1972), generally finding improvement in over 50% of subjects.

Two double-blind placebo-controlled studies reported the superiority of imipramine to placebo in treating hospitalized prepubertal children with a DSM-III or RDC diagnosis of major depressive disorder (Petti & Law, 1982; Puig-Antich et al., 1979). In the Puig-Antich study, imipramine in doses up to 5 mg/kg/day strongly supports efficacy for imipramine over placebo when the total TCA plasma level is in the range of 200 ng/ml, with a positive response in many children at or above 150 ng/ml.

In the Petti and Law study, seven children were randomly administered either placebo or imipramine in doses of 5 mg/kg/day, with significant advantage for improvement in the imipramine treated children. The authors acknowledged the limitations in generalization imposed by the small sample size and some imperfections in the degree of matching between the two groups.

Reported side effects include:

1. Anorexia and weight loss; insomnia; an increase in heart rate and in systolic and diastolic blood pressure; stomachaches and tearfulness (Rapoport et al., 1974; Greenberg et al., 1975).

2. Anticholinergic effects of dry mouth, constipation, and blurring of vision.

3. Precipitation of seizures (Brown, Winsberg, Bialer, & Press, 1973; Petti & Campbell, 1975).

4. Cardiotoxic effect at doses approaching 5 mg/kg/day are reported by Winsberg, Goldstein, Yepes, and Perel (1975), with EKG changes including three with a first-degree atrioventricular block. The Federal Drug Administration now recommends EKG monitoring of children on doses of imipramine approaching

5 mg/kg/day. One sudden cardiaclike death is reported in a 6-year-old girl receiving imipramine at a dosage of 200 mg/day (14.7 mg/kg/day)(Saraf, Klein, Gittelman-Klein, & Groff, 1974).

5. Withdrawal symptoms include abdominal pain, nausea, vomiting, drowsiness, decreased appetite, tearfulness, and agitation. Gradual tapering may require several weeks (Petti & Law, 1982).

Lithium

Large-scale studies in the United States demonstrating the efficacy of lithium treatment in adults with affective disorders began in the late 1960s. Case studies of children and adolescents with possible bipolar disorder treated with lithium were reported throughout the 1970s. Van Krevelen and Van Voorst in 1959 (Campbell, Fish, Korein, et al., 1972, p. 235) reported on a retarded adolescent boy with alternating depression and hypomanic states who responded to lithium. Annell (1969) reported on 15 patients ages 10 to 18 with serious emotional disorders of an episodic nature who responded favorably to lithium. Kelly, Koch, and Buegel (1976) and Horowitz (1977) reported adolescents with bipolar illness who responded to lithium. Youngerman and Canino (1978) reviewed the literature and analyzed 46 cases, of which approximately two-thirds responded to lithium treatment. A positive family history for affective disorder and a strong affective component as part of presenting symptoms appeared to be related to a positive lithium response.

Carlson and Strober (1979) described nine adolescents with manic-depressive disorder where the diagnosis was previously missed because of the following: insufficient inquiry into signs and symptoms, irritability and manic lability being interpreted as adolescent turmoil, and depressive or grandiose delusions being interpreted as schizophrenia. Six of the nine responded well to treatment programs that included lithium.

Although bipolar illness in prepubertal children appears to be quite rare, there are some clinical reports of positive responses to lithium. Brumback and Weinberg (1977) described five such children where adult therapeutic plasma levels yielded positive results.

Studies of lithium treatment for severely hyperactive children were negative (Greenhill, Rieder, Wender, Bucksbaum, & Zahn, 1973). Studies on psychotic children yielded weak or negative results. Gram and Rafaelsen (1972) described a significant decrease in disturbed activity, mood and aggressiveness, whereas Campbell, Fish, Korein, et al., (1972) in a study of severely disturbed preschool children, did not obtain significant improvement.

During the latter part of the 1970s, lithium's effectiveness in reducing aggressiveness was studied in various types of patients and in scientifically controlled studies. Clinical reports on mentally retarded aggressive and/or self-mutilating children and adolescents related a positive response to lithium (Goetzl & Berkowitz, 1977; Dostal & Zvolsky, 1970). Sheard, Marini, and Bindger (1976) in a double-blind placebo-controlled study of chronically aggressive, antisocial teenagers in a correctional facility demonstrated that lithium treatment reduced the number of reported aggressive incidents and decreased self-reported aggressive affect.

1980 TO THE PRESENT

The 1970s were marked by an accelerated search for efficacy and comparative effects. The 1980s became the decade for reflection and reevaluation.

In the society at large, groups with conflicting opinions, such as the Scientologists, generated a revival of the opposition to drug treatment, equating it with memories of the ill-termed "better living through chemistry" philosophy of the 1960s. The strident high-profile opposition campaign acted as catalyst for the reaction of the scientific community. Data emerging from ongoing studies and the advent of DSM-III (1980) and DSM-III-R (1987) allowed a frame of reference in which comparative studies were possible and meta-analysis feasible. One focus of investigation became medication's safety. Researchers increased their attempts to assess the short- and long-term risks of the pharmacological interventions and to review the reliability of the treatments developed over the past 25 years (Werry, 1993).

STIMULANTS

In the 1980s and partway through the 1990s, there has been an explosive increase in both scientific studies and general use of stimulant medication in the treatment of children and adolescents, as major advances occur in neurochemistry, neurophysiology, and brain-imaging techniques. Improved standardized diagnostic evaluations and rating instruments combined with increased financial research support have enabled a sharp increase in the performance of more sophisticated controlled stimulant psychopharmacological studies. These scientific advances have been mirrored by the increasing acceptance, especially by the general public, that ADHD is a specific disorder and that medication has a special role in its treatment.

Efficacy Studies

A number of studies continue to demonstrate efficacy under various circumstances. Gittelman (1980a) points out that studies with more restrictive diagnostic selection criteria yield more significant drug effects. Other factors affecting results are therapeutic dosage range and timing of observations within the period of drug efficacy, rather than more than 4 to 6 hours after dosage.

A number of studies in the 1970s found little support for stimulant effects directly on learning and academic performance. Gadow (1981, 1983) proposed that the samples studied included hyperactive children who were nondrug responders or who were under- or overmedicated. Other studies on learning-disabled (LD) and reading-disordered children who do not have behavior problems (LD but no ADD) show no positive effects from treatment with stimulants (Aman & Werry, 1982; Gittelman, 1980b).

Since a significant number of ADD children also appear to have specific learning disabilities (Silver, 1981), stimulant treatment alone will treat only the attention span-behavior impulsivity symptoms and not the learning disability. The learning disability needs to be remediated by special education. This aspect may account for the poor results on academic achievement and also the relatively poor results of most long-term follow-up studies. In contrast to these poor outcome studies, a follow-up study of up to 3 years indicated that multimodality treatment led to improvement in a number of areas including decreased antisocial behavior, improved academic performance, and improved adjustment at home and at school (Satterfield, Satterfield, & Cantwell, 1981). In this study of ADD-hyperactive children, stimulant medication plus other therapies (e.g., education therapy, family therapy, parent training, individual or group therapy) were administered according to the child's needs.

In contradistinction to the findings of dosage level relating to clinical effects, studies on plasma levels have not yielded a relationship to clinical effects. Brown, Ebert, Mikkelsen, and Hunt (1980) were not able to correlate a specific plasma level of amphetamine to clinical response, and Gualtieri et al. (1982) found a wide range of both inter- and intraindividual variations in serum levels on different days. Also MPH serum levels did not differentiate responders from nonresponders.

Whereas previous studies on activity levels of hyperactive children have yielded mixed results, Porrino et al. (1983) studied this issue using a solid-state activity monitor worn on a belt. This study of twelve matched 6 to 12-year-olds in their natural environments, demonstrated that hyperactive children show consistently and substantially higher levels of motor movement in many diverse settings including sleep. Administration of dextroamphetamine decreased the activity level down to, but not below, the activity level of the normal boys. Motor activity was most strikingly decreased during structured classroom activity. As the drug effects diminished, a distinct behavioral rebound occurred.

The issue of state dependent learning continues to be studied. A recent study suggested that although stimulants enhanced the acquisition of information and its retrieval 24 hours later, there was no evidence of poorer retrieval of information learned in a state different from the retrieval state (Weingartner, Langer, Gria, & Rapoport, 1982).

Multimodal treatment involving psychotherapies, psychosocial interventions, and psychopharmacological treatment now is the standard treatment for attention deficit hyperactivity disorder (American Academy of Child and Adolescent Psychiatry, 1991). Prevalence rates in some studies (Szatmari, 1992), indicate that ADHD is one of the most common disorders of childhood. Well over a half-million children were treated with stimulants for this disorder in 1988 (Safer & Kroger, 1988). Schedule II drugs are manufactured in limited amounts each year. Toward the end of 1993, the supply of methylphenidate (Ritalin) was depleted, and many ADHD children and adolescents were switched to amphetamines or pemoline or received nonscheduled trials off medication. A similar phenomenon occurred in mid-1994, related to the limited supply of Dexedrine spansules. Increased acceptance in the general population of the diagnosis of ADHD and the use of stimulant medication has been enhanced by the activities of CHADD (Children and Adults with Attention Deficit Disorders), a national advocacy and support association. CHADD's national, state, and local community meetings in almost every state in the United States have fostered improved awareness and services.

Another major movement of the 1990s, which may be the most significant in publicizing ADHD and medication treatment, is the recognition of ADHD in adults. The criteria for adult ADHD were described by Wender in 1987. During the first half of the 1990s, awareness of adult ADHD increased to the point of making the cover of *Time* magazine on July 18, 1994. The first page of this article stated: "Disorganized? Distracted? Discombobulated? Doctors say you may have Attention Deficit Disorder. It's not just kids who suffer from it" (p. 43). This balanced article (Wallis, 1994) presented the positive effects of stimulants along with side effects and possible overprescription. Positive results of medication treatment of adult ADHD have substantiated the role of pharmacological treatment of ADHD in children and adolescents.

Since the mid-1980s, scientific articles have studied various facets of stimulant metabolism, efficacy, and side effects. The following paragraphs summarize the major recent representative studies.

Dulcan (1990) describes psychostimulants as the most studied and most used medications in child psychiatry. She describes ADHD in children, adolescents, or adults to be the established indication for psychostimulant treatment. ADHD in preschool children, children with fragile X syndrome and children and adolescents with mental retardation are listed as probable indications.

Clinically effective dosage varies with each individual, and therapeutic effects appear to relate to the rate of increase of blood level and not the final plasma level (Perel, Greenhill, Curran, et al., 1990). Numerous treatment studies demonstrate that approximately 75% of ADHD children show significant improvement (compared with 2%–39% placebo response) in short-term studies of up to a few months (Greenhill, 1992). Cognitive processing including sustained attention, distractibility, impulsivity, and short-term memory are improved. An early report of a dose-related dissociation between cognitive and behavioral effects has not been confirmed by further studies (Pelham, 1986). Excessive motor activity is decreased. Efficiency and productivity in academics is improved but not reading retardation (Pelham, 1986). ADHD children who respond to medication had more positive and less critical interactions with their mothers (Schachar et al., 1987). Friction with siblings is also decreased, but changes in peer interactions appear to be less strongly affected (Whalen et al., 1989).

Whereas short-term stimulant studies with ADHD children show positive effects on behavior and the cognitive processes of attention and short-term memory, long-term stimulant treatment studies have not demonstrated lasting improvement in academic performance or delinquent behavior (Jacobvitz, Scrouge, Stewart, & Leffert, 1990). Explanations for this include the methodological problems of no measure of drug compliance, high attrition rates, lack of random assignment and inclusion of medication nonresponsers. Other possible explanations include diagnostic heterogeneity of children studied and the possibility of the development of tolerance (Jacobvitz et al., 1990).

Greenhill (1992) summarized 16 stimulant treatment studies published in the previous 4 years and found that tolerance did not develop in longer controlled treatment studies. Dulcan (1990) indicates that the long-term studies included comorbid conduct disorders and that continuing medication effects should not be expected after the medication is stopped. In addition, the presence of specific learning disabilities, which require educational remediation and are not improved by stimulant medication, will affect long-term results if the only treatment modality used is medication. In contrast to these poor outcome medication-alone studies, Satterfield's (Satterfield et al., 1981; Satterfield, Satterfield, & Schell, 1987) multimodal studies, which used stimulant medications plus other psychological/educational therapies according to the child's needs, demonstrated significantly decreased delinquency and improved adjustment. Other studies of combined therapy have been reported. Cognitive behavioral training with medication was not more effective than medication alone (Horn, Islongo, Pascoe, et al., 1991). Behavior modification may enhance the positive stimulant effects (Dulcan, 1990). More studies are needed to further define and specify what treatments in combination are helpful for which children. A major advance in diagnostic specificity during the past few years has been the recognition of comorbid disorders. ADHD is frequently comorbid with conduct disorders, depressive disorders, and anxiety disorders. Pliazka (1989), in a double-blind trial of methylphenidate, found a significantly poorer stimulant response if overanxious disorder was comorbid, whereas comorbid conduct disorder did not affect the response. This indicates the importance of defining comorbid conditions that may affect treatment response and long-term outcome.

Side Effects

The issue of growth inhibition has been further studied during the past several years. A study by Mattes and Gittelman-Klein (1983), using revised growth charts, demonstrated a significant decrease in weight and height percentile. After controlling for age and pretreatment height and weight, MPH dosage accounted for only 2% of the variance in final height, indicating the magnitude of the drug effect is small. Although growth velocity may be slowed during stimulant treatment, a growth rebound effect occurs when medication is stopped (Gittelman-Klein, Landa, Mattes, & Klein, 1988). In addition, adult height of treated children did not differ from a control group (Gittelman-Klein & Mannuzza, 1988). These studies indicate minimal growth suppression effect during stimulant treatment in childhood, but studies where stimulant medication is continued for several years through adolescence have not been done.

It has been believed that the presence of motor tics or Tourette's syndrome is a contraindication to stimulant treatment, but some recent studies have questioned whether this is absolute. Whereas Lowe, Cohen, Detlor, Kremenitzer, and Shaywitz (1982) showed that stimulants can induce or precipitate Tourette's syndrome, Gadow, Sverd, and Nolan (1992) present evidence that in some children (20%) with Tourette's syndrome and ADHD, stimulant medication may decrease the tics. Relatively few children were studied, however, and larger studies would need to be done to establish the safety of this use.

Although dextroamphetamine and methylphenidate may be abused during adolescence, there are only two case reports in the literature (Jaffe, 1991) where teenagers have become addicted to their prescribed methylphenidate. Long-term follow-up studies indicate that prescribing stimulants in childhood does not increase the risk of drug abuse in adolescence (Hechtman & Weiss, 1986).

There are currently no reports in the literature of death in children or adolescents receiving therapeutic doses of methylphenidate or dextroamphetamine, indicating a relatively high degree of safety.

The 1990s are being marked by major changes in the delivery of psychiatric care. Managed care, with an emphasis on short-term inexpensive treatment procedures, is increasingly affecting psychiatric treatment delivery. We would predict that with these changes in treatment availability, the efficacy and relative safety of stimulant medication will continue to make them the most prescribed medications in child and adolescent psychiatry and one of the most used treatment modalities.

Early in the 1980s, the first substantive contraindication for the use of stimulants was described when Lowe et al. (1982) presented evidence that stimulant medication might precipitate onset of Tourette's syndrome. Because of this possibility, they recommended that the appearance of motor tics in a child receiving stimulant medication would be a clear indication for discontinuation of stimulant medication. Similarly stimulants would be contraindicated or used with caution in a child with a history of motor tics, a diagnosis of Tourette's syndrome, and/or a family history of tics or Tourette's syndrome.

ANTIDEPRESSANTS

Major Depressive Disorder

The 1980s into the 1990s are highlighted by the development, extensive marketing and widespread use of a new class of antidepressants—the selective serotonin reuptake inhibitors (SSRIs). Further, scientifically sophisticated studies have been done on the use of tricyclic antidepressants in children and adolescents. This time period also has been marked by major safety concerns, as a number of sudden deaths of children who were taking desipramine (Norpramin) were reported.

Studies on the biological correlates of childhood depression are early in development but support the validity of the diagnosis and its continuity with the adult disorder. Reports in prepubertal depressed children include cortisol hypersecretion in two of four children (Puig-Antich et al., 1981), a reduction in urinary MHPG excretion (McKnew & Cytryn, 1979), a decreased response of growth hormone using the insulin tolerance test (Puig-Antich et al., 1981), and a response similar to that in adults to the dexamethasone suppression test (Poznanski et al., 1982).

Improved assessment and rating instruments and more reliable and valid criteria for the diagnosis of depression have led to more rigorous studies of the efficacy of tricyclics in children and adolescents. Open clinical trials of depressed adolescent outpatients (Ryan et al., 1986) and depressed adolescent inpatients (Strober, Freeman, & Rigali, 1990) treated with imipramine yielded improvement in 44% and 38%. However, placebo-controlled double-blind studies (Geller, Coopec, Graham, Marsteller, & Bryant, 1990; Kutcher, et al., 1994) have not demonstrated that tricyclic medication is superior to placebo for the treatment of major depressive disorder in adolescents. These negative findings may relate to methodological issues such as variable washout periods, a high spontaneous and placebo response rate, and insufficient duration of medication treatment (Ambrosini, Bianchi, Rabinovich, & Elia, 1993a). As other possible factors, Kutcher et al. (1994) suggest developmental factors such as hormonal levels, or that adolescent depressives may be a more variable symptom population than depressive adults. Further research is needed. Strober, Freeman, Rigali, Schmidt, and Diamond (1992) reported positive results for lithium augmentation in tricyclic-resistant depressed inpatient adolescents.

An open study reports significant efficacy for imipramine in a group of 20 hospitalized prepubertal children carefully diagnosed by DSM-III criteria for a major depressive episode (Weller, Preskorn, Weller, & Croskell, 1983). In this study, all children who responded had a total TCA level between 125 and 225 ng/ml, without benefit from either lower or higher levels.

Similar to the adolescent studies, tricyclic antidepressants have not been demonstrated to be superior to placebo in treating prepubertal major depressive disorder (Ambrosini et al., 1993a; Ryan, 1990). Although there was no difference between imipramine and placebo in the double-blind placebo-controlled study by Puig-Antich, Perel, Lupatkin, et al. (1987), those children with at least a plasma level of 200 ng/ml responded best. Another possibly important finding reported by Preskorn, Weller, Hughes, et al. (1987) was that hospitalized depressed children with a positive DST (dexamethasone suppression test) responded better to imipramine than placebo. During the past several years, tricyclic antidepressants have been widely used for depressed children and adolescents even though there is as yet little research support for this clinical practice.

Enuresis

Earlier reports on the clinical efficacy of tricyclics in treating enuresis have been confirmed by numerous other double-blind clinical studies (Ambrosini, Bianchi, Rabinovich, & Elia, 1993b). There is no delay in medication response and over two-thirds will show over a 50% decrease in wetting. The mechanism of action continues to be unknown. Fritz, Rockney, and Young (1994) reported that a higher tricyclic serum level was associated with a better response, but there was at least a 700% variation in serum level among subjects at each weight-determined dosage.

Enuresis remains an established indication for treatment with tricyclic antidepressants.

"School Phobia"

Although an initial controlled study of separation anxiety disorder (school phobia) showed children treated with imipramine and psychotherapy returned to school sooner than those treated with placebo and psychotherapy (Gittelman-Klein & Klein, 1970), a recent study (Klein, Koplewicz, & Kanner, 1992) did not replicate these initial positive medication effects. In this latter study, the anxiety rating scale used did not provide clinically meaningful information. The development of valid instruments for anxiety levels is needed for medication studies in this area.

By contrast to these negative findings, recent double-blind placebo-controlled studies of clomipramine in children and adolescents with obsessive-compulsive disorder showed medication to be superior to placebo (DeVeaugh-Geiss et al., 1992).

Anorexia Nervosa

Contrary to earlier reports (see 1970s), more recent double-blind placebo-controlled studies fail to demonstrate any significant advantage over placebo for antidepressant medication (Lacey & Crisp, 1980; Biederman et al., 1982).

Attention Deficit Hyperactivity Disorder

Within the practice parameters of the American Academy of Child and Adolescent Psychiatry for the treatment of ADHD (1991), imipramine and desipramine are listed as possible medication treatments secondary to the stimulants. Beginning in the 1970s, the tricyclic antidepressant medications were shown to be superior to placebo for ADHD children. These early findings have been subsequently confirmed in double-blind placebo-controlled trials (Biederman, Baldessarini, Wright, Knee, & Harmatz, 1989; Ambrosini et al., 1993b). Long-term efficacy has not been demonstrated, and the stimulants are still considered the drugs of first choice for ADHD.

Side Effects

Ambrosini et al. (1993b) summarized the reported side effects of the tricyclics, including induction of seizures, occurrence of an acute brain syndrome associated with high serum levels, anticholinergic symptoms, and precipitation of manic episodes. Cardiovascular abnormalities include PR prolongation, QRS widening, and lengthening of the QT_c (Puig-Antich et al., 1987). Biederman, Baldessarini, Wright, Knee, Harmatz, and Goldblatt (1989) have described right bundle branch block and AV block, which are more common with higher plasma levels.

Of major concern in the past few years are the reports of nonoverdose sudden death in children taking desipramine. This was first reported to the medical community in 1990 when *The Medical Letter on Drugs and Therapeutics* (Abramowicz, 1990) listed three cases of sudden death in prepubertal children who were receiving desipramine (Norpramin). A fourth death was reported in 1993 (Riddle, Geller, & Ryan, 1993) and a fifth by Brian Yimnitzky, M.D., at the scientific program of the 1994 meeting of the American Psychiatric Association. In three of these cases, the child was being treated for ADHD and in one for depression. Two died shortly after exercise and all were taking desipramine. Available serum levels were subtherapeutic. Riddle et al. (1993) hypothesize that the development of a prolonged QT complex leading to *torsades do pointes* (a form of ventricular tachyarrhythmia) may be the mechanism involved. Further understanding of this safety issue is imperative.

A major advance in the past several years has been the development of the SSRIs. Fluoxetine (Prozac) was introduced in 1988 and rapidly became the most widely prescribed antidepressant. Sertraline (Zoloft) and parolitine (Paxil) are similarly being widely marketed and used. Specific safety factors make this class of antidepressants potentially extremely useful in children and adolescents. There is a lack of lethality after intentional overdose, and there are no anticholinergic or cardiac side effects. Controlled clinical trials have demonstrated clinical efficacy in adults with major depressive disorder and obsessive-compulsive disorder. Clinical studies in children and adolescents with depression and obsessive-compulsive disorder (Riddle, Scahill, King, et al., 1992) and ADHD (Barrickman, Noyes, Kuperman, Schumacher, & Verda, 1991) report positive results. Side effects include rash, precipitation of mania, irritability, and gastrointestinal upset (Greenhill & Setterberg, 1993).

Because of the sudden deaths in children in desipramine and the apparent efficacy and relative safety of the SSRIs, it is likely that the SSRIs will become the medication of first choice for major depression and obsessive-compulsive disorder in children and adolescents. Clinical use in ADHD, anxiety disorders, and other nonpsychotic psychiatric disorders looks promising but requires further study.

NEUROLEPTICS

In 1980, Gualtieri and coworkers published a review and their own studies concerning movement disorders in children treated with neuroleptics

(Gualtieri, Barnhill, et al., 1980; Gualtieri & Hawk, 1980). They classified the disorders in four broad groups:

1. *Withdrawal emergent symptoms (WES)* included the dyskinetic movements developed by a child withdrawn from neuroleptics, which remitted within 12 weeks.

2. *Tardive dyskinesia (TD)* was characterized by late-onset abnormal movements of the face, limbs, and trunk, varying in severity and not always reversible.

3. *Acute extrapyramidal symptoms (EPS)* grouped manifestations similar to those found in adults (oculogyric crisis, akathisia, pseudoparkinsonism, drug-induced catatonia, and acute dystonia).

4. *Dyskinesia* associated with other medications such as stimulants, carbamazepine, and antihistamines.

Six case-reports were described, illustrating TD, WES, combinations with Sydenham's chorea, and two instances of acute late-onset dyskinesia. The authors found that there was no way to predict which children were more likely to develop acute EPS, WES, or TD, and that abrupt withdrawal from high-potency neuroleptics was a frequent factor in the development of WES. Also cited was research that did not support the idea that organic brain syndrome would predispose to TD and caution about the pre-existing movement disorders in children who were likely to be treated with neuroleptic drugs. In that respect, they (the authors) referred to the choreoathetoid movements of the cerebral palsy and the hyperactive children, as well as the posturing and mannerisms of the childhood psychoses.

In 1984, Gualtieri evaluated 41 subjects, ages 3 to 21 years old, who were withdrawn from chronic neuroleptic treatment. The duration of dosage of the various neuroleptics ranged from 1 to 132 months. The mean cumulative dose was 235+/-338 grams of chlorpromazine equivalents. The patients were followed after withdrawal for 3 months to 3 years, with findings that 18 of the 41 subjects (44%) developed one or more of four syndromes: 3 cases of tardive dyskinesia; 9 cases of withdrawal dyskinesia; 3 cases of ambiguous dyskinesia that had to resume neuroleptic treatment within 16 weeks, precluding diagnosis; 5 cases of nondyskinetic withdrawal; and 4 cases of neuroleptic-withdrawal-induced acute behavioral deterioration. All the cases remitted within 8 weeks of withdrawal except the three tardive dyskinesia. Two remitted within 9 months and one persisted after 12 months of follow-up. Gualtieri found that facial movements were more frequent than limb choreoathetosis.

Two years later, the same author conducted a systematic neuroleptic withdrawal study in 38 mentally retarded children, adolescents, and young adults. His findings were consistent with the ones described earlier with transient and tardive dyskinesia in 34% of the cases.

Campbell, Adams, Small, et al. (1988) published a prospective study on tardive and withdrawal dyskinesia in autistic children treated with neuroleptics. The research documented rates as high as 30% of TD, appearing about 2 weeks after drug discontinuation. All the cases reverted during the first 9 months after stopping the neuroleptic administration (see also Campbell, Grega, Green, & Bennett, 1983; Locascio, Malone, Campbell, et al., 1991).

Tardive dystonia and tardive Tourette's syndrome, along with tardive dyskinesia (TD), were reviewed by Wolf and Wagner (1993). They summarized and tabulated the findings of their search including 1966 to 1993. The data in TD was consistent with that described earlier in this chapter. Tardive dystonia, a sustained involuntary muscular contracture secondary to neuroleptic exposure, was described by the investigators as severe and incapacitating, with poor response to treatment and lasting from 5 months to 2 years. The tardive Tourette's syndrome involved tic and dyskineticlike symptoms associated with vocal phenomena, appearing after at least 3 months of treatment with major tranquilizers. As with the other syndromes depicted, no irreversible cases were found by the reviewers.

Neuroleptic malignant syndrome (NMS) is a potentially fatal side effect of the treatment with major tranquilizers (Caroff et al., 1991; Joshi, Capozzoli, & Coyle, 1991; Merry et al., 1985). A review of the English literature about the disease (Steingard et al., 1992) identified descriptions of 34 cases in children and adolescents . The publication also reported a new case occurred on a 16-year-old male treated with a combination of trifluoperazine and lithium after being admitted to a psychiatric hospital with diagnoses of acute manic episode. The authors found that almost two-thirds of the cases were males and an additional two-thirds had received more than one neuroleptic at the time of onset. The syndrome developed within 2 weeks of the initiated neuroleptic treatment, and the symptoms were similar to those classically shown by adults: altered mental status, fever, rigidity, and autonomic instability, accompanied by leukocytosis and increased creatinphosophokinase levels. This review found that five patients (14%) died, but could identify no distinction with the survivors in terms of neuroleptics, coadjuvant agents, or complication treatments. A significant difference with adult reports was the finding that NMS could ensue after a single exposure to the neuroleptics. Latz and McCracken reported two more cases in 1992, and found 49 cases in their own review of the literature, by including cases of lethal catatonia in the search. The writers cautioned about a much higher incidence of death (27%) in patients age 12 or younger. The publications by Steingard and Latz coincided on describing discontinuation of neuroleptic and supportive measures as the mainstay of the treatment for the NMS.

Mikkelsen, Detlor, and Cohen (1981) described phobic-spectrum side effects for neuroleptics. School phobia and work avoidance were described in 15 patients with Tourette's syndrome treated with haloperidol. The symptoms appeared at low doses (1–7.5 mg/day) and in several cases within few weeks from starting the neuroleptic. All the cases reverted after discontinuation or reduction of the neuroleptic's dose. A report by Linet (1984) extended this side effect to pimozide. Linet described an 11-year-old boy with Tourette's who developed school phobia each of the three times that the drug was administered to him in attempts to control the tic symptomatology. The patient had previous history of similar symptomatology accompanied by suicidal thoughts during an earlier trial with haloperidol.

Clinicians had observed psychotic symptoms in children, despite the scarcity of diagnosed schizophrenia in the prepubertal group (Mikkelsen, 1982). Seeking alternative treatments, thiothixene, and thioridazine were compared by Realmuto, Erickson, Yellin, Hopwood, and Greenberg (1984) in a single-blind study of 21 schizophrenic adolescents, 12 to 18 years old. The subjects were assigned randomly to either of the groups and participated in a 4- to 6-week trial with doses determined by the patient's psychiatrist. The two drugs were similar in their efficacy, response latency, and side effects. The high levels of sedation encountered limited the therapeutic response and suggested that high-potency neuroleptics might be preferable in that population. Klein (1990) compared the cognitive effects of thioridazine in children diagnosed with attention deficit hyperactivity disorder. Thirty-six children were treated with the active drug in mean doses of 193 mg (25–300mg), and 40 received placebo in a double-blind design of 4 weeks' duration, followed by 8 weeks' treatment in a nonblind manner. The report found no differences between the two groups at 4 and 12 weeks, in contrast with previous findings, but coincided with them in the finding of substantial drowsiness. Aman, Marks, et al. (1991) validated Realmuto's results, in a research comparing methylphenidate and thioridazine.

Research on Tourette's syndrome increased the knowledge on pimozide as an alternative treatment with potentially fewer side effects than haloperidol (Shapiro & Shapiro, 1982; Bruun, 1984, 1988). Sallee, Pollack, Stiller, et al. (1987) studied the pharmacokinetics of the drug on 7 adults and 4 children receiving a single oral dose of 2 mg of pimozide. The results showed the half-life of the drug as being 66 hours in children compared with 111 hours in adults with significant interindividual variability for both groups.

Shapiro and Shapiro (1984) conducted a double-blind study comparing placebo with pimozide for the treatment of 13 males and 7 females, 11 to 53 years old, with DSM-III (1980) diagnosis of Tourette's syndrome.

Shapiro, Shapiro, et al. (1989) compared pimozide with haloperidol and placebo for Tourette's patients. The double-blind study evaluated 57 patients between the ages of 8 and 65 years treated with pimozide up to 20 mg/day or haloperidol up to 10 mg/day. They found haloperidol to be only slightly superior in suppressing the motor and vocal manifestations of the illness. Pimozide caused less extrapyramidal side effects but was also found to produce EKG alterations, including QT_c prolongation in up to 25% of the cases. In 1992, Ernst published a study on pimozide in autistic children. A year later, he reported on acute dystonic reactions suffered by a 6-year-old boy treated with low doses of pimozide (0.09 and 0.03 mg/kg/day). Ernst wrote that the same patient had had a similar reaction when he was receiving thioridazine. The author theorized about the sensitivity to neuroleptics demonstrated by some individuals.

The research on the atypical neuroleptics was impulsed by the findings of good clinical response in previously treatment-resistant patients as well as the reduced risk of tardive dyskinesia. In Germany, Siefen and Remschmidt (1986) performed a retrospective study of clozapine administration to 21 schizophrenics (18 adolescents) with poor response or intolerable extrapyramidal side effects when treated with classic neuroleptics. The doses ranged from 225 to 800 mg/day.

They found 11 patients markedly improved and 6 with partial alleviation of symptoms, without unacceptable side effects including hematological changes.

Birmaher, Baker, Kapur, et al. (1992) reported on three cases of schizophrenic adolescents successfully treated with clozapine after the failure of conventional neuroleptics. Two patients were 17 years old and one was 18 years old. The doses of clozapine varied from 100 to 400 mg/day. In all three cases, the authors indicated clinical improvement as measured by the reduction of positive and negative signs of schizophrenia, the increase in alertness, and the return of the adolescents to their families and school. They also reported the alleviation of dyskinetic symptoms in one patient during clozapine treatment. The most common complaints were drowsiness and hypersalivation. Although the authors acknowledged an adult incidence of 1% to 2% for agranulocytosis, as established by other investigators, none of the cases reported suffered more than a mild and transient drop on the neutrophils.

Several authors published their research on adolescents and clozapine recently. In Germany, Remschmidt, Schultz, et al. (1994) conducted a retrospective study of open trials with the atypical neuroleptic in 36 adolescent inpatients with schizophrenia, according with ICD-10 criteria. The inclusion criteria were nonresponse to treatment with at least two conventional neuroleptics; symptom deterioration during prior treatment with typical neuroleptics; and significant adverse effects during treatment with conventional neuroleptics. The mean dose of clozapine used was 330 mg/day (50–800 mg/day). The mean duration of treatment was 154 days (*SD* 93 days). The authors found that 11% of the patients showed total symptomatic remission, 75% had ". . . some degree of clinical improvement . . . and became able to participate in a comprehensive rehabilitation program." Only 8% of the subjects did not show response to the clozapine trial. The authors stated that patients exhibiting predominantly positive signs of schizophrenia were more responsive to the treatment. Among the side effects, the trials had to be discontinued in 6 out of 36 cases (17%) due to severe reactions. One patient became stuporous, two developed leukopenia, two had hypertension and EKG changes, and two showed up to tenfold elevation of liver transaminases. Remschmidt disclosed that four of the patients developed akathisia and one, a coarse tremor. He concluded, "It can no longer be stated that clozapine is completely free of extrapyramidal side effects."

Towbin, Dykens, et al. (1994) reported on the outcome of the use of clozapine on a 10-year-old Latino boy diagnosed with childhood-onset schizophrenia. The child suffered repeated hospitalizations, with larger doses of haloperidol each time, and the development of TD, gynecomastia, and mild liver alterations. Clozapine was gradually increased to 500 mg/day. A 15-month follow-up rated the child as moderately improved, with a broader affective range and better environmental awareness. No serious side effects were found during this trial.

Mandoki (1993) described the successful treatment with clozapine of two schizophrenic adolescents (14 and 16 years old) who had been resistant to the classic neuroleptics. Clozapine was used in doses of 300 and 400 mg/day. The younger patient had predominantly negative signs of schizophrenia (isolation, mutism, amotivation). The treatment with clozapine improved him to a level that allowed discharge from the hospital and return to school. The side effects suffered by the patient after 3 years of follow-up were weight gain (53 kg in 3 years), hypersalivation, and drowsiness. The older child presented florid psychotic symptoms (hallucinations, disorganization, incoherence) that improved within a week of clozapine addition to his thiotixene regimen. After discharge, the thiotixene was discontinued without deleterious effects. This patient did not report any side effects of the clozapine.

Jacobsen, Walker, et al. (1994) described the clozapine treatment of a 13-year-old schizophrenic girl. The doses were incremented by 12.5 mg every 5 to 7 days up to a maximum of 550 mg/day. The authors found decreased hallucinatory and bizarre activity and improved socialization, with steady gains during the 14-month follow-up.

The side effects described included sialorrhea, weight gain, and transient enuresis, which abated with reduction of the daily dose to 500 mg.

An open trial of clozapine in 11 adolescents with childhood-onset schizophrenia was conducted by Frazier, Gordon, et al. (1994) as part of an ongoing double-blind study. Eight males and three females, ages 12 to 17 years old received 6 weeks of treatment after a 4-week washout period from previous medication. Clozapine was started on 12.5 or 25 mg/day and increased by one or two times every four days. The maximum possible dose, 900 mg/day, was limited by the side effects, primarily tachycardia and sedation. Other significant findings were sialorrhea, weight gain, enuresis, and constipation. No agranulocytosis or leucopenia occurred. The authors found that all the patients improved compared with the nondrug state, and all but three improved when compared with their condition while taking admission medication.

Mozes, Toren, Chernauzen, et al. (1994) reported 3 cases of schizophrenic children ages 10, 11, and 12 who were unresponsive to typical neuroleptics or who developed severe akhatisia, parkinsonism, and TD at suboptimal doses, preventing an effective treatment.

The group at the New York University Medical Center, headed by Dr. Campbell, studied the effects that major tranquilizers had on aggressive children, in a series of articles. Campbell, Small, Green, et al. (1984) reviewed the literature on pharmacological treatment of aggression and presented a double-blind pilot study comparing lithium carbonate, haloperidol, and chlorpromazine in aggressive, hospitalized children. Fifteen male patients, 6 to 12 years old, completed the study. After reaching optimum dosages, the levels were maintained for three weeks. A final week of placebo treatment finalized the design. The authors found no significant differences between the three drugs' ability to improve the aggressive behavior. Chlorpromazine, though, led to excessive sedation at relatively low doses. Two years later, Campbell et al. compared behavioral effects of lithium carbonate, haloperidol, and placebo in a double-blind study involving 61 treatment-resistant hospitalized children, whereas Platt et al. (1981, 1984) compared the cognitive effects of those three drugs. The findings corroborated that both drugs were superior to placebo for aggression control. Haloperidol, however, produced significant decrease of cognition, as measured by the response to the Porteus Maze test, and increased the reaction time of the subjects.

Research about the use of neuroleptics on autism and pervasive developmental disorders was also pursued during this period (Mikkelsen, 1982; Sloman, 1991). Anderson et al. (1984) studied 40 autistic children between 2 and 7 years old treated with haloperidol. The double-blind, placebo-controlled design used the neuroleptic in doses between 0.5 and 4 mg/day. The authors concluded that haloperidol resulted in clinical improvement as measured by a decrease in behavioral symptoms and facilitation of discriminative learning. No adverse effects were observed at the doses used.

Joshi, Capozzoli, and Coyle (1988) reported on an open study using low doses of haloperidol and fluphenazine hydrochloride (0.5–2.0 mg/day) on 12 consecutively hospitalized children between 7 and 12 years old with diagnosis of pervasive developmental disorder. They observed significant reduction of aggressiveness and hyperactivity and improvement in peer relations and reality testing, with minimal side effects.

Anderson, Campbell, et al. (1989) published the results of a double-blind, placebo-controlled, crossover trial of haloperidol in discrimination learning and behavioral symptoms in 45 autistic children, ages 2 to 7 years old. This study confirmed the value of neuroleptics in the treatment of some of the most severe symptoms associated with autism rather than in affecting the disease itself. Hyperactivity, withdrawal, aggressivity, and stereotypies were decreased by haloperidol (see also Campbell, Kafantaris, Malone, et al., 1991). The study could not find a direct facilitating effect on discrimination learning, agreeing with results found by Erickson, Yellin, Hopwood, et al. (1984) and by Klein (1990).

Also, Perry, Campbell, et al. (1989) validated the efficacy of long-term therapy with haloperidol and addressed the issue of continuous versus discontinuous treatment regimen. The study group comprised 60 autistic children, 48 males and 12 females, aged 2.3 to 7.9 years. They were randomly assigned to 2 groups. Group 1 received the drug on a continuous basis. Group 2 was on a schedule of 5 days of active drug and 2 days of placebo per week. A month with placebo followed 6 months of neuroleptic treatment. The authors concluded that haloperidol remained effective on a long-term basis, with enduring therapeutic effect up to four weeks after drug withdrawal. No differences on efficacy or side effects were found when continuous or discontinuous administration was considered.

The first half of the 1990s has seen relentless efforts to develop new neuroleptics that enable effective and safe treatment of different disorders found in childhood and adolescence. Besides the trials with clozapine, already described, other atypical drugs are currently under research worldwide. Risperidone and remoxipride specially have occupied the most recent literature in adult patients, but no publications to our knowledge have yet addressed their use in children (Marder, 1992).

BENZODIAZEPINES

The use of benzodiazepines in adults has been a standard, well-supported practice for over three decades. Conversely, in the younger segments of the population, the research had been very limited (Biederman, 1990;

Coffey, 1990). Benzodiazepines have mostly been applied in children in relationship to seizures and anesthesia, although anxiety disorders and sleep disorders had long been recognized in this group (Dupont & Saylor, 1992; Moreau et al., 1989). The process from DSM-III (1980) and its revision, to the recent DSM-IV (1994), allowed the progressive clarification of the diagnostic confusion that separated the pathology on adults and children, redefining it as spectrum disorders. This new approach stimulated the trial of different drugs on the younger population.

Benzodiazepine mechanism of action seems to be related to potentiation of GABA (gamma-aminobutyric acid)-ergic activity, the main inhibitory neurotransmitter of the central nervous system (CNS). The neuronal receptors are concentrated predominantly in the limbic system, cortex, and hippocampus. As happened with other psychotropics, benzodiazepine pharmacokinetics revealed increased hepatic metabolism and renal clearance in children (Coffey, 1990).

Lorazepam, a short-acting benzodiazepine, has been used in conjunction with neuroleptics to treat agitated psychosis. Lorazepam allowed reductions in the dose of neuroleptics along with improved symptomatic control as compared with neuroleptics employed alone (Bodkin, 1990; Busch et al., 1989). Catatonia also proved responsive to this benzodiazepine (Greenfield et al., 1987; Salam et al., 1987, 1988). Marneros and Jagger (1993) reported on a 14-year-old boy with catatonic stupor who responded to 2 mg of oral lorazepam with recovery within 40 minutes of the administration of the drug.

Clonazepam, a long-acting benzodiazepine, had been studied extensively as an anticonvulsant since the 1960s. Studies in children with seizure disorder proved it safe and without serious side effects at therapeutic doses. Clonazepam had demonstrated efficacy on the treatment of manic states and panic disorder, and as coadjuvant in acute psychosis, obsessive-compulsive disorder, and neuroleptic-induced akathisia (Leonard & Rapoport, 1989; Leonard et al., 1994; Biederman, 1990). As with other drugs of this group, clonazepam's potential drawbacks include excessive sedation, depressogenic action, and behavioral disinhibition with paradoxical excitement (Graae, 1990; Graae & Milner, 1994; Maoris, Maoris, Rachel, & Biggio, 1987).

Biederman (1987) published a report on three cases of prepubertal children with paniclike symptoms, treated with clonazepam. The first patient was an 11-year-old boy with history of separation anxiety and school refusal since age 4, who developed discrete anxiety attacks in fifth grade. The treatment with clonazepam up to 1 mg/day allowed complete remission without adverse side effects. The patient remained symptom-free at the 5-month follow-up. The second subject was an 11-year-old girl who presented signs of anxiety since early childhood and anxiety attacks since third grade. Her mother was being treated for panic disorder with agoraphobia and had responded well to clonazepam. After unsuccessful attempts at monotherapy with imipramine at doses of 4 mg/kg/day, clonazepam 0.5 mg/day was added to the regimen. The author described progressive symptomatic improvement and no side effects at the 3-year follow-up. The third patient was an 8-year-old boy with history of fear development since age 6 and episodes of panic twice daily. His mother had been diagnosed with panic disorder and had responded well to alprazolam and phenelzine. The child was treated initially with alprazolam, following the mother's positive response to it, in doses up to 3 mg/day. The symptoms remitted only partially and alprazolam was replaced by clonazepam. At doses of 3 mg/day of clonazepam, the child became asymptomatic. Two years later, he was still free of panic attacks and without adverse effects.

Panic disorder in children and adolescents also was reported by Vitiello, Behar, et al. (1990), among several authors. Hayward et al. (1989) conducted a survey of 106 ninth graders from three schools in northern California. The authors found that 11.6% of the girls and 6.1% of the boys had experienced at least one panic attack. Moreau et al. (1989) found panic disorder in 7 out of 220 subjects studied (6–23 years old). Vitiello et al. (1990) reported on six cases of panic disorder in prepubertal children and recommended the use of antidepressants and benzodiazepines for their treatment.

Pfefferbaum, Overall, et al. (1987) studied alprazolam as treatment of anticipatory anxiety in children with cancer. A total of 13 children between 7 and 16 years completed the design. The patients were administered alprazolam up to 0.06 mg/day for three days before and on the day of bone marrow or lumbar puncture. Children were evaluated using the State Trait Anxiety Inventory for Children, the Clinical Global Distress and Clinical Global Anxiety scales. Nine of the patients responded at least partially to the drug. The authors concluded that alprazolam could be a beneficial anxiolytic agent with minimal side effects, in agreement with the conclusions published by Simeon, Ferguson, et al. (1992) regarding alprazolam administration in overanxious children.

Two studies were conducted by Bernstein et al. (1990) comparing imipramine and alprazolam as treatment for school refusal. The first design was an open trial on 17 subjects recruited from the School Refusal Outpatient Clinic at the University of Minnesota. The children were placed on a comprehensive school reentry program that included alprazolam in doses ranging up to 4 mg/day or imipramine between 50 and 150 mg/day. The authors reported global improvement and return to school after about 8 weeks of treatment. The second phase described in the publication studied a group of 24 children (7–18 years old). Bernstein compared alprazolam, imipramine, and placebo using a double-blind design. The dose of alprazolam was adjusted to 0.03 mg/kg/day.

Imipramine was administered at 3 mg/kg/day. After 8 weeks of treatment, the subjects were tapered off the medication to avoid rebound and withdrawal phenomena. The monitoring of the results was evaluated by anxiety and depression scales (ARC, CDI, CDS; see chapter 4). The data did not support significant differences between the drugs at the fourth week of treatment, but at the eighth week, alprazolam patients demonstrated the greater symptomatic improvement, followed by imipramine and placebo.

Simeon, Ferguson, et al. (1992) studied the effects of alprazolam treatment in 30 children diagnosed with overanxious and avoidant disorders. The authors could not demonstrate significant differences between placebo and the benzodiazepine in terms of anxiolytic properties.

ADRENERGIC BETA BLOCKERS

Propranolol has had ample use in adults in cardiology and neurology. Psychopharmacologically, it has been used to treat aggressive patients, whether alone or in conjunction with neuroleptics, anticonvulsants, lithium carbonate, and clonidine. Beta blockers have also been helpful in the treatment of neuroleptic-induced akathisia (Lipiski, Zubenko, & Cohen, 1984; Wells et al., 1991) and in reducing the symptomatology of some anxiety disorders and its somatic manifestations (Melbach, Dunner, Wilson, et al., 1987).

Although the literature regarding the utilization of these agents is profuse, the pediatric applications in psychiatry are not as extensively documented (Connor, 1993).

Williams et al. (1982) conducted a study in 30 patients with uncontrolled rage outbursts associated with organic brain syndrome. The group consisted of 11 children, 15 adolescents, and 4 adults, ranging from 7 to 35 years. It was composed mainly of males (26). Two-thirds were outpatients. Diagnostically, the ample majority (26) met criteria for conduct disorder, 15 also had ADHD, and 13 were described as having had some degree of mental retardation. Eleven patients suffered from uncontrolled seizures at the time of being included in the trials and three others had a seizure disorder controlled with anticonvulsants. Before receiving propranolol, the patients had been treated with a multidisciplinary approach including psychotherapy and pharmacological interventions (neuroleptics, stimulants, and anticonvulsants). The authors noted that during the beta-blocker trial, other medications were in several instances reduced or discontinued if the patient responded. Propranolol was started at doses of 10 or 20 mg, 3 or 4 times a day and increased every 3 days by 30 to 80 mg if the blood pressure was greater than 90/50 and the pulse was above 55. The total dose range was 50 to

1600 mg/day. The data on the patient's response to the trial were collected retrospectively from the medical records. Williams found that 75% of the patients showed moderate or marked improvement, maintained during the follow-up period. The side effects recorded in the publication included somnolence and lethargy, hypotension, bradycardia, depression, and bronchospasm. All of them were dose-dependent and rapidly reversible. Although this study presented various methodological limitations, it helped to establish propranolol as an accepted alternative to treat aggression in the pediatric population (see also Connor, 1993).

Propranolol also demonstrated efficacy in the treatment of self-injurious behavior, as a coadjuvant to the mainstay drugs (neuroleptics, lithium carbonate, carbamazepine), or when they have proven ineffective or have unacceptable side effects. (Lang & Remington, 1994; Sandman, 1990).

Metoprolol and Nadolol, Beta-1 adrenergic blockers, have also been found useful in reducing rage outbursts in children. Kastner et al. (1990) published a report on two cases of mentally retarded patients treated with metoprolol. The first case was a 26-year-old severely retarded man with long history of self-injurious and assaultive behaviors. He had been treated with thiordazine since age 13. At the time of the trial, metoprolol was selected because the patient had history of asthma. The authors described that within 6 months of starting with the beta blocker, thioridazine was discontinued without loss in behavioral control. The second case described was a 16-year-old boy with severe mental retardation, autism, and cerebral palsy who would exhibit aggressive behavior in response to frustration. The patient was receiving alprazolam 0.5 mg/day. Kastner described that the addition of metoprolol in increasing doses up to 200 mg/day resulted in a dramatic improvement of the aggressive behavior. The authors recommended that metoprolol should be considered among the drugs for the treatment of aggression, akathisia, and anxiety in mentally retarded and autistic populations.

The therapeutic action of beta blockers on pediatric anxiety manifestations was explored by Famularo, Kinscherff, and Fenton (1988). They conducted a pilot study in 4 boys and 7 girls diagnosed with post-traumatic stress disorder (PTSD), using propranolol in doses up to 2.5 mg/day. The children were treated for 4 weeks and evaluated at the end of the trial and a month after discontinuation of the drug. The results of the study suggested that propranolol could be an effective agent in the treatment of PTSD, acute type, in children. Three years later, Faigel (1991) proposed the use of propranolol to treat stress-induced cognitive dysfunction in adolescents. He administered 40 mg of the drug to 32 high school students, one hour before they retook the Scholastic Achievement Test (SAT). The subjects had self-reported "test-anxiety" symptoms. The results of this trial, as stated in the paper, indicated that the mean improvement in SAT scores was 50 for the verbal part and 80 for the math section.

CLONIDINE

Clonidine is an alpha 2-adrenergic agent with agonist action specially on presynaptic receptors in the central nervous system. Its action tends to decrease neuronal release of norepinephrine, therefore reducing noradrenergic activity. It has been used as an effective antihypertensive agent and was also recognized as useful in the treatment of opiate withdrawal (Hunt, Capper, et al., 1990).

Cohen, Detlor, et al. (1980) conducted a study of clonidine in Tourette's patients who had not responded to haloperidol, or who could not tolerate it due to cognitive blunting, depression, or social phobia development. The group included a total of 25 patients, 11 studied directly by the authors and 14 on which the researchers acted as consultants. The patients ranged in age from 9 to 50 years old. The trial started with clonidine at doses of 0.05 mg in one or two daily intakes. The drug was increased 0.05 mg every 4 to 7 days up to a maximum of 0.3 mg/day for the directly supervised patients, while the charts reviewed on the 14 consulted-on patients revealed maximum doses of 0.6 mg/day. Cohen described a transient hypotension lasting up to 3 hours after the first oral intake of clonidine. He also recorded tiredness and sleepiness in almost all patients throughout the treatment around 40 to 50 minutes from the successive doses. After following the subjects up to 26 months, the authors concluded that 70% of the patients had benefited from the clonidine treatment and divided the therapeutic response in five phases:

1. Within hours or days, the patients became calmer and less irritable.

2. Three to four weeks into the treatment, the compulsive behavior and the vocal and motor tics diminished.

3. The third month marked the achievement of the therapeutic plateau.

4. At about the fifth month after the beginning of the treatment, the subject required an increase in dosages.

5. Some patients developed resistance to the clonidine. The study did not find serious side effects, describing only mild blood pressure and pulse changes, sedation, and xerostomia.

Shapiro and Shapiro (1982), reported on the treatment of 36 Tourette's patients with clonidine. The data evaluated only the motoric and phonic response to the treatment. They found improvement in 25% of the patients but no changes or worsening in the balance, addressing the differences identified within the Tourette's population.

Clonidine was also assayed to treat children with attention deficit hyperactivity disorder. The observations of the arousal-dampening effects of clonidine and its mild side effect profile postulated the adrenergic drug as an alternative for those patients who did not respond to stimulants or who developed intolerable adverse reactions to them. Hunt, Minderaa, and Cohen (1985) published a double-blind placebo-controlled study of 10 children diagnosed with ADHD. The children had been off medication for a month prior to the study. Clonidine was administered with increases of 0.05 mg/day up to a total dose of 0.2 mg, for 8 weeks and then was replaced by a placebo phase. The children were evaluated by teachers, parents, and clinicians at two- and four-week intervals. The results showed that clonidine significantly reduced the impulsivity, inattention, and hyperactivity in about half the patients. The drug could be used in children with tic disorder, insomnia, excessive rebound phenomena on stimulants, or growth retardation. The authors postulated that clonidine acted predominantly to improve frustration tolerance while methylphenidate effected distractibility. Similar results were demonstrated a year later by Hunt in a study of 10 children.

Hunt (1987) compared oral and transdermal clonidine in 10 children with ADHD in an open design. He found that both routes of administration were equally effective, although the transdermal form required higher doses for equivalent effects. Typically, a child responding to 0.2 mg of oral clonidine would need 0.3 mg patches. He also observed that the patches had to be changed every 5 days instead of every week as was the manufacturer's claim.

Steingard, Biederman, et al. (1994) examined retrospectively the records on 54 patients treated with clonidine. The group was divided into ADHD children with and without tic disorders. The drug was effective in 70% of the sample, but the group that showed greater improvement corresponded to those subjects with comorbid tics. Sedation was the most common side effect and in 5 children motivated the discontinuation of the drug. Another publication by Steingard, Goldberg, et al. (1994) a year later highlighted the value of clonazepam as a coadjuvant in the treatment of comorbid ADHD and tic disorders. These findings were corroborated by the group led by Biederman (1990) at Massachusetts General Hospital. They also identified clonidine as useful in the treatment of spontaneous or stimulant-induced sleep disturbances in children with diagnosis of ADHD (Steingard, Biederman, et al., 1994; Wilens et al., 1994).

Jaselskis, Cook, Fletcher, et al. (1992) conducted a double-blind, crossover, placebo-controlled study in 8 autistic children (5–11 years old) with hyperactivity symptoms. The writers found improvement over 6 weeks in the irritability and hyperactivity of some children, but in half of them, clonidine had to be discontinued for intense sedation or hypotension.

Indications that hyperarousal could play a role in some of the manifestations of autism led Frankhauser, Karumanchi, German, et al. (1992), to a trial of clonidine in children with said disease. The sample included nine males, 5 to 33 years old, who were treatment-free at the beginning of the study. The clonidine dose was calculated at a rate of 0.005 mg/kg/day and was delivered transdermally. The active phase of the trial was 4 weeks, and was followed by a 2-week washout period before crossover with placebo patches. The children were rated by parents and clinicians using semistructured interviews, the Clinical Global Impression scale, and the Ritvo-Freeman Real Life Rating Scale. Eight out of the nine patients improved significantly with decreased motor reactivity, less affective lability, and improved social relationships. Similarly, Kemph, DeVane, et al. (1993) conducted an open trial of clonidine in 17 chronically violent children from 5 to 13 years of age. Their findings also were positive and encouraged further research on the role of clonidine in the treatment of aggression in children.

ANTICONVULSANTS

Early in the development of medicine, physicians noticed the relationship between epilepsy and behavioral disorders. During the middle part of this century, as new pharmacological agents were developed and tried for the treatment of seizure disorders, researchers realized that the drugs themselves had mood and behavioral repercussions. The application of these agents to adult patients affected by psychiatric illnesses proved the efficacy of carbamazepine and valproic acid in a number of cases of psychosis, mood disorders, and aggressive dyscontrol (Evans & Gualtieri, 1987; Evans et al., 1985; Kafantaris et al., 1992; Klein, Bental, et al., 1984; Mandoki et al., 1992). Their beneficial effect occurred disregarding the existence of comorbid EEG alterations. Cowdry and Gardner (1988) described the uses of carbamazepine in the treatment of dyscontrol paroxysms in the context of borderline personality disorder.

Post and colleagues (Post, 1988), in reference to the neurobiology of affective disorder, postulated that environmental stressors would determine permanent genetic and morphological changes in the nervous system. Said changes would modify the response of the patients to the classic drug approach, rendering lithium less effective. A number of those cases could be treated with carbamazepine and valproic acid, either in mono- or polytherapeutic regimes (Papatheodorou & Kutchee, 1993). They also highlighted that there were no predictors for cross-reactivity among the anticonvulsants.

Different authors reviewed the actions of carbamazepine and valproic acid in the acute and prophylactic phases of mania, especially on those patients presenting atypical manic variants with dysphoria, or rapid cycling, or those without a familial history of bipolar disorder (Lapierre and Roval, 1989; McElroy et al., 1992). The adult studies also described mood-elevating properties of carbamazepine, along with its potential to induce or maintain manic episodes in some patients. These effects derived from the structural similarities of carbamazepine to the tricyclic antidepressants.

Kastner, Friedman, et al. (1990) described the successful use of valproic acid to treat mood symptoms in three mentally retarded children. The maximum doses administered ranged between 1500 and 3000 mg/day, with documented blood levels up to 111 micrograms/ml. In their study, they found no serious side effects. The authors stated that carbamazepine had become their drug of first choice in the treatment of dysphoria in the mentally retarded. Valproic acid represented an alternative option for the cases of inadequate or undesired response to carbamazepine. The basis for their preference for the anticonvulsants in this population was the potential increased disability caused by the effects that lithium carbonate had on cognition, tremor, and urinary continence.

Two years later, Kastner and Friedman (1992) reported on the successful use of valproic acid and verapamil to treat a severely mentally retarded 18-year-old blind boy with chronic history of sleep disturbance and self-injurious behavior. The symptoms had failed to improve with thioridazine, chloral hydrate, carbamazepine, and imipramine, and the author's explanation proposed that the last two agents were maintaining manic phases on the patient which resolved with the valproic-calcium channel blocker combination.

The behavioral effects of different anticonvulsants were also studied in autistic children who had seizure disorder. Gillberg (1991) reviewed the treatment records of 66 reports on this comorbidity. He concluded that two-thirds of the cases had been treated with carbamazepine. This group obtained not only good seizure control but also "clear psychotropic effect" defined as improvement in attention deficit and autistic symptoms, as spontaneously reported by the caregivers. Valproic acid was used in 26% of the children. The seizure control and beneficial psychotropic effect, as previously defined, were slightly less good than with carbamazepine. Gillberg reported that 20% of the valproic-treated children showed severe side effects, described by caregivers to include somnolence for over a month, increased autistic behavior, and unmalleable hyperactivity or irritability. A benzodiazepine anticonvulsant, clonazepam, used in 23% of the cases, was accompanied by severe side effects, according with the definition rendered for valproic acid. Phenytoin and barbiturates also produced "severe aggravation of autistic symptomatology, confusion and hyperactivity" (see also Berg et al., 1993).

Aman, Werry, et al. (1987, 1990) published two studies describing the cognitive effects of valproate and carbamazepine in children. The authors concluded that neither drug decreased the intellectual performance of the subjects. Actually the measurements used showed improvement in direct correlation with the blood levels obtained for carbamazepine and valproic acid. The psychotropic properties of both drugs were as described by Trimble (1990 a & b) and Vining (1987).

Among the side effects seen with carbamazepine, the initial concern with bone marrow depression (aplastic anemia, agranulocytosis, and thrombocytopenia) decreased as studies demonstrated that serious, irreversible phenomena were very infrequent (Hart & Easton, 1982; Joffe, Post, et al., 1988; Sabotka, Alexander, & Cooke, 1990). Less threatening events, such as gastrointestinal phenomena, tics, drowsiness, skin reactions, and blurred vision were much more common and sometimes required discontinuation of the treatment (Pellock, 1987; Robertson, Garofalo, et al., 1993).

A study by Domizio and Verrotti (1993) analyzed 300 children between 3 and 15 years undergoing antiepileptic therapy. Approximately two-thirds were treated with phenobarbital and the rest with other anticonvulsants (". . . valproic acid, carbamazepine, etc."). The authors evaluated the patients for hyperactivity, irritability, dyssomnias, and drowsiness. The results of the study determined that 76% of the children receiving phenobarbital versus 31% of those under other drug treatments showed behavioral disturbances, with hyperactivity being the most frequent one. One year later, Mitchell, Zhou, et al. (1993) measured reaction time, attention, and impulsivity in children receiving antiepileptic drugs. The group studied comprised 111 children, aged 5 to 13 years. Carbamazepine was found to improve reaction time performance and decreased omission errors, while phenobarbital had the contrary effect.

Valproic acid carries more potential for gastrointestinal disturbance, sedation, and distal tremor than carbamazepine. Although pancreatic and liver toxicity becomes extremely rare in children older than 3 years old, it requires regular monitoring of blood enzymatic levels.

The anticonvulsants were found to interact extensively with different systems changing the bioavailability of themselves or other drugs. Trimble cautioned readers of his 1990 review of anticonvulsants regarding important interactions among psychotropics, noting that both antidepressants and neuroleptics can reduce or increase blood levels of anticonvulsants, and that adding carbamazepine or phenytoin will usually reduce the effects of neuroleptics, antidepressants and benzodiazepines.

LITHIUM

Case reports on the use of lithium in bipolar children and adolescents began in the 1970s. McKnew et al. (1981) described two latency-age children with bipolar disorder who were part of a double-blind placebo-controlled crossover study and responded positively to lithium. Puig-Antich (1980) stated that enough pilot work had accumulated so that properly controlled studies of bipolar disorder in children and adolescents should now be undertaken. By 1994, nine double-blind, placebo-controlled studies were reviewed (Alessi, Naylor, Ghaziuddin, & Zubieta, 1994).

The clearest indication for the use of lithium in childhood and adolescent disorders is bipolar disorder in adolescence. Not only is lithium carbonate often effective for the active illness, but Strober, Morrell, Lampect, and Burroughs (1990) have shown that continued lithium treatment may prevent or decrease relapses. Adolescents who continued lithium for 18 months had a decreased incidence of illness compared with baseline and had significantly fewer relapses compared with non-completers. Bipolar adolescents with "mixed mania" are likely to be resistant to lithium treatment (Himmelback & Garfinkel, 1986).

Bipolar disorder in prepubertal children has been recognized with increasing frequency during the past several years. Weller, Weller, and Tucker (1986) applied DSM-III (1980) diagnostic criteria to case reports of psychotic children and found that 50% of those meeting clear criteria for mania had been given different diagnoses. Delong and Aldershof (1987) described long-term lithium treatment of 196 children who were treated for up to 10 years. Open discontinuation trials were done for all, and some had double-blind placebo-controlled discontinuation trials. For the 59 diagnosed with childhood bipolar affective disorder, 66% were treated successfully with lithium.

Lithium augmentation of tricyclic antidepressants in refractory depressed adults has been reported since the early 1980s (Heninger, Charney, & Sternberg, 1983). Strober et al. (1992) reported some modest positive results with this treatment strategy in tricyclic-resistant depressed hospitalized adolescents. Among 24 patients, 2 had a dramatic response to lithium augmentation and 8 had partial improvement.

Alessi et al. (1994) describes aggression " to be the most widely supported clinical diagnostic entity for which lithium is indicated" (p. 293). In an early major double-blind placebo-controlled study by Campbell et al. (1984), children hospitalized with the diagnosis of undersocialized aggressive conduct disorder were treated with lithium, haloperidol, or placebo. Lithium was as effective as haloperidol in reducing aggressiveness and temper outbursts. In a series of further studies, Campbell, Gonzales, and Silva (1992) studied 48 children, ages 5 to 12, who were diagnosed with conduct disorder with extreme aggression and explosiveness. Under double-blind conditions, lithium was clinically and statistically superior to placebo and had fewer side effects than haloperidol. Impulsive explosive aggression is the target symptom affected by lithium. Under double-blind placebo-controlled conditions, Sheard et al. (1976) reported decreased aggressive incidents and self-reported aggressive affect in aggressive antisocial teenagers in a correctional facility. Although this is an extremely important area in need of further studies, the authors have not found any further research on the effect of lithium in delinquent populations. There are a few reports of lithium being effective in decreasing aggressive outbursts in children and adolescents with mental retardation or developmental disorders (Campbell, Gonzalez, & Silva, 1992).

Lithium has not been reported helpful in ADHD or eating disorders but has been reported to be effective in the acute treatment of Klein-Levin syndrome (Alessi et al. 1994). Significant advances in understanding the neurochemistry of lithium's mechanism of action are also summarized by Alessi et al. (1994). Scientific studies to aid understanding of the basic mechanisms of action are progressing, and lithium has become part of the standard treatments available in clinical child and adolescent psychiatry.

OTHER MEDICATIONS

Triiodothyronine (T3)

A report by Sherwin, Flach, and Stokes (1958) noted improvement in two euthyroid autistic boys after receiving triiodothyronine. Campbell, Fish, David, et al. (1972) administered triiodothyronine (T3) to an inpatient population of 16 euthyroid preschool autistic-schizophrenic children with severe developmental deviations. On a daily dose of 12.5 to 75 mg of T3, marked improvement was noted in 11 children consisting of changes in affect, social responsiveness, language production, and self-initiated activity; with decreases in stereotypy, hyperactivity, distractibility, and so on. Blind ratings, using treatment results with dextroamphetamine as the control, indicated statistically significant improvement with T3 in overall symptomatology. This study has important methodological limitations, and a subsequent double-blind placebo-controlled study failed to demonstrate any significant superiority for T3 over placebo in the treatment of 30 young euthyroid children with autism (Campbell, Small et al., 1978).

Lysergic Acid Diethylamide (LSD)

In two papers published in 1962 and 1963, Bender and colleagues reported on the use of LSD-25 in the treatment of hospitalized, severely disturbed children with diagnoses of schizophrenia and autism. Favorable results reported included mood elevations, spontaneous play with adults and other children, improvement in social relatedness, responsiveness to contact and affection, and reduced rhythmic and whirling behavior. The dosage was 100 mg of LSD-25, with the response lasting over several hours beginning 30 to 40 minutes after ingestion. The drug was given one to three times per week over a 6-week period. The methodology and data were not presented.

Simmons, Leiken, Lovaas, Schaeffer, and Perioff (1966), commenting on the methodological limitations of the earlier studies, administered LSD to a pair of identical male twins, aged 4 years 9 months, using an intrasubject replication design with LSD interspersed with control and placebo observations and objective behavior records. Both twins satisfied the diagnostic criteria for childhood autism. Changes included an increase in social behaviors with better eye-to-face contact and responsiveness to adults, an increase in smiling and laughing behavior indicating a pleasurable affective state, and a decrease in self-stimulation behavior. They found the drug responses to be consistent with those reported by Bender, and mentioned unpublished data from a population of 18 psychotic children to whom LSD was also administered. In this more heterogeneous population, there was a tendency for the autisticlike children to respond as described, whereas the less retarded schizophrenic children became more withdrawn and disorganized. The effects of the LSD were transient and required continued administration.

Despite these relatively optimistic findings, there are no further reports or follow-up on these studies.

Anticonvulsants

Merritt and Putnam (1938) reported on the efficacy of diphenylhydantoin in the treatment of convulsive disorders. Since that time, reports of its effect on children with emotional or behavioral problems have intermittently occurred. Lindsley and Henry (1942) described that diphenylhydantoin improved the behavior scores of 13 behavior problem children, but there was no significant difference in mean scores between diphenylhydantoin and no drug at the conclusion of the study. Brown and Solomon (1942) administered diphenylhydantoin for 7 weeks to seven behavior-disordered adolescents with grossly abnormal EEGs at a state training school and described improvement in three of them. Walker and Kirkpatrick (1947) administered diphenylhydantoin to 10 behavior-disordered children with abnormal EEGs and described improvement during the 9–18-month outpatient follow-up. Pasamanick (1951) reported little positive effect of diphenylhydantoin in 21 hospitalized behavior-disordered children aged 6 to 13 years with abnormal EEGs. One improved slightly with diphenylhydantoin; another improved markedly on trimethadione. Gross and Wilson (1964) studied 48 hyperactive children with abnormal EEGs who were treated with medication. Diphenylhydantoin was rarely effective. A child with severe temper tantrums and an EEG with left temporal spikes responded dramatically to Celontin. Looker and Conners (1970) reported three cases of children who responded to diphenylhydantoin following nonresponse to stimulant medication. Because these three children had in common a history of violent temper outbursts, 17 children, aged 5 ½ to 14 ½ years, with a history of periodic outbursts of violent temper were studied in a 9-week double-blind placebo-controlled crossover trial of diphenylhydantoin. The authors reported no statistically significant group changes attributable to drug effect, and concluded that diphenylhydantoin was of little clinical benefit in a group of children characterized by severe temper tantrums. All of these children subsequently improved with dextroamphetamine or methylphenidate. Millichap (1973), in a study of 22 children with learning and behavior disorders, reported a significant elevation of the auditory perception quotient following treatment with diphenylhydantoin in a group of children with paroxysmal dysrhythmia. Wender (1971) reported on four children with periodic rather than continuous MBD symptoms who failed to respond to amphetamines, but responded dramatically to diphenylhydantoin. Thus, individual case reports with marked improvement in response to diphenylhydantoin continue to be reported, although controlled studies demonstrating positive effects do not exist.

Carbamazepine is established in the treatment of seizure disorders, with apparent special usefulness in temporal lobe seizures and so-called psychomotor epilepsy. There is also an established relationship in some children between epilepsy and learning and behavior disorders (Stores, 1978). Furthermore, carbamazepine is considered to have independent psychotropic properties and is reported effective in the treatment of affective disorders in adults. Based on these factors, a number of studies report efficacy for carbamazepine in the treatment of a variety of symptoms occurring both with and without evidence of association with a seizure disorder. These symptoms include hyperactivity, aggressive behaviors, and mood disturbances. These studies vary greatly in the quality of design and methodology and their results are not consistent; so although the use of carbamazepine in childhood disorders is promising, it is so far not established (see review by Remschmidt, 1976). An extended discussion of this issue is presented in Chapter 5.

ETHNIC CONSIDERATIONS IN CHILD PSYCHOPHARMACOTHERAPY

"An understanding of ethnicity and its psychopharmacological and psychobiological correlates is vital for ensuring quality psychiatric care for the ethnic minority population in this country" (Lin, Poland, & Nakasaki, 1993, p. 4). In addition to considering diverse ethnic groups in the United States, Lin notes, "80% of all people live outside North America and Western Europe" and "the introduction of psychopharmacotherapy and biological psychiatry has encountered little if any resistance in cross-cultural and cross-national dissemination," (p. 4), even though little psychopharmacological research has been conducted with these populations. The findings discussed in this section pertain to adult pharmacology. Psychopharmacological research pertaining to infants, children, and adolescents remains limited. However, extrapolation from adult research often has been useful in pediatric and child psychiatric treatment. Cautions suggested by these findings also may be helpful in considering psychopharmacological treatment of children. As research efforts continue and methodologies become more refined in child psychopharmacology, issues of race and ethnicity also should be considered.

Lawson (1986) indicates a trend toward disregarding racial and ethnic issues in psychiatric research. However, Kalow (1982) observes that interethnic differences in drug-metabolizing capacity may be sufficient to warrant attention in research. He describes differences related to variations in the amount of accessible enzymes, differences in enzyme molecular structure, and effects of modifiers of enzyme activity. It is established that children and adolescents respond differently to psychotropic medications than do adults (Riddle, 1991), but an understanding of possible differences in responses to psychotropics among diverse groups of children and adolescents based on race and ethnicity is not empirically established.

Lawson (1986) states:

> *Racial and ethnic differences in response to various nonpsychotropic medications are well known. (p. 50)*

Empirical studies confirming clinical impressions and elucidating the underlying mechanisms have been reported for psychotropic medication only quite recently. It is well known that dosage levels of neuroleptic medication in the Third World are far lower than in the United States . . . Asians require lower dosages or have side effects at lower dosages than whites for a variety of different medications, including lithium, antidepressants, and neuroleptics.

Many reports suggest pharmacological differences between ethnic groups (Bond, 1991; Johnson, 1993; Lin et al., 1989; Lin et al., 1993; Rudorfer, 1993; Strickland et al., 1991; Strickland et al., 1993; Zhou, Adedoyin, & Wilkinson, 1990). Rudorfer (1993) points to differences in metabolism between Chinese and whites, noting, "Recent studies have shown that racial and ethnic background can significantly affect both the pharmacokinetic and pharmacodynamic actions of a number of psychotropic drugs" (p. 53). Rudorfer further states, "The clinical implications are that dosing with hepatically metabolized drugs like desipramine may need to be reduced in at-risk populations like Orientals and that plasma monitoring should be carried out during treatment" (p. 53).

Strickland et al. (1991) reviewed several studies pertaining to tricyclic antidepressants (TCAs) and differential responses between whites and blacks. Although he notes methodological problems in the studies, he concludes that they "consistently suggest that Black patients with depression may be more sensitive to the effect of TCAs. Findings derived from some of these studies further suggest that this may be mediated through ethnic differences in TCA pharmacokinetics" (p. 443). However, Bond (1991) cautions against treatment recommendations based on current comparative TCA studies, noting:

> *Pharmacokinetic and pharmacodynamic investigations with larger patient samples and control of dosage for body weight, drug interactions, and environmental variables such as diet, smoking, and alcohol use are needed before the existence of ethnic differences in antidepressant metabolism and response can be definitively determined. (p. 468)*

There is evidence that major differences exist between Caucasian and Asian patients regarding therapeutic dosages of antipsychotic medication associated with pharmacokinetic and pharmacodymanic factors (Lin et al., 1989; Bond, 1991). These findings are supported by "pharmacokinetic studies of haloperidol that report higher plasma or serum drug concentrations in Asian patients, even when differences in weight and body surface area are controlled" (Bond, 1991, p. 467). A comparative controlled study of Asian and white patients indicated that "Asian psychotic patients need a significantly lower dose of neuroleptics than whites to control the psychopathology to the same degree. . . . extrapyramidal symptoms occurred at a lower dose in Asian patients" (Lin & Finder, 1983, p. 491).

Strickland et al. (1991) notes that black patients tend to receive higher dosages of neuroleptics, questioning, among other factors, if ethnic differences in the utilization of these medications influence the dosage.

Differences in pharmacokinetics also have been shown regarding lithium. The literature suggests significant variation in responses to lithium among Asian, African American, and Caucasian groups (Strickland et al., 1993), which is thought to be related to the red cell membrane.

> It has been demonstrated that intra-RBC (red blood cell) lithium levels and RBC/plasma lithium ratios are different between black Americans and those from other ethnic backgrounds. This in turn has been shown to be due, at least in part, to a less efficient lithium-sodium countertransport system among black Americans. These differences might be important for the clinical management of black patients with bipolar illness. (Strickland et al., 1991, p. 445)

It is recognized that additional research is needed to explore these findings.

Strickland also reports findings of racial differences in metabolism of carbamazepine that suggest "a difference in the mono-oxygenase enzyme activity" (Strickland et al., 1991, p. 446) and may account for significantly lower carbamazepine metabolite levels in blacks involved in the study.

Zhou et al. (1991) reports:

> Dissimilar plasma concentration-time profiles between Oriental subjects and Caucasians given the same dose of drug have also been reported for diazepam, haloperidol, diphenhydramine, and desipramine. For these and other compounds that are extensively bound in plasma, differences in the pharmacokinetics of total (unbound plus bound) drug may occur because of differences in the extent of such binding. (pp. 10–11)

Johnson (1993), also looking at differences between black and white subjects in response to beta-blockers in vitro, shows that "lymphocyte B-receptors from whites were more sensitive to B-blockade than those from blacks" (p. 304).

Price (1991) notes an increased incidence of clozapine-induced agranulocytosis in Finnish and Jewish patients and urges research for possible genetic and environmental differences as causative.

> The ethnic background of patients needs to be considered in the design of clinical investigations of the safety and efficacy of psychotropic drugs. The influence of ethnicity on psychotropic drug disposition and effect will become increasingly important in clinical practice, given the continued immigration to the United States of large numbers of people of different ethnic backgrounds. (Bond, 1991, p. 469)

SUMMARY

The use of psychoactive medication for the treatment of childhood psychiatric disorders began with Benzedrine during the 1930s. Little was added until the onset of the "biological revolution" in psychiatry beginning in the 1950s. This decade and the next witnessed a steadily progressive increase in reports of efficacy for antipsychotic, antidepressant, "minor tranquilizer," and stimulant medications for a wide variety of childhood disorders.

Almost without exception, methodological limitations compromise the interpretation of the results reported in these studies. These include diagnostic heterogeneity, the absence of a standardized diagnostic classification system, inadequate attention to control groups, absence of double-blind procedures, the unavailability of standardized assessment instruments, and variable dosage schedules.

Nonetheless, evidence accumulated for the efficacy of drugs in certain childhood disorders: stimulants for "hyperactive" children, the antidepressant imipramine for enuresis, antipsychotic medication for psychosis and aggressive behaviors in children and adolescents, and early reports on the treatment of depression in children.

During the 1970s, several major changes dramatically affected the field of childhood psychopharmacology:

1. The introduction and gradual acceptance by 1980 of agreed on diagnostic criteria for psychiatric disorder (RDC and DSM-III).

2. An increasing number of child psychiatry research scientists sophisticated in the application of scientific methodology.

3. The development of a number of reliable assessment instruments.

4. An increasing knowledge about pharmacokinetics of psychoactive medications.

5. A growing attention to and concern about immediate and long-term adverse effects of medications.

6. A considerable broadening of the conditions considered responsive to medication and/or appropriate for drug trials, including depressive disorders, bipolar disorders, Tourette's syndrome, eating disorders, aggressive conduct disorders, and separation anxiety disorders (school phobia).

The 1980s into the 1990s built on the diagnostic and epidemiological data stimulated by DSM-III (1980) and DSM-III-R (1987) to explore further and expand the knowledge base on indications, contraindications, efficacy, pharmacokinetics and adverse effects of the various categories of drugs. Significant work occurred on efficacy and limitations of

stimulant medications alone, and tic and Tourette's disorders were identified as likely contraindications for the use of stimulants in treating
ADHD.

The dyskinetic side effects of neuroleptic use in children and adolescents were described and clarified. The use of psychoactive medications—neuroleptics, lithium, anticonvulsants, and benzodiazepines—in
controlling or modifying aggressive behaviors, anxiety disorders (especially obsessive-compulsive disorder and Tourette's disorder), and other
symptomatic behaviors continued to be actively explored and expanded.

The 1980s saw the introduction of a new category of antidepressants—the serotonin reuptake inhibitor group—with demonstrated efficacy and an advantageous side-effect profile in treating depressive
and some anxiety disorders in adults. The results from double-blind
placebo-controlled studies in children are still in process, although
these medications are being used clinically in treating depressive disorders and ADHD in children and adolescents. Likewise, controlled
studies are underway but not yet reported for the use of the newer generation of antipsychotic drugs—clozaril and resperidone—in childhood and adolescent psychotic disorders.

A reflection of the growing substance of the field of psychopharmacology in childhood and adolescent disorders is the presence of a journal
devoted exclusively to this topic—*The Journal of Childhood and Adolescent
Psychopharmacology*, which began quarterly publication in 1990. Another
is the increasing presence and sophistication of articles on psychopharmacology accepted for publication in the *Journal of the American Academy
of Child and Adolescent Psychiatry*, which increased to monthly publication
in 1995.

Finally, the publication of the fourth edition of the *Diagnostic and
Statistical Manual of Mental Disorders* (DSM-IV; APA, 1994) builds on the
remarkable advances stimulated by its predecessors (DSM-III, & DSM-
III-R) in providing more reliable and valid diagnostic classifications
and therefore more relevant and specific studies on the efficacies of
various treatments, on comparative efficacies, and especially on the efficacies of combined psychopharmacology and psychotherapy for various disorders.

The field of childhood psychopharmacology is actively exploring the
indications, contraindications, efficacy, pharmacokinetics, and adverse
effects of several groups of drugs: stimulants, antidepressants, the newer
antipsychotics, lithium, anticonvulsants (carbamazepine), and benzodiazepines.

Concurrently, studies are underway to refine the reliability and validity of diagnostic criteria, assessment instruments, dosage/plasma
level relationships, the genetics of childhood and adolescent disorders
and their continuity or discontinuity with adult conditions, and the comparative efficacy of different treatment approaches.

Taken together, these studies, often complementary and overlapping, represent a solid, vigorous, and exciting area for continued research.

REFERENCES

Abramowicz, M. (Ed.). (1990). Sudden death in children treated with a tricyclic antidepressant. *Medical Letter on Drugs and Therapeutics, 32,* 53.

Alderton, H. R., & Hoddinott, B. A. (1964). A controlled study of the use of thioridazine in the treatment of hyperactive and aggressive children in a children's psychiatric hospital. *Canad. Psych. J.,* 239–247.

Alessi, N., Naylor, M. W., Ghaziuddin, M., & Zubieta, J. D. (1994). Update on lithium carbonate therapy in children and adolescents. *Journal of the American Academy of Child and Adolescent Psychiatry 33,* 291–304.

Alexandris, A., & Lundell, F. W. (1968). Effect of thioridazine, amphetamine, and placebo on the hyperkinetic syndrome and cognitive area in mentally deficient children. *Canadian Medical Association Journal, 98,* 92–96.

Aman, M. G. (1980). Psychotropic drugs and learning problems, a selective review. *Journal of Learning Disabilities, 13*(2), 87–97.

Aman, M. G., & Werry, J. S. (1982). Methylphenidate and diazepam in severe reading retardation. *Journal of the American Academy of Child Psychiatry, 1,* 31–37.

Aman, M., Marks, R., et al. (1991). Methylphenidate and thioridazine in the treatment of intellectually subaverage children: Effects on cognitive-motor performance. *Journal of the American Academy of Child and Adolescent Psychiatry, 30,* 816–824.

Aman, M., Werry, J., et al. (1987). Effects of carbamazepine on psychomotor performance in children as a function of dose, fluctuations in concentration and diagnosis, *Epilepsia, 28,* 115–124.

Aman, M., Werry, J., et al. (1990). Effects of sodium valproate on psychomotor performance in children as a function of drug concentration seizure type, and time of medication, *Epilepsia, 31,* 51–60.

Ambrosini, P. J., Bianchi, M. D., Rabinovich, H., & Elia, J. (1993a). Antidepressant treatments in children and adolescents I. Affective disorders. *Journal of the American Academy of Child and Adolescent Psychiatry 32,* 1–6.

Ambrosini, P. J., Bianchi, M. D., Rabinovich, H., & Elia, J. (1993b). Antidepressant treatments in children and adolescents II. Anxiety, physical and behavioral. *Journal of the American Academy of Child and Adolescent Psychiatry 32,* 483–493.

American Academy of Child and Adolescent Psychiatry. (1991). Practice parameters for the assessment and treatment of attention deficit hyperactivity disorder. *Journal of the American Academy of Child and Adolescent Psychiatry, 30,* i–iii.

American Psychiatric Association. (1980). *Diagnostic and statistical manual of mental disorders* (3rd ed.). Washington, DC: Author.

American Psychiatric Association. (1987). *Diagnostic and statistical manual of mental disorders* (3rd ed., rev.). Washington, DC: Author

American Psychiatric Association. (1994). *Diagnostic and statistical manual of mental disorders* (4th ed.). Washington, DC: Author.

Anderson, L. T., Campbell, M., Grega, D. M., Perry, R., Small, A. M., & Green, W. H. (1984). Haloperidol in infantile autism: Effects on learning and behavioral symptoms. *American Journal of Psychiatry, 141,* 1195–1202.

Anderson, L. T., Campbell, M., et al. (1989). The effects of haloperidol on discrimination learning and behavioral symptoms in autistic children. *Journal of Autism and Developmental Disorders, 19,* 227–239.

Annell, A. L. (1969). Manic-depressive illness in children and effects of treatment with lithium carbonate. *Acta Paedopsychiatrica, 36,* 282–301.

Bair, H. V., & Herold, W. (1955). Efficacy of chlorpromazine in hyperactive mentally retarded children. *Archives of Neurology and Psychiatry, 74,* 363.

Barker, P., & Fraser, I. A. (1968). A controlled trial of haloperidol in children. *British Journal of Psychiatry, 114,* 855–857.

Barkley, R. A. (1977). A review of stimulant drug research with hyperactive children. *Journal of Child Psychology and Psychiatry, 18,* 137–166.

Barkley, R. A., & Cunningham, C. E. (1978). Do stimulant drugs improve the academic performance of hyperkinetic children? *Clinical Pediatrics, 17,* 85–92.

Barrickman, L., Noyes, R., Kuperman, S., Schumacher, E., & Verda, M. (1991). Treatment of ADHD with fluoxetine: A preliminary trial. *Journal of the American Academy of Child and Adolescent Psychiatry, 30,* 762–767.

Beaudry, P., & Gibson, D. (1960). Effect of trifluoperazine on the behavior disorders of children with malignant emotional disturbances. *American Journal of Mental Deficiency, 64,* 823.

Bender, L., & Cottington, F. (1942). The use of amphetamine sulfate (Benzedrine) in child psychiatry. *American Journal of Psychiatry, 99,* 116–121.

Bender, L., Faretra, F., & Cobrink, L. (1963). LDS and UML treatment of hospitalized disturbed children. *Recent Advances in Biological Psychiatry, 5,* 84–92.

Bender, L., Goldschmidt, L., & Siva Shanka, D. V. (1962). Treatment of autistic schizophrenic children with LSD-25 and UML-491. *Recent Advances in Biological Psychiatry, 4,* 170–177.

Bender, L., & Nichtern, S. (1956). Chemotherapy in child psychiatry. *New York State Journal of Medicine, 56,* 2791–2796.

Berg, I., Butler, A., Ellis, M., et al. (1993). Psychiatric aspect of children treated with carbamazepine, phenytoin or sodium valproate. A random trial. *Developmental Medicine and Child Neurology, 35,* 149–157.

Bernstein, G. A., Garfinkel, B., et al. (1990). Comparative studies of pharmacotherapy for school refusal. *Journal of the American Academy of Child and Adolescent Psychiatry, 29,* 773–781.

Biederman, J. (1987). Clonazepam in the treatment of prepubertal children with panic-like symptoms. *Journal of Clinical Psychiatry, 48*(Suppl.), 38–42.

Biederman, J. (1990). Diagnosis and treatment of adolescent anxiety disorders. *Journal of Clinical Psychiatry, 51*(May Suppl.), 20–26.

Biederman, J., Baldessarini, F. J., Wright, V., Knee, D., & Harmatz, J. S. (1989). A double-blind placebo-controlled study of desipramine in the treatment of ADD: I. Efficacy. *Journal of the American Academy of Child and Adolescent Psychiatry, 28,* 777–784.

Biederman, J., Baldessarini, R. J., Wright, V., Knee, D., Harmatz, J. S., & Goldblatt, A. (1989). A double-blind placebo-controlled study of desipramine in the treatment of ADD: II. Serum drug levels and cardiovascular findings. *Journal of the American Academy of Child and Adolescent Psychiatry, 28,* 903–911.

Biederman, J., Herzig, D. B., Rivinus, T., Haber, G., Feber, R., Rosenbaum, J., Harmatz, J. S., Tandorf, R., Orsulak, P., & Schildkraut, J. (1982, October). *Amitriptyline in the treatment of anorexia nervosa: A double blind placebo controlled study.* Paper presented at the annual meeting of the American Academy of Child Psychiatry, Washington, DC.

Bindelglass, P. M., Dec, G. H., & Enos, F. A. (1968). Medical and psychosocial factors in enuretic children treated with imipramine hydrochloride. *American Journal of Psychiatry, 124*(8), 1107–1112.

Birmaher, B., Baker, R., Kapur, S., et al. (1992). Clozapine for the treatment of adolescents with schizophrenia. *Journal of the American Academy of Child and Adolescent Psychiatry, 31,* 160–164.

Bodkin, J. (1990). Emerging uses for high potency benzodiazepines in psychotic disorders. *Journal of Clinical Psychiatry, 51*(Suppl. 5), 41–46.

Bond, W. S. A. (1991). Ethnicity and psychotropic drugs. *Clinical Pharmacy, 10,* 467–470.

Bradley, C. (1937). The behavior of children receiving Benzedrine. *American Journal of Psychiatry, 94,* 577–585.

Bradley, C. (1950). Benzedrine and dexedrine in the treatment of children's behavior disorders. *Pediatrics, 5,* 24–37.

Bradley, C., & Bowen, M. (1940). School performance of children receiving amphetamine (benzedrine) sulfate. *American Journal of Orthopsychiatry, 10,* 782–788.

Bradley, C., & Bowen, M. (1941). Amphetamine (benzedrine) therapy of children's behavior disorders. *American Journal of Orthopsychiatry, 11,* 92–103.

Bradley, C., & Green, E. (1940). Psychometric performance of children receiving amphetamine (benzedrine) sulfate. *American Journal of Psychiatry, 97,* 388–394.

Breger, E. (1961, October). Meprobamate in the management of enuresis. *Journal of Pediatrics,* 571–576.

Brown, D., Winsberg, B. G., Bialer, I., & Press, M. (1973). Imipramine therapy and seizures: Three children treated for hyperkinetic behavior disorders. *American Journal of Psychiatry, 130,* 210–212.

Brown, G. L., Ebert, M. H., Mikkelsen, E. J., & Hunt, R. D. (1980). Behavior and motor activity response in hyperactive children and plasma amphetamine levels following a sustained release preparation. *Journal of the American Academy of Child Psychiatry, 19,* 225–239.

Brown, R. T., & Sleator, E. K. (1979). Methylphenidate in hyperkinetic children: Differences in dose effect on impulsive behavior. *Pediatrics, 64,* 408–411.

Brown, W. T., & Soloman, C. I. (1942). Delinquency and the electroencephalogram. *American Journal of Psychiatry, 98,* 499–503.

Brumback, R. A., & Weinberg, W. A. (1977). Mania in childhood. *American Journal of Diseases in Children, 131,* 1122–1126.

Bruun, R. D. (1984). Gilles de la Tourette's syndrome: An overview of clinical experience. *Journal of the American Academy of Child Psychiatry, 23,* 126–133.

Bruun, R. D. (1988). Subtle and unrecognized side effects of neuroleptic treatment in children with Tourette's disorder. *American Journal of Psychiatry, 145,* 621–624.

Busch, F., Miller, F., et al. (1989). A comparison of two adjunctive treatments in acute mania. *Journal of Clinical Psychiatry, 50,* 453–455.

Campbell, M. (1975). Pharmacotherapy in early infantile autism. *Biological Psychiatry, 10*(4), 399–423.

Campbell, M., Adams P., Small, A. M., et al. (1988). Tardive and withdrawal dyskinesia in autistic children. A prospective study. *Psychopharmacology Bulletin, 24,* 251–255.

Campbell, M., Anderson, L. T., Meier, M., Cohen, I. L., Small, A. M., Sanit, C., & Sachar, E. J. (1978). A comparison of haloperidol and behavior therapy and their interaction in autistic children. *Journal of the American Academy of Child Psychiatry, 17,* 640–655.

Campbell, M., Cohen, I. L., & Small, A. M. (1982). Drugs in aggressive behavior. *Journal of the American Academy of Child Psychiatry, 21,* 107–117.

Campbell, M., Fish, B., David, R., Shapiro, T., Collins, P., & Koh, C. (1972). Response to triiodothyronine and dextroamphetamine: A study of preschool schizophrenic children. *Journal of Autism and Childhood Schizophrenia, 2,* 343–358.

Campbell, M., Fish, B., Korein, J., Shapiro, T., Collins, P., & Koh, C. (1972). Lithium and chlorpromazine: A controlled crossover study of hyperactive severely disturbed young children. *Journal of Autism and Childhood Schizophrenia, 2,* 234–263.

Campbell, M., Fish, B., Shapiro, T., & Floyd, A. (1970). Thiothixene in young disturbed children. *Archives of General Psychiatry, 23,* 70–72.

Campbell, M., Fish, B., Shapiro, T., & Floyd, A. (1971). Imipramine in preschool autistic and schizophrenic children. *Journal of Autism and Childhood Schizophrenia, 3,* 260–282.

Campbell, M., Fish, B., Shapiro, T., & Floyd, A. (1972). Acute responses of schizophrenic children to a sedative and a "stimulating" neuroleptic: A pharmacologic yardstick. *Current Therapy Research, 14,* 759.

Campbell, M., Gonzalez, N. M., & Silva, R. R. (1992). The pharmacologic treatment of conduct disorders and rage outbursts. *Psychiatric Clinics of North America, 15,* 69–85.

Campbell, M., Grega, D. N., Green, W. H., & Bennett, W. G. (1983). Neuroleptic induced dyskinesia in children. *Clinical Neuropharmacology, 6,* 207–222.

Campbell, M., Kafantaris, V., Malone, R. P., et al. (1991). Diagnostic and assessment issues related to pharmacotherapy for children and adolescents with autism. *Behavioral Modification, 15,* 326–354.

Campbell, M., Perry, R., & Green, W. H. (1984). Use of lithium in children and adolescents. *Psychosomatics, 25,* 95–106.

Campbell, M., Schulman, D., & Rapoport, J. L. (1978). The current status of lithium therapy in child and adolescent psychiatry. *Journal of the American Academy of Child Psychiatry, 17,* 717–720.

Campbell, M., Small, A. M., & Green, W. H. (1982). Lithium and haloperidol in hospitalized aggressive children. *Psychopharmacological Bulletin, 18,* 126–130.

Campbell, M., Small, A. M., Green, W. H., Jennings, S. J., Perry, R., Bennett, W. G., & Anderson, L. (1984). Behavioral efficacy of haloperidol and lithium carbonate. *Archives of General Psychiatry, 41,* 650–656.

Campbell, M., Small, A. M., Hollander, C. S., Korein, J., Cohen, I., Kalmijn, M., & Ferris, S. (1978). A controlled crossover study of triiodothyronine in autistic children. *Journal of Autism and Childhood Schizophrenia, 8*(4), 371–381.

Carlson, G. A., & Cantwell, D. P. (1979). A survey of depressive symptoms in a child and adolescent psychiatric population. *Journal of the American Academy of Child Psychiatry, 18,* 587–599.

Carlson, G. A., & Cantwell, D. P. (1980). Unmasking masked depression in children and adolescents. *American Journal of Psychiatry, 137,* 445–449.

Carlson, G. A., Rapport, M. D., Kelly, K. L., & Pataki, C. S. (1992). The effects of methylphenidate and lithium on attention and activity level. *Journal of the American Academy of Child and Adolescent Psychiatry, 31,* 262–270.

Carlson, G. A., & Strober, M. (1979). Affective disorders in adolescence. *Psychiatric Clinics of North America, 2*(3), 511–525.

Caroff, S., Mann, S., et al. (1991). Neuroleptic malignant syndrome: Diagnostic issues. *Psychiatric Annals, 21,* 130–147.

Carter, C. H., & Maley, M. C. (1957). Chlorpromazine therapy in children at the Florida Farm Colony. *American Journal of Medical Science, 233,* 131.

Claghorn, J. L. (1972). A double-blind comparison of haloperidol (Haldol) and thioridazine (Mellaril) in outpatient children. *Current Therapy and Research, 14,* 785–789.

Coffey, B. (1990). Anxiolytics for children and adolescents: Traditional and new drugs. *Journal of Child and Adolescent Psychopharmacology, 1,* 57–83.

Cohen, I. L., Campbell, M., Posner, B. A., Small, A. M., Triebel, D., & Anderson, L. T. (1980). Behavioral effects of haloperidol in young autistic children. *Journal of the American Academy of Child Psychiatry, 19,* 655–677.

Cohen, D., Detlor, J., Young, J. G., & Shaywity, B. A. (1980). Clonidine ameliorates Gilles de la Tourette Syndrome. *Archives of General Psychiatry, 37,* 1350–1357.

Cohen, N. J., Douglas, C. I., Weiss, G., & Minde, K. K. (1971). Attention in hyperactive children and the effect of methylphenidate. *Journal of Child Psychology and Psychiatry, 12,* 129–139.

Conners, C. K. (1969). The teacher rating scale for use in drug studies with children. *American Journal of Psychiatry, 126,* 884–888.

Conners, C. K. (1970). Symptom patterns in hyperkinetic neurotic and normal children. *Child Development, 41,* 667–682.

Conners, C. K. (1972). Psychological effects of stimulant drugs in children with minimal brain dysfunction. *Pediatrics, 49,* 702–708.

Conners, C. K., & Eisenberg, L. (1963). The effect of methylphenidate on symptomatology and learning in disturbed children. *American Journal of Psychiatry, 120,* 458–463.

Conners, C. K., Eisenberg, L., & Barcai, A. (1967). Effect of dextroamphetamine on children. *Archives of General Psychiatry, 17,* 478–485.

Conners, C. K., Rothchild, G., Eisenberg, L., Schwartz, L. S., & Robinson, E. (1969). Dextroamphetamine sulfate in children with learning disorders. *Archives of General Psychiatry, 21,* 182–190.

Conners, C. K., & Taylor, E. (1980). Pemoline, methylphenidate and placebo in children with minimal brain dysfunction. *Archives of General Psychiatry, 37,* 922–930.

Connor, D. (1993). Beta blockers for aggression: A review of the pediatric experience. *Journal of Child and Adolescent Psychopharmacology, 3,* 99–114.

Cowdry, R. W., & Gardner, D. L. (1988). Pharmacotherapy of borderline personality disorder: Alprazolam, carbamazepine, trifluoperazine and tranylcypromine. *Archives of General Psychiatry, 45,* 111–119.

Cunningham, M. A., Pillai, V., & Rogers, W. J. B. (1968). Haloperidol in the treatment of children with severe behavior disorders. *British Journal of Psychology, 114,* 845–854.

Cutts, K. K., & Jasper, H. H. (1939). Effect of benzedrine sulfate and phenobarbital on behavior problem children with abnormal electroencephalograms. *Archives of Neurology and Psychiatry, 41,* 1138–1145.

Cytryn, L., Gilbert, A., & Eisenberg, L. (1960). The effectiveness of tranquilizing drugs plus supportive psychotherapy in treating behavior disorder of children: A double-blind study of eighty outpatients. *American Journal of Orthopsychiatry, 30,* 113–129.

Cytryn, L., McKnew, D. H., Jr., & Bunney, W. E., Jr., (1980). Diagnosis of depression in children: A reassessment. *American Journal of Psychiatry, 137,* 22–25.

Delay, J., & Deniker, P. (1952, July). *Reactions biologiques observees au cours du traitement par le chlorthydrate de dimethylaminopropyl-N-chlorophenothiazine (4560 r.p.),* Congres des psychiatres de langue francaise, Luxembourg.

Delay, J., Dendiker, P., & Harl, J. M. (1952). Traitement des etats d'excitation et d'agitation par une methode medicamenteuse derivee de l'hibernotherapie. *Annales Medico-Psychologiques, 110,* 267–273.

Delong, G. R., & Aldershof, A. L. (1987). Long-term experience with lithium treatment in childhood: Correlation with clinical diagnosis. *Journal of the American Academy of Child and Adolescent Psychiatry, 26,* 389–394.

Denhoff, E., & Holden, R. H. (1955). The effectiveness of chlorpromomazine (Thorazine) with cerebral palsied children. *Journal of Pediatrics, 47,* 328–332.

DeVeaugh-Geiss, J., Moroz, G., Biederman, J., Cantwell, D., Fontaine, R., Greist, J. H., Reichler, R., Katz, R., & Landau, P. (1992). Clomipramine hydrochloride in childhood and adolescent obsessive-compulsive disorder—a multi-center trial. *Journal of the American Academy of Child and Adolescent Psychiatry 31,* 45–49.

DiMascio, A. (1970). Classification and overview of psychotropic drugs. In A. DiMascio & R. I. Shader (Eds.), *Clinical handbook of psychopharmacology* (pp. 3–15). New York: Aronson.

Domizio, S., & Verrotti, A. (1993). Antiepileptic treatment and behavioral disturbances in children. *Children Nervous System, 9,* 272–274.

Dostal, T., & Zvolsky, P. (1970). Antiaggressive effects of lithium salts in severely mentally retarded adolescents. *International Pharmacopsychiatry, 5,* 203–207.

Dulcan, M. K. (1990). Using psychostimulants to treat behavioral disorders in children and adolescents. *Journal of Child and Adolescent Psychopharmacology, 1,* 7–20.

Dundee, J. W. (1954). A review of chlorpromazine hydrochloride. *British Journal of Anaesthesia, 26,* 357–379.

Dupont, R. L., & Saylor, K. E. (1992). Depressant substances in adolescent medicine. *Pediatric Review, 13,* 381–386.

Effron, A. S., & Freedman, A. M. (1953). The treatment of behavior disorders in children with Benadryl: A preliminary report. *Journal of Pediatrics, 42,* 261.

Eisenberg, L., Gilbert, A., Cytryn, L., & Molling, P. A. (1961). The effectiveness of psychotherapy alone and in conjunction with perphenazine or placebo in the treatment of neurotic and hyperkinetic children. *American Journal of Psychiatry, 117,* 1088–1093.

Eisenberg, L., Lackman, R., Molling, P. A., Lockner, A., Mizelle, J. D., & Conners, C. K. (1963). A psychopharmacologic experiment in a training school for delinquent boys: Methods, problems, findings. *Journal of Orthopsychiatry, 33,* 431–447.

Engelhardt, D. M., & Polizos, P. (1978). Adverse effects of pharmacotherapy in childhood psychosis. In M. A. Lipton, A. Di Mascio, & K. F. Killam (Eds.), *Psychopharmacology: A generation of progress.* New York: Raven.

Engelhardt, D. M., Polizos, P., Waizer, J., & Hoffman, S. P. (1973). A double-blind comparison of fluphenazine and haloperidol in outpatient schizophrenic children. *Journal of Autistic and Child Schizophrenia, 3,* 128–237.

Erickson, W. D., Yellin, A. M., Hopwood, J. H., et al. (1984). The effects of neuroleptics on attention in adolescent schizophrenics. *Biological Psychiatry, 19,* 745–753.

Ernst, M., Gonzalez, N. M., & Campbell, M. (1993). Acute dystonic reaction with low-dose pimozide. *Journal of the American Academy of Child and Adolescent Psychiatry, 32,* 640–642.

Ernst, M., Magee, H. J., Campbell, M., et al. (1992). Pimozide in autistic children. *Psychopharmacology Bulletin, 28,* 187–191.

Evans, R. W., & Gualtieri, C. T. (1987). Carbamazepine in pediatric psychiatry. *Journal of the American Academy of Child and Adolescent Psychiatry, 26,* 2–8.

Evans, R. W., Gualtieri, C. T., et al. (1985). Carbamazepine: A neuropsychological and psychiatric profile. *Clinical Neuropharmacology, 8,* 221–241.

Eveloff, H. H. (1966). Psychopharmacologic agents in child psychiatry. *Archives of General Psychiatry, 14,* 472–481.

Faigel, H. (1991). The effect of Beta blockade on stress-induced cognitive dysfunction in adolescents. *Clinical Pediatrics, 30*(7), 441–445.

Famularo, R., Kinscherff, R., & Fenton, T. (1988). Propranolol treatment for childhood post-traumatic stress disorder, acute type. A pilot study. *American Journal of Diseases of Children, 142,* 1244–1247.

Faretra, G., Dooher, L., & Dowling, J. (1970). Comparison of haloperidol and fluphenazine in disturbed children. *American Journal of Psychiatry, 126,* 1670–1673.

Firestone, P., Davey, J., Goodman, J. T., & Peters, S. (1978). The effects of caffeine and methylphenidate on hyperactive children. *Journal of the American Academy of Child Psychiatry, 17,* 445–456.

Firestone, P., Kelly, M. J., Goodman, J. T., & Davey, J. (1980). Differential effects of parent training and stimulant medication. *Journal of the American Academy of Child Psychiatry, 20,* 135–147.

Fish, B. (1960a). Drug therapy in child psychiatry: Pharmacological aspects. *Comprehensive Psychiatry, 1,* 212–227.

Fish, B. (1960b). Drug therapy in child psychiatry: Psychological aspects. *Comprehensive Psychiatry, 1,* 55–61.

Fish, B., Campbell, M., Shapiro, T., & Floyd, A. (1969). Comparison of trifluperidol, trifluoperazine, and chlorpromazine in preschool, schizophrenic children: The value of less sedative antipsychotic agents. *Current Therapeutic Research, 11,* 589–595.

Fish, B., & Shapiro, T. (1965). A typology of children's psychiatric disorders. Its application to a controlled evaluation of treatment. *Journal of the American Academy of Child Psychiatry, 4,* 32–52.

Fish, B., Shapiro, T., & Campbell, M. (1966). Long term prognosis and the response of schizophrenic children to drug therapy: A controlled study of trifluoperazine. *American Journal of Psychiatry, 123,* 32–39.

Fisher, K. C., & Wilson, W. P. (1971). Methylphenidate and the hyperkinetic state. *Diseases of the Nervous System,* 695–698.

Flaherty, J. A. (1955). Effect of chlorpromazine medication on children with severe emotional disturbance. *Delaware State Medical Journal, 27,* 180–184.

Foster, P. (1967). Treatment of childhood depression. *Newton Wellsley Medical Bulletin, 19,* 33–36.

Frankhauser, M. P., Karumanchi, V. C., German, M. L., et al. (1992). A double-blind, placebo-controlled study of the efficacy of transdermal clonidine in autism. *Journal of Clinical Psychiatry, 53,* 77–82.

Frazier, J., Gordon, C. T., et al. (1994). An open trial of clozapine in 11 adolescents with childhood-onset schizophrenia. *Journal of the American Academy of Child and Adolescent Psychiatry, 33,* 658–663.

Freed, H., & Peifer, C. A. (1956). Treatment of hyperkinetic emotionally disturbed children with prolonged administration of chlorpromazine. *American Journal of Psychiatry, 113,* 22–26.

Freedman, A. M. (1958). Drug therapy in behavior disorders. *Pediatric Clinics of North America, 5,* 573–594.

Freedman, A. M., Effron, A. S., & Bender, L. (1955). Pharmacotherapy in children with psychiatric illness. *Journal of Nervous and Medical Diseases, 122,* 479–486.

Freedman, A. M., Kremer, M. W., Robertiello, R. C., & Effron, A. S. (1955). The treatment of behavior disorders in children with tolserol. *Journal of Pediatrics, 47,* 369–372.

Fritz, G. D., Rockney, R. M., & Yeung, A. S. (1994). Plasma levels and efficacy of imipramine treatment for enuresis. *Journal of the American Academy of Child and Adolescent Psychiatry, 33,* 60–64.

Frommer, E. A. (1967). Treatment of childhood depression with antidepressant drugs. *British Medical Journal, 1,* 729–732.

Frommer, E. A. (1972). Indications for antidepressant treatment with special reference to depressed preschool children. In A. L. Annell (Ed.), *Depressive states in childhood and adolescence.* Stockholm: Almquist & Wiksell.

Gadow, K. D. (1981). Effects of stimulant drugs on attention and cognitive deficits. *Exceptional Education Quarterly, 2*(3), 83–93.

Gadow, K. D. (1983). Effects of stimulant drugs on academic performance in hyperactive and learning disabled children. *Journal of Learning Disabilities, 16,* 290–300.

Gadow, K. D., Sverd, J., & Nolan, E. E. (1992). Methylphenidate in hyperactive boys with comorbid tic disorder: II. Short term behavioral effects in school settings. *Journal of the American Academy of Child and Adolescent Psychiatry, 31,* 462–471.

Garfield, S. L., Helper, M. M., Wilcott, R. C., & Murrly, R. (1962). Effects of chlorpromazine on behavior in emotionally disturbed children. *Journal of Nervous Mental Diseases, 135,* 147–154.

Gatski, R. L. (1955). Chlorpromazine in the treatment of emotionally maladjusted children. *Journal of the American Medical Association, 157,* 1298–1300.

Geller, B., Coopec, T. B., Graham, D. L., Marsteller, F. A., & Bryant, D. M. (1990). Double-blind placebo-controlled study of nortriptyline in depressed adolescents using a "fixed plasma level" design. *Psychopharmacology Bulletin, 26,* 85–90.

Gillberg C. (1991). The treatment of epilepsy in autism. *Journal of Autism and Developmental Disorders, 21,* 61–77.

Gittelman, R. (1980a). Diagnosis and drug treatment of childhood disorders. In D. F. Klein et al. (Eds.), *Diagnosis and drug treatment of psychiatric disorders: Adults and children* (2nd ed., pp. 590–776). Baltimore: Williams & Wilkins.

Gittelman, R. (1980b). Indications for the use of stimulant treatment in learning disorders. *Journal of the American Academy of Child Psychiatry, 19,* 623–636.

Gittelman-Klein, R. (1977). Definitional and methodological issues concerning depressive illness in children. In J. G. Schulterbrandt & A. Raskin (Eds.), *Depression in childhood: Diagnosis, treatment, and conceptual models.* New York: Raven.

Gittelman-Klein, R., Abikoff, H., Pollack, E., Klein, D., Katz, S., & Mattes, J. (1980). A controlled trial of behavior modification and methylphenidate in hyperactive children. In C. Whalen & B. Henker (Eds.), *Hyperactive children: The social ecology of identification and treatment.* New York: Academic.

Gittelman-Klein, R., & Klein, D. F. (1970). Controlled imipramine treatment of school phobia. *Archives of General Psychiatry, 25,* 204–207.

Gittelman-Klein, R., Klein, D. F., Katz, S., Saraf, K., & Pollack, E. (1976). Comparative effects of methylphenidate and thioridazine in hyperkinetic children. *Archives of General Psychiatry, 33,* 1217–1231.

Gittelman-Klein, R., Landa, B., Mattes, J. A., & Klein, D. F. (1988). Methylphenidate and growth in hyperactive children: A controlled withdrawal study. *Archives of General Psychiatry, 45,* 1127–1130.

Gittelman-Klein, R., & Mannuzza, S. (1988). Hyperactive boys almost grown up. III. Methylphenidate effects on ultimate height. *Archives of General Psychiatry, 45,* 1131–1134.

Gordon, D. A., Forehand, R., & Picklesimer, D. K. (1978). The effects of dextroamphetamine on hyperactive children using multiple outcome measures. *Journal of Clinical Child Psychology, 7,* 125–128.

Goetzl, U., & Berkowitz, B. (1977). Lithium carbonate in the management of hyperactive aggressive behavior of the mentally retarded. *Comprehensive Psychiatry, 18,* 599–606.

Graae, F. (1990). High anxiety in children. *Journal of Clinical Psychiatry, 51*(Suppl. 18-9), 50–53.

Graae, F., & Milner, J. (1994). Clonazepam in childhood anxiety disorders. *Journal of the American Academy of Child and Adolescent Psychiatry, 33,* 372–376.

Gram, L. F., & Rafaelsen, O. J. (1972). Lithium treatment of psychotic children and adolescents. *Acta Psychiatrica Scandinavica, 48*(3), 253–260.

Greenberg, L. M., Deens, M. A., & McMahon, A. (1972). Effects of dextroamphetamine, chlorpromazine, and bydroxyzine on behavior and performance in hyperactive children. *American Journal of Psychiatry, 129,* 532–539.

Greenberg, L. M., Yellin, A., Spring, C., & Metcalf, M. (1975). Clinical effect of imipramine and methylphenidate in hyperactive children. In R. Gittelman-Klein (Ed.), *Recent advances in child psychopharmacology.* New York: Human Science Press.

Greenfield, D., Conrad, C., et al. (1987). Treatment of catatonia with low dose lorazepam. *American Journal of Psychiatry, 144,* 1224–1225.

Greenhill, L. L. (1992). Pharmacotherapy: Stimulants. In G. Weiss (Ed.), *Attention deficit hyperactivity disorder. Child and Adolescent Psychiatric Clinics of North America, 1,* 411–447.

Greenhill, L. L., Rieder, R. O., Wender, P. H., Bucksbaum, M., & Zahn, T. P. (1973). Lithium carbonate in the treatment of hyperactive children. *Archives of General Psychiatry, 28,* 636–640.

Greenhill, L. L., & Setterberg, S. (1993) Pharmacotherapy of disorders of adolescents. *Psychiatric Clinics of North America, 16,* 793–814.

Gross, M. D. (1976). Growth of hyperkinetic children taking methylphenidate, dextroamphetamine or imipramine/desipramine. *Pediatrics, 58,* 423.

Gross, M. D., & Wilson, W. C. (1964). Behavior disorders of children with cerebral dysrhythmia. *Archives of General Psychiatry, 11,* 610–619.

Gualtieri, C. T., Barnhill, J., et al. (1980). Tardive kyskinesia and other movement disorders in children treated with psychotropic drugs. *Journal of the American Academy of Child and Adolescent Psychiatry, 19,* 491–510.

Gualtieri, C. T., & Hawk, B. (1980). Tardive dyskinesia and other drug-induced movement disorders among handicapped children and youth. *Applied Research in Mental Retardation, 1,* 55–69.

Gualtieri, C. T., Quade, D., Hicks, R. E., et al. (1984). Tardive dyskinesia and other clinical consequences of neuroleptic treatment in children and adolescent. *American Journal of Psychiatry, 141,* 20–23.

Gualtieri, C. T., Schroeder, S. R., Hicks, R. E., & Quade, D. (1986). Tardive kyskinesia in young mentally retarded individuals. *Archives of General Psychiatry, 43,* 335–340.

Gualtieri, C. T., Wargin, W., Kanoy, R., Patrick, K., Shen, C., Youngblood, W., Mueller, R., & Breese, G. (1982). Clinical studies of methylphenidate serum levels in children and adults. *Journal of the American Academy of Child Psychiatry, 21,* 19–26.

Halliday, R., Gnanck, K., Rosenthal, J. R., McKibben, J. L., & Callaway, E. (1980). The effect of methylphenidate dosage on school and home behaviors of the hyperactive child. In R. M. Knight & D. J. Bakker (Eds.), *Treatment of learning disabilities.* Baltimore: University Park Press.

Hart, R. G., & Easton, J. D. (1982). Carbamazepine and hematologic monitoring. *Annals of Neurology, 11,* 309–312.

Hayward, C., Killen, J., et al. (1989). Panic attacks in young adolescents. *American Journal of Psychiatry, 146,* 1061–1062.

Hechtman, L., & Weiss, G. (1986). Controlled perspective fifteen year follow-up of hyperactives as adults: Non-medical drug and alcohol use and anti-social behavior. *Canadian Journal of Psychiatry, 31,* 557–567.

Heninger, G. R., Charney, D. S., & Sternberg, D. E. (1983). Lithium carbonate augmentation of antidepressant treatment. *Archives of General Psychiatry, 40,* 1336–1342.

Heuyer, G., Dell, C., & Prinquet, G. (1956). Emploi de la chlorpromazine en neuropsychiatric infantile. *Encephale, 45,* 576–578.

Heuyer, G., Gerard, G., & Galibert, J. (1953). Traitement de l'exitation psychometrics chez l'enfant pare (13456 r.p.). *Archives Francaises de pediatrie, 9,* 961.

Himmelback, J. M., & Garfinkel, M. E. (1986). Mixed mania: Diagnosis and treatment. *Psychopharmacological Bulletin, 22,* 603–620.

Horn, W. F., Islongo, N. S., Pascoe, J. M., et. al. (1991). Additive effects of psychostimulants, parent training, and self-control therapy with ADHD children. *Journal of the American Academy of Child and Adolescent Psychiatry, 30,* 233–240.

Horowitz, H. A. (1977). Lithium and the treatment of adolescent manic-depressive illness. *Diseases of the Nervous System, 37,* 90–92.

Huestis, R. D., Arnold, L. E., & Smeltzer, D. J. (1975). Caffeine versus methylphenidate and D-amphetamine in minimal brain dysfunction: A double-blind comparison. *American Journal of Psychiatry, 132,* 868–870.

Hunt, B. R., Frank, T., & Krush, T. P. (1956). Chlorpromazine in the treatment of severe emotional disorders of childhood. *Journal of the Diseases of Children, 9,* 268–277.

Hunt, R. D. (1987). Treatment effects of oral and transdermal clonidine in relation to methylphenidate: An open pilot study in ADD-H. *Psychopharmacology Bulletin, 23,* 111–114.

Hunt, R. D., Capper, L., et al. (1990). Clonidine in child and adolescent psychiatry. *Journal of Child and Adolescent Psychopharmacology, 1,* 87–102.

Hunt, R. D., Cohen, D. J., Shaywitz, D. E., & Shaywitz, B. A. (1982). Strategies for study of neurochemistry of attention deficit disorder in children. *Schizophrenia Bulletin, 8*, 236–252.

Hunt, R. D., Minderaa, R., & Cohen, D. J. (1985). Clonidine benefits children with attention deficit disorder and hyperactivity: Report of a double-blind placebo-crossover therapeutic trial. *Journal of the American Academy of Child and Adolescent Psychiatry, 24*, 617–629.

Hunt, R. D., Minderaa, R., & Cohen, D. J. (1986). The therapeutic effect of clonidine in attention deficit disorder with hyperactivity: A comparison with placebo and methylphenidate. *Psychopharmacology Bulletin, 22*, 229–236.

Jacobsen, L., Walker, M., et al. (1994). Clozapine in the treatment of a young adolescent with schizophrenia. *Journal of the American Academy of Child and adolescent Psychiatry, 33*, 645–650.

Jacobvitz, D., Scrouge, L. A., Stewart, M., & Leffert, N. (1990). Treatment of attentional and hyperactivity problems in children with sympathomimetic drugs: A comprehensive review. *Journal of the American Academy of Child and Adolescent Psychiatry, 29*, 677–688.

Jaffe, S. L. (1991). Intranasal use of prescribed methylphenidate by an alcohol and drug abusing adolescent with ADHD. *Journal of the American Academy of Child and Adolescent Psychiatry, 30*, 773–775.

Jaselskis, C. A., Cook, E. H., Fletcher, K. E., et al. (1992). Clonidine treatment of hyperactive and impulsive children with autistic disorder. *Journal of Clinical Psychopharmacology, 12*, 322–327.

Joffe, R. T., Post, R. M., et al. (1985). Hematological effects of carbamazepine in patients with affective illness. *American Journal of Psychiatry, 142*, 1196–1199.

Johnson, J. A. (1993). Racial differences in lymphocyte beta-receptor sensitivity to propranolol. *Life Sciences, 53*, 297–304.

Joshi, P. T., Capozzoli, J. A., & Coyle, J. T. (1988). Low dose neuroleptic therapy for children with childhood onset pervasive developmental disorder. *American Journal of Psychiatry, 145*, 335–338.

Joshi, P. T., Capozzoli, J. A., & Coyle, J. T. (1991). Neuroleptic malignant syndrome: Life-threatening complication of neuroleptic treatment in adolescents with affective disorder. *Pediatrics, 87*, 235–239.

Kafantaris, V., Campbell, M., Small, A. M., et al. (1992). Carbamazepine in hospitalized aggressive conduct disorder children: An open study. *Psychopharmacology Bulletin, 28*, 193–199.

Kalow, W. (1982). Ethnic differences in drug metabolism. *Clinical Pharmacokinetics, 7*, 373–400.

Kanner, L. (1935). *Child psychiatry* (p. 133). Springfield: Charles C. Thomas.

Kanner, L. (1957). *Child psychiatry* (2nd ed.). Springfield: Charles C. Thomas.

Kaplan, S. L., Busner, J., Kupiety, S., et al. (1990). Effects of methylphenidate on adolescents with aggressive conduct disorder and ADHD: A preliminary report. *Journal of the American Academy of Child and Adolescent Psychiatry, 29*, 719–723.

Kastner, T., Burlingham, K., et al. (1990). Metoprolol for aggressive behavior in persons with mental retardation. *American Family Physician, 42*, 1585–1588.

Kastner, T., Finesmith, R., et al. (1993). Long-term administration of valproic acid in the treatment of affective symptoms in people with mental retardation. *Journal of Clinical Psychopharmacology, 13*, 448–451.

Kastner, T., & Friedman, D. (1992). Verapamil and valproic acid treatment of prolonged mania. *Journal of the American Academy of Child and Adolescent Psychiatry, 31,* 271–275.

Kastner, T., Friedman, D. L., Plummer, A. T., et al. (1990). Valproic acid for the treatment of children with mental retardation and mood symptomatology. *Pediatrics, 86,* 467–472.

Kelly, J. T., Koch, M., & Buegel, D. (1976). Lithium carbonate in juvenile manic-depressive illness. *Diseases of the Nervous System, 37,* 90–92.

Kemph, J., DeVane, L., et al. (1993). Treatment of aggressive children with clonidine: Results of an open study. *Journal of the American Academy of Child and Adolescent Psychiatry, 32,* 577–581.

Klein, R. (1990). Thioridazine effects on the cognitive performance of children with attention deficit hyperactivity disorder. *Journal of Child and Adolescent Psychopharmacology, 1,* 263–270.

Klein, E., Bental, E., et al. (1984). Carbamazepine and haloperidol vs. placebo and haloperidol in excited psychoses. *Archives of General Psychiatry, 41,* 165–170.

Klein, R., Koplewicz, H. S., & Kanner, A. (1992). Imipramine treatment of children with separation anxiety disorder. *Journal of the American Academy of Child and Adolescent Psychiatry, 31,* 21–28.

Knobel, M. (1962). Psychopharmacology for the hyperkinetic child. *Archives of General Psychiatry, 6,* 30–34.

Kraft, I. A., Ardali, C., Duffy, J., Hart, J., & Pearce, P. R. (1966). Use of amitriptyline in childhood behavior disturbances. *International Journal of Neuropsychiatry, 2,* 611–614.

Kraft, I. A., Marcus, I. M., Wilson, W., Swander, D. V., Rumage, N. W., & Schulhoffer, E. (1959). Methodological problems in studying the effect of tranquilizers in children with specific reference to meprobamate. *Southern Medical Journal, 52,* 179–185.

Krakowski, A. J. (1965). Amitriptyline in treatment of hyperkinetic children: A double-blind study. *Psychosomatics, 6,* 355–360.

Kuhn, V., & Kuhn, R. (1972). Drug therapy for depression in children. Indications and methods. In A. L. Annell (Eds.), *Depressive states in childhood and adolescents.* Stockholm: Almquist & Wiksell.

Kurtis, L. B. (1966). Clinical study of the response to nortriptyline on autistic children. *International Journal of Neuropsychiatry, 2,* 298–301.

Kutcher, S., Boulos, C., Ward, B., Marton, P., Simeon, J., Ferguson, H. B., Szalai, J., Katic, M., Roberts, N., Dubois, C., & Reed, K. (1994). Response to desipramine treatment in adolescent depression; a fixed dose, placebo controlled trial. *Journal of the American Academy of Child and Adolescent Psychiatry, 33,* 686–694.

Kutcher, S., & Marton, P. (1989) Parameters of adolescent depression. *Psychiatric Clinics of North America, 12,* 895–918.

Kydd, R. R., & Werry, J. S. (1982). Schizophrenia in children under 16 years. *Journal of Autism and Development Disorders, 12*(4), 343–356.

Lacey, J. H., & Crisp, A. H. (1980). Hunger, food intake and weight: The impact of clomipramine on a refeeding anorexia nervosa population. *Postgraduate Medical Journal, 56*(Suppl. 1), 79–85.

Lang, C., & Remington, D. (1994). Treatment with propranolol of severe self injurious behavior in a blind, deaf, retarded adolescent. *Journal of the American Academy of Child and Adolescent Psychiatry, 33,* 265–269.

Lapierre, Y. D., & Roval, K. J. (1989). Pharmacotherapy of affective disorders in children and adolescents. *Psychiatric Clinics of North America, 12,* 951–961.

Latz, S., & McCracken, J. (1992). Neuroleptic malignant syndrome in children and adolescents: Two case reports and a warning. *Journal of Child and Adolescent Psychopharmacology, 2,* 123–129.

Laufer, M., Denhoff, E., & Solomons, G. (1957). Hyperkinetic impulse disorder in children's behavior problems. *Psychosomatic Medicine, 19,* 38–49.

La Veck, G. D., De La Crug, F., & Simundson, E. (1960). Fluphenazine in the treatment of mentally retarded children with behavior disorders. *Diseases of the Nervous System, 23,* 82–85.

Lawson, W. B. (1986). Racial and ethnic factors in psychiatric research. *Hospital and Community Psychiatry, 37*(1), 50–54.

Leckman, F. F., Cohen, D. J., & Detlor, J. (1982). Clonidine in the treatment of Tourette syndrome: A review of the data. In A. J. Friedhoff & T. N. Chase (Eds.), *Gilles de la Tourette Syndrome.* New York: Raven.

Lehmann, H. E., & Hanrahan, G. E. (1954). Chlorpromazine, new inhibiting agent for psychomotor excitement and manic states. *Archives of Psychiatry and Neurology, 71,* 227–237.

Leonard, H., Topol, D., et al. (1994). Clonazepam as an augmenting agent in the treatment of childhood-onset obsessive-compulsive disorder. *Journal of the American Academy of Child and Adolescent Psychiatry, 33,* 792–794.

Leonard, H. L., Rapoport, J. L. (1989). Pharmacotherapy of childhood obsessive compulsive disorder. *Psychiatric Clinics of North America, 12,* 963–970.

Lerer, R. J., Lerer, M. P., & Artner, J. (1977). The effects of methylphenidate on the handwriting of children with minimal brain dysfunction. *Journal of Pediatrics, 91,* 127–132.

Le Vann, L. J. (1961). Thioridazine, a psychosedative virtually free of side-effects. *Alberta Medical Bulletin.*

Le Vann, L. J. (1969). Haloperidol in the treatment of behavioral disorders in children and adolescents. *Canadian Psychiatric Association Journal, 14,* 217–220.

Lin, K. M., & Finder, E. (1983). Neuroleptic dosage for Asians. *American Journal of Psychiatry, 140*(4), 409–491.

Lin, K. M., Poland, R. E., & Nakasaki, G. (1993). Introduction: Psychopharmacology, psychobiology, and ethnicity. In K. M. Lin, R. Poland, & G. Nakasaki (Eds.), *Psychopharmacology and psychobiology of ethnicity.* Washington, DC: American Psychiatric Press.

Lin, K. M., Poland, R. E., Nuccio, I., et al. (1989). A longitudinal assessment of haloperidol doses and serum concentrations in Asian and Caucasian schizophrenic patients. *American Journal of Psychiatry, 146*(10), 1307–1311.

Lindsley, D. B., & Henry, C. E. (1942). The effects of drugs on behavior and the electroencephalograms of children with behavior disorders. *Psychosomatic Medicine, 4,* 140–149.

Linet, L. (1984). Tourette syndrome, pimozide and school phobia: The neuroleptic separation anxiety syndrome. *American Journal of Psychiatry, 142,* 613–615.

Lipinski, J. F., Jr., Zubenko, G. S., & Cohen, B. M. (1984). Propranolol in the treatment of neuroleptic-induced akathisia. *American Journal of Psychiatry, 141,* 412–415.

Lipman, R. S. (1973). NIMH-PRB support of research in minimal brain dysfunction and other disorders of childhood. *Psychopharmacology Bulletin* [Special issue]. Pharmacotherapy of children. (pp. 1–8) (DHEW Publication No. HSM 73–9002).

Litchfield, H. R. (1957). Clinical evaluation of meprobamate in disturbed and prepsychotic children. *Annals of the New York Academy of Science, 67,* 828–832.

Locascio, J. J., Malone, R. P., Campbell, M., et al. (1991). Factors related with haloperidol responses and dyskinesias in autistic children. *Psychopharmacology Bulletin, 27,* 119–126.

Looker, A., & Conners, C. K. (1970). Diphenylhydantoin in children with severe temper tantrums. *Archives of General Psychiatry, 23,* 80–89.

Lowe, T. L., Cohen, D. J., Detlor, J., Kremenitzer, M. W., & Shaywitz, B. A. (1982). Stimulant medications precipitate Tourette's syndrome. *Journal of the American Medical Association, 247,* 1729–1731.

Lucas, A. P., Lockett, H. J., & Grimm, F. (1965). Amitriptyline in childhood depression. *Diseases of the Nervous System, 28,* 105–113.

MacLean, R. E. G. (1960). Imipramine hydrochloride (Tofranil) and enuresis. *American Journal of Psychiatry, 117,* 551.

Malmquist, C. P. (1971). Depressions in childhood and adolescence. *New England Journal of Medicine, 284,* 887–893.

Mandoki, M. (1993). Clozapine for adolescents with psychosis: Literature review and two case reports. *Journal of Child and Adolescent Psychopharmacology, 3,* 213–221.

Mandoki, M., Summer, G., et al. (1992). Evaluation and treatment of rage in children and adolescents. *Child Psychiatry and Human Development, 22,* 227–235.

Maoris, F., Maoris, G., Rachel, M. G., & Biggio, G. (1987). Paradoxical reactions elicited by diazepam in children with classic autism. *Functional Neurology, 2,* 355–361.

Marder, S. (1992). Risperidone: Clinical development: North American results. *Clinical Neuropharmacology, 15*(Suppl.), 92A–93A.

Marneros, A., & Jagger, A. (1993). Treatment of catatonic stupor with oral orazepam in a 14-year-old psychotic boy. *Pharmacopsychiatry, 26,* 259–260.

Mattes, J., & Gittelman-Klein, R. (1983). Growth of hyperactive children on a maintenance regimen of methylphenidate. *Archives of General Psychiatry, 40,* 317–321.

Mattson, R. H., & Calverley, J. R. (1968). Dexrtroamphetamine sulfate induced dyskinesias. *Journal of the American Medical Association, 205,* 400–402.

McAndrew, J. B., Case, Q., & Treffert, D. (1972). Effects of prolonged phenothiazine intake on psychotic and other hospitalized children. *Journal of Autistic and Child Schizophrenia, 2,* 75.

McElroy, S., Pope, H., et al. (1992). Clinical and research implications of the diagnosis of dysphoric or mixed mania or hypomania. *American Journal of Psychiatry, 149,* 1633–1644.

McKnew, D. H., Jr., & Cytryn, L. (1979). Urinary metabolites in chronically depressed children. *Journal of the American Academy of Psychiatry, 18,* 608–615.

McKnew, D. H., Jr., Cytryn, L., Buschbaum, M. S., Hamovit, J., Lamour, M., Rapoport, J. L., & Gershon, E. S. (1981). Lithium in children of lithium-responding parents. *Psychiatry Research, 4,* 171–180.

Melbach, R. C., Dunner, D., Wilson, L. G., et al. (1987). Comparative efficacy of propanolol, chloriazepoxide and placebo in the treatment of anxiety: A double-blind trial. *Journal of Clinical Psychiatry, 48,* 355–358.

Merritt, H. H., & Putnam, T. J. (1938). Sodium diphenylhydantoinate in treatment of convulsive disorders. *Journal of the American Medical Association, 111,* 1068–1073.

Merry, S., Werry, S., et al. (1985). The neuroleptic malignant syndrome in an adolescent. *Journal of the American Academy of Child and Adolescent Psychiatry, 25,* 284–286.

Meyerson, A. (1936). Effect of benzedrine sulfate on mood and fatigue in normal neurotic persons. *Archives of Neurology and Psychiatry, 36,* 816–822.

Meyerson, A., Lomar, J., & Dameshek, W. (1936). Physiological effects of benzedrine and its relationship to other drugs affecting the autonomic nervous system. *American Journal of Medical Science, 192,* 560–574.

Mikkelsen, E. J. (1982). Efficacy of neuroleptic medication in pervasive development disorders of childhood. *Schizophrenic Bulletin, 8*(2), 320–332.

Mikkelsen, E. J., Detlor, J., & Cohen, D. J. (1981). School avoidance and social phobia triggered by haloperidol in patients with Tourette's disorder. *American Journal of Psychiatry, 138,* 1572–1576.

Mikkelson, E. J., Rapoport, J., Nee, L., Grunenau, C., Mendelson, W., & Gillin, J. C. (1980). Childhood enuresis I. Sleep patterns and psychopathology. *Archives of General Psychiatry, 37,* 1139–1144.

Miksztal, M. W. (1956). Chlorpromazine (Thorazine) and reserpine in residential treatment of neuropsychiatric disorders in children. *Journal of Nervous and Mental Disease, 123,* 477–479.

Millichap, J. G. (1973). Drugs in management of minimal brain dysfunction. *Annals of the New York Academy of Science, 205,* 321–334.

Millichap, J. G., Aymat, F., Sturgis, L. H., Larsen, K. W., & Egan, R. A. (1968). Hyperkinetic behavior and learning disorders III. Battery of neuropsychological tests in controlled trial of methlphenidate. *American Journal of the Diseases of Children, 166,* 235–244.

Mills, I. H. (1976). Amitriptyline therapy in anorexia nervosa (letter). *Lancet, 2,* 687.

Mitchell, W. G., Zhou, Y., et al. (1993). Effects of antiepileptic drugs on reaction time, attention and impulsivity in children. *Pediatrics, 91,* 101–105.

Molitch, M., & Eccles, A. K. (1937). The effect of benzedrine sulfate on the intelligence scores of children. *American Journal of Psychiatry, 94,* 587–590.

Molitch, M., & Poliakoff, S. (1937). The effect of benzedrine sulfate on enuresis. *Archives of Pediatrics, 54,* 499–501.

Molitch, M., & Sullivan, J. P. (1937). The effect of benzedrine sulfate on children taking the new Stanford Achievement Test. *American Journal of Orthopsychiatry, 7,* 519–522.

Moreau, D., Weissman, M., et al. (1989). Panic disorder in children at high risk for depression. *American Journal of Psychiatry, 146,* 1059–1060.

Morselli, P. L., Bianchertti, G., Durand, G., Le Huzey, M. F., Zarifian, E., & Dugas, M. (1979). Haloperidol plasma level monitoring in pediatric patients. *Therapeutic Drug Monitoring, 1,* 35–46.

Mozes, T., Toren, P., Chernauzan, N., et al. (1994). Clozapine treatment in very early onset schizophrenia. *Journal of the American Academy of Child and Adolescent Psychiatry, 33,* 65–70.

Munster, A. J., Stanley, A. M., & Saunders, J. C. (1961). Imipramine (Tofranil) in the treatment of enuresis. *American Journal of Psychiatry, 118,* 76–77.

Needleman, H. L., & Waber, D. (1977). The use of amitriptyline in anorexia nervosa. In R. Vigersky (Ed.), *Anorexia nervosa* (pp. 341–348). New York: Raven.

Ney, P. G. (1967). Psychosis in a child associated with amphetamine administration. *Canadian Medical Association Journal, 97,* 1026–1029.

Oettinger, L., Jr. (1962). Chlorprothixene in the management of problem children. *Diseases of the Nervous System* (October), 568–571.

Oettinger, L., Jr., & Simonds, R. (1962). The use of thioridazine in the office management of children's behavior disorders. *Medical Times, 90,* 596–604.

Page, J. G., Janicki, R. S., Bernstein, J. E., Curran, C. F., & Michelli, F. A. (1974). Pemoline in the treatment of childhood hyperkinesis. *Journal of Learning Disorders, 7,* 498–503.

Papatheodorou, B., & Kutchee, S. P. (1993). Divalproex sodium treatment in late adolescents and young adults acute mania. *Psychopharmacology Bulletin, 29,* 213–219.

Pasamanick, B. (1951). Anticonvulsant drug therapy of behavior problem with abnormal electroencephalograms. *Archives of Neurology and Psychiatry, 65,* 752–766.

Pelham, W. (1986). The effects of psychostimulant drugs on learning and academic achievement in children with attention deficit disorders and learning disabilities. In J. Torgesen & B. Wong (Eds.), *Psychological and educational perspectives on learning disabilities* (pp. 259–295). New York: Academic Press.

Pellock, J. M. (1987). Carbamazepine side effects in children and adolescents. *Epilepsia, 28*(Suppl. 3), 64–70.

Perel, J., Greenhill, L. L., Curran, S., et al. (1990). Correlates of pharmacokinetics and attentional measures in methylphenidate treated hyperactive children. *Journal of Clinical Pharmacology, 49,* 160–161.

Perry, R., Campbell, M., et al. (1989). Long term efficacy of haloperidol in autistic children: Continuous vs. discontinuous drug administration. *Journal of the Academy of Child and Adolescent Psychiatry, 28,* 187–192.

Petti, T. A., & Campbell, M. (1975). Imipramine and seizures. *American Journal of Psychiatry, 132,* 538–540.

Petti, T. A., & Law, W., III. (1982). Imipramine treatment of depressed children: A double-blind pilot study. *Journal of Clinical Psychopharmacology, 2*(2), 107–110.

Pfefferbaum, B., Overall, J., et al. (1987). Alprazolam in the treatment of anticipatory and acute situational anxiety in children with cancer. *Journal of the American Academy of Child and Adolescent Psychiatry, 26,* 532–535.

Platt, J. E., Campbell, M., Green, W. H., et al. (1981). Effects of lithium carbonate and haloperidol on cognition in aggressive hospitalized school-age children. *Journal of Clinical Psychopharmacology, 1,* 8–13.

Platt, J. E., Campbell, M., Green, W. H., et al. (1984). Cognitive effects of lithium carbonate and haloperidol in treatment-resistant aggressive children. *Archives of General Psychiatry, 41,* 657–662.

Pliazka, S. R. (1989). Effect of anxiety on cognition, behavior and stimulant response in ADHD. *Journal of the American Academy of Child and Adolescent Psychiatry, 28,* 882–887.

Polizos, P., Engelhardt, D. M., Hoffman, S. P., & Waizer, J. (1973). Neurological consequences of psychotropic drug withdrawal in schizophrenic children. *Journal of Autism and Childhood Schizophrenia, 3,* 247.

Porrino, L. J., Rapoport, J. L., Behan, D., Scevy, W., Ismond, D. R., & Bunney, W. E. (1983). A naturalistic assessment of the motor activity of hyperactive boys. *Archives of General Psychiatry, 40,* 681–687.

Post, R. M., (1988). Time course of clinical effects of carbamazepine: Implication for mechanism of action. *Journal of Clinical Psychiatry, 49*(Suppl.), 35–46.

Post, R. M. (1992). Transduction of psychosocial stress into the neurobiology of recurrent affective disorder. *American Journal of Psychiatry, 149,* 999–1010.

Poussaint, A. F., & Ditman, K. S. (1965). A controlled study of imipramine (Tofranil) in the treatment of childhood enuresis. *Journal of Pediatrics, 67,* 283–290.

Poznanski, E. O., Carroll, B. J., Banegas, M. C., et al. (1982). The dexamethasone suppression test in prepubertal depressed children. *American Journal of Psychiatry, 139,* 321–324.

Preskorn, S. H., Weller, E. B., Hughes, C. W., et al. (1987). Depression in prepubertal children: Dexamethasone nonsuppression predicts differential response to imipramine vs. placebo. *Psychopharmacology Bulletin, 23,* 128–133.

Price, K. O. (1991). Ethnicity and clozapine-induced agranulocytosis. *Clinical Pharmacy, 10,* 743–744.

Psychopharmacology Bulletin. (1973). Pharmacotherapy of children [Special issue]. (NIMH, DHEW Publication No. HSM 73–9002).

Puig-Antich, J. (1980). Affective disorders in childhood. *Psychiatric Clinics of North America, 3,* 403–424.

Puig-Antich, J., Blau, S., Marx, N., Greenhill, L. L., & Chambers, W. J. (1978). Prepubertal major depressive disorder. A pilot study. *Journal of the American Academy of Child Psychiatry, 17,* 695–707.

Puig-Antich, J., Perel, J. M., Lupatkin, W. M., et al. (1987). Imipramine in prepubertal major depressive disorders. *Archives of General Psychiatry 46,* 406–420.

Puig-Antich, J., Perel, J. M., Lupatkin, W. J., Shea, C., Tabrizi, M. A., & Stiller, R. (1979). Plasma levels of imipramine (IMI) and desmethylimipramine (DMI) and clinical response in prepubertal major depressive disorder. A preliminary report. *Journal of the American Academy of Child Psychiatry, 18,* 616–627.

Puig-Antich, J., Tabrizi, M. A., Davies, M., Goetz, R., Chambers, W. J., Halapern, F., & Sachar, E. J. (1981). Prepubertal endogenous major depressive hyposecrete growth hormone in response to insulin-induced hypoglycemia. *Biological Psychiatry, 16,* 801–807.

Quinn, P., & Rapoport, J. L. (1975). One year follow-up of hyperactive boys treated with imipramine or methylphenidate. *American Journal of Psychiatry, 132,* 241–245.

Rapoport, J. (1965). Childhood behavior and learning problems treated with imipramine. *International Journal of Neuropsychiatry, 1,* 635–642.

Rapoport, J. L., Buchsbaum, M. S., Zahn, T. P., Weingartner, H., Ludlow, C., & Mirkkelser, E. L. (1978). Dextroamphetamine: Cognitive and behavioral effects in normal prepubertal boys. *Science, 199,* 560–562.

Rapoport, J., Mikkelson, E. J., Zavadil, A., Nee, L., Gruenau, C., Mendelson, W., & Gillin, J. C. (1980). Childhood enuresis II. *Archives of General Psychiatry, 37,* 1146–1152.

Rapoport, J. L., Quinn, P. O., Bradbard, G., Riddle, D., & Brooks, E. (1974). Imipramine and methylphenidate treatments of hyperactive boys. *Archives of General Psychiatry, 30,* 789–793.

Realmuto, G. M., Erickson, W. D., Yellin, A. M., Hopwood, J. H., & Greenberg, L. M. (1984). Clinical comparison of thiotixene and thioridazine in schizophrenic adolescents. *American Journal of Psychiatry, 141,* 440–442.

Remschmidt, H. (1976). The psychotropic effect of carbamazepine in non-epileptic patients with particular reference to problems posed by clinical studies in children with behavior disorders. In W. Birkmayer (Ed.), *Epileptic seizures-behavior-pain* (pp. 253–258). Baltimore: University Park Press.

Remschmidt, H., Schultz, E., et al. (1994). An open trial of clozapine in thirty-six adolescents with schizophrenia. *Journal of Child and Adolescent Psychopharmacology, 4,* 31–41.

Rettig, J. H. (1955). Chlorpromazine for the control of psychomotor excitement in the mentally deficient. *Journal of Nervous and Mental Disease, 122,* 190.

Riddle, M. A. (1991). Pharmacokinetics in children and adolescents. In M. Lewis (Ed.), *Child and adolescent psychiatry: A comprehensive textbook.* Baltimore, MD: Williams & Wilkins.

Riddle, M. A., Geller, B., & Ryan, N. (1993). Another sudden death in a child treated with desipramine. *Journal of the American Academy of Child and Adolescent Psychiatry, 32,* 792–797.

Riddle, M. A., Scahill, L., King, R., et al. (1992). Double-blind crossover trial of fluoxetine and placebo in children and adolescents with obsessive compulsive disorder. *Journal of the American Academy of Child and Adolescent Psychiatry, 31,* 1062–1070.

Robertson, P. L., Garofalo, E. A., et al. (1993). Carbamazepine-induced tics. *Epilepsia, 34,* 965–968.

Rogers, W. J. B. (1965). Use of haloperidol in children's psychiatric disorders. *Clinical Trials Journal, 2,* 162–164.

Rosenblum, S., Buoniconto, P., & Graham, B. D. (1960). "Campazine" vs. placebo: A controlled study with educable, emotionally disturbed children. *American Journal of Mental Deficiency, 64,* 713.

Rudorfer, M. V. (1993). Pharmacokinetics of psychotropic drugs in special populations. *Journal of Clinical Psychiatry, 54*(Suppl. 9), 50–54.

Ryan, N. D. (1990). Heterocyclic antidepressants in children and adolescents. *Journal of Child and Adolescent Psychopharmacology, 26,* 85–90.

Ryan, N. D., Puig-Antich, J., Cooper, T., et al. (1986). Imipramine in adolescent major depression: Plasma level and clinical response. *Acta Psychiatra Scandanavia, 73,* 275–288.

Sabotka, J. C., Alexander, B., & Cook, B. C. (1990). A review of carbamazepine's hematologic reactions and monitoring recommendations. *DICP Annals of Pharmacotherapy, 24,* 1214–1219.

Safer, D., Allen, R., & Barr, E. (1972). Depression of growth in hyperactive children on stimulant drugs. *New England Journal of Medicine, 287,* 217–220.

Safer, D. J., & Kroger, J. M. (1988). A survey of medication treatment for hyperactive/inattentive students, *Journal of the American Medical Association, 260,* 2256–2258.

Salam, S., Kilzieh, N., et al. (1988). Lorazepam for psychogenic catatonia: An update. *Journal of Clinical Psychiatry, 49*(Suppl. 12), 16–21.

Salam, S., Pillai, A., et al. (1987). Lorazepam for psychogenic catatonia. *American Journal of Psychiatry, 144,* 1082–1083.

Saletu, B., Simeon, J., Saletu, M., Itil, T. M., & DaSilva, J. (1974). Behavioral and visual evoked potential investigations during trihexyphenidyl and thiothixene treatment in psychotic boys. *Biological Psychiatry, 8,* 177–189.

Salgado, M. A., & Kierdel-Vegas, O. (1963). Treatment of enuresis with imipramine. *American Journal of Psychiatry*, 119–990.

Sallee, F. R., Pollock, B. G., Stiller, R. L., et al. (1987). Pharmacokinetics of pimozide in adults and children with Tourette's syndrome. *Journal of Clinical Pharmacology, 27*, 776–781.

Sandman, C. (1990). The opiate hypothesis in autism and self-injury. *Journal of Child and Adolescent Psychopharmacology, 1*, 237–248.

Saraf, K., Klein, D., Gittelman-Klein, R., & Groff, S. (1974). Imipramine side effects in children. *Psychopharmacologia, 37*, 265–274.

Sargant, W., & Blackburn, J. M. (1936). The effect of benzedrine on intelligence scores. *Lancet*, December 12, 1385–1387.

Satterfield, J. B., Satterfield, B. T., & Cantwell, D. P. (1981). Three years multimodality treatment study of 100 hyperactive boys. *Journal of Pediatrics, 98*, 650–655.

Satterfield, J. B., Satterfield, B. T., & Schell, A. M. (1987). Therapeutic interventions to prevent delinquency in hyperactive boys. *Journal of the American Academy of Child and Adolescent Psychiatry, 26*, 56–64.

Schachar, R., Taylor, E., Wieselberg, M., et al. (1987). Changes in family function and relationships in children who respond to methylpenidate. *Journal of the American Academy of Child and Adolescent Psychiatry, 26*, 728–732.

Schain, R. J., & Reynard, C. L. (1975). Observations on effects of a central stimulant drug (methylphenidate) in children with hyperactive behavior. *Pediatrics, 55*, 709–716.

Seignot, J. J. N. (1961). A case of the syndrome of tics of Gilles de la Tourette controlled by R1625. *Annales Medico-psychologiques, 1961*, 119, 578–579.

Shaffer, D., Costello, A. J., & Hill, I. D. (1968). Control of enuresis with imipramine. *Archives of Diseases in Children, 43*, 665–671.

Shapiro, A. K., & Shapiro, E. (1981). Do stimulants provoke, cause or exacerbate tics or Tourette's syndrome. *Comprehensive Psychiatry, 22*, 265–273.

Shapiro, A. K., & Shapiro, E. (1982). *Clinical efficacy of haloperidol, pimozide, fenfluridol, and clonidin in the treatment of Tourette syndrome*. New York: Raven.

Shapiro, A. K., & Shapiro, E. (1984). Controlled study of pimozide vs. placebo in Tourette's syndrome. *Journal of the American Academy of Child and Adolescent Psychiatry, 23*, 161–173.

Shapiro, E., Shapiro, A. K., et al. (1989). Controlled study of haloperidol, pimozide and placebo for the treatment of Gilles de la Tourette's syndrome. *Archives of General Psychiatry, 46*, 722–730.

Shapiro, A. K., Shapiro, E., & Wayne, H. (1973). Treatment of Tourette's syndrome. *Archives of General Psychiatry, 28*, 92–97.

Shaw, C. R., Lockett, H. J., Lucas, A. R., Lamontagne, C. H., & Crimm, F. (1963). Tranquilizer drugs in the treatment of emotionally disturbed children: I. Inpatients in a residential treatment center. *Journal of the American Academy of Child Psychiatry, 2*, 725–742.

Sheard, M. H., Marini, J. L., & Bindger, C. I. (1976). The effect of lithium on impulsive aggressive behavior in man. *American Journal of Psychiatry, 133*, 1409–1413.

Sherwin, A. C., Flach, F. F., & Stokes, P. E. (1958). Treatment of psychosis in early childhood with triiodothyronine. *American Journal of Psychiatry, 115*, 166–167.

Siefen, G., & Reinschmidt, H. (1986). Results of the treatment with clozapine in schizophrenic children. *Kinder Jungenpsychiatry, 14*, 245–257.

Silver, A. A. (1955). Management of children with schizophrenia. *American Journal of Psychotherapy, 9,* 196.

Silver, L. B. (1981). The relationship between learning disabilities, hyperactivity, distractibility and behavior problems, a clinical analysis. *Journal of the American Academy of Child Psychiatry, 20,* 385–397.

Simeon, J., Ferguson, H., et al. (1992). Clinical, cognitive and neurophysiological effects of alprazolam in children and adolescents with overanxious and avoidant disorders. *Journal of the American Academy of Child and Adolescent Psychiatry, 31,* 29–33.

Simeon, J. G., & Ferguson, H. B. (1987). Alprazolam effects in children with anxiety disorders. *Canadian Journal of Psychiatry, 32,* 570–574.

Simeon, J. G., & Knott, V. S. (1992). Pharmacotherapy of childhood anxiety disorders. *Clinica Neuropharmacologica, 15*(Suppl. 1, Pt. A), 229–300.

Simmons, J. Q., III, Leiken, S. J., Lovaas, O. I., Schaeffer, B., & Perioff, B. (1966). Modification of autistic behavior with LSK-25. *American Journal of Psychiatry, 122,* 1201–1211.

Sloman, L. (1991). Use of medication in pervasive developmental disorders. *Psychiatric Clinics of North America, 14,* 165–183.

Sprague, R. L., & Sleator, E. K. (1977). Methylphenidate in hyperkinetic children: Differences in dose effects on learning and social behavior. *Science, 198,* 1274–1276.

Steingard, R., Biederman, J., et al. (1994). Comparison of clonidine response in the treatment of attention deficit hyperactivity disorder with and without comorbid tic disorders. *Journal of the American Academy of Child and Adolescent Psychiatry, 32*(2), 350–353.

Steingard, R. J., Goldberg, M., Lee, D., et al. (1994). Adjunctive clonazepam treatment of tic symptoms in children with co-morbid tic disorders and ADHD. *Journal of the American Academy of Child and Adolescent Psychiatry, 33,* 394–399.

Steingard, R., Khan, A., et al. (1992). Neuroleptic malignant syndrome: Review of experience with children and adolescents. *Journal of Child and Adolescent Psychopharmacology, 3,* 183–198.

Stores, G. (1978). School children with epilepsy at risk for learning and behavior problems. *Developmental Medicine and Child Neurology, 20,* 302–308.

Strickland, T. L., Lawson, W., Lin, M. K., et al. (1993). Interethnic variation in response to lithium therapy among African-American and Asian-American populations. In K. M. Lin, R. Poland, & G. Nakasaki (Eds.), *Psychopharmacology and psychobiology of ethnicity.* Washington, DC: American Psychiatric Press.

Strickland, T. L., Vijay, R., Lin, M. K., et al. (1991). Psychopharmacologic considerations in the treatment of Black American populations. *Psychopharmacology Bulletin, 27*(94), 441–448.

Strober, M., Freeman, R., & Rigali, J. (1990). The pharmacotherapy of depressive illness in adolescence: An open trial of imipramine. *Psychopharmacology Bulletin, 26,* 80–84.

Strober, M., Freeman, R., Rigali, J., Schmidt, S., & Diamond, R. (1992). The pharmacotherapy of depressive illness in adolescence: II. Effects of lithium augmentation in nonresponders to imipramine. *Psychopharmacology Bulletin, 31,* 16–20.

Strober, M., Morrell, W., Lampect, C., & Burroughs, J. (1990). Relapse following discontinuation of lithium maintenance therapy in adolescents with bipolar illness: A naturalistic study. *American Journal of Psychiatry, 147,* 457–461.

Swanson, J., Kinsbourne, M., Roberts, W., & Zucker, K. (1978). Dose response analysis of the effect of stimulant medication on the learning ability of children referred for hyperactivity. *Pediatrics, 61,* 21–29.

Sykes, D. H., Doyles, V. I., Weiss, G., & Minde, K. K. (1971). Attention in hyperactive children and the effect of methylphenidate. *Journal of Child Psychology and Psychiatry, 12,* 129–139.

Szatmari, P. (1992). The epidemiology of attention deficit hyperactivity disorders. *Child and Adolescent Psychiatric Clinics of North America, 1,* 361–371.

Tarjan, G., Lowery, V. E., & Wright, S. W. (1957). Use of chlorpromazine in two hundred seventy-eight mentally deficient patients. *American Journal of Diseases of Children, 94,* 294–300.

Towbin, K., Dykens, E., et al. (1994). Clozapine for early developmental delays with childhood-onset schizophrenia: Protocol and 15-month outcome. *Journal of the American Academy of Child and Adolescent Psychiatry, 33,* 651–657.

Trimble, M. (1990a). Anticonvulsants in children and adolescents. *Journal of Child and Adolescent Psychopharmacology, 1,* 107–124.

Trimble, M. (1990b). Antiepileptic drugs, cognitive function and behavior in children: Evidence from recent studies. *Epilepsia, 31*(Suppl.), S30–S34.

Ucer, E., & Kreger, D. C., (1969). A double-blind study comparing haloperidol and thioridazine in emotionally disturbed, mentally retarded children. *Current Therapeutic Research, 11,* 278–283.

Varanka, T. M., Weller, R. A., Weller, E. B., & Fristad, M. A. (1988). Lithium treatment of manic episodes with psychotic features in prepubertal children. *American Journal of Psychiatry 145,* 1557–1559.

Vining, E. P. G., Mellits, E. D., et al. (1987). Psychological and behavioral effects of anticonvulsants in children: A double-blind comparison of phenobarbital and valproate. *Pediatrics, 30,* 165–174.

Vitiello, B., Behar, D., et al. (1990). Diagnosis of panic disorder in prepubertal children. *Journal of the American Academy of Child and Adolescent Psychiatry, 29,* 782–784.

Waizer, J., Hoffman, S. P., Polizos, P., & Engelhardt, D. M. (1974). Outpatient treatment of hyperactive school children with imipramine. *American Journal of Psychiatry, 131,* 587–591.

Waizer, J., Polizos, P., Hoffman, S. P., Engelhardt, D. M., & Margolis, R. A. (1972). A singleblind evaluation of thiothixene with outpatient schizophrenic children. *Journal of Autism and Childhood Schizophrenia, 2,* 378–386.

Walker, C. F., & Kirkpatrick, B. B. (1947). Dilantin treatment for behavior problem children with abnormal electroencephalograms. *American Journal of Psychiatry, 103,* 484–492.

Wallis, C. (1994, July 18). Life in Overdrive. *Time,* pp. 43–50.

Weinberg, W. A., Rutman, J., & Sullivan, L. (1973). Depression in children referred to an educational diagnostic center: Diagnosis and treatment. *Journal of Pediatrics, 83,* 1065–1072.

Weingartner, H., Langer, D., Gria, J., & Rapoport, J. L. (1982). Acquisition and retrieval of information in amphetamine-treated hyperactive children. *Psychiatry Research 6,* 21–26.

Weiss, G., Werry, J., Minde, K., Douglas, V., & Sykes, K. (1968). Studies on the hyperactive child V: The effects of dextroamphetamine and chlorpromazine on behavior and intellectual functioning. *Journal of Child Psychology and Psychiatry, 9,* 145–156.

Weller, E. B., Preskorn, S. H., Weller, R. A., & Croskell, M. (1983). Childhood depression: Imipramine levels and response. *Psychopharmacology Bulletin, 19*(1), 59–62.

Weller, E. B., Weller, R. A., & Tucker, S. G. (1986). Mania in prepubertal children; has it been underdiagnosed? *Journal of Affective Disorders, 11,* 151–154.

Wells, B., Cold, J., et al. (1991). A placebo-controlled trial of nadolol in the treatment of neuroleptic induced akathisia. *Journal of Clinical Psychiatry, 52,* 255–260.

Wender, P. H. (1971). *Minimal brain dysfunction in children.* New York: Wiley.

Wender, P. H. (1987). *The hyperactive child, adolescent, and adult: Attention deficit disorder through the life span.* New York: Wiley.

Werry, J. S. (1993). Long-term drug use in psychiatric disorders in children. Facts, controversies and the future. *Acta Paedopsychiatrica, 56,* 113–118.

Werry, J. S., Weiss, G., Douglas, V., & Martin, J. (1966). Studies on the hyperactive child III: The effect of chlorpromazine upon behavior and learning ability. *Journal of the American Academy of Child Psychiatry, 5,* 292–312.

Whalen, C. K., Henker, B., Buhrmester, D., Hinshaw, S. P., Huber, A., & Loski, K. (1989). Does stimulant medication improve the peer status of hyperactive children? *Journal of Consulting Clinical Psychology, 57,* 545–549.

White, J. H., & Schnaulty, N. L. (1977). Successful treatment of anorexia nervosa with imipramine. *Diseases of the Nervous System, 38,* 567–568.

Wilens, T., Biederman, J., et al. (1994). Clonidine for sleep disturbances associated with attention deficit hyperactivity disorder. *Journal of the American Academy of Child Psychiatry, 33*(3), 424–426.

Williams, D., Mehl, R., et al. (1982). The effect of propranolol on uncontrolled rage outbursts in children and adolescents with organic brain dysfunction. *Journal of the American Academy of Child Psychiatry, 21,* 129–135.

Winchell, R., & Stanley, M. (1991). Self-injurious behavior: Our view of the behavior and biology of self-mutilation. *American Journal of Psychiatry, 148,* 306–317.

Winsberg, B. G., Beater, I., Kupietz, S., & Tobias, J. (1972). Effects of imipramine and dextroamphetamine on behavior of neuropsychiatrically impaired children. *American Journal of Psychiatry, 128,* 1425–1431.

Winsberg, B. G., Goldstein, S., Yepes, L. E., & Perel, J. M. (1975). Imipramine and electrocardiographic abnormalities in hyperactive children. *American Journal of Psychiatry, 132,* 542–545.

Wolf, D., & Wagner, K., (1993). Tardive dyskinesia, tardive dystonia and tardive Tourette's syndrome in children and adolescents. *Journal of Child and Adolescent Psychopharmacology, 3,* 175–198.

Wolpert, A., Hagamen, M. B., & Merlis, S. (1966). A pilot study of thiothixene in childhood schizophrenia. *Current Therapeutic Research, 8,* 617–620.

Wolpert, A., Hagamen, M. B., & Merlis, S. (1967). A comparative study of thiothixene and trifluoperazine in childhood schizophrenia. *Current Therapeutic Research, 9,* 482–485.

Wolpert, A., Quintos, A., White, L., & Merlis, S. (1968). Thiothixene and chlorprothixene in behavior disorder. *Current Therapeutic Research, 10,* 566–569.

Yepes, L., Balka, B., Winsberg, B., & Bialer, I. (1977). Amitriptyline and methylphenidate treatment of behaviorally disordered children. *Journal of Child Psychology and Psychiatry, 18,* 39–52.

Youngerman, J., & Canino, I. A. (1978). Lithium carbonate use in children and adolescents. *Archives of General Psychiatry, 35,* 216–224.

Zier, A. (1959). Meprobamate (Miltown) as an aid to psychotherapy in an outpatient child guidance clinic. *American Journal of Orthopsychiatry, 29,* 377–382.

Zhou, H. H., Adedoyin, A., & Wilkinson, G.R. (1990). Differences in plasma binding of drugs between Caucasians and Chinese subjects. *Clinical Pharmacology and Therapeutics, 48*(1), 10–17.

Zimmerman, F. T., & Burgemeister, B. B. (1958). Action of methylphenidate (Ritalin) and reserpine in behavior disorders in children and adults. *American Journal of Psychiatry, 115,* 323–328.

A Review of DSM-IV Categories

JERRY M. WIENER, M.D.

In each clinical chapter of this book, the diagnostic criteria used throughout are from the *Diagnostic and Statistical Manual of Mental Disorders,* Fourth Edition DSM-IV; (American Psychiatric Association [APA], 1994). As in the two previous editions (DSM-III and DSM-III-R), relevant disorders in DSM-IV are listed in two ways: some under Disorders Usually First Diagnosed in Infancy, Childhood or Adolescence (pp. 13–14, 37–122), and others in the following sections applicable to all age groups and using the same diagnostic criteria as for adults (e.g., as in affective, schizophrenic, and anxiety disorders).

The section on Childhood and Adolescent Disorders was developed by 1 of 13 Task Forces and was led by Drs. David Shaffer and Magda Campbell along with 14 other senior clinicians and researchers representing a wide range of backgrounds and interests, including international perspectives. In addition, the reviews and reports of the Task Force involved participation and consultation with a much larger number of advisers from the field, chosen to represent a broad diversity.

The intent from the beginning was to base DSM-IV on empirical evidence to the maximum extent possible (see DSM-IV, pp. XV–XXV), and to reflect and benefit from the research-based advances in diagnosis largely stimulated by DSM-III (APA, 1980) and DSM-III-R (APA, 1987). To this end, a systematic and explicit process was developed to construct and document anew each category and diagnosis. This process then included the following staged approach:

1. A systematic and comprehensive literature review of each diagnostic question or topic.

2. Analysis and reanalysis of previous and new data sets.

3. Extensive field trials at more than 70 sites involving diverse and representative populations that tested the proposals and changes for clinical usefulness.

What follows is a systematic listing, with some annotation, of changes made in DSM-IV from DSM-III-R in the categories of "First Diagnosed in Infancy, Childhood or Adolescence" and in a few other areas of special relevance for childhood and adolescent onset (see Tables 2.1 and 2.2).

I. The overarching category of "Developmental Disorders" coded on Axis II is dropped.

II. *Mental Retardation* remains essentially the same with some modifications for compatibility with the American Association of Mental Retardation and continues to be coded on Axis II (along with Personality Disorders).

Table 2.1.   *Disorders New to DSM-IV*

Rett's Disorder

Childhood Disintegrative Disorder

Asperger's Disorder

Feeding Disorder of Infancy or Early Childhood

Delirium due to Multiple Etiologies

Catatonic Disorder due to a General Medical Condition

Bipolar II Disorder

Acute Stress Disorder

Sexual Dysfunction due to a General Medical Condition

Substance-Induced Sexual Dysfunction

Narcolepsy

Breathing-Related Sleep Disorder

From DSM-IV, p. 789.

III.   *Pervasive Developmental Disorders* (PDD), *Learning Disorders* (LD, formerly Academic Skills Disorders), *Motor Skills Disorder,* and *Communication Disorders* (formerly Language and Speech Disorders) all are now coded on *Axis I,* rather than on Axis II as was the case in DSM-III-R.

    A.   Pervasive Developmental Disorders (PDD) in DSM-III-R included Autistic Disorder and PDD Not Otherwise Specified (NOS). PDD in DSM-IV now includes:

        1.   Autistic Disorder.

        2.   Rett's Disorder—a syndrome with onset after a period of normal development, associated with severe

Table 2.2.   *DSM-III Disorders Deleted or Subsumed in DSM-IV*

Cluttering

Overanxious Disorder of Childhood

Avoidant Disorder of Childhood

Undifferentiated Attention-Deficit Disorder

Identity Disorder

Transsexualism

Idiosyncratic Alcohol Intoxication

Passive-Aggressive Personality Disorder

From DSM-IV, p. 789.

mental retardation and progressive loss of function (DSM-IV, pp. 71–73).

3. Childhood Disintegrative Disorder—a syndrome of marked regression and loss of function following at least 2 years of apparently normal functioning, also termed "Heller's syndrome" and "infantile dementia" (DSM-IV, pp. 73–75).

4. Asperger's Disorder—a syndrome very similar to Autism but differing in the absence of any clinically significant delay in development of language, communication, cognitive skills, or age-appropriate self-help and adaptive skills (DSM-IV, pp. 75–77).

5. PDD NOS.

B. Learning Disorders now includes, in order, Reading Disorder (previously Developmental Reading Disorder), Mathematics Disorder (previously Developmental Arithmetic Disorder), and Disorders of Written Expression (previously Developmental Expressive Writing Disorder), and LDNOS. The diagnostic criteria remain essentially the same; the terminology is simplified, and the exclusion criteria have been modified to allow for the presence of a neurological condition.

C. Motor Skills Disorders is essentially unchanged.

D. Communication Disorders now includes the previous two DSM-III-R categories of Language and Speech Disorders and Speech Disorders not Elsewhere Classified.

1. Expressive Language Disorders (previously Developmental Expressive Language Disorders).

2. Mixed Receptive—Expressive Language Disorder (replacing Developmental Receptive Language Disorder).

3. Phonological Disorder (formerly Developmental Articulation Disorder).

4. Stuttering, including an expanded criteria set and discussion (DSM-IV, pp. 63–65); the term "Cluttering" from DSM-III-R has been eliminated.

5. Communication Disorder NOS.

IV. *Attention Deficit* and *Disruptive Behavior Disorders* (DBD) replaces the previously simplified category of DBD. This category now includes:

    A.   Attention Deficit/Hyperactivity Disorder (ADHD) now includes the "Undifferentiated" type (see Item X). ADHD may be subclassified as

        1. Combined Type.

        2. Predominantly Inattentive Type.

        3. Predominantly Hyperactive-Impulsive Type.

    B.   ADHD NOS.

    C.   Conduct Disorder (CD), drops the DSM-III-R categories of group, solitary, and undifferentiated in favor of childhood-onset or adolescent-onset (after age 10 years) types with mild, moderate, and severe specifiers. The criteria are reorganized into thematically related groups and "staying out at night" and "intimidating others" have been added.

    D.   Oppositional-Defiant Disorder.

    E.   DBD NOS is added.

  V. Anxiety Disorders of Childhood or Adolescence is eliminated as a category and subsumed under "Other Disorders . . ." (see Item X) and Anxiety Disorders.

 VI. *Feeding and Eating Disorders of Infancy or Early Childhood* is a name change and new category, reflecting the displacement of Anorexia Nervosa and Bulimia Nervosa to a separate Eating Disorders section (see Item XI) and allowing for a broader inclusion of early onset eating problems. This new category now includes:

    A.   Pica.

    B.   Rumination Disorder.

    C.   Feeding Disorder of Infancy or Early Childhood—the persistent failure to eat adequately with weight loss or failure to gain weight and a number of associated features (DSM-IV, pp. 98–100).

VII. The category of Gender Identity Disorders (GID) has been removed from this section and reclassified under the larger heading of *Sexual and Gender Identity Disorders,* with categories of "in childhood" and "in adolescents or adults" and NOS. The category per se of Transsexualism has been dropped from DSM-IV and is subsumed under GID with specifiers (DSM-IV, pp. 532–538).

VIII.   *Tic Disorders* is left essentially unchanged in DSM-IV, with only a drop in the upper limit of age of onset from 21 to 18, and includes:

   A.   Tourette's Disorder.

   B.   Chronic Motor or Vocal Tic Disorder.

   C.   Transient Tic Disorder.

   D.   Tic Disorder NOS.

IX.   *Elimination Disorders* includes some relatively minor changes in duration specifiers and terminology:

   A.   Encopresis (formerly "Functional Encopresis").

   1.   With constipation and Overflow Incontinence.

   2.   Without Constipation and Overflow Incontinence.

   B.   Enuresis (formerly "Functional Enuresis"): Specify Nocturnal Only/Diurnal Only/Nocturnal and Diurnal.

X.   *Other Disorders of Infancy, Childhood or Adolescence* in DSM-III-R included, in order, Elective Mutism, Identity Disorder, Reactive Attachment Disorder, Stereotypy/Habit Disorder. This last category now has been incorporated into ADHD.

   This category has been reorganized in DSM-IV and now includes:

   A.   Separation-Anxiety Disorder (see Item V).

   B.   *Selective* Mutism—includes a number of new provisions to reduce false-positive diagnoses.

   C.   Reactive Attachment Disorder of Infancy or Early Childhood adds two subtypes—the inhibited type and the disinhibited type (indiscriminate and diffuse attachments)—to allow for compatibility with ICD-10.

   D.   Stereotypic Movement Disorder (formerly Stereotypy/Habit Disorder) adds the specifier "With Self-Injurious Behavior" if the behavior results in self-damage requiring treatment.

   E.   NOS.

XI.   *Eating Disorders* is now a separate category in DSM-IV, incorporating Anorexia Nervosa and Bulimia Nervosa from the Section on "Disorders Usually First Diagnosed in Infancy, Childhood or Adolescence" in DSM-III-R. The category of

Anorexia Nervosa now includes types of *Restricting* versus *Binge Eating/Purging*. Bulimia Nervosa is not given if the behavior occurs during episodes of Anorexia Nervosa. Subtypes include purging and nonpurging types.

XII. *Anxiety Disorders*

    A. Social Phobia now subsumes Avoidant Disorder of Childhood or Adolescence from DSM-III-R. DSM-IV includes criteria and discussion for childhood onset (pp. 411–417).

    B. Generalized Anxiety Disorder now subsumes Overanxious Disorder of Childhood from DSM-III-R and requires "excessive" anxiety and worry rather than "unrealistic" worries as in DSM-III-R. The DSM-IV discussion of diagnostic features, age features and criteria includes considerations specific or relevant to childhood onset (pp. 432–436).

Finally, there is a significant change in the use of Axis IV, which in DSM-III-R is termed Severity of Psychosocial Stressors and included severity ratings, coding and types of stressors to be considered. DSM-IV conceptualizes Axis IV as Psychosocial and Environmental Problems, grouped together as indicated in Table 2.3.

The description and criteria for their use are included in DSM-IV (pp. 29–30). Coding and severity rating scales are dropped from DSM-IV.

Table 2.3. Axis IV—Psychosocial and Environmental Problems

Problems with primary support group

Problems related to the social environment

Educational problems

Occupational problems

Housing problems

Economic problems

Problems with access to health-care services

Problems related to interaction with the legal system/crime

Other psychosocial and environmental problems

REFERENCES

American Psychiatric Association. (1980). *Diagnostic and statistical manual of mental disorders* (3rd ed.). Washington, DC: Author.

American Psychiatric Association. (1987). *Diagnostic and statistical manual of mental disorders* (3rd ed., rev.). Washington, DC: Author.

American Psychiatric Association. (1994). *Diagnostic and statistical manual of mental disorders* (4th ed.). Washington, DC: Author.

Developmental Considerations in Psychopharmacology: The Interaction of Drugs and Development

THEODORE SHAPIRO, M.D.

THE CHILD AND ADOLESCENT PSYCHIATRIST
AND MEDICATION

Enormous changes in the clinical practice of child and adolescent psychiatry over the past 30 years have kept apace of the pharmacological revolution in general psychiatry. Child and adolescent psychiatrists now use multiple drugs, alone and in combination, to help patients cope with their symptoms and achieve better adaptation. The focus of treatment is improved adaptive functioning and resumption of developmental progress expressed in behaviorally appropriate achievement of milestones.

Nonetheless, the child and adolescent psychiatrist's use of medication is different from that of the general psychiatrist because the former's patients are progressing rapidly in their biological maturation and increasing in their behavioral complexity. The child and adolescent psychiatrist must be expert about every level of organization—biological, social, and intrapsychic. In this sense, most child psychiatrists consider themselves practitioners of developmental psychiatry, suited by their training to deal with the interplay of drugs with changing behavior. Physiological concepts such as "inhibition" and "disinhibition" are too mechanistically gruff in a human context. The notion of "modulating" behavior to encourage a new adaptive state or developmental phase is more salutary to our practice.

These preliminary comments highlight the difficulty of defining an appropriate framework for the use of medication for children, requiring the integration of language from disciplines learned during medical training with the language of developmental propositions that are the major scaffolding of child psychiatry. In using pharmacological agents, we attempt to change some substrate, thereby tacitly accepting a mechanistic contribution to the emergence of behavior. On the other hand, day-to-day work with children requires an observational stance that accounts for psychosocial and dynamic factors in change.

During the first 10 years of active psychopharmacological research with children, there was a tendency toward polarization among child psychiatrists, similar to that which occurred among certain general psychiatrists. Some claimed to be childhood psychopharmacologists, whereas others resisted prescribing a medication because they believed they did not know enough about pharmacological action.

During the next 20 years, there was greater acceptance that the use of medicines did not compromise psychological understanding and that the interplay among substrate, behavior, and environment was essential to therapeutic progress. The antagonism has proved to be spurious.

Phrases such as "clinical psychopharmacology" are attempts to solve the potential conflicts. A breakdown of that term may help us define the problem and the task ahead: Pharmacology pertains to the rational use of medicines in biological systems and the study of their rates of absorption, excretion, sites of action, toxicity, and so on; "psycho" refers to the mind; and "clinical" to ministrations at the bedside. Joined together, these parts form a compound term that attests to the Anglo-Saxon, Latin, and Greek origins of our English language and the reconciliation of skills that demands the most from us.

Physicians treating children not only must bring together mind, body, and behavior, but also must bring together these sectors in relation to a growing organism in a changing social milieu, with different requirements at different stages of the life cycle. The latter is what renders the developmental point of view unique from others and warrants a separate disciplinary definition of child and adolescent psychiatry. *Development* includes concepts such as growth, differentiation, and maturation. The first two terms are borrowed from biology, the third is a fiction of heuristic value. *Growth* pertains to the accretion of cells and changing size or mass; *differentiation* refers to specialization of more general cellular elements or differentiation of behavior from more global, syncretic beginnings to more highly specialized and articulated functions. *Maturation* refers to the natural unfolding of genetic potentials in "average expectable environments" (Hartmann, Kris, & Lowenstein, 1947).

Development refers not only to maturation but also to the milieu in which maturation emerges. As such, development pertains to the species-specific potentials of an organism, and also to the variation in the environment at different stages. The hierarchical structuralization of mind is the synthesis of all these forces impinging on the organism and serves as the basis for creative and new behaviors in aging systems. In addition, child psychiatry as a clinical discipline includes affective components in its view of development, unlike some cognitive psychologies that exclude such factors to decrease the number of parameters in their experimental work.

Although these general principles clarify the conceptual framework of developmental psychiatrists, they do not cover the methodological biases that are inherent in the techniques used to study development. We can look at development from the standpoint of cross-sectional norms, which refer to expected weight and height or behavior at such and such an age. These normative approaches are characteristic of testing devices used to arrive at intelligence or developmental quotients. Normalizing developmentalists utilize bell-shaped distribution curves showing the relative presence or absence of behaviors in relation to chronological age. Such approaches usually are not interested in the structural underpinnings of changing capacity. Also there are longitudinal techniques designed to alert us to the sequences and precursors of behavior as development progresses toward its ends as highly integrated and differentiated behaviors.

In addition to these approaches, child psychiatrists also utilize the concepts of "developmental lines" and "aims of development" outlined in terms of more general concepts of maturity not based on the usual, but on the desirable and adaptive. Anna Freud's (1965) scheme of developmental lines is one such program. Erikson (1963) offers another. He refers to the reconciliations that individuals are expected to make at each stage of development between their concomitant needs and capacities to adapt in an ecological balance with the rest of society and nature. These schemes utilize behaviors cataloged in descriptive assessments as indicators of selective or global advance.

Our discussion to this point presents us not only with the problem of bringing together substrate with behavior and epiphenomena of mind in consideration of the use of pharmacological agents, but also with various views of development that may not converge at the same focus. How can we reconcile these into a holistic program so that the child psychiatrist still can maintain the distinctiveness of his or her essential training as a developmental clinician? In practice we see children with actual worries and wishes in real or imagined trouble with a real environment of parents and society with similar or dissimilar desires and concerns. How can we succeed therapeutically using the enabling principles of our training?

One such reconciliation can be seen in the multiaxial approach of the latest editions of the *Diagnostic and Statistical Manual of Mental Disorders* (DSM-III & DSM-IV; American Psychiatric Association [APA], 1980, 1994). Another is seen in the dynamic formulation that does a relative weighting of all sectors including the diagnosis to arrive at a feasible intervention in clinic that may or may not employ medication (Shapiro, 1989).

DEVELOPMENTAL VIEW IN THEORY AND PRACTICE

We are all trained dualistically in medical schools as applied physiologists: We believe in the possibility of altering structure or function through mechanistic means, while we depend heavily on the doctor-patient relationship and the capacity of individuals to respond to talking, relationship, and insight therapies that range from psychoanalysis to transactional analysis. It is exactly here that the developmental principles not only tolerate the presumed dualism, but offer theoretical reconciliations. Developmental observation does not permit a stance that is either all nature or all nurture. To make the variety of disorders we see in childhood understandable, we are trained to be alert to factors that we may (for the sake of ease) call inner and outer influences. The weight we give to each sector is highly dependent on the existing knowledge available within our science and information we receive from patients.

Freud's early interest in distinguishing "actual" neuroses from psychoneuroses reflected a strongly organic bias. On the other hand, the insistence on trauma as real and external showed his willingness to shift his focus to the external world as a source of pathological influence. These concepts only came together when he explicated the notion of psychic reality and could postulate the possibilities of exploring the person who behaved neurotically. Furthermore, when he made the etiologic inferences about causes in the past, his guidelines for practice were posed as hypotheses yet to be tested by clinical observation.

Similarly, concepts within child psychiatry have undergone change. The early diagnosis of "minimal brain dysfunction" (MBD) is but one example of where we hedged our bets in reasoning by analogy to the presenting clinical picture of known organic mental syndromes with actual tissue damage. Yet, as child psychiatrists, we were aware that children bearing this formidable diagnosis could be helped clinically by a number of techniques that included substrate manipulation (medication) as well as learning techniques (tutoring) and, frequently, psychotherapy. Indeed, no one treatment was generally sufficient. When confronted by reality we are practical empiricists. DSM-III (APA, 1980) is an apt testimony to this idea insofar as it helped take the onus off the brain by changing MBD to Attention Deficit Disorder (ADD). Attention became the most important behavior to be considered, not hyperactivity, and the brain, though involved, was now out of the name. The change in emphasis furthermore made us honest. Although we presume a substrate and developmental immaturity to be at fault, we cannot make a one-to-one correlation between brain and behavior yet.

The adaptive point of view proposes that a child with at least average endowment is fitted to adaptation in the ecological interplay within the family and the smaller community as well as the larger community. And currently, developmental knowledge suggests a great deal more "prewiring" than we ever suspected. There is continuous interplay between soma, psyche, and society. Drug therapy applies knowledge and skills to one or more sectors but may not be sufficient by itself to affect all systems uniformly or beneficially. Multiple approaches sometimes are needed.

To explicate these developmental principles, let us look at a number of practical examples commonly seen in child psychiatry and how the use of medication may alter the vital balance within and between subsystems and also require other therapeutic considerations.

During the second year of life, many children show interrupted sleep. Should such children be given some mild bedtime medication such as diphenhydramine (Benadryl), if to do so might interfere with working out and arriving at a satisfactory resolution of a phase-specific adaptation to parental requirements? In some children, a need to establish control, perhaps in response to toilet training or as a feature of the new negativism that emerges at the end of the second year is clearly operative. Although the drug may interfere with the mother-infant interface stimulated by a new training demand, the parents and the child are also in a balance socially. If the sleep disturbance interferes with the mother's sense of well-being and affects her attitudes and concerns about the child, how will she respond to the continuing nighttime intrusions and will they evolve into a battle? A sadomasochistic model could ensue, as well as one where control is offered by a drug. A developmental psychopharmacologist asks if a mild sedative would change the scenario to the developmental advantage of the infant at that level of patterning and have salutary influence on the mother-infant pair as well.

At a still simpler level, we have been told that attention deficit/hyperactivity disorder (ADHD) is influenced favorably by the use of stimulant drugs. In fact, some argue that it may be reprehensible to withhold such medication from a child who needs help in focusing attention and increasing learning potential. Not only do the matters that concern the mother-child interface apply, as in the first instance, but we are aware also that the medication itself may affect the growth potential of the child (Safer & Allen, 1973) and that interfering with a biological system must be considered in light of the benefits that the medication might offer. Moreover the drug is not specific to the disorder and may help anyone to achieve better attention (Rapoport, Buchsbaum, Weingartner, et al., 1978). There is further evidence that—while the drug effect is large—it can be even more effective if used in combination with educational and psychological treatments (Firestone, 1982).

The more extreme circumstance of childhood psychosis provides the example of a child who behaves bizarrely and also has tantrums. The child may be using the only adaptive means available to attract the caretaker's attention or may be responding to internal stimuli generated by brain irritability. We may be tempted to interfere with the radical behaviors, frequently at the behest of distraught parents. Should we do so if these are the child's *only* human interactions? Such an intervention (if it were possible to be handled with medication) would quiet the child, to be sure. However, we could not be certain that while the complaining environment might welcome the quieting, it might also deprive the child of the only interaction he is, at that juncture, able to elicit. So often, medication is wrongly used to quiet so as not to disturb, rather than as an adjunct to, or concomitant with, other methods designed to enhance developmental progress. These examples and others are presented as a reminder to those who work with children and families that medication alone is rarely sufficient. Parents and children's shorthand designations such as a "reading pill" are just as bad as the physician's "he'll grow out of it," because each implies a unitary cause or the sufficiency of one therapeutic intervention.

The fact is that neither is adequate in itself but requires adjunctive help for other developmental systems in producing a well-functioning child in an adapted state with a minimum of anxiety.

The organismic view of development does not easily accede to dividing functions simply into varying sectors, but some more clarity may be gained by discussing each level of the human organization separately. This is done with the general caution that there is no mind without a brain, there is little behavior without stimuli, and the dynamics of childhood dependency is a feature of human development as taught by evolutionary biological theorists. These factors notwithstanding, we can look in a rational way at the individual child in relation to these various sectors to explicate aspects of drug use according to known developmental principles.

We will first address biological development. We will then look at developmental lines as the significant feature of the ego's adaptive organization and consider the influence of medication on these functions. Finally, we will take those functions that are largely under the sway of the imaginative eye of children and look at the influence of drugs on fantasy formation. Within each sector, we will try to attend to the interactional homeostasis of the child at each stage of development with reference to his or her caretakers, ranging from mother through teacher and reaching to the extended community. Their developmental expectations and normative values will be looked at as feeding back to and influencing the developing child. The changing meaning of the maturing child to parents and community as well as the changing meaning of varying techniques available for modulating development will be examined with special reference to the use of medication.

INDEPENDENT AND INTEGRATED SECTORS OF DEVELOPMENT

Biological Features

The child is in a biological process of growth, maturation, and development. These may be measured by height and weight curves; physiological responses that clinically include blood pressure, pulse rate, and temperature control; and at the biochemical level, by techniques for observing the changes that occur, for example, in liver, thyroid, and corticosteroid function with progressive chronological maturation. In addition, whatever organ system is potentially affected by a medication can itself be monitored along with behavior. To keep close track of developmental biological issues, one must have a working knowledge and empirical understanding of the supposed sites of action of each drug as well as their potential side effects, and utilize available measures for monitoring drug dosage, potential side effects, and effectiveness. Because we are interested in behavioral alterations, it is all too easy to forget that the medication itself works on a biochemical substrate and that the substrate alteration may be sufficiently distressing to warrant changing either the drug used or its dosage.

A developmentally alert clinician also attends to biological sectors because slow psychological development may be secondary to slow physical maturation. When looking for target symptoms to influence by drug use, the clinician must consider the organism's developmental underpinnings. For example, it has been shown that early adolescent development of secondary sexual characteristics influences social competence (McCandless, 1960).

Another important developmental factor to be considered is that although medication may alter an undesirable developmental trait, secondary or long-term effects of the drug may be less desirable. Antipsychotic neuroleptics are useful, but many lower the seizure threshold, may be sedating at therapeutic dosage levels, may interfere with learning, and may give rise to tardive dyskinesia in some children.

The third factor to be considered concerns the natural thrust of maturation itself, which is relatively independent of external environmental influences. We must always ask whether it is medication that is providing the change or do we have development and maturation on our side to do the job? Our models must include "developmental boosters" designed to prod development along, "developmental sustainers" designed to modulate development on a continuous basis, and placebos that function as "environmental suggestives" to permit auxiliary support to children in human milieus.

Even a biological view of development depends on behavioral evidence of effectiveness. As physicians, we know it is not enough to treat the diabetic's urine but the patient with diabetes. We may look at children as having a number of characteristics from infancy on that require monitoring. Past investigators have chosen their own favorites (Fish, 1967; Fries & Woolf, 1953; Thomas, Chess, Birch, Hertzig, & Korn, 1963). I would choose four as having particularly biological significance: Anergy-energy, modulated-unmodulated, attention-inattention, and predictive patterning-randomness. From the developmental point of view, each of these features may be a factor in temperamental and characterological disposition.

When using medication, the practitioner must have in mind some developmental norms but also be prepared to allow for individual stylistic variation. For example, the attention span of an infant of 6 months is clearly shorter than the attention span of a 2-year-old. Yet such a child's attention disposition may be insufficiently responsive to society's demands as compared with the attention span available to a 4-year-old who is expected to cooperate in a nursery program. Clinicians would have to take into account the richness of variation in children's behavior that might be based on maturational factors, as well as on other influences when they consider whether or not to use a medication. They would not want incorrectly to interpret exuberance as hyperactivity, because exuberance is desirable whereas hyperactivity is definitionally fraught with undesirable connotations.

Behavioral Measures

Now we must again confront the difficulty alluded to before of assaying which method or model of development we should use as a yardstick to measure drug effect on behavior. Many global severity rating scales are available; there are also symptom checklists and there is the developmental lines vantage point. We also can break development into hypothetical stages. Any or all of these methods have and may be used to verify change, but we ought to recognize that changes that take place at one stage of development might not be considered desirable or may even be undesirable at another, and also that any checklist or global scale omits features present in others. For example, many checklists have an item for "separating easily from the parent." This is desirable at 4 years if the nursery school is the order of the day, but the clinician would like to see protest and separation anxiety in an 8-month-old as an index of attachment behavior, which is a significant precursor of future object relations (Ainsworth, Blehar, & Water, 1978).

From a developmental standpoint, the issue is one of distinguishing a lag in maturation from a fixed or developmental "lesion." For example, there is evidence that appropriate tutoring in appropriately diagnosed learning-disabled children without ADHD is not enhanced by medication (Gittelman, Klein, & Feingold, 1983).

Nonnormative Developmental Lines Approach

Generally, child psychiatrists utilize a broader definition of developmental disorders than the simple normative index of the presence of symptoms or cognitive deficits. Some functions are clearly in the biological maturational scheme of things, but these also interact with other psychic and social structures. A developmental position within psychiatry views transient symptom formation as way stations in solving conflicts not only with the external world, but also within. Transient identifications or transient compromises may result in new ego adaptations.

Enuresis provides an interesting example of a common symptom that may have a number of roots and may be examined developmentally. Some families insist that the child be placed on the potty as soon as he or she can sit and use "gastrocolic reflexology" as their ally in toilet training, figuring that bladder training follows bowel training. Other families, on the advice of "enlightened" physicians who insist that the "myelinization route" be followed, do not put pressure on a child until 18 months of age when the sphincter is supposedly innervated. Other families who feel children should never be coerced do not really toilet train their children and trust that somehow the socialization process will include toilet training by shame or social constraint. With this variability of possible environmental impositions, the central notion of the move to body control as a developmental line has gained in attractiveness to developmentally alert clinicians. "When is the child able to participate in the control of his bowels and bladder for his own purposes?" becomes the central query for such a frame of reference. On the other hand, the force of numbers should not hold sway. It is estimated that seven-eighths of the world's children are reflexly toilet trained, yet that does not recommend it to all cultures. To reduce psychopharmacology to absurdity would recommend that we toilet train by using imipramine which is helpful in treating enuresis.

In still another vein, at what stage and in what kind of community should we expect the child to have less separation anxiety rather than more, and in what communities would it be wiser if the child stuck close to an adult's side because of actual environmental dangers? To what degree should a child be expected to yield egocentric wishes and move toward more cooperative approaches? However, maturation also may make children more capable of moving away from their own primary demands toward social demands. If we accept Piaget's frame of reference, it is a distinct step in development when the child can decenter and cognitively take the other individual's vantage point. Does this achievement itself influence the capacity to move out of the egocentric position or is it a prerequisite to achieving the social step of cooperation?

This brief excursion into the developmentalists' conceptual framework now permits a better basis for understanding drug use in children.

If parents and/or schools ask for drugs as an adjunct in helping the overassertive, egocentric, unsocialized child, they may in fact be asking for a drug to increase the speed of development of a cognitive process that may be slower in this specific child on a maturational basis. It may be that the use of the drug for nonpharmacological effects in quieting the complaining community or school may influence the child indirectly by a trickle-down effect resulting in a less threatened and anxious child. The facts are that ego developmental lines or ego functions themselves will be only secondarily influenced by medication, insofar as medications somehow affect the substrate, the background music, the noise factor, and/or the resultant anxiety that underlies the symptoms that may accrue. On the other hand, a relieved community puts less pressure on a child and permits self-realization.

The developmental line of movement from body to toy to work enables us to observe a gradual reorganization of a child's thinking as well as the encroachment of reality factors on pleasure factors. These can be directly inferred clinically from the vantage point of "capacity to attend to play." This could lead us to a method of understanding how a drug modulates wishes and what the balance is in a regression-progression continuum. Moreover, such observation can be used to infer how the child distortedly or realistically interprets the medication itself and how it fits into the child's fantasies as an aid or enemy.

First, we may inquire on a cognitive level whether the child is using predominantly mediational or associational thinking, and whether the level is appropriate for the stage of development. Second, we may assay the "relative abundance" of aggressive themes. Third, is there ample modulation of affect? Moreover, we can observe how much of a child's fantasy life is tolerated as opposed to dampened and inhibited, and how this expression emerges relative to expectations at each developmental stage. As clinicians, we have certain normative standards of how well a child ought to be able to control or express his or her fantasies. All in all, we are looking for the happy balance at each stage and age that represents an appropriate equilibrium between drive factors and their organization in goal-oriented wishes in an adaptive relationship with the requirements of the child's community.

For some children, the pressures of wishes may be insistent, persistent, and oppressive to their own sense of well-being. For other children, inhibitions may be strong, because of excessive social demands. Either of these states (too much or too little) may lead the clinician to prescribe medication. Usually, in neurotic compromises there is a tendency to dampen excessively and create substitutive symptoms that in themselves reveal a pressure similar to the drives, as in obsessional questioning or tics. However, when drives in the form of bizarre fantasies encroach on reality, a child may act in an uninhibited manner that tends to disrupt his relationships to peers and adults alike. Clinicians should be neither activity "makers" nor "dampeners," but should seek to establish better homeostatic mechanisms from within that ultimately can be trusted. The developmental notion that modulation from without has to be replaced by controls from within is another form of this developmental proposition. We assume that as ego apparatuses develop, gratification becomes possible in and along socially acceptable channels and that each stage of development has its appropriate pleasures and controls.

Descriptive Diagnoses and Development

Yet another area of developmental concern that has recently arisen involves comparing childhood disorders with adult disorders. There is much controversy regarding whether we see the same symptomatology in childhood as we do in adults. One view suggests that each developmental stage will provide a different manifestation of a disorder, and the practitioner has to consider the stage-phase related capacities for social response as more central to phenomenology than the issue of whether a descriptive syndrome can be identified as such. Two examples may provide some light.

The offspring of manic-depressive families have been studied (Kestenbaum, 1982; Kron, Decina, Kestenbaum, et al., 1982). The progeny of bipolar parents suggest some abnormality and unusual behavior, but little that corresponds to what mania looks like in adulthood. Similar questions have been raised with respect to the early manifestations of frank depressive disorders. Many (Carlson & Cantwell, 1979, 1980, 1982; Cytryn & Bunney, 1980; Puig-Antich, 1982) have shown that we do have both pubertal and prepubertal depression. Assessment instruments (Pozanski, Cook, & Carroll, 1979; Puig-Antich, 1982) can certainly pick up such children. The criteria of each assessment instrument are somewhat different, but even using careful assessment instruments does not uncover a high prevalence of frank depressive disorders in the prepubertal years. Indeed, even those conduct disorders that may respond to antidepressants (Puig-Antich, 1982) must satisfy research criteria for depression (RDC) to be considered for drug trials.

Thus, the landscape is somewhat muddied by the developmental process, because each stage of development will provide its own repertoire of behaviors that can be affected by whatever disorder intervenes. From a psychopharmacological vantage, we still struggle to show that tricyclics or selective serotonin reuptake inhibitors (SSRIs) are effective in childhood or adolescent depression, but to no avail. So even though adults with the same clinical picture respond to these agents, there is, as yet, no double-blind, placebo study that sustains such evidence in children.

The general trends described make it difficult to study forms of adult disorder in childhood if we continue to require the simpleminded notion that children have to show the same characteristics as the adults. Instead developmental propositions provide us with a new research line that suggests we need some method or metric of detecting diathesis, the biological or genetic factors as they interact with social and behavioral observations during the early life cycle. Moreover, recent determination of high rates of comorbidity confound our quest even more.

The Meaning of Taking Drugs

We are not only what we eat or how we eat. Instead, we also are as our fantasies dictate.

For children whose fantasies are laden with aggression and fears of penetration and/or oral impregnation, a medication taken by mouth may be fraught with unhappy adultomorphic meaning. According to their capacity for reality testing, such children may fancy that they are being poisoned, that someone is putting foreign substances into them, that they are being given a magical strengthening potion, and so on. If the mother is in charge of the drug administration, she may be looked on as the object from whom the evil or balm is dispensed. Giving medication also may be perceived according to prior patterns of interaction in families; for example, as a continuation of an earlier pattern of oral assault—being forced to eat, or being duped into a dishonest relationship. The background of basic trust may have to be assessed before deciding who is to administer the medication. If the level of conflict is centered around toilet training, giving drugs can deteriorate into a sadomasochistic struggle, or taking medicine can be construed as pleasing mother by being submissive. Conversely, administration of drugs may become a nonparticipating pseudoalliance enveloped in denial or passivity.

Giving medication by injection or in suppository form offers even more possibility for misinterpretation. Anal sadistic assault is easily read into such routes. Phallic level interpretations may be dominant no matter what the route of administration. The notion of being intruded on, seduced, or having one's manhood taken away or femininity mocked are all possible modes of interpretation for a vulnerable child who has been made to feel less than adequate by whatever symptom he or she has that requires pharmacological treatment.

The hope that fantasy life and reality organization will become modulated by the administration of medication also depends on what life problems have to be solved by the child at what stage of development.

Although we all know about the placebo effect of giving a medication or any substitute, we are not so well schooled in the issue of compliance. The latter is a major issue both in research and at clinic. This area has been studied extensively and more focally in the use of psychostimulants for ADHD (Brown, Borden, Wynne, et al., 1988; Firestone, 1982; Sleator, Ullmann, & Von Neumann, 1982). The problems that are described are not unique in this disorder, but common enough for both short- and long-term use of medication where the meaning of the use of the drug to parent and child may undermine the study of its effectiveness. It is suspected that more drug studies probably are confounded by premature discontinuation than by poor pharmacological effect. Noncompliance in psychostimulant use has been reported in the range between 20% and 68%. Firestone's one-year study showed that the falloff in medicine use was 20% by 4 months and 44% by 10 months. Parents reported they were not comfortable continuing the drug or that the children refused the medicine. A more recent study by Pelham, Murphy, Vannatta et al. (1992) showed that when children on methylphenidate were asked why they were doing better at school they attributed the result to their own abilities.

SUMMARY

A drug used to treat a target symptom without some understanding of the nature of the disorder in developmental terms is not only poor clinical practice, but also antithetical to the developmental propositions that guide the work of the child and adolescent psychiatrists. These developmental principles mesh with the pharmacological rule of thumb that suggests using the appropriate drug in the appropriate dose for the right child who has a given symptom that is the target for a desired effect. Developmentally, we must add the caution that the drug should be used for as long a time as necessary and titrated to the current needs of our patients based on what is know to be different about them because they are children.

Not only must a child be considered at each stage of development or maturity in accepting the medication, but also for the maturity of the child's detoxification methods—his or her routes of absorption and excretion and end-organ responses. The therapeutic effects expected must be potentially better than the toxic or side effects and the therapeutic/toxic ratio must be satisfactory for the stage of development of the young patient. Clinicians cannot simply compare the responses of adults with the responses of children. We must take into account the "paradoxical" differences that accrue at different stages of development and that may be very discreetly demarcated by chronological (maturational) age (Fish, 1967). Extrapolation of dose by body weight does not apply simply in children, just as indexes of severity are more important than diagnosis per se in some instances. Level of IQ may also be determining because as psychic organization becomes more complex, drug effect is less clearly dependent on simple biological effect. Developmentally, we must look at toxicity not only in terms of the physiological biological system, but in the sense of behavioral deterioration that interferes with the desired "good functioning" of the child (Fish & Shapiro, 1964). Again, this diversion into biology amidst a discussion of psychological factors points up the need to look for developmental balance, not simple effects on one sector of behavior. Parents must be guided not only by their wish that the child lose a symptom, but by the fact that the symptom may signify developmental turmoil or temperamental variety as well as pathology.

Clinicians must also keep in mind that medication is something that is neither desirable or undesirable in itself according to preconceived notions, but a therapeutic agent that may help a child accept available educational and social opportunities. If a clinician can bring a parent into cooperative participation, drug therapy will be much more successful and less prone to failure due to conflict between the child and parents or parents and physician. To encourage compliance, the physician should try to defuse erroneous ideas and superfluous meaning about drug use. Although physicians may have authority on their side and want to provide placebo effect by lending the weight of that authority, they must remember that overselling a medication leads to disappointments for the parents as well as the children and discourages confidence for future therapeutic enterprises.

The developmentally alert clinician should maximize the therapeutic relationship before prescribing any medication. This requires careful and prolonged consultation as well as accurate dose regulation in a particular child. Now, because an increasing number of pharmacological agents are touted as effective for troubled behavior, children will be subjected to an increasing likelihood of drugs recommended to take care of their problems by psychiatrically unsophisticated practitioners. If the public mind associates giving drugs to children with the illegal and illicit "drug scene," a detrimental effect is projected onto the possibility of influencing the therapy of children who need medication and who may otherwise be subjected to prolonged suffering. Moreover, if a contaminated view of drug administration prevails within the family, the developmental effect on the growing child will be to establish attitudes against a "pill-pushing" culture. On the other hand, drug administration in the context of the developmental principles outlined should make giving medicines to children more reasonable and provide a framework of limits, aims, and constraints as well as a well-tempered appropriate optimism.

REFERENCES

Ainsworth, M. D. S., Blehar, M. D., & Water, E. (1978). *Patterns of attachment: A psychological study of the strange situation.* Hillsdale, NJ: Erlbaum.

American Psychiatric Association. (1980). *Diagnostic and statistical manual of mental disorders* (3rd ed.). Copyright Division of Public Affairs, APA, 1700 18th Street, N.W., Washington, DC.

American Psychiatric Association. (1994). *Diagnostic and statistical manual of mental disorders* (4th ed.). Washington, DC: Author.

Brown, R., Borden, K., Wynne, E., et al. (1988). Compliance with pharmacological and cognitive treatments for attention deficit disorder. *Journal of the American Academy of Child and Adolescent Psychiatry, 26*(4), 521–526.

Carlson, G. A., & Cantwell, D. P. (1979). A survey of depressive symptoms in a child and adolescent psychiatric population. *Journal of the American Academy of Child Psychiatry, 18*, 587–599.

Carlson, G. A., & Cantwell, D. P. (1980). Unmasking masked depression in children and adolescents. *American Journal of Psychiatry, 137,* 445–449.

Carlson, G. A., & Cantwell, D. P. (1982). Diagnosis of childhood depression: A comparison of the Weinberg and DSM-III criteria. *Journal of the American Academy of Child Psychiatry, 21*(3), 247–250.

Cytryn, L., & Bunney, W. (1980). Diagnosis of depression in children: Reassessment. *American Journal of Psychiatry, 137,* 22–25.

Erikson, E. H. (1963). *Childhood and society* (2nd ed., pp. 247–274). New York: Norton.

Firestone, P. (1982). Factors associated with children's adherence to stimulant medication. *American Journal of Orthopsychiatry, 52,* 447–457.

Fish, B. (1967). Methodology in child psychopharmacology. In D. H. Efron et al. (Eds.), *Psychopharmacology, review of progress.* Public Health Publication No. 1836.

Fish, B., & Shapiro, T. (1964). A descriptive typology of children's psychiatric disorders, II. A behavioral classification in child psychiatry. *American Psychiatric Association Research, 18,* 75–86.

Freud, A. (1965). The concept of developmental lines. *Normality and pathology in childhood: Assessment of development* (pp. 56–92). New York: International Universities Press.

Fries, M., & Woolf, P. (1953). Some hypotheses on the role of congenital activity type in personality development. *Psychoanalytic study of the child.* New York: International Universities Press, 8, 48–62.

Gittelman, R., Klein, D. F., & Feingold, I. (1983). Children with reading disorders, II. Effects of methylphenidate in combination with reading remediation. *Journal of Child Psychology and Psychiatry, 24*(2), 193–212.

Hartmann, H., Kris, E., & Lowenstein, R. M. (1947). Comments on the formation of psychic structure. *Psychoanalytic study of the child* (pp. 11–38). New York: International Universities Press.

Kestenbaum, C. J. (1982). Children and adolescents at risk for manic-depressive illnesses: Introduction and overview. *Adolescent Psychiatry: Development and Clinical Studies* (Vol. X, pp. 245–255). Chicago: The University of Chicago Press.

Kron, L., Decina, P., Kestenbaum, C. J., et al. (1982). The offspring of bipolar manic depressives: Clinical features. *Adolescent Psychiatry: Developmental and Clinical Studies* (Vol. X, pp. 273–291). Chicago: The University of Chicago Press.

McCandless, B. (1960). Rate of development: Body build and personality. *Child Development and Child Psychiatry. American Psychiatric Association Research, 13,* 42.

Pelham, W. E., Murphy, D. A., Vannatta, K., et al. (1992). Methylphenidate and attributions in boys with attention-deficit hyperactivity disorder. *Journal of Consulting and Clinical Psychology, 60*(2), 282–292.

Poznanski, E. O., Cook, S. C., & Carroll, B. J. (1979). A depression rating scale for children. *Pediatrics, 64,* 442–450.

Puig-Antich, J. (1982). Major depression and conduct disorder in prepuberty. *Journal of American Academy of Child Psychiatry, 21,* 118–128.

Rapoport, J., Buchsbaum, M., & Weingartner, H., et al. (1978). Dextroamphetamine: Behavioral and cognitive effects in normal prepubertal boys. *Science, 199,* 560–563.

Safer, D. J., & Allen, R. P. (1973). Factors influencing the suppressant effects of two stimulant drugs on the growth of hyperactive children. *Pediatrics, 51,* 660–667.

Shapiro, T. (1989). The Psychodynamic formulation in child and adolescent psychiatry. *Journal of the American Academy of Child and Adolescent Psychiatry, 28,* 675–680.

Sleator, E. K., Ullmann, R. K., & Von Neumann, A. (1982). How do hyperactive children feel about taking stimulants and will they tell their doctors? *Clinical Pediatrics, 21,* 474–479.

Thomas, A., Chess, S., & Birch, H. G. (1968). *Temperament and behavior disorders in children.* New York: New York University Press.

Thomas, A., Chess, S., Birch, H. G., Hertzig, M. E., & Korn, S. (1963). *Behavioral individuality in early childhood.* New York: International Universities Press.

Methodological and Assessment Issues in Pediatric Psychopharmacology

DREW ERHARDT, Ph.D. and C. KEITH CONNERS, Ph.D.

We are not free from the techniques, the methods, from the means by which we know, we see.

—Mahasi Sayadaw

We gratefully acknowledge the assistance of Elizabeth Sparrow and Jennie Treeger in the preparation of this chapter.

Other contributors to this volume have documented the enormous growth over the past decade in the field of child and adolescent psychopharmacology. This growth has been accompanied and, to some extent, driven by an increase in the number and sophistication of research reports on the effects and mechanisms of psychoactive medications. However, the pace with which an ever-expanding array of drugs is applied to a widening class of childhood psychiatric disorders far exceeds that which is justifiable on the basis of scientific advances in our knowledge about these medications.

Indeed, word of mouth, anecdotal reports, clinical lore, speculations drawn from the adult treatment literature, serendipity, aggressive marketing by pharmaceutical companies, and market pressures to deliver increasingly efficacious and cost-effective treatments all continue to play important roles in determining current practices in child psychopharmacology. As a result, drugs are administered to children and adolescents without empirically demonstrated efficacy or safety or FDA approval for use with certain disorders (Gadow, 1993). Although some applications of this sort are justified by the gap between real-world clinical demands and the boundaries of our scientific knowledge, they should nonetheless be limited as they increase the likelihood of drawing erroneous conclusions regarding drug effects along with subsequent over- or underprescription and misuse. Wherever possible, decisions regarding pharmacotherapy for children or adolescents should be based on the results of controlled scientific studies. Highlighting some of the issues involved in the design and implementation of appropriate methods for such studies is the focus of this chapter.

DESIGN ISSUES

Fortunately, as technical knowledge related to pharmacokinetics and cellular action of psychoactive medications expands at a dizzying pace, the basic methodology underlying a sound clinical study remains constant. At the broadest level, all scientific investigations attempt to carefully arrange observations so that relationships between variables of interest can be identified. In doing so, all research designs must strive to establish adequate control over experimental variables so as to minimize the number of alternative explanations for observed results. Uniformity in the process of drawing conclusions from those results is achieved by applying rules of causal inference that are fundamentally *statistical* (Russell, 1948) (not to be confused with the mistaken conclusion that *inferential statistics* are always required in a scientific study).

However, to point out that the principles underlying adequate research design are clear and static is not to say that designing an appropriate study is a simple endeavor. Classic approaches to methodology espoused in textbooks or courses often seem unfeasible when applied to real-world clinical problems (see Kraemer, 1981, for a discussion of practical solutions to coping with common design and analysis dilemmas). Furthermore, the researcher is faced with the challenge of selecting a design from a range of options including between-group, within-group, and single-subject experimental procedures.*

Research design is ultimately a decision-making process and every choice is associated with unique costs and benefits. A timeless illustration of this point and of the factors that influence causal inferences in clinical research is provided by Campbell and Stanley (1966). They make the distinction between experimental and quasi-experimental designs and point out that behavioral science offers a wide continuum of designs, depending on which sources of error the researcher is willing to tolerate in a particular investigation. Some of these sources of error are described in Tables 4.1 and 4.2.

Therefore, it is important at the outset to eschew the temptation to opt for the *one* right design, dosage, response measure, or subject selection procedure. The kind of methodological imperialism which decrees that a particular strategy of investigation of drug effects is superior usually arises from a disease that Donald Klein has referred to as "premature hardening of the categories." Good methodology, like life, ought to be a dance that skillfully adjusts to the changing nature of the problem. As pointed out by Kraemer (1981), "Every design/analysis dyad is (a) optimal under certain circumstances, (b) acceptable under a somewhat broader range of circumstances, and (c) invalid under other circumstances" (p. 315).

Although the circumstances within which a study is to be conducted will always introduce practical, administrative, and ethical demands that constrain methodological choice, the appropriateness of a particular design is best thought of as being dictated by the specific experimental question being posed. For instance, determining whether a pharmacological agent represents a generally effective and safe treatment for a particular symptom or diagnostic group is best addressed through a double-blind, placebo-controlled clinical trial, comprising the random

---

* Single-subject experimental designs are also referred to as single-subject designs, intensive designs, and intrasubject-replication designs. As pointed out by Kazdin (1980), the latter term is most accurate because it avoids the mistaken implication that these designs need to be restricted to the individual subject. We chose the term "single-subject experimental designs" because, both historically and currently, it is the most commonly employed descriptor for these procedures in the treatment outcome literature. However, we caution the reader to be aware that such designs may be employed with groups of subjects.

Table 4.1.   Threats to Internal Validity as Related to Therapy Outcome Research

Threat	Definition	Examples	
		General	Specific Instance
History	Events other than therapy that occur during the time period when therapy is provided; simultaneous occurrence of extratherapy events.	Informal counseling by peers; important lifestyle change.	A long phone call from a former roommate relieves a client's depression and gives a new meaning to his life. The phone call comes about the time that the therapist begins an important part of treatment. The depression is relieved.
Maturation	Psychological or biological changes that appear to occur naturally with the passage of time.	Children's development of the capacity for abstract thought; menopausal effects.	The normal cognitive development of a child may result in an increased ability to take another person's perspective and therefore behave in a more sensitive and empathic manner. The child displays less aggression.
Testing	The impact of repeated exposure to the assessment measures.	Increased skill due simply to the practice provided by repeated testing; reduced anxiety due to repeated exposure to the feared stimulus; increased self-disclosure due to multiple instances of asking personal questions.	A client becomes more interpersonally skilled in social situations as a result of the researcher's role-play tests. Performing the role-play tests over and over has beneficial effects. The client more comfortably interacts with members of the opposite sex.
Instrumentation	Decay in the sensitivity-accuracy of the assessment instruments.	Fatigue on the part of observers; decreased sensitivity of psychophysiological equipment due to usage.	Children's attentiveness in the classroom appears to show less off-task behavior due to the observers paying less attention after having observed for several weeks. The observers are not seeing or recording the off-task behavior. The child appears to be paying more attention, but only because the off-task behavior is not being noticed.

Table 4.1.   *(Continued)*

Threat	Definition	Examples	
		General	Specific Instance
Statistical Regression	The tendency for persons whose initial scores on assessment measures are extreme (high or low) to have later scores that drift toward the mean.	Extreme depression (bottom of the scale) is more likely to rise, since it cannot drop further; hyperactive children are more likely to show less activity.	A client who scores particularly high on a measure of anxiety before therapy is statistically more likely to score nearer the mean on a second testing than to score even higher.
Mortality	Attrition of participants-clients.	Clients who drop out from therapy and for whom posttherapy assessments are not available.	Clients in a study of the treatment of depression terminate prematurely. Their data are lost, even though they may have terminated because of a sense of already achieved relief. The client has not returned to complete the assessments.
Selection	Utilization of participants-clients who might appear to change simply because of personal factors that predispose them to do so rather than due to the intervention.	Clients who volunteer for a therapy program advertised in a local newspaper may be on the verge of changing due to a high level of personal motivation.	Using adolescents in studies of peer pressure or persuasion. The characteristics of adolescent subjects tend to make them especially susceptible to peer pressure and persuasive maneuvers.

Source: P.C. Kendall and L.N. Butcher, (Eds.). (1982). *Handbook of research methods in clinical psychology* (pp. 438–439). New York: Wiley. Copyright © 1982 by John Wiley & Sons, Inc. Reprinted by permission.

Table 4.2.   Threats to External Validity as Related to Therapy Outcome Research

		Examples	
Threat	Definition	General	Specific Instance
Interactions of the environment and testing	Preintervention assessments may sensitize clients to the intervention, thus potentiating the intervention's influence.	When clients who are to receive a therapy for fear are asked to role-play the feared situation, this action may increase their motivations to change.	An otherwise ineffective treatment may appear to alleviate fear, but the fear reduction is due to increased motivation from some aspect of the study. This increased motivation would not be present when the treatment is provided outside the context of a study and would then be ineffective.
Interaction of selection and intervention	If all clients selected are a special subgroup who are particularly amenable to participation, these clients cannot be considered comparable to the rest of the population.	If only two of the four clinics that are asked to be involved in a therapy outcome study agree to do so, the results cannot be generalized to all clinics. The two that refused might be significantly different from the two that agreed.	A project designed to compare psychological therapy, medications, and a control condition for the treatment of hyperactivity requires parents to give their informed consent. Many parents refuse to participate, not wanting their child assigned to the control condition. This selection problem reduces the researcher's ability to generalize the results to all hyperactive children.
Reactive arrangements	Clients may change due to a reaction to the fact of participating in a novel experience, rather than due to the therapy interaction.	Clients may change due to an expectancy on their parts or on the part of their therapist. Therapy must, or should, cause change, and clients change simply because they expect they ought to.	A father's physical abuse of family members is reduced by therapy: not as a result of the therapist's actions but a function of the father's belief that going to therapy will make him stop being abusive.

Table 4.2. *(Continued)*

		Examples	
Threat	Definition	General	Specific Instance
Multiple intervention interference	When several kinds of intervention are combined in one experience, the total effect may be very different from the outcome of any one of them in isolation.	Clients involved in multicomponent therapies may fail to change because the plethora of intervention obscures the positive impacts of each separate component.	A child's acting-out, aggressive behavior pattern elicits aggression from his father, rewarding attention from his mother and his peers, and attempts at rational discussion by school authorities. A single consistent approach designed to reduce the aggression would be more effective when not interfered with by other efforts.

Source: P.C. Kendall and L.N. Butcher, (Eds.). (1982). *Handbook of research methods in clinical psychology* (p. 440). New York: Wiley. Copyright © 1982 by John Wiley & Sons, Inc. Reprinted by permission.

assignment of subjects to treatment and control groups (Klerman, 1986). These studies, however, are often predicated on promising results from single or time-limited multiple dose open trials or single-blind studies.

The double-blind, placebo-controlled group designs have the advantage of controlling for multiple threats to internal validity and reducing alternative explanations for observed results. Thus, these designs have generally dominated investigations of the effects of psychoactive drugs (Gitlin, 1990). As noted by Sprague and Werry (1971), accepted minimal requirements for studies in this field include random assignment of subjects to drug groups, placebo controls, standardized doses, blind evaluations of drug effects to minimize bias, the use of standardized measures of drug effect, and the appropriate use of inferential statistics to evaluate the significance of observed changes. A thorough review of both experimental and quasi-experimental between-group designs, along with their indications and limitations, is provided by Kazdin (1980). Whalen and Henker (1986) tailor their excellent comprehensive discussion of group designs to the study of medication effects.

Conclusions drawn from group studies apply to many individuals, on the *average,* and thus may obscure potentially important individual outcomes. More specifically, the frequently idiosyncratic nature of drug response in an individual patient may be disguised by the average effects obtained in large numbers. Therefore, other than identifying the universe of potentially efficacious agents and specifying broad dose ranges, the results of such group studies may be of limited value to the individual clinician. This relates to the practitioner's need to know what drug at what dosage is optimal for *this particular* child, whereas the results of a group study apply only to a *sample* that represents some theoretical population.

At the other end of the methodological spectrum is the case study, which involves the intensive but uncontrolled observation of the individual subject over time. Because almost all sources of possible error are unprotected in the typical case study, it represents an unacceptable method for drawing scientifically valid inferences regarding treatment effects. However, the case study can be of value in *generating* (rather than *testing*) hypotheses, evaluating rare phenomena, providing contrary evidence to well-established assumptions, and exploring innovative treatments (Kazdin, 1980, 1981). On the other hand, many sources of error can be controlled in the single subject by the application of single-subject experimental designs. Although they are used extensively in the behavioral treatment literature, single-subject experimental designs have been underutilized in psychopharmacological research. Yet, a review of these studies as applied to psychopharmacology shows that some important discoveries as well as answers to clinical problems have been made using these designs (Conners & Wells, 1982). Tables 4.3 and 4.4 review applications of single-subject designs for drug studies of depression and hyperactivity in children. They are highlighted here because of their relative neglect in the literature.

Single-subject experimental designs comprise a variety of methods, including A-B-A withdrawal (and its variants), multiple-baseline, multiple-treatment, and changing-criterion designs. All involve a specified intervention, clear treatment targets, the delineation of distinct phases or periods, and repeated measures of the same individual over a period of time. The essentials of single-subject experimental methodology have been reviewed by a number of authors (see, e.g., Barlow & Hersen, 1984; Hays, 1981; Kazdin, 1982). Following is a typical stepwise sequence of experimental phases found in drug studies:

1. No drug (A).
2. Placebo (A_1).
3. Active drug (B).
4. Placebo (A_1).
5. Active drug.

Such designs permit the researcher to examine possible placebo effects, active drug effects, and when expanded, combined effects of drugs

Table 4.3. Single-Case Design for Drug Studies of Hyperactive Children

Study	Ss	Design	Dependent Measures	Distinctive Findings	Drugs
Martin, 1971	1	A-B₁-B-C (B = drug C = token program)	*Behavioral:* 1. Appropriate and inappropriate social behavior *Task performance:* 2. Pegboard, stimulus matching, block design, picture naming	Decrease in appropriate behavior on placebo. Increase in rate and variability of appropriate social behavior on drug. Increased variability in task performance on drug.	Dexedrine: 5 mg b.i.d.
Ayllon et al., 1975	3	Combined design: Multiple baseline across behaviors on ABA design (B = drugs)	*Behavioral:* 1. "Hyperactivity," for example, gross motor behavior, noise. *Academic:* 2. Percentage of correct math and reading responses	Hyperactivity increased when drug withdrawn and decreased when academic responses reinforced.	S₁: Ritalin: 5 mg q.i.d. S₂: Ritalin: 5 mg b.i.d. S₃: Ritalin: 5 mg t.i.d.
Stableford et al., 1976	2	S₁:B₃-B₂-B₁-A₁-A-C (B₃-B₁ = decreasing doses of drug C = behavioral program) S₂:B₅-B₄-B₃-B₂-B₁-A₁-A (B₅-B₁ = decreasing dose of drug)	*Behavioral:* 1. Out of seat 2. On task 3. Appropriate 4. Inappropriate	Behavior did not deteriorate till placebo removed in A phase. 1 primary observer not blind. No dramatic increase in negative behavior when drug decreased. Decrease when pills withdrawn.	Ritalin: 15, 10, 5 mg Dexedrine: 25, 20, 15, 10, 5 mg

(Continued)

Table 4.3. (*Continued*)

Study	Ss	Design	Dependent Measures	Distinctive Findings	Drugs
Wells et al., 1981	1	A-B-A-C-CD-A$_1$D-CD (B = Dexedrine C = Ritalin D = self-control program)	*Behavioral:* 1. Off task 2. Gross motor 3. Deviant behavior *Physiological:* 1. Finger temperature 2. EMG	Combination better than either alone on behavioral measures. Only study to collect physiological measures. Helped in decision as to effectiveness of Ritalin over Dexedrine.	Ritalin: 15 mg b.i.d. Dexedrine: 5 mg, b.i.d.
Horn et al., 1983	1	A-A$_1$-B$_1$-A$_1$-C-B$_1$C-B$_2$C-A$_1$C-B$_1$C-B$_2$C (B = Dexedrine program)	*Behavioral:* 1. Off task 2. Gross motor 3. Noise and vocalization *Teacher Report:* 1. Conners teacher questionnaire *Academic Measures:* 1. Math performance 2. Spelling performance *Laboratory Measures:* 1. Continuous performance test	Dexedrine and self-control best. Equivocal effects. Equivocal effects. Drug and self-control best. Direct reinforcement only produced effects. Dexedrine alone best.	Dexedrine: B$_1$ = titrating drug, B$_2$ = 10 mg
Rose, 1978	2	A-A$_1$-B-A$_1$-B-A$_1$ (B = food additives, tartrazine #5)	*Behavioral:* 1. Out of seat 2. On task 3. Aggression	Increased. Decreased. Unclear.	Tartrazine #5; 0.5 mg/kg
Wulbert & Diries, 1977	1	B-A$_1$-B-A$_1$ (B = drug)	*Behavioral:* 1. Rituals 2. Aggressive behavior	No drug effects on behavior in clinic. Increased aggression and increased ritualistic behavior in home.	Ritalin: 10 mg q.i.d.

Study		Design	Measures	Results	Drug/dose
Shafto & Sulzbacher, 1977	1	A-B₂-B₂C-A-B₁-B₃-C-A Alternating tx design phase in an additive design (B = drug C = behavioral intervention)	*Behavioral:* 1. Activity changes 2. Nondirected or indistinct verbals 3. Isolate play 4. Wandering 5. Attending 6. Compliance	Both together better than either alone. Increased during drug. Decreased during behavioral intervention. Equivocal. Decreased with behavioral intervention. Increased with drug. Increased with low dose drug.	Ritalin: $B_1 = 5$ mg, $B_2 = 10$ mg, $B_3 = 15$ mg
Pelham, 1977	1	BC-C (B = drug C = behavioral program)	*Teacher report:* 1 IMH Global rating scale	Continued improvement with behavior program after drug withdrawn.	Ritalin: 10 mg
Williamson et al., 1981	1	A-B-A-B-BC-BCD-BCDEF (B = drug C = instructions D = practice E = feedback F = reinforcement)	*Behavioral:* 1. On task 2. Gross motor 3. Appropriate *Monitor:* 1. Arm activity 2. Foot activity	Increased best with drug Decreased best with Dexedrine, feedback and reinforcement. Equivocal. Decreased best with Dexedrine, feedback and reinforcement. Decreased best as above.	Dexedrine: increased to 20 mg

Note: The authors are indebted to Karen C. Wells, Ph.D. for the compilation of this table.

Table 4.4. Single-Case Design for Drug Studies of Depressed Children

Study	Ss	Design	Dependent Measures	Distinctive Findings	Drugs
Petti et al., 1980	1	AB (B = drug)	*Ward observations:*		Imipramine: 100 mg
			1. CBI total deviant	Decrease	
			Behavioral analog measures:		
			1. Eye contact	Increase	
			2. Smiles	Increase	
			3. Speech duration	Increase	
			4. Requests for new behavior	Increase	
Petti & Unis, 1981	1	$A-A_1-B_1-B_2-B_1-A_1-B_2$ (B = drug)	*Behavioral:*		Imipramine: $B_2 = 125$ mg/day, full dose; $B_1 =$ titrating up and down.
			1. Adaptive peer	Increase	
			2. Bizarre vocalizations	Decrease	
			3. Unusual movements	Decrease	
			4. Activities of daily living	Increase	
			5. Adaptive mealtime behavior	Increase	
			6. Compliance	Increase	
			7. Number of seclusion orders	Decrease	
Michelson et al., 1984	1	A-B-A	*Behavioral:*		Imipramine: 150 mg
			1. On task in class	Increase; no reversal	
			2. Disruptive in class	Decrease; no reversal	
			3. Activities of daily living	Increase; no reversal	
			4. Enuretic episodes	Decrease; no reversal	

Note: The authors are indebted to Karen C. Wells, Ph.D. for the compilation of this table.

and behavioral interventions (Barlow & Hersen, 1984; Liberman, Davis, Moon, & Moore, 1973).

Because they permit experimental work to be conducted in clinical settings where between-group research may be unfeasible, single-subject designs are of particular value to individual practitioners in their efforts to assess a patient's response to medication or to titrate dosage. For example, in place of the subjective and unsystematic methods routinely applied in practice, a number of authors have relied on single-subject experimental methodology to develop more rigorous multimethod protocols for evaluating and monitoring individual children's response to stimulant medication in clinic (Fischer & Newby, 1991), day treatment (Pelham & Hoza, 1987), and school (Gadow, Nolan, Paolicelli, & Sprafkin, 1991) settings.

Typical problems encountered with the application of single-subject designs in psychopharmacology are carryover effects of treatments that occur in reversal designs, indeterminate interaction effects among successive treatment conditions, difficulties establishing double-blind procedures with certain designs, and the inability to evaluate Subject Characteristic X Treatment interactions. Problems of external validity (generalizing findings to other subjects) are, of course, intrinsic to these designs. Multiple baseline designs—in which subjects are given a staggered start with the treatment—have seldom been used in psychopharmacology but might be particularly useful in clinical settings where placebos cannot be used or where the condition mitigates against reversal of the experimental treatment. Much research is not done because of the ethical problems of using placebos, and the single-subject designs offer some advantage under these conditions. Barlow and Hersen (1984, pp. 183–192) provide a cogent discussion of the application of single-subject designs to psychopharmacological research.

Once the efficacy of individual treatments has been established for a particular disorder or symptom, whether through group comparison or single-subject methods, there is a logical progression toward comparing alternative treatments, both alone and in combination with one another. Indeed, the examination of multimodal treatment strategies, combining psychopharmacological and psychosocial interventions is an emerging area in child psychiatry. Methodologically, such studies typically require, at minimum, a four-group factorial design in which two treatments are evaluated against each other, against the control group, and against their combination (see Figure 4.1). As noted by Klerman (1986), the advantage of such factorial designs is that they provide a simultaneous "comparison of drugs against [psychosocial therapy] and against a control group, as well as a constructive strategy to assess the possible advantage of combining drugs and [psychosocial therapy]" (p. 793). A discussion of design options and related issues when evaluating multiple treatments is also provided by Kazdin (1986).

	Psychosocial Treatment	
Pharmacotherapy	Combined Treatment Group	Psychosocial Treatment Group
	Drug Treatment Group	Control Group

Figure 4.1.   Four-group factorial design for evaluating combined treatment.

Because of the well-established, short-term efficacy of both stimulant medications (Gadow, 1992) and behavioral interventions (Hinshaw & Erhardt, 1993; Pelham & Hinshaw, 1992) in the treatment of attention-deficit/hyperactivity disorder (ADHD), investigators in that field are leading the way in designing comparative treatment studies involving pharmacotherapy, behavioral interventions, and their combination (Abikoff, 1991; see Pelham & Murphy, 1986, for review). Although multi-modal treatment packages comprising carefully titrated stimulant medication and psychosocial interventions are emerging as the treatment of choice for ADHD, the empirical basis for such practice is still incomplete. The significant methodological barriers to definitively determining the relative efficacy of psychosocial treatments and medication in ADHD children have been enumerated and discussed by a number of authors (Conners et al., 1994; Whalen & Henker, 1991). Of note is the recently initiated NIMH collaborative study on the multimodal treatment of children with ADHD. Because of its careful design and statistical power, this project, which comprises a randomized one-way design with four groups (medication treatment alone, psychosocial treatment alone, combination of medication and psychosocial treatments, and a community comparison group), should provide the most definitive determination to date of which treatment interventions (alone and in combination) work best for which children in which settings, and for how long.

ORGANISMIC VARIABLES

Subject Selection

DSM-IV and Diagnosis.   Interview methods for clinical diagnosis have long formed the foundation of research in child psychiatry. The publication of the third edition of the *Diagnostic and Statistical Manual of*

Mental Disorders (DSM-III: American Psychiatric Association [APA], 1980) marked a major advance in terms of providing detailed criteria for diagnosing child psychiatric disorders (Cantwell & Baker, 1988) and led to a growing reliance among researchers on structured and semistructured interviews.

A complete discussion of the clinical and methodological issues associated with interviewing is beyond the scope of this chapter, but two excellent general sources are chapters by Costello (1991) and Hodges and Zeman (1993). As was the case with the revised third edition of the DSM (DSM-III-R; APA, 1987), the recently published DSM-IV (APA, 1994) has introduced new disorders and subgroups in the pediatric arena while revising or deleting others. These new diagnostic rules, derived in part from extensive field trials, will certainly have an important effect on psychopharmacological research. Ideally, revised diagnostic criteria will yield more homogeneous samples and result in more informative therapeutic drug trials.

Conversely, the results of such trials may either support or cast doubt on the validity of new diagnostic distinctions, although the use of drug response as a diagnostic validator can only be carried so far in light of the nonspecific nature of current psychopharmacology (Orvaschel, Ambrosini, & Rabinovich, 1993).

Reliability is a critical requisite of any categorical classification system such as the DSM (Quay, 1979). Threats to reliability in psychiatric diagnosis include variance related to information obtained, criteria employed, and the use of different informants (e.g., parent vs. child), as well as true differences that children with disorders will exhibit over time (Volkmar, 1991). Studies on previous versions of the DSM have found interdiagnostician reliability to be acceptable for the broadly defined major categories of disorder (Rutter & Shaffer, 1980; Volkmar, 1991). Thus, some of the categories of most interest to pediatric psychopharmacologists, such as Attention-Deficit/Hyperactivity Disorder, Conduct Disorder, Major Depressive Disorder, and Anxiety disorders have satisfactory reliability (see, e.g., Schwab-Stone et al., 1993; Shaffer et al., 1993).

However, reliability has generally been consistently lower for less common disorders or subcategories (Werry, Methven, Fitzpatrick, & Dixon, 1983). For example, it is known that aggressive behavior is a highly important predictor of outcome in children that respond to stimulant treatment (Hinshaw, 1991). Yet DSM subcategories of Conduct Disorder that have attempted to capture this critical dimension have proven to be highly unreliable. Socialized Aggressive Conduct Disorder, for instance, was found in one study (Werry et al., 1983) to have a Kappa reliability of −0.04! Additionally, the DSM-III-R Conduct Disorder category of Solitary Aggressive Type was abandoned in DSM-IV (which simply distinguishes Conduct Disorder on the basis of childhood or adolescent onset), presumably due in part to its poor reliability. As pointed out by Hinshaw (1991), the low base rates associated with aggressive behaviors make reliable measurement difficult and categorical diagnostic approaches may have to give way to adult ratings or data from behavior observations to properly select aggressive subjects for pharmacological investigations.

Data pertaining to the reliability of child diagnostic categories as defined by DSM-IV are not yet widely available but should be included in the soon-to-be-published *Sourcebooks* that will detail relevant field trials and data-analyses. It will be important to examine how the system's reliability will vary as a function of a number of variables, including the training of the raters, the age of the subjects, the setting, and the type, range, and severity of psychopathology. With respect to the diagnosis of ADHD, for instance, it appears on the basis of field trials that the DSM-IV is superior to its predecessor in terms of (a) providing criteria that yield diagnoses that agree with those made by clinicians using all available information, and (b) test-retest reliability over a 2-week period (McBurnett, Lahey, & Pfiffner, 1993).

Structured Interviews.   Although certain sources of unreliability are beyond methodological control, the variance attributable to the clinical interviewing method, criteria employed for various disorders, and diagnostic thresholds can all be minimized by using a structured interview. These interviews, which include both semistructured and highly structured types, are increasingly relied on methods for subject selection in pharmacological research. As noted by Hodges (1993), standardized questions and procedures for making diagnoses should result in research samples that are more homogeneous within studies and more comparable across studies. In addition to being more reliable than traditional interviews (Werry, 1992), structured approaches, by systematically covering a variety of diagnoses, provide data on comorbidity, which is increasingly recognized as having important implications for treatment response (Orvaschel et al., 1993; Pliszka, 1991).

A number of structured interviews tied to DSM criteria have been developed that provide a research basis for psychopharmacology studies within the prepubertal and adolescent age-range (see Costello, 1991; Hodges, 1993; Hodges & Zeman, 1993; Orvaschel, 1985, for reviews). The predominant interviews in current use include the Child Assessment Schedule (CAS: Hodges & Fitch, 1979), Child and Adolescent Psychiatric Assessment (CAPA: Angold, Cox, Prendergast, Rutter, & Simonoff, 1987), Diagnostic Interview for Children and Adolescents (DICA: Herjanic, Herjanic, Brown, & Wheatt, 1975; DICA-R: Reich & Welner, 1988), Diagnostic Interview Schedule for Children (DISC: Costello, Edelbrock, Dulcan, Kalas, & Klaric, 1984; DISC-R: Shaffer et al., 1993), the Interview

Schedule for Children (ISC: Kovacs, 1983, 1985), and the Schedule for Affective Disorders and Schizophrenia for School Aged Children (K-SADS-III-R: Ambrosini, 1986; K-SADS: Puig-Antich & Chambers, 1978).

All these interviews can be used to generate diagnoses for the major child and adolescent categories of most interest to psychopharmacological researchers including Attention-Deficit/Hyperactivity Disorder, Oppositional Defiant Disorder, Conduct Disorder, Major Depressive and Dysthymic Disorders, Overanxious Disorder, Separation Anxiety Disorder, Phobias, and Obsessive Compulsive Disorder. Many also permit additional diagnoses (e.g., schizophrenic spectrum disorders, Bipolar Disorder, elimination disorders, eating disorders). The CAS, CAPA, DICA, and DISC provide computerized scoring algorithms that can be used to generate diagnoses. Certain interviews, such as the CAS, DISC, and K-SADS also provide continuous symptom scale scores grouped by diagnosis. Common to all these measures is the availability of both parent and child versions. Although adult informants are generally more reliable than their younger counterparts (Edelbrock, Costello, Dulcan, Kalas, & Conover, 1985), children may provide more accurate data on internalizing symptoms such as those related to depressive and anxious disorders (Herjanic et al., 1975). For most research purposes, it is recommended to obtain both child and parent reports of symptoms (Hodges, 1993).

Although it is tempting to view the available structured interviews as competing measures, they are in fact alternative tools with profiles of strengths and weaknesses that make them more of less suitable to a particular research application. A key dimension on which they vary involves the degree of structure present, with respect to the exact wording and ordering of questions, methods of recording responses, and procedure for generating diagnoses. Although distinctions along this domain are at times blurred, the more highly structured measures include the DICA, CAPA, and DISC. Such highly structured interviews have shown good reliability (Werry, 1992), high degrees of sensitivity (Costello, 1991), minimize subjective clinical judgment, and may be administered by trained lay interviewers or clinicians. However, they also may be cumbersome, less "user friendly," lengthy, and highly demanding of data processing resources.

Additionally, in certain instances, the meaningfulness and validity of results emerging from structured interviews can be called into question when the data are not filtered through the knowledge base of an experienced clinician. For example, an inner-city boy who endorses items related to having been "followed," "attacked," or the belief that "someone is out to hurt me" may be accurately conveying the realities of his environment. Yet, in the context of a completely objective system that removes clinical judgment, such a child may be misdiagnosed as suffering from paranoid delusions. The risk of such errors highlights the importance of careful interviewer training, even for measures that appear to be highly straightforward.

The most frequently used semi-structured interviews in research settings include K-SADS, ISC, and the CAS. Advantages that may be associated with the use of semi-structured measures include greater flexibility, increased rapport with subjects, brevity, and possibly higher levels of diagnostic specificity. However, they require the interviewer to be knowledgeable and experienced with respect to the assessment and diagnosis of child psychopathology. Although the CAS, like more structured interviews, provides algorithms and computer software for generating diagnoses, classifications derived from the K-SADS and ISC are based on clinical judgment.

The degree to which the psychometric properties of interviews are influenced by the level of structure in their format or the clinical expertise of the interviewer remains unclear. Reliability data have been generated for all of the interviews discussed here and most have been the subject of some validity studies. However, because these instruments undergo frequent changes, it is difficult to make final recommendations based on these factors. An analysis of such psychometric data is beyond the scope of this chapter as it is complicated by issues such as the multiple types of reliability and validity to be considered, the absence of a "gold standard" with respect to psychiatric diagnosis, and differing findings depending on the version of a particular interview used or whether the informant was a parent or child. However, the psychometric properties of most of these interviews has been reviewed by a number of authors (see Costello, 1991; Hodges, 1993; Hodges & Zeman, 1993; Orvaschel, 1985).

As is the case with any decision regarding research methods, the selection of the most appropriate interview will depend on a number of factors including the question of interest to the investigator, the nature and extent of available resources, and the extent to which a measure has demonstrated reliability and validity for the specific population and outcome variables being assessed. Thus, if the researcher is blessed with a cadre of well-trained clinician interviewers and is investigating childhood mood disorders, the K-SADS may represent the "best" choice. If, however, the researcher is conducting an epidemiological study with lay interviewers, the DISC would be more appropriate. A revision of the DISC (NIMH DISC-3) keyed to DSM-IV symptoms is currently being developed and will be field tested over the next year. Because it provides comprehensive coverage of symptomatology, well-standardized algorithms for classification, and computer-based programs for administration, scoring, and assigning diagnoses, the DISC is likely to remain a frequently employed interview in child psychopharmacological research. Because it is the most recently introduced interview and continues to be underutilized, it is worth noting that the CAPA is the most clinically thorough of the available measures and well suited to making highly sensitive and valid diagnoses (albeit at the cost of extensive interviewer training). The CAPA also has been updated to yield DSM-IV diagnoses. All told, despite their limitations, structured interviews have brought improved comparability and order into methods of subject selection for psychopharmacology with children.

Dimensional Methods. Whereas structured interviews tend to be relied on for determining categorical diagnoses among research subjects, the *continuous* measure of symptoms provided by rating scales is an equally important component of subject selection. Although the use of dimensional measures as outcome variables will be described in a later section, their value as part of a battery of subject selection techniques lies in providing information on the *range* and *degree* of pathology, typically on the basis of normative comparisons. Additional advantages associated with rating scales include their brevity, low cost, ease of administration and scoring, aggregation of an informant's experience with a child across time and settings, potential for assessing low frequency behaviors, and capacity to measure both broadly and narrowly defined areas of disturbance.

Indeed, following the publication by the National Institute of Mental Health (NIMH, 1973, 1985) of two *Psychopharmacology Bulletin* special issues on assessment instruments for children, the use of rating scales for subject selection, sample description, and drug response became commonplace. The *Psychopharmacology Bulletin* special issue (NIMH, 1985), soon to be updated, remains an invaluable compendium of measures in this area. A number of reviews pertaining to child and adolescent rating scales have appeared more recently, including Piacentini (1993) on the most widely used broad- and narrow-band scales, Barkley (1990) on measures for children with ADHD, Wells (1995) on scales for the assessment of children with conduct disorder, along with Conners (1994a) and Achenbach (1994) providing detailed reviews of the Conners Rating Scales and Child Behavior Checklist (and related measures), respectively. The reader is referred to these sources for detailed information on the content and psychometric properties of the primary scales employed in child psychopharmacology research.

Given the prevalence of drug treatment studies for the disruptive behavior disorders, one of the most important historical subject selection issues has been whether there are in fact separate syndromes of hyperactivity and conduct disorder. The high degree of correlation among rating scale factor dimensions of conduct disorder and hyperactivity/inattention had led some (Lahey, Green, & Forehand, 1980; Quay, 1979; Shaffer & Greenhill, 1979) to question the existence of separate syndromes.

Consensus has since emerged, however, that the dimensions of inattention/hyperactivity and conduct problems/aggression are at least partially independent (Hinshaw, 1987). Nevertheless, the fact that aggressive and hyperactive/inattentive symptoms frequently co-occur in clinical samples and that such comorbidity is associated with poorer outcome (Loeber, 1990; Rutter, 1989) argues for the importance of careful sampling and/or the statistical separation of these two sources of variance in drug outcome studies. The teacher-completed, 10-item Iowa-Conners Rating Scale (Loney & Milich, 1982) addresses this issue in that it was constructed to allow for the identification of children who are purely aggressive, purely hyperactive, or who have a mixed syndrome.

As was noted in the discussion of selecting a structured interview, the specific aims of the investigation will determine which is the most appropriate rating scale for subject selection. Wells (1995) highlights this fact, pointing out, for instance, that multidimensional scales are indicated when screening for a wide array of presenting problems or for patterns of comorbidity. These include the Achenbach-Conners-Quay Questionnaire (ACQ: Achenbach, Conners, & Quay, 1983; Achenbach, Conners, Quay, Verhulst, & Howell, 1992), Child Behavior Checklist (CBCL: Achenbach & Edelbrock, 1983), Conners Parent and Teacher Rating Scales (CPRS, CTRS: Conners, 1969, 1970, 1994a), and the Revised Behavior Problem Checklist (Quay & Peterson, 1983).

Pharmacology studies have also relied heavily upon the NIMH-developed Children's Psychiatric Rating Scale (CPRS: Fish, 1985) for assessing behavioral profiles in a variety of subject groups. In studies involving adolescents with ADHD, parent and teacher rating scales should be augmented by self-report scales, such as the Youth Self-Report (CBCL-YSR: Achenbach & Edelbrock, 1987), the ADD/H Adolescent Self-Report Scale (ADD/HSRS: Conners & Wells, 1985), and the Brown Attention-Activation Disorder Scale (BAADS: Brown, Gammon, & Barua, 1992) (for a review of the latter two measures, see Robin, 1994). If social and behavioral competencies, as well as symptomatic features, are a focus of assessment, the CBCL should be chosen. Research aimed at assessing pharmacological treatment effects where repeated measurements over time are necessary requires scales that are both brief and established to be drug sensitive (e.g., Conners Abbreviated Symptom Questionnaire, CPRS, CTRS). Of note is that the Conners Scales are currently undergoing a large national restandardization.

There is considerably less research data available to guide the researcher in choosing appropriate scales with which to select subjects or measure drug effects for children with depression or anxiety disorders (Aman, 1993). Scales applicable to depressed children include the Child Depression Inventory (CDI: Kovacs, 1992), the Reynolds Scales (Reynolds,

1981; Reynolds, Anderson, & Bartell, 1985), the Children's Depression Scale (CDS: Lang & Tisher, 1978), the Depressive Self-Rating Scale (Birleson, 1981), and the Emotional Disorders Rating Scale (EDRS: Kaminer, Feinstein, Seifer, Stevents, & Banett, 1990). Aman (1993) reviews the extant scales for assessing anxious symptoms and specific anxious disorders in children and adolescents. The Multidimensional Anxiety Scale for Children (MASC: March, Stallings, Parker, Terry, & Conners, 1994) is a promising new measure that may yield subscales more sensitive to drug effects than its predecessors (J. March, personal communication, June 1994). The special issue of *Psychopharmacology Bulletin* (1985) as well as Aman (1993) describe scales for potential use for monitoring drug effects in children with other disorders, including schizophrenia, tic disorder and Tourette's syndrome, mental retardation, and autism.

Objective Laboratory Methods. Zametkin and Yamada (1993) review the medical history data and baseline physical examination measures necessary to collect before any clinical or research application of psychoactive drugs in children. Given some of the potential biases and other limitations associated with the subjective reports of informants (whether gathered through interviews or rating scales), there has been increasing interest in developing more objective measures of identifying subjects and assessing the presence and severity of symptoms. Such measures include direct observations, objective recording devices, and computerized performance tests.

Although they are more frequently used as a method of assessing the effects of drugs in research studies, systematic behavioral observations can also be employed in natural or clinic-analogue settings in the assessment and diagnosis of children. Observational procedures vary considerably but tend to share common features, including a priori determination of behavioral categories of interest, the use of a systematic coding system, observation periods of predetermined length, and the incorporation of reliability checks. Advantages associated with these methods include their high degree of objectivity, potential for ecological validity (especially when conducted in natural settings), and adaptability to a wide variety of pathology and settings. Moreover, they can be repeated without practice effects (Aman & White, 1986). Disadvantages include the potential for reactivity effects, the lack of normative data for most systems (Barkley, 1990), the insensitivity to drug effects of behavior categories that are either too broadly or too narrowly defined, and their expense and logistical demands. Barios (1993) provides a review of the development, implementation, and evaluation of behavior observation methods.

The type of observation employed will be dictated by the nature of the target behaviors and the limits of available resources. For example, a *response duration* measure may be indicated when assessing the total hours of sleep obtained by a depressed child or the extended tantrums of a child with oppositional-defiant disorder. On the other hand, *interval recording* would be preferred when the goal is to simultaneously measure a number of distinct categories (e.g., noncompliance, aggression, prosocial behaviors, social isolation). Phobias can be assessed with an observationally based *Behavioral Avoidance Test* that measures the degree to which the child will approach a feared stimulus. Mash and Terdal's (1988) edited volume on behavioral assessment provides descriptions of a variety of observational measures for various childhood disorders. Barkley (1990) critically reviews extant observational procedures for children with ADHD and concludes that, despite their limitations, "behavioral observations—when combined with parent, child, and teacher interviews and rating scales—can add greater validity, integrity, and rigor to the clinical diagnostic process" (p. 352).

Much of the activity in developing objective laboratory based assessment measures for children has occurred in the area of ADHD. Although mechanical measures of activity level are available (e.g., wrist-, ankle-, or waist-bound actometers, specialized seat cushions or floor pads), they have not achieved widespread use either in clinic or research settings, in part because of concerns about reliability and external validity (Barkley, 1988). On the other hand, computer-based Continuous Performance Tests (CPT), which provide an attentional performance measure of vigilance or attention span, have become widely used measures both among ADHD researchers and others studying pediatric psychopharmacology.

Numerous versions of the CPT are available, but most require a child to monitor a display for a target stimulus (e.g., the letter *X*, or *X* only when preceded by *A*) which occurs infrequently among a series of nontargets. The value of these measures in providing a sensitive index of drug effects will be discussed below. However, they also are being used increasingly as a component of diagnostic or subject selection test batteries (Barkley, 1990). Although reviews have shown inconsistent results with regard to discriminative validity (Lovejoy & Rasmussen, 1990) and evidence for a vigilance decrement as measured by the CPT in ADHD children (Corkum & Siegel, 1993), these findings appear, at least in part, to be artifacts of specific test parameters such as *target frequency* and *interstimulus interval* (Davies & Parasuraman, 1982). Conners (1994b) recently reported data suggesting that CPT procedures that involve increased response frequencies on the part of subjects and analysis of reaction time and variability measures in addition to errors appear to yield improved diagnostic sensitivity for discriminating between normal subjects and those with ADHD. Barkley (1994) has recently reviewed the use of the CPT and other neuropsychological tests in the diagnosis of ADHD.

The Independent Variable

Irrespective of the particular research design that is chosen, it behooves researchers to keep in mind Mill's canon regarding experiments; that a valid comparison among treatments requires that we manipulate the variable of interest (e.g., pharmacological treatment), and nothing else. To do this, those designing experiments must first define what the treatment consists of, both in terms of what is required to be present and what must be absent. Over the past decade, these definitions have increasingly been codified in treatment manuals.

Whether applied to pharmacological or psychosocial interventions, treatment manuals detail the goals, specific procedures, and sequence of intervention components, often operationalizing the therapy through definitions, case examples, and therapist "scripts" (Klerman, 1986). Algorithms for clinical decision making are frequently included in treatment manuals. They also explicitly *proscribe* interventions or procedures that do not constitute part of treatment and that would, if included, introduce an experimental confound. For example, in a study comparing the effects of stimulant medication to comprehensive behavior therapy for children with ADHD, the pharmacotherapy manual should explicitly prohibit the pharmacotherapist from teaching parents to institute "Time-Out," a token economy, or other systematic behavioral interventions. Because subjects in a drug trial are receiving their treatment in the context of a human interaction rather than through some automatic dispensing of medication, the interpersonal context also should be addressed in pharmacotherapy manuals, with attention to issues such as therapeutic tone, the structure and format of sessions, and forming a therapeutic alliance.

Once treatment has been "manualized," procedures can be instituted to assess therapist adherence to the protocol. As noted by Waltz, Addis, Koerner, and Jacobson (1993), "Successful tests of treatment integrity include both an assessment of therapist adherence to the treatment protocol and a determination that the interventions are being performed competently" (p. 620). A number of different approaches may be used to assess treatment fidelity, including live monitoring or audiotapes of subject-therapist interactions that are rated for adherence by a third party, group supervision of therapists to ensure uniformity of procedures, and direct measures (e.g., serum or blood levels).

Compliance. In most psychopharmacological studies, the independent variable of interest is the level of the drug. Ultimately, brain levels rather than blood levels or dosage are of interest, but one usually settles for the latter two in human studies. Although merely prescribing the drug has often been assumed to be a sufficient condition to ensure that the appropriate variable is being manipulated, studies of drug noncompliance make it increasingly clear that this is not the case.

Noncompliance with pharmacological treatment is a serious but often neglected problem in both clinical and research studies, where it can seriously distort findings. In both contexts, the failure of the child to take the medication as prescribed represents a common cause of absent, unexpectedly poor, or highly variable response (Campbell, Green, & Deutsch, 1985; Zametkin & Yamada, 1993). It is estimated that approximately one-half of all patients in chronic drug treatment do not adhere to their prescribed regimens (Epstein & Cluss, 1982). In an earlier well-known survey, Solomons (1973) reports that only about 43% of children receiving stimulants were being properly monitored.

In an important study, 12 male hyperactive children 6 to 12 years of age, were randomly assigned to placebo, dextroamphetamine, or methylphenidate (MPH) for 6 weeks in a triple-blind crossover design (Kauffman, Smith-Wright, Reese, Simpson, & Jones, 1981). Weekly urine samples were obtained and assayed for MPH and dextroamphetamine. Individual compliance varied from 0% to 100%, with a mean of 67%, with the percentage of patients compliant for a given week varying from 55% to 80% (mean of 67%). More interestingly, significant *positive noncompliance* was found in that MPH was found in the urine of 5 of the 12 subjects during what was supposedly their placebo period. As the authors correctly note:

> *Failure of the patient to take medication as dictated by the investigational protocol has gone totally unrecognized as a potential contributor to the confusion and contradiction among studies. . . . The relatively high rate of noncompliance observed in this study raises serious questions regarding the reliability of behavioral and learning data obtained from even relatively well-controlled studies. (p. 236)*

Firestone (1982) investigated several variables that might relate to patient noncompliance with medication requirements. He followed 76 families over a 10-month period. Children were randomly assigned to either MPH treatment or a behavior modification program. By the end of the 10 months, 44% of the children were no longer taking medication. "Nonadherents" tended to be slightly younger and less intelligent, but no significant pretreatment factors were found that were characteristic of these children. It appeared that families of female rather than male children were more likely to discontinue medication. No differences in family psychopathology were found, but nonadherent parents were significantly younger and showed a trend to being less intelligent on a standardized measure. These predictors are similar to those previously found in studies of adherence to behavioral programs. Other variables found to influence the likelihood of noncompliance include the type of medication, drug efficacy, the presenting disorder, treatment environment, and the degree to which compliance is emphasized by the pharmacologist (Moore & Klonoff, 1986; Poling, Gadow, & Cleary, 1991).

Another important finding of the Firestone (1982) study was that 26% of the parents originally assigned medication refused this treatment. This could be an extremely important biasing factor for subject selection in drug studies. Noncompliance in many studies may represent resistance to subtle coercion to be in a drug study in the first place. There seems to be little doubt that compliance with a drug regimen may be one of the most significant variables in the outcome of pediatric drug trials, particularly among outpatients.

Any research design in pediatric psychopharmacology should include measures of treatment compliance. Sleator (1985) reviews both direct (e.g., blood levels, urinary excretion of drug or metabolite) and indirect (e.g., pill counts, interviews) measures of medication compliance. Moore and Klonoff (1986) provide a thorough discussion of assessing compliance in pharmacological research and propose that a biopsychosocial perspective is necessary to achieve a more complete understanding of this phenomenon.

Drug Plasma Levels

Stimulants. The psychostimulants have demonstrated efficacy in yielding short-term improvements in the behavioral, social, and academic functioning of children with ADHD. They have been established to be rapidly metabolized agents with relatively short half-lives. Although the considerable intersubject variability with respect to pharmacokinetics must be kept in mind, peak plasma levels for dextroamphetamine are generally reached within 2 to 3 hours of ingestion with a plasma half-life between 4 and 6 hours. Methylphenidate (MPH) reaches peak plasma levels within 1.5 to 2.5 hours and has a typical plasma half-life between 2 and 3 hours (Barkley, DuPaul, & Costello, 1993; Diener, 1991).

The relationship between drug plasma levels of MPH and clinical response in hyperactive children has been a matter of considerable scientific interest and some mixed findings. If drug plasma levels could be shown to be highly predictive of clinical response, it would have important implications for both research and clinical issues with this drug. With respect to the effects of stimulants on behavior, it does not appear that MPH plasma concentration provides a better prediction of clinical response than knowledge of oral dose alone (Gualtieri et al., 1982; Kupietz, 1991). On the other hand, a limited number of studies suggest that changes in learning performance on laboratory tasks may correspond more closely to plasma concentrations (Kupietz, 1991). Although such findings raise the possibility that blood levels may provide a useful index of learning performance and thus may be of benefit in establishing a therapeutic range, the high rates of inter- and intrasubject variability in response would appear to limit such applications. At present, there is insufficient evidence to recommend the use of blood levels to guide pharmacotherapy with the stimulants (Greenhill, 1992; Shaywitz & Shaywitz, 1991).

Antidepressants. Despite widespread clinical use and belief in their effectiveness, no controlled studies to date have found antidepressants to be superior to placebo in the treatment of depressed children or adolescents (for reviews, see Gadow, 1992; Pliszka, 1991; Ryan, 1992; Viesselman, Yaylayan, Weller, & Weller, 1993). There are convincing well-controlled single-subject design studies that strongly support, but do not confirm, the value of this treatment modality (Petti & Unis, 1981; Petti, Bornstein, Delamater, & Conners, 1980). Additionally, positive results from uncontrolled "open label" trials with imipramine (Preskorn, Weller, & Weller, 1982; Puig-Antich, Perel, & Lupatkin, 1979) had indicated relationships between plasma levels and response similar to those seen in adults. In a controlled study conducted by Simeon, Dinicola, Ferguson, and Copping (1990) with depressed adolescents, groups receiving fluoxetine and placebo both improved, with no superiority found for the active medication. Similarly, no double-blind, placebo-controlled studies of tricyclics for children (Geller, Cooper, McCombs, Graham, & Wells, 1989; Kashani, Shekin, & Reid, 1984; Petti & Law, 1982; Puig-Antich et al., 1987) or adolescents (Geller, Cooper, Graham, Marsteller, & Bryant, 1990; Kramer & Feiguine, 1981) have yielded favorable results for medication (Gadow, 1992).

Despite the negative findings from controlled studies and the possibility that various biological and developmental factors do indeed render the antidepressants less effective with younger subjects, the question of whether these agents are effective treatments for depressed youngsters must remain open. Conners (1992) has discussed the methodological problems (including placebo response rates, comorbidity, small sample size, and other design features) that limit the conclusions that can be drawn from these studies. With respect to blood levels, Gadow (1992) concludes that "the findings from blood level-therapeutic response analyses are too contradictory to offer sound clinical recommendations for either children or adolescents" (p. 159).

Neuroleptics. Across individuals, identical doses of antipsychotic agents are associated with extremely variable blood levels. These variations, along with the absence of a clear relationship between blood levels and therapeutic response, suggest little clinical indication for measuring blood levels except when (a) high doses have no clinical effect and (b) low doses lead to toxicity (Campbell, Gonzalez, Ernst, Silva, & Werry, 1993).

Data pertaining to the relationship between neuroleptic blood levels and clinical response in children and adolescents is sparse and somewhat mixed. Although, compared with adults, children and adolescents typically require larger weight-adjusted doses of psychoactive medications to achieve comparable therapeutic effects, this does not appear to be the case for the antipsychotics (Jatlow, 1987; Whitaker & Rao, 1992). Rivera-Calimlim and colleagues (Rivera-Calimlim, 1982; Rivera-Calimlim, Griesbach, & Perlman, 1979) found that children require larger doses of chlorpromazine (CPZ) than adults to achieve comparable plasma concentrations. However, the apparent therapeutic plasma concentration in children (estimated at about 40–80 ng/ml) is lower than that reported for adults (50–300 ng/ml) (Rivera-Calimlim et al., 1979). A similar pattern of results, suggesting greater neuroleptic sensitivity among children, has been reported for haloperidol (Moreselli, Bianchetti, & Dugas, 1982). However, data inconsistent with these findings was reported by Geller (1991), who found a therapeutic response to CPZ at 6–11 ng/ml in a group of adolescents with psychotic depression. Plasma concentrations appear to decline in many children despite maintaining the same dosage level, perhaps because of autoinduction of CPZ metabolism.

Thorough discussions of the uses of neuroleptics for children and adolescents are provided by Campbell et al. (1993), Gadow (1992), and Whitaker and Rao (1992). Included in these reviews are extensive discussions of toxic reactions to neuroleptics in children, which appear to be closely related to plasma concentrations (Teicher & Baldessarini, 1987; Tsujimoto, Tsujimoto, Ishizaki, Nakasawa, & Ichihashi, 1982). Important developments in the assessment of neuroleptic-related dyskinesias and other adverse effects have come from the NIMH Psychopharmacology Branch (see *Psychopharmacology Bulletin,* 1985, for review).

Dosage. Drug research with children suggests that dosage effects of drugs are complex. Such effects may be linear, curvilinear, or threshold responsive, depending on the agent, dose, and type of measure (Barkley, DuPaul, & Costello, 1993; Rapport, 1990). In ADHD research, Sprague and Sleator (1977) were first to suggest that the optimal dosage of stimulant medication for one domain of functioning may be detrimental to performance in another domain. Specifically, they concluded that the dose of MPH required to achieve optimal effect for social behavior (1mg/kg) is higher than that required for cognitive functioning and learning (0.3 mg/kg). These highly influential findings resulted in something of a *de facto* standard of dosing in treatment studies. However, this important work was never replicated by the authors, using the same measures, and considerable contrary evidence now exists. More recent studies have generally found linear dose-response relationships, with performance on a variety of cognitive, learning, and behavioral measures improving in a dose-related fashion within a range of 0.3–1.0 mg/kg (Barkley, DuPaul, & Costello, 1993; Charles, Schain, & Zelniker, 1981; Cunningham, Siegel, & Offord, 1985; Douglas, Barr, Amin, O'Neill, & Britton, 1988; Rapport, DuPaul, Stoner, Birmingham, & Masse, 1985; Rapport & Kelly, 1991; Sebrechts et al., 1986; Shaywitz & Shaywitz, 1991; Solanto, 1991). Of course, such findings represent group means and belie significant intersubject variability in dose-response relationships. This individual heterogeneity of response has led some researchers to report both group effects (e.g., ANOVAS yielding significant effects for medication status) and data analyzed at the level of the individual subject (e.g., 15 of 20 subjects being judged to be positive responders to a particular dosage) (see, e.g., Hinshaw, Henker, Whalen, Erhardt, & Dunnington, 1989; Pelham, Vodde-Hamilton, Murphy, Greenstein, & Vallano, 1991; Rapport, 1990).

On the other hand, some well-designed studies continue to find that key attentional and academic measures show a quadratic ("U-shaped") relationship of dose and effect (Rapport, DuPaul, Stoner, & Jones, 1986), and recent reviews express concern regarding "cognitive toxicity" of high doses, particularly when the laboratory or academic task is effortful or complex (Aman & Rojahn, 1992; Swanson, Cantwell, Lerner, McBurnett, & Hanna, 1991; however, see studies by Rapport, 1991, for contradictory findings). Swanson and colleagues (1991) have suggested that the relationship of dose to performance may be quadratic or linear, depending on the complexity or "effort-load" of the task.

In a critical review, Pelham (1986) carefully reexamines the relationship between dosage and a number of other methodological factors as they relate to academic achievement in stimulant drug studies with hyperactive children. He concludes with a tongue-in-cheek set of recommendations on how *not* to find a drug treatment effect on academic measures:

> (a) Select a group of HA (hyperactive) children, some of whom are also LD and/or have academic deficits and need an academic intervention and some of whom do not; (b) administer a psychostimulant drug to all of these children at a dose that is 2 to 5 times higher than the level known to maximize improvement in cognition in most children. If doses are individually titrated, make certain that they are titrated on measures of global improvement rather than measures of cognition, thereby insuring that the majority of children in the study will be overmedicated with respect to cognitive performance; (c) entrust drug administration to the children's parents, thus guaranteeing that more than half of the children will not follow the prescribed regimen; (d) administer the medication in such a way that there is very little overlap between

the medication's time of peak effectiveness and the child's performance of daily academic tasks; (e) do not systematically arrange for concurrent interventions and instructional conditions that will maximize potential drug effects; (f) utilize dependent measures that are not sensitive to treatment effects; (g) finally, ignore individual differences in drug and dose response, academic deficits, and all other relevant dimensions, and average results across all of these variables, thus obscuring any positive results that would otherwise have been evident. (pp. 32–33)

These conditions continue to merit consideration among those investigating the effects of stimulants and other psychopharmacological agents in children. Discussions pertaining to dosage for other primary psychoactive drugs used with children and adolescents may be found in Shaffer (1992) and Werry and Aman (1993).

SETTING VARIABLES

Scant attention has been paid to the interaction of the drug effects and the social or stimulus environment of the child treated with drugs. Indeed, awareness of these variables arrived late on the adult scene as well until an important stimulus was given by the findings with adult schizophrenics that significant drug treatment variance is accounted for by aspects of the social environment in aftercare (Hogarty, Goldberg, Schooler, & Ulich, 1974).

In an extended multiple-treatment single-subject design, Wells, Conners, Imber, and Delamater (1981) showed an interaction between drug treatment, behavioral treatment (self-control), and stimulus setting. The drug treatment (MPH) and the behavioral treatment had different effects on behavior, depending on whether classroom or ward settings were examined.

The impact of the setting in which drug effects are *assessed* also must be considered, along with the attendant demand characteristics. For instance, the conditions in which ratings are made (e.g., classroom vs. playground, clinic vs. home) may markedly influence drug response (Campbell, Green, & Deutch, 1985). This point was made cogently by Rapport (1990) who found poor correspondence between the results of standardized measures of drug response administered in a highly controlled laboratory environment and those derived from teacher ratings, direct observations, and academic measures collected in actual classrooms. Unlike classrooms, controlled clinic settings do not contain multiple children engaged in a variety of diverse activities. Rapport astutely concluded that "high correlations between performance on experimental tasks . . . and classroom behavior and learning will likely occur to the extent that the former mimic the complex and multifaceted dimensions of the latter" (p. 106).

An important point regarding comparative efficacy studies of antidepressants and stimulants is made by Garfinkel, Wender, Sloman, and O'Neill (1983). They found that although MPH is generally superior in the treatment of ADD, TCAs had more effect on mood and provided more improvement across settings because of the longer half-life of these drugs compared with MPH. Comparative studies need to consider the impact of different dose-time-action profiles as they relate to when and where a particular target symptom will be observed.

DEPENDENT VARIABLES

Decisions regarding outcome measures in pediatric psychopharmacology tend all too often to be based on convenience or tradition. Demonstration of a relationship between a drug or dosage and clinical effects will often depend on a careful selection of dependent variables. Poor decisions regarding these measures can further obscure an already abstruse picture regarding the efficacy of psychoactive drugs in children and adolescents.

In part, the problem arises from the field's "growing pains" as it struggles with the issue of whether our pharmacologic treatments are directed at *disorders* or more specific *target symptoms.* Although some discern a trend toward disorder-specific pharmacotherapy (Aman, 1993), drug treatments continue to be aimed, in both research and clinical practice, at a more molecular level. Even in the few instances where a diagnostic category has come to imply an indication for a particular agent, treatment goals continue to be defined at the symptom level. For instance, a diagnosis of ADHD readily and appropriately leads to a consideration of psychostimulant therapy; yet our goals for the medication may involve various combinations of sharpening attention span, reducing impulsivity, calming motor behavior, improving compliance, decreasing aggression, raising academic productivity, or bolstering peer acceptance, depending on the particular presentation of the child or teen.

Given the relative nonspecificity of drug effects to current psychiatric diagnostic categories, mistakes can occur when the investigator operates at the level of a disorder and uses global-dependent measures that do not adequately assess target symptoms or are relatively insensitive to drug effects (Gadow, 1992). In his review of pediatric psychopharmacology, Gadow (1992) refers to a "desperate need for researchers to describe in greater detail response to medication in terms of specific target behaviors" (p. 181). Similarly, Barkley (1991) speaks of the potential for global rating scales to either add little to our current knowledge base regarding drug effects on children or to mislead us regarding their effects on a particular domain.

Many of the subject selection measures discussed earlier also may be used to assess drug effects. This is not always the case, however, and investigators must carefully consider their choice of dependent variable on the basis of (a) "goodness of fit" to the primary study questions, (b) psychometric properties, (c) appropriateness to the developmental range of subjects, (d) ecological validity, and (e) evidence of sensitivity to drug effects. Because clinical problems of interest are often multifaceted and require attention to the patterning of drug effects across different symptoms or domains of functioning, multiple dependent measures are typically necessary. Among these need to be methods of assessing for adverse side effects that are administered during both baseline and treatment phases to control for symptoms that could be occurring in the absence of treatment. Issues related to the assessment of adverse effects and specific side effects are discussed by Barkley (1990), Campbell, Green, and Deutsch (1985), Campbell and Palij (1985), and Zametkin and Yamada (1993).

Space permits only brief comments to be made here regarding specific outcome measures for drug studies with children. For thorough reviews of these methods, the reader is referred to Aman (1993), Barkley (1990), and the special issue of the *Psychopharmacology Bulletin* (NIMH, 1985). Newman and Ciarlo (1994) propose a set of generic criteria for researchers to use when selecting measures for assessing treatment outcome.

Although the categorical distinctions made by structured interviews make them generally more appropriate for subject selection and description procedures, the continuous measures (e.g., symptom scales) now included in many of these instruments may provide useful change measures (Hodges, 1993). Rating scales continue to be a mainstay for monitoring drug effects. The NIMH Clinical Global Impressions (CGI) scale (NIMH, 1985) provides a quick and simple measure that captures a clinician's judgments regarding severity of illness, improvement, and efficacy (which incorporates both therapeutic effects and side effects). Although widely used and sensitive to drug-induced changes (Campbell, Green, & Deutsch, 1985), the CGI is problematic due to its highly general nature, the unknown criteria employed by its users, lack of comparability across studies, and likely poor psychometric properties (Aman, 1993). For childhood disruptive behavior disorders, the Conners scales (viz., CPRS, CTRS, and Abbreviated Symptom Questionnaire) (Conners, 1969, 1970, 1994a), Iowa-Conners Rating Scale (Loney & Milich, 1982), ADHD Rating Scale (DuPaul, 1991), Home Situation Questionnaire (HSQ: Barkley, 1990), and School Situation Questionnaire (SSQ: Barkley, 1990) continue to be recommended due to their brevity, amenability to repeated administrations, and well-established sensitivity to drug effects (Aman, 1993; DuPaul & Stoner, 1994).

The need to augment measures based on subjective report with more objective methods applies as much to outcome assessment as to subject selection. Research studies commonly employ direct behavioral observations to assess the effects of drugs, and a variety of coding systems geared toward different settings or domains of functioning have been developed (for reviews see Aman, 1993; Barkley, 1990; DuPaul & Stoner, 1994). For example, reliable and drug-sensitive codes have been used to assess both the classroom behavior (Abikoff & Gittelman, 1985) and playground social functioning (Hinshaw et al., 1989) of children with ADHD. Barkley's important work on the impact of stimulant medication on parent-child interactions relied on observational methods (Barkley, 1989). In finding that both child compliance and negative parenting behaviors improved following the introduction of MPH, these studies helped to discredit theories connecting parenting style to the onset of ADHD (Barkley, 1990).

The steadily growing interest in the effects of psychoactive medications on cognitive functions and learning, along with the ascendancy of the microcomputer, has led to the increasing use of automated performance tests as dependent variables (see Aman, 1991, 1993, for reviews). Measures such as the Paired Associate Learning task (PAL; Swanson, 1985) and certain versions of the CPT (Conners, 1994b; Coons, Klorman, & Borgstedt, 1987; Garfinkel et al., 1986) have proven to be sensitive to the effects of drugs, although concerns related to external validity persist. The CPT has generated particular interest due not only to its diagnostic and treatment sensitivity, but also because a vigilance measure has great theoretical relevance to disorders such as ADHD and schizophrenia.

An encouraging trend in child and adolescent psychopharmacology studies is the attention being paid to a broadening array of dependent variables. Indeed, this represents an area of significant creativity in research design as investigators devise new ways to assess the effects of psychotropic medications. Examples include the use of an engaging space adventure board game to assess the social, ecological impact of stimulant medication (Whalen & Henker, 1980), measurement of attention during baseball games (Pelham et al., 1990), sociometric measures (Whalen et al., 1989), thought disturbance task and rating scales (developed by Caplan, Perdue, Tanguay, & Fish, 1990, cited in Barkley, 1991), objective measures of classroom desk organization (Atkins, Pelham, & Licht, 1989), paradigms to assess covert antisocial acts such as cheating, stealing, and property destruction (Hinshaw, Heller, & McHale, 1992), and a variety of innovative academic measures, including curriculum-based measurement (Shinn, 1989; see reviews in DuPaul

& Stoner, 1994; Gadow & Swanson, 1986). As pointed out by Barkley (1991), there is a pressing need not only to broaden dependent measures across domains, but also to extend them across time in order to assess how the short-term effects of medications alter long-term outcome in a variety of spheres.

STATISTICAL ISSUES

Unlike research design options, which remain relatively static over time, statistical techniques for analyzing data are subject to constant development and advancement. As noted by Kraemer (1981), "[Statistical] tools that were best 10 or 20 years ago may be either obsolete or superseded by newer, better, or more powerful tools" (p. 318). A detailed discussion of data-analytic methods is beyond the scope of this chapter. However, a number of excellent general references exist on statistical issues associated with evaluating treatment-related change (see, e.g., Collins & Horn, 1991; Francis, Fletcher, Stuebing, Davidson, & Thompson, 1991; Newman, 1994; Whalen & Henker, 1986). A few statistical issues relevant to psychopharmacological outcome research are highlighted in the following sections.

Placebo Contingency

It has been repeatedly shown that a powerful predictor of drug response is the baseline or placebo rate of the behavior of interest. This phenomenon, know as *rate dependency* or *placebo contingency,* occurs across a wide variety of species, behaviors, and pharmacological agents, but has been most extensively documented for stimulant drugs. This effect was first reported for ADHD/LD children by Conners (1972) in a controlled study comparing dextroamphetamine, methylphenidate, and placebo.

Regression analyses showed that the best predictor of any drug-related changes in several different domains was always the initial rate or level of the behavior, even when controlled for regression-to-mean effects. In a clinical sample of hyperactive children, Hicks, Gualtieri, Mayo, Schreder, and Lipton (1985) found drug effects to be inversely related to placebo scores for an extensive array of dependent measures including activity measures, rating scales, continuous performance test scores, and direct observations. Kinsbourne (1985) reported similar rate-dependency drug effects on hyperactive children's performance on cognitive tasks (e.g., Matching Familiar Figures Test).

The applicability of rate dependency drug effects to social, cognitive, and academic measures indicates that baseline or placebo behavior rates may be useful in predicting which dose is most effective for which domain of behavior. As noted elsewhere (Conners, 1994a), these effects suggest that it is reasonable in drug studies to use the most elevated scales on rating measures as predictors of drug treatment outcome, as well as primary target behaviors for medication effects. With respect to the Conners Rating Scales, high scores on the 10-item Hyperactivity Index as well as on the Conduct Disorder, Hyperactivity, and Inattention scales have been found to be good indicators of likely improvement with drug therapy.

Data Analysis

Statistical analyses need to be appropriate to the research question posed, the study design, and the nature of the data collected. Rather than deferral to the end of a study, decisions regarding data analysis should be an integral part of the research design stage. In planning research, the investigator must make informed judgments about a variety of statistical matters, including the likely size of the drug effect being studied, the level of Type I error risk that will be tolerated ("alpha-level"), the desired and anticipated sample size, and the preferred level of power (Cohen, 1990). Additional data-analytic considerations meriting early attention include how problems associated with subject attrition and missing data will be addressed, the robustness of chosen procedures to violations of assumptions regarding the nature of the data (such as those related to normality, homogeneity of variances, and linearity of effects), and whether the design and analytic strategies will be sufficient to detect interaction effects of interest.

Statistical power, which refers to the likelihood of detecting a genuine difference between experimental conditions, merits special attention because it continues to be neglected by researchers and many studies are compromised by inadequate power (see Cohen, 1990; Rosnow & Rosenthal, 1989; Sedlmeier & Gigerenzer, 1989, for more extensive discussions of this issue). Conners (1992) addressed the relevance of power issues to the negative findings of antidepressant drug trials for depressed adolescents. Kraemer and Thiemann (1987) present a helpful method enabling researchers to calculate power and determine approximate sample sizes for a wide variety of research designs.

As noted earlier, single-subject experimental designs are underutilized in psychopharmacology research. Although the analysis of these designs most frequently involves visual-inspection methods applied to graphic displays of the data, statistical tests (e.g., t and F tests, time series-analysis, randomization tests, R_n ranking test, split middle technique) can also be applied. Kazdin (1982, 1984) provides detailed discussions of data-analytic methods for single-subject research designs.

Nevertheless, most pharmacological researchers will be faced with the need to develop data-analytic strategies appropriate to group comparison designs. One of the most common issues in the analysis of drug-placebo effects is how to handle the scores that characterize the pre- to postdrug and pre- to postplacebo change effects. Simple difference scores represent a basic unit of analysis; yet, they have been the subject of considerable controversy. Criticism has focused on two issues: (a) the inverse relation between the reliability of the difference score and the correlation between pre- and posttreatment measures, and (b) the correlation between the difference score and the pretest measure (Francis et al., 1991). On the other hand, Newman (1994) cites others (e.g., Rogosa & Willett, 1983; Willett, 1988; Zimmerman & Williams, 1982) who have provided arguments and empirical support contrary to these criticisms and challenged the merit of proposed solutions (e.g., residualized change scores, Webster & Bereiter, 1963). Following an extensive discussion of the issue, Newman (1994) concludes that the difference score may be appropriately applied when the research question is simply stated (e.g., "Is there a change related to treatment?") but inadequate when considering more complex questions such as treatment interactions with subject characteristics or maintenance of effects over time.

A multitude of authors have discussed the advantages and limitations of the traditionally applied analytic methods for examining between-group differences in change over time (see, e.g., Francis et al., 1991; Friedman, Furberg, & DeMets, 1985; Kraemer, 1981; Newman, 1994; Whalen & Henker, 1986). Among the methods are these frequently used repeated measures: analysis of variance (ANOVA or MANOVA when applied to multivariate designs) and analysis of covariance (ANCOVA, MANCOVA). Although they may be adequate for addressing broad research questions at the level of group trends and main effects (Newman, 1994), these procedures often entail restrictive design requirements and assumptions that are frequently violated in typical drug studies (e.g., differential dropout in drug and placebo groups due to side effects can lead to inequality of regression slopes in the two treatment conditions, a fundamental violation of required assumptions).

Moreover, these traditional analytic procedures may not be optimal for drug studies designed to detect interactions of treatment with other variables. Smith and Sechrest (1991) argue that regression methods or individual growth curve analyses are better suited to the detection of interaction effects. Francis et al. (1991) provide an extensive discussion of the more recent individual growth curves approach to the study of change, which permits analysis of research questions aimed at both individual and group levels of change. Noting the applicability of this approach to the evaluation of treatment outcomes, including medication effects, Francis et al. (1991) cite advantages over traditional analysis of variance methods including greater flexibility, less restrictive assumptions, and greater tolerance for missing data and for uneven or variably spaced repeated measures across subjects. Additionally, both Francis et al. (1991) and Newman

(1994) suggest that growth curve analysis may provide a better means to uncover treatment by subject characteristic interaction effects, which hold such importance for pharmacotherapy. Although structural equation modeling techniques can also be used to assess the pattern of influence among multiple variables related to treatment outcome, the required sample sizes are prohibitively large for the typical drug study.

Another data analysis problem involves detecting patterns of effect of a drug in clinical laboratory measures. Typically, drug studies will examine the impact of a drug on renal, hepatic, hematological, endocrine, or other variables one at a time, counting the number of patients showing an abnormality, or the number of abnormalities in drug versus placebo conditions. This method is obviously meaningless with respect to the issue of the *pattern* of effect that a drug might have. The problem is more akin to detecting the difference between individuals by their fingerprints than by a list of independent characteristics. Moreover, much of the information is lost since each laboratory value is counted only in terms of its normal-to-abnormal classification rather than its actual level.

Ryback, Eckardt, Rawlings, and Rosenthal (1982) demonstrated that quadratic discriminant analysis is a useful method for discriminating among medical conditions that are symptomatically very similar. The technique "is a nonlinear form of discriminant analysis which does not assume that the variability present in the discriminating variables (e.g., clinical laboratory tests) is the same for each medical condition but rather takes into account the finding that heterogeneity is very common in medical data" (p. 2342). This technique has been successfully used to demonstrate subtle clinical laboratory differences between alcoholics and nonalcoholics. However, it appears to be ideally suited as a method of examining the impact of a drug compared with a placebo on the overall pattern of side effects in a drug study.

Quitkin and colleagues (Quitkin, Rabkin, Ross, & McGrath, 1984; Quitkin, Rabkin, Ross, & Stewart, 1984) have shown how traditional pre-post change measures may obscure the effect of pharmacological agents that are slow-acting and affect only a subgroup of responders. They provide simple methods of pattern analysis that clarify the effects in samples containing true responders to an antidepressant. Such methods have typically been ignored in childhood studies.

The statistical criteria commonly employed to evaluate change in any treatment outcome study, including those involving pharmacological agents, inform us as to the likelihood that observed differences between groups represent chance findings. However, they may tell us very little about whether such differences are *meaningful* in a practical or clinical sense. The goal of pharmacotherapy, after all, is not to produce nonrandom changes in scores on symptom rating scales or laboratory measures, but to effect meaningful change in the subject's life, whether that change be reflected in normalized functioning, elimination or significant amelioration of target symptoms, or the perception of improvement by significant others.

Treatment outcome researchers are increasingly being encouraged to attend to the *clinical significance* of their findings. Whalen and Henker (1986), for example, propose, "It is incumbent upon each investigator who reports significant findings to demonstrate not only that $p < .05$, but also that the documented changes or differences have real-life meanings" (p. 215). Although no consensus has yet emerged as to the optimal method of determining clinical significance of findings, a number of options have been proposed (e.g., see Wittenborn, 1978 for a discussion of criteria for clinical significance in drug trials). A method introduced by Jacobson and Truax (1991) is particularly intriguing in that it entails a statistical approach to operationalizing clinical significance. The procedure combines assessing change in terms of a subject's level of functioning relative to the mean of the normal or dysfunctional population and introduces a statistic (RCI: Reliable Change Index) designed to reflect meaningful levels of improvement.

A final comment regarding analysis pertains to the use of meta-analytic techniques. *Meta-analysis* entails applying quantitative procedures to summarize the results of a body of individual studies (see Bangert-Drowns, 1986; Cooper, 1989; Kazdin, 1986, for discussions of the method). Meta-analysis is increasingly being applied to the treatment outcome literature and is highly indicated for drug outcome research in light of the frequency of divergent results across individual studies and the rarity of strict replication studies. The research on stimulant effects on children with ADHD, for instance, has been subject to a number of meta-analyses (see review by Swanson et al., 1993).

ETHICAL ISSUES

Despite the rapid growth of pediatric psychopharmacology, the ethics of medicating minors for their behavioral and emotional problems continues to be a matter of considerable debate. However, it is important to distinguish the broad issues associated with the clinical practice of child psychopharmacology from the ethical concerns involved in conducting a research investigation on medication effects in a pediatric population. Schouten and Duckworth (1993) provide a review of current medicolegal and ethical issues encountered by practitioners who prescribe psychoactive medications to children.

The most common ethical dilemmas facing psychopharmacological researchers often involve the need to strike a delicate balance between ensuring conscientious clinical management of patients and preserving a research design capable of providing meaningful and unambiguous data. For instance, can one ethically withhold a potentially efficacious treatment from a subject who is experiencing both distress and impairment in order to establish a placebo control group? Should a researcher, at the conclusion of the active phase of a medication trial, provide the subject with referrals for additional treatments even though those interventions may confound the results of subsequent follow-up data? What are the experimenter's clinical obligations to subjects who violate treatment protocols such that they are no longer providing useful data for the trial?

Specific answers to questions such as these must be derived in the context of the unique circumstances of each clinical trial (Hill, 1971). However, general guidelines exist to assist researchers in adhering to ethical standards while conducting studies with human subjects. Examples include the most recent ethical code issued by the American Psychological Association (1992) and United States Department of Health and Human Services (DHHS) guidelines regarding the protection of children involved as subjects in research (see Reatig, 1985a). Such guidelines prioritize the protection and safety of individual subjects and specify researchers' ethical responsibilities with respect to issues such as institutional approval, informed consent, privacy, confidentiality, inducements for subject participation, deception, debriefing participants, and reporting results. Ceci, Peters, and Plotkin (1985) describe and evaluate the process by which institutional review boards (IRBs) or human subject committees evaluate research proposals. Reatig (1985b) has compiled a bibliography of sources pertaining to ethical issues in research with children. An additional excellent resource on the subject is Imber et al. (1986). The authors provide a comprehensive review of ethical issues arising in clinical trials and describe practical solutions that are likely to have common applications across a wide variety of drug studies.

The process of informed consent involves apprising subjects (or their guardians) of study aims, procedures, potential risks and benefits, alternative treatments, and all other factors that may affect their willingness to participate in a research study. Although it is critical to the ethical conduct of all human subject research, truly informed consent is of particular importance in psychopharmacological research with children, given the extent of what is unknown about such interventions with respect to effectiveness, specific mechanisms of action, effects on developing central nervous systems, and the potential for short- and long-term adverse effects (Petti & Sallee, 1986). Bukstein (1993, p. 26) provides some guidelines for obtaining informed consent for medication trials. Barkley (1991) has noted the promise of standardized, intelligibly worded, and up-to-date consent forms for specific drugs or drug classes for improving the informed consent process in psychopharmacological research with children.

DHHS guidelines stipulate that children must give *assent,* whereas parents or guardians must give *permission.* The age and capability of the child to give assent is determined by the IRB on an individual basis. If there is direct benefit to the child only through the research or if the child is not capable of assent, the IRB may decide that assent is not required.

One advantage of these regulations is that they require investigators to assure that children are more psychologically involved and agreeable to participation when they are in drug studies, possibly one of the important variables relating to whether the child adheres to the treatment protocol. Obvious problems occur when the cognitive limitations of the child render assent meaningless, but IRBs must now make a more discriminating evaluation of how pediatric drug protocols relate to the well-being and trust of the children serving as study subjects.

REFERENCES

Abikoff, H. (1991). Interaction of methylphenidate and multimodal therapy in the treatment of attention deficit-hyperactive behavior disorder. In L. Greenhill & B. O. Osman (Eds.), *Ritalin: Theory and patient management* (pp. 147–154). New York: Mary Ann Liebert.

Abikoff, H., & Gittelman, R. (1985). The normalizing effects of methylphenidate on the classroom behavior of ADDH children. *Journal of Abnormal Child Psychology, 13,* 33–44.

Achenbach, T. M. (1994). Child Behavior Checklist and related instruments. In M. E. Maruish (Ed.), *The use of psychological testing for treatment planning and outcome assessment* (pp. 517–549). Hillsdale, NJ: Erlbaum.

Achenbach, T. M., Conners, C. K., & Quay, H. C. (1983). *The ACQ behavior checklist.* Burlington: University of Vermont Department of Psychiatry.

Achenbach, T. M., Conners, C. K., Quay, H. C., Verhulst, F. C., & Howell, C. T. (1992). Replication of empirically derived syndromes as a basis for taxonomy of child/adolescent psychopathology. *Journal of Abnormal Child Psychology, 17,* 299–323.

Achenbach, T. M., & Edelbrock, C. S. (1983). *Manual for the child behavior checklist and revised child behavior profile.* Burlington: University of Vermont, Department of Psychiatry.

Achenbach, T. M., & Edelbrock, C. S. (1987). *Manual for the child behavior checklist—youth self report.* Burlington: University of Vermont, Department of Psychiatry.

Aman, M. G. (1991). Applications of computerized cognitive-motor measures to the assessment of psychoactive drugs. In W. E. Dodson, M. Kinsbourne, & B. Hiltbrunner (Eds.), *The assessment of cognitive function in epilepsy* (pp. 69–96). New York: Demos.

Aman, M. G. (1993). Monitoring and measuring drug effects. II. Behavioral, emotional, and cognitive effects. In J. S. Werry & M. G. Aman (Eds.), *Practitioner's guide to psychoactive drugs for children and adolescents* (pp. 99–159). New York: Plenum.

Aman, M. G., & Rojahn, J. (1992). Pharmacological intervention. In N. N. Singh & I. L. Beale (Eds.), *Learning disabilities: Nature, theory, and treatment* (pp. 478–525). New York: Springer-Verlag.

Aman, M. G., & White, A. J. (1986). Measures of drug change in mental retardation. In K. D. Gadow (Ed.), *Advances in learning and behavioral disabilities* (Vol. 5, pp. 157–202). Greenwich, CT: JAI Press.

Ambrosini, P. J. (Ed.). (1986). *Schedule for affective disorders and schizophrenia for school age children (6–18 yrs.) (K-SADS-IIIR)*. Unpublished manuscript.

American Psychiatric Association. (1980). *Diagnostic and statistical manual of mental disorders* (3rd ed.). Washington, DC: Author.

American Psychiatric Association. (1987). *Diagnostic and statistical manual of mental disorders* (3rd ed. rev.). Washington, DC: Author.

American Psychiatric Association. (1994). *Diagnostic and statistical manual of mental disorders* (4th ed.). Washington, DC: Author.

American Psychological Association. (1992). *Ethical principles of psychologists and code of conduct.* Washington, DC: Author.

Angold, A., Cox, A., Prendergast, M., Rutter, M., & Simonoff, E. (1987). The child and adolescent psychiatric assessment (CAPA). Unpublished manuscript.

Atkins, M. S., Pelham, W. E., & Licht, M. H. (1989). The differential validity of teacher ratings of inattention/overactivity and aggression. *Journal of Abnormal Child Psychology, 17,* 423–435.

Ayllon, T., Layman, D., & Kandel, H. J. (1975). A behavioral-educational alternative to drug control of hyperactive children. *Journal of Applied Behavior Analysis, 8,* 137–146.

Bangert-Drowns, R. L. (1986). Review of developments in meta-analytic method. *Psychological Bulletin, 99,* 388–399.

Barios, B. A. (1993). Direct Observation. In T. H. Ollendick & M. Hersen (Eds.), *Handbook of child and adolescent assessment* (pp. 140–164). Needham Heights, MA: Allyn and Bacon.

Barkley, R. A. (1988). Attention deficit disorder with hyperactivity. In E. J. Mash & L. G. Terdal (Eds.), *Behavioral assessment of childhood disorders* (2nd ed., pp. 69–104). New York: Guilford.

Barkley, R. A. (1989). Hyperactive girls and boys: Stimulant drug effects on mother-child interactions. *Journal of Child Psychology and Psychiatry, 30,* 379–390.

Barkley, R. A. (1990). *Attention deficit hyperactivity disorder.* New York: Guilford.

Barkley, R. A. (1991). Introduction to the special issue: Child psychopharmacology. *Journal of Clinical Child Psychology, 20,* 226–231.

Barkley, R. A. (1994, February). Can neuropsychological tests help diagnose ADD/ADHD? *The ADHD Report,* 1–3.

Barkley, R. A., DuPaul, G. J., & Costello, A. (1993). Stimulants. In J. S. Werry & M. G. Aman (Eds.), *Practitioner's guide to psychoactive drugs for children and adolescents* (pp. 205–237). New York: Plenum.

Barlow, D. H., & Hersen, M. (1984). *Single case experimental designs* (2nd ed.). New York: Pergamon.

Birleson, P. (1981). The validity of depression in childhood and the development of a self-rating scale: A research report. *Journal of Child Psychology and Psychiatry, 22,* 73–88.

Brown, T. E., Gammon, G. D., & Barua, G. (1992, May). *Attention-activation disorder in high IQ.* Paper presented at American Psychiatric Association Conference, Washington, DC.

Bukstein, O. G. (1993). Overview of pharmacological treatment. In V. B. Van Hasselt & M. Hersen (Eds.), *Handbook of behavior therapy and pharmacotherapy for children: A comparative analysis* (pp. 13–32). Needham Heights, MA: Allyn and Bacon.

Campbell, D. T., & Stanley, J. C. (1966). *Experimental and quasi-experimental design for research.* Chicago: Rand McNally.

Campbell, M., Gonzalez, N. M., Ernst, M., Silva, R. R., & Werry, J. S. (1993). Antipsychotics (neuroleptics). In J. S. Werry & M. G. Aman (Eds.), *Practitioner's guide to psychoactive drugs for children and adolescents* (pp. 269–296). New York: Plenum.

Campbell, M., Green, W. H., & Deutsch, S. I. (1985). *Child and adolescent psychopharmacology.* Beverly Hills, CA: Sage.

Campbell, M., & Palij, M. (1985). Measurement of side effects including tardive dyskinesia. *Psychopharmacology Bulletin, 21,* 1063–1082.

Cantwell, D., & Baker, L. (1988). Issues in the classification of child and adolescent psychopathology. *Journal of the American Academy of Child and Adolescent Psychiatry, 27,* 521–533.

Caplan, R., Perdue, S., Tanguay, P. E., & Fish, B. (1990). Formal thought disorder in childhood onset schizophrenia and schizotypal personality disorder. *Journal of Child Psychology and Psychiatry, 31,* 1103–1114.

Ceci, S. J., Peters, D., & Plotkin, J. (1985). Human subjects review, personal values, and the regulation of social science research. *American Psychologist, 40,* 994–1002.

Charles, L., Schain, R., & Zelniker, T. (1981). Optimal dosages of methylphenidate for improving the learning and behavior of hyperactive children. *Journal of Developmental and Behavioral Pediatrics, 2,* 27–81.

Cohen, J. (1990). Things I have learned (so far). *American Psychologist, 45,* 1304–1312.

Collins, L. M., & Horn, J. L. (Eds.). (1991). *Best methods of the analysis of change: Recent advances, unanswered questions, future directions.* Washington, DC: American Psychological Association.

Conners, C. K. (1969). A teacher rating scale for use in drug studies with children. *American Journal of Psychiatry, 126,* 884–888.

Conners, C. K. (1970). Symptom patterns in hyperkinetic, neurotic, and normal children. *Child Development, 41,* 667–682.

Conners, C. K. (1972). Stimulant drugs and cortical evoked responses in learning and behavior disorders in children. In W. L. Smith (Ed.), *Drugs, development and cerebral function.* Springfield, IL: Charles C. Thomas.

Conners, C. K. (1992). Methodology of antidepressant drug trials for treating depression in adolescents. *Journal of Child and Adolescent Psychopharmacology, 2,* 11–22.

Conners, C. K. (1994a). Conners Rating Scales. In M. E. Maruish (Ed.), *The use of psychological testing for treatment planning and outcome assessment* (pp. 550–576). Hillsdale, NJ: Erlbaum.

Conners, C. K. (1994b, August). *The Continuous Performance Test (CPT): Use as a diagnostic tool and measure of treatment outcome.* Paper presented at the annual convention of the American Psychological Association, Los Angeles, CA.

Conners, C. K., & Wells, K. C. (1982). Single-subject designs in psychopharmacology. In A. E. Kazdin & A. H. Tuma (Eds.), *New directions for methodology of social and behavioral sciences: Single-subject research designs, Number 13.* San Francisco: Jossey-Bass.

Conners, C. K., & Wells, K. C. (1985). ADD-H Adolescent Self-Report Scale. *Psychopharmacology Bulletin, 21,* 921–922.

Conners, C. K., Wells, K. C., Erhardt, D., March, J. S., Schulte, A., Osborne, S., Fiore, C., & Butcher, A. T. (1994). Multimodality therapies: Methodologic issues in research and practice. In L. Greenhill (Ed.), *Child and adolescent psychiatric clinics of North America: Disruptive disorders* (pp. 361–377). Philadelphia, PA: W. B. Saunders.

Coons, H. W., Klorman, R., & Borgstedt, A. D. (1987). Effects of methylphenidate on adolescents with a childhood history of ADD: II. Information processing. *Journal of the American Academy of Child and Adolescent Psychiatry, 26,* 368–374.

Cooper, H. M. (1989). *Integrating research: A guide for literature reviews* (2nd ed.). Newbury Park, CA: Sage.

Corkum, P. V., & Siegel, L. S. (1993). Is the continuous performance task a valuable research tool for use with children with attention-deficit-hyperactivity disorder? *Journal of Child Psychology and Psychiatry, 34,* 1217–1239.

Costello, A. J. (1991). Structured interviewing. In M. Lewis (Ed.), *Child and adolescent psychiatry: A comprehensive textbook* (pp. 463–472). Baltimore, MD: Williams & Wilkins.

Costello, A. J., Edelbrock, L. S., Dulcan, M. K., Kalas, R., & Klaric, S. H. (1984). *Report on the NIMH Diagnostic Interview Schedule for Children (DISC).* Washington, DC: National Institute of Mental Health.

Cunningham, C. E., Siegel, L. S., & Offord, D. R. (1985). A developmental dose-response analysis of the effects of methylphenidate on the peer interactions of attention deficit disordered boys. *Journal of Child Psychology and Psychiatry, 26,* 955–971.

Davies, D. R., & Parasuraman, R. (1982). *The psychology of vigilance.* New York: Academic Press.

Diener, R. M. (1991). Toxicology of ritalin. In L. L. Greenhill & B. B. Osman (Eds.), *Ritalin: Theory and patient management* (pp. 34–43). New York: Mary Ann Liebert.

Douglas, V. I., Barr, R. G., Amin, K., O'Neill, M. E., & Britton, B. G. (1988). Dosage effects and individual responsivity to methylphenidate in attention deficit disorder. *Journal of Child Psychology and Psychiatry and Allied Disciplines, 29,* 453–475.

DuPaul, G. J. (1991). Parent and teacher ratings of ADHD symptoms: Psychometric properties in a community-based sample. *Journal of Clinical Child Psychology, 20,* 245–253.

DuPaul, G. J., & Stoner, G. (1994). *ADHD in the schools: Assessment and intervention strategies.* New York: Guilford.

Edelbrock, C., Costello, A. J., Dulcan, M. K., Kalas, R., & Canover, N. (1985). Age differences in the reliability of the psychiatric interview of the child. *Child Development, 56,* 265–275.

Epstein, L. H., & Cluss, P. A. (1982). A behavioral medicine perspective on adherence to long-term medical regimens. *Journal of Consulting and Clinical Psychology, 50,* 950–971.

Firestone, P. (1982). Factors associated with children's adherence to stimulant medication. *American Journal of Orthopsychiatry, 52,* 447–457.

Fischer, M., & Newby, R. F. (1991). Assessment of stimulant response in ADHD children using a refined multimethod clinical protocol. *Journal of Clinical Child Psychology, 20,* 232–244.

Fish, B. (1985). Children's Psychiatric Rating Scale. *Psychopharmacology Bulletin, 21,* 753–770.

Francis, D. J., Fletcher, J. M., Stuebing, K. K., Davidson, K. C., & Thompson, N. M. (1991). Analysis of change: Modeling individual growth. *Journal of Consulting and Clinical Psychology, 59,* 27–37.

Friedman, L. M., Furberg, C. D., & DeMets, D. L. (1985). *Fundamentals of clinical trials* (2nd ed.). Littleton, MA: PSG Publishing.

Gadow, K. D. (1992). Pediatric psychopharmacotherapy: A review of recent research. *Journal of Child Psychology and Psychiatry, 33,* 153–195.

Gadow, K. D. (1993). Prevalence of drug therapy. In J. S. Werry & M. G. Aman (Eds.), *Practitioner's guide to psychoactive drugs for children and adolescents* (pp. 57–74). New York: Plenum.

Gadow, K. D., Nolan, E. E., Paolicelli, L. M., & Sprafkin, J. (1991). A procedure for assessing the effects of methylphenidate on hyperactive children in public school settings. *Journal of Clinical Child Psychology, 20,* 268–276.

Gadow, K. D., & Swanson, H. L. (1986). Assessing drug effects on academic performance. In K. D. Gadow & A. Poling (Eds.), *Advances in learning and behavioral disabilities (Supplement 1, 1986: Methodological issues in human psychopharmacology)* (pp. 247–279). Greenwich, CT: JAI Press.

Garfinkel, B. D., Brown, W. A., Klee, S. H., Braden, W., Beauchesne, H., & Shapiro, S. K. (1986). Neuroendocrine and cognitive responses to amphetamine in adolescents with a history of attention deficit disorder. *Journal of the American Academy of Child Psychiatry, 25,* 503–508.

Garfinkel, B. D., Wender, P. H., Sloman, L., & O'Neill, I. (1983). Tricyclic antidepressants and methylphenidate treatment of attention deficit disorder in children. *Journal of the American Academy of Child Psychiatry, 22,* 343–348.

Geller, B. (1991). Psychopharmacology of children and adolescents: Pharmacokinetics and relationships of plasma/serum levels to response. *Psychopharmacology Bulletin, 27,* 401–409.

Geller, B., Cooper, T. B., Graham, D. L., Marsteller, F. A., & Bryant, D. M. (1990). Double-blind placebo-controlled study of nortriptyline in depressed adolescents using a "fixed plasma level" design. *Psychopharmacology Bulletin, 26,* 85–90.

Geller, G., Cooper, T. B., McCombs, H. G., Graham, D., & Wells, J. (1989). Double-blind placebo-controlled study of nortriptyline in depressed children using a "fixed plasma level" design. *Psychopharmacology Bulletin, 25,* 101–108.

Gitlin, M. J. (1990). *The psychotherapist's guide to psychopharmacology.* New York: Free Press.

Greenhill, L. L. (1992). Pharmacologic treatment of attention deficit hyperactivity disorder. In D. Shaffer (Ed.), *The psychiatric clinics of North America: Pediatric psychopharmacology* (pp. 1–27). Philadelphia, PA: W. B. Saunders.

Gualtieri, C. T., Wargin, W., Kanoy, R., Patrick, K., Shen, C. D., Youngblood, W., Mueller, R. A., & Reese, G. (1982). Clinical studies of methylphenidate serum levels in children and adults. *Journal of the American Academy of Child Psychiatry, 21,* 19–26.

Hays, S. C. (1981). Single case experimental design and empirical clinical practice. *Journal of Consulting and Clinical Psychology, 49,* 193–211.

Herjanic, B., Herjanic, M., Brown, F., & Wheatt, T. (1975). Are children reliable reporters? *Journal of Abnormal Child Psychology, 3,* 41–48.

Hicks, R. E., Gualtieri, C. T., Mayo, J. P., Schroeder, S. R., & Lipton, M. A. (1985). Methylphenidate and homeostatis: Drug effects on the cognitive performance of hyperactive children. In L. M. Bloomingdale (Ed.), *Attention deficit disorder: Identification, course, and treatment rationale* (pp. 131–141). Jamaica, NY: Spectrum.

Hill, A. B. (1971). *Principles of medical statistics.* New York: Oxford University Press.

Hinshaw, S. P. (1987). On the distinction between attentional deficits/hyperactivity and conduct problems/aggression in child psychopathology. *Psychological Bulletin, 101,* 443–463.

Hinshaw, S. P. (1991). Stimulant medication and the treatment of aggression in children with attention deficits. *Journal of Clinical Child Psychology, 20,* 301–312.

Hinshaw, S. P., & Erhardt, D. (1993). Attention-deficit hyperactivity disorder: Behavioral interventions. In V. B. Van Hasselt & M. Hersen (Eds.), *Handbook of behavior therapy and pharmacotherapy with children: A comparative analysis* (pp. 233–250). Needham Heights, MA: Allyn and Bacon.

Hinshaw, S. P., Heller, T., & McHale, J. (1992). Covert antisocial behavior in boys with attention-deficit hyperactivity disorder: External validation and effects of methylphenidate. *Journal of Consulting and Clinical Psychology, 60,* 274-281.

Hinshaw, S. P., Henker, B., Whalen, C. K., Erhardt, D., & Dunnington, R. E., Jr. (1989). Aggressive, prosocial, and nonsocial behavior in hyperactive boys: Dose effects of methylphenidate in naturalistic settings. *Journal of Consulting and Clinical Psychology, 57,* 636–643.

Hodges, K. (1993). Structured interviews for assessing children. *Journal of Child Psychology and Psychiatry, 34,* 49–68.

Hodges, K., & Fitch, P. (1979). *Development of a mental status examination interview for children.* Paper presented at the meeting of the Missouri Psychological Association, Kansas City, MO.

Hodges, K., & Zeman, J. (1993). Interviewing. In T. H. Ollendick & M. Hersen (Eds.), *Handbook of child and adolescent assessment* (pp. 65–81). Needham Heights, MA: Allyn and Bacon.

Hogarty, G. E., Goldberg, S. C., Schooler, N. R., & Ulich, R. F. (1974). Drug and sociotherapy in the aftercare of schizophrenic patients. II. Two year relapse rates. *Archives of General Psychiatry, 31,* 603–608.

Horn, W. F., Chatoor, I., & Conners, C. K. (1983). Additive effects of dexedrine and self-control training: A multiple assessment. *Behavior Modification, 7*(3), 383–402.

Imber, S. D., Glanz, L. M., Elkin, I., Sotsky, S. M., Boyer, J. L., & Leber, W. R. (1986). Ethical issues in psychotherapy research: Problems in a collaborative clinical trials study. *American Psychologist, 41,* 137–146.

Jacobson, N. S., & Truax, P. (1991). Clinical significance: A statistical approach to defining meaningful change in psychotherapy research. *Journal of Consulting and Clinical Psychology, 59,* 12–19.

Jatlow, P. I. (1987). Psychotropic drug disposition during development. In C. Popper (Ed.), *Psychiatric pharmacosciences of children and adolescents: Progress in psychiatry* (pp. 27–44). Washington, DC: American Psychiatric Press.

Kaminer, Y., Feinstein, C., Seifer, R., Stevents, L., & Banett, R. (1990). An observationally based scale for affective symptomatology in child psychiatry. *Journal of Nervous and Mental Disease, 178,* 750–754.

Kashani, J. H., Shekin, W. O., & Reid, J. C. (1984). Amitriptyline in children with major depressive disorder: A double-blind crossover pilot study. *Journal of the American Academy of Child Psychiatry, 23,* 348–351.

Kauffman, R. E., Smith-Wright, D., Reese, C. A., Simpson, R., & Jones, F. (1981). Medication compliance in hyperactive children. *Pediatric Pharmacology, 1,* 231–237.

Kazdin, A. E. (1980). *Research design in clinical psychology.* New York: Harper & Row.

Kazdin, A. E. (1981). Drawing valid inferences from case studies. *Journal of Consulting and Clinical Psychology, 49,* 183–192.

Kazdin, A. E. (1982). Single-case research designs: Methods for clinical and applied settings. New York: Oxford University Press.

Kazdin, A. E. (1984). Statistical analysis for single-case experimental designs. In D. H. Barlow & M. Hersen (Eds.), *Single case experimental designs* (2nd ed., pp. 285–324). New York: Pergamon.

Kazdin, A. E. (1986). The evaluation of psychotherapy: Research design and methodology. In S. L. Garfield & A. E. Bergin (Eds.), *Handbook of psychotherapy and behavior change* (pp. 23–68). New York: Wiley.

Kinsbourne, M. (1985). Base-state dependency of stimulant effects on the cognitive performance of hyperactive children. In L. M. Bloomingdale (Ed.), *Attention deficit disorder: Identification, course, and treatment rationale* (pp. 143–154). Jamaica, NY: Spectrum.

Klerman, G. L. (1986). Drugs and psychotherapy. In S. L. Garfield & A. E. Bergin (Eds.), *Handbook of psychotherapy and behavior change* (pp. 777–818). New York: Wiley.

Kovacs, M. (1983). *The Interview Schedule for Children (ISC): Interrater and parent-child agreement.* Unpublished manuscript.

Kovacs, M. (1985). The Interview Schedule for Children (ISC). *Psychopharmacology Bulletin, 21,* 991–994.

Kovacs, M. (1992). *Children's depression inventory manual.* North Tonawanda, NY: Multi-Health Systems.

Kraemer, H. C. (1981). Coping strategies in psychiatric clinical research. *Journal of Consulting and Clinical Psychology, 49,* 309–319.

Kraemer, H. C., & Thiemann, S. (1987). *How many subjects? Statistical power analysis in research.* Newbury Park, CA: Sage.

Kramer, A. D., & Feiguine, R. J. (1981). Clinical effect of amitriptyline in adolescent depression: A pilot study. *Journal of the American Academy of Child Psychiatry, 20,* 636–645.

Kupietz, S. S. (1991). Ritalin blood levels and their correlations with measures of learning. In L. L. Greenhill & B. B. Osman (Eds.), *Ritalin: Theory and patient management* (pp. 247–265). New York: Mary Ann Liebert.

Lahey, B., Green, K. D., & Forehand, R. (1980). On the independence of hyperactivity, conduct problems and deficits in children: A multiple regression analysis. *Journal of Consulting and Clinical Psychology, 44,* 286–296.

Lang, M., & Tisher, M. (1978). *Children's depression scale.* Melbourne: Australian Council for Educational Research.

Liberman, R. P., Davis, J., Moon, W., & Moore, J. (1973). Research design for analyzing drug-environment-behavior interactions. *Journal of Nervous and Mental Disease, 156,* 432–439.

Loeber, R. (1990). Development and risk factors of juvenile antisocial behavior and delinquency. *Clinical Psychology Review, 10,* 1–41.

Loney, J., & Milich, R. (1982). Hyperactivity, inattention, and aggression in clinical practice. In M. Wolraich & D. Routh (Eds.), *Advances in developmental and behavioral pediatrics* (Vol. 3, pp. 113–147). Greenwich, CT: JAI Press.

Lovejoy, C., & Rasmussen, N. H. (1990). The validity of vigilance tasks in differential diagnosis of children referred for attention and learning problems. *Journal of Abnormal Child Psychology, 18,* 671–682.

March, J., Stallings, P., Parker, J., Terry, R., & Conners, C. (1994). *The multidimensional anxiety scale for children (MASC): Factor structure and external validity.* Manuscript submitted for publication.

Martin, M. (1971). Single-subject designs for assessment of psychotropic drug effects in children. *Child Psychiatry and Human Development, 2,* 102–115.

Mash, E. J., & Terdal, L. G. (Eds.). (1988). *Behavioral assessment of childhood disorders* (2nd ed.). New York: Guilford.

McBurnett, K., Lahey, B. B., & Pfiffner, L. J. (1993). Diagnosis of attention deficit disorders in DSM-IV: Scientific basis and implications for education. *Exceptional Children, 60,* 108–117.

Michelson, L., DeLorenzo, T., & Petti, T. (1984). *Behavioral assessment of imipramine effects in a depressed child.* Unpublished manuscript.

Moore, D. J., & Klonoff, E. A. (1986). Assessment of compliance: A systems perspective. In K. D. Gadow & A. Poling (Eds.), *Methodological issues in human psychopharmacology (Advances in learning and behavioral disabilities, Suppl. 1)* (pp. 223–246). Greenwich, CT: JAI Press.

Morselli, P. L., Bianchetti, G., & Dugas, M. (1982). Haloperidol plasma monitoring in neuropsychiatric patients. *Therapeutic Drug Monitoring, 4,* 51–58.

National Institute of Mental Health (NIMH). (1973). Pharmacotherapy of children [Special issue]. *Psychopharmacology Bulletin.*

National Institute of Mental Health (NIMH). (1985). Rating scales and assessment instruments for use in pediatric psychopharmacology research [Special issue]. *Psychopharmacology Bulletin, 21*(4).

Newman, F. L. (1994). Selection of design and statistical procedures for progress and outcome assessment. In M. E. Maruish (Ed.), *The use of psychological testing for treatment planning and outcome assessment* (pp. 111–134). Hillsdale, NJ: Erlbaum.

Newman, F. L., & Ciarlo, J. A. (1994). Criteria for selecting psychological instruments for treatment outcome assessment. In M. E. Maruish (Ed.), *The use of psychological testing for treatment planning and outcome assessment* (pp. 98–110). Hillsdale, NJ: Erlbaum.

Orvaschel, H. (1985). Psychiatric interviews suitable for use in research with children and adolescents. *Psychopharmacology Bulletin, 21,* 737–745.

Orvaschel, H., Ambrosini, P., & Rabinovich, H. (1993). Diagnostic issues in child assessment. In T. H. Ollendick & M. Hersen (Eds.), *Handbook of child and adolescent assessment* (pp. 26–40). Needham Heights, MA: Allyn and Bacon.

Pelham, W. E. (1977). Withdrawal of a stimulant drug and concurrent behavioral intervention in the treatment of a hyperactive child. *Behavior Therapy, 8,* 473–479.

Pelham, W. E. (1986). The effects of psychostimulant drugs on learning and academic achievement in children with attention deficit disorders and learning disabilities. In J. Tageson & B. Wong (Eds.), *Psychological and educational perspectives on learning disabilities* (pp. 259–295). New York: Academic Press.

Pelham, W. E., & Hinshaw, S. P. (1992). Behavioral intervention for ADHD. In S. M. Turner, K. S. Calhoun, & H. E. Adams (Eds.), *Handbook of clinical behavior therapy* (2nd ed., pp. 259–283). New York: Wiley.

Pelham, W. E., & Hoza, B. (1987). Behavioral assessment of psychostimulant effects on ADD children in a summer day treatment program. In J. Prinz (Ed.), *Advances in behavioral assessment of children and families* (Vol. 3, pp. 3–33). Greenwich, CT: JAI Press.

Pelham, W. E., McBurnett, K., Harper, G. W., Milich, R., Murphy, D. A., Clinton, J., & Thiele, C. (1990). Methylphenidate and baseball playing in ADHD children: Who's on first? *Journal of Consulting and Clinical Psychology, 58,* 130–133.

Pelham, W. E., & Murphy, H. A. (1986). Behavioral and pharmacological treatment of attention deficit and conduct disorders. In M. Hersen (Ed.), *Pharmacological and behavioral treatment: An integrative approach* (pp. 108-148). New York: Wiley.

Pelham, W. E., Vodde-Hamilton, M., Murphy, D. A., Greenstein, J., & Vallano, G. (1991). The effects of methylphenidate on ADHD adolescents in recreational, peer group, and classroom settings. *Journal of Clinical Child Psychology, 20,* 293–300.

Petti, T., Bornstein, M., Delamater, A., & Conners, C. K. (1980). Evaluation and multimodality treatment of a depressed prepubertal girl. *Journal of the American Academy of Child Psychiatry, 19,* 690–702.

Petti, T. A., & Law, W. (1982). Imipramine treatment of depressed children: A double-blind pilot study. *Journal of Clinical Psychopharmacology, 2,* 107–110.

Petti, T. A., & Sallee, R. (1986). Issues in childhood and adolescent psychopharmacology. In K. D. Gadow & A. Poling (Eds.), *Advances in learning and behavioral disabilities, Supplement 1: Methodological issues in human psychopharmacology* (pp. 281–311). Greenwich, CT: JAI Press.

Petti, T. A., & Unis, A. (1981). Imipramine treatment of borderline children: Case reports with a controlled study. *American Journal of Psychiatry, 138,* 515–518.

Piacentini, J. (1993). Checklists and rating scales. In T. H. Ollendick & M. Hersen (Eds.), *Handbook of child and adolescent assessment* (pp. 82–97). Needham Heights, MA: Allyn and Bacon.

Pliszka, S. R. (1991). Antidepressants in the treatment of child and adolescent psychopathology. *Journal of Clinical Child Psychology, 20,* 313–320.

Poling, A., Gadow, K. D., & Cleary, J. (1991). *Drug therapy for behavior disorders: An introduction.* New York: Pergamon Press.

Preskorn, S. H., Weller, E. B., & Weller, R. A. (1982). Depression in children: Relationship between plasma imipramine levels and response. *Journal of Clinical Psychiatry, 43,* 450–453.

Puig-Antich, J., & Chambers, W. (1978). *The Schedule for Affective Disorders and Schizophrenia for School-Age Children (Kiddie-SADS).* New York: New York State Psychiatric Institute.

Puig-Antich, J., Perel, J. M., & Lupatkin, W. (1979). Plasma levels of imipramine (IMI) and desmethylimipramine (DMI) and clinical response in prepubertal major depressive disorder. *Journal of the American Academy of Child Psychiatry, 18,* 616–627.

Puig-Antich, J., Perel, J. M., Lupatkin, W., Chambers, W. J., Tabrizi, M. A., King, J., Goetz, R., Davies, M., & Stiller, R. L. (1987). Imipramine in prepubertal major depressive disorders. *Archives of General Psychiatry, 44,* 81–89.

Quay, H. C. (1979). Classification. In H. C. Quay & J. S. Werry (Eds.), *Psychopathological disorders of children* (2nd ed.). New York: Wiley.

Quay, H. C., & Peterson, D. R. (1983). *Interim manual for the revised behavior problem checklist.* Unpublished manuscript, University of Miami, FL.

Quitkin, F. M., Rabkin, J. G., Ross, D., & McGrath, P. J. (1984). Duration of antidepressant drug treatment: What is an adequate trial? *Archives of General Psychiatry, 41,* 238–245.

Quitkin, F. M., Rabkin, J. G., Ross, D., & Stewart, J. W. (1984). Identification of true drug response to antidepressants: Use of pattern analysis. *Archives of General Psychiatry, 41,* 782–786.

Rapport, M. D. (1990). Controlled studies of the effects of psychostimulants on children's functioning in clinic and classroom settings. In C. K. Conners & M. Kinsbourne (Eds.), *ADHD: Attention Deficit Hyperactivity Disorder* (pp. 77–111). Munich: MMV Medizin Verlag Munchen.

Rapport, M. D., DuPaul, G. J., Stoner, G., Birmingham, B. K., & Masse, G. (1985). Attention deficit disorder with hyperactivity: Differential effects of methylphenidate on impulsivity. *Pediatrics, 76,* 938–943.

Rapport, M. D., DuPaul, G. J., Stoner, G., & Jones, J. T. (1986). Comparing classroom and clinic measures of attention deficit disorder: Differential, idiosyncratic, and dose-response effects of methylphenidate. *Journal of Consulting and Clinical Psychology, 54,* 334–341.

Rapport, M. D., & Kelly, K. L. (1991). Psychostimulant effects on learning and cognitive function: Findings and implications for children with attention deficit hyperactivity disorder. *Clinical Psychology Review, 11,* 61–92.

Reatig, N. (1985a). DHHS internal policies for reviewing protections to human subjects in research: Children. *Psychopharmacology Bulletin, 21,* 1100–1104.

Reatig, N. (1985b). Ethical issues in research with children: A bibliography. *Psychopharmacology Bulletin, 21,* 1105–1107.

Reich, W., & Welner, Z. (1988). *Diagnostic interview for children and adolescents.* Unpublished manuscript, Washington University School of Medicine, St. Louis.

Reynolds, W. M. (1981). *Reynolds adolescent depression scale.* Unpublished manuscript, University of Wisconsin, Madison.

Reynolds, W. M., Anderson, G., & Bartell, N. (1985). Measuring depression in children: A multimethod assessment investigation. *Journal of Abnormal Child Psychology, 13,* 513–526.

Rivera-Calimlim, L. (1982). Problems in therapeutic monitoring of chlorpromazine. *Therapeutic Drug Monitoring, 4,* 41–49.

Rivera-Calimlim, L., Griesbach, P. H., & Perlmutter, R. (1979). Plasma chlorpromazine concentrations in children with behavioral disorders and mental illness. *Clinical Pharmacology and Therapeutics, 26,* 114–121.

Robin, A. L. (1994, April). Adolescent self-report of ADHD symptoms. *The ADHD Report,* 4–6.

Rogosa, D. R., & Willett, J. B. (1983). Demonstrating the reliability of the difference score in the measurement of change. *Journal of Educational Measurement, 20,* 335–343.

Rose, T. L. (1978). The functional relationship between artificial food colors and hyperactivity. *Journal of Applied Behavior Analysis, 11*(4), 439–446.

Rosnow, R. L., & Rosenthal, R. (1989). Statistical procedures and the justification of knowledge in psychological science. *American Psychologist, 44,* 1276–1284.

Russell, B. (1948). *Human knowledge: Its scope and limits.* London: George Allen and Unwin, Ltd.

Rutter, M. (1989). Attention deficit disorder/hyperkinetic syndrome: Conceptual and research issues regarding diagnosis and classification. In T. Sagvolden & T. Archer (Eds.), *Attention deficit disorder: Clinical and basic research* (pp. 1–24). Hillsdale, NJ: Erlbaum.

Rutter, M., & Shaffer, D. (1980). DSM-III: A step forward or back in terms of the classification of child psychiatric disorders. *Journal of the American Academy of Child Psychiatry, 3,* 371–394.

Ryan, N. D. (1992). The pharmacologic treatment of child and adolescent depression. In D. Shafer (Ed.), *The psychiatric clinics of North America: Pediatric psychopharmacology* (pp. 29–40). Philadelphia, PA: W. B. Saunders.

Ryback, R. S., Eckardt, M. J., Rawlings, R. R., & Rosenthal, L. S. (1982). Quadratic discriminant analysis as an aid to interpretive reporting of clinical laboratory tests. *Journal of the American Medical Association, 248,* 2342–2345.

Schouten, J. D., & Duckworth, K. S. (1993). Medicolegal and ethical issues in the pharmacologic treatment of children. In J. S. Werry & M. G. Aman (Eds.), *Practitioner's guide to psychoactive drugs for children and adolescents* (pp. 161–178). New York: Plenum.

Schwab-Stone, M., Fisher, P., Piacentini, J., Shaffer, D., Davies, M., & Briggs, M. (1993). The diagnostic interview schedule for children—revised version (DISC-R): II. Test-retest reliability. *Journal of the American Academy of Child and Adolescent Psychiatry, 32,* 651–657.

Sebrechts, M. M., Shaywitz, S. E., Shaywitz, B. A., Jatlow, P., Anderson, G. M., & Cohen, D. J. (1986). Components of attention, methylphenidate dosage, and blood levels in children with attention deficit disorder. *Pediatrics, 77,* 222–228.

Sedlmeier, P., & Gigerenzer, G. (1989). Do studies of statistical power have an effect on the power of studies? *Psychological Bulletin, 105,* 309–316.

Shaffer, D. (Ed.). (1992). *The psychiatric clinics of North America: Pediatric psychopharmacology.* Philadelphia, PA: W. B. Saunders.

Shaffer, D., & Greenhill, L. A. (1979). A critical note on the predictive validity of the hyperkinetic syndrome. *Journal of Child Psychology and Psychiatry, 20,* 60–72.

Shaffer, D., Schwab-Stone, M., Fisher, P., Cohen, P., Piacentini, J., Davies, M., Conners, C. K., & Regier, D. (1993). The diagnostic interview schedule for children—revised version (DISC-R): I. Preparation, field testing, interrater reliability, and acceptability. *Journal of the American Academy of Child and Adolescent Psychiatry, 32,* 643–650.

Shafto, F., & Sulzbacher, S. (1977). Comparing treatment tactics with a hyperactive preschool child: Stimulant medication and programmed teacher intervention. *Journal of Applied Behavior Analysis, 10,* 13–20.

Shaywitz, S. E., & Shaywitz, B. A. (1991). Attention deficit disorder: Diagnosis and role of Ritalin in management. In L. L. Greenhill & B. B. Osman (Eds.), *Ritalin: Theory and patient management* (pp. 45–67). New York: Mary Ann Liebert.

Shinn, M. R. (Ed.). (1989). *Curriculum-based measurement: Assessing special children.* New York: Guilford.

Simeon, J. G., Dinicola, V. F., Ferguson, B. H., & Copping, W. (1990). Adolescent depression: A placebo-controlled fluoxetine treatment study and follow-up. *Progress in Neuropsychopharmacology and Biological Psychiatry, 14,* 791–795.

Sleator, E. K. (1985). Measurement of compliance. *Psychopharmacology Bulletin, 21,* 1089–1093.

Smith, B., & Sechrest, L. (1991). Treatment of aptitude X treatment interactions. *Journal of Consulting and Clinical Psychology, 59*, 233–244.

Solanto, M. V. (1991). Dosage effects of ritalin on cognition. In L. L. Greenhill & B. B. Osman (Eds.), *Ritalin: Theory and patient management* (pp. 233–245). New York: Mary Ann Liebert.

Solomons, G. (1973). Drug therapy: Initiation and follow-up. *Annals of the New York Academy of Sciences, 205*, 335–344.

Sprague, R. L., & Sleator, E. K. (1977). Methylphenidate in hyperkinetic children: Differences in dose effects on learning and social behavior. *Science, 198*, 1274–1276.

Sprague, R. L., & Werry, J. S. (1971). Methodology of psychopharmacological studies with the retarded. In N. R. Ellis (Ed.), *International review of research in mental retardation* (Vol. 5, pp. 147–210). New York: Academic.

Stableford, W., Butz, R., Hasazi, J., Leitenberg, H., & Peyser, J. (1976). Sequential withdrawal of stimulant drugs and use of behavior therapy with two hyperactive boys. *American Journal of Orthopsychiatry, 46*, 302–312.

Swanson, J. M. (1985). Measures of cognitive functioning appropriate for use in pediatric psychopharmacology research studies. *Psychopharmacology Bulletin, 21*, 887–892.

Swanson, J., Cantwell, D., Lerner, M., McBurnett, K., & Hanna, G. (1991). Effects of stimulant medication on learning in children with ADHD. *Journal of Learning Disabilities, 24*, 219–230.

Swanson, J. M., McBurnett, K., Wigal, T., Pfiffner, L., Lerner, M. A., Williams, L., Christian, D. L., Tamm, L., Willcutt, E., Crowley, K., Clevenger, W., Khouzam, N., Woo, C., Crinella, F. M., & Fisher, T. D. (1993). Effect of stimulant medication on children with attention deficit disorder: A "review of reviews." *Exceptional Children, 60*, 154–162.

Teicher, M. H., & Baldessarini, R. J. (1987). Developmental pharmacodynamics. In C. Popper (Ed.), *Psychiatric pharmacosciences of children and adolescents* (pp. 45–80). Washington, DC: American Psychiatric Press.

Tsujimoto, A., Tsujimoto, G., Ishizaki, T., Nakasawa, S., & Ichihashi, Y. (1982). Toxic haloperidol reactions with observation of serum haloperidol concentration in two children. *Developmental Pharmacological Therapy, 4*, 12–17.

Viesselman, J. O., Yaylayan, S., Weller, E. B., & Weller, R. A. (1993). Antidysthymic drugs (antidepressants and antimanics). In J. S. Werry & M. G. Aman (Eds.), *Practitioner's guide to psychoactive drugs for children and adolescents* (pp. 239–268). New York: Plenum.

Volkmar, F. (1991). Classification in child and adolescent psychiatry: Principles and issues. In M. Lewis (Ed.), *Child and adolescent psychiatry: A comprehensive textbook* (pp. 415–421). Baltimore, MD: Williams & Wilkins.

Waltz, J., Addis, M. E., Koerner, K., & Jacobson, N. S. (1993). Testing the integrity of a psychotherapy protocol: Assessment of adherence and competence. *Journal of Consulting and Clinical Psychology, 61*, 620–630.

Webster, H., & Bereiter, C. (1963). The reliability of changes measured by mental test scores. In C. W. Harris (Ed.), *Problems in measuring change* (pp. 39–59). Madison: University of Wisconsin Press.

Wells, K. C. (1995). Rating scales for assessment of conduct disorder in children and adolescents. In G. P. Sholevar (Ed.), *Conduct disorders in children and adolescents: Assessment and intervention*. Washington, DC: APPI Press.

Wells, K. C., Conners, C. K., Imber, L., & Delamater, A. (1981). Use of single-subject methodology in clinical decision making with a hyperactive child on the psychiatric inpatient unit. *Behavioral Assessment, 3,* 359–369.

Werry, J. S. (1992). Child psychiatric disorders: Are they classifiable? *British Journal of Psychiatry, 161,* 472–480.

Werry, J. S., & Aman, M. G. (Eds.). (1993). *Practitioner's guide to psychoactive drugs for children and adolescents.* New York: Plenum.

Werry, J. S., Methven, R. J., Fitzpatrick, J., & Dixon, H. (1983). The interrater reliability of DSM-III in children. *Journal of Abnormal Child Psychology, 11,* 341–354.

Whalen, C. K., & Henker, B. (1980). *Hyperactive children: The social ecology of identification and treatment.* New York: Academic.

Whalen, C. K., & Henker, B. (1986). Group designs in applied psychopharmacology. In K. D. Gadow & A. Poling (Eds.), *Advances in learning and behavioral disabilities, Supplement 1: Methodological issues in human psychopharmacology* (pp. 137–222). Greenwich, CT: JAI Press.

Whalen, C. K., & Henker, B. (1991). Therapies for hyperactive children: Comparisons, combinations, and compromises. *Journal of Consulting and Clinical Psychology, 59,* 126–137.

Whalen, C. K., Henker, B., Buhrmester, D., Hinshaw, S. P., Huber, A., & Laski, K. (1989). Does stimulant medication improve the peer status of hyperactive children? *Journal of Consulting and Clinical Psychology, 57,* 545–549.

Whitaker, A., & Rao, U. (1992). Neuroleptics in pediatric psychiatry. In D. Shafer (Ed.), *The psychiatric clinics of North America: Pediatric psychopharmacology* (pp. 243–276). Philadelphia, PA: W. B. Saunders.

Willet, J. B. (1988). Questions and answers in the measurement of change. In E. Z. Rothkopf (Ed.), *Review of research in education* (Vol. 15, pp. 345–422). Washington, DC: American Educational Research Association.

Williamson, D. A., Calpin, J. P., DiLorenzo, T. M., Garris, R. P., & Petti, T. A. (1981). Treating hyperactivity with dexedrine and activity feedback. *Behavior Modification, 5,* 399–416.

Wittenborn, J. R. (1978). Guidelines for clinical trials in psychopharmacology. In M. A. Lipton, A. DiMascio, & K. F. Killam (Eds.), *Psychopharmacology: A generation of progress* (pp. 833–840). New York: Raven.

Wulbert, M., & Dries, R. (1977). The relative efficacy of methylphenidate (Ritalin) and behavior modification technique in the treatment of a hyperactive child. *Journal of Applied Behavior Analysis, 10*(1), 21–31.

Zametkin, A. J., & Yamada, E. M. (1993). Monitoring and measuring drug effects. I. Physical measures. In J. S. Werry & M. G. Aman (Eds.), *Practitioner's guide to psychoactive drugs for children and adolescents* (pp. 75–97). New York: Plenum.

Zimmerman, D. W., & Williams, R. H. (1982). Gain scores in research can be highly reliable. *Journal of Educational Measurement, 19,* 149–154.

Diagnosis and Treatment

Autism and Pervasive Developmental Disorders

MAGDA CAMPBELL, M.D.*, JEANETTE E. CUEVA, M.D., and ALEJANDRA HALLIN, M.D.

This work was supported in part by USPHS Grants MH-32212 and MH-40177 (Dr. Campbell) and MH-18915 (Drs. Campbell and Cueva) from the National Institute of Mental Health; the Hirschell and Deanna E. Levine Foundation, The Marion O. and Maximilian E. Hoffman Foundation, Inc., and The Beatrice and Samuel A. Seaver Foundation.
*Reprint requests to Dr. Campbell, Department of Psychiatry, New York University Medical Center, 550 First Avenue, New York, NY 10016, telephone: 212-263-6206; fax: 212-263-8135.

CLASSIFICATION OF PERVASIVE DEVELOPMENTAL DISORDERS (PDD) AND DEFINITION OF AUTISTIC DISORDER

The pervasive developmental disorders are a class of disorders characterized by impairments in several areas of development and deviant behavior in the areas of social interaction, language and communication and play, as well as stereotyped activities and interests. This group of disorders was first introduced in the third *Diagnostic and Statistical Manual of Mental Disorders* (DSM-III) of the American Psychiatric Association (APA, 1980). Both classification and definition underwent changes in the revised third edition (DSM-III-R; APA, 1987) and in the fourth edition (DSM-IV; APA, 1994). DSM-III contained Infantile Autism (Full Syndrome Present; Residual State) with onset before 30 months of age; Childhood Onset Pervasive Developmental Disorder (Full Syndrome Present; Residual State); and Atypical Pervasive Development Disorder, all of these coded on Axis I. DSM-III-R (APA, 1987) required coding of PDD on Axis II and included Autistic Disorder, an ahistorical diagnosis with specification if childhood onset (after 36 months of age); and Pervasive Developmental Disorder Not Otherwise Specified (PDDNOS).

DSM-IV (APA, 1994) introduces numerous changes in the PDD category, although the criteria for Autistic Disorder remained in essence unchanged from Kanner's (1943) first report of "Early Infantile Autism." These changes and revisions from DSM-III-R to DSM-IV were based on literature review (Szatmari, 1992), field trials, compliance with ICD-10 and because of clinical utility (the number of criteria for Autistic Disorder were excessive and some were cumbersome to use).

The DSM-IV Autism/PDD Field Trial was a collaborative international multicenter effort designed to answer specific questions (Volkmar et al., 1994). The entire sample participating in the field trial consisted of 977 carefully diagnosed subjects, whose ages ranged from infancy to approximately 25 years; every effort was made to obtain nonautistic PDD subjects: specifically Rett's Disorder, Childhood Disintegrative Disorder, and Asperger's Disorder. In this sample, 454 subjects were clinically diagnosed as autistic disorder (mean age 8.99 years ± 7.18; 54% were mute); 240 were clinically diagnosed as nonautistic or other PDDs (mean age, 9.68 ± 6.57 years, 33% were mute); Rett's Disorder = 13; Childhood Disintegrative Psychosis = 16; Asperger's Disorder = 48; Atypical Autism = 47; and PDDNOS = 116); and 283 subjects (mean age, 9.72 ± 8.26 years; 35% mute) were diagnosed as non-PDD (including mentally retarded = 132; language disorder = 88). In general, the results obtained from the DSM-IV Autism/Field Trial confirmed that the age of onset of autistic disorder in the vast majority of cases is before the age of 3 years; the DSM-III-R definition of Autistic Disorder was too broad and the criteria for Autistic Disorder were overinclusive, yielding a high percentage of false positive cases. The number of the proposed DSM-IV criteria was reduced, and the wording was revised and simplified. The proposed ICD-10 criteria also underwent changes so that a high degree of compatibility was reached between the two systems. The validity of these "final" DSM-IV criteria for Autistic Disorder (shown in Table 5.1) was tested in randomly picked subjects from 16 sites of the total 21 sites, and was also tested against the reduced ICD-10 criteria; there was a high agreement between the two sets of criteria.

Perhaps the major change in the PDD's group in DSM-IV was the splitting of the PDDNOS into three separate diagnostic categories: Rett's Disorder, Childhood Disintegrative Disorder, and Asperger's Disorder (Tables 5.2–5.4). The PDDNOS remains in DSM-IV and includes Atypical Autism (Table 5.5), which is a separate diagnostic entity in ICD-10.

RETT'S DISORDER

This rare disorder was first described by Andreas Rett (1966) and was based on 22 females. It is a progressive neurodegenerative disorder and it appears that only females are affected. Head circumference is normal at birth but growth decelerates between 5 months and 48 months of age. Arrests (slowing) of development and loss of certain functions take place along with social withdrawal and ataxia/apraxia of extremities and trunk with typical jerky movements of the trunk. Characteristically, midline handwashing, handwringing stereotypies and wetting hands with saliva result in skin lesions. Disturbances of gait and breathing are associated features; spasticity, scoliosis, and immobility may be the final stage. However, withdrawal is transient and some degree of social relatedness is not uncommon in later childhood. Rett's Disorder is differentiated from Autistic Disorder and Childhood Disintegrative Disorder (Volkmar et al., 1994) by characteristic midline hand stereotypies, early development, and course. Social withdrawal is usually less severe than in Autistic Disorder and mental retardation is usually severe or profound. The validity of Rett's Disorder is supported by the literature (approximately 330 articles in the English language) (for review, see Tsai, 1992) and by the DSM-IV Autism/PDD Field Trial which, as previously noted, contained 13 subjects, all females (Volkmar et al., 1994). Rett's Disorder is a rare condition and the estimated prevalence is one in 10,000 to 15,000 females (Rett Syndrome Diagnostic Criteria Work Group, 1988).

Table 5.1.   *Pervasive Developmental Disorders*

299.00 Autistic Disorder

A.   A total of six (or more) items from (1), (2), and (3), with at least two from (1), and one each from (2) and (3):

    (1)   qualitative impairment in social interaction, as manifested by at least two of the following:

        (a)   marked impairment in the use of multiple nonverbal behaviors such as eye-to-eye gaze, facial expression, body postures, and gestures to regulate social interaction

        (b)   failure to develop peer relationships appropriate to developmental level

        (c)   a lack of spontaneous seeking to share enjoyment, interests, or achievements with other people (e.g., by a lack of showing, bringing, or pointing out objects of interest)

        (d)   lack of social or emotional reciprocity

    (2)   qualitative impairments in communication as manifested by at least one of the following:

        (a)   delay in, or total lack of, the development of spoken language (not accompanied by an attempt to compensate through alternative modes of communication such as gesture or mime)

        (b)   in individuals with adequate speech, marked impairment in the ability to initiate or sustain a conversation with others

        (c)   stereotyped and repetitive use of language or idiosyncratic language

        (d)   lack of varied, spontaneous make-believe play or social imitative play appropriate to developmental level

    (3)   restricted repetitive and stereotyped patterns of behavior, interest, and activities, as manifested by at least one of the following:

        (a)   encompassing preoccupation with one or more stereotyped and restricted patterns of interest that is abnormal either in intensity or focus

        (b)   apparently inflexible adherence to specific, nonfunctional routines or rituals

        (c)   stereotyped and repetitive motor mannerisms (e.g., hand or finger flapping or twisting, or complex whole-body movements)

        (d)   persistent preoccupation with parts of objects

B.   Delays or abnormal functioning in at least one of the following areas, with onset prior to age 3 years: (1) social interaction, (2) language as used in social communication, or (3) symbolic or imaginative play.

C.   The disturbance is not better accounted for by Rett's Disorder or Childhood Disintegrative Disorder.

Source: *Diagnostic and Statistical Manual of Mental Disorders* (4th ed.), Washington, DC: American Psychiatric Association, permission granted, pp. 70–71.

Table 5.2.   299.80 Rett's Disorder

A. All of the following:

    (1) apparently normal prenatal and perinatal development

    (2) apparently normal psychomotor development through the first 5 months after birth

    (3) normal head circumference at birth

B. Onset of all of the following after the period of normal development:

    (1) deceleration of head growth between ages 5 and 48 months

    (2) loss of previously acquired purposeful hand skills between ages 5 and 30 months with the subsequent development of stereotyped hand movements (e.g., hand-wringing or hand washing)

    (3) loss of social engagement early in the course (although often social interaction develops later)

    (4) appearance of poorly coordinated gait or trunk movements

    (5) severely impaired expressive and receptive language development with severe psychomotor retardation

Source: Diagnostic and Statistical Manual of Mental Disorders (4th ed.), Washington, DC: American Psychiatric Association, permission granted, pp. 72–73.

CHILDHOOD DISINTEGRATIVE DISORDER

Childhood Disintegrative Disorder is a very rare condition described first by Heller (1908) as "dementia infantilis," based on 6 cases. There have been approximately 90 cases reported in the literature since that time. Following an apparent normal pregnancy, birth, and development in the first 2 to 3 years of life, there is regression and cognitive deterioration with autisticlike behavioral symptoms and loss of sphincter control. In the DSM-IV Autism/PDD Field Trial, 16 persons received the clinical diagnosis of Childhood Disintegrative Disorder (Volkmar et al., 1994). Both the literature review (Volkmar, 1992) and the results of the Field Trial supported the validity of this disorder, which is included in ICD-10.

Childhood Disintegrative Disorder differs from autism in age of onset, course of illness, and a lower IQ (Volkmar et al., 1994). The patients who participated in the Field Trial tended to be mute, they were placed in a residential treatment center, with a static or progressive course.

Table 5.3.   299.10 Childhood Disintegrative Disorder

A.   Apparently normal development for at least the first 2 years after birth as manifested by the presence of age-appropriate verbal and nonverbal communication, social relationships, play, and adaptive behavior.

B.   Clinically significant loss of previously acquired skills (before age 10 years) in at least two of the following areas:

   (1)   expressive or receptive language

   (2)   social skills or adaptive behavior

   (3)   bowel or bladder control

   (4)   play

   (5)   motor skills

C.   Abnormalities of functioning in at least two of the following areas:

   (1)   qualitative impairment in social interaction (e.g., impairment in nonverbal behaviors, failure to develop peer relationships, lack of social or emotional reciprocity)

   (2)   qualitative impairments in communication (e.g., delay or lack of spoken language, inability to initiate or sustain a conversation, stereotyped and repetitive use of language, lack of varied make-believe play)

   (3)   restricted, repetitive, and stereotyped patterns of behavior, interests, and activities, including motor stereotypies and mannerisms

D.   The disturbance is not better accounted for by another specific Pervasive Developmental Disorder or by Schizophrenia.

Source: Diagnostic and Statistical Manual of Mental Disorders (4th ed.), Washington, DC: American Psychiatric Association, permission granted, pp. 74–75.

ASPERGER'S DISORDER

This condition was first described by Asperger (1944) as "autistic psychopathy." It remained largely unknown until Wing (1981) published a paper on relatively high-functioning persons with marked impairments in social interaction. This syndrome has been referred to in the literature as "high-functioning autism," schizoid personality disorder, and atypical children. The validity of Asperger's Disorder has not been well established in the literature (Szatmari, 1992; Rutter & Schopler, 1992) nor by the DSM-IV Field Trial. Asperger's Disorder does share some features with autism: It is characterized by impairment in social interaction, stereotyped and repetitive behaviors, activities, and interests. These behaviors exist in the presence of normal cognitive development and no delay in language development, though speech is reported to be pedantic, tangential, and repetitive (Wing, 1981). In addition to a lack

Table 5.4.   299.80 Asperger's Disorder

A. Qualitative impairment in social interaction, as manifested by at least two of the following:

    (1) marked impairment in the use of multiple nonverbal behaviors such as eye-to-eye gaze, facial expression, body postures, and gestures to regulate social interaction

    (2) failure to develop peer relationships appropriate to developmental level

    (3) a lack of spontaneous seeking to share enjoyment, interests, or achievements with other people (e.g., by a lack of showing, bringing, or pointing out objects of interest to other people)

    (4) lack of social or emotional reciprocity

B. Restricted, repetitive, and stereotyped patterns of behavior, interests, and activities, as manifested by at least one of the following:

    (1) encompassing preoccupation with one or more stereotyped and restricted patterns of interest that is abnormal either in intensity or focus

    (2) apparently inflexible adherence to specific, nonfunctional routines or rituals

    (3) stereotyped and repetitive motor mannerisms (e.g., hand or finger flapping or twisting, or complex whole-body movements)

    (4) persistent preoccupation with parts of objects

C. The disturbance causes clinically significant impairment in social, occupational, or other important areas of functioning.

D. There is no clinically significant general delay in language (e.g., single words used by age 2 years, communicative phrases used by age 3 years).

E. There is no clinically significant delay in cognitive development or in the development of age-appropriate self-help skills, adaptive behavior (other than in social interaction), and curiosity about the environment in childhood.

F. Criteria are not met for another specific Pervasive Developmental Disorder or Schizophrenia.

Source: Diagnostic and Statistical Manual of Mental Disorders (4th ed.), Washington, DC: American Psychiatric Association, permission granted, p. 77.

of significant delay in cognitive and language development, Asperger's Disorder differs from autism in that it has higher verbal IQ scores than performance scores. Motor delays, clumsiness, and isolated special skills are reported to be more common in Asperger's Disorder than in Autistic Disorder; furthermore, the age of onset (or recognition of the disorder) is later and anxiety is frequently present.

Though the validity of this diagnostic concept as an independent entity remains controversial, the field trial gave some evidence for the

Table 5.5.   299.80 Pervasive Developmental Disorder Not Otherwise Specified (including Atypical Autism)

This category should be used when there is a severe and pervasive impairment in the development of reciprocal social interaction or verbal and nonverbal communication skills, or when stereotyped behavior, interests, and activities are present, but the criteria are not met for a specific Pervasive Developmental Disorder, Schizophrenia, Schizotypal Personality Disorder, or Avoidant Personality Disorder. For example, this category includes "atypical autism"—presentations that do not meet the criteria for Autistic Disorder because of late age at onset, atypical symptomatology, or subthreshold symptomatology, or all of these.

Source: Diagnostic and Statistical Manual of Mental Disorders (4th ed.), Washington, DC: American Psychiatric Association, permission granted, pp. 77–78.

validity and distinctiveness (separateness) from autism. Furthermore, there were compelling clinical/service reasons, research issues (to differentiate Asperger's Disorder from schizoid personality disorder and other schizophrenia spectrum disorders), as well as the issue of compatibility with ICD-10 that justified the inclusion of this disorder in DSM-IV as a separate diagnostic entity.

INDICATIONS FOR PHARMACOTHERAPY

All autistic children require some type of treatment intervention, or a combination of treatments. The type of treatment or treatment combination needed depends on several factors including the individual's chronological age (CA); level of intellectual and language functioning (most autistic children function on a retarded level, and 50% are nonverbal at 4–5 years of age); and types of prominent maladaptive behaviors. Treatment modalities include special education, speech and language therapy, communication therapy, behavior modification, social skills training, group and individual psychotherapy, and pharmacotherapy.

In the subgroup of children and adolescents with autism requiring pharmacotherapy in addition to other treatment modalities, pharmacotherapy may play an important or an essential role in augmenting response to other types of treatments. The goal of all treatment interventions, including pharmacotherapy, is to promote normal development and acquisition of skills, and to reduce or to eliminate maladaptive behaviors.

Target symptoms for which medication is indicated vary depending on the chronological age of the individual, level of cognitive functioning, and also on environmental and psychosocial factors. Temper tantrums, hyperactivity, inability to focus, stereotypies, aggression, agitation, and self-injurious behavior (SIB) are the target symptoms for pharmacotherapy. Maladaptive behaviors frequently encountered in younger autistic children include temper tantrums, hyperactivity, inattention and stereotypies, while aggression and SIB are perhaps more frequent in older children. When these behaviors are severe and unresponsive to other treatment modalities (e.g., behavior modification), medication should be considered. In addition, an autistic adolescent or adult may have a superimposed psychiatric disorder such as major depression, or obsessive-compulsive disorder, which requires pharmacotherapy.

Treatment with an appropriate psychoactive agent can make an autistic child with severe behavior problems more amenable to other treatment interventions, including special education. The only enduring effects of pharmacotherapy are due to conjoint psychosocial interventions (Irwin, 1968).

METHODOLOGICAL ISSUES: PATIENTS, DESIGN, AND ASSESSMENTS

For a critical assessment of efficacy and safety of a psychoactive agent in Autistic Disorder or the other specific PDDs, the following are required: a representative and adequate sample size of carefully diagnosed patients using accepted diagnostic criteria; a relatively narrow age range of subjects with moderate to severe target symptoms that may be reduced by an appropriate drug; and a design that is appropriate for a chronic and rare condition such as autism, preferably a parallel groups design (Campbell, Green, & Deutsch, 1985). The length of treatment period should be adequate but not excessive. A placebo baseline period is required to achieve a stable baseline, and to eliminate possible placebo responders. Appropriate rating instruments are required reflecting change due to a drug and with a moderate but not excessive number of behavioral items (for review, see Campbell & Palij, 1985a). The number of assessments (frequency) and the number of instruments employed should not be excessive; the child should be evaluated in multiple settings and by multiple raters, independently. Studies relying exclusively on ratings of videotapes are of limited value (Sanchez et al., 1995).

A variety of instruments are available for use in this population. Some are diagnostic or specifically developed for autistic children, adolescents or adults: the Autism Diagnostic Interview (ADI; Le Couteur et al., 1989), the Autism Diagnostic Observation Schedule (ADOS; Lord et al., 1989) and the Childhood Autism Rating Scale (CARS; Schopler, Reichler, & Renner, 1988) are among these measures (these and other measures are detailed in Campbell, Kafantaris, Malone, Kowalik, & Locascio, 1991). Several objective rating scales recording the frequency of target symptoms in a specified period of time are also available; this group includes the Ritvo-Freeman Real Life Rating Scale (Freeman, Ritvo, Yokota, & Ritvo, 1986), a measure that was used in a multicenter clinical drug trial of fenfluramine (Ritvo et al., 1986) and was adapted from the Behavioral Observation System (BOS; Freeman, Ritvo, & Schroth, 1984). Two general-purpose instruments, the Children's Psychiatric Rating Scale (CPRS) and the Clinical Global Impressions (CGI), were most commonly employed in clinical drug trials involving autistic children.

Unlike in ADHD, no specific behavioral scale is being employed across studies in this population. In the past two decades, the first 28 items of the CPRS (Campbell & Palij, 1985a; Guy, 1976) have been used in clinical drug trials involving autistic children.

Other instruments were also used in studies with a small number of subjects or in uncontrolled studies and their utility cannot be evaluated (for review, see Campbell, 1987; Campbell & Palij, 1985a; Campbell, Kafantaris, et al., 1991). The ADOS developed by Lord et al. (1989), a widely used instrument in the diagnostic evaluation of children, has not yet been tested in clinical drug trials.

An instrument was developed for rating stereotypies, the Timed Stereotypies Rating Scale (TSRS) (Campbell, 1985c, p. 1082; also see Locascio et al., 1991) and was found to be useful. The Abnormal Involuntary Movement Scale (AIMS) (NIMH, 1995) has been useful in young autistic children (Golden, Campbell, & Perry, 1987) and, following a protocol, feasible to administer (Campbell, 1985a, p. 1081). The AIMS differentiated the profile of neuroleptic-related dyskinesias from baseline stereotypies in autistic children who were rated independently and blindly by raters (Shay et al., 1993).

Drug effects on performance and learning were assessed in short-term studies (Anderson et al., 1984, 1989; Campbell et al., 1978) as well as an effect on IQ or DQ in long-term studies (Shell et al., 1987). The choice of measures is important and practice effect has to be avoided (for example, see Ritvo, Freeman, Geller, & Yuwiler, 1983). These issues were reviewed elsewhere (Campbell, 1987; Campbell & Palij, 1985a).

Untoward effects of drugs should be carefully monitored employing appropriate instruments (see Campbell & Palij, 1985b; Campbell, Green, & Deutsch, 1985) or side effect checklists developed specifically for the drug under investigation. A clinical drug trial and the report of the trial is incomplete without adequate and appropriate laboratory monitoring. Drug level determination in blood (or saliva) is a useful measure of drug compliance. Patient status (inpatient vs. outpatient) may affect the outcome as well as compliance.

For a review of methodological issues, Chapter 4 in this book is recommended; other suggested readings are Campbell (1987), Campbell and Palij (1985a, 1985b), Campbell et al. (1985), Fish (1968), and Grof et al. (1993). For readings on ethical issues, a recently published book by Hattab (1994) is recommended, and a chapter specifically addressing issues involving psychopharmacology in children (Small, Campbell, Shay, & Goodman, 1994).

REVIEW OF THE LITERATURE

Autism

Neuroleptics. The earlier literature has been summarized in Chapter 1 in this book and elsewhere (Campbell, 1985b; Campbell, 1987; Campbell & Schopler, 1989). The early reports all suffer from methodological flaws and, therefore, definite conclusions cannot be based on those reports. The only exceptions are a carefully designed study by Fish, Shapiro, and Campbell (1966) on trifluoperazine and systematic studies on the efficacy and safety of haloperidol.

Studies found 0.25 to 4.0 mg/day (mean, 0.844–1.65 mg/day, or 0.016–0.217 mg/kg/day) to be therapeutic in hospitalized children, ages 2 to 8 years (Anderson et al., 1984, 1989; Campbell et al., 1978; Cohen et al., 1980; Perry et al., 1989) or even older (Armenteros, Adams, & Campbell, 1995). In the Engelhardt, Polizos, Waizer, and Hoffman (1973) study, administration of haloperidol was associated with a number of untoward effects even at therapeutic doses, but in the preceding studies at conservative therapeutic doses, which were individually regulated, untoward effects were rated only above therapeutic doses (Anderson et al., 1984, 1989; Campbell et al., 1978; Cohen et al., 1980; Perry et al., 1989). This important finding indicates that minimum effective doses of haloperidol should be employed. The doses were individually regulated, starting with 0.25 or 0.5 mg in a single morning dose; increments were made twice a week, on Tuesday and Thursday, until side effects occurred, but not exceeding 4.0 mg/day. When side effects developed, the next lower dose or a lower dose was judged to be the therapeutic dose and was always free of side effects. Both the short- and long-term efficacy and safety of this drug were evaluated, and its clinical effectiveness was also shown. In these studies (Table 5.6), the therapeutic doses of haloperidol ranged from 0.25 to 4.0 mg/d, median, 1.0 mg/d (0.016–0.184 mg/kg/day) in children ages 2 to 8 years, all of whom were hospitalized (Anderson et al., 1984, 1989; Campbell et al., 1978; Cohen et al., 1980).

The most common side effects with neuroleptics are excessive sedation and, in one study, acute dystonic reaction (Anderson et al., 1984). Acute dystonic reaction was relieved by Benadryl, 25 mg orally or, if necessary, given intramuscularly. Parkinsonian side effects are almost nonexistent, whereas behavioral toxicity (worsening of preexisting symptoms or

Table 5.6. Double-blind, Placebo-Controlled Studies of Haloperidol with Randomization in Autistic Disorder

Author(s) and Year	Sample	Age in Years	Design	Dosage mg/d (mg/kg/d)	Measures	Clinical Effects	
						Therapeutic	Untoward
Campbell et al., 1978	$N = 40$	2.6–7.2	Factorial design	0.5–4.0 mean, 1.65	CPRS; CBI; CGI; NGI; DOTES; TESS-Write-In	Significant decreases of stereotypies and withdrawal by haloperidol (in subjects ≥ 4.5 years old); facilitation of acquisition of speech in combination with language therapy	Sedation, excitement-agitation, acute dystonic reaction ($N = 2$)
Cohen et al., 1980	$N = 10$	2.1–7.0	Crossover, ABA BAB	1.78	Timed Rating Scale; Look At Me Scale	Significant decrease in stereotypies; facilitation of the orienting reaction to the request "Look at me"	Sedation, irritability and hypoactivity, acute dystonic reaction ($N = 1$)
Anderson et al., 1984	$N = 40$	2.33–6.92	ABA	0.5–3.0, mean, 1.11 (0.019–0.217; mean, 0.05)	CPRS; CGI; PTQ; DOTES; TESS-Write-In; AIMS; ADS; discrimination learning; motor activity and duration of stereotypies in a computerized laboratory; side effects checklist	Significant decreases of withdrawal, stereotypies, hyperactivity, abnormal object relationships, fidgetiness, negativism, angry and labile affect (CPRS); facilitation of discrimination learning in the computerized laboratory; CGI Severity of Illness ($p < .001$), Improvement ($p < .001$) & Efficacy ($p < .03$)	Sedation, irritability, acute dystonic reaction ($N = 11$), tremor, decreased motor activity

Study	N		Design	Measures	Results	Side Effects
Anderson et al., 1989	$N = 45$	2.02–7.58	Crossover	CPRS; CGI; PTQ; TESS; side effects checklist; discrimination learning; motor activity and duration of stereotypies in a computerized laboratory	Significant reduction of CPRS Autism, Hyperactivity, and Conduct Problem Factors (Overall & Campbell, 1988); CGI Severity of Illness ($p < .0001$), Improvement ($p < .0001$) & Efficacy ($p < .0001$); PTQ Temper outbursts item	Excessive sed tion, acute d tonic reactio
		0.25–4.0 mean, 0.844 (0.016–0.184; mean, 0.047)				
Perry et al., 1989	$N = 60$	2.3–7.9	Open; double-blind, placebo-controlled random assignment to continuous versus discontinuous administration of haloperidol[a]	CPRS; CGI; AIMS; ADS; TSRS	Significant decreases in fidgetiness, withdrawal, stereotypies, and speech deviancies; improved spontaneous relation to examiner (CPRS); significant reduction of the CPRS Autism Factor (Overall & Campbell, 1988); CGI Severity of Illness ($p < .0001$)	Haloperidol-related dyski sias ($N = 12$) 3 while on haloperidol a while on plac
		0.5–4.0 (0.016–0.209)				

Note: ADS: Abbreviated Dyskinesia Scale (Simpson, Lee, Zoubok, & Gardos, 1979); AIMS: Abnormal Involuntary Movement Scale; CBI: Clinic havior Inventory; CGI: Clinical Global Impressions; CPRS: Clinical Psychiatric Rating Scale; DOTES: Dosage Record and Treatment Emergent toms; NGI: Nurses' Global Impressions; PTQ: Conners Parent-Teacher Questionnaire (Guy, 1976, p. 300); TESS-Write-In: Treatment-Eme Symptom Scale-Write-In; TSRS: Timed Stereotypies Rating Scale.

[a]Subjects received haloperidol for 6 months; one group received haloperidol every day on a continuous basis; the other group received drug days and placebo for 2 days; the 2-day placebo periods varied and were randomly assigned.

symptoms de novo) are frequently observed above therapeutic doses. At therapeutic doses, administration of haloperidol is associated with clinically and statistically significant reduction of hyperactivity, temper tantrums, irritability, stereotypies, and withdrawal (Anderson et al., 1984, 1989; Campbell et al., 1978; Cohen et al., 1980). Attention span increases, and in some children aggressiveness and self-injurious behavior (SIB) decreases. All children were rated in several and different settings by multiple raters, including teachers. Only normo- or hyperactive children were included in these studies, because administration of haloperidol to predominantly or exclusively hypoactive children was associated with sleepiness, without any reduction of symptoms. Not only are behavioral symptoms reduced at therapeutic doses, but in two studies learning was facilitated in the laboratory. Acquisition of words was increased when haloperidol was combined with behavior therapy focusing on language acquisition (Campbell et al., 1978). In another double-blind, placebo-controlled study, discrimination learning was facilitated by haloperidol in a computerized laboratory employing auditory and visual stimuli (Anderson et al., 1984). In a third study, employing only visual stimuli in the same laboratory, the effect of haloperidol on discrimination learning did not differ from that of placebo (Anderson et al., 1989).

These short-term studies confirmed the earlier findings of Faretra, Dooher, and Dowling (1970) and of Engelhardt et al. (1973).

Although the sample sizes of three short-term studies of haloperidol were relatively large, each consisting of 40 to 45 children, we were unable to define haloperidol responders except that in one study, the older children, those over 4.5 years of age (4.5–7.2) responded to haloperidol alone in terms of decreases of stereotypies and withdrawal, but not the younger children (ages 2.6–4.5 years). As noted earlier, we also made the clinical observation that the predominately hypoactive children or exclusively hypoactive children get only excessively sedated (sleepy) without any beneficial effect on haloperidol; therefore, such children were excluded from clinical trials involving this drug.

To define haloperidol responders and to be able to predict response to haloperidol, data were pooled from three studies (Anderson et al., 1984, 1989; Campbell et al., 1978) and a secondary analysis of the data was performed (Locascio et al., 1991). These secondary analyses showed that, in general, there was a significantly greater response to haloperidol than to placebo as measured by the CGI, the mean scores of the 14 selected CPRS items (Campbell & Palij, 1985a), and the 4 factors derived from the 14 selected CPRS items (Overall & Campbell, 1988). The four factors are Autism, Anger/Uncooperativeness, Hyperactivity, and Speech deviance. As in the single study (Campbell et al., 1978), secondary data analyses ($N = 125$) showed that older children respond to haloperidol itself, whereas higher intellectual functioning and greater baseline severity of illness and symptoms tended to respond, in general, to both haloperidol and to placebo in these short-term clinical trials (Locascio et al., 1991).

The long-term efficacy of haloperidol was shown in a prospective study consisting of 60 outpatients, ages 2.3 to 7.9 years (Perry et al., 1989). All children enrolled in this study were responders to haloperidol and remained so, but the drug was particularly effective in those who were uncooperative and had a labile and angry affect on baseline. At daily doses ranging from 0.5 to 4.0 mg (0.016–0.209 mg/kg), the only side effects associated with haloperidol at the end of the 6-month treatment period and during the 4-week posttreatment placebo period were drug related dyskinesias in 12 of the children (Perry et al., 1989). Administration of haloperidol, over a period of one year, did not appear to affect adversely intellectual functioning.

Fenfluramine. In search for a more rational pharmacotherapy in autism, and because of neuroleptic-related dyskinesias, two other psychoactive agents were explored in pilot studies (fenfluramine) or acute dose range tolerance trials (naltrexone), as well as double-blind, placebo-controlled clinical trials; the patient samples ranged from small to a relatively large size. In addition, fenfluramine was investigated in a large multicenter study, though each site had a small sample, ranging from 8 to a maximum of 15 patients, and, in most, the age ranges were excessively wide.

Several studies have shown that abnormalities of the serotonergic system exist in a subsample of autistic children (Ritvo et al., 1970; for review, Campbell & Shay, 1994; Lotspeich, 1995) and that this may be the basis of behavioral deviances and cognitive deficits in autism. Ritvo hypothesized that an agent with antiserotonergic properties, such as fenfluramine, by reducing hyperserotonemia (one-third of autistic children were reported to have hyperserotonemia), will also reduce behavioral symptoms characteristic of autistic children. An overview of the representative literature is given in Table 5.7.

Early reports were favorable, but several later reports failed to demonstrate efficacy greater than placebo. Reports on fenfluramine still appear in the literature: the study of Leventhal et al. (1993), involving 15 children of a relatively narrow age range, was also largely negative. A critical review of the literature on fenfluramine through early 1987 is available (Campbell, 1988). In a double-blind, placebo-controlled study, fenfluramine failed to reach superiority over placebo; side effects were frequent and fenfluramine had a retarding effect on discrimination learning in the laboratory (Campbell, Adams, Small, et al., 1988). Furthermore, in

Table 5.7.   Double-blind, Placebo-Controlled Studies of Fenfluramine in Autistic Disorder

Author(s) and Year	Sample	Age in Years	Design	Dosage mg/d (mg/kg/d)	Measures	Clinical Effects Therapeutic	Clinical Effects Untoward
Ritvo et al., 1986	N = 81[a] (Rett's Disorder N = 1)	2.75–24	Multicenter, crossover; not all were randomized	(1.5)	Alpern-Boll Developmental Profile; RLRS; monthly parental reports, serial cognitive testing	33% strong responders; 52% moderate responders (by clinical consensus)	Irritability, lethargy, insomnia, initially anorexia (N = 16)
Campbell, Adams, Small, et al., 1988	N = 28	2.56–6.66	Parallel groups design, randomized	(1.250–2.068; mean, 1.747)	CPRS; CGI; PTQ; AIMS; ADS; TSRS; discrimination learning and measurement of motor activity and stereotypies in a computerized laboratory	Decreases of Fidgetiness, Withdrawal (CPRS), and Restlessness (PTQ)	Loss of weight, sedation, irritability, loose bowel movements and increased aggressiveness; retarding effect on discrimination learning in the computerized laboratory
Leventhal et al., 1993	N = 15	3–12.5	ABA crossover (for 30 wks) with additional crossover phase (for 32 wks)	(1.5)	CTQ; PTQ; RLRS	Modest decrease of hyperactivity (PTQ) particularly during the first period of treatment with fenfluramine; small decreases in sensory motor abnormalities (RLRS)	Weight loss during first fenfluramine phase

Note: ADS: Abbreviated Dyskenesia Scale (Simpson et al., 1979); AIMS: Abnormal Involuntary Movement Scale; CPRS: Clinical Psychiatric Rating Scale; CTQ: Conners Teacher Questionnaire (Guy, 1976, p. 288); PTQ: Conners Parent-Teacher Questionnaire (Guy, 1976, p. 300); RLRS: Real-Life Rating Scale for Autism (Freeman et al., 1986); TSRS: Timed Stereotypies Rating Scale (Campbell, 1985c).
[a] Three subjects dropped out; in 2 cases parents complained of irritability, anorexia, weight loss, and insomnia; in one case the parents moved.

individual responders to fenfluramine, the therapeutic gains declined or were lost after approximately 2 months of treatment (Campbell et al., 1986).

Naltrexone.   Naltrexone was explored because it was hypothesized that there is an analogy between behavioral deviances and other abnormalities in autism (e.g., associated seizure disorder), and symptoms in patients addicted to opiates; behaviors in animals receiving opiates, and symptoms in newborns of opiate addict mothers (Panksepp, 1979). This hypothesis, based on studies with laboratory animals, was supported by some evidence from studies with autistic children suggesting that abnormalities of the endogenous opioid system may exist in a subgroup (Gillberg, Terenius, & Lonnerholm, 1985; Weizman et al., 1984, 1988). It should be noted that these studies consisted of small sample sizes, with a wide age range of subjects and without adequate controls. However, naltrexone was explored because it was reported to be a potent opioid antagonist, relatively safe and presumably without the problem of associated tardive dyskinesia, a problem that neuroleptics shared.

In two acute dose range tolerance trials involving autistic children, naltrexone appeared to be a therapeutically promising and safe agent, at doses ranging from 0.5 to 2.0 mg/kg/day (Campbell et al., 1989; Herman et al., 1986). However, only the reduction of hyperactivity by naltrexone was confirmed in a subsequent large clinical trial of naltrexone, consisting of 41 hospitalized children, ages 2.9 to 7.8 years, with daily administration of medication over a period of 3 weeks (Campbell, Anderson, et al., 1993). Naltrexone was given in a single morning dose, 1.0 mg/kg/day (initial dose 0.5 mg/kg/day), as previously noted, over a period of 3 weeks. In this study, naltrexone's effect did not differ from that of placebo on discrimination learning in the automated laboratory. A subsample of the 41 patients had SIB on baseline ($N = 21$), as measured by the Aggression Scale. The effect of naltrexone on SIB was not different from placebo though there was a suggestion that it had beneficial effect in individual children. A total of 10 children with SIB were in the naltrexone group.

Untoward effects associated with naltrexone were transient and minimal on daily doses of 0.5 and 1.0 mg/kg; mainly sedation ($N = 3$), decrease of appetite ($N = 2$), and vomiting ($N = 3$) were seen. There was no relationship between naltrexone levels in plasma and clinical response (Gonzalez et al., 1994).

The reduction of hyperactivity by naltrexone was also reported in an acute dose range tolerance trial conducted by Herman et al. (1991) in 13 outpatients, ages 3 to 12 years. Table 5.8 lists the major studies with naltrexone.

Table 5.8. Studies of Naltrexone in Autistic Disorder

Author(s) and Year	Sample	Age in Years	Design	Dosage mg/d (mg/kg/d)	Measures	Clinical Effects	
						Therapeutic	Untoward
Herman et al., 1986	$N = 5$	4–12	Open, administered once per week with placebo "surrounds"	(0.5, 1.0, 1.5, 2.0)	BRC Autism scale; BRC Social Proximity test; BOS scale	Decreases in hand flapping and whirling and increase in social behavior	None
Herman et al., 1987	$N = 3$ heterogenous (autistic disorder and profound MR = 1, Tourette's disorder = 1, autistic behaviors and profound MR = 1)	10–17	Open, acute dose range tolerance trial with placebo "surrounds"	(0.5, 1.0, 1.5, 2.0)	Experimental self-injury test (used to evaluate frequency)	Significant decrease in frequency of self-injurious behavior (no effect at 2.0 mg/kg/d)	Not listed
Herman et al., 1991	$N = 13$	3–12	Open, acute dose range tolerance trial	(0.5, 1.0, 1.5, 2.0)	BRC Social Proximity Test; AAM; CP-TRS; CARS	Significant reduction of CARS scores and of hyperactivity, as measured by number of squares crossed (BRC Social Proximity Test) and computerized activity monitor counts (AAM)	Not listed

Study	N	Age	Design	Dose	Measures	Results	Side Effects
Leboyer et al., 1992	N = 4[a]	4–19	Double-blind, placebo-controlled, crossover	(0.5, 1.0, 2.0) each dose administered for one week	CGI; BSE; SIB scale (by parental report as rated by the investigators)	Significant reduction of SIB, temper tantrums, resistance to change, and restlessness; improved attention, verbalization and explorative behavior; CGI Efficacy ($p < .05$)[b]	No "troublesome" (p. 316) side effects
Campbell et al., 1993	N = 41	2.9–7.8	2-week placebo baseline, double-blind, placebo-controlled random assignment; one week posttreatment placebo	(1.0) administered for 3 weeks	CPRS; CGI; NGI; PTQ; ARS; AIMS; TSRS; Global Clinical Consensus Rating; discrimination learning and measurement of motor activity and duration of stereotypies in computerized laboratory	Significant decrease in hyperactivity ($p = 0.006$) and increase in hypoactivity ($p = 0.003$) (CPRS); decrease of motor activity as measured by carpet activity in the computerized laboratory ($p < 0.045$); on PTQ Demands must be met ($p = 0.035$) & restless (overactive, $p = 0.09$)	Excessive sedation, decreased appetite and vomiting?

Note: ARS: Aggressive Rating Scale; AIMS: Abnormal Involuntary Movement Scale; BOS: Behavioral Observation Scale; BSE: Behavior Summarized Evaluation (Barthelemy et al., 1990); CARS: Children's Autism Rating Scale; CGI: Clinical Global Impressions; CPRS: Clinical Psychiatric Rating Scale; CP-TRS: Conners Parent-Teacher Rating Scale; PTQ: Conners Parent-Teacher Questionnaire (Guy, 1976, p. 300); NGI: Nurses' Global Impression; SIB: Self-Injurious Behavior; TSRS: Timed Stereotypies Rating Scale (Campbell, 1985c).

[a] One subject was on antipsychotic agent.

[b] Clear behavioral improvements seen with low (0.5 mg/kg/d) and high (2.0 mg/kg/d) doses in the 3 subjects who had elevated B-endorphin.

Though naltrexone was reported to reduce SIB in a few case reports (for review, see Campbell, Anderson, et al., 1993; Deutsch, 1986), no definite conclusions can be made at the present time because of insufficient information. Aman (1993) analyzed and reviewed the literature critically on the effectiveness of naltrexone as well as other psychoactive agents in reducing SIB in developmental disabilities including autism. He came to the conclusion that naltrexone may have reduced SIB in about half of the 54 reported cases he reviewed, but the effect was small, though statistically significant (Aman, 1993). Table 5.9 represents an overview of the pertinent literature on the effect of naltrexone on SIB; 32 subjects with SIB were diagnosed with autism. The efficacy of naltrexone on SIB requires a critical assessment.

Stimulants. There is a disagreement about the effects of stimulants in autism, though all reports have some methodological flaws and/or the findings are based on open studies with a small number of subjects. Birmaher, Quintana, and Greenhill (1988) found improvement in 8 of 9 outpatients, ages 4 to 6 years, on daily doses of 10 to 50 mg of methylphenidate. Geller, Guttmacher, and Bleeg (1981) found dextroamphetamine to be therapeutic in 2 children.

A mixture of therapeutic effects and side effects associated with dextroamphetamine (1.25 to 10 mg/day) was reported by Campbell, Fish, David, Shapiro, Collins, and Koh (1972). Although decrease of hyperactivity and increase of attention span were rated, these therapeutic effects were outweighed by side effects in 16 hospitalized children, ages 3 to 6 years. Most common side effects were irritability, hyperactivity, worsening of withdrawal, worsening of stereotypies, stereotypies de novo, and loss of appetite (Campbell, Fish, David, et al., 1972). In an open trial of methylphenidate in 2 autistic children, there was no change of hyperactivity in one, and worsening of hyperactivity in the other child, in addition to other behavioral toxicity (Realmuto et al., 1989). A third child had a history of "facial and eye twitches" associated both with methylphenidate and dextroamphetamine (Realmuto, August, & Garfinkel, 1989, p. 124).

Clomipramine. Clomipramine, a tricyclic and 5-HT uptake inhibitor, also was explored and studied in autism, (see Table 5.10), the rationale being that there may be a relationship between compulsions/rituals in autism and certain repetitive behaviors which are reduced by clomipramine (Gordon, State, Nelson, Hamburger, & Rapoport, 1993). It was thought that stereotypies seen in young autistic children may change into obsessive-compulsive phenomena in adolescence in autism (Sanchez, Campbell, Small, Cueva, Armenteros, & Adams, in press). Abnormalities of the serotonergic system were thought to be underlying behavioral abnormalities in autism (for review, see Campbell & Shay, 1994).

Table 5.9. Naltrexone and Self-Injurious Behavior: Overview of the Representative Literature[a]

Author(s)	N	Age Range in Years	Diagnosis	Design	Daily Dose in mg (mg/Kg)	Duration	Results
Szymanski et al., 1987	2	21, 29	MR	ABAB,[b] double-blind, placebo-controlled	50; 100	3 weeks	Negative
Sandman, 1988	4	23–26	MR	Latin square, double-blind, placebo-controlled	0, 25, 50, or 100	2 days	Positive
Barrett et al., 1989	1	12	Autism	Crossover, double-blind, placebo-controlled	50 (1.2)	12 days	Positive
Lienemann & Walker, 1989b	1	50	Depression with SIB	Open	50	28 days	Positive
Lienemann & Walker, 1989a	1	27	Autism	Open	50	1 year	Positive
Luiselli et al., 1989	1	16	MR	Crossover, double-blind, placebo-controlled	50	10 days; 5 days	Negative
Sandman et al., 1990	4		MR	Latin square, crossover, double-blind, placebo?	0, 25, 50, and 100	2 doses/week	Positive
Walters et al., 1990	1	14	Autism	Crossover, double-blind, placebo-controlled	(1.0)	21 days	Positive
Kars et al., 1990	6	15–31	MR	Crossover, double-blind, placebo-controlled	50	21 days	Positive (N = 2); Slight (N = 1); Negative (N = 2)
Knabe et al., 1990	2	27, 46	Autism	Open	(2.0)	15–30 days	Positive

(Continued)

Table 5.9. (Continued)

Author(s)	N	Age Range in Years	Diagnosis	Design	Daily Dose in mg (mg/Kg)	Duration	Results
Leboyer et al., 1992	4	4–19	Autism	Crossover (3 doses) double-blind, placebo-controlled[c]	(0.5, 1.0, and 2.0)	7 days, each dose	Positive
Taylor et al., 1991	1	20	Autism? micro-cephaly	Crossover (3 doses), partially blinded, placebo-controlled[b]	(0.5, 1.0, and 2.0)	each dose 1 week	Positive
Panksepp & Lensing, 1991	2 (of 4)	5–21	Autism	Open	(0.4–0.5 every third day	?	Positive
Campbell, Anderson, et al., 1993	21 (of 41)	2.9–7.8	Autism	Parallel groups design, double-blind, placebo-controlled, randomized	(1.0)	3 weeks	Negative except in a few individuals
Sandman et al., 1993	24 (2 with autism)	13–67	MR/Hetere-ogeneous	Double-blind, placebo-controlled, random-ized	(0.5, 1.0, 2.0)	Each dose 1 week, total of 3 weeks	Positive
Johnson et al., 1994	1	7	MR	Crossover, placebo-controlled, and behav-ioral treatment	50 mg b.i.d. (3.8)	2 weeks	Negative
Zingarelli et al., 1992	8 (6 with SIB)	19–39	Autism DSM-III	Double-blind, placebo-controlled, crossover (baseline, ABAB)	50 mg (0.63–1.14, mean = 0.78)	17 weeks; each period 3 weeks (daily)	Negative

[a] Acute dose range studies excluded.
[b] Neuroleptic treatment continued.
[c] Neuroleptic treatment continued in one case.

Table 5.10. Clomipramine in Autistic Children

Author(s) and Year	Sample	Age in Years	Design	Dosage mg/d (mg/kg/d)	Measures	Clinical Effects Therapeutic	Clinical Effects Untoward
Garber et al., 1992	$N = 11$[a] Heterogeneous (4 with autism)	10–20	Open	(25–125; mean, 70)	Staff report based on frequency of each target symptom (SIB and stereotypies)	Marked decreases of SIB and stereotypies	Constipation, enuresis, rash, aggression, hypomania, sedation, worsening of stereotypies ($N = 1$), new onset aggression
Gordon et al., 1993	$N = 24$	6–18	Double-blind, placebo-controlled, randomized ($N = 12$); double-blind comparison of clomipramine & desipramine ($N = 12$) crossover, randomized	152 (4.3)	CPRS; CGI; Modified NIMH OCD Scale; Modified NIMH Global OCD & Anxiety scales; modified CPRS OCD subscale; TESS	Significant decreases in the CPRS Autism Relevant Subscale; autism, hyperactivity, and anger/uncooperativeness (CPRS); significant decreases in compulsive and ritualized behaviors (CPRS OCD subscales; Modified NIMH OCD and global OCD scales); reduction of SIB[b]	Insomnia, constipation, sedation, twitching, tremor, flushing, dry mouth, decreased appetite, nausea, prolonged QT interval ($N = 1$), "severe" tachycardia ($N = 1$), grand mal seizures ($N = 1$; dropped from study)
Brasic et al., 1994	$N = 5$	6–12	Open	200	AIMS; RSTD; TSRS; HAS; RSDIA; GCAA; TSGS; YGTSS; CGI-TS	"Marked to moderate" decreases of general dyskinesias (AIMS, RSTD, TSRS), akathisias (HAS, RSDIA) and tics (TSGS,	Not listed

(Continued)

173

Table 5.10. *(Continued)*

Author(s) and Year	Sample	Age in Years	Design	Dosage mg/d (mg/kg/d)	Measures	Clinical Effects	
						Therapeutic	Untoward
Sanchez et al., in press; Sanchez, unpublished data	$N = 8$	3.5–8.7	Open	50–175 mean, 103.57 (2.5–4.65; mean, 3.44)	CPRS; CGI; PTQ; NGI	Moderate improvement seen in one subject (decrease in hyperactivity and aggression and increase in attention span); worsening in 6; one dropped	Acute urinary retention on 2 occasions ($N = 1$); constipation; behavioral toxicity

Note: AIMS: Abnormal Involuntary Movement Scale; CGI: Clinical Global Impressions; CGI-TS: Clinical Global Impressions for Tourette's Syndrome; CPRS: Clinical Psychiatric Rating Scale; GCAA: Global Clinical Assessment of Akathisia; HAS: Hillside Akathisia Scale; NIMH OCD Scale: National Institute of Mental Health Obsessive-Compulsive Disorder Scale; PTQ: Conners Parent-Teacher Questionnaire; RSDIA: Rating Scale for Drug-Induced Akathisia; RSTD: Rating Scale for Tardive Dyskinesia; TESS: Subjective Treatment Emergent Symptoms Scale; TSGS: Tourette Syndrome Global Scale; TSRS: Timed Stereotypies Rating Scale; YGTSS: Yale Global Tic Severity Scale.

[a] Most subjects including 3 of the 4 autistic subjects were on other medication.

[b] SIB (self-injurious behavior) was "markedly diminished" (p. 446) for the 4 subjects who exhibited SIB.

Clomipramine was superior to placebo and to desipramine in reducing withdrawal and stereotypies (behavioral items included in the Autism Factor of the 14 selected items of the CPRS) and compulsive behaviors in a sample of 24 autistic subjects ages 6 to 18 years (Gordon et al., 1993). This was a double-blind randomized crossover study, each treatment period of 5 weeks' duration; the mean daily dose of clomipramine was 152 mg (4.3 mg/kg). Both active drugs (imipramine at mean daily dose of 127 mg, or 4.0 mg/kg) were superior to placebo in reducing hyperactivity.

Reduction of "adventitious movements" (Brasic et al., 1994, p. 1309) and compulsions were reported in an open study of clomipramine, administered in a single evening dose (200 mg/d; 3.0–5.0 mg/kg/day) to 5 subjects, ages approximately 5 to 12 years. The nature of abnormal movements is unclear; whether akathisia, reduced by clomipramine, was due to an antipsychotic received prior to clomipramine, or whether it was preexisting hyperactivity in these outpatients.

Clonidine. Reduction of hyperactivity along with other symptoms was reported to be associated with administration of clonidine (see Table 5.11) in two small samples of patients. Ghaziuddin, Tsai, and Ghaziuddin (1992) used 0.15 to 0.20 mg/day in outpatients (mean age 6.5 years) who failed to respond to other drugs previously; Jaselskis, Cook, Fletcher, and Leventhal (1992) employed similar doses of clonidine in outpatients whose ages ranged from 5 to 13.4 years. Side effects were reported and included hypotension.

Beta Blockers. This class of drugs was reported to be effective in decreasing aggression and SIB, as well as other behavioral symptoms in 7 of 8 adult patients (Ratey et al., 1987). A critical review of the literature indicates that in mental retardation and in developmentally disordered persons small doses of beta-blockers may be adequate (sufficient) for therapeutic effect (Arnold & Aman, 1991).

Fluoxetine. Fluoxetine was explored in autism (see Table 5.12) because of its effect on the serotonergic system, and on obsessive-compulsive symptoms (Pigott et al., 1990). There are several reports, as shown in Table 5.12; all with small samples of patients and/or open case reports.

Reduction of a variety of symptoms or global improvement was reported to be associated with administration of fluoxetine. Only Bregman, Volkmar, and Cohen (1991) conducted a double-blind study, employing a crossover design in 7 subjects with severe obsessive-compulsive behavior. It is not clear what type of control was employed.

Buspirone. Buspirone is an agonist at postsynaptic serotonergic receptors. Because of the effect of buspirone on the serotonergic system,

Table 5.11. *Studies of Clonidine in Autistic Disorder*

Author(s) and Year	Sample	Age in Years	Design	Dosage mg/d (mg/kg/d)	Measures	Clinical Effects Therapeutic	Clinical Effects Untoward
Fankhauser et al., 1992	$N = 9$	5–33	Double-blind, placebo-controlled, crossover, randomized	Transdermal clonidine; mean, 0.16 ± 0.09 (mean, 0.0036)	CGI; RLRS; PTQ	Significant decreases of sensory responses (RLRS); CGI Global Improvement ($p < .0001$), CGI Efficacy ($p = .0003$)	Drowsiness and fatigue
Ghaziuddin et al., 1992	$N = 7$	4–8	Open	0.05–0.25	PTQ; Parents' and teachers' reports; Clinical observation	PTQ ($p < 0.01$); marked improvement ($N = 2$); moderate ($N = 3$); slight ($N = 1$)	Sedation
Jaselskis et al., 1992	$N = 8$	5.0–13.4	Double-blind, placebo-controlled, crossover, randomized	0.15–0.20	PTQ-Abbreviated; HSS; SC; ACTeRs; ABC; CPRS; CGI; CGAS	Significant decreases of irritability, hyperactivity, inappropriate speech, and stereotypies (ABC); decrease of oppositional behavior (ACTeRs) no significant difference between drug and placebo in the clinical ratings; CGAS, CGI, and modified CPRS	Drowsiness, hypotension (2), crying spells, irritability, and decrease in activity level

Note: ABC: Aberrant Behavior Checklist; ACTeRs: Attention deficit disorder with hyperactivity Comprehensive Teacher's Rating Scale (Ullman, Sleator, and Sprague, 1984); CGAS: Clinical Global Assessment Scale (Shaffer et al., 1973); CGI: Clinical Global Impressions; CPRS: Children's Psychiatric Rating Scale; HSS: Home Situational Scale (Barkley, 1983); PTQ: Conners Parent-Teacher Questionnaire; SC: Symptom Checklist; RLRS: Real-Life Rating Scale (Freeman et al. 1986).

Table 5.12. **Studies of Fluoxetine in Autistic Children**

Author(s) and Year	Sample	Age in Years	Design	Dosage mg/d (mg/kg/d)	Measures	Clinical Effects Therapeutic	Clinical Effects Untoward
Cook et al., 1992	$N = 23$	7.5–28.8	Open	10–80[a]	CGI	Decreases of rituals & compulsions, & a variety of symptoms (clinically); reduction of CGI Severity of Illness ($p < 0.002$)	Hyperactivity, agitation, decreased appetite, insomnia, "elevated affect" (p. 743)
Bregman et al., 1991	$N = 7$	Children and young adults	Double-blind crossover (5 months) followed by an open continuation trial	20–60	YBOCS	"Clear" improvement in only one case	None
Mehlinger et al., 1990	$N = 1$	26	Case report	20 (every other day)	None	Decreases of stereotypies, temper tantrums, and ritualistic behavior; Improvement in mood, social behavior, and language use	Increase in stereotypies and anxiety[b]

(Continued)

177

Table 5.12. (*Continued*)

Author(s) and Year	Sample	Age in Years	Design	Dosage mg/d (mg/kg/d)	Measures	Clinical Effects	
						Therapeutic	Untoward
Ghaziuddin et al., 1991	$N = 4$	13–21	Case report	20–40[c]	None	Decreases of compulsive behavior, irritability, agitation, and crying spells; improvement in mood	Agitation and "nervousness"
Todd, 1991	$N = 4$	8–19	Case report	20–30	None	Decreases of temper tantrums, ritualistic behavior, and stereotypies; improvement in tolerance to changes	None

Note: CGI: Clinical Global Impressions; YBOCS: Yale Brown Obsessive Compulsive Scale.

[a] Most patients were taking neuroleptics as well as fluoxetine.

[b] Side effects seen when dose increased to 20 mg/d.

[c] One case received clomipramine as well.

Realmuto et al. (1989) explored this drug in 4 autistic subjects (see Table 5.13). Decrease of hyperactivity was the main finding.

Rett's Disorder

To the best of our knowledge, there are only three studies involving psychoactive agents in Rett's disorder. It should be noted that only in the past decade has interest developed in Rett's disorder (see Hagberg, Aicardi, Dias, & Ramos, 1983; Olsson & Rett, 1990; for review, Tsai, 1992), even though it was first described in 1966 by Rett.

Bromocriptine.   Bromocriptine, an ergot derivative, and a potent dopamine receptor agonist, was explored in an open study ($N = 13$; Zappella, Genazzani, Facchinetti, & Hayek, 1990) and in a double-blind, placebo-controlled crossover study, involving 10 children, ages ranging from 3 years 5 months to 14 years 10 months (Zappella, 1990). Bromocriptine was investigated because of the suggestion that in persons with Rett's disorder a reduction of biogenic amines exists in several regions of the brain.

Two of 10 children improved moderately, one minimally, and 7 showed no change in response to bromocriptine (1.25–3.75 mg/day in divided doses) (Zappella, 1990). Fine and gross motor functioning, and cognitive and social behavior improved, as well as sleep patterns, after 4 months of administration of bromocriptine. Blood pressure, complete blood count, and liver enzymes remained unchanged; vomiting was the only side effect.

Naltrexone.   Naltrexone was investigated in 25 subjects; 22 subjects, ages 2.0 to 15.7 years, completed the study (Percy et al., 1994). The authors hypothesized that naltrexone, a potent opiate antagonist, should be of therapeutic value, because there was supportive evidence that an elevation of beta-endorphin exists in this condition (Myer, Tripathi, Brase, & Dewey, 1992; Percy et al., 1994). A variety of biological and behavioral measures were employed in this double-blind, placebo-controlled crossover study. Although naltrexone had a therapeutic effect on respiratory disturbance and pattern, this was outweighed by significant deleterious effects on various developmental parameters including motor behavior. Naltrexone advanced (worsened) clinical Rett stage (Percy et al., 1994).

Haloperidol had a positive effect in a 6-year-old child, at daily doses of 1.75 mg (divided in 3 or 4 doses); hand stereotypies (wringing), teeth grinding and mouthing decreased as well as the skin lesions on hands (Campbell, 1995). There was an improvement in social behavior, the child was "more happy, more available, and more focused." The child

Table 5.13. *Reports on Busiprone in Autistic Children*

Author(s) and Year	Sample	Age in Years	Design	Dosage mg/d (mg/kg/d)	Measures	Clinical Effects	
						Therapeutic	Untoward
Realmuto et al., 1989	N = 4	9.1–10.5	Open trial	15	ABC; Sensory Motor Behavior Checklist;[a] Social Awareness Inventory,[a] CTRS	Decreases in hyperactivity, aggression, and stereotypies (clinically)	Not specified
Ratey et al., 1989	N = 14 heterogenous[b] (3 autistic)	23–63	Case report	15–45	None	Decrease of aggression and SIB (N = 9), improvement in cognitive tasks and language production (N = 4)	Sedation and over-arousal

Note: ABC: Aberrant Behavior Checklist (Aman & Singh, 1986); CTRS: Conners Teacher's Rating Scale; SIB: Self-Injurious Behavior.

[a] August, Raz, & Baird (1987).

[b] Most patients were on other psychoactive agents.

was very sensitive even to minimal increase or decrease of haloperidol dose. Improvements were seen both in school and at home.

DRUGS OF CHOICE AND CLINICAL USAGE

Since most experience in this population of children is with haloperidol, this is the drug of choice when intervention with a psychoactive agent is required for the reduction of target symptoms, such as hyperactivity, temper tantrums, stereotypies, aggressiveness, and SIB. The starting dose should be low, 0.25 mg/day or 0.25 mg b.i.d.; increments should be small and gradual, not more frequent than twice a week, to avoid an acute dystonic reaction. Slow dosage increase also permits detection of therapeutic effects at the lowest effective dose. If long-term administration of haloperidol is required, medication should be discontinued every 6 months, for a period of 4 weeks, to determine whether the patient requires continued pharmacotherapy and to detect withdrawal dyskinesias. When hypoactivity is prominent, haloperidol should not be prescribed. In these cases, low doses of pimozide are suggested (3.0–6.0 mg/day and not exceeding 3.0 mg/kg/day).

If haloperidol is not effective in reducing SIB, lithium carbonate (see Campbell, Fish, Korein, Shapiro, Collins, & Koh, 1972) or naltrexone should be given a trial.

Naltrexone (0.5–2.0 mg/kg/day) is indicated in children with the prominent symptom of hyperactivity in the absence of other disruptive behavior that interferes with the child's functioning. Liver enzymes should be monitored.

Prior to a trial of a psychoactive agent, an adequate clinical and laboratory workup of the patient should be carried out including a behavioral evaluation with specification of target symptoms. The type and extent of workup will be influenced by the nature of the specific psychoactive agent. For example, the use of a tricyclic drug will require a baseline ECG and monitoring with ECG, whereas an associated seizure disorder would be a contraindication for a tricyclic. Prior to treatment with any psychoactive agent, an assessment of abnormal movements should be carried out, preferably employing the Abnormal Involuntary Movement Scale (AIMS) (Campbell, 1985a; NIMH, 1985). This is to obtain a baseline and to be able to differentiate (baseline) stereotypies from later developing tardive or withdrawal dyskinesias associated with administration of a psychoactive agent. Furthermore, withdrawal dyskinesias are to be differentiated from stereotypies reemerging after withdrawal of a neuroleptic. Differentiation of these two types of movements may be difficult in some cases (Campbell, Adams, Perry, Spencer, &

Overall, 1988; Campbell, Grega, Green, & Bennett, 1983; Campbell et al., 1990; Meiselas et al., 1989; Shay et al., 1993).

SIDE EFFECTS (UNTOWARD EFFECTS)

At certain dose levels and/or under certain conditions, all psychoactive agents have side effects (see Campbell et al., 1985). Some of the variables that may influence the development of side effects are duration of treatment (cumulative or total exposure to drug), age, diagnosis, degree of central nervous system (CNS) dysfunction, and drug level in plasma or serum. Prescribing daily dose or dose per body weight should be guided by recommendations of the Food and Drug Administration (e.g., tricyclics, see Hayes, Logan, Panitch, & Barker, 1975), most recent *Physicians' Desk Reference,* and sound research. Polypharmacy and unnecessary dose escalation should be avoided.

Baseline assessments should include a carefully taken history (including history of febrile seizures or seizure disorders); prior medication history; unusual reactions to drugs; height; and weight. Which baseline laboratory tests, including ECG, are required will depend on the type of psychoactive agent prescribed; administration of lithium will require white count, thyroid, liver, and kidney function tests, as well as monitoring lithium levels in blood. The use of specific side effect checklists is most helpful and highly recommended.

For a detailed review of side effects associated with administration of psychoactive agents, a book by Rosenberg, Holttum, and Gershon (1994) is recommended; for assessment instruments, Campbell and Palij (1985a, 1985b) and Campbell et al. (1985) are recommended. In this book, Chapter 3 is recommended; in this chapter, see Tables 5.6–5.8 and 5.10–5.13. Untoward effects of neuroleptics are detailed in a chapter by Campbell, Gonzalez, Ernst, Silva, and Werry (1993); untoward effects of lithium are discussed by Campbell, Silva, et al. (1991); Campbell et al. (1995); Silva et al. (1992); and Silva, Ernst, and Campbell (1993).

NEUROLEPTIC-RELATED TARDIVE AND WITHDRAWAL DYSKINESIAS

Tardive and withdrawal dyskinesias are reported in children and adolescents of normal intelligence with psychiatric disorders and in the mentally retarded (Gualtieri, Quade, Hicks, Mayo, & Schroeder, 1984; Gualtieri, Schroeder, Hicks, & Quade, 1986; Richardson, Haugland, & Craig, 1991). Richardson et al. (1991) studied 104 subjects, ages 10 to 18 years (mean, 15.2); 41 of the 104 received neuroleptics continuously for

3 months (or longer). Of the 41, tardive dyskinesias developed in 5 (12%). These data are based on retrospective and neuroleptic withdrawal studies.

Prospective and long-term studies of haloperidol have been conducted in autistic children, all outpatients, ages 2.3 to 10.3 years (Armenteros et al., 1995; Campbell et al., 1983, 1988, 1990; Malone, Ernst, Godfrey, Locascio, & Campbell, 1991; Meiselas et al., 1989; Shay et al., 1993). The design was as follows: Children who responded to haloperidol received the drug for 6 months, followed by abrupt withdrawal of haloperidol and placement on placebo for 4 weeks (Perry et al., 1989). If the child required further pharmacotherapy, haloperidol was administered for another 6 months. Assessment of stereotypies and other abnormal movements was carried out twice on baseline, while receiving placebo; at the end of the 6-month treatment with haloperidol, and weekly, during the 4-week posttreatment period, after drug withdrawal (Campbell, Adams, Perry, et al., 1988). In addition to behavioral rating scales (Perry et al., 1989) abnormal movements were assessed employing the Timed Stereotypies Rating Scale (TSRS; Campbell, 1985c) as well as the Abnormal Involuntary Movement Scale (AIMS, NIMH, 1985), employing a specified protocol (Campbell, 1985a) and videotaping the patients (Campbell et al., 1983; Campbell, Adams, Perry, et al., 1988; Meiselas et al., 1989; Shay et al., 1993). Approximately 26% (Campbell, Adams, Perry, et al., 1988) to 33.9% (Armenteros et al., 1995) of children developed dyskinesias, mainly withdrawal dyskinesias (Campbell, Adams, Perry, et al., 1988). As in adult psychiatric patients, most commonly the muscles of tongue, mouth, and jaws are involved, followed by muscles of upper and then lower extremities (including ataxia) and trunk. Blinking was also rated on haloperidol withdrawal, as well as involvement of laryngeal muscles or diaphragm, resulting in development of bizarre sounds (Campbell et al., 1983; Golden et al., 1987). The duration of movements with spontaneous cessation ranged from 1 week up to 7 ½ months. The relationship between dyskinesias and several parameters, including daily dose and cumulative dose of haloperidol was tested (Campbell, Adams, Perry, et al., 1988). Only complications of pregnancy and birth as measured by the Rochester Research Obstetrical Scale (ROS, Zax, Sameroff, & Babigian, 1977) had an effect. The mean total ROS score and the mean ROS delivery score differentiated the children who developed dyskinesias related to haloperidol from those who did not develop movements (Armenteros et al., 1995). The sample in this prospective long-term study of haloperidol included 118 autistic children, ages ranging from 2.3 to 8.2 years (mean, 4.98). Of the 118 children, 35 developed withdrawal dyskinesias and a few of these 45 while receiving haloperidol (Armenteros et al., 1995). Because drug-related dyskinesias are often difficult to differentiate from preexisting stereotypies (Campbell et al.,

1983), particularly in the absence of past drug history or when ratings are based exclusively on blind ratings of videotapes (Meiselas et al., 1989; Shay et al., 1993), children should be rated for abnormal movements on the AIMS prior to prescribing a neuroleptic or any other psychoactive agent. Repeated development of dyskinetic movements was also reported (Campbell, Adams, Perry et al., 1988; Malone et al., 1991).

REFERENCES

Aman, M. G. (1993). Efficacy of psychotropic drugs for reducing self-injurious behavior in the developmental disabilities. *Annals of Clinical Psychiatry, 5,* 171–188.

Aman, M. G., & Singh, N. (1986). *Aberrant behavior checklist.* New York: Slosson Educational Publication.

American Psychiatric Association (APA). (1980). *Diagnostic and statistical manual of mental disorders* (DSM-III-R) (3rd ed.). Washington, DC: Author.

American Psychiatric Association (APA). (1987). *Diagnostic and statistical manual of mental disorders* (DSM-III-R) (3rd ed. rev). Washington, DC: Author.

American Psychiatric Association (APA). (1994). *Diagnostic and statistical manual of mental disorders* (DSM-IV) (4th ed.). Washington, DC: Author.

Anderson, L. T., Campbell, M., Adams, P., Small, A. M., Perry, R., & Shell, J. (1989). The effects of haloperidol on discrimination learning and behavioral symptoms in autistic children. *Journal of Autism and Developmental Disorders, 19,* 227–239.

Anderson, L. T., Campbell, M., Grega, D. M., Perry, R., Small, A. M., & Green, W. H. (1984). Haloperidol in infantile autism: Effects on learning and behavioral symptoms. *American Journal of Psychiatry, 141,* 1195–1202.

Armenteros, J. L., Adams, P. B., Campbell, M., & Eisenberg, Z. W. (1995). Haloperidol related dyskinesias and pre- and perinatal complications in autistic children. *Psychopharmacology Bulletin, 31*(2), 361–367.

Arnold, L. E., & Aman, M. G. (1991). Beta blockers in mental retardation and developmental disorders. *Journal of Child and Adolescent Psychopharmacology, 1,* 361–373.

Asperger, H. (1944). Die "autistischen Psychopathen" im Kindersalter. *Archiv fur Psychiatrie und Nervenkrakheiten, 117,* 76.

August, G., Raz, N., & Baird, T. (1987). Fenfluramine response in high and low functioning autistic children. *Journal of the American Academy of Child and Adolescent Psychiatry, 3,* 342–346.

Barkley, R. A. (1983). *Hyperactive Children.* New York: Guilford.

Barrett, R. P., Feinstein, C., & Hole, W. T. (1989). Effects of naloxone and naltrexone on self-injury: A double-blind, placebo-controlled analysis. *American Journal of Mental Retardation, 93,* 644–651.

Barthelemy, C., Adrien, J. L., Tanguay, P., Garreau, B., Fermanian, J., Roux, S., Sauvage, D., & Lelord, G. (1990). The behavioral summarized evaluation: Validity and reliability of a scale for the assessment of autistic behaviors. *Journal of Autism and Developmental Disorders, 20,* 189–203.

Birmaher, B., Quintana, H., & Greenhill, L. L. (1988). Methylphenidate treatment of hyperactive autistic children. *Journal of the American Academy of Child and Adolescent Psychiatry, 27,* 248–251.

Brasic, J. R., Barnett, J. Y., Kaplan, D., Sheitman, B. B., Aisemberg, P., Lafargue, R. T., Kowalik, S., Clark, A., Tsaltas, M. O., & Young, J. G. (1994). Clomipramine ameliorates adventitious movements and compulsions in prepubertal boys with autistic disorder and severe mental retardation. *Neurology, 44,* 1309–1312.

Bregman, J., Volkmar, F., & Cohen, D. (1991, October 15–20). Fluoxetine in the treatment of autistic disorder. *Scientific Proceedings,* American Academy of Child and Adolescent Psychiatry, Vol. VII, p. 52.

Campbell, M. (1985a). Protocol for rating drug-related AIMS, stereotypies, and CPRS assessments. *Psychopharmacology Bulletin, 21*(4), 1081.

Campbell, M. (1985b). Schizophrenic disorders and pervasive development disorders/infantile autism. In J. M. Wiener (Ed.), *Diagnosis and psychopharmacology of childhood and adolescent disorders* (pp. 113–150). New York: Wiley.

Campbell, M. (1985c). Times stereotypies rating scale. *Psychopharmacology Bulletin, 21*(4), 1082.

Campbell, M. (1987). Drug treatment of infantile autism: The past decade. In H. Y. Meltzer (Ed.), *Psychopharmacology: The third generation of progress* (pp. 1225–1231). New York: Raven.

Campbell, M. (1988). Fenfluramine treatment of autism. Annotation. *Journal of Child Psychology and Psychiatry, 29*(1), 1–10.

Campbell, M. (1995). Haloperidol in a child with Rett's Disorder. Unpublished manuscript.

Campbell, M., Adams, P., Perry, R., Spencer, E. K., & Overall, J. E. (1988). Tardive and withdrawal dyskinesia in autistic children: A prospective study. *Psychopharmacology Bulletin, 24*(2), 251–255.

Campbell, M., Adams, P., Small, A. M., Curren, E. L., Overall, J. E., Anderson, L. T., Lynch, N., & Perry, R. (1988). Efficacy and safety of fenfluramine in autistic children. *Journal of the American Academy of Child and Adolescent Psychiatry, 27,* 434–439.

Campbell, M., Adams, P. B., Small, A. M., Kafantaris, V., Silva, R. R., Shell, J., Perry, R., & Overall, J. E. (1995). Lithium in hospitalized aggressive children with conduct disorder: A double-blind and placebo controlled study. *Journal of the American Academy of Child and Adolescent Psychiatry, 34,*(4), 445–453.

Campbell, M., Anderson, L. T., Meier, M., Cohen, I. L., Small, A. M., Samit, C., & Sachar, E. J. (1978). A comparison of haloperidol, behavior therapy and their interaction in autistic children. *Journal of the American Academy of Child Psychiatry, 17,* 640–655.

Campbell, M., Anderson, L. T., Small, A. M., Adams, P., Gonzalez, N. M., & Ernst, M. (1993). Naltrexone in autistic children: Behavioral symptoms and attentional learning. *Journal of the American Academy of Child and Adolescent Psychiatry, 32*(6), 1283–1291.

Campbell, M., Fish, B., David, R., Shapiro, T., Collins, P., & Koh, C. (1972). Response to triiodothyronine and dextroamphetamine: A study of preschool schizophrenic children. *Journal of Autism and Childhood Schizophrenia, 2,* 343–358.

Campbell, M., Fish, B., Korein, J., Shapiro, T., Collins, P., & Koh, C. (1972). Lithium and chlorpromazine: A controlled crossover study of hyperactive severely disturbed young children. *Journal of Autism and Childhood Schizophrenia, 2,* 234–263.

Campbell, M., Gonzalez, N. M., Ernst, M., Silva, R. R., & Werry, J. S. (1993). Antipsychotics (Neuroleptics). In J. S. Werry & M. G. Aman (Eds.), *Practioner's guide to psychoactive drugs for children and adolescents* (pp. 269–296). New York: Plenum Medical.

Campbell, M., Green, W. H., & Deutsch, S. I. (1985). *Child and Adolescent Psychopharmacology.* Beverly Hills: Sage.

Campbell, M., Grega, D. M., Green, W. H., & Bennett, W. G. (1983). Neuroleptic-induced dyskinesias in children. *Clinical Neuropharmacology, 6,* 207–222.

Campbell, M., Kafantaris, V., Malone, R. P., Kowalik, S. C., & Locascio, J. J. (1991). Diagnostic and assessment issues related to pharmacotherapy for children and adolescents with autism. Behavior modification [Special issue]. In J. K. Luiselli & N. N. Singh (Eds.), *Current Perspectives in the Diagnosis, Assessment, and Treatment of Child and Adolescent Disorders, 15*(3), 326–354. London: Sage.

Campbell, M., Locascio, J. J., Choroco, M. C., Spencer, E. K., Malone, R. P., Kafantaris, V., & Overall, J. E. (1990). Stereotypies and tardive dyskinesia: Abnormal movements in autistic children. *Psychopharmacology Bulletin, 26*(2), 260–266.

Campbell, M., Overall, J. E., Small, A. M., Sokol, M. S., Spencer, E. K., Adams, P., Foltz, R. L., Monti, K. M., Perry, R., Nobler, M., & Roberts, E. (1989). Naltrexone in autistic children: An acute open dose range tolerance trial. *Journal of the American Academy of Child and Adolescent psychiatry, 28,* 200–206.

Campbell, M., & Palij, M. (1985a). Behavioral and cognitive measures used in psychopharmacological studies of infantile autism. *Psychopharmacology Bulletin, 21*(4), 1047–1053.

Campbell, M., & Palij, M. (1985b). Measurement of untoward effects including tardive dyskinesia. *Psychopharmacology Bulletin, 21*(4), 1063–1082.

Campbell, M., Perry, R., Polonsky, B. B., Deutsch, S. I., Palij, M., & Lukashok, D. (1986). Brief report: Fenfluramine in hospitalized young autistic children: An open study. *Journal of Autism and Developmental Disorders, 16,* 495–506.

Campbell, M., & Schopler, E. (Co-Chairpersons). (1989). *Pervasive developmental disorders.* In T. B. Karasu (Chairperson), *Treatments of psychiatric disorders. A Task Force Report of the American Psychiatric Association* (Vol. 1, pp. 179–294). Washington, DC, American Psychiatric Association.

Campbell, M., & Shay, J. (1994). The pervasive developmental disorders. In H. I. Kaplan & B. J. Sadock (Eds.), *Comprehensive textbook of psychiatry/VI.* Baltimore, MD: Williams & Wilkins.

Campbell, M., Silva, R. R., Kafantaris, V., Locascio, J. J., Gonzalez, N. M., Lee, D., & Lynch, N. S. (1991). Predictors of side effects associated with lithium administration in children. *Psychopharmacology Bulletin, 27*(3), 373–380.

Cohen, I. L., Campbell, M., Posner, D., Small, A. M., Triebel, D., & Anderson, L. T. (1980). Behavioral effects of haloperidol in young autistic children: An objective analysis using a within-subjects reversal design. *Journal of the American Academy of Child Psychiatry, 19,* 665–677.

Cook, E. H., Jr., Rowlett, R., Jaselskis, C., & Leventhal, B. L. (1992). Fluoxetine treatment of children and adults with autistic disorder and mental retardation. *Journal of the American Academy of Child and Adolescent Psychiatry, 31,* 739–745.

Deutsch, S. I. (1986). Rationale for the administration of opiate antagonists in treating infantile autism. *American Journal of Mental Deficiency, 90,* 631–635.

Engelhardt, D. M., Polizos, P., Waizer, J., & Hoffman, S. P. (1973). A double-blind comparison of fluphenazine and haloperidol in outpatient schizophrenic children. *Journal of Autism and Childhood Schizophrenia, 3,* 128–137.

Faretra, G., Dooher, L., & Dowling, J. (1970). Comparison of haloperidol and fluphenazine in disturbed children. *American Journal of Psychiatry, 126,* 1670–1673.

Fankhauser, M. P., Karumanchi, V. C., German, M. L., Yates, A., & Karumanchi, S. D. (1992). A double-blind, placebo-controlled study of the efficacy of transdermal clonidine in autism. *Journal of Clinical Psychiatry, 53,* 77–82.

Fish, B. (1968). Methodology in child psychopharmacology. In D. H. Efron, J. O. Cole, J. Levine, & J. R. Wittenborn (Eds.), *Psychopharmacology, a review of progress, 1957–1967* (pp. 989–1001). Public Health Service Publication No. 1836. Washington, DC: U.S. Government Printing Office.

Fish, B., Shapiro, T., & Campbell, M. (1966). Long term prognosis and the response of schizophrenic children to drug therapy: A controlled study of trifluoperazine. *American Journal of Psychiatry, 123,* 32–39.

Freeman, B. J., Ritvo, E. R., & Schroth, P. C. (1984). Behavioral observation system. *Journal of the American Academy of Child Psychiatry, 23,* 588–594.

Freeman, B. J., Ritvo, E. R., Yokota, A., & Ritvo, A. (1986). A scale for rating symptoms of patients with the syndrome of autism in real life settings. *Journal of the American Academy of Child Psychiatry, 25*(1), 130–136.

Garber, H. J., McGonigle, J. J., Slomka, G. T., & Monteverde, E. (1992). Clomipramine treatment of stereotypic behaviors and self-injury in patients with developmental disabilities. *Journal of the American Academy of Child and Adolescent Psychiatry, 31*(6), 1157–1160.

Geller, B., Guttmacher, L., & Bleeg, M. (1981). The coexistence of childhood onset pervasive developmental disorder and attention deficit disorder with hyperactivity. *American Journal of Psychiatry, 38,* 338–339.

Ghaziuddin, M., Tsai, L. Y., & Ghaziuddin, N. (1991). Fluoxetine in autism with depression. *Journal of the American Academy of Child and Adolescent Psychiatry, 30,* 508–509.

Ghaziuddin, M., Tsai, L. Y., & Ghaziuddin, N. (1992). Clonidine for autism [letter]. *Journal of Child Adolescent Psychopharmacology, 2*(4).

Gillberg, C., Terenius, L., & Lonnerholm, G. (1985). Endorphin activity in childhood psychosis: Spinal fluid levels in 24 cases. *Archives of General Psychiatry, 42,* 780–783.

Golden, R. R., Campbell, M., & Perry, R. (1987). A taxometric method for diagnosis of tardive dyskinesia. *Journal of Psychiatric Research, 21*(3), 233–241.

Gonzalez, N. M., Campbell, M., Small, A. M., Shay, J., Bluhm, L. D., Adams, P. B., & Foltz, R. L. (1994). Naltrexone plasma levels, clinical response and effect on weight in autistic children. *Psychopharmacology Bulletin, 30*(2), 203–208.

Gordon, C. T., State, R. C., Nelson, J. E., Hamburger, S. D., & Rapoport, J. L. (1993). A double-blind comparison of clomipramine, desipramine, and placebo in the treatment of autistic disorder. *Archives of General Psychiatry, 50,* 441–447.

Grof, P., Akhter, M. I., Campbell, M., Gottfries, C. G., Khan, I., Lapierre, Y., Lemberger, L., Müller-Oerlingshausen, B., & Woggon, B. (1993). *Clinical evaluation of psychotropic drugs for psychiatric disorders. Principles and proposed guidelines.* WHO Expert Series on Biological Psychiatry, Volume 2. Published on behalf of the World Health Organization by Hogrefe & Huber Publishers, Bern.

Gualtieri, C. T., Quade, D., Hicks, R. E., Mayo, J. P., & Schroeder, S. R. (1984). Tardive dyskinesia and other clinical consequences of neuroleptic treatment in children and adolescents. *American Journal of Psychiatry, 141,* 20–23.

Gualtieri, C. T., Schroeder, S. R., Hicks, R. E., & Quade, D. (1986). Tardive dyskinesia in young mentally retarded individuals. *Archives of General Psychiatry, 43,* 335–340.

Guy, W. (1976). ECDEU Assessment Manual for Psychopharmacology, Revised. Rockville, MD: National Institute of Mental Health.

Hagberg, B., Aicardi, J., Dias, K., & Ramos, O. (1983). A progressive syndrome of autism, dementia, ataxia, and loss of purposeful hand use in girls: Rett's syndrome: Report of 35 cases. *Annals of Neurology, 14,* 471–479.

Hattab, J. Y. (1994). *Ethics & child mental health.* Hewlett, NY: Gefen Books.

Hayes, T. A., Logan Panitch, M., & Barker, E. (1975). Imipramine dosage in children: A comment on "imipramine and electrocardiographic abnormalities in hyperactive children." *American Journal of Psychiatry, 132,* 546–547.

Heller, T. (1908). Dementia infantilis. *Zeitschrift fur die Erforschung und Behandlung des Jugenlichen Schwachsinns, 2,* 141–165.

Herman, B. H., Asleson, G. S., Borghese, I. F., Chatoor, I., Benoit, M. B., Powell, A., Papero, P., Allen, R. P., & McNulty, G. (1991, October 15–20). Acute naltrexone in autism: Selective decreases in hyperactivity (p. 52). *Scientific Proceedings,* 38th Annual Meeting of the American Academy of Child and Adolescent Psychiatry, San Francisco, CA.

Herman, B. H., Hammock, M. K., Arthur-Smith, A., Egan, J., Chatoor, I., Werner, A., & Zelnik, N. (1987). Naltrexone decreases self-injurious behavior. *Annals of Neurology, 22,* 550–552.

Herman, B. H., Hammock, M. K., Arthur-Smith, A., Egan, J., Chatoor, I., Zelnik, N., Applegate, K., & Boeckx, R. L. (1986, October 15–19). Effects of naltrexone in autism: Correlation with plasma opioid concentrations. *Scientific Proceedings,* (Vol. II, pp. 11–12) 33rd Annual Meeting of the American Academy of Child and Adolescent Psychiatry, Los Angeles, CA.

ICD-10. *The ICD-10 Classification of Mental and Behavioural Disorders.* (1992). Clinical descriptions and diagnostic guidelines. Geneva: World Health Organization.

Irwin, S. (1968). A rational framework for the development, evaluation, and use of psychoactive drugs. *American Journal of Psychiatry, 124*(Suppl.), 1–19.

Jaselskis, C. A., Cook, E. H., Jr., Fletcher, K. E., & Leventhal, B. L. (1992). Clonidine treatment of hyperactive and impulsive children with autistic disorder. *Journal of Clinical Psychopharmacology, 12,* 332–327.

Johnson, K., Johnson, C. R., & Sahl, R. A. (1994). Behavioral and naltrexone treatment of self-injurious behavior. *Journal of Developmental and Physical Disabilities, 6*(6), 193–202.

Kanner, L. (1943). Autistic disturbances of affective contact. *Nervous Child, 8,* 477–479.

Kars, H., Broekema, W., Glaudemans-van Gelderen, I., Verhoeven, W. M. A., & van Ree, J. M. (1990). Naltrexone attenuates self-injurious behavior in mentally retarded subjects. *Biological Psychiatry, 27,* 741–746.

Knabe, R., Schulz, P., & Richard, J. (1990). Letter to the editor, Initial aggravation of self-injurious behavior in autistic patients receiving naltrexone treatment. *Journal of Autism and Developmental Disorders, 20*(4), 591–593.

Leboyer, M., Bouvard, M. P., Launay, J-M., Tabuteau, F., Waller, D., Dugas, M., Kerdelhue, B., Lensing, P., & Panksepp, J. (1992). Brief report: A double-blind study of naltrexone in infantile autism. *Journal of Autism and Developmental Disorders, 22,* 309–319.

Le Couteur, A., Rutter, M., Lord, C., Rios, P., Robertson, S., Holdgrafer, M., & McLennan, J. D. (1989). Autism diagnostic interview. *Journal of Autism and Developmental Disorders, 19,* 363–387.

Leventhal, B. L., Cook, E. H., Jr., Morford, M., Ravitz, A. J., Heller, W., & Freedman, D. X. (1993). Clinical and neurochemical effects of fenfluramine in children with autism. *Journal of Neuropsychiatry, 5,* 307–315.

Lienemann, J., & Walker, F. D. (1989a). Naltrexone for treatment of self-injury. *American Journal of Psychiatry, 146,* 1639–1640.

Lienemann, J., & Walker, F. D. (1989b). Reversal of self-abusive behavior with naltrexone. *Journal of Clinical Psychopharmacology, 9*(6), 448–449.

Locascio, J. J., Malone, R. P., Small, A. M., Kafantaris, V., Ernst, M., Lynch, N. S., Overall, J. E., & Campbell, M. (1991). Factors related to haloperidol response and dyskinesias in autistic children. *Psychopharmacology Bulletin, 27*(2), 119–126.

Lord, C., Rutter, M., Goode, S., Heembsbergen, J., Jordan, H., Mawhood, L., & Schopler, E. (1989). Autism diagnostic observation schedule: A standardized observation of communicative and social behavior. *Journal of Autism and Developmental Disorders, 19,* 185–212.

Lotspeich, L. J. (1995). Autism and pervasive developmental disorders. In F. E. Bloom & D. J. Kupfer (Eds.), *Psychopharmacology: The fourth generation of progress.* New York: Raven.

Luiselli, J. K., Beltis, J. A., & Bass, J. (1989). Clinical analysis of naltrexone in the treatment of self-injurious behavior. *Journal of the Clinical Handicapped Persons, 2*(1), 43–50.

Malone, R. P., Ernst, M., Godfrey, K. A., Locascio, J. J., & Campbell, M. (1991). Repeated episodes of neuroleptic-related dyskinesias in autistic children. *Psychopharmacology Bulletin, 27*(2), 113–117.

Mehlinger, R., Scheftner, W. A., & Poznanski, E. (1990). Fluoxetine and autism. *Journal of the American Academy of Child and Adolescent Psychiatry, 29,* 985.

Meiselas, K., Spencer, E. K., Oberfield, R., Peselow, E. D., Angrist, B., & Campbell, M. (1989). Differentiation of stereotypies from neuroleptic-related dyskinesias in autistic children. *Journal of Clinical Psychopharmacology, 9*(3), 207–209.

Myer, E. C., Tripathi, H. L., Brase, D. A., & Dewey, W. L. (1992). Elevated CSF beta-endorphin immunoreactivity in Rett's syndrome: Report of 158 cases and comparison with leukemic children. *Neurology, 42,* 357–360.

Olsson, B., & Rett, A. (1990). A review of the Rett syndrome with a theory of autism. *Brain Development, 12,* 11–15.

Overall, J. E., & Campbell, M. (1988). Behavioral assessment of psychopathology in children: Infantile autism. *Journal of Clinical Psychology, 44,* 708–716.

Panksepp, J. (1979). A neurochemical theory of autism. *Trends Neuroscience, 2,* 174–177.

Panksepp, J., & Lensing, P. (1991). Naltrexone treatment of autism. A synopsis of an open-trial with four children. *Journal of Autism and Developmental Disorders, 21,* 135–141.

Percy, A. K., Glaze, D. G., Schultz, R. J., Zoghbi, H. Y., Williamson, D., Frost, J. D., Jr., Jankovic, J. J., del Junco, D., Skender, M., Waring, S., & Myer, E. C. (1994). Rett syndrome: Controlled study of an oral opiate antagonist, naltrexone. *Annals of Neurology, 35,* 464–470.

Perry, R., Campbell, M., Adams, P., Lunch, N., Spencer, E. K., Curren, E. L., & Overall, J. E. (1989). Long-term efficacy of haloperidol in autistic children: Continuous vs. discontinuous drug administration. *Journal of the American Academy of Child and Adolescent Psychiatry, 28,* 87–92.

Physicians' Desk Reference. (1994). Montvale, NJ: Medical Economics Data Production Company.

Pigott, T. A., Pato, M. T., Bernstein, S. E., Grover, G. N., Hill, J. L., Tolliver, T. J., & Murphy, D. L. (1990). Controlled comparisons of clomipramine and fluoxetine in the treatment of obsessive-compulsive disorder: Behavioral and biological results. *Archives of General Psychiatry, 47,* 926–932.

Ratey, J. J., Bemporad, J., Sorgi, P., Bick, P., Polakoff, S., O'Driscoll, G., & Mikkelsen, E. (1987). Brief report: Open trial effects of beta-blockers on speech and social behaviors in 8 autistic adults. *Journal of Autism and Developmental Disorders, 17,* 439–446.

Ratey, J. J., Sovner, R., Mikkelsen, E., & Chmielinski, H. E. (1989). Buspirone therapy for maladaptive behavior and anxiety in developmentally disabled persons. *Journal of Clinical Psychiatry, 50,* 382–384.

Realmuto, G. M., August, G. J., & Garfinkel, B. D. (1989). Clinical effect of buspirone in autistic children. *Journal of Clinical Psychopharmacology, 9,* 122–125.

Rett, A. (1966). Uber ein eigenartiges hirnatrophisches Syndrom bei Hyperammoniamie im Kindesalter. *Wiener Medizinische Wochenschrift, 116,* 723–738.

The Rett Syndrome Diagnostic Criteria Work Group. (1988). Diagnostic criteria for Rett syndrome. *Annals of Neurology, 23,* 425–428.

Richardson, M. A., Haugland, G., & Craig, T. J. (1991). Neuroleptic use, parkinsonian symptoms, tardive dyskinesia, and associated factors in child and adolescent psychiatric patients. *American Journal of Psychiatry, 148,* 1322–1328.

Ritvo, E. R., Freeman, B. J., Geller, E., & Yuwiler, A. (1983). Effects of fenfluramine on 14 outpatients with the syndrome of autism. *Journal of the American Academy of Child Psychiatry, 22,* 549–558.

Ritvo, E. R., Freeman, B. J., Yuwiler, A., Geller, E., Schroth, P., Yokota, A., Mason-Brothers, A., August, G. T., Klykylo, W., Leventhal, B., Lewis, V., Piggott, L., Realmuto, G., Stubbs, G., & Umansky, R. (1986). Fenfluramine treatment of autism: UCLA collaborative study of 81 patients at nine medical centers. *Psychopharmacology Bulletin, 22*(1), 133–140.

Ritvo, E. R., Yuwiler, A., Geller, E., Ornitz, E. M., Saeger, K., & Plotkin, S. (1970). Increased blood serotonin and platelets in early infantile autism. *Archives of General Psychiatry, 23,* 566–572.

Rosenberg, D. R., Holttum, J., & Gershon, S. (1994). *Textbook of pharmacotherapy for child and adolescent psychiatric disorders.* New York: Brunner/Mazel.

Rutter, M., & Schopler, E. (1992). Classification of pervasive developmental disorders: Some concepts and practical consideration. *Journal of Autism and Developmental Disorders, 22,* 459–482.

Sanchez, L. E., Adams, P. B., Uysal, S., Hallin, A., Campbell, M., & Small, A. M. (1995). A comparison of live and videotape ratings: Clomipramine and haloperidol in autism. *Psychopharmacology Bulletin, 31*(2).

Sanchez, L. E., Campbell, M., Small, A. M., Cueva, J. E., Armenteros, J. L., & Adams, P. B. (in press). A pilot study of clomipramine in young autistic children. *Journal of the American Academy of Child and Adolescent Psychiatry.*

Sandman, C. A. (1988). B-endorphin disregulation in autistic and self-injurious behavior: A neurodevelopmental hypothesis. *Synapse, 2,* 193–199.

Sandman, C. A., Barron, J. L., & Colman, H. (1990). An orally administered opiate blocker, naltrexone, attenuates self-injurious behavior. *American Journal of Mental Retardation, 95*(1), 93–102.

Sandman, C. A., Hetrick, W. P., Taylor, D. V., Barron, J. L., Touchette, P., Lott, I., Crinella, F., & Martinazzi, V. (1993). Naltrexone reduces self-injury and improves learning. *Experimental and Clinical Psychopharmacology, 1,* 242–258.

Schopler, E., Reichler, R. J., & Renner, B. R. (1988). *The childhood autism rating scale (CARS).* Los Angeles: California Western Psychological Services.

Shaffer, D., Gould, M., Brasic, J., Ambrosini, P., Fisher, P., Bird, H., & Aluwahlia, S. (1973). The Children's Global Assessment Scale (CGAS): Adapted from Global Assessment Scale for Adults. *Archives of General Psychiatry, 40,* 1228–1231.

Shay, J., Sanchez, L. E., Cueva, J. E., Armenteros, J. L., Overall, J. E., & Campbell, M. (1993). Neuroleptic-related dyskinesias and stereotypies in autistic children: Videotaped ratings. *Psychopharmacology Bulletin, 29*(3), 359–363.

Shell, J., Spencer, E. K., Curren, E. L., Perry, R., Die Trill, M. L., Lynch, N., Polonsky, B. B., & Campbell, M. (1987). Long-term haloperidol administration and intellectual functioning in autistic children. *Scientific Proceedings,* 34th Annual Meeting of the American Academy of Child and Adolescent Psychiatry, Washington, DC, NR-47.

Silva, R. R., Campbell, M., Golden, R. R., Small, A. M., Pataki, C. S., & Rosenberg, C. R. (1992). Side effects associated with lithium and placebo administration in aggressive children. *Psychopharmacology Bulletin, 28*(3), 319–326.

Silva, R. R., Ernst, M., & Campbell, M. (1993). Lithium and conduct disorder. *L'Encèphale, XIX,* 585–590.

Simpson, G. M., Lee, J. H., Zoubok, B., & Gardos, G. (1979). A rating scale for tardive dyskinesia. *Psychopharmacology (Berlin), 64*(2), 171–179.

Small, A. M., Campbell, M., Shay, J., & Goodman, I. S. (1994). Ethical guidelines for psychopharmacological research in children. In J. Y. Hattab (Ed.), *Ethics & child mental health* (pp. 244–253). Hewlett, NY: Gefen Books.

Szatmari, P. (1992). A review of the DSM-III-R criteria for autistic disorder. *Journal of Autism and Development Disorders, 22,* 507–523.

Szatmari, P. (1992). The validity of autistic spectrum disorders: A literature review. *Journal of Autism and Developmental Disorders, 22,* 583–600.

Szymanski, L., Kedesdy, J., Sulkes, S., & Cutler, A. (1987). Naltrexone in treatment of self-injurious behavior: A clinical study. *Research in Developmental Disabilities, 8,* 179–190.

Taylor, D. V., Hetrick, W. P., Neri, C. L., Touchette, P., Barron, J. L., & Sandman, C. A. (1991). Effect of naltrexone upon self-injurious behavior, learning and activity: A case study. *Pharmacology Biochemistry and Behavior, 40,* 79–82.

Todd, R. D. (1991). Fluoxetine in autism. *American Journal of Psychiatry, 148,* 1089.

Tsai, L. Y. (1992). Is Rett Syndrome a subtype of pervasive developmental disorders? *Journal of Autism and Developmental Disorders, 22,* 551–561.

Ullmann, R. K., Sleator, E. K., & Sprague, R. L. (1984). A new rating scale for diagnosis and monitoring of ADD children. *Psychopharmacology Bulletin, 20,* 160–164.

Volkmar, F. R. (1992). Childhood disintegrative disorder: Issues for DSM-IV. *Journal of Autism and Developmental Disorders, 22,* 625–642.

Volkmar, F. R., Cicchetti, D. V., Bregman, J., & Cohen, D. J. (1992). Three diagnostic systems for autism: DSM-III, DSM-III-R, and ICD-10. *Journal of Autism and Developmental Disorders, 22,* 483–492.

Volkmar, F. R., Klin, A., Siegel, B., Szatmari, P., Lord, C., Campbell, M., Freeman, B. J., Cicchetti, D. V., Rutter, M., Kline, W., Buitelaar, J., Hattab, Y., Fombonne, E., Fuentes, J., Werry, J., Stone, W., Kerbeshian, J., Hoshino, Y., Bregman, J.,

Loveland, K., Szymanski, L., & Towbin, K. (1994). Field trial for autistic disorder in DSM-IV. *American Journal of Psychiatry, 151,* 1361–1367.

Walters, A. S., Barrett, R. P., Feinstein, A. M., & Hole, W. T. (1990). A case report of naltrexone treatment of self-injury and social withdrawal in autism. *Journal of Autism and Developmental Disorders, 20*(2), 169–176.

Weizman, R., Gil-Ad, I., Dick, J., Tyano, S., Szekely, G. A., & Laron, Z. (1988). Low plasma immunoreaction beta-endorphin levels in autism. *Journal of the American Academy of Child and Adolescent Psychiatry, 27,* 430–433.

Weizman, R., Weizman, A., Tyano, S., Szekely, G., Weissman, B. A., & Sarne, Y. (1984). Humoral-endorphin blood levels in autistic, schizophrenic and healthy subjects. *Psychopharmacology (Berlin) 82,* 368–370.

Wing, L. (1981). Asperger's syndrome: A clinical account. *Psychological Medicine, 11,* 115–130.

Zappella, M. (1990). A double blind trial of bromocriptine in the Rett syndrome. *Brain Development, 12,* 148–150.

Zappella, M., Genazzani, A., Facchinetti, F., & Hayek, G. (1990). Bromocriptine in the Rett syndrome. *Brain Development, 12*(2), 221–225.

Zax, M., Sameroff, A. J., & Babigian, H. M. (1977). Birth outcomes in the offspring of mentally disordered women. *American Journal of Orthopsychiatry, 47*(2), 218–230.

Zingarelli, G., Ellman, G., Hom, A., Wymore, M., Heidorn, S., & Chicz-DeMet, A. (1992). Clinical effects of naltrexone on autistic behavior. *American Journal on Mental Retardation, 97,* 57–63.

Schizophrenia and Other Psychotic Disorders

MAGDA CAMPBELL, M.D.* and
JORGE L. ARMENTEROS, M.D.[†]

This work was supported in part by USPHS Grants MH-32212 and MH-40177 (Dr. Campbell) and MH-18915 (Drs. Campbell and Armenteros) from the National Institute of Mental Health; the Hirschell and Deanna E. Levine Foundation, The Marion O. and Maximilian E. Hoffman Foundation, Inc., and The Beatrice and Samuel A. Seaver Foundation.
*Reprint requests to Dr. Campbell, Department of Psychiatry, New York University Medical Center, 550 First Avenue, New York, NY 10016, telephone: 212-263-6206.
[†]At the time this work was conducted, Dr. Armenteros was Research Fellow and Clinical Instructor, Department of Psychiatry, New York University Medical Center (Program Director, Dr. Campbell).

The existence of childhood-onset schizophrenia has been recognized since the first two decades of this century (Bleuler, 1911/1951; DeSanctis, 1906; Kraepelin, 1899/1919) and it has been known that most patients develop schizophrenia in adolescence and young adulthood. Employing DSM-III criteria, Loranger (1984) reported that the cumulative percentage of schizophrenia for males by the age of 19 years was 49%. Even so, until a few years ago very little systematic research was conducted in children, and particularly in adolescents with schizophrenia (for review, see Campbell, Spencer, Kowalik, & Erlenmeyer-Kimling, 1991; Werry & Taylor, 1994). The June 1994 issue of the *Journal of the American Academy of Child & Adolescent Psychiatry* contained six articles on this topic (Caplan, 1994b; Frazier et al., 1994; Jacobsen, Walker, Edwards, Chappell, & Woolston, 1994; McClellan & Werry, 1994; McKenna et al., 1994; Towbin, Dykens, & Pugliese, 1994) and the November 1994 issue of *Schizophrenia Bulletin* is devoted to research on this topic (Asarnow, Asamen et al., 1994; Asarnow & Asarnow, 1994; Asarnow, Tompson, & Goldstein, 1994; Caplan, 1994a; Gordon et al., 1994; Remschmidt, Schulz, Martin, Warnke, & Trott, 1994; Russell, 1994; Strandburg, Marsh, Brown, Asarnow, & Guthrie, 1994; Werry, McClellan, Andrews, & Ham, 1994).

Schizophrenia in children was defined in a variety of ways over time (Asarnow & Asarnow, 1994; Bender, 1942; Campbell et al., 1991; Fish & Ritvo, 1979; Kolvin, 1971; Rutter, 1972).

DeSanctis (1906) described dementia precocissima, and both Kraepelin (1899/1919) and Bleuler (1911) recognized that in a low percentage of cases the onset of dementia praecox or schizophrenia was before the age of 15 years. Whereas Bender (1942) believed that autism was the earliest expression of schizophrenia (childhood schizophrenia), Kanner (1943), with the exception of one paper (Kanner, 1949), considered early infantile autism to be a separate diagnostic entity from childhood-onset schizophrenia. Kolvin (1971) and Rutter (1972) and later Green et al. (1984) have shown that the two disorders are separate diagnostic entities. Rutter argued that because "childhood schizophrenia" was used as a generic term, included a variety of disorders, including autism and schizophrenia, and in addition, has been used in various ways by child psychiatrists, it should be no longer employed and should become history (Rutter, 1972).

To be diagnosed with schizophrenia in DSM-III (APA, 1980), DSM-III-R (APA, 1987) or DSM-IV (APA, 1994) children had to meet the criteria for schizophrenic disorder developed for adult patients. As shown in Table 6.1, some changes and revisions took place in the diagnostic criteria for schizophrenia in DSM-III-R and DSM-IV.

The literature on schizophrenia with onset in childhood or in adolescence as diagnosed by DSM-III or DSM-III-R criteria is limited (see

Table 6.1. A Comparison of DSM-III, DSM-III-R, and DSM-IV Diagnostic Criteria for Schizophrenia

DSM-III (1980) Schizophrenic Disorder	DSM-III-R (1987) Schizophrenia	DSM-IV (1994) Schizophrenia
A. At least one of the following during a phase of the illness: (1) bizarre delusions (content is patently absurd and has *no* possible basis in fact), such as delusions of being controlled, thought broadcasting, thought insertion, or thought withdrawal (2) somatic, grandiose, religious, nihilistic, or other delusions without persecutory or jealous content (3) delusions with persecutory or jealous content if accompanied by hallucinations of any type (4) auditory hallucinations in which either a voice keeps up a running commentary on the individual's behavior or thoughts or two or more voices converse with each other (5) auditory hallucinations on several occasions with content of more than one or two words having no apparent relation to depression or elation	A. Presence of characteristic psychotic symptoms in the active phase: either (1), (2), or (3) for at least one week (unless the symptoms are successfully treated): (1) two of the following: (a) delusions (b) prominent hallucinations (throughout the day for several days or several times a week for several weeks, each hallucinatory experience not being limited to a few brief moments) (c) incoherence or marked loosening of associations (d) catatonic behavior (e) flat or grossly inappropriate affect (2) bizarre delusions (i.e., involving a phenomenon that the person's culture would regard as totally implausible, e.g., thought broadcasting, being controlled by a dead person)	A. *Characteristic symptoms:* Two (or more) of the following, each present for a significant portion of time during a 1-month period (or less if successfully treated): (1) delusions (2) hallucinations (3) disorganized speech (e.g., frequent derailment or incoherence) (4) grossly disorganized or catatonic behavior (5) negative symptoms, i.e., affective flattening, alogia, or avolition *Note:* Only one Criterion A symptom is required if delusions are bizarre or hallucinations consist of a voice keeping up a running commentary on the person's behavior or thoughts, or two or more voices conversing with each other.

(Continued)

195

Table 6.1. (Continued)

DSM-III (1980) Schizophrenic Disorder	DSM-III-R (1987) Schizophrenia	DSM-IV (1994) Schizophrenia
(6) incoherence, marked loosening of associations, markedly illogical thinking, or marked poverty of content of speech if associated with at least one of the following: (a) blunted, flat, or inappropriate affect (b) delusions or hallucinations (c) catatonic or other grossly disorganized behavior	(3) prominent hallucinations [as defined in (1b) above] of a voice with content having no apparent relation to depression or elation, or a voice keeping up a running commentary on the person's behavior or thoughts, or two or more voices conversing with each other	
B. Deterioration from a previous level of functioning in such areas as work, social relations, and self-care.	B. During the course of the disturbance, functioning in such areas as work, social relations, and self-care is markedly below the highest level achieved before onset of the disturbance (or, when the onset is in childhood or adolescence, failure to achieve expected level of social development).	B. *Social/occupational dysfunction:* For a significant portion of the time since the onset of the disturbance, one or more major areas of functioning such as work, interpersonal relations, or self-care are markedly below the level achieved prior to the onset (or when the onset is in childhood or adolescence, failure to achieve expected level of interpersonal, academic, or occupational achievement).

C. Duration: Continuous signs of the illness for at least 6 months . . . . .

D. The full depressive or manic syndrome (criteria A and B of major depressive or manic episode), if present, developed after any psychotic symptoms, or was brief in duration relative to the duration of the psychotic symptoms in A.

C. Schizoaffective Disorder and Mood Disorder with Psychotic Features have been ruled out, i.e., if a Major Depressive or Manic Syndrome has ever been present during an active phase of the disturbance, the total duration of all episodes of a mood syndrome has been brief relative to the total duration of the active and residual phases of the disturbance.

D. Continuous signs of the disturbance for at least 6 months. The six-month period must include an active phase (of at least one week, or less if symptoms have been successfully treated) during which there were psychotic symptoms characteristic of Schizophrenia (symptoms in A), with or without a prodromal or residual phase . . . .

C. *Duration:* Continuous signs of the disturbance persist for at least 6 months. This 6-month period must include at least 1 month of symptoms (or less if successfully treated) that meet Criterion A (i.e., active-phase symptoms) . . . .

D. *Schizoaffective and Mood Disorder exclusion:* Schizoaffective Disorder and Mood Disorder with Psychotic Features have been ruled out . . . .

(Continued)

Table 6.1. *(Continued)*

DSM-III (1980) Schizophrenic Disorder	DSM-III-R (1987) Schizophrenia	DSM-IV (1994) Schizophrenia
E. Onset of prodromal or active phase of the illness before age 45.	E. It cannot be established that an organic factor initiated and maintained the disturbance.	E. *Substance/general medical condition exclusion:* The disturbance is not due to the direct physiological effects of a substance (e.g., a drug of abuse, a medication) or a general medical condition.
F. Not due to any Organic Mental Disorder or Mental Retardation.	F. If there is a history of Autistic Disorder, the additional diagnosis of Schizophrenia is made only if prominent delusions or hallucinations are also present.	F. *Relationship to a Pervasive Developmental Disorder:* If there is a history of Autistic Disorder or another Pervasive Developmental Disorder, the additional diagnosis of Schizophrenia is made only if prominent delusions or hallucinations are also present for at least a month (or less if successfully treated).

Source: Diagnostic and Statistical Manual of Mental Disorders (3rd ed., 1980), pp. 188–190; (3rd ed.-rev, 1987), pp. 194–195; (4th ed., 1994), pp. 285–286.

Werry, 1992) and little is known about the reliability of the symptoms and diagnosis, particularly in clinical practice. Some investigators find that schizophrenia with childhood onset has been overdiagnosed or used overinclusively (McKenna et al., 1994). Hallucinations in children are frequently ill-defined and occur in non-psychotic children (Kotsopoulos, Kanigsberg, Cote, & Fiedorowicz, 1987; Pilowsky & Chambers, 1986); the same is true for illogical thinking. Though loosening of associations is an essential feature of schizophrenia (Bleuler, 1911/1951), Arboleda and Holzman (1985) were the first to conduct studies of thought disorder in children employing a valid and reliable instrument as well as controls. The definition of formal thought disorder in this age group was studied systematically by Caplan (for review, see Caplan, 1994b) based on DSM-III (1980) criteria and on an instrument developed by Andreasen (1979).

CLINICAL CRITERIA AND DIAGNOSTIC ISSUES PER DSM-IV

In developing DSM-IV, the following questions were addressed:

1. Is schizophrenia with onset in childhood diagnostically the same clinical entity as schizophrenia with onset in adulthood (as stated by DSM and ICD).

2. Do maturational/developmental influences affect the phenomenology of schizophrenia and if so, are amendments to diagnostic criteria required for children.

3. If schizophrenia with onset in childhood is the same disorder as schizophrenia with onset in adulthood, but with some differences, will it require a separate developmental subcategory?

4. Will some children who probably have schizophrenia be excluded if employing criteria for schizophrenia developed for adults (false negatives)? (Campbell, Ernst, Setterberg & Shaffer, 1993; Shaffer et al., 1989; Werry, 1992).

A critical review of the literature revealed that the diagnostic criteria employed (including between 1960 and 1980) were vague, overinclusive, unclear, or nonexistent (Werry, 1992). Only six studies were qualified for review (Eggers, 1978, 1989; Green & Padron-Gayol, 1986; Green et al., 1984; Makita, 1966; Kolvin, 1971; Volkmar, Cohen, Hoshino, Rende, & Paul, 1988; Werry, McClellan, & Chard, 1991).The seventh set of data was derived from a group of papers referred to as the UCLA Group (Asarnow, Asarnow, & Strandburg, 1989; Asarnow & Ben-Meir, 1988; Asarnow, Goldstein, & Ben-Meir, 1988; Caplan, Guthrie,

Fish, Tanguay, & David-Lando, 1989; Russell, Bott, & Sammons, 1989; Watkins, Asarnow, & Tanguay, 1988; Werry, 1992). The studies reviewed contained a total of 212 to 229 subjects whose ages ranged from 3 to 15 years; the sex ratio (M/F) ranged from 1:1.28 to 2.66:1. Most studies represented chart reviews. All reports were in agreement that schizophrenia can be diagnosed in children between ages 6 and 12 years employing Bleulerian, Schneiderian, DSM-III (1980) or DSM-III-R (1987) criteria developed for adult patients with schizophrenia, thus strongly supporting the notion that schizophrenia with onset in childhood is diagnostically the same disorder as schizophrenia with onset in adulthood. Though maturational/developmental age-dependent differences were found in children's phenomenology, these were mainly quantitative and not qualitative and therefore a separate subcategory for children and adolescents was not required. Some studies suggested that well-organized delusions are less frequent in children than in adults; and that there are differences in type of thought disorder. A low base rate of incoherence and poverty of content of thought, as measured by the Kiddie Formal Thought Disorder Rating Scale, developed by Caplan et al. (1989) was also reported in children. The phenomenology in this group of patients was often found to be undifferentiated, particularly in children, and the disorder is more common in males (Werry, 1992); Eggers' report is the only exception (M/F = 1:1.28). The review of the literature indicates that in adolescence, the M/F ratio is closer to 1:1 (Werry et al., 1991) though a recent study is in disagreement reporting an M:F ratio of 2.33:1 in patients ages 11 to 17 admitted to an acute psychiatric hospital (Armenteros, Fennelly, Hallin et al., 1995).

The DSM-IV Work Group and the Advisers were also concerned about false negatives because of (a) immature language or absence of language in young children and (b) frequency of insidious onset, particularly in children under 13 years of age. It was suggested that the age of 7 years represents the maturational/developmental cognitive cutoff for both illogical thinking and loose association in children of normal intelligence and free of psychiatric disorders (Caplan et al., 1989; Caplan, Perdue, Tanguay, & Fish, 1990; for review, Caplan, 1994b). Concerning insidious onset, and the difficulty of ascertaining the point (in time) when psychosis developed for the duration of illness criterion and for the criterion deterioration from a previous level of functioning, it was felt that this problem also exists in some adults with schizophrenia and that not all studies involving children and adolescents with schizophrenia found this to be an issue (Werry, 1992). The diagnosis cannot be made reliably in children below age 5 and in young children whose intellectual functioning is subnormal.

The DSM-IV diagnostic criteria for schizophrenia are listed in Table 6.2.

Table 6.2. *Diagnostic Criteria for Schizophrenia*

A. *Characteristic symptoms:* Two (or more) of the following, each present for a significant portion of time during a 1-month period (or less if successfully treated):

(1) delusions

(2) hallucinations

(3) disorganized speech (e.g., frequent derailment or incoherence)

(4) grossly disorganized or catatonic behavior

(5) negative symptoms, i.e., affective flattening, alogia, or avolition

Note: Only one Criterion A symptom is required if delusions are bizarre or hallucinations consist of a voice keeping up a running commentary on the person's behavior or thoughts, or two or more voices conversing with each other.

B. *Social/occupational dysfunction:* For a significant portion of the time since the onset of the disturbance, one or more major areas of functioning such as work, interpersonal relations, or self-care are markedly below the level achieved prior to the onset (or when the onset is in childhood or adolescence, failure to achieve expected level of interpersonal, academic, or occupational achievement).

C. *Duration:* Continuous signs of the disturbance persist for at least 6 months. This 6-month period must include at least 1 month of symptoms (or less if successfully treated) that meet Criterion A (i.e., active-phase symptoms) and may include periods of prodromal or residual symptoms. During these prodromal or residual periods, the signs of the disturbance may be manifested by only negative symptoms or two or more symptoms listed in Criterion A present in an attenuated form (e.g., odd beliefs, unusual perceptual experiences).

D. *Schizoaffective and Mood Disorder exclusion:* Schizoaffective Disorder and Mood Disorder With Psychotic Features have been ruled out because either (1) no Major Depressive, Manic, or Mixed Episodes have occurred concurrently with the active-phase symptoms; or (2) if mood episodes have occurred during active-phase symptoms, their total duration has been brief relative to the duration of the active and residual periods.

E. *Substance/general medical condition exclusion:* The disturbance is not due to the direct physiological effects of a substance (e.g., a drug of abuse, a medication) or a general medical condition.

F. *Relationship to a Pervasive Developmental Disorder:* If there is a history of Autistic Disorder or another Pervasive Developmental Disorder, the additional diagnosis of Schizophrenia is made only if prominent delusions or hallucinations are also present for at least a month (or less if successfully treated).

(Continued)

Table 6.2. *(Continued)*

Classification of longitudinal course (can be applied only after at least 1 year has elapsed since the initial onset of active-phase symptoms):

Episodic With Interepisode Residual Symptoms (episodes are defined by the reemergence of prominent psychotic symptoms); *also specify if:* **With Prominent Negative Symptoms**

Episodic With No Interepisode Residual Symptoms

Continuous (prominent psychotic symptoms are present throughout the period of observation); *also specify if:* **With Prominent Negative Symptoms**

Single Episode In Partial Remission; *also specify if:* **With Prominent Negative Symptoms**

Single Episode In Full Remission

Other or Unspecified Pattern

Source: *Diagnostic and Statistical Manual of Mental Disorders* (4th ed., 1994), pp. 285–286.

The schizophrenia subtypes in DSM-IV are Paranoid Type, Disorganized Type, Catatonic Type, Undifferentiated Type and Residual Type, as shown in Tables 6.3–6.7. It is unclear how frequently these subtypes occur in children and adolescents (Werry, 1992). The same is true for other psychotic disorders: Schizophreniform Disorder (Table 6.8), Schizoaffective Disorder (Table 6.9); Delusional Disorder (Table 6.10), Brief Psychotic Disorder (Table 6.11), Shared Psychotic Disorder (Folie á Deux) (Table 6.12), Psychotic Disorder due to a Medical Condition (Table 6.13), Substance-Induced Psychotic Disorder (Table 6.14), and Psychotic Disorder Not Otherwise Specified (Table 6.15).

Recent Studies

After the DSM-IV Work Group completed deliberations regarding schizophrenia, several new reports on the subject appeared. The findings of Green, Padron-Gayol, Hardesty, & Bassiri (1992) are the same as in the original study with 24 schizophrenic children (Green et al., 1984).

Table 6.3. *Diagnostic Criteria for 295.30 Paranoid Type*

A type of Schizophrenia in which the following criteria are met:

A.   Preoccupation with one or more delusions or frequent auditory hallucinations.

B.   None of the following is prominent: disorganized speech, disorganized or catatonic behavior, or flat or inappropriate affect.

Source: *Diagnostic and Statistical Manual of Mental Disorders* (4th ed., 1994), p. 287.

Table 6.4. *Diagnostic Criteria for 295.10 Disorganized Type*

A type of Schizophrenia in which the following criteria are met:

- A. All of the following are prominent:
    - (1) disorganized speech
    - (2) disorganized behavior
    - (3) flat or inappropriate affect
- B. The criteria are not met for Catatonic Type.

Source: Diagnostic and Statistical Manual of Mental Disorders (4th ed., 1994), p. 288.

Table 6.5. *Diagnostic Criteria for 295.20 Catatonic Type*

A type of Schizophrenia in which the clinical picture is dominated by at least two of the following:

- (1) motoric immobility as evidenced by catalepsy (including waxy flexibility) or stupor
- (2) excessive motor activity (that is apparently purposeless and not influenced by external stimuli)
- (3) extreme negativism (an apparently motiveless resistance to all instructions or maintenance of a rigid posture against attempts to be moved) or mutism
- (4) peculiarities of voluntary movement as evidenced by posturing (voluntary assumption of inappropriate or bizarre postures), stereotyped movements, prominent mannerisms, or prominent grimacing
- (5) echolalia or echopraxia

Source: Diagnostic and Statistical Manual of Mental Disorders (4th ed., 1994), p. 289.

Table 6.6. *Diagnostic Criteria for 295.90 Undifferentiated Type*

A type of Schizophrenia in which symptoms that meet Criterion A are present, but the criteria are not met for the Paranoid, Disorganized, or Catatonic Type.

Source: Diagnostic and Statistical Manual of Mental Disorders (4th ed., 1994), p. 289.

Table 6.7. *Diagnostic Criteria for 295.60 Residual Type*

A type of Schizophrenia in which the following criteria are met:

- A. Absence of prominent delusions, hallucinations, disorganized speech, and grossly disorganized or catatonic behavior.
- B. There is continuing evidence of the disturbance, as indicated by the presence of negative symptoms or two or more symptoms listed in Criterion A for Schizophrenia, present in an attenuated form (e.g., odd beliefs, unusual perceptual experiences).

Source: Diagnostic and Statistical Manual of Mental Disorders (4th ed., 1994), p. 290.

Table 6.8.   Diagnostic Criteria for 295.40 Schizophreniform Disorder

A. Criteria A, D, and E of Schizophrenia are met.

B. An episode of the disorder (including prodromal, active, and residual phases) lasts at least 1 month but less than 6 months. (When the diagnosis must be made without waiting for recovery, it should be qualified as "Provisional.")

Specify if:

Without Good Prognostic Features

With Good Prognostic Features: as evidenced by two (or more) of the following:

(1) onset of prominent psychotic symptoms within 4 weeks of the first noticeable change in usual behavior or functioning

(2) confusion or perplexity at the height of the psychotic episode

(3) good premorbid social and occupational functioning

(4) absence of blunted or flat affect

Source: Diagnostic and Statistical Manual of Mental Disorders (4th ed., 1994), pp. 291–292.

Table 6.9.   Diagnostic Criteria for 295.70 Schizoaffective Disorder

A. An uninterrupted period of illness during which, at some time, there is either a Major Depressive Episode, a Manic Episode, or a Mixed Episode concurrent with symptoms that meet Criterion A for Schizophrenia.

Note: The Major Depressive Episode must include Criterion A1: depressed mood.

B. During the same period of illness, there have been delusions or hallucinations for at least 2 weeks in the absence of prominent mood symptoms.

C. Symptoms that meet criteria for a mood episode are present for a substantial portion of the total duration of the active and residual periods of the illness.

D. The disturbance is not due to the direct physiological effects of a substance (e.g., a drug of abuse, a medication) or a general medical condition.

Specify type:

Bipolar Type: if the disturbance includes a Manic or a Mixed Episode (or a Manic or a Mixed Episode and Major Depressive Episodes)

Depressive Type: if the disturbance only includes Major Depressive Episodes

Source: Diagnostic and Statistical Manual of Mental Disorders (4th ed., 1994), pp. 295–296.

Table 6.10.   Diagnostic Criteria for 297.1 Delusional Disorder

A.   Nonbizarre delusions (i.e., involving situations that occur in real life, such as being followed, poisoned, infected, loved at a distance, or deceived by spouse or lover, or having a disease) of at least 1 month's duration.

B.   Criterion A for Schizophrenia has never been met. **Note:** Tactile and olfactory hallucinations may be present in Delusional Disorder if they are related to the delusional theme.

C.   Apart from the impact of the delusion(s) or its ramifications, functioning is not markedly impaired and behavior is not obviously odd or bizarre.

D.   If mood episodes have occurred concurrently with delusions, their total duration has been brief relative to the duration of the delusional periods.

E.   The disturbance is not due to the direct physiological effects of a substance (e.g., a drug of abuse, a medication) or a general medical condition.

Specify type (the following types are assigned based on the predominant delusional theme):

Erotomanic Type: delusions that another person, usually of higher status, is in love with the individual

Grandiose Type: delusions of inflated worth, power, knowledge, identity, or special relationship to a deity or famous person

Jealous Type: delusions that the individual's sexual partner is unfaithful

Persecutory Type: delusions that the person (or someone to whom the person is close) is being malevolently treated in some way

Somatic Type: delusions that the person has some physical defect or general medical condition

Mixed Type: delusions characteristic of more than one of the above types but no one theme predominates

Unspecified Type

Source: Diagnostic and Statistical Manual of Mental Disorders (4th ed., 1994), p. 301.

Armenteros, Fennelly, Hallin et al. (1995) reported a good agreement between the DSM-III-R, DSM-IV, and ICD-10 diagnostic criteria for schizophrenia in a sample of 30 hospitalized patients with psychotic disorders whose ages ranged from 11 to 17 years (mean, 14.44). The clinical diagnosis of Psychotic Disorder NOS was overinclusive and had poor agreement between diagnostic systems. There was no significant relationship between the frequency or type of symptoms and the age or sex of subjects; the data were based on a retrospective chart review.

A group of children and adolescents with transient psychotic symptoms have been labeled as "multidimensionally impaired" because of failure to meet the criteria for schizophrenia or any other DSM-III-R psychiatric disorder (McKenna et al., 1994). The 21 multidimensionally

Table 6.11.   Diagnostic Criteria for 298.8 Brief Psychotic Disorder

A. Presence of one (or more) of the following symptoms:

    (1) delusions

    (2) hallucinations

    (3) disorganized speech (e.g., frequent derailment or incoherence)

    (4) grossly disorganized or catatonic behavior

    Note: Do not include a symptom if it is a culturally sanctioned response pattern.

B. Duration of an episode of the disturbance is at least 1 day but less than 1 month, with eventual full return to premorbid level of functioning.

C. The disturbance is not better accounted for by a Mood Disorder With Psychotic Features, Schizoaffective Disorder, or Schizophrenia and is not due to the direct physiological effects of a substance (e.g., a drug of abuse, a medication) or a general medical condition.

Specify if:

    With Marked Stressor(s) (brief reactive psychosis): if symptoms occur shortly after and apparently in response to events that, singly or together, would be markedly stressful to almost anyone in similar circumstances in the person's culture

    Without Marked Stressor(s): if psychotic symptoms do *not* occur shortly after, or are not apparently in response to events that, singly or together, would be markedly stressful to almost anyone in similar circumstances in the person's culture

    With Postpartum Onset: if onset within 4 weeks postpartum

Source: Diagnostic and Statistical Manual of Mental Disorders (4th ed., 1994), p. 304.

Table 6.12.   Diagnostic Criteria for 297.3 Shared Psychotic Disorder

A. A delusion develops in an individual in the context of a close relationship with another person(s), who has an already-established delusion.

B. The delusion is similar in content to that of the person who already has the established delusion.

C. The disturbance is not better accounted for by another Psychotic Disorder (e.g., Schizophrenia) or a Mood Disorder With Psychotic Features and is not due to the direct physiological effects of a substance (e.g., a drug of abuse, a medication) or a general medical condition.

Source: Diagnostic and Statistical Manual of Mental Disorders (4th ed., 1994), p. 306.

Table 6.13.   Diagnostic Criteria for 293.xx Psychotic Disorder Due to . . . [Indicate the General Medical Condition]

A.   Prominent hallucinations or delusions.

B.   There is evidence from the history, physical examination, or laboratory findings that the disturbance is the direct physiological consequence of a general medical condition.

C.   The disturbance is not better accounted for by another mental disorder.

D.   The disturbance does not occur exclusively during the course of a delirium.

Code based on predominant symptom:

   .81 With Delusions: if delusions are the predominant symptom

   .82 With Hallucinations: if hallucinations are the predominant symptom

   Coding note: Include the name of the general medical condition on Axis I, e.g., 293.81 Psychotic Disorder Due to Malignant Lung Neoplasm, With Delusions; also code the general medical condition on Axis III (see Appendix G for codes).

   Coding note: If delusions are part of a preexisting dementia, indicate the delusions by coding the appropriate subtype of the dementia if one is available, e.g., 290.20 Dementia of the Alzheimer's Type, With Late Onset, With Delusions.

Source: Diagnostic and Statistical Manual of Mental Disorders (4th ed., 1994), pp. 309–310.

impaired subjects (mean age 11.8 ± 2.9) represented part of a larger sample ($N = 71$) screened for a study of schizophrenia with onset in childhood. Seventy-five children, ages 8 to 17 years, were asked to be interviewed; 71 were interviewed and 19 received the diagnosis of schizophrenia with childhood onset. The 21 multidimensionally impaired subjects differed from those with schizophrenia on several variables. More common in multidimensionally impaired subjects were affective instability (in 100% of cases vs. 52.2% in childhood-onset schizophrenia), immature social interactions (95.2% vs. 5.3%) and comorbid attention-deficit hyperactivity disorder (85% vs. 31%). Visual hallucinations (78.9% vs. 42.9%), auditory hallucinations (100% vs. 76.2%) and delusions were more common in schizophrenia than in multidimensionally impaired individuals who failed to meet the strict DSM-III-R criteria for schizophrenia. Furthermore, these children failed to respond to neuroleptics. Research is still required concerning the phenomenology and diagnosis of schizophrenia and other psychotic disorders in children and adolescents.

Table 6.14. *Diagnostic Criteria for Substance-Induced Psychotic Disorder*

A. Prominent hallucinations or delusions. **Note:** Do not include hallucinations if the person has insight that they are substance induced.

B. There is evidence from the history, physical examination, or laboratory findings of either (1) or (2):

   (1) the symptoms in Criterion A developed during, or within a month of, Substance Intoxication or Withdrawal

   (2) medication use is etiologically related to the disturbance

C. The disturbance is not better accounted for by a Psychotic Disorder that is not substance induced. Evidence that the symptoms are better accounted for by a Psychotic Disorder that is not substance induced might include the following: the symptoms precede the onset of the substance use (or medication use); the symptoms persist for a substantial period of time (e.g., about a month) after the cessation of acute withdrawal or severe intoxication, or are substantially in excess of what would be expected given the type or amount of the substance used or the duration of use; or there is other evidence that suggests the existence of an independent non-substance-induced Psychotic Disorder (e.g., a history of recurrent non-substance-related episodes).

D. The disturbance does not occur exclusively during the course of a delirium.

Note: This diagnosis should be made instead of a diagnosis of Substance Intoxication or Substance Withdrawal only when the symptoms are in excess of those usually associated with the intoxication or withdrawal syndrome and when the symptoms are sufficiently severe to warrant independent clinical attention. . . .

Specify if . . .

   With Onset During Intoxication: if criteria are met for Intoxication with the substance and the symptoms develop during the intoxication syndrome

   With Onset During Withdrawal: if criteria are met for Withdrawal from the substance and the symptoms develop during, or shortly after, a withdrawal syndrome

Source: *Diagnostic and Statistical Manual of Mental Disorders* (4th ed., 1994), pp. 314–315.

EPIDEMIOLOGY

Childhood-onset schizophrenia before the age of 13 is rare (for review, see Campbell et al., 1991; Werry & Taylor, 1994). Of 2,199 children ages 10 and 11 years who were screened, not a single child had schizophrenia, though 126 had a psychiatric disorder (Rutter, Tizard, & Whitmore, 1970); in a prospective longitudinal study of 792 children no case of schizophrenia was reported at age 11 years (Anderson, Williams, McGee, & Silva, 1987), so the condition is rare. The point prevalence rate of schizophrenia was calculated to be 0.19 in 10,000 for

Table 6.15.   *298.9 Psychotic Disorder Not Otherwise Specified*

This category includes psychotic symptomatology (i.e., delusions, hallucinations, disorganized speech, grossly disorganized or catatonic behavior) about which there is inadequate information to make a specific diagnosis or about which there is contradictory information, or disorders with psychotic symptoms that do not meet the criteria for any specific Psychotic Disorder.

Examples include:

1. Postpartum psychosis that does not meet criteria for Mood Disorder With Psychotic Features, Brief Psychotic Disorder, Psychotic Disorder Due to a General Medical Condition, or Substance-Induced Psychotic Disorder

2. Psychotic symptoms that have lasted for less than 1 month but that have not yet remitted, so that the criteria for Brief Psychotic Disorder are not met

3. Persistent auditory hallucinations in the absence of any other features

4. Persistent nonbizarre delusions with periods of overlapping mood episodes that have been present for a substantial portion of the delusional disturbance

5. Situations in which the clinician has concluded that a Psychotic Disorder is present, but is unable to determine whether it is primary, due to a general medical condition, or substance induced

Source: *Diagnostic and Statistical Manual of Mental Disorders* (4th ed., 1994), p. 315.

children 2 to 12 years of age in an epidemiological study of Burd and Kerbeshian (1987).

Of 664 children ages 12 years or younger, who were hospitalized in an acute care psychiatric hospital, 38 children (5.7%), ages 5 years 7 months to 11 years 11 months, were diagnosed with schizophrenia (Green et al., 1992). These figures represent admissions over a period of 8 years and one month with an average of 4.7 children with schizophrenia per year.

The rate of schizophrenia subtypes in children and adolescents is not known, though catatonic behavior and paranoid delusions were reported in prospective studies of carefully diagnosed patients (McKenna et al., 1994). In a report based on a retrospective chart review, of 30 hospitalized and clinically psychotic adolescents, 9 were diagnosed with Schizophrenia, 4 with Schizophreniform Disorder, one with Delusional Disorder, and 10 with Psychotic Disorder Not Otherwise Specified (NOS) employing DSM-IV criteria (Armenteros, Fennelly, Hallin et al., 1995). Clinically, 16 of the 30 subjects were given the diagnosis of Psychotic Disorder NOS. Another report, also based on a retrospective chart review, showed a high number of adolescents diagnosed with Psychotic Disorder NOS; of 34 hospitalized psychotic adolescents, 9 were given the clinical diagnosis of schizophrenia and 16 Psychotic Disorder NOS (Kafantaris, Ernst, Locascio, & Campbell, 1990). This study also revealed that subjects diagnosed as Psychotic Disorder NOS tended to have more acute stressors than those diagnosed with schizophrenia or mood disorder with psychotic features (Kafantaris et al., 1990). Patients with Psychotic Disorder NOS were less likely to present blunted or inappropriate affect and were more likely to have comorbid personality disorders than those with schizophrenia.

PSYCHOPHARMACOLOGY

In the past two decades there have been only a few reports and still fewer studies on the efficacy and safety of psychoactive agents in children and adolescents with schizophrenia. Pool, Bloom, Mielke, Roniger, and Gallant (1976) conducted a well-designed double-blind and placebo-controlled study comparing haloperidol to loxapine in 75 hospitalized adolescents, with acute schizophrenia or exacerbation of chronic schizophrenia. Both drugs were superior to placebo in these hospitalized patients, diagnosed by DSM-III criteria. The first study of this type conducted in children ages 5 to 11 years, all hospitalized, meeting DSM-III-R criteria for schizophrenia, is an ongoing study and the preliminary findings, demonstrating the superiority of haloperidol over placebo, were reported recently ($N = 12$, Spencer, Kafantaris, Padron-Gayol, Rosenberg, & Campbell, 1992; $N = 16$, Spencer & Campbell, 1994). The remaining reports, all involving antipsychotics, are open trials, case reports or retrospective chart reviews, as shown in Table 6.16.

Classes of Neuroleptics and Effects

The classes of neuroleptics studied in this age group of patients with schizophrenia are listed in Table 6.17. For a more detailed review and information on chemical properties, metabolism and absorption, a chapter by Campbell et al. (1993) and a textbook by Rosenberg et al. (1994) are recommended.

Phenothiazines.   Thioridazine is the only agent from the class of phenothiazines studied in this population. In a small sample of adolescents ($N = 8$), it had no advantage over thiothixene and appeared to be more sedating (Realmuto, Erickson, Yellin, Hopwood, & Greenberg, 1984). The response to both psychoactive agents was unsatisfactory.

Thioxanthenes.   The response of adolescents with chronic schizophrenia ($N = 13$) to thiothixene was inadequate as previously indicated.

Table 6.16. Neuroleptics in Children and Adolescents with Schizophrenia

Author(s) and Year	Sample	Age in Years	Drug and Dosage, mg/day (mg/kg/day)	Design	Measures
Realmuto et al., 1984	$N = 21$ Chronic schizophrenia DSM-III criteria	11.75–18.75	Thioridazine, 92–228, mean = 178 vs. thiothixene 4.8–42.6, mean = 16.2	Single blind, randomized	BPRS, CGI
Pool et al., 1976	$N = 75$ Acute schizophrenia or exacerbation of chronic DSM-III criteria	13–18	Haloperidol, mean = 9.8, maximum 16 vs. loxapine, mean = 87.5, maximum 200	Double-blind, placebo-controlled, randomized, parallel groups	BPRS, CGI, NOSIE
Versiani et al., 1978	$N = 50$ DSM-II criteria all subtypes (17 hebephrenic and 17 catatonic)	13–18 mean, 16	Loxapine, mean = 70.4 Haloperidol, mean = 7.6	Double-blind, randomized	BPRS, NOSIE, CGI
Spencer & Campbell, 1994 (Spencer et al., 1992)	$N = 16$ DSM-III-R criteria	5.5–11.75	Haloperidol, 0.5–3.5, mean = 1.77 (0.02–0.12, mean = 0.058)	Double-blind, placebo-controlled, randomized, crossover	DICA-R, CPRS, BPRS, CGI, CPTQ, Global Clinical Judgments
Frazier et al., 1994	$N = 11$ DSM-III-R criteria	12–17	Clozapine, 125–825, mean = 370.5	Open	BPRS, CGI, Bunney Hamburg Rating Scale, CGAS, SAPS, SANS
Blanz & Schmidt, 1993	$N = 57$ ($N = 53$ with schizophrenia) ICD-9 criteria	10–21	Clozapine, 75–800, mean = 285	Open	Target symptoms

(Continued)

211

Table 6.16. *(Continued)*

Author(s) and Year	Sample	Age in Years	Drug and Dosage, mg/day (mg/kg/day)	Design	Measures
Levkovitch et al., 1994	$N = 13$ criteria	14–17	Clozapine, mean = 240	Open	BPRS
Siefen & Remschmidt, 1986	$N = 21$ Paranoid type ($N = 15$) ICD-9 criteria	Mean, 18 (12 under 18 years)	Clozapine, 150–800	Retrospective chart review	67-item rating scale developed by the authors
Birmaher et al., 1992	$N = 3$ DSM-III-R criteria	17–18	Clozapine, 100–400	Open	Target symptoms
Jacobsen et al., 1994	$N = 1$	13.5	Clozapine, 500–550 (starting dose 12.5 mg BID)	Open	Clinical
Towbin et al., 1994	$N = 1$	11.5	Clozapine, 400–500 (starting dose 12.5)	Open	BPRS, CGI, AIMS

Note: AIMS: Abnormal Involuntary Movement Scale; BPRS: Brief Psychiatric Rating Scale; CGAS: Children's Global Assessment Scale; CGI: Clinical Global Impressions; CPRS: Children's Psychiatric Rating Scale; CPTQ: Conners Parent-Teacher Questionnaire; DICA-R: Diagnostic Interview for Children and Adolescents-Revised; NOSIE: Nurse's Observation Scale for Inpatient Evaluation; SANS: Scale for the Assessment of Negative Symptoms; SAPS: Scale for the Assessment of Positive Symptoms.

Table 6.17. Classes of Neuroleptics Studied in Children and Adolescents with Schizophrenia

Class	Published Studies/Reports
Phenothiazines	
Thioridazine	Realmuto et al., 1984
Thioxanthenes	
Thiothixene	Realmuto et al., 1984
Butyrophenones	
Haloperidol	Pool et al., 1976
	Spencer et al., 1992
	Spencer & Campbell, 1994
Dibenzoxapines	
Loxapine	Pool et al., 1976
Clozapine	Frazier et al., 1994
	Blanz & Schmidt, 1993
	Siefen & Remschmidt, 1986
	Levkovitch et al., 1994
	Birmaher et al., 1992
	Jacobsen et al., 1994
	Towbin et al., 1994

Seven of the 13 patients experienced drowsiness by the 12th day of administration of thiothixene, in addition to extrapyramidal side effects (Realmuto et al., 1984).

Butyrophenones. Haloperidol, a potent psychoactive agent, is the drug that has been most extensively investigated in schizophrenia with onset in childhood and adolescence (Pool et al., 1976; Spencer & Campbell, 1994; Versiani, Da Silva, Frota, & Mundim, 1978). As shown in Table 6.16, the efficacy and safety of haloperidol was critically assessed in a total of 141 hospitalized patients with schizophrenia, ages 5.5 to 18 years. In 91 of the 141 patients, diagnosis was made by DSM-III or DSM-III-R criteria for schizophrenia, and placebo was used as a control (Pool et al., 1976; Spencer et al., 1992; Spencer & Campbell, 1994).

Haloperidol was shown to be clinically and statistically superior to placebo and, in general, was effective in reducing psychotic symptoms at relatively conservative doses, as shown in Table 6.16. The advantage of haloperidol, as of other high-potency neuroleptics, is in its low sedative and anticholinergic properties; however, extrapyramidal side effects are frequently associated with the administration of this agent.

Spencer et al.'s (1992) ongoing clinical drug trial of haloperidol is the only published double-blind, placebo-controlled study of a psychoactive agent in prepubertal children with schizophrenia. The children, all hospitalized, are diagnosed employing DSM-III-R criteria for schizophrenia. To date, 16 patients have completed the study (Spencer & Campbell, 1994) but results are detailed only for 12 children (Spencer et al., 1992). Of the 12 children, 9 were males and 3 were females; their ages ranged from 5.5 to 11.75 years (mean, 8.78). A crossover design is employed: Following a 2-week placebo baseline period, subjects are randomly assigned to either haloperidol for 4 weeks followed by placebo for 4 weeks, or, first to placebo for 4 weeks followed by haloperiodol for 4 weeks. Dosage is individually titrated starting at 0.5 mg/day guided by therapeutic response and the emergence of untoward effects. Assessment instruments include the Brief Psychiatric Rating Scale for Children (BPRS-C; Gale, Pfefferbaum, Suhr, & Overall, 1986), Children's Psychiatric Rating Scale (CPRS; Guy, 1976); Clinical Global Impressions (CGI; National Institute of Mental Health [NIMH], 1985), a Global Clinical Judgment consensus rating (as adapted from Campbell et al., 1984), and the Abnormal Involuntary Movements Scale (AIMS; NIMH, 1985). Haloperidol, at optimal doses, ranging from 0.5 to 3.5 mg/day, mean, 2.02 (0.02-0.12 mg/kg/day), was clinically and statistically superior to placebo in the reduction of the following CPRS symptoms: "Ideas of Reference" ($p = .04$), "Persecutory Ideation" ($p = .01$), "Other Thinking Disorders" ($p = .04$), and "Hallucinations" ($p = .04$). Though the CPRS items of "Suspicious Affect," "Blunted Affect" "Delusions" and "Peculiar Fantasies" appeared to be reduced by haloperidol, the difference between active drug and placebo was not statistically significant. Haloperidol showed a significant reduction of the CGI "Severity of Illness" item ($p = .001$) and had a positive effect on the "Global Improvement" ($p = .02$) items as well as on the Global Clinical Judgment consensus scale by staff.

In these children, who were carefully monitored on a 24-hour basis, the most common untoward effects associated with haloperidol treatment were drowsiness ($N = 8$), drooling, dizziness, and acute dystonic reactions ($N = 2$) (Spencer et al., 1992). These untoward effects occurred during drug titration and resolved during dosage maintenance or with dosage reduction. No subject was dropped from the study as a result of side effects. The benefits of haloperidol were sustained and all subjects continued to receive the medication on discharge.

Dibenzoxapines

Loxapine. Loxapine, as shown in Table 6.16, was evaluated in two large double-blind clinical drug trials involving adolescents with schizophrenia, a total of 135 patients. In both studies, loxapine was compared with haloperidol (Pool et al., 1976; Versiani et al., 1978); the efficacy of the two agents did not differ significantly, though sleepiness was more common in the patients who were receiving loxapine. Both loxapine and haloperidol were better than placebo in reducing hallucinatory behavior and loxapine had a greater effect than placebo in reducing thinking disorder, as measured on the Brief Psychiatric Rating Scale (BPRS) (Overall & Gorham, 1962). However, a strong superiority of the two psychoactive agents over placebo was not evident, and did not reach significance for either drug on the Clinical Global Impressions Scale (CGI) (Pool et al., 1976.)

Clozapine. The recognition that some patients do not improve with conventional neuroleptics and that side effects, particularly extrapyramidal side effects including tardive dyskinesia, often result in serious impairment, generated an interest in new neuroleptics. Clozapine, an "atypical" neuroleptic, differs both biochemically and pharmacologically from the typical, standard neuroleptics (for review, see Jacobsen, Walker, Edwards, Chappell, & Woolston, 1994; Kane, Honigfeld, Singer, & Meltzer, 1988; Rapoport, 1994). It is an alternative for adults with treatment-resistant schizophrenia. Unlike typical neuroleptics, clozapine is rarely associated with extrapyramidal side effects; however, the risk for agranulocytosis (2% of patients) exceeds the risk associated with other neuroleptics (Kane et al., 1988). Several studies demonstrated a significant improvement with clozapine in 30% to 60% of adult patients with schizophrenia who failed to respond to typical neuroleptics (Kane et al., 1988; Pickar et al., 1992). Currently, clozapine is used clinically only in patients who are treatment resistant or who have developed side effects from typical neuroleptics, particularly in those with tardive dyskinesia.

Because of its potential benefit for nonresponders, and because it has extrapyramidal side effects only infrequently, clozapine appears as a treatment alternative for children and adolescents with schizophrenia. The experience with clozapine in this age group of patients with schizophrenia is almost exclusively limited to open studies (Blanz & Schmidt, 1993; Frazier et al., 1994) or to case reports (Birmaher, Baker, Kapur, Quintana, & Ganguli, 1992; Remschmidt, Schulz & Martin, 1992, 1994; Remschmidt, Schulz, Martin, Warnke et al., 1994; Siefen & Remschmidt, 1986). There is currently an ongoing double-blind study of clozapine employing haloperidol as a control (Gordon et al., 1994).

Siefen and Remschmidt (1986) reported on an open study of clozapine in 21 inpatients (12 under age 18 years) nonresponsive to typical neuroleptics. The authors described a "marked improvement" in 11 subjects and "some improvement" in 6. Reported side effects such as fatigue, dizziness, orthostatic hypotension, and increased salivation were transient. The data are based on a retrospective chart review. A subsequent report was based on a retrospective study involving 36 adolescents ages 14 to 22 years (Remschmidt, Schulz, & Martin, 1994). Of the

36 patients, 27 responded to clozapine (50 to 800 mg/d, mean 330); and 3 were nonresponders. Clozapine was discontinued in 6 patients because of severe side effects; these included extrapyramidal side effects, leukopenia ($N = 3$), hypertension, tachycardia, ECG abnormalities ($N = 2$) and marked elevation of serum glutamic oxaloacetic transaminase (SGOT) and serum glutamic pyruvic transaminase (SGPT) ($N = 1$). Clozapine was reported to be more effective in reducing positive than negative symptoms.

Birmaher et al. (1992) treated three adolescents with clozapine who were previously partial responders to typical neuroleptics. At a dose of 300 mg/day, clozapine improved the patients' functioning. In this report, no assessment scales were employed. Increased salivation and sedation were experienced by all three subjects and two had a transient decrease in white blood count (WBC).

Blanz and Schmidt (1993) evaluated 57 "predominantly" schizophrenic adolescents treated with clozapine after failure to respond to a combination of other neuroleptics or after having developed side effects. The authors found a significant improvement in 67% of patients and partial improvement in 21% (average daily dose 285 mg). Tachycardia, fatigue, increased salivation, and orthostatic hypotension were common. Extrapyramidal side effects occurred in 9 (16%) of patients. Another report of 13 adolescent nonresponders to typical neuroleptics showed that 10 of these improved significantly on clozapine as measured by a 50% decline in BPRS scores (Levkovitch et al., 1994). The average dose of clozapine was 240 mg/day and side effects were fatigue, increased salivation, and elevation in temperature. There was no decrease in WBCs in any subject.

The study of Frazier et al. (1994) represents an open trial of clozapine in 11 patients with schizophrenia, ages 12 to 17 years, all nonresponders to at least two neuroleptics prior to the trial with clozapine. The mean daily therapeutic dose of clozapine was 370.5 mg/day, a higher dose than reported by other investigators. Half of the sample was rated as improved, with a 30% decline in their BPRS scores. The patients appeared to respond better to clozapine than to haloperidol.

Gordon et al. (1994) reported on an ongoing double-blind comparison of clozapine and haloperidol in a carefully diagnosed sample ($N = 16$) with a mean age of 14.1 years. Findings in 8 subjects randomized to clozapine and of 4 who received clozapine on an open basis suggest that clozapine is "possibly efficacious" (Gordon et al., 1994, p. 706). Some patients have shown a dramatic improvement in response to clozapine (mean daily dose, 366.7 mg; maximum dose for clozapine, 900 mg/day; maximum dose for haloperidol, 36 mg/day). Side effects in the 12 subjects receiving clozapine included weight gain (mean 14.4 lbs in 6 weeks), transient neutropenia ($N = 2$), and recurrent neutropenia requiring discontinuation of drug ($N = 2$). Furthermore, 2 patients developed grand mal seizures that did not respond to treatment with anticonvulsants (Gordon et al., 1994).

Benzisoxazole Derivatives

Risperidone. Another novel antipsychotic agent, risperidone, is a potent serotonin (5-HT$_2$) and dopamine-D$_2$ receptor antagonist (Janssen et al., 1988). In adults with schizophrenia, administration of risperidone was associated with significant decreases of both positive and negative symptoms, less parkinsonian side effects than haloperidol, under double-blind, placebo-controlled conditions, with therapeutic effect on tardive dyskinesia (Chouinard et al., 1993). The doses of risperidone employed were 2.0, 6.0, 10.0, and 16.0 mg/day, and the sample in this multicenter study consisted of 135 inpatients with chronic schizophrenia, ages 19 to 67 years (mean, 37 ± 10). In an ongoing pilot study of hospitalized adolescents, risperidone appears to be effective at doses ranging from 4.0 to 8.0 mg/day and it is well tolerated (Armenteros et al., 1995). To date, there are no published reports on the efficacy and safety of risperidone in children and adolescents. Because of the potential effectiveness of this agent in nonresponders to other neuroleptics, reduction of both positive and negative symptoms, and low frequency of extrapyramidal side effects, risperidone warrants a critical assessment in this age group.

Drugs of Choice and Clinical Usage

As indicated earlier, haloperidol is the most extensively studied neuroleptic in children and adolescents with schizophrenia, and it is the drug of choice for the treatment of this age group. Haloperidol has been studied in other psychiatric disorders as well, including autism, conduct disorder, Tourette's disorder, and attention deficit disorder with hyperactivity (for review, see Campbell, Gonzalez, Ernst, Silva, & Werry, 1993). Thus data have accumulated concerning both the short-term and long-term efficacy, and, more importantly, the short- and long-term safety of this agent in children (for review, see Campbell et al., 1993).

In children, the recommended starting dose of haloperidol is 0.25 mg/day or 0.25 mg BID, with gradual increments, not more frequently than twice weekly. The therapeutic dose range is shown in Table 6.16. In adolescents, 1.0 mg/day to 1.0 mg t.i.d. is recommended as a starting dose, and approximately 0.02 to 0.15 mg/kg/day will be adequate for most patients who will show a response to haloperidol. Dosage escalation will not result necessarily in greater clinical improvement. Minimum effective dose should be the guide in careful titration of haloperidol. Benadryl, 25 mg orally or intramuscularly, and up to 50 mg, will relieve acute dystonic reactions.

Clozapine should be prescribed only if the patient fails to respond to haloperidol or other typical neuroleptics, or in case of severe side effects associated with administration of a typical neuroleptic (e.g., tardive dyskinesia). When prescribed, a careful laboratory and clinical assessment on baseline and weekly monitoring throughout treatment is required, with particular attention to the white blood count. (WBC).

Before a trial of a neuroleptic, a history of prior treatment with psychoactive agents and other medications is to be taken. A history of allergy or hypersensitivity to a drug requires serious consideration. A careful clinical examination and laboratory workup of the patient is required, including the following: complete blood count (CBC) and differential, liver function tests (SGOT, SGPT), electrocardiogram (ECG), urinalysis, weight, height, blood pressure and pulse rate, and examination for abnormal movements. Assessment of abnormal movements should be carried out preferably by employing the Abnormal Involuntary Movement Scale (AIMS) (*Psychopharmacology Bulletin,* No. 4, 1985; see Campbell, 1985a).

Side Effects of Neuroleptics

Early and Short-Term Side Effects.   Sedation is one of the most common side effects associated with this class of drugs. Maculopapular skin rash, an allergic type of reaction, may occur with neuroleptics.

Extrapyramidal side effects include acute dystonic reaction, parkinsonian side effects, akathisia, and akinesia. Acute dystonic reactions usually develop early during treatment with neuroleptics, in the first few days, or even a few hours after the first dose. They are more frequently associated with the administration of high-potency neuroleptics than with low-potency neuroleptics. Oculogyric crisis and opisthotonos are most common, in addition to cramps of tongue, jaw, and back; muscles of the esophagus can be affected also. Diphenhydramine 25 mg, administered orally or intramuscularly, can relieve this adverse effect; if necessary, the dose can be repeated. In addition, the dose of neuroleptic should be lowered (or discontinued for a day or two) and smaller and more gradual increments are recommended.

Parkinsonian side effects develop usually after 2 to 3 weeks of administration of a neuroleptic agent. They include cogwheel-phenomenon, tremor, masked facies, drooling, and bradykinesia. Drugs with anticholinergic properties are used for treatment of parkinsonian side effects (e.g., benztropine), or lowering of the neuroleptic's dose is recommended.

Anticholinergic side effects include dry mouth, blurred vision, constipation, increased heart rate, and difficulty in urination; they are common with low-potency neuroleptics (chlorpromazine and thioridazine) and with clozapine.

Neuroleptic malignant syndrome, a potentially life threatening condition, is estimated to develop in approximately 0.5% to 1.0% of patients receiving neuroleptic treatment (Rosenberg & Green, 1989); it usually occurs early in treatment. This condition has been reported in children and in adolescents (Geller & Greydamus, 1979; Klein, Levinsohn, & Blumer, 1985). Mortality in adults ranges from 11% to 22 % and even up to 50%. Neuroleptic malignant syndrome is manifested as hyperthermia, severe muscular rigidity, parkinsonian symptoms, alteration of mental status, hypertension or hypotension, diaphoresis, pallor, tachypnea, tachycardia, abnormal blood pressure fluctuations, elevation of creatinine phosphokinase (CPK) (due to breakdown of muscles), elevation of white blood count and liver enzymes. Catatonia and delirium may also develop. Treatment consists of discontinuation of all medications, careful medical evaluation, cardiac and renal monitoring, and vigorous supportive measures including hydration. Although bromocriptine and/or dantrolene sodium were employed in the treatment of neuroleptic malignant syndrome, there are no data based on well-controlled studies supporting the usefulness of these drugs (Rosebush & Stewart, 1989). High neuroleptic dose, change of neuroleptic dose, and intramuscular administration of neuroleptic have been associated with the development of neuroleptic malignant syndrome.

Other side effects associated with administration of neuroleptics are behavioral toxicity, endocrine effects (weight gain, galactorrhea, and gynecomastia) and cardiovascular effects (tachycardia, orthostatic hypotension, and lengthening of the QTR interval). For pimozide, a pretreatment ECG is recommended and a dosage not to exceed 0.3 mg/kg/day. QT prolongation and arrhythmia were reported with both pimozide and with thioridazine.

Sudden (cardiac) death has been reported in association with neuroleptic administration though causal relationship has not been firmly demonstrated (Simpson et al., 1988). Sudden unexpected death was known to exist prior to the advent of neuroleptics even in young persons with schizophrenia (Simpson et al., 1988).

Hepatic toxicity is associated with chlorpromazine. Increased risk for seizures or increase in frequency of preexisting seizures is associated especially with chlorpromazine (Tarjan, Lowery, & Wright, 1957); leukopenia and agranulocytosis are associated mainly with phenothiazines (less than 1 in 2,000 cases). However, leukopenia and agranulocytosis occur with greater frequency in patients treated with clozapine (Gordon et al., 1994; Kane et al., 1988; Remschmidt, Schulz, & Martin,

1994); fatalities were reported (in adults) and therefore weekly monitoring of WBC is mandatory.

Pigmentary retinopathy has been associated with administration of thioridazine, particularly with higher doses; photosensitivity of skin (to sunlight) may be associated with all neuroleptics, particularly with aliphatic phenothiazines (chlorpromazine or triflupromazine).

Long-Term Side Effects. The rabbit syndrome and tardive and withdrawal dyskinesias are the extrapyramidal long-term side effects. In addition to these, weight gain is commonly seen.

The rabbit syndrome is manifested in rapid and fine movements of lips; it is reported in approximately 4% of patients receiving neuroleptics (Yassa et al., 1986). Unlike tardive dyskinesias, these movements can be reduced by anticholinergic agents.

Tardive dyskinesia, a relatively common side effect associated with long-term administration of neuroleptics, has not been studied in children and adolescents with schizophrenia. Most of the information involving children and adolescents is derived from two studies. One study involves a sample of 104 subjects, ages 9 to 18 years (mean, 14.9 ± 2.2); of the 104 subjects, 15 were diagnosed as schizophrenia (DSM-III criteria). Mean continuous days of neuroleptic administration prior to assessments was 92.4 ± 111.0 (Richardson et al., 1991). The other, a prospective long-term study of haloperidol, involves 82 children diagnosed with autistic disorder (DSM-III) ages 2.3 to 8.2 years (Campbell et al., 1988). This second study employs the following design: baseline assessments, haloperidol administration for periods of 6 months followed by periods of placebo for 4 weeks; the length of cumulative exposure to haloperidol prior to the development of movements ranged from 56 to 1,266 days. In the sample of 82 children, 29.27% developed dyskinesias ($N = 24$); 19 children had withdrawal dyskinesias and 5 had dyskinesias while receiving haloperidol. The median daily dose of haloperidol was 1.0 mg; all dyskinesias were reversible. Preliminary analyses of a larger sample of children with autism, employing the same design as in the sample of 82 children (Campbell et al., 1988) indicates that 40 of 118 developed withdrawal dyskinesias or tardive dyskinesias (Armenteros, Adams, Campbell, & Eisenberg, 1995).

Perhaps these data, derived from an autistic population, are not applicable to schizophrenia, a different diagnostic entity. However, Richardson et al. (1991) do not specify in their report whether 1 or 2 of the 15 subjects with schizophrenia developed tardive dyskinesia, or none. The report is based on careful assessment of subjects, employing, as did Campbell et al. (1988) the Abnormal Involuntary Movement Scale (AIMS) and the Simpson Abbreviated Dyskinesia Scale and, in addition, the Simpson-Angus Neurological Rating Scale. However, the findings are not based on a prospective study, lacking a specific design; instead they are based on a single evaluation. Five subjects (12%) developed treatment-emergent tardive dyskinesia while receiving neuroleptics (Richardson et al., 1991), perhaps a greater occurrence than in the sample of Campbell et al. (1988) during haloperidol administration (6%). Of these 5 subjects, 3 were diagnosed conduct disorder or adjustment disorder, and 2 with psychosis or affective disorder. As in the Campbell et al. (1988) study, no association was found between neuroleptic-related dyskinesias and several parameters, including age, daily dose of neuroleptic, and number of continuous days of treatment with a neuroleptic prior to assessment (Richardson et al., 1991).

Short- and long-term side effects of neuroleptics (including tardive dyskinesia) are also discussed in Chapter 5 of this volume. For a detailed discussion on tardive dyskinesia, a report of the APA Task Force is recommended (Kane, 1992); on sudden death with neuroleptics, an APA Task Force report is suggested (Simpson, Davis, Jefferson, & Perez-Cruet, 1988). A chapter of Campbell et al. (1993) covers the side effects associated with neuroleptics; for measurement of side effects Campbell, Green, and Deutsch (1985) and Campbell and Palij (1985) are recommended. In addition, a textbook by Rosenberg, Holttum, and Gershon (1994) is most useful.

REFERENCES

American Psychiatric Association (APA). (1980). *Diagnostic and statistical manual of mental disorders* (DSM-III). (3rd ed.). Washington, DC: Author.

American Psychiatric Association (APA). (1987). *Diagnostic and statistical manual of mental disorders* (DSM-III-R). (3rd ed. rev.). Washington, DC: Author.

American Psychiatric Association (APA). (1994). *Diagnostic and statistical manual of mental disorders* (DSM-IV). (4th ed.). Washington, DC: Author.

Anderson, J. C., Williams, S., McGee, R., & Silva, P. A. (1987). DSM-III disorders in preadolescent children. *Archives of General Psychiatry, 44,* 69–76.

Andreasen, N. C. (1979). Thought, language, and communication disorders. I. Clinical assessment, definition of terms, and evaluation of their reliability. *Archives of General Psychiatry, 36,* 1315–1323.

Arboleda, C., & Holzman, P. S. (1985). Thought disorder in children at risk for psychosis. *Archives of General Psychiatry, 42,* 1004–1013.

Armenteros, J. L., Adams, P. B., Campbell, M., & Eisenberg, Z. W. (1995). Haloperidol related dyskinesias and pre- and perinatal complications in autistic children. *Psychopharmacology Bulletin, 31*(2), 361–367.

Armenteros, J. L., Fennelly, B. W., Hallin, A., Campbell, M., Pomerantz, P., Michell, M., & Sanchez, L. E. (1995). Schizophrenia in hospitalized adolescents: Clinical diagnosis, DSM-III-R, DSM-IV and ICD-10 criteria. *Psychopharmacology Bulletin, 31*(2).

Armenteros, J. L., Whitaker, A. H., Joachim, N., & Gorman, J. (1995). Open trial of risperidone in adolescents with schizophrenia. Final Programme, International Academy for Biomedical and Drug Research. Florence, Italy, pp. 176–177.

Asarnow, J. R., & Ben-Meir, S. (1988). Children with schizophrenia spectrum and depressive disorders: A comparative study of premorbid adjustment, onset pattern, and severity of impairment. *Journal of Child Psychology and Psychiatry, 29,* 477–488.

Asarnow, J. R., Goldstein, M. J., & Ben-Meir, S. (1988). Parental communication deviance in childhood onset schizophrenia spectrum and depressive disorders. *Journal of Child Psychology and Psychiatry, 29,* 825–838.

Asarnow, J. R., Tompson, M. C., & Goldstein, M. J. (1994). Childhood-onset schizophrenia: A followup study. *Schizophrenia Bulletin, 20,* 599–617.

Asarnow, R. F., Asamen, J., Granholm, E., Sherman, T., Watkins, J. M., & Williams, M. E. (1994). Cognitive/neuropsychological studies of children with a schizophrenic disorder. *Schizophrenia Bulletin, 20,* 647–669.

Asarnow, R. F. & Asarnow, J. R. (1994). Childhood-onset schizophrenia: Editors' introduction. *Schizophrenia Bulletin, 20,* 591–597.

Asarnow, R. F., Asarnow, J. R., & Strandburg, R. (1989). Schizophrenia: A developmental perspective. In D. Cicchetti (Ed.), *Rochester symposium on developmental psychology* (pp. 189–220). New York: Cambridge University Press.

Bender, L. (1942). Childhood schizophrenia. *Nervous Child, 1,* 138–140.

Birmaher, B., Baker, R., Kapur, S., Quintana, H., & Ganguli, R. (1992). Clozapine for the treatment of adolescents with schizophrenia. *Journal of the American Academy of Child and Adolescent Psychiatry, 31,* 160–164.

Blanz, B., & Schmidt, M. H. (1993). Letter to the editor, Clozapine for schizophrenia. *Journal of the American Academy of Child and Adolescent Psychiatry, 32,* 223–224.

Bleuler, E. (1951). *Dementia praecox of the group of schizophrenias.* Monograph Series on Schizophrenia. No. 1. Translated by J. Zinkin. New York: International Universities Press. (Original work published 1911)

Burd, L., & Kerbeshian, J. (1987). A North Dakota prevalence study of schizophrenia presenting in childhood. *Journal of the American Academy of Child and Adolescent Psychiatry, 26,* 347–350.

Campbell, M. (1985a). Protocol for rating drug-related AIMS, stereotypies, and CPRS assessments. *Psychopharmacology Bulletin, 21*(3), 1081.

Campbell, M. (1985b). Schizophrenic disorders and pervasive developmental disorders/infantile autism. In J. M. Wiener (Ed.), *Diagnosis and psychopharmacology of childhood and adolescent disorders* (pp. 113–150). New York: Wiley.

Campbell, M., Adams, P., Perry, R., Spencer, E. K., & Overall, J. E. (1988). Tardive and withdrawal dyskinesia in autistic children: A prospective study. *Psychopharmacology Bulletin, 24*(2), 251–255.

Campbell, M., Ernst, M., Setterberg, S. R., & Shaffer, D. (1993). Proposed changes in the DSM-IV criteria for child psychiatry. In D. L. Dunner (Ed.), *Current psychiatric therapy* (pp. 418–420). Philadelphia, PA: W. B. Saunders.

Campbell, M., Gonzalez, N. M., Ernst, M., Silva, R. R., & Werry, J. S. (1993). Antipsychotics. In J. S. Werry & M. G. Aman (Eds.), *Practitioner's guide to psychoactive drugs for children and adolescents* (pp. 269–296). New York: Plenum.

Campbell, M., Green, W. H., & Deutsch, S. I. (1985). *Child and adolescent psychopharmacology.* Beverly Hills, CA: Sage.

Campbell, M., & Palij, M. (1985). Measurement of untoward effects including tardive dyskinesia. *Psychopharmacology Bulletin, 21*(4), 1063–1082.

Campbell, M., Small, A. M., Green, W. H., Jennings, S. J., Perry, R., Bennett, W. G., & Anderson, L. (1984). Behavioral efficacy of haloperidol and lithium carbonate. A comparison in hospitalized aggressive children with conduct disorder. *Archives of General Psychiatry, 41,* 650–656.

Campbell, M., & Spencer, E. K. (1988). Review article. Psychopharmacology in child and adolescent psychiatry: A review of the past five years. *Journal of the American Academy of Child and Adolescent Psychiatry, 27,* 269–279.

Campbell, M., Spencer, E. K., Kowalik, S. C., & Erlenmeyer-Kimling, L. (1991). Schizophrenia and psychotic disorders. In J. M. Wiener (Ed.), *Textbook of child and adolescent psychiatry* (pp. 223–258). Washington, DC: APPI.

Caplan, R. (1994a). Communication deficits in childhood schizophrenia spectrum disorders. *Schizophrenia Bulletin, 20,* 671–683.

Caplan, R. (1994b). Thought disorder in childhood. *Journal of the American Academy of Child and Adolescent Psychiatry, 33,* 605–615.

Caplan, R., Guthrie, D., Fish, B., Tanguay, P. E., & David-Lando, G. (1989). The Kiddie Formal Thought Disorder Rating Scale: Clinical assessment, reliability, and validity. *Journal of the American Academy of Child and Adolescent Psychiatry, 28,* 408–416.

Caplan, R., Perdue, S., Tanguay, P. E., & Fish, B. (1990). Formal thought disorder in childhood onset schizophrenia and schizotypal personality disorder. *Journal of Child Psychology & Psychiatry 31,* 1103–1114.

Chouinard, G., Jones, B., Remington, G., Bloom, D., Addington, D., MacEwan, G. W., Labelle, A., Beauclair, L., & Arnott, W. (1993). A Canadian multicenter placebo-controlled study of fixed doses of risperidone and haloperidol in the treatment of chronic schizophrenic patients. *Journal of Clinical Psychopharmacology, 13,* 25–40.

DeSanctis, S. (1906). On some variations of dementia praecox. *Revista Sperimentali di Frenciatria, 32,* 141–165.

Eggers, C. (1978). Course and prognosis in childhood schizophrenia. *Journal of Autism and Childhood Schizophrenia, 8,* 21–36.

Eggers, C. (1989). Schizoaffective psychoses in childhood: A follow-up study. *Journal of Autism and Developmental Disorders, 19,* 327–342.

Fish, B., & Ritvo, E. R. (1979). Psychoses of childhood. In J. D. Noshpitz (Ed.), *Basic handbook of child psychiatry, Volume Two, Disturbances in development.* New York: Basic Books.

Frazier, J. A., Gordon, C. T., McKenna, K., Lenane, M. C., Jih, D., & Rapoport, J. L. (1994). An open trial of clozapine in 11 adolescents with childhood-onset schizophrenia. *Journal of the American Academy of Child and Adolescent Psychiatry, 33,* 658–663.

Gale, J., Pfefferbaum, B., Suhr, M. A., & Overall, J. E. (1986). The Brief Psychiatric Rating Scale for Children: A reliability study. *Journal of Clinical Child Psychology, 15,* 341–345.

Geller, B., & Greydanus, D. E. (1979). Haloperidol-induced comatose state with hyperthermia and rigidity in adolescence: Two case reports with a literature review. *Journal of Clinical Psychiatry, 40,* 102–103.

Gordon, C. T., Frazier, J. A., McKenna, K., Giedd, J., Zametkin, A., Zahn, T., Hommer, D., Hong, W., Kaysen, D., Albus, K. E., & Rapoport, J. L. (1994). Childhood-onset schizophrenia: An NIMH study in progress. *Schizophrenia Bulletin, 20,* 697–712.

Green, W. H., Campbell, M., Hardesty, A. S., Grega, D. M., Padron-Gayol, M., Shell, J., & Erlenmeyer-Kimling, L. (1984). A comparison of schizophrenic and autistic children. *Journal of the American Academy of Child Psychiatry, 23,* 399–409.

Green, W. H., & Padron-Gayol, M. (1986). Schizophrenic disorder in childhood: Its relationship to DSM-III criteria. In C. Shagass, R. C. Josiassen, W. H. Bridger, K.J. Weiss, D. Stoff, & G. M. Simpson (Eds.), *Biological psychiatry 1985* (pp. 1484–1486). New York: Elsevier.

Green, W. H., Padron-Gayol, M., Hardesty, A. S., & Bassiri, M. (1992). Schizophrenia with childhood onset: A phenomenological study of 38 cases. *Journal of the American Academy of Child and Adolescent Psychiatry, 31,* 968–976.

Guy, W. (Ed.). (1976). *ECDEU assessment manual for psychopharmacology* (rev.). DHEW Publication No. ADM 76-338. Rockville, MD: National Institute of Mental Health.

Jacobsen, L. K., Walker, M. C., Edwards, J. E., Chappell, P. B., & Woolston, J. L. (1994). Case Study: Clozapine in the treatment of a young adolescent with schizophrenia. *Journal of the American Academy of Child and Adolescent Psychiatry, 33,* 645–650.

Janssen, P. A. J., Niemegeers, C. J. E., Awouters, F. H. L., Schellekens, K. H. L., Megens, A. A. H. P., & Meert, T. F. (1988). Pharmacology of risperidone (R 64766), a new antipsychotic with serotonin-S_2 and dopamine-D_2 antagonistic properties. *Journal of Pharmacology and Experimental Therapy, 244*(2), 685–693.

Kafantaris, V., Ernst, M., Locascio, J., & Campbell, M. (1990, October 24–28). Psychotic disorder not otherwise specified in hospitalized adolescents. *Scientific Proceedings* (Vol. VI, p. 65) 37th Annual Meeting of the American Academy of Child and Adolescent Psychiatry, Chicago, IL.

Kane, J. M. (Chairperson) (1992). *Tardive dyskinesia: A task force report of the American Psychiatric Association.* Washington, DC: American Psychiatric Association.

Kane, J., Honigfeld, G., Singer, J., & Meltzer, H. (1988). Clozapine for the treatment-resistant schizophrenic: A double-blind comparison with chlorpromazine. *Archives of General Psychiatry, 45,* 789–796.

Kanner, L. (1943). Autistic disturbances of affective contact. *Nervous Child, 8,* 477–479.

Kanner, L. (1949). Problems of nosology and psychodynamics of early infantile autism. *American Journal of Orthopsychiatry, 19,* 416–426.

Klein S. K., Levinsohn, M. W., & Blumer, J. L. (1985). Accidental chlorpromazine ingestion as a cause of neuroleptic malignant syndrome in children. *Journal of Pediatrics, 107*(6), 970–973.

Kolvin, I. (1971). Studies in the childhood psychoses. *British Journal of Psychiatry, 118,* 381–419.

Kotsopoulos, S., Kanigsberg, J., Cote, A., & Fiedorowicz, C. (1987). Hallucinatory experiences in nonpsychotic children. *Journal of the American Academy of Child and Adolescent Psychiatry, 26,* 375–380.

Kraepelin, E. (1919). Dementia praecox and paraphrenia. In R. M. Barclay (Trans.), *Textbook of psychiatry* (8th ed.). Edinburgh: Livingstone. (Original work published 1899)

Levkovitch, Y., Kaysar, N., Kronnenberg, Y., Hagai, H., & Ganoi, B. (1994). Clozapine for schizophrenia. *Journal of the American Academy of Child and Adolescent Psychiatry, 33,* 431.

Loranger, A. W. (1984). Sex differences in age at onset of schizophrenia. *Archives of General Psychiatry, 41,* 157–161.

Makita, K. (1966). The age of onset of childhood schizophrenia. *Folia Psychiatrica et Neurologica Japonica, 20,* 111–121.

McClellan, J., & Werry, J. (1994). Practice parameters for the assessment and treatment of children and adolescents with schizophrenia. *Journal of the American Academy of Child & Adolescent Psychiatry, 33,* 616–635.

McKenna, K., Gordon, C. T., Lenane, M., Kaysen, D., Fahey, K., & Rapoport, J. L. (1994). Looking for childhood-onset schizophrenia: The first 71 cases screened. *Journal of the American Academy of Child and Adolescent Psychiatry, 33,* 636–644.

National Institute of Mental Health. (1985). Rating scales and assessment instruments for use in pediatric psychopharmacology research [Special issue]. *Psychopharmacology Bulletin, 21*(4).

National Institute of Mental Health. (1993). Schizophrenia 1993 [Special issue]. *Schizophrenia Bulletin, 19.*

Overall, J. E., & Gorham, D. R. (1962). The brief psychiatric rating scale. *Psychological Report, 10,* 799–812.

Pickar, D., Owen, R. R., Litman, R. E., Konizki, E., Gutierrez, R., & Rapoport, M. H. (1992). Clinical and biological response to clozapine in patients with schizophrenia. *Archives of General Psychiatry, 49,* 345–353.

Pilowsky, D., & Chambers, W. J. (Eds.). (1986). *Hallucinations in childhood.* Washington, DC: American Psychiatric Press.

Pool, D., Bloom, W., Mielke, D. H., Roniger, J. J., & Gallant, D. M. (1976). A controlled evaluation of loxitane in seventy-five adolescent schizophrenic patients. *Current Therapeutic Research, 19,* 99–104.

Rapoport, J. L. (1994). Clozapine and child psychiatry [Editorial]. *Journal of Child and Adolescent Psychopharmacology, 4*(1), 1–3.

Realmuto, G. M., Erickson W. D., Yellin, A. M., Hopwood, J. H., & Greenberg, L. M. (1984). Clinical comparison of thiothixene and thioridazine in schizophrenic adolescents. *American Journal of Psychiatry, 141,* 440–442.

Reich, W., & Weiner, Z. (1990). *Diagnostic interview for children and adolescents-revised.* St. Louis, MO: Washington University Press.

Remschmidt, H., Schulz, E., & Martin, M. (1992). Die Behandlung schizophrener Psychosen in der Adoleszenz mit Clozapin (Leponex). In D. Naber & F. Muller-Spahn (Eds.), *Clozapin. Pharmakologie and klinik eines atypischen neuroleptikums—eine kritische bestandsaufnahme* (pp. 99–119). New York: Schattauer.

Remschmidt, H., Schulz, E., & Martin, M. (1994). An open trial of clozapine in thirty-six adolescents with schizophrenia. *Journal of Child and Adolescent Psychopharmacology, 4,* 31–41.

Remschmidt, H. E., Schulz, E., Martin, M., Warnke, A., & Trott, G. E. (1994). Childhood-onset schizophrenia: History of the concept and recent studies. *Schizophrenia Bulletin, 20,* 727–745.

Richardson, M. A., Haugland, G., & Craig, T. J. (1991). Neuroleptic use, Parkinsonian symptoms, tardive dyskinesia, and associated factors in child and adolescent psychiatric patients. *American Journal of Psychiatry, 148,* 1322–1328.

Rosebush, P. I., & Stewart, T. D. (1989). A prospective analysis of 24 episodes of nuroleptic malignant syndrome. *American Journal of Psychiatry, 146,* 717–725.

Rosenberg, D. R., Holttum, J., & Gershon, S. (1994). *Textbook of pharmacotherapy for child and adolescent psychiatric disorders.* New York: Brunner/Mazel.

Rosenberg, M. R., & Green, M. (1989). Neuroleptic malignant syndrome. Review of response to therapy. *Archives of Internal Medicine, 149*(9), 1927–1931.

Russell, A. T. (1994). The clinical presentation of childhood-onset schizophrenia. *Schizophrenia Bulletin, 20,* 631–646.

Russell, A. T., Bott, L., & Sammons, C. (1989). The phenomenology of schizophrenia occurring in childhood. *Journal of the American Academy of Child and Adolescent Psychiatry, 28,* 399–407.

Rutter, M. (1972). Childhood schizophrenia reconsidered. *Journal of Autism and Childhood Schizophrenia, 2,* 315–337.

Rutter, M., Tizard, J. & Whitmore, K. (Eds.). (1970). Education, health and behavior. London: Longman.

Shaffer, D., Campbell, M., Cantwell, D., Bradley, S., Carlson, G., Cohen, D., Denckla, M., Frances, A., Garfinkel, B., Klein, R., Pincus, H., Spitzer, R. L., Volkmar, F., & Widiger, T. (1989). Brief communication. Child and adolescent psychiatric disorders in DSM-IV: Issues facing the work group. *Journal of the American Academy of Child and Adolescent Psychiatry, 28,* 830–835.

Siefen, G., & Remschmidt, H. (1986). Behandlungsergebnisse mit Clozapine bei schizophrenen Jugendlichen, *Z. Kinder-Jugendpsychiat, 14,* 245–257.

Simpson, G. M., Davis, J., Jefferson, J. W., & Perez-Cruet, J. F. (1988). *Sudden death in psychiatric patients: The role of neuroleptic drugs.* (Task Force Report 27). Washington, DC: American Psychiatric Association.

Simpson, G. M., Lee, J. H., Zoubok, B., & Gardos, G. (1979). A rating scale for tardive dyskinesia. *Psychopharmacology (Berlin), 64,* 171–179.

Spencer, E. K., & Campbell, M. (1994). Children with schizophrenia: Diagnosis, phenomenology, and pharmacotherapy. *Schizophrenia Bulletin, 20,* 713–725.

Spencer, E. K., Kafantaris, V., Padron-Gayol, M. V., Rosenberg, C. R., & Campbell, M. (1992). Haloperidol in schizophrenic children: Early findings from a study in progress. *Psychopharmacology Bulletin, 28*(2), 183–186.

Strandburg, R. J., Marsh, J. T., Brown, W. S., Asarnow, R. F., & Guthrie, D. (1994). Information-processing deficits across childhood- and adult-onset schizophrenia. *Schizophrenia Bulletin, 20,* 685–695.

Tarjan, C., Lowery, V. E., & Wright, S. W. (1957). Use of chlorpromazine in 278 mentally deficient patients. *American Medical Association Journal of Disturbed Children, 94,* 294–300.

Towbin, K. E., Dykens, E.M., & Pugliese, R. G. (1994). Case study: Clozapine for early developmental delays with childhood-onset schizophrenia: Protocol and 15-month outcome. *Journal of the American Academy of Child and Adolescent Psychiatry, 33,* 651–657.

Versiani, M., Da Silva, J. A. R., Frota, L. H., & Mundim, F. D. (1978). Double-blind comparison between loxapine and haloperidol in the treatment of adolescent schizophrenic patients. *Current Therapeutic Research, 24,* 556–559.

Volkmar, F. R., Cohen, D. J., Hoshino, Y., Rende, R. D., & Paul, R. (1988). Phenomenology and classification of the childhood psychoses. *Psychological Medicine, 18,* 191–201.

Volkmar, F. R., Klin, A., Siegel, B., Szatmari, P., Lord, C., Campbell, M., Freeman, B. J., Cicchetti, D. V., Rutter, M., Kline, W., Buitelaar, J., Hattab, Y., Fombonne, E., Feuentes, J., Werry, J., Stone, W., Kerbeshian, J., Hoshino, Y., Bregman, J., Loveland,

K., Szymanski, L., & Towbin, K. (1994). Field trial for autistic disorder in DSM-IV. *American Journal of Psychiatry, 151,* 1361–1367.

Watkins, J. M., Asarnow, R. F., & Tanguay, P. (1988). Symptom development in childhood onset schizophrenia. *Journal of Child Psychology and Psychiatry, 29,* 865–878.

Werry, J. S. (1992). Child and adolescent (early onset) schizophrenia: A review in light of DSM-III-R. *Journal of Autism and Developmental Disorders, 22,* 601–624.

Werry, J. S., McClellan, J. M., Andrews, L. K., & Ham, M. (1994). Clinical features and outcome of child and adolescent schizophrenia. *Schizophrenia Bulletin, 20,* 619–630.

Werry, J. S., McClellan, J. M., & Chard, L. (1991). Childhood and adolescent schizophrenia, bipolar and schizoaffective disorders: A clinical and outcome study. *Journal of the American Academy of Child and Adolescent Psychiatry, 30,* 457–465.

Werry, J. S., & Taylor, E. (1994). Schizophrenic and allied disorders. In M. Rutter, E. Taylor, & L. Hersov (Eds.), *Child and adolescent psychiatry: Modern approaches* (3rd ed., pp. 594–615). Oxford: Blackwell Scientific Publications.

Whitaker, A., & Rao, U. (1992). Neuroleptics in pediatric psychiatry. *Pediatric Psychopharmacology, 15,* 243-276.

Yassa, R., & Lal, S. (1986). Prevalence of the rabbit syndrome. *American Journal of Psychiatry, 143,* 656–657.

Affective/Mood Disorders

JAVAD H. KASHANI, M.D. and JYOTSNA NAIR, M.D.

Mood disorders in childhood and adolescence have received increasing recognition in recent decades from both researchers and clinicians after years of debate and controversy. According to psychoanalytic thinking, children's superego structures were too immature to sustain either severe depression or its defense, mania. Affective disorders were unknown in childhood because the immature personality structure of the infant or the older child was thought to be incapable of producing a state of depression and hence, mood disorders could not exist in the younger age group (Mahler, 1961). Other researchers such as Anthony and Scott (1960) described a set of criteria that had to be met before making the diagnosis of manic-depression. They reviewed the earlier 63 cases published in prepubertal children and only three met their criteria. They also described a 12-year-old boy who continued to have episodes of mania and depression into adulthood supporting their notion of Bipolar Disorder in children being an early-onset variant of the adult form.

Psychoanalytic theories underwent revision over the years, and the advent of a biochemical theory of depression resulted in an increasing acceptance of childhood mood disorders. The catecholamine deficiency hypothesis was based on observations that many antidepressant drugs increased the synaptic concentration of norepinephrine, whereas catecholamine-depleting drugs such as reserpine seemed to cause depressionlike symptoms (Bunney & Davis, 1965; Schildkraut, 1965). The indolamine hypothesis postulated that a deficit in brain serotonin was responsible for depression because drugs that increased synaptic serotonin such as monoamine oxidase inhibitors or serotonin precursors such as 5-hydroxytryptophan and L-tryptophan relieved depression (Coppen, 1967; Lapin & Oxenkrug, 1969). The observation that children and adults were more similar physiologically than in their emotional maturity level paved the way for increasing acceptance of the concept of mood disorders in children and adolescents.

Along with the changing attitudes, researchers moved toward a more empirical course, utilizing standardized methods such as structured interviews and rating scales to aid in diagnosis, to ensure uniformity, and to increase the reliability and validity of their results. Diagnostic criteria have been revised and improved. This is important since not only are the mood disorders quite prevalent, but they may go undetected and untreated for prolonged periods unless active measures are taken. Since depression affects many areas of functioning and in some cases can be life threatening, both early recognition and treatment are important, even more so since the sufferers usually do not draw attention to themselves. The clinician may not readily observe the symptoms of feeling hopeless, miserable, tired; having difficulty sleeping; and lowered self-esteem. If there is no intervention, long-term problems may result in impaired functioning and possible suicidal behavior.

230

In the past twenty-five years, extensive research has been conducted into the psychopharmacological treatment of mood disorders but with mixed results. Even though the criteria for diagnosing these disorders in children and adolescents are almost identical to adults, the two groups differ in their response to the medications commonly used to treat adults.

In this chapter, we review the existing literature on the diagnosis, epidemiology, and pharmacological treatment of mood disorders and discuss the various options available to clinicians when contemplating treatment. Results of various drug studies will also be described along with the newer medications being used for treatment.

CLINICAL CRITERIA AND DIAGNOSTIC ISSUES PER DSM-IV

General Considerations

Mood disorders are known to occur in all age groups. The diagnosis of mood disorders is made using the *Diagnostic and Statistical Manual of Mental Disorders* (DSM-IV; American Psychiatric Association [APA], 1994).

DSM-I did not include psychiatric disorders of children (APA, 1952). DSM-II included an overall category of behavioral disorders of children and adolescents with several subtypes (APA, 1968). DSM-III (APA, 1980) provided a fairly comprehensive classification of the various psychiatric disorders present in infants, children, and adolescents, along with a multiaxial system of diagnosis and a description of the clinical picture. The revised form, DSM-III-R was released in 1987 (APA, 1987). In DSM-III and DSM-III-R, the criteria for making the diagnosis of mood disorders in the younger age group were similar to the ones used for adults with some changes to account for the developmental differences in the two age groups.

The organization of the Mood Disorders section was changed in DSM-IV, providing for a complete description of depression followed by Bipolar Disorder, adding clarity and making the book easier to use. We will describe the changes made in DSM-IV as compared with DSM-III-R in this section.

Major Depressive Episode

The description of a Major Depressive Episode in DSM-III-R required the presence of at least five of nine symptoms for a minimum duration of 2 weeks (see Table 7.1). These nine symptoms were depressed mood, loss of interest or pleasure, increase or decrease in weight, disturbance in sleep pattern, psychomotor retardation or agitation, feelings of tiredness

Table 7.1. *Major Depressive Episode*

(1)	Presence of five or more of nine symptoms listed, for a two week period, with one symptom being either depressed (irritable in children and adolescents) mood or loss of interest or pleasure. The symptoms are: depressed mood, loss of interest, change in weight, insomnia or hypersomnia, psychomotor agitation or retardation, loss of energy, feeling of guilt or worthlessness, decreased concentration and recurrent thoughts of death.
(2)	The symptoms do not meet the guidelines for a Mixed Episode.
(3)	Clinically significant distress or impairement of functioning present.
(4)	Symptoms not attributable directly to substance use or medical conditions.
(5)	The presence of symptoms is not better accounted for by Bereavement.

Note: Underline indicates changes made in DSM-IV as compared with its predecessor DSM-III-R.

and loss of energy, feelings of worthlessness or excessive/inappropriate guilt, decreased ability to think or concentrate, and recurrent thoughts of death. At least one of the five symptoms was either depressed mood or loss of interest or pleasure. However, in children and adolescents, irritable mood could substitute for depressed mood. Organicity and uncomplicated bereavement were to be ruled out. Hallucinations or delusions should not have occurred in the absence of prominent mood symptoms for two weeks nor should the process be superimposed on Schizophrenia, Schizophreniform Disorder, Delusional Disorder, or Psychotic Disorder Not Otherwise Specified.

Major Depressive Episode was rated on its severity, presence of psychotic features, and the state of remission. Diagnostic criteria were listed separately for Melancholic type of depression and for the presence of a seasonal pattern.

In addition to the preceding, DSM-IV includes the presence of clinically significant distress in social, occupational, or other areas of functioning. DSM-IV criteria further clarify that the symptoms should not be the direct result of substance use or a general medical condition. Substance use was not specifically addressed in DSM-III-R in the context of depression.

Dysthymic Disorder

In DSM-III-R, Dysthymic Disorder was described as depressed mood for most of the day, on more days than not, for a duration of 2 years, and could have been a subjective feeling of sadness. Two out of the six symptoms were required to make the diagnosis. The symptom-free period was limited to 2 months. Major depressive, manic or hypomanic episodes should not have occurred. The same exclusionary criteria applied as in major depressive episode. Dysthymic Disorder was further subtyped into primary or secondary and also had either an early or late onset.

In children and adolescents, irritable mood could be substituted for depressed mood and the disturbance of mood could have lasted for 1 year instead of 2 years.

In the DSM-IV, the term used is Dysthymic Disorder instead of Dysthymia as in DSM-III-R. The criteria for the duration are the same as DSM-III-R. The diagnosis of depression in the younger age group can be made in the presence of an irritable mood instead of depressed mood, failure to maintain expected weight gain instead of weight loss, drop in school performance instead of decreased occupational functioning and a lack of interest in friends and play when considering loss of interest or pleasure, as well as the required duration of 1 year and not 2 years for Dysthymic Disorder. These modifications and interpretations of the criteria make the diagnosis more relevant to the younger age group.

Bipolar Disorder

The description of Bipolar Disorder has changed in DSM-IV as compared with its predecessor. Hypomanic episode is included as a separate entity and not as a mild form of a full-blown manic episode. Bipolar Disorder has further been classified into Bipolar I and Bipolar II. Bipolar I is the presence of full-blown manic and depressive episodes while Bipolar II requires the presence of hypomanic episodes. The diagnosis of Bipolar I and Bipolar II can be further clarified using longitudinal course and describing the most recent episode, providing a more comprehensive picture.

Manic Episode. In DSM-IV, Manic Episode is a distinct period of persistently abnormal expansive, elevated or irritable mood for one week unless hospitalization is required (see Table 7.2). Of the following symptoms, three should be present with expansive mood and four symptoms should occur with irritable mood. The symptoms are inflated self-esteem or grandiosity, decreased need for sleep, more talkative than usual and pressured speech, racing thoughts or flight of ideas, distractibility, increased goal-directed activity or psychomotor agitation and excessive involvement in pleasurable activities with a high potential for painful consequences. Occupational, social, or relationship impairment occurs as a result of mood change. During the periods of mood disturbance, there are no prominent hallucinations or delusions without mood symptoms for as long as 2 weeks. Mood disturbance should not be

Table 7.2.   Manic Episode

(1)   Presence of elevated, irritable, or expansive mood for <u>at least one week or any duration if hospitalization</u> is required.

(2)   Presence of three or more of seven symptoms listed: inflated self-esteem or grandiosity, decreased need for sleep, pressured speech, flight of ideas or feeling that thoughts are racing, distractibility, increased goal directed activity or psychomotor agitation and excessive involvement in pleasurable activities.

(3)   The symptoms do not meet the guidelines for a Mixed Episode.

(4)   Clinically significant distress or impairement of functioning present.

(5)   Symptoms not attributable directly to substance use or medical conditions.

Note: Underline indicates changes made in DSM-IV as compared with its predecessor DSM-III-R.

superimposed on Schizophrenia, Schizoaffective Disorder, Delusional Disorder, or Psychotic Disorder NOS. No organic cause should initiate it or maintain it. An antidepressant's precipitation of manic episodes does not count toward the diagnosis of Bipolar Disorder.

Hypomanic Episode.   DSM-IV describes Hypomanic Episode in a separate section, as the presence of elevated, expansive, or irritable mood for at least 4 days (see Table 7.3). If the mood is elevated, at least three of the seven symptoms should occur. In irritable mood, however, at least four of the seven symptoms should be present. The symptoms are

Table 7.3.   Hypomanic Episode

(1)   Presence of elevated, irritable, or expansive mood for at least <u>four days</u> clearly different from the usual nondepressed mood.

(2)   Presence of <u>three or more of seven symptoms</u> listed: inflated self-esteem or grandiosity, decreased need for sleep, pressured speech, flight of ideas or feeling that thoughts are racing, distractibility, increased goal directed activity or psychomotor agitation and excessive involvement in pleasurable activities.

(3)   <u>Change in functioning not characteristic of the person when asymptomatic.</u>

(4)   <u>Change in functioning observable by others.</u>

(5)   <u>Impairment of functioning present but not enough to need hospitalization.</u>

(6)   <u>Symptoms not attributable directly to substance use or medical conditions.</u>

Note: Underline indicates changes made in DSM-IV as compared with its predecessor DSM-III-R.

the same as those for a manic episode. The change in mood should be observable by others. Marked impairment in functioning should not be present. No organic or medical condition may be related to the episodes and episode precipitation by antidepressant treatment does not count toward the diagnosis of Bipolar II.

Cyclothymia.   In DSM-IV, Cyclothymia should be present for at least 2 years in adults with numerous hypomanic and depressive episodes. Hypomanic episodes do not have the occupational and social impairment associated with a manic episode. The depressive episodes are not Major Depressive Episodes. During the 2 years, the symptom-free period should not exceed 2 months. In the first 2 years, no clear evidence of a Major Depressive Episode or a Manic Episode should be present. In adolescents and children the duration of the mood disturbance is reduced to 1 year.

Subtypes of Bipolar Disorder in DSM-IV.   The classification of Bipolar Disorder is more detailed in DSM-IV, using the concept of Bipolar I and Bipolar II. Bipolar I is the presence of depressive and manic episodes, whereas Bipolar II involves the presence of hypomanic episodes along with depressive episodes. A single manic episode with no depressive episodes is described as Bipolar I Disorder, Single Manic Episode. Bipolar I disorder where the most recent episode is hypomanic, manic, mixed, depressed, or unspecified is described as Bipolar I Disorder, Most Recent Episode.

Bipolar II is similar to Bipolar I except that hypomanic episodes substitute for manic episodes, along with major depressive episodes. Again, one can specify if the most recent episode was hypomanic or depressed. Another diagnosis included in this section is that of Bipolar Disorder, Not Otherwise Specified, and it includes all the conditions that do not meet the specific criteria described previously.

Mood Disorder Due to General Medical Condition.   DSM-IV has added a new diagnosis. Mood Disorder Due to a General Medical Condition is disturbance of mood etiologically related to a medical condition with significant impairment in functioning. One can specify whether the disturbance is manic, depressive, or mixed in nature.

Substance-Induced Mood Disorder.   Substance-Induced Mood Disorder is similar to the one described earlier where the causative agent is substance use. This diagnosis is exclusive to DSM-IV. One can specify whether manic, depressed, or mixed features are present and also if the onset was during intoxication or withdrawal.

Mood Disorders Not Otherwise Specified.   Mood Disorders Not Otherwise Specified include the disorders that do not meet any specific criteria and that present difficulty in choosing between Bipolar Disorder NOS or Depressive Disorder NOS.

Cross-Sectional Symptom Features.   This is a new section that has been added to the diagnostic criteria in DSM-IV, enabling the clinician to describe any special features such as melancholic, atypical, and catatonic features occurring in the depressive or manic episodes.

- *With Melancholic Features* Melancholic Features can be applied to major depressive, Bipolar I disorder and Bipolar II disorder. Melancholic Features include either loss of pleasure or the lack of reactivity to pleasurable stimuli and at least three of the following six symptoms: a distinct quality of the depressed mood, worse in the morning, early morning awakening, marked psychomotor agitation or retardation, significant anorexia or weight loss, and excessive or inappropriate guilt.

- *With Atypical Features* This involves mood reactivity, does not meet the criteria of melancholic features and two of the following four features should be present for 2 weeks: significant weight gain or increased appetite, hypersomnia, leaden paralysis, and a long-standing pattern of interpersonal rejection-sensitivity resulting in significant impairment.

- *With Catatonic Features* The clinical picture of this subtype consists of at least two of the five symptoms of motoric immobility or stupor, excessive motor activity, extreme negativism or mutism, peculiar voluntary movements, such as posturing and grimacing, and echolalia and echopraxia.

Course Specifiers.   To further improve the description of mood disorders, DSM-IV has included the following criteria to specify the course of Bipolar Disorder:

- *With Rapid Cycling* Rapid cycling is applied to Bipolar I or II Disorders with four or more manic, hypomanic or depressive episodes in the past 12 months and the presence of either switch or remission in between episodes.

- *With Seasonal Pattern* Seasonal pattern implies a temporal relationship between the time of the year and the onset of Bipolar I, Bipolar II, or Major Depressive Disorder. Full remissions or switches occur at characteristic times of the year. At least two episodes should have occurred in the past 2 years to define the temporal relationship, and no nonseasonal episodes should have occurred. Seasonal episodes far outnumber the nonseasonal episodes in the individual's lifetime.

- *With Postpartum Onset* If the mood disturbance occurs within 4 weeks postpartum then postpartum onset can be specified.

Longitudinal Course Specifiers for Major Depressive Disorder and Bipolar I Disorder. In contrast to DSM-III-R, DSM-IV also describes the longitudinal course specifiers for major depressive disorders and Bipolar I Disorder. The longitudinal course can be drawn pictorially and the presence of full interepisode recovery depicted. This improves the clinicians' understanding of the pattern of the individual's illness and the response to medications. Recurrence is also clearly represented. The diagrams have a baseline of functioning that is represented as a straight line and depression or manic episodes are shown as curves either below or above this baseline respectively. If a full recovery has not occurred, then a deterioration will be seen.

On the whole, DSM-IV has made significant changes in the diagnosis of mood disorders, adding both a longitudinal and a cross-sectional dimension to the diagnosis. This dimension was lacking in the earlier criteria and adds to the amount of information conveyed through the diagnosis.

EPIDEMIOLOGY

The prevalence of mood disorders varies in the different age groups and depends on the sample characteristics, diagnostic criteria, and the subject age range.

The diagnosis of depression in preschoolers using the adult criteria is infrequent (Kashani, Holcomb, & Orvaschel, 1986; Kashani & Carlson, 1987) but substantial evidence has been provided for the existence of major depressive disorder in preschoolers as young as three years of age (Kashani, Ray, & Carlson, 1984; Kashani & Carlson, 1987). Two samples of preschoolers from the community were reported with 1 depressed preschooler among 350 preschoolers and a rate of depression of 0.3% in this age group (Kashani & Ray, 1983; Kashani, Holcomb, & Orvaschel, 1986) indicating that depression is a rare finding in preschoolers.

Two studies of preadolescents, both in the general population, in the United States and New Zealand conducted by Kashani and colleagues (Kashani et al., 1983; Kashani & Simmonds, 1979) indicated the prevalence of Major Depressive Disorder to be 1.8% with no gender difference.

The rate increases in clinically referred samples, whether inpatient or outpatient.

The prevalence of depression increases in the adolescent age group. In a study of 14- to 16-year-olds, the prevalence of Major Depressive Disorder was 4.7%, more than double the prevalence in preadolescence. This study also showed that more girls than boys had depressive symptomatology (Kashani, Beck, et al., 1987). Gender differences were also observed by Baron and Perron (1986) and Connelly, Johnston, Brown, Mackay, and Blackstock (1993). In contrast, no gender difference was observed by Teri (1982) and Sullivan and Engin (1986). However, Kashani et al. used structured interviews for making the diagnosis in contrast to the other studies, which utilized the Beck Depression Inventory to detect depression.

Rutter (1986) and others (Teri, 1982; Sullivan & Engin, 1986) observed that approximately one-third of nonclinical samples of adolescents endorsed some depressive symptoms in a community-based sample.

Connelly et al. (1993), using the Beck Depression Inventory, observed a shift toward the more severe category of depression with increasing age and peaks in the rate of depression at age 16 and age 19.

Depression has been shown to be related more frequently to substance abuse in adolescents (Kashani et al., 1985). Geller, Chestnut, Miller, Price, and Yates (1985) demonstrated an association between Major Depressive Disorder and antisocial behavior.

In this age group, manic episodes are rare compared with the depressive disorders. In adults, the lifetime prevalence of manic episodes is 0.6% to 1% and 4.1% to 7.5% for Major Depressive Episode (Robins, Helzer, & Weissman, 1984).

Mania may be underdiagnosed in children and adolescents due to the difficulty in differential diagnosis from attention deficit/hyperactivity disorder (Coll & Bland, 1979; Bowring & Kovacs, 1992). Twenty five percent of the children diagnosed with depression may present an early onset of manic illness (Kovacs & Gastonis, 1989). Attention deficit/hyperactivity disorder exhibits some symptoms similar to mania such as mood lability, temper outbursts, and distractibility. In about half of the attention deficit disorder cases, the age of onset is prior to the age of 4 years and elevated mood is usually absent. Mania, has a later age of onset and the presence of elevated mood.

Weller, Weller, Tucker, and Fristad (1986), in a retrospective study, found that approximately half the children who fulfilled the diagnostic criteria for mania had received another diagnosis, suggesting that the clinicians' expectations had a role in the apparent underdiagnosis. Bowden and Sarabia (1980) emphasized the tendency of clinicians to choose diagnoses to avoid the use of medications and to avoid labeling the person. Ballenger, Reus, and Post (1982) found a higher frequency of psychotic symptoms in bipolar adolescents and noted the need to keep open the possibility of a Bipolar Disorder in psychotic children and adolescents.

Carlson and Kashani (1988) used a structured interview (Diagnostic Interview for Children and Adolescents) in 150 nonpsychiatrically referred adolescents to determine the frequency of Bipolar Disorder. Life time prevalence was reported as 0.6%. Life time rate for Major Depression was 4.7%.

Hence, in contrast to depression, Bipolar Disorder is uncommon and is a diagnostic problem both due to the symptom complex and the perceptions of the clinicians with regards to the effect of the diagnosis on the future of the individual.

PSYCHOPHARMACOLOGY

Depressive disorders are encountered more commonly than Bipolar Disorders. Pharmacological treatment options include tricyclic antidepressants, lithium augmentation of tricyclics, monoamine oxidase inhibitors, seretonin reuptake inhibitors, lithium, anticonvulsants, and electroconvulsive therapy. The different classes of antidepressants will be described and the effects and the dosage shall be discussed. Side effects of the class will be mentioned as a group.

Tricyclic Antidepressants

Tricyclic antidepressants are the oldest and best studied medications for depression. Individual drugs are placed in different groups based on the number of methyl groups on the nitrogen atom of the side chain of the three-ringed nucleus. Imipramine, amitriptyline, clomipramine, and doxepin are called tertiary amines because there are two methyl groups on the nitrogen atom of the side chain. Desipramine, nortriptyline, and protriptyline are named secondary amines because there is only one methyl group in that position. The tertiary amines are metabolized by demethylation to the corresponding secondary amines in the body. The tricyclic nucleus is oxidized in the liver, conjugated with glucoronic acid, and then excreted.

Studies investigating the efficacy and side effects of tricyclics in the younger age group have been done mainly for imipramine, desipramine, amitriptyline, and nortriptyline. These medications were used to treat depression in the younger age group because of their demonstrated therapeutic effect in adults.

Effectiveness of Individual Tricyclic Antidepressants

Imipramine. Imipramine, a tertiary amine, inhibits the reuptake of norepinephrine and serotonin. Imipramine is demthylated to desipramine in the body, which does not inhibit the reuptake of serotonin. Imipramine administration also results in some muscarinic blockade in contrast to its metabolite desipramine.

Imipramine has been commonly researched in children and adolescents and has the most information available. Earlier open-labeled drug trials demonstrated the effectiveness of imipramine in depressive disorders in children and adolescents (Frommer, 1967; Petti & Conners, 1983; Preskorn, Weller, & Weller, 1982; Puig-Antich et al., 1978, 1979; Ryan et al., 1986).

Further investigations utilizing the double-blind method had a limited number of participants in pilot studies. Petti and Law (1982) conducted a double-blind trial on Imipramine with 7 children; imipramine demonstrated improvement while the placebo group had minimal changes in depressive symptoms.

The study that raised doubts about the effectiveness of imipramine in the younger age group was reported by Puig-Antich et al. in 1987. Fifty-three outpatient prepubertal children with major depressive disorder participated in the drug study, using a double-blind, placebo-controlled design, including the correlation of plasma level of the drug to its observed clinical response and no placebo washout period. Placebo response rate was found to be 68%, and the response to imipramine was 56%. In contrast, a placebo washout period of 2 weeks was included in an inpatient double-blind study by Preskorn, Weller, Hughes, Weller, and Boltek (1987) with imipramine, and by the end of the study, imipramine had only a marginal superiority over placebo.

Puig-Antich et al. (1987) noted that the plasma level of imipramine correlated linearly with clinical response, in contrast with Preskorn et al. (1982) who described an inhibiting effect of the higher plasma levels of imipramine in reducing depression. Ryan et al. (1986) did not observe a relationship between plasma level of imipramine and clinical response in 34 adolescents in an open-label study of depressed outpatient adolescents. Puig-Antich et al. (1987) did not find any relationship between the dose of imipramine and plasma level, whereas other studies have reported a high correlation between the two (Preskorn, Bupp, Weller, & Weller, 1989; Sallee, Stiller, Perel, & Rancurello, 1986).

From the information available on imipramine, no definite conclusions about its effectiveness can be drawn because of high response to placebo.

Amitriptyline. Amitriptyline is a tertiary amine that mostly inhibits the reuptake of serotonin. Nortriptyline is its active metabolite, and it inhibits the reuptake of norepinephrine. Amitriptyline also has strong muscarinic blockade activity. Amitriptyline has not been well studied and there are few well-controlled studies available at this time in addition to the open drug trials described.

Kramer and Feiguine (1981) found mixed results in an amitriptyline versus placebo study with both groups showing improvement but little qualitative difference between the two groups after 6 weeks. Kashani, Shekim, and Reid (1984) in a double-blind crossover design reported a favorable response in 6 of the 9 children being treated with amitriptyline, while two responded to placebo.

Due to the limited research on amitriptyline, the results are inconclusive with regard to its effectiveness. The availability of compounds with fewer side effects has resulted in a waning of interest in this particular compound in the younger age group.

Nortriptyline. Nortriptyline is a secondary amine that inhibits the reuptake of norepinephrine and blocks the reuptake of muscarinic receptors at a low level. As a result, it is less sedating and has lower orthostatic and anticholinergic effects as compared with amitriptyline and imipramine.

Nortriptyline was of particular interest due to its adrenergic mode of action. Geller, Perel, Knitter, Lyacaki, and Farroki (1983) found a significant improvement in 8 out of the 12 participants within 2 to 8 weeks of achieving a therapeutic plasma level of nortriptyline in an open drug trial. A double-blind, placebo-controlled study, using a 2-week placebo washout period and a fixed plasma level design, was reported by Geller et al. (1992). The 50 prepubertal participants met the criteria of Major Depressive Disorder and had not been on any medication for depression in the past. The response rate of 30.8% for nortriptyline and 16.7% for placebo was not statistically significant. No significant difference was found in the mean dose administered to responders versus nonresponders. This study was remarkable for its design, using the fixed plasma level, eliminating the possibility of nonresponse as a result of insufficient dosage or low plasma drug levels. Geller, Cooper, Graham, Marsteller, and Bryant (1990) also studied post-pubertal adolescents in a double-blind, placebo-controlled study, and found such a low rate of response that the study was terminated early.

The preceding well-controlled drug trials indicate that children and adolescents do not have a clear-cut response to tricyclic antidepressants in contrast to adults.

Lithium Augmentation of Tricyclic Antidepressants. Lithium augmentation involves using a low dose of lithium along with tricyclics in patients who have demonstrated poor response to tricyclics alone. Ryan, Meyer, Dachille, Mazzie, and Puig-Antich (1988) used lithium at a level of 0.6 m Eq/L to augment the medication regimen of 14 non-bipolar depressed. Of the sample, 36% showed no improvement, but 43% had marked improvement and 21% had intermediate improvement. The improvement was gradual. Hence, lithium augmentation has had demonstrated some efficacy in the studies reported to date in adolescents and is a useful strategy.

Dosage/Clinical Usage of Tricyclic Antidepressants

The Food and Drug Administration has approved the use of tricyclic antidepressants in children and adolescents over the age of 12 except imipramine, which is approved for children over the age of 6 years for enuresis. Imipramine has been used in the younger age group to treat depression based on the studies described earlier.

The recommended dose of imipramine is up to a maximum of 2.5 mg/kg/day according to the manufacturer's recommendations (*Physicians Desk Reference,* 1995). Imipramine should be started in a dose of 1.5 mg/kg/day, in divided doses and increased in increments of 0.5 to 1 mg/kg/day every 3 to 4 days. Therapeutic drug level monitoring, with the blood draw 10 to 12 hours after the last dose, is done after one week of the initiation of therapy and then following every dose change. Once a steady state level has been obtained, the monitoring can be spaced out to every month and then every 3 months. There is a correlation between the higher dose and the clinical response in prepubertal children, but not between dose and the plasma level (Puig-Antich et al., 1987). After the dose of 5 mg/kg/day or 300 mg/day has been reached, further increases require careful monitoring of side effects, drug level, and response. Adolescents can tolerate a combined single daily dose of imipramine (Ryan et al., 1987).

Prior to initiating therapy, complete blood count including differential, serum electrolytes, thyroid function tests, blood urea nitrogen, liver function tests, urinalysis, and a baseline EKG should be obtained. Repeat EKG after the daily dose has reached 3 mg/kg, and every dose change thereafter.

Nortriptyline is not recommended for the age group under 12 years by the Food and Drug Administration. Nortriptyline should be started in a daily dose of 25 mg/day in children and 50 mg/day in adolescents; plasma drug level should be obtained. The dose should be titrated upward gradually based on the clinical response.

Amitriptyline is used rarely and can be started in a dose of 25 mg/day and titrated upward in increments of 25 mg based on clinical response and drug levels.

It is generally recommended that the drugs in this group be withdrawn gradually rather than abruptly to avoid the effects of gastrointestinal distress, vivid dreams, and initial and middle insomnia with abrupt termination. These characteristics have been attributed to the anticholinergic effects of the tricyclics (Dilsaver & Greden, 1984).

Side Effects of Tricyclic Antidepressants

Tricyclic antidepressants are metabolized much more rapidly by children than by adults and adolescents. They are highly protein bound and have an extensive first-pass metabolism in the liver. They are metabolized by oxidation, aromatic hydroxylation, and demethylation in the liver. Due to the different rates of metabolism, a wide variation in the plasma level may occur in children and adolescents (Preskorn, Weller, Weller, & Glotzbach, 1983; Ryan et al., 1987).

Tricyclic antidepressants are not selective in their action on the various receptors, resulting in a varied side-effect profile. Secondary amines such as nortriptyline and desipramine are better tolerated than tertiary amines such as amitriptyline and imipramine because of their differences in binding affinity for the muscarinic acetylcholine receptors, histamine receptors, and α-adrenergic receptors (Preskorn, 1989).

Sedation is an unpleasant effect that occurs initially and wears off gradually. The sedative side effects could be due to histaminergic, muscarinic, and α1-adrenergic activity. The anticholinergic side effects of this group are dry mouth, difficulty passing urine, sexual dysfunction, dyspepsia, constipation, and an increased risk of developing narrow-angle glaucoma in susceptible individuals. Geller et al. (1992) noted that children did not have complaints of the preceding symptoms as compared with adults. She attributed the difference in response to developmental reasons.

Decreased seizure threshold is a rare but important complication related to the use of tricyclics, and caution should be exercised in the use of tricyclics in susceptible individuals (Jabbari, Bryan, Mars, & Gunderson, 1985).

Long-term use of tricyclics has been associated with hyperphagia and weight gain in adults and can also occur with low doses of the medication (Paykel, Mueller, & De La Vesgne, 1973). The mechanism of the weight gain is not clear but it could be due to the histaminergic effects of the group (Preskorn, 1989).

Another very uncommon side effect is the development of hypomania, which reverses after the discontinuation of the agent. Kashani, Hodges, and Shekim (1980) reported a case of an 11-year-old with depression and maternal history of bipolar depression who developed a hypomanic episode on amitriptyline that improved on tapering the dose.

When using tricyclic antidepressants in the younger age group, the cardiac effects of the drugs need to be closely monitored. Baldessarini (1990) suggested that children can be particularly vulnerable to the cardiotoxic effects of tricyclics by converting tricyclics to their potentially toxic 2-OH metabolites and their increased sensitivity to the same effects. Dugas et al. (1980) recommend divided doses in children in doses above 1 mg/kg/day to minimize the cardiotoxicity of tricyclics. Ryan et al. (1987) suggest that the immaturity of the cardiac system renders it more susceptible to the cardiotoxic effects of tricyclics.

Puig-Antich et al. (1987) noted that practically every child on imipramine presented at least minor EKG changes as compared with baseline. The following guidelines are recommended for termination of therapy: heart rate more than 130 beats/minute, QRS interval more than 30% plus baseline, and PR interval more than 0.21 seconds. In a report by Biederman et al. (1993), echocardiograms and EKG changes were studied along with monitoring of the plasma levels of desipramine. The associated effects on cardiac function were quite benign, and the only association detected was between paired premature atrial contractions and desipramine levels. The reports of sudden death in children taking desipramine demonstrates the need for research in this area (Biederman, 1991; Riddle, Geller, & Ryan, 1993).

Incidences of deliberate or accidental overdose are of grave concern due to these side effects. Fatality results from intractable arrhythmia, asystole, or hypotension. In these cases, cardiovascular support and monitoring are crucial.

Hence, precautions should be taken when using this group of antidepressants. Some of the side effects can be treated symptomatically such as sugar-free candy or gum for dry mouth, stool softeners or increased dietary fiber for constipation, and either decreasing the dose or using bethanechol for urinary hesitancy.

Contraindications to the use of tricyclics are hypersensitivity, cardiac conduction problems, use of monoamine oxidase inhibitors within the previous 2 weeks, and susceptibility to seizures. The last one is a relative contraindication. The combination of monoamine oxidase inhibitors and tricyclics can lead to hyperpyretic crises or severe convulsive seizures. Using antipsychotics with tricyclics can lead to the possibility of anticholinergic toxicity due to the effect on muscarinic receptors of both the drugs. Tricyclics decrease the efficacy of some antihypertensive agents by their affinity for the α-adrenergic receptors. Thus, tricyclics, which are the oldest group of antidepressants available, have numerous side effects that should be considered in their use.

Monoamine Oxidase Inhibitors

Monoamine oxidase inhibitors are compounds that inhibit the enzyme monoamine oxidase. This enzyme is responsible for the breakdown of monoamines, which are important in neurotransmission. Monoamine oxidase enzyme is of two types—A and B. The MAO-A enzyme selectively deaminates serotonin and norepinephrine and MAO-B selectively deaminates benzylamine and phenylethylamine. Tyramine, tryptamine, and dopamine are deaminated by both types of enzymes. Type B is found mainly in the central nervous system while type A is found mainly in the gut. Administration of monoamine oxidase inhibitors leads to the increase in the levels of the monoamines.

The monoamine oxidase inhibitors available at present are irreversible inhibitors of the enzyme. When the treatment ceases, a new enzyme has to be synthesized before the levels of monoamine oxidase return to normal. The half-life of the monoamine oxidase inhibitors is short but the half-life of the inhibition is about 2 weeks because it takes about that long to get the enzyme synthesized.

The monoamine oxidase inhibitors that have been used in the younger age group include clorgyline, which is a selective monoamine oxidase A inhibitor; phenelzine and tranylcypromine, which are mixed monoamine oxidase A and B inhibitors; and L-deprenyl, which is a selective monoamine oxidase B inhibitor. The compounds which are in the process of being developed are now both selective and reversible giving them the advantage of decreased dietary restrictions. Diet is a major factor in the administration and usage of this class of medications in the younger age group.

Effects of Monoamine Oxidase Inhibitors

Drug studies utilizing monoamine oxidase inhibitors are rare in the younger age group and we are not aware of any double-blind, placebo-controlled drug study. Ryan et al. (1988) conducted an open trial of 23 adolescents treated with either monoamine oxidase inhibitors alone or in combination with tricyclic antidepressants. Dietary noncompliance was one of the most significant issues noted with treatment. Known noncompliance with diet occurred in 7 of the 23 participants and the medication had to be discontinued in 5 of the 23 despite adequate response. Some good responders had to be taken off the medication due to dietary problems. In the final analysis, 48% had both a good response and good compliance with the diet, 13% had good response but poor dietary compliance. Thus monoamine oxidase inhibitors have a role to play in some patients who suffer from refractory depression but the importance and ability to follow the diet regimen needs to be considered.

Dosage/Clinical Usage of Monoamine Inhibitors

The Food and Drug Administration has approved isocarboxazid and phenelzine sulfate for use in patients over 16 years of age and the use of tranylcypromine sulfate in adults only. Due to the potentially serious side effects following dietary noncompliance, the use of monoamine inhibitors in routine clinical practice is not recommended in children and adolescents.

Side Effects of Monoamine Inhibitors

In general, monoamine oxidase inhibitors are well tolerated except for the concerns with diet and drug interactions, which can be life threatening. Hypotension is one side effect that occurs in the absence of dietary problems. Regular monitoring of blood pressure until the dose is established is recommended.

Hypertensive crisis occurs after the drugs in this group interact with either tyramine containing foods or sympathomimetic drugs. This is a rare occurrence, but is potentially life threatening. The crisis occurs as a result of inhibition of monoamine oxidase in the gut, liver, and the blood vessels. When exogenous amines in the form of tyramine containing foods or sympathetic amines are ingested, they are not destroyed. Central monoamine stores are also full and hence a hypertensive event can be precipitated. Detailed patient education regarding the possible dietary and medication interactions should be a requirement in every case.

Hyperserotonergic syndrome or central serotonin syndrome has been described when fluoxetine is stopped and monoamine oxidase inhibitors are started without waiting for at least 5 weeks. This syndrome has also been described with the use of tricyclics, clomipramine, dextromorphan, meperidine, and tryptophan. Details of the symptoms and signs of this syndrome are described in the following section, Selective Serotonin Reuptake Inhibitors.

These medications can also result in weight gain. Since they do not affect the cholinergic receptors, constipation, dry mouth, and blurred vision are not associated with their use. Urinary hesitancy occurs due to their adrenergic effects.

Monoamine oxidase inhibitors do not have direct cardiac effects and thus provide a safer alternative to the patients who are unable to take tricyclics due to conduction problems.

Hepatotoxicity has been described with the use monoamine oxidase inhibitors. Bilirubin and serum transaminases are elevated with anorexia, weakness, jaundice, and malaise. This reaction may be initially confused with the worsening of the depressive symptoms if the clinician does not have a high index of suspicion.

Like other antidepressants, monoamine oxidase inhibitors can precipitate hypomanic episode in some individuals. Confusional states have been described. They have also been reported to cause psychotic reactions as in the case of a child being treated for lymphoma with procarbazine (Pfefferbaum, Pack, & Van Eys, 1989).

Thus in general, this group of drugs can be used as a last resort in cases where other regimens have not been effective. Contraindications include liver disease, kidney disease, pheochromocytoma, hypertension, cardiovascular disease, asthma, and chronic bronchitis. Some of the diseases have been listed because they may require the use of sympathomimetic amine to keep the symptoms under adequate control.

Selective Serotonin Reuptake Inhibitors (SSRI)

In the past two decades increasing interest has been generated by the possibility that serotonin neurotransmission is decreased during an episode of depression. Earlier observations that serotonin precursors such as L-tryptophan and 5-hydroxytryptophan had antidepressant effects, whereas norepinephrine precursor and L-dopa did not, were the basis of the search for antidepressants that affected this system. Serotonin receptors have been subtyped and their detailed molecular structure is being determined. The three known families of receptors are $5-HT_1$, $5-HT_2$, and $5-HT_3$. The $5-HT_1$ family is further divided into $5-HT_{1A}$, $5-HT_{1B}$, $5-HT_{1C}$, $5-HT_{1D}$, and 5-HTlike subgroups based on their biochemical and physiological characteristics (Hartig, 1989; Pertouka, 1988; Van, Wijngaarden, Tulp, & Soudijn, 1990). The receptors that have been implicated in the pathophysiology of depression are the 5-HT uptake site and $5-HT_{1A}$ receptor.

Some of the biochemical evidence that links the disturbance of the serotonin system to depression comes from studies in suicide victims and suicide attempters. Decreased concentrations of 5-hydroxyindole acetic acid in the cerebrospinal fluid of patients who attempted to kill themselves was noted to be a consistent finding (Roy, DeJong, & Linnoilla, 1989). Postmortem studies of brains of suicide victims showed a decrease in the brain stem concentrations of 5-hydroxytryptamine and 5-hydroxyindole acetic acid. Increased 5-HT2 receptors was reported in the neocortex of suicide victims (Arora & Meltzer, 1989; Mann, Arango, Mazuk, Theccanat, & Reis, 1989; Stanley, Vergillio, & Gershon, 1982). Since a large number of those who commit suicide suffer from major depressive disorders, there is evidence that dysfunction in the serotonin system would be involved in the pathophysiology of depression.

Selective serotonin reuptake inhibitors have been under investigation for years, and since 1988 three have been released in the United States. The drugs that belong to this class are remarkable because they are chemically unrelated to tricyclics and were developed specifically for their effect on the 5-hydroxytryptamine receptors. Fluoxetine was the first to be released in this country in 1988, followed by sertraline in 1992, and paroxetine in 1993. In adults, these drugs have antidepressant effects comparable to the tricyclic antidepressants and superior to placebo but with lesser side effects.

Effects of Serotonin Reuptake Inhibitors

Because the serotonin reuptake inhibitors have been developed and released for general use only in the past several years, limited data are available regarding their use in children and adolescents. Joshi, Walkup, Capozzoli, Detrinis, and Coyle (1989) reported improvement with fluoxetine in the depressive symptoms of 71.4% of children and adolescents within 6 weeks with few side effects. Simeon, Dinicola, Ferguson, and Copping (1990) conducted a placebo-controlled study of fluoxetine in depression in 13 to 18-year-old outpatients with 31 patients participating, and concluded that the drug effect was indistinguishable from placebo with two-thirds of the adolescents responding in each group. As in the case of tricyclics, the high placebo-response rate has made it difficult to draw any conclusions from these drug studies.

Dosage/Clinical Usage of Serotonin Reuptake Inhibitors

Serotonin reuptake inhibitors are approved for use in adults and older adolescents for depression. Their safety and efficacy in the younger age group has not been established. The dosage for fluoxetine is 5–20 mg per day with monitoring for response over several weeks prior to further dose adjustment. Sertraline can be given in the dosage of 50 mg daily with the amount being adjusted every two weeks. Paroxetine has a starting dose of 20 mg/day and the response can be monitored.

Fluoxetine has an active metabolite norfluoxetine, which results in its longer half-life and the time to reach steady state. The half-life of norfluoxetine varies from 7 to 9 days and the half-life of fluoxetine is 2 to 3 days. The other two medications in this group do not have an active metabolite and hence reach steady state much faster.

Serotonin reuptake inhibitors have a flat dose response curve. Therefore, as the dosage increases, the response does not increase but the side effects go up. This is the rationale behind waiting 2 to 4 weeks prior to changing the dose for fluoxetine and a week for sertraline (Janicak, Davis, Preskorn, & Ayd, 1993).

As a group, these drugs have a wider margin of safety as compared with the tricyclics and the monoamine oxidase inhibitors and hence are recommended in the group at high risk for suicide. These drugs do not affect the histaminergic, muscarinic, and adrenergic receptors to the extent that tricyclics do and have an increased margin of safety and a better side-effect profile.

Because of the safer and more acceptable side-effect profile, these medications may become the first line of choice for depression in the younger age group. At the present time, sertraline may be preferred to fluoxetine and paroxetine due to its lack of effect on the cytochrome P450IID6. The long-term effects of this inhibition are not known, and subsequently it is prudent to choose an antidepressant with minimal side effects and good efficacy.

Side Effects of Serotonin Reuptake Inhibitors

Serotonin reuptake inhibitors lack the serious side effects of the tricyclic antidepressants such as the cardiac conduction delays, induction of seizures, postural hypotension, and the fatality rate in overdose. This gives them an advantage over the tricyclic group. The most frequent side effects of this group include headache, dizziness, nausea, loose stools, somnolence, insomnia, sweating, tremors, dry mouth, anxiety, and restlessness. The infrequent side effects include weight gain, inhibition of ejaculation, and myoclonus. Most of these are dose related and thus can be avoided by increasing the dose slowly. Riddle et al. (1991) have described the behavioral side effects including motor restlessness, sleep disturbance, social disinhibition, or a subjective sensation of excitation, seen in 12 of the 24 children and adolescents, aged 8 to 16 years, who were treated with fluoxetine.

Another concern with fluoxetine has been the reported emergence of self-destructive and suicidal behavior in adults. This aspect of fluoxetine has received extensive coverage in the national and international media and has been frequently presented to the practitioner as a concern by the patients and their guardians. Analysis of the data has indicated that this is not a serious concern despite the initial appearance of case reports in this regard.

Serotonin reuptake inhibitors alter the metabolism of other drugs by affecting liver enzymes, and the extent of this effect varies in individual members of the group. The order of the drugs affecting the liver enzyme systems was paroxetine followed by fluoxetine followed by sertraline (Crewe, Lennard, Tucker, Woods, & Haddock, 1992). The in vitro effect of fluoxetine of inhibiting CYPIID6 raises the plasma concentration of a variety of medications being used concurrently. These include tricyclic antidepressants, bupropion, diazepam, alprazolam, and some antipsychotics. These interactions can result in toxicity. A demonstration of the preceding interactions was shown in a study by Preskorn and Fast (1992). Healthy volunteers were asked to take a combination of either desipramine and fluoxetine or desipramine and sertraline in a double-blind, parallel design. Fluoxetine caused a 350% increase in the concentration of desipramine compared with 30% increase with sertraline. The fluoxetine effect lasted longer than sertraline which resolved in 7 days of discontinuation of the drug. Paroxetine had results similar to fluoxetine in another study (Brosen, Gram, Sindrup, Skjelbo, & Neilsen, 1992).

Special precautions should also be taken when switching from serotonin reuptake inhibitors and fluoxetine to a monoamine oxidase inhibitor. Central serotonin syndrome is a hyperserotonergic reaction, in which there are serious gastrointestinal, neurological, cardiovascular, psychiatric, and autonomic symptoms. The features of this syndrome include bloating, diarrhea, tremors, incoordination, headache, dysarthria, tachycardia, hypotension, hypertension, disorientation, confusion, pressured speech, hypomanic symptoms, hyperthermia, hyperreflexia, cardiovascular collapse, and death. It is advisable to wait for at least 5 weeks after discontinuing fluoxetine before switching to a monoamine oxidase inhibitor. Three deaths have been reported in a switch from fluoxetine to tranylcypromine (Feighner, Boyer, Tyler, & Nebrosky, 1990).

In conclusion, SSRI are a fairly safe group of antidepressants with a reasonable side-effect profile for treatment of mood disorders. The clinician, however needs to be aware of the possible drug interactions.

Lithium Carbonate

The mechanism of action of lithium is not clear but it acts on many neurotransmitter systems. Lithium has been reported to affect the serotonin neurotransmitter system, adrenergic receptors, β-adrenoceptors, α-adrenoceptors, and dopamine receptors. Some of the possible modes of action include reduced catacholamine transmission and an increased transport of sodium across the neuronal membranes, reduced second messenger cyclic adenosyl monophosphate concentrations, and an effect on the levels of the second messengers diacylglycerol and inositol triphosphate by inositol-1-phophatase blocking (Alessi, Naylor, Ghazinddin, & Zubieta, 1994). It has also been known to block the release of thyroid hormone, and this may in part be responsible for its mechanism of action in a susceptible subgroup of patients suffering from Bipolar Disorder when excessive thyroid activity may be precipitating manic episodes.

Effects of Lithium Carbonate

In children and adolescents, lithium has been used for treating Bipolar Disorder and to augment the antidepressant effect of tricyclics in cases of depression not responding or partially responding to tricyclic antidepressants alone.

Since lithium has been available and known to be effective in manic episodes in adults, clinical trials in children and adolescents have been reported. The earlier drug studies are difficult to interpret due to the lack of clarity in the patient selection and the diagnostic criteria being used for Bipolar Disorder. Many case reports describing the effectiveness of lithium carbonate in the offsprings of lithium-responsive parents suffering from Bipolar Disorder have also appeared over the years. Akiskal et al. (1985) describe the effectiveness of lithium in treating tricyclic-induced mania in siblings of manic depressives. They described two cases of a 14- and a 16-year-old with good results.

Brumback and Weinberg (1977) described a clinical trial with lithium in 6 children diagnosed manic by their criteria who responded to lithium at levels over 0.8 mEq/L but 5 out of the 6 suffered from recurrent depression and 3 out of the 6 had to be taken off the medication. Varanka, Weller, Weller, and Fristad (1988) conducted an open trial of lithium carbonate in 10 children, aged 6 to 12 years, and improvement was seen in an average of 11 days. Blood levels ranged from 0.6 to 1.4 mEq/L on a dose of approximately 40 mg/kg/day.

McKnew et al. (1981) studied 6 children, aged 6 through 12 years, whose parents were lithium responders. They used a double-blind, crossover design and found 2 children responded to lithium. Unlike the nonresponders, these 2 subjects had clear-cut symptoms suggestive of cyclothymia.

Lithium is also effective in prophylaxis or maintenance of Bipolar Disorder. Strober, Morrell, Lampert, and Burroughs (1990) reported that rate of relapse in noncompleters in an 18-month trial was three times that in completers of the study.

Dosage/Clinical Usage of Lithium Carbonate

Lithium should be started in a dose of 600 mg/day in divided doses and titrated up gradually monitoring the response, side effects, and therapeutic level. The same dose of lithium can produce widely different serum levels due to individual variations. The therapeutic level varies between 0.6 to 1.2 mEq/L. The half-life of lithium is shorter in children, and the renal clearance of lithium is greater than that of adults (Vitiello et al., 1988).

Prior to initiating therapy a complete blood count, serum electrolytes, pregnancy test, serum creatinine, urinalysis, thyroid function tests, and EKG should be obtained to establish a baseline. Lithium level should be checked twice weekly followed by weekly monitoring until a safe steady-state level has been reached. Then the level can be monitored monthly for 3 months followed by a level check every 3 months. Renal status, thyroid function, EKG, and height and weight measurements should be recorded at quarterly intervals along with serum chemistry. This regimen would help in monitoring for side effects.

Monitoring the level of lithium in saliva has been proposed as an alternative to blood level due to the younger age groups' difficulty with venipuncture. However, serum levels continue to be the technique of choice due to the lack of consistent parameters and the reported variability in the ratios of the level of lithium in saliva and blood (Vitiello et al., 1988).

Side Effects of Lithium Carbonate

Lithium use in children results in side effects similar to those seen in adults. Mild tremors, metallic taste, transient gastrointestinal symptoms, polyuria, and polydypsia have been reported (Campbell, Perry, & Green, 1984). Weight gain has been noted, but the etiology is unclear. Nausea and malaise are common complaints. In the child and adolescent age group, side effects were milder than those reported in adults (Siassi, 1982; Varanka et al., 1988).

Lithium toxicity can be precipitated after the onset of dehydration, and hence parents and the patients both should be instructed to stop lithium intake in the case of gastrointestinal upset. Khandelwal, Varma, and Murthy (1984) studied four children and adolescents for effects of lithium on renal functioning and no effects were noted after 3 to 4 years.

Lithium has some antithyroid effects that may result in complaints of tiredness. Hair loss, dry or rough hair, and hoarseness are other common signs.

A concern that lithium may affect the bone growth in children and adolescents remains unresolved because there are no radiological studies of bone development in children receiving lithium.

Intake of nonsteroidal antiinflammatory agents that are available over the counter and are used commonly by female adolescents could lead to an increased level of lithium in the blood. This is due to the interference in renal excretion of lithium by these agents (Jefferson, Greist, & Baudhiun, 1981).

There are no reported interactions between illegal drugs and lithium that would limit the dose of lithium (Jefferson et al., 1981).

In pregnancy, the clearance of lithium increases and drops abruptly after childbirth. A 50% dose reduction in the dosage is required a week or more prior to delivery to avoid postpartum toxicity in mother and in the neonate who has a much lower rate of renal clearance of lithium. Lithium has been reported to have a teratogenic effect, and it crosses the placenta. Congenital cardiovascular malformations such as right-sided heart damage and malformations and Ebstein's anomaly have been reported. It can be toxic to the neonates and may result in weak cry, poor sucking capacity, hypotonia, lethargy, weakness, cyanosis, hypothermia, and EKG changes. Some infants may present with goiter. Because lithium is present in breast milk in high concentrations, breast feeding should be discouraged.

Anticonvulsants

Anticonvulsants have been used in recent years to treat Bipolar Disorder as an alternative to lithium. The rationale behind this increased use could be the kindling hypothesis, which has been proposed for both mania and Bipolar Disorder. However, other mechanisms of actions cannot be ruled out (Post, 1988). The anticonvulsants used are carbamazepine, valproic acid, and clonazepam.

Carbamazepine is related structurally to tricyclic antidepressants, and this similarity may be related to its effectiveness. Valproic acid is similar to fatty acids and clonazepam is a member of the benzodiazepine subgroup.

Effects of Anticonvulsants

Open and double-blind studies in the adult population have demonstrated the efficacy of carbamazepine in prophylaxis and treating manic episodes in patients where lithium has not been effective (Ballenger & Post, 1978; Post & Uhde, 1985). For treating Bipolar Disorder, we are not aware of any controlled studies demonstrating efficacy in the younger population. Valproic acid has been used in adults with Bipolar Disorder, but controlled studies in adolescents with Bipolar Disorder are lacking. Based on experience with adult populations, clinicians can use anticonvulsants in the adolescent population in similar conditions. One reason for the lack of controlled studies in this area could be the difficulty encountering enough children and adolescents with Bipolar Disorder to make the study possible. In the case of epilepsy, there is a demonstrated relationship between efficacy and response, but this has not been demonstrated in psychiatric disorders in children and adolescents.

Dosage/Clinical Usage of Anticonvulsants

Anticonvulsants have a shorter half-life and higher renal clearance in the younger age group than they do in adults. As a result, the mg/kg dose requirement is higher in this group than in adults (Trimble, 1990). The initial dose of valproic acid is about 15 mg/kg/day and can be increased to 30–60 mg/kg/day. Side effects and tolerance determine the final dose. Carbamazepine is given in a dose of up to 10–50 mg/kg/day and the therapeutic blood level should be within the range of 4–12 μg/ml. Clonazepam is used in a starting dose of 0.01–0.03 mg/kg/day, and the maintenance dose is 0.1–0.2 mg/kg/day.

The Food and Drug Administration guidelines state that carbamazepine should be used for ages more than 6 years. The dose limit recommended is 1000 mg/day by age 15 years and 1200 mg/day after that. Bipolar Disorder is not one of the indications mentioned in the guidelines. There is no age guideline for valproic acid, but the dose is limited to 60 mg/kg/day and it is approved for seizures. Carbamazepine has linear kinetics resulting in a predictable rise in blood level with the increase in dose, and hence drug-monitoring frequency can safely be performed every 3 months once steady state has been achieved.

Carbamazepine induces its own enzymatic metabolism. This autoinduction starts when the treatment is initiated and continues for about 6 weeks leading to up to a 50% decrease in the serum levels. Monitoring closely and readjusting the dose in the first 2 months can help in drug therapy (Levy & Pitlick, 1982). Carbamazepine induces the liver enzymes and increases the metabolism of many drugs (Trimble, 1990).

Valproic acid has a shorter half-life and a longer duration of action leading to a prolonged effect even when the drug has cleared the blood. It is mostly cleared from the kidneys (Trimble, 1990).

To minimize the adverse effects, the strategy used is to start treatment at a low dose and increase it gradually. Education regarding side effects helps in the early reporting of such effects. Involvement of the family in the treatment process assists in closer monitoring of the symptoms as they develop.

Side Effects of Anticonvulsants

Anticonvulsants have a well-defined, side-effect profile with variations from drug to drug because the medications in this group are structurally variable. Carbamazepine adverse effects will be described followed by the side effects of valproic acid and clonazepam.

The common side effects of carbamazepine are drowsiness, light-headedness, clumsiness, and mild nausea at the beginning of the treatment, but these wear off as time progresses. Blurred vision, nystagmus, and leukopaenia are other frequently occurring side effects. Rare but serious side effects are agranulocytosis and aplastic anemia, antidiuretic effect, severe skin rashes, hepatotoxicity, and aggravation of psychosis. Carbamazepine also reportedly aggravates anxiety, agitation, and impulsive behavior in some patients as well as neurotoxicity and hypocalcaemia (Trimble, 1990).

Carbamazepine should not be used in known cases of hypersensitivity to tricyclics or bone marrow depression. Renal disease and liver dysfunction are relative contraindications to therapy with carbamazepine and valproic acid.

The common side effects of valproic acid are nausea, vomiting and gastrointestinal upset, sedation, weight gain, and tremors. Its serious side effects include neutropenia, thrombocytopenia, chemical hepatitis, liver failure, and possible fatal hepatotoxicity especially in children younger than 3 years. Hair loss and stupor have been reported as well (Trimble, 1990).

The common side effects of clonazepam are sedation, drowsiness, confusion, ataxia, muscle weakness, palpitations, and transient liver function test elevations. Elevated liver function tests return to the normal range with prolonged treatment.

Valproic acid and carbamazepine levels can be increased by drugs like tricyclic antidepressants, phenothiazine antipsychotics, methylphenidate, cimetidine, and macrolide antibiotics (e.g., erythromycin). Clonazepam has additive central nervous system effects with tricyclic antidepressants, alcohol, and barbiturates.

Electroconvulsive Therapy

Electroconvulsive therapy was used much more frequently in the younger population in the past. Multiple case reports have appeared in the literature on patients who received electroconvulsive therapy and improved. Most of them had affective disorders (Berman & Wolport, 1987; Black, Wilcox, & Stewart, 1985; Campbell, 1952; Carr, Dorrington, Schader, & Wale, 1983; Hassanyeh, 1980; Mansheim, 1983; Warneke, 1975). Other reports questioned the effectiveness of ECT. Guttmacher and Cretella (1988) reported two cases of depression treated with ECT and only one improved. One case of schizophrenia and one of Tourette's failed to show any improvement.

Reports about effectiveness in schizophrenia, autism, and anorexia nervosa are variable and need further clarification because the number of case reports is limited (Bertagnoli & Borchardt, 1990). After the other modes of treatment have been explored and found to be ineffective, then one can consider ECT in treatment-resistant cases of mood disorders.

PROGNOSIS

In view of the reported association of suicidal thoughts with depression, the long-term outcome and natural history of mood disorders gain importance. In Bipolar Disorder, long-term morbidity is a concern in terms of its early onset. Carlson et al. (1977) reported that 60% of the adolescents with Bipolar Disorder had favorable social functioning on a 20-year follow-up. McGlashen (1988) divided his patients into early and late onset bipolar and noted more psychiatric problems in the early onset group even though they had better social interactions. Rates of hospitalization and suicide remained the same.

McGee and Williams (1988) followed 121 children from a New Zealand cohort who were diagnosed at age 9 with current depression, past depression, and no depression. At ages 11 and 13, the currently depressed group had more behavioral and emotional problems compared with other groups. Almost one-third of the currently depressed group continued to be depressed at the time of follow-up.

In a 5-year longitudinal study of depressed children and their families, Kovacs, Feinberg, Crouse-Novak, Paulauskas, and Finkelstein (1984a) examined the characteristics and diagnostic validity of Major Depressive Disorder (MDD), Dysthymic Disorder (DD), and Adjustment Disorder with Depressed Mood (ADDM). The study included a population of 65 children, aged 8 to 13 years at initial diagnosis, who were evaluated using semistructured interviews. All met DSM-III diagnostic criteria for a depressive disorder. A companion group of 49 children were psychiatric outpatients whose research diagnoses were not depressive disorders. Differences were noted for MDD, DD, and ADDM children for age of onset and pattern of recovery variables.

For MDD and DD children, earlier age of onset denoted a more lengthy recovery period, whereas the children with a later age of onset appeared to recover more rapidly. However, for ADDM, age of onset was not related to the time of recovery. Earliest overall age of onset occurred among the DD children. Time of recovery from the onset of depression was shortest for ADDM children with an average recovery period of 25 weeks with 90% remission rate within 9 months. For the children with the diagnosis of MDD, the recovery average was about 32 weeks. For DD children, average recovery time was about 3 years, with an 89% remission rate during 6 years.

Thus, in the case of Bipolar Disorder, prognosis is related to the age of onset and preexisting psychopathology. Outcome reports have varied with favorable results in 15% to 60% of cases studied. Strober et al. (1990) reported decreased relapse rates in the adolescents who continued to be maintained on lithium. On the other hand, in the case of depressive disorders, the recovery is longest for dysthymia and the shortest for adjustment disorders. Hence, the clinician may consider intervention early in dysthymia in an attempt to shorten the period of the disturbance.

REFERENCES

Akiskal, H. S., Down, J., Jordan, P., Watson, J., Daugherty, D., & Pruitt, D. K. (1985). Affective disorders in referred children and younger siblings of manic-depressives. *Archives of General Psychiatry, 42,* 996–1009.

Alessi, N., Naylor, M. W., Ghaziuddin, M., & Zubieta, J. K. (1994). Update on lithium carbonate therapy in children and adolescents. *Journal of the American Academy of Child and Adolescent Psychiatry, 33,* 291–304.

American Psychiatric Association. (1952). *Diagnostic and statistical manual of mental disorders* (1st ed.). Washington, DC: American Psychiatric Association.

American Psychiatric Association. (1968). *Diagnostic and statistical manual of mental disorders* (2nd ed.). Washington, DC: American Psychiatric Association.

American Psychiatric Association. (1980). *Diagnostic and statistical manual of mental disorders* (3rd ed.). Washington, DC: American Psychiatric Association.

American Psychiatric Association. (1987). *Diagnostic and statistical manual of mental disorders* (3rd ed. rev.). Washington, DC: American Psychiatric Association.

American Psychiatric Association. (1994). *Diagnostic and statistical manual of mental disorders* (4th ed.). Washington, DC: American Psychiatric Association.

Anthony, E. J., & Scott, P. (1960). Manic depressive psychosis in childhood. *Journal of Child Psychology and Psychiatry, 1,* 53–72.

Arora, R. C., & Meltzer, H. Y. (1989). Serotonergic measures of the brains of suicide victims: 5-HT2 binding sites in the frontal cortex of suicide victims and controls. *American Journal of Psychiatry, 146,* 730–736.

Baldessarini, R. J. (1990). Drugs and the treatment of psychiatric disorders. In A. F. Gilman, T. W. Rall, A. S. Neis, & P. Taylor (Eds.), *Goodman and Gilman's The pharmacological basis of therapeutics* (8th ed.) (pp. 383–435). New York: Pergamon.

Ballenger, J. C., & Post, R. M. (1978). Therapeutic effects of carbamezapine in affective illness: A preliminary report. *Communications in Psychopharmacology, 2,* 159–175.

Ballenger, J. C., Reus, V. I., & Post, R. M. (1982). The "atypical" picture of adolescent mania. *American Journal of Psychiatry, 139,* 602–606.

Baron, P., & Perron, L. M. (1986). Sex differences in Beck Depression Inventory Scores of adolescents. *Journal of Youth and Adolescence, 15,* 165–171.

Berman, E., & Wolport, E. (1987). Intractable manic-depressive psychosis with rapid cycling in 18-year-old woman successfully treated with ECT. *Journal of Nervous and Mental Diseases, 175,* 236–239.

Bertagnoli, M. W., & Borchardt, L. M. (1990). A review of ECT for children and adolescents. *Journal of the American Academy of Children and Adolescents, 29,* 302.

Biederman, J. (1991). Sudden death in children treated with a tricyclic antidepressant. *Journal of the American Academy of Child and Adolescent Psychiatry, 30,* 495–498.

Biederman, J., Baldessarini, R. J., Goldblatt, A., Lapey, K. A., Doyle, A., & Hesslein, P. S. (1993). A naturalistic study of 24-hour electrocardiographic recordings and echocardiographic findings in children and adolescents treated with desipramine. *Journal of the American Academy of Child and Adolescent Psychiatry, 32,* 805–813.

Black, D. W., Wilcox, J. A., & Stewart, M. (1985). The use of ECT in children: Case report. *Journal of Clinical Psychiatry, 46,* 98–99.

Bowden, C. L., & Sarabia, F. (1980). Diagnosing manic-depressive illness in adolescents. *Comprehensive Psychiatry, 21,* 263–269.

Bowring, M. A., & Kovacs, M. (1992). Difficulties in diagnosing manic disorders among children and adolescents. *Journal of the American Academy of Child and Adolescent Psychiatry, 31,* 611–614.

Brosen, K., Gram, L., Sindrup, S., Skjelbo, E., & Neilsen, K. (1992). Pharmacogenetics of tricyclic antidepressants and novel antidepressants: Recent developments. *Clinical Neuropharmacology, 15*(Suppl.), 80A–81A.

Brumback, R. A., & Weinberg, W. A. (1977). Mania in childhood. II. Therapeutic trial of 1 lithium carbonate and further description of manic-depressive illness in children. *American Journal of Diseases of the Child, 131,* 1122–1126.

Bunney, W. E., Jr., & Davis, J. M. (1965). Norepinephrine in depressive reactions: A review. *Archives of General Psychiatry, 13,* 483–494.

Campbell, J. D. (1952). Manic-depressive psychosis in children—report of 18 cases. *Journal of Nervous and Mental Diseases, 116,* 424–439.

Campbell, M., Perry, R., & Green, W. H. (1984). Use of lithium in children and adolescents. *Psychosomatics, 25,* 95–106.

Carlson, G. A., Davenport, Y. B., & Jamison, K. (1977). A comparison of outcome in adolescent and late-onset bipolar manic-depressive illness. *American Journal of Psychiatry, 134,* 919–922.

Carlson, G. A., & Kashani, J. H. (1988). Manic symptoms in a non-referred adolescent population. *Journal of Affective Disorders, 15,* 219–226.

Carr, V., Dorrington, C., Schader, G., & Wale, J. (1983). The use of ECT in Bipolar Disorder. *British Journal of Psychiatry, 143,* 411–415.

Coll, P. G., & Bland, R. (1979). Manic depressive illness in adolescents and childhood. *Canadian Journal of Psychiatry, 24,* 255–263.

Connelly, B., Johnston, D., Brown, I. D. R., Mackay, S., & Blackstock, E. G. (1993). The prevalence of depression in a High School Population. *Adolescence, 28,* 149–158.

Coppen, A. (1967). The biochemistry of affective disorders. *British Journal of Psychiatry, 113,* 1237–1264.

Crewe, H. K., Lennard, M. S., Tucker, G. T., Woods, F. R., & Haddock, R. E. (1992). The effect of select reuptake inhibitors on cytochrome P450IID6 (CYP2D6) activity in human liver microsomes. *British Journal of Clinical Pharmacology, 34,* 262–265.

Dilsaver, S. C., & Greden, J. F. (1984). Antidepressant withdrawal phenomena. *Biological Psychiatry, 19,* 237–256.

Dugas, M., Zarifian, E., Leheuzey, M-F., Rovei, V., Durand, G., & Morselli, P. L. (1980). Preliminary observations of the significance of monitoring tricyclic antidepressant plasma levels in the paediatric patient. *Therapeutic Drug Monitoring, 2,* 307–314.

Feighner, J. P., Boyer, W. F., Tyler, D. L., & Nebrosky, R. J. (1990). Adverse consequences of fluoxetine-MAOI combination therapy. *Journal of Clinical Psychiatry, 51,* 222–225.

Frommer, E. A. (1967). Treatment of childhood depression with antidepressant drugs. *British Medical Journal, 1,* 729–732.

Geller, B., Chestnut, E. C., Miller, M. D., Price, D. T., & Yates, E. (1985). Preliminary data on DSM-III associated features of major depressive disorder in children and adolescents. *American Journal of Psychiatry, 142,* 643–644.

Geller, B., Cooper, T. B., Graham, D. L., Fetner, H. H., Marsteller, F. A., & Wells, J. M. (1992). Pharmacokinetically designed double-blind placebo-controlled study of nortriptyline in 6- to 12-year olds with major depressive disorder. *Journal of the American Academy of Child and Adolescent Psychiatry, 31,* 34–44.

Geller, B., Cooper, T. B., Graham, D. L., Marstellar, F. A., & Bryant, D. M. (1990). Double-blind placebo-controlled study of nortriptyline in depressed adolescents using a "fixed plasma level" design. *Psychopharmacology Bulletin, 26,* 85–90.

Geller, B., Perel, J. M., Knitter, E. F., Lyacaki, H., & Farroki, Z. Q. (1983). Nortriptyline in major depressive disorder in children: Response steady-state plasma levels, predictive kinetics, and pharmacokinetics. *Psychopharmacology Bulletin, 19,* 62–65.

Guttmacher, L. B., & Cretella, H. (1988). Electroconvulsive therapy in one child and three adolescents. *Journal of Clinical Psychiatry, 49,* 20–22.

Hartig, P. R. (1989). Molecular biology of 5-HT receptors. *Trends in Pharmacological Science, 10,* 64–69.

Hassanyeh, F. (1980). Bipolar affective psychosis with onset before age 16. *British Journal of Psychiatry, 137,* 530–539.

Jabbari, B., Bryan, G., Mars, L. E. E., & Gunderson, C. H. (1985). Incidence of seizures with tricyclic and tetracyclic antidepressants. *Archives of Neurology, 42,* 480–481.

Janicak, P. J., Davis, J. M., Preskorn, S. H., & Ayd, F. J., Jr. (1993). Treatment with antidepressants. In *Principles and Practice of Psychopharmacotherapy* (pp. 209–292). Baltimore: Williams and Wilkins.

Jefferson, J. W., Greist, J. H., & Baudhiun, M. (1981). Lithium interactions with other drugs. *Journal of Clinical Psychopharmacology, 1,* 124–134.

Joshi, P. T., Walkup, J. T., Capozzoli, J. A., Detrinis, R. B., & Coyle, J. T. (1989, October 11–15). *The use of fluoxetine in the treatment of major depressive disorder in children and adolescents.* Paper presented at the 36th Annual Meeting of the American Academy of Child and Adolescent Psychiatry, New York.

Kashani, J. H., Beck, N. C., Hoeper, E. W., Fallahi, C., Corcoran, C. M., McAllister, J. A., Rosenberg, T. K., & Reid, J. C. (1987). Psychiatric disorders in a community sample of adolescents. *American Journal of Psychiatry, 144,* 584–589.

Kashani, J. H., & Carlson, G. A. (1987). Seriously depressed preschoolers. *American Journal of Psychiatry, 144,* 348–350.

Kashani, J. H., Carlson, G. A., Beck, N. C., Hoeper, E. W., Corcoran, C. M., McAllister, J. A., Fallahi, C., Rosenberg, T. K., & Reid, J. C. (1987). Depression, depressive symptoms and depressed mood among a community of adolescents. *American Journal of Psychiatry, 144,* 931–934.

Kashani, J. H., Hodges, K. K., & Shekim, W. O. (1980). Hypomanic reaction to amitriptyline in a depressed child. *Psychosomatics, 21,* 867–868.

Kashani, J. H., Holcomb, W. R., & Orvaschel, H. (1986). Depression and depressive symptomatology in preschool children from the general population. *American Journal of Psychiatry, 143,* 1138–1143.

Kashani, J. H., Keller, M. B., Solomon, N., Reid, J. C., Mazzola, D. (1985). Double depression in adolescent substance users. *Journal of Affective Disorders, 8,* 153–157.

Kashani, J. H., McGee, R. O., Clarkson, S. E., Anderson, J. C., Walton, L. A., Williams, S., Silva, P. A., Robins, A. J., Cytryn, L., & McKnew, D. H. (1983). Depression in a sample of 9-year-old children prevalance and associated characteristics. *Archives of General Psychiatry, 40,* 1217–1223.

Kashani, J. H., & Ray, J. S. (1983). Depressive symptoms among preschool-age children. *Child Psychiatry and Human Development, 13,* 233–238.

Kashani, J. H., Ray, J. S., & Carlson, G. A. (1984). Depression and depression like states in preschool-age children in a child development unit. *American Journal of Psychiatry, 141,* 1397–1402.

Kashani, J. H., Shekim, W. O., & Reid, J. C. (1984). Amitriptyline in children with major depressive disorder: A double-blind crossover pilot study. *Journal of the American Academy of Child Psychiatry, 23,* 348–351.

Kashani, J., & Simmonds, J. F. (1979). The incidence of depression in children. *American Journal of Psychiatry, 136,* 1203–1205.

Khandelwal, S. K., Varma, V. K., & Murthy, R. S. (1984). Renal function in children receiving long-term lithium prophylaxis. *American Journal of Psychiatry, 141,* 278–279.

Kovacs, M., Feinberg, T. L., Crouse-Novak, M. A., Paulauskas, S. L., & Finkelstein, R. (1984a). Depressive disorders in childhood. I. A longitudinal prospective study of characteristics and recovery. *Archives of General Psychiatry, 41,* 229–237.

Kovacs, M., Feinberg, T. L., Crouse-Novak, M. A., Paulauskas, S. L., & Finkelstein, R. (1984b). Depressive disorders in childhood. II. A longitudinal study of the risk for a subsequent major depression. *Archives of General Psychiatry, 41,* 643–649.

Kovacs, M., & Gastonis, C. (1989). Stability and change in childhood onset depressive disorders: Longitudinal course in a diagnostic validator. In L. N. Robins & J. E. Barrett (Eds.), *The validity of psychiatric diagnosis* (pp. 57–76). New York: Raven.

Kramer, A. D., & Feiguine, R. J. (1981). Clinical effects of amitriptyline in adolescent depression: A pilot study. *Journal of the American Academy of Child Psychiatry, 20,* 636–644.

Lapin, I. P., & Oxenkrug, G. F. (1969). Intensification of central serotonergic processes as a possible determinant of the thermoleptic effect. *Lancet, 1,* 132–136.

Levy, R., & Pitlick, W. H. (1982). Carbamazepine: Interactions with other drugs. In D. M. Woodbury, J. K. Penry, & C. E. Pippenger (Eds.), *Antiepileptic drugs* (pp. 497–505). New York: Raven.

Mahler, M. G. (1961). On sadness and grief in infancy and childhood: Loss and restoration of symbiotic love object. *Psychoanalytic Study Child, 16,* 332–351.

Mann, J. J., Arango, V., Mazuk, M. P., Theccanat, S., & Reis, D. J. (1989). Evidence for the 5-HT hypothesis of suicide: A review of the post-mortem studies. *British Journal of Psychiatry, 155*(Suppl. 8), 7–14.

Mansheim, P. (1983). ECT in the treatment of depressed adolescent with meningomyelocele hydrocephalus and seizures. *Journal of Clinical Psychiatry, 44,* 386.

McGee, R., & Williams, S. (1988). A longitudinal study of depression in nine year old children. *Journal of the American Academy of Child and Adolescent Psychiatry, 27,* 342–348.

McGlashen, T. H. (1988). Adolescent versus adult onset mania. *American Journal of Psychiatry, 145,* 221–224.

McKnew, D. H., Cytryn, L., Buchsbaum, M. S., Hamovit, J., Lamour, M., Rapoport, J. L., & Gershon, E. S. (1981). Lithium in children of lithium-responding parents. *Psychiatry Research, 4,* 171–180.

Paykel, E. S., Mueller, P. S., & De La Vesgne, P. M. (1973). Amitriptyline, weight gain and carbohydrate craving: A side effect. *British Journal of Psychiatry, 123,* 501–507.

Pertouka, S. (1988). 5-hydroxytryptamine receptors subtypes. Molecular, biochemical, and physiological characterization. *Trends in Neuroscience, 11,* 496–500.

Petti, T. A., & Conners, C. K. (1983). Changes in behavioral ratings of depressed children treated with imipramine. *Journal of the American Academy of Child Psychiatry, 22,* 355–360.

Petti, T. A., & Law, W. (1982). Imipramine treatment of depressed children: A double blind pilot study. *Journal of Clinical Psychopharmacology, 2,* 107–110.

Pfefferbaum, B., Pack, R., & Van Eys, J. (1989). Monoamine oxidase inhibitor toxicity. *Journal of the American Academy of Child and Adolescent Psychiatry, 28,* 954–955.

Physicians' desk reference (49 ed.). Oradell, NJ: Medical Economics Co.

Post, R. M. (1988). Effectiveness of carbamazepine in the treatment of bipolar affective disorder. In S. L. McElroy & H. G. Pope, Jr. (Eds.), *Use of anticonvulsants in psychiatry: Recent advances,* (pp. 1–24). Clifton, NJ: Oxford Health Care.

Post, R. M., & Uhde, T. W. (1985). Carbamazepine in bipolar illness. *Psychopharmacology Bulletin, 21,* 10–17.

Preskorn, S. (1989). Tricyclic antidepressants: The whys and hows of therapeutic drug monitoring. *Journal of Clinical Psychiatry, 50,* 34–42.

Preskorn, S. H., Bupp, S. J., Weller, E. B., & Weller, R. A. (1989). Plasma levels of imipramine and metabolites in 68 hospitalized children. *Journal of the American Academy of Child and Adolescent Psychiatry, 28,* 373–375.

Preskorn, S. H., Weller, E. B., Hughes, C. W., Weller, R. A., Boltek, K. (1987). Depression in prepubertal children: Dexamethasone nonsuppression predicts differential response in imipramine versus placebo. *Psychopharmacology Bulletin, 23,* 128–133.

Preskorn, S. H., Weller, E. B., & Weller, R. A. (1982). Depression in children: Relationship between plasma imipramine levels and response. *Journal of Clinical Psychiatry, 43,* 450–453.

Preskorn, S. H., Weller, E. B., Weller, R. A., & Glotzbach, E. (1983). Plasma levels of imipramine and adverse effects in children. *American Journal of Psychiatry, 140,* 1332–1335.

Puig-Antich, J., Blau, S., Marx, N., Greenhill, L. L., & Chambers, W. J. (1978). Prepubertal major depressive disorder: A pilot study. *Journal of the American Academy of Child and Adolescent Psychiatry, 17,* 695–707.

Puig-Antich, J., Perel, J. M., Lupatkin, W., Chambers, W. J., Shea, C., Tabrizi, M. A., & Stiller, R. L. (1979). Plasma levels of imipramine (IMI) and desmethylimipramine (DMI) and clinical response in prepubertal major depressive disorder: A preliminary report. *Journal of the American Academy of Child and Adolescent Psychiatry, 18,* 616–627.

Puig-Antich, J., Perel, J. M., Lupatkin, W., Chambers, W. J., Tabrizi, M. A., King, J., Goetz, R., Davies, M., & Stiller, R. L. (1987). Imipramine in prepubertal major depressive disorders. *Archives of General Psychiatry, 44,* 81–89.

Riddle, M. A., Geller, B., & Ryan, N. (1993). Another sudden death in a child treated with desipramine. *Journal of the American Academy of Child and Adolescent Psychiatry, 32,* 792–797.

Riddle, M. A., King, R. A., Hardin, M. T., Scahill, L., Ort, S. I., Chappell, P. B., Rasmusson, A. M., & Leckman, J. F. (1991). Behavioral side effects of fluoxetine in children and adolescents. *Journal of Child and Adolescent Psychopharmacology, 1,* 193–198.

Robins, L. N., Helzer, J. E., & Weissman, M. M. (1984). Lifetime prevalence of specific psychiatric disorders at three sites. *Archives of General Psychiatry, 41,* 949–958.

Roy, A., DeJong, J., & Linnoilla, M. (1989). Cerebral spinal fluid monoamine metabolites and suicidal behavior in depressed patients. *Archives of General Psychiatry, 46,* 609–612.

Rutter, M. (1986). Developmental psychopathology of depression: Issues and perspectives. In M. Rutter, C. E. Izard, & P. B. Read (Eds.), *Depression in young people: Developmental and clinical perspectives* (pp. 3–30). New York: Guilford.

Ryan, N. D., Meyer, V., Dachille, S., Mazzie, D., & Puig-Antich, J. (1988). Lithium antidepressant augmentation in TCA-refractory depression in adolescents. *Journal of the American Academy of Child and Adolescent Psychiatry, 27,* 371–376.

Ryan, N. D., Puig-Antich, J., Cooper, T. B., Rabinovich, H., Ambrosini, P., Davies, M., King, J., Torres, D., & Fried, J. (1986). Imipramine in adolescent major depression: Plasma level and clinical response. *Acta Psychiatrica Scandinavia, 73,* 275–288.

Ryan, N. D., Puig-Antich, J., Cooper, T. B., Rabinovich, H., Ambrosini, P., Fried, J., Davies, M., Torres, D., & Suckow, R. F. (1987). Relative safety of single versus divided dose imipramine in adolescent major depression. *Journal of the American Academy of Child and Adolescent Psychiatry, 26,* 400–406.

Ryan, N. D., Puig-Antich, J., & Rabinovich, H. (1988). MAOIs in adolescent major depression unresponsive to tricyclic antidepressants. *Journal of the American Academy of Child and Adolescent Psychiatry, 27,* 755–758.

Sallee, F., Stiller, R., Perel, J., & Rancurello, M. (1986). Targeting imipramine dose in children with depression. *Clinical Pharmacology and Therapy, 40,* 8–13.

Schildkraut, J. J. (1965). The catacholamine hypothesis of affective disorders: A review of supporting evidence. *American Journal of Psychiatry, 122,* 509–522.

Siassi, I. (1982). Lithium treatment of impulsive behavior in children. *Journal of Clinical Psychiatry, 43,* 482–484.

Simeon, J. C., Dinicola, V. F., Ferguson, H. B., & Copping, W. (1990). Adolescent depression: A placebo-controlled fluoxetine treatment study and follow-up. *Progress in Neuropsychopharmacology & Biological Psychiatry, 14,* 791–795.

Stanley, M., Vergillio, J., & Gershon, S. (1982). Tritiated imipramine binding sites are decreased in the frontal cortex of suicides. *Science, 216,* 1337–1339.

Strober, M., Morrell, W., Lampert, C., & Burroughs, J. (1990). Relapse following discontinuation of lithium maintenance therapy in adolescents with bipolar illness: A naturalistic study. *American Journal of Psychiatry, 147,* 457–461.

Sullivan, W. O., & Engin, A. W. (1986). Adolescent depression: Its prevalence in High School students. *Journal of School Psychology, 24,* 103–109.

Teri, L. (1982). The use of Beck Depression Inventory with adolescents. *Journal of Abnormal Child Psychology, 10,* 277–284.

Trimble, M. R. (1990). Anticonvulsants in children and adolescents. *Journal of Child and Adolescent Psychopharmacology, 2,* 107–124.

Van, V., Wijngaarden, I., Tulp, M., & Soudijn, W. (1990). The concept of selectivity in 5-HT receptor research. *European Journal of Pharmacology, 188,* 301–312.

Varanka, T. M., Weller, R. A., Weller, E. B., & Fristad, M. A. (1988). Lithium treatment of manic episodes with psychotic features in prepubertal children. *American Journal of Psychiatry, 145,* 1557–1559.

Vitiello, B., Behar, D., Malone, R., Delaney, M. A., Ryan, P. J., & Simpson, E. M. (1988). Pharmacokinetics of lithium carbonate in children. *Journal of Clinical Psychopharmacology, 8,* 355–359.

Warneke, L. (1975). A case of manic-depressive illness in childhood. *Canadian Journal of Psychiatry, 20,* 195–200.

Weller, R. A., Weller, E. B., Tucker, S. G., & Fristad, M. A. (1986). Mania in prepubertal children: Has it been underdiagnosed? *Journal of Affective Disorders, 11,* 151–154.

Attention-Deficit/ Hyperactivity Disorder

JUDITH L. RAPOPORT, M.D. and
F. XAVIER CASTELLANOS, M.D.

Please address correspondence to Dr. Castellanos. Mailing address for both authors: Child Psychiatry Branch, NIMH, Bldg 10, Room 6N240, 10 CENTER DR MSC 1600, BETHESDA MD 20892-1600.

DEFINITION

Attention-Deficit/Hyperactivity Disorder (ADHD) in *Diagnostic and Statistical Manual of Mental Disorders* (DSM-IV; American Psychiatric Association [APA], 1994), as in DSM-III-R, is brought together under one heading—Attention Deficit and Disruptive Behavior Disorders—together with Oppositional Defiant Disorder and Conduct Disorder. This was done because of the high comorbidity and close relationship among these three diagnostic groups. Although this chapter deals with ADHD, it is important to recognize that often there will be features of or dual diagnosis with one of the other two disorders.

The DSM-IV subdivisions of ADHD are Attention-Deficit/Hyperactivity Disorder, Combined Type (both inattention and hyperactivity-impulsivity), Predominantly Inattentive Type, and Predominantly Hyperactive-Impulsive Type. This current subdivision follows years of research documenting the major contribution of motor restlessness and impulsivity to the syndrome with the relatively difficult to define and less predictive symptoms of inattention being a part of the definition but not necessarily the core defining feature.

The current definition of ADHD remains largely the same as in previous DSM versions: the essential feature is a persistent pattern of inattention and/or hyperactivity-impulsivity that is more frequent and severe than is typically observed in individuals of the same age. The symptoms must cause impairment and be apparent before age 7:

> *Inattention* is often manifested by failure to give close attention to details. Typically, ADHD children have trouble persisting with effortful tasks until completion and appear as if their mind is elsewhere. They may avoid situations in which close attention to details or organizational skill is needed. A pattern of losing necessary objects or forgetfulness is generally observed.

> *Hyperactivity* may be manifested by fidgetiness, excessive running or climbing, by constantly appearing to be "on the go," or by excessive talking. This is the symptom complex that most often improves with age, manifesting in adolescence or adulthood generally as a subjective sense of restlessness.

> *Impulsivity* may be manifested by impatience, difficulty in delaying responses, blurting out answers, and trouble waiting one's turn. Impulsivity and hyperactivity must be apparent in more than one setting including home, school, work, and social situations. Associated with the disorder are poor social functioning, low self-esteem, specific developmental disorders, and academic difficulties (APA, 1994).

DIAGNOSTIC CONSIDERATIONS AND VARIATIONS

Before its DSM-III designation in 1980 as Attention Deficit Disorder, this syndrome (or syndromes) was popularly referred to as minimal brain damage, minimal brain dysfunction, the hyperactive child syndrome, and by the DSM-II label of Hyperkinetic Reaction of Childhood (Barkley, 1990). These groups of behavioral difficulties and abnormal clinical signs are similar to each other and ADHD, but not necessarily in all aspects. The change in terminology resulted from a belief that attention deficit was invariably present, and was the core symptom, while motor restlessness was not. Although never part of official terminology, the term "minimal brain damage/dysfunction" was deliberately avoided. Since the publication of DSM-III-R in 1987, however, a number of anatomic MRI studies (Castellanos et al., 1994; Giedd et al., 1994; Hynd, Semrud-Clikeman, Lorys, Novey, & Eliopulos, 1990; Hynd, Semrud-Clikeman, et al., 1991; Hynd et al., 1993; Semrud-Clikeman et al., 1994) have in fact documented minimal but significant brain anatomical deviations—ironically, minimal brain dysfunction now takes on new meaning!

DSM-III-R returned *Hyperactivity* into the title Attention-Deficit/Hyperactivity Disorder, where it remains in DSM-IV. Later research and the DSM-IV field trials continued to support the relative importance of motor restlessness and impulsivity for this syndrome, at least in school-age boys (Halperin, Matier, Bedi, Sharma, & Newcorn, 1992; Porrino et al., 1983b). Extensive DSM-IV field trials in school-aged children found that symptoms of hyperactivity/impulsivity are the main contributors to the diagnosis of ADHD, and that the diagnosis is virtually independent of the symptoms of inattention (Carlson, Lahey, & Frick, 1994; Frick et al., 1994). There is now one set of criteria with subtypes that allow the clinician to note the predominance of either symptoms of inattention or of hyperactivity/impulsivity.

The DSM-IV field trials (Frick et al., 1994) not only clarified the basis on which clinicians actually make the diagnosis but stressed separation from both Conduct Disorder and Oppositional Defiant Disorder (see Rapoport & Ismond, in press). Controversies still remain over the boundaries of ADHD, and over its evident heterogeneity. We expect that with newer imaging and genetic techniques and more thoughtful prospective follow-up, the refinement of the diagnosis will continue.

EPIDEMIOLOGY

The epidemiology of ADHD has been recently reviewed (Szatmari, 1992). Community-based studies confirm that ADHD is one of the most prevalent psychiatric disorders in childhood and adolescence, with estimates of 3% to 5% in the elementary school population.

PSYCHOPHARMACOLOGY

Pharmacological treatments for the behaviors encompassed by ADHD have been well documented for over 25 years. The major class of drugs indicated for ADHD is the central nervous system (CNS) stimulants, especially methylphenidate (MPH) and dextroamphetamine (DEX). This chapter also will discuss antidepressants and antihypertensives, but many other possible agents are omitted because they either were not well documented or because treatment effect size appeared unimpressive. Diet is mentioned briefly.

Stimulants

Pharmacology.   Stimulants are drugs that have significant CNS excitatory actions, in addition to other central and peripheral effects. The most commonly used are dextroamphetamine, MPH, and magnesium pemoline. Amphetamine, which is similar in structure to norepinephrine, comes in three isomeric forms: dextroamphetamine (Dexedrine), levoamphetamine (no longer marketed), and racemic amphetamine (Benzedrine). The least used sympathomimetic, methamphetamine, has been reviewed elsewhere (Wender, 1993) and will not be further discussed here. The amphetamines have CNS stimulant and peripheral α and β sympathomimetic actions. The *d*-isomer is three to four times more potent than the *l*-isomer in terms of CNS effects, but has less potent cardiovascular effects (Hoffman & Lefkowitz, 1990).

The amphetamines are well absorbed when taken orally, achieve peak plasma levels in children in two to three hours, easily cross the blood brain barrier, and have a half-life in children of 4 to 6 hours with large interindividual variation (Elia, 1991). Amphetamines are potent releasers of cytoplasmic dopamine as well as blockers of dopamine, norepinephrine, and serotonin reuptake (Rebec & Segal, 1978; Snyder & Meyerhoff, 1973). Amphetamines also inhibit monoamine oxidase, although this latter action is weak (Creese, 1983; Hoffman & Lefkowitz, 1990). Subjective clinical effects seem to peak earlier than plasma levels, at approximately 1 to 3 hours (Ebert, van Kammen, & Murphy, 1976). Chronic use for 6 or more months yields a steady state half-life of about 10 hours (Greenhill et al., 1984). These drugs are mainly metabolized via oxidative deamination to benzoic acid and hippuric acid (which are inactive). Given an acid urine and normal renal function, about one-third to one-half of the drugs is excreted unchanged (Ebert, van Kammen, & Murphy, 1976; Saunders, 1974).

Methylphenidate (MPH) is a piperidine derivative with structural and pharmacological properties similar to amphetamines, though its mode of action is different. Methylphenidate does not release dopamine in the absence of nerve impulses, but it is an effective blocker of cate-cholamine reuptake, with stronger effects on dopamine than on norepi-nephrine (Butcher, Liptrot, & Aburthnott, 1991). In children, it is easily absorbed after oral administration, is poorly bound to plasma proteins, readily crosses the blood brain barrier, reaches peak plasma levels in 1 to 2 hours and has a half-life of 2 to 3 hours. Its clearance also shows large in-terindividual and intraindividual variability (Gualtieri & Hicks, 1985; Kupietz, 1991). Serum levels correspond approximately to the time course of clinical effects (Gualtieri et al., 1982; Swanson, Sandman, Deutsch, & Baren, 1983; Wargin et al., 1983) but their inter- and intrasubject variabil-ity is too large for clinical utility (Gualtieri, Hicks, Patrick, Schroeder, & Breese, 1984). Methylphenidate is chiefly deesterified to ritalinic acid, which accounts for about 80% of the oral dose. The remainder is metabo-lized to parahydroxymethylphenidate, which is potent, and to oxoritalinic acid and oxomethylphenidate, which are weakly active. Essentially none of the drug appears unchanged in the urine (Ebert, van Kammen, & Mur-phy, 1976; Hoffman & Lefkowitz, 1990; Saunders, 1974).

Magnesium pemoline is also believed to block dopamine reuptake like MPH, though it has minimal sympathomimetic effects and is dissim-ilar in structure to the other stimulants. It reaches peak serum level in children in 2 to 4 hours; its half-life is 12 hours. Its onset of action ap-pears to be about as rapid as the other stimulants when therapeutic doses are used (Collier et al., 1985; Sallee, Stiller, & Perel, 1992; Sallee, Stiller, Perel, & Bates, 1985).

Physiological and Psychophysiological Effects. Centrally, stimulants excite the medullary respiratory center, though without significant ef-fects on respiratory rate. They stimulate the reticular activating system, sometimes resulting in insomnia, and this mechanism may account for part of their effects on attention and task performance (Mefford & Pot-ter, 1989; Zametkin & Rapoport, 1987b). Sleep physiology and EEG ar-chitecture may be altered, though sleep research findings have not been consistent (Collier et al., 1985; Greenhill, Puig-Antich, Goetz, Hanlon, & Davies, 1983; Sallee, Stiller, & Perel, 1992; Sallee, Stiller, Perel, & Bates, 1985; Tirosh, Sadeh, Munvez, & Lavie, 1993; Trommer, Hoeppner, Rosenberg, Armstrong, & Rothstein, 1988). There is depression of ap-petite, perhaps secondary to effects on the lateral hypothalamic center. In addition, methylphenidate and amphetamine have been shown to have differential neuroendocrine effects. Acute use of MPH increases growth hormone and minimally decreases prolactin. Chronic use yields increased growth hormone and unchanged prolactin levels. Chronic am-phetamine use is associated with decreased prolactin and unchanged growth hormone (Greenhill et al., 1984; Shaywitz et al., 1990; Shaywitz et al., 1982).

Peripherally, stimulants mildly elevate systolic and diastolic blood pressure, as well as heart rate, though the clinical significance of this is not clear. They also relax bronchial smooth muscle, cause some contraction of the urinary bladder sphincter, and have unpredictable gastrointestinal effects (Hoffman & Lefkowitz, 1990).

Behavioral Effects. Many careful studies demonstrate that dextroamphetamine and MPH consistently, readily, and sometimes quite dramatically improve the behaviors of ADHD. This clinical effect occurs even when subject groups are *not* strictly defined, the sample sizes are small, and the drug dosages span a wide range. Most likely to improve are hyperactive, restless, impulsive, disruptive, aggressive, socially inappropriate behaviors (Allen, Safer, & Covi, 1975; Gadow, Nolan, Sverd, Sprafkin, & Paolicelli, 1990; Hinshaw, Henker, Whalen, Erhardt, & Dunnington, 1989; Klein, 1993; Murphy, Pelham, & Lang, 1992). A large number of studies show improvement on global impression, on parent, and on teacher scales (Conners, Eisenberg, & Barcai, 1967; Conners, Taylor, Meo, Kurtz, & Fournier, 1972; Firestone, Davey, Goodman, & Peters, 1978; Gittelman-Klein, Klein, Katz, Saraf, & Pollack, 1976; Rapoport, Quinn, Bradbard, Riddle, & Brooks, 1974; Sykes, Douglas, Weiss, & Minde, 1971; Weiss, Werry, Minde, Douglas, & Sykes, 1968; Werry & Aman, 1975). There also are positive changes with drug treatment in mother-child and teacher-child interactions, and normalization of social behavior (making hyperactive children indistinguishable from their peers) (Barkley, Karlsson, Strzelecki, & Murphy, 1984; Buhrmester, Whalen, Henker, MacDonald, & Hinshaw, 1992; Whalen et al., 1987; Whalen & Henker, 1991). Though dextroamphetamine and MPH seem to be equally effective in achieving these results in the general population of ADHD children, not all children respond equally well to both, and about one-quarter will respond favorably to one or the other but not both (Elia, Borcherding, Rapoport, & Keysor, 1991).

Magnesium pemoline is also clinically effective, though probably less so than these other stimulants (Conners, Taylor, Meo, Kurtz, & Fournier, 1972; Conners & Taylor, 1980). One recent short-term trial found it comparable in efficacy to long-acting formulations of MPH and dextroamphetamine (Pelham et al., 1990) and another found its onset of efficacy to be as rapid as other stimulants on measures of attention (Sallee, Stiller, & Perel, 1992). In a recent cross-over comparison, it was the preferred medication for only 1 of 16 who received all three stimulants in double-blind trials (Castellanos et al., in press).

There has also been much attention to stimulant drug effects on cognition, academic achievement, mood, and motor behavior. Dextroamphetamine and MPH have been shown to improve performance on many cognitive tests of attention, vigilance, reaction time, visual and verbal learning, and short-term memory (Callaway, 1983; Charles, Schain, Zelniker, & Guthrie, 1979; de Sonneville, Njiokiktjien, & Hilhorst, 1991; Elia, Welsh, Gullotta, & Rapoport, 1993; Evans, Gualtieri, & Amara, 1986; Flintoff, Barron, Swanson, Ledlow, & Kinsbourne, 1982; Keith & Engineer, 1991; Klein, 1991; Rapoport et al., 1980; Sostek, Buchsbaum, & Rapoport, 1980; Weingartner, Langer, Grice, & Rapoport, 1982). There is some evidence that the improvement is due to increased concentration or vigilance, through both more focused attention and less distraction by extraneous stimuli (Balthazor, Wagner, & Pelham, 1991; Richardson, Kupietz, Winsberg, Maitinsky, & Mendell, 1988; Sergeant & Van der Meere, 1991). However, in spite of better performance on particular measures, children's overall academic performance and achievement have not been shown to be enhanced over the long term (Hechtman, Weiss, & Perlman, 1984; Rapport & Kelly, 1991).

Stimulant effect on mood is of interest, and much further research is needed in this area. Following a single-dose challenge with amphetamine, no euphoria was found in normal or hyperactive prepubertal children, whereas normal young adults reported significant euphoria (Rapoport et al., 1980). In fact, complaints of dysphoric mood or flattening of affect are not uncommon, though they usually respond to a decrease in dose or a change to an alternative stimulant (Elia, Borcherding, Rapoport, & Keysor, 1991) or to a nonstimulant.

Motor activity is another important variable in the study of ADHD. Generally, stimulants have been found to decrease activity levels in structured settings, while yielding inconsistent results for less restricted situations. A naturalistic study using 24-hour activity monitors, showed that dextroamphetamine significantly decreased activity in the structured classroom and significantly increased activity during physical recreation times. The overall decrease lasted about 8 hours and was followed by a slight "rebound" increase in motor activity (Porrino, Rapoport, Behar, Ismond, & Bunney, 1983a; Porrino et al., 1983b).

Of note is that stimulant actions are not specific for the population of children with ADHD. They have been shown to have similar cognitive and behavioral effects on normal children and adults (Rapoport et al., 1978; Rapoport et al., 1980).

Clinical Usage. Stimulants are indicated for the treatment of ADHD. Not all children with ADHD, however, need to take medication. A careful psychiatric and physical evaluation is made. The decision to employ medication is a clinical one, based on severity of symptoms, preferences of the child and parents, ability of the child, parents, and school to cope with the problem behaviors, and success and failure of previous treatment. Contraindications to drug use are the presence of psychosis or a thought disorder. Relative contraindications may be the presence of tics, extreme anxiety, or any medical condition precluding the use of sympathomimetics. Use with the child who has tics or anxiety is controversial (Denckla, Bemporad, & MacKay, 1976; Gadow & Sverd, 1990; Golden, 1986; Lowe, Cohen, Detlor, Kremenitzer, & Shaywitz, 1982; Sleator, 1980). Since tricyclic antidepressants (Hoge & Biederman, 1986; Spencer, Biederman, Wilens, Steingard, & Geist, 1993) and clonidine (Cohen, Riddle, & Leckman, 1992; Leckman et al., 1991) have been found to benefit both ADHD symptoms and tics they are usually considered first. However, some children with severe ADHD and Tourette's syndrome may not worsen or may even improve on stimulants and individual trials may be indicated (Castellanos et al., 1993; Gadow, Nolan, & Sverd, 1992; Gadow, Nolan, Sverd, Sprafkin, & Paolicelli, 1990). In some cases, deprenyl (5–15 mg/day) also may be a useful alternative when ADHD and Tourette's co-occur (Jankovic, 1993), although controlled trials are not yet completed.

ADHD children who also are mentally retarded benefit substantially from stimulants if their mental age is over 5 or their IQ over 55. Patients with more severe mental retardation have a lower response rate and a higher rate of side effects (Aman, Marks, Turbott, Wilsher, & Merry, 1991; Handen et al., 1992), as do preschool-age children (Schleifer et al., 1975). Adolescents respond comparably to younger children, although compliance may be much more difficult, in part due to stigma (Stine, 1994). It is not unusual for adolescents to become more sensitive to side effects, and to benefit from *decreased* dosages or sustained-release preparations (Kelly & Aylward, 1992; Klein, 1987; Klein, 1993; Klorman, Brumaghim, Fitzpatrick, & Borgstedt, 1991; Waltz, 1990).

In spite of much research, there is no reliable method to predict which children will respond to or benefit from medication. This is not surprising in view of the nonspecificity of the effect. More importantly, almost all children respond when a wide range of doses *and* both methylphenidate and dextroamphetamine are tried (Elia, Borcherding, Rapoport, & Keysor, 1991). Medication benefits are usually more robust on behavioral symptoms than on academic efficiency (Rapport, Denney, DuPaul, & Gardner, 1994; Swanson et al., 1993). There is a paucity of information on issues of compliance, but some authors suggest that this may be a significant problem with maintenance medication (Firestone, 1982; Sleator, Ullmann, & von Neumann, 1982).

MPH and dextroamphetamine are the drugs of choice, followed by pemoline. Increasing attention to comorbidity has resulted in more frequent use of more than one psychotropic medication at a time. Most often, a stimulant is combined with clonidine or a tricyclic (Hunt, Lau,

& Ryu, 1991; Pataki, Carlson, Kelly, Rapport, & Biancaniello, 1993), or a serotonergic agent such as fluoxetine (Gammon & Brown, 1993).

Dosages for the most commonly used agents are given in Table 8.1. The usual beginning dose of dextroamphetamine is 5 mg q.d. or b.i.d. (for ages 6 or older), of MPH is 5 mg b.i.d., and of pemoline is 37.5 mg q.d. The medication is increased gradually every 3 to 5 days until therapeutic effect or adverse effects occur. Different dosages may be optimum for different behaviors (lower for cognitive improvement versus higher for overall clinical improvement) (Rapport, Denney, DuPaul, & Gardner, 1994; Sprague & Sleator, 1977). Dosages must be reevaluated as the child grows, with increases through childhood corresponding to increases in lean body weight (Safer & Allen, 1989), with dosage decreases often necessary after puberty (Waltz, 1990). Timing of doses is based on duration of drug action, which is relatively short for MPH and dextroamphetamine and longer for pemoline. There are sustained-release preparations of dextroamphetamine and MPH, but their superiority has not been demonstrated (Fitzpatrick, Klorman, Brumaghim, & Borgstedt, 1992), perhaps owing to a lack of real pharmacokinetic differences (Birmaher, Greenhill, Cooper, Fried, & Maminski, 1989). Alternatively, some practitioners have successfully used the short-acting preparations on a once-a-day regimen. More commonly, a third, generally smaller, dose of a short-acting stimulant is given after school to support homework completion and after-school behavior.

There is some evidence (Chan et al., 1983; Swanson, Sandman, Deutsch, & Baren, 1983) that drug effects are similar when stimulants are taken in a fasting or fed state, with absorption actually faster in the latter. This has the added benefit of minimizing anorexic effects and may decrease the incidence of stomachaches.

Table 8.1.   ***Dosage of Commonly Used Medications in ADHD***

Drug	Starting Dose	Maximum Range Daily Dose	
		(mg)	(mg/kg)
Dextroamphetamine	5 mg q.d. or b.i.d. (age 6 or older) 2.5 mg q.d. (ages 3–5)	40	0.15–0.5/dose
Methylphenidate	5 mg b.i.d.	60	0.3–1.0/dose
Pemoline	37.5 mg q.d.	112.5	0.5–2.0/day
Desipramine or Imipramine	10 mg b.i.d.		3–5 mg/kg/day
Clonidine	0.025 mg q.h.s.		3–5 mcg/kg/day

The development of true tolerance in children to stimulants is extremely rare, and dependence and abuse have been almost nonexistent (Gittelman, 1983; Goyer, Davis, & Rapoport, 1979; Safer & Allen, 1989).

Combining medication with other treatments is usual. Parent counseling and modification of the school milieu are almost always indicated. In most research investigations, however, stimulants alone have been more effective than other treatments alone (Abikoff & Gittelman, 1985; Gittelman-Klein et al., 1976). Some data suggest that the combination of a moderate dose of a stimulant with behavior therapy is comparable in the short term to the effects of a higher dose of a stimulant alone (Carlson, Pelham, Milich, & Dixon, 1992; Christensen & Sprague, 1973; Horn et al., 1991; Pelham et al., 1993; Wolraich, Drummond, Salomon, O'Brien, & Sivage, 1978). There is as yet no evidence that multimodal intervention is superior once stimulant medication is withdrawn (Abikoff, 1991; Ialongo et al., 1993).

The decision of when to discontinue stimulants is a clinical one, also. Lack of improvement after 2 weeks at maximum dosage of dextroamphetamine and MPH or 5 weeks of pemoline is an indication to stop. Dosage can usually be lowered for most side effects, though more severe adverse effects might necessitate ending that treatment. Weekend or vacation "drug holidays" must be individualized when home problems are prominent and dramatically improved on drug. The drug should be discontinued at least once a year to assess continued need for treatment. A fairly high percentage of children do not need to resume treatment when this is done (Ialongo et al., 1993). Drugs have not been shown to produce long-term benefits for factors such as better life adjustment or better jobs (Charles & Schain, 1981; Gittelman, Mannuzza, Shenker, & Bonagura, 1985; Hechtman, 1985; Klein & Mannuzza, 1991; Mannuzza, Klein, Bessler, Malloy, & LaPadula, 1993; Riddle & Rapoport, 1976; Weiss, 1985; Weiss, Hechtman, Milroy, & Perlman, 1985; Weiss, Kruger, Danielson, & Elman, 1975).

Adverse Effects.   The most common short-term adverse effects are anorexia and insomnia. Less common are weight loss, abdominal pain, and headache. These are generally short-lived and rarely require the stopping of medication. Drowsiness, dizziness, mood changes, dyskinesias, and toxic psychosis are rare (Ahmann et al., 1993; Burd & Kerbeshian, 1991; Fine & Johnston, 1993; Jaffe, 1991; Young, 1981). Idiosyncratic responses do occur, such as the development of blood dyscrasias. Relatively few side effects occur with dosages below 0.5 mg/kg of dextroamphetamine or 1 mg/kg of MPH per day.

Suppression of growth in weight and height has been found in short-term treatment with dextroamphetamine, MPH, and pemoline. Though growth suppression is generally thought to be temporary (Klein, Landa,

Mattes, & Klein, 1988; Satterfield, Cantwell, Schell, & Blaschke, 1979), there are reports of small but statistically significant decreases in height and weight percentiles with chronic DEX and MPH treatment that might prove important for specific individuals (Mattes & Gittelman, 1983; Safer, Allen, & Barr, 1972; Spencer, Biederman, Wright, & Danon, 1992).

Pemoline carries a risk of chemical hepatitis that may be as high as 3%, so monitoring of liver function tests is necessary at initiation and every 6 months (Nehra, Mullick, Ishak, & Zimmerman, 1990). Routine blood tests are not necessary with the other stimulants in the absence of symptoms.

Concern that stimulants may produce permanent movement disorders such as tics or Tourette's syndrome led to the relabeling of MPH by its manufacturer, with a history of tics in the individual or in the family being classified as an absolute contraindication (Lowe, Cohen, Detlor, Kremenitzer, & Shaywitz, 1982; Medical Economics Data, 1994). Although stimulants can exacerbate tics in some patients, the description of six pairs of identical twins, concordant for TS but discordant for prior exposure to MPH, cast doubt on the hypothesis that stimulants were necessary or sufficient for the de novo production of tic disorders (Price, Leckman, Pauls, Cohen, & Kidd, 1986). Subsequent controlled trials have found that children with ADHD and a tic disorder can benefit behaviorally from the stimulant without a statistically significant effect on tic severity (Sverd, Gadow, & Paolicelli, 1989; Gadow, Nolan, & Sverd, 1992), and that a short course of high-dose MPH produces an inverted-U dose response curve, with most children subsequently tolerating stimulants with minimal effects on tics (Castellanos et al., 1993). Nevertheless, the small number of children studied systematically (less than 60 total in two centers), and the known variable course of tic disorders makes the presence of a known tic disorder a *relative* contraindication for stimulant use (Cohen & Leckman, 1989). Lack of benefit from or intolerance to other treatments, and the degree of morbidity associated with ADHD must be weighed in the balance, and parents must be fully informed of the continuing uncertainty in this area. Long-term tic disorders such as Tourette's must be distinguished from the mild transient tics that are common when stimulants are begun (Borcherding, Keysor, Rapoport, Elia, & Amass, 1990; Ickowicz, Tannock, Fulford, Purvis, & Schachar, 1992).

Antidepressants: Behavioral Effects of Clinical Usage

This discussion is limited to the effects of antidepressants in ADHD. Other aspects of antidepressants are presented in Chapter 7.

Tricyclic antidepressants (TCA) have shown clinical efficacy in several studies (Biederman, Baldessarini, Wright, Knee, & Harmatz, 1989;

Donnelly et al., 1986; Rapoport, Quinn, Bradbard, Riddle, & Brooks, 1974; Spencer, Biederman, Wilens, Steingard, & Geist, 1993). Improvement is as rapid and sometimes as striking as with the stimulants. However, the effects seem to be short-lived for some subjects. Dosages may vary widely around an average of 3 mg/kg/day, divided into two or three doses. Anticholinergic side effects are well tolerated by children but they increase in a dose-dependent manner. Due to very large intersubject variability of serum levels, their utility in guiding initial dosing is limited, but they may be of value when doses about 3 mg/kg/day are contemplated.

The use of TCAs in children has received heightened attention following recent reports of sudden death in five children who were taking desipramine (Abramowicz, 1990; Riddle et al., 1991; Riddle, Geller, & Ryan, 1993; Zimnitzky & Popper, 1994). Careful scrutiny by the American Academy of Child and Adolescent Psychiatry's Work Group on Research (Biederman et al., 1989) revealed that the rate of the four deaths (the fifth had not been reported at the time) on desipramine was not clearly increased over the incidence of sudden death in the general population. The report concluded that there was minimal or no increased risk of sudden death in children on desipramine. However, the cases led to much commentary and controversy about the relative risks of prescribing TCAs, particularly desipramine, to children (Ambrosini, Bianchi, Rabinovich, & Elia, 1994; Geller, 1991; Popper & Elliott, 1990; Riddle, Geller, & Ryan, 1994; Werry, 1994). Riddle et al. (1993) reviewed the four cases and found a paucity of data and concluded that "considerable uncertainty remains about the basis of the apparent association between the use of desipramine and the sudden deaths." Any association would presumably be secondary to cardiac toxicity in susceptible individuals (Vincent, Jaiswal, & Timothy, 1991). Since stimulants appear to be more effective in the classroom (Garfinkel, Wender, Sloman, & O'Neill, 1983; Pliszka, 1987; Rapport, Carlson, Kelly, & Pataki, 1993; Rapoport, Quinn, Bradbard, Riddle, & Brooks, 1974) and lack this concern, antidepressants are generally considered second-line drugs for ADHD. When they are used, the standard of care includes monitoring the electrocardiogram before and during treatment (see Chapter 7 for a more detailed discussion).

Monoamine oxidase inhibitors (MAOI) have stimulant effects, and some studies have suggested benefits in ADHD (Trott, Friese, Menzel, & Nissen, 1992; Wender, Wood, Reimherr, & Ward, 1983; Zametkin, Rapoport, Murphy, Linnoila, & Ismond, 1985). Concern over dietary restrictions in impulsive individuals has limited their utility. One open trial found the selective MAOI deprenyl useful in ADHD combined with Tourette's syndrome (Jankovic, 1993). Serotonin-specific antidepressants have not been evaluated in controlled trials, but even anecdotal evidence for their utility is lacking, except for one open trial with fluoxetine (Barrickman, Noyes, Kuperman, Schumacher, & Verda, 1991). The decreased anticholinergic side effects of the newer agents in this class makes them potentially useful adjunctives to stimulants in co-morbid cases (Gammon & Brown, 1993).

Other Drugs/Diet

A wide variety of drugs have been tried in ADHD, but generally the stimulants have been the clear winners (Zametkin & Rapoport, 1987a). Several studies, using different classes of *antipsychotics*, have shown improvement in various symptoms of ADHD. However, overall clinical efficacy is not as striking as with stimulants (Gittelman-Klein, Klein, Katz, Saraf, & Pollack, 1976; Werry, Aman, & Lampen, 1976), and their use is limited because of concern over adverse effects. Besides potential long-term tardive dyskinesia, antipsychotics produce a decrease in cognitive function (Gualtieri, Quade, Hicke, Mayo, & Schroeder, 1984). Antipsychotic medications are discussed in more detail in Chapter 6.

Clonidine is an antihypertensive agent with alpha-2 agonist activity. Though it has been studied in only two small controlled trials (Hunt, Minderaa, & Cohen, 1985, 1986), it is widely used in ADHD, especially when comorbid with tics or Tourette's syndrome (Cohen, Riddle, & Leckman, 1992; Leckman et al., 1991; Steingard, Biederman, Spencer, Wilens, & Gonzalez, 1993). Adding clonidine ameliorates stimulant-induced insomnia (Rubinstein, Silver, & Licamele, 1994; Wilens, Biederman, & Spencer, 1994), can decrease "rebound" effects, and may decrease aggressive behavior (Kemph, DeVane, Levin, Jarecke, & Miller, 1993; Schvehla, Mandoki, & Sumner, 1994). The principal side effect is sedation, which is minimized by gradually titrating the dosage increase, starting with bedtime doses as small as 0.025 mg. Total daily doses of 0.003–0.005 mg/kg/day must be divided into two or preferably three doses (Hart-Santora & Hart, 1992). When a stable response is reached, transdermal administration may be used (Hunt, 1987), although the patches usually need to be changed every 5 days rather than 7 days, as recommended for adults. Local irritation is common and is generally what limits this mode of administration. Patients and parents must be warned not to discontinue treatment suddenly, since rebound hypertension and increases in symptoms may occur (Leckman et al., 1986). Also, clonidine patches must be disposed of safely, as a near-fatal intoxication took place in a toddler who retrieved a patch from a waste receptacle (Caravati & Bennett, 1988).

The issue of dietary treatment in ADHD is no longer "hot" and the majority of controlled trials of food additives or sugar, for example, have been negative (Kruesi & Rapoport, 1986; Kruesi et al., 1987; Wolraich et al., 1994). In individual cases, however, there is some evidence that elimination diets may be helpful (Boris & Mandel, 1994; Egger, Stolla, & McEwen, 1992). These are tedious and costly undertakings, and much more study must be undertaken before such diets are incorporated into standard clinical practice.

Attention-Deficit/Hyperactivity Disorder, Predominantly Inattentive Type. The changes in DSM-IV, with specific criteria for what was previously termed ADD without hyperactivity is expected to assist research into the prevalence and optimal treatment of these individuals. The few studies to date suggest that while stimulants are often helpful, there may be a higher incidence of dose-related side effects, as well as of comorbidity with learning disabilities and anxiety disorders (Cantwell & Baker, 1992; Hynd, Lorys, et al., 1991; Lahey, Schaughency, Hynd, Calrson, & Nieves, 1987; Lahey, Schaughency, Strauss, & Frame, 1984; Lahey et al., 1988; McBurnett, Lahey, & Swanson, 1991; Shaywitz et al., 1983). Because by definition these individuals are not predominantly disruptive, diagnosis is often delayed or missed altogether. For example, the mean age of presentation of this subtype of ADHD at the Massachusetts General Hospital was 14 years (T. Wilens, personal communication, August 1994).

Adult Attention-Deficit/Hyperactivity Disorder. The diagnosis of ADHD in adulthood remains controversial but important. Research has had mixed results in defining and validating the disorder, as well as in evaluating treatments (Fargason & Ford, 1994; Shaffer, 1994; Shekim, Asarnow, Hess, Zaucha, & Wheeler, 1990; Silver, 1992; Ward, Wender, & Reimherr, 1993; Wender, Wood, & Reimherr, 1984, 1993). A recent controlled trial of MPH in doses up to 1 mg/kg/day found a marked therapeutic response comparable to that obtained in children (Spencer et al., 1995). Tricyclics and monoamine oxidase inhibitors may also be of some benefit.

ASSESSMENT

Assessment of treatment begins with a careful diagnostic evaluation, with particular attention to the presence or absence of learning disabilities, and to comorbidity with the other disruptive behavior disorders, anxiety, affective, and substance abuse disorders. The diagnosis is made exclusively by history, and this is aided substantially by the use of teacher and parent rating scales, such as the Child Attention Problems scale, or the updated Conners Parent and Teacher Rating Scales (Schaughency & Rothlind, 1991). A psychoeducational evaluation comprising an IQ test such as the Wechsler Intelligence Scale for Children–III (Wechsler, 1991) and achievement testing such as the Woodcock Johnson Psychoeducational

Battery (Woodcock & Johnson, 1977) should be considered, but may be best deferred until optimal pharmacological treatment is instituted. Other types of psychological tests such as projective or personality inventories should not be used indiscriminately. The Continuous Performance Test is available in various commercial formats, but should not be used to "make" the diagnosis, since the test lacks sufficient sensitivity or specificity.

PROGNOSIS

The prognosis of ADHD appears to depend largely on associated comorbid conditions. Earlier age of onset is associated with more pervasive and severe symptoms, and with greater comorbidity (McGee et al., 1992). Long-term follow-up studies indicate that as many as 25% of adults diagnosed with ADHD as children will continue to have substantial psychiatric morbidity, chiefly substance abuse and antisocial personality disorder. For the remaining majority, global functioning falls within the normal range (Mannuzza, Klein, Bessler, Malloy, & LaPadula, 1993; Mannuzza, Klein, Konig, & Giampino, 1989; Weiss, 1985). Factors predicting long-term outcome are being examined in an ongoing multisite NIMH-funded study.

SUMMARY

1. Attention-Deficit/Hyperactivity Disorder is still evolving as a diagnostic entity. Validation of the syndrome, particularly in older subjects, remains a major outstanding issue.

2. The pharmacological treatment of ADHD is one of the best described and researched treatments in child psychiatry. Stimulants, in particular dextroamphetamine and methylphenidate, remain the drugs of choice. Their short-term benefits are well documented. Long-term benefits from drug (or any other) treatment are unclear.

3. Much remains to be learned about the clinical use of pharmacological agents in ADHD. However, enough is known presently for safe and effective use. Short-term adverse effects are rarely of major clinical significance. Long-term adverse effects on growth and learning are still of interest.

4. The additive value of combined behavioral/cognitive and family therapy is an area of intense scrutiny but the cost-benefit value of practical implementation remains unclear.

REFERENCES

Abikoff, H. (1991). Cognitive training in ADHD children: Less to it than meets the eye. *Journal of Learning Disabilities, 24,* 205–209.

Abikoff, H., & Gittelman, R. (1985). Hyperactive children treated with stimulants. Is cognitive training a useful adjunct? *Archives of General Psychiatry, 42,* 953–961.

Abramowicz, M. (1990). Sudden death in children treated with a tricyclic antidepressant. *Medical Letter on Drugs and Therapeutics, 32,* 53.

Ahmann, P. A., Waltonen, S. J., Olson, K. A., Theye, F. W., Van Erem, A. J., & LaPlant, R. J. (1993). Placebo-controlled evaluation of ritalin side effects. *Pediatrics, 91,* 1101–1106.

Allen, R. P., Safer, D., & Covi, L. (1975). Effects of psychostimulants on aggression. *Journal of Nervous and Mental Disease, 160,* 138–145.

Aman, M. G., Marks, R. E., Turbott, S. H., Wilsher, C. P., & Merry, S. N. (1991). Clinical effects of methylphenidate and thioridazine in intellectually subaverage children. *Journal of the American Academy of Child and Adolescent Psychiatry, 30,* 246–256.

Ambrosini, P. J., Bianchi, M. D., Rabinovich, H., & Elia, J. (1994). The safety of desipramine [Reply to letter]. *Journal of the American Academy of Child and Adolescent Psychiatry, 33,* 590.

American Psychiatric Association. (1994). *Diagnostic and statistical manual of mental disorders* (4th ed.). Washington, DC: American Psychiatric Association.

Balthazor, M. J., Wagner, R. K., & Pelham, W. E. (1991). The specificity of the effects of stimulant medication on classroom learning-related measures of cognitive processing for attention deficit disorder children. *Journal of Abnormal Child Psychology, 19,* 35–52.

Barkley, R. A. (1990). *Attention-deficit hyperactivity disorder: A handbook for diagnosis and treatment* (2nd ed.). New York: Guilford.

Barkley, R. A., Karlsson, J., Strzelecki, E., & Murphy, J. (1984). Effects of age and Ritalin dosage on the mother-child interactions of hyperactive children. *Journal of Consulting and Clinical Psychology, 52,* 750–758.

Barrickman, L., Noyes, R., Kuperman, S., Schumacher, E., & Verda, M. (1991). Treatment of ADHD with fluoxetine: A preliminary trial. *Journal of the American Academy of Child and Adolescent Psychiatry, 30,* 762–767.

Biederman, J., Baldessarini, R. J., Wright, V., Knee, D., & Harmatz, J. S. (1989). A double-blind placebo-controlled study of desipramine in the treatment of ADD: I. Efficacy. *Journal of the American Academy of Child and Adolescent Psychiatry, 28,* 777–784.

Birmaher, B., Greenhill, L. L., Cooper, T. B., Fried, J., & Maminski, B. (1989). Sustained release methylphenidate: Pharmacokinetic studies in ADHD males. *Journal of the American Academy of Child and Adolescent Psychiatry, 28,* 768–772.

Borcherding, B. G., Keysor, C. S., Rapoport, J. L., Elia, J., & Amass, J. (1990). Motor/vocal tics and compulsive behaviors on stimulant drugs: Is there a common vulnerability? *Psychiatry Research, 33,* 83–94.

Boris, M., & Mandel, F. S. (1994). Foods and additives are common causes of the attention deficit hyperactive disorder in children. *Annals of Allergy, 72,* 462–468.

Buhrmester, D., Whalen, C. K., Henker, B., MacDonald, V., & Hinshaw, S. P. (1992). Prosocial behavior in hyperactive boys: Effects of stimulant medication and comparison with normal boys. *Journal of Abnormal Child Psychology, 20,* 103–121.

Burd, L., & Kerbeshian, J. (1991). Stuttering and stimulants. *Journal of Clinical Psychopharmacology, 11*, 72–73.

Butcher, S. P., Liptrot, J., & Aburthnott, G. W. (1991). Characterisation of methylphenidate and nomifensine induced dopamine release in rat striatum using in vivo brain microdialysis. *Neuroscience Letters, 122*, 245–248.

Callaway, E. (1983). The pharmacology of human information processing. *Psychophysiology, 20*, 359–370.

Cantwell, D. P., & Baker, L. (1992). Attention deficit disorder with and without hyperactivity: A review and comparison of matched groups. *Journal of the American Academy of Child and Adolescent Psychiatry, 31*, 432–438.

Caravati, E. M., & Bennett, D. L. (1988). Clonidine transdermal patch poisoning. *Annals of Emergency Medicine, 17*, 175–176.

Carlson, C. L., Lahey, B. B., & Frick, P. J. (1994). Attention deficit disorders: A review of research relevant to diagnostic classification. In T. A. Widiger, A. J. Frances, W. Davis, & M. First (Eds.), *DSM-IV sourcebook*. Washington, DC: American Psychiatric Press.

Carlson, C. L., Pelham, W. E., Jr., Milich, R., & Dixon, J. (1992). Single and combined effects of methylphenidate and behavior therapy on the classroom performance of children with attention-deficit hyperactivity disorder. *Journal of Abnormal Child Psychology, 20*, 213–232.

Castellanos, F. X., Elia, J., Kruesi, M. J. P., Marsh, W. L., Gulotta, C. S., Potter, W. Z., Ritchie, G. F., Hamburger, S. D., & Rapoport, J. L. (in press). Cerebrospinal homovanillic acid predicts behavioral response to stimulants in 45 boys with attention-deficit/hyperactivity disorder. *Neuropsychopharmacology*.

Castellanos, F. X., Giedd, J. N., Eckburg, P., Marsh, W. L., Vaituzis, A. C., Hamburger, S. D., & Rapoport, J. L. (1994). Quantitative morphology of the caudate nucleus in attention-deficit hyperactivity disorder. *American Journal of Psychiatry, 151*, 1791–1796.

Castellanos, F. X., Gulotta, C. S., Tanaka, J., Ritchie, G. F., Elia, J., & Rapoport, J. L. (1993). Stimulant treatment of pediatric Tourette's disorder and ADHD. *Biological Psychiatry,* (Suppl. 33), 42A–43A.

Chan, Y. P., Swanson, J. M., Soldin, S. S., Thiessen, J. J., MacLeod, S. M., & Logan, W. (1983). Methylphenidate hydrochloride given with or before breakfast: II. Effects on plasma concentration of methylphenidate and ritalinic acid. *Pediatrics, 72*, 56–59.

Charles, L., & Schain, R. (1981). A four-year follow-up study of the effects of methylphenidate on the behavior and academic achievement of hyperactive children. *Journal of Abnormal Child Psychology, 9*, 495–505.

Charles, L., Schain, R. J., Zelniker, T., & Guthrie, D. (1979). Effects of methylphenidate on hyperactive children's ability to sustain attention. *Pediatrics, 64*, 412–418.

Christensen, D. E., & Sprague, R. L. (1973). Reduction of hyperactive behavior by conditioning procedures alone and combined with methylphenidate (Ritalin). *Behavior Research and Therapy, 11*, 331–334.

Cohen, D. J., & Leckman, J. F. (1989). Commentary on "Methylphenidate treatment of attention-deficit hyperactivity disorder in boys with Tourette's syndrome." *Journal of the American Academy of Child and Adolescent Psychiatry, 28*, 580–582.

Cohen, D. J., Riddle, M. A., & Leckman, J. F. (1992). Pharmacotherapy of Tourette's syndrome and associated disorders. *Psychiatric Clinics of North America, 15*, 109–129.

Collier, C. P., Soldin, S. J., Swanson, J. M., MacLeod, S. M., Weinberg, F., & Rochefort, J. G. (1985). Pemoline pharmacokinetics and long term therapy in children with attention deficit disorder and hyperactivity. *Clinical Pharamacokinetics, 10,* 269–278.

Conners, C. K., Eisenberg, L., & Barcai, A. (1967). Effect of dextroamphetamine on children. Studies on subjects with learning disabilities and school behavior problems. *Archives of General Psychiatry, 17,* 478–485.

Conners, C. K., & Taylor, E. (1980). Pemoline, methylphenidate, and placebo in children with minimal brain dysfunction. *Archives of General Psychiatry, 37,* 922–930.

Conners, C. K., Taylor, E., Meo, G., Kurtz, M. A., & Fournier, M. (1972). Magnesium pemoline and dextroamphetamine: A controlled study in children with minimal brain dysfunction. *Psychopharmacologia, 26,* 321–336.

Creese, I. (Ed.). (1983). *Stimulants: Neurochemical, behavioral, and clinical perspectives.* New York: Raven.

Denckla, M. B., Bemporad, J. R., & MacKay, M. C. (1976). Tics following methylphenidate administration. A report of 20 cases. *Journal of the American Medical Association, 235,* 1349–1351.

de Sonneville, L. M., Njiokiktjien, C., & Hilhorst, R. C. (1991). Methylphenidate-induced changes in ADHD information processors. *Journal of Child Psychology & Psychiatry & Allied Disciplines, 32,* 285–295.

Donnelly, M., Zametkin, A. J., Rapoport, J. L., Ismond, D. R., Weingartner, H., Lane, E., Oliver, J., Linnoila, M., & Potter, W. Z. (1986). Treatment of childhood hyperactivity with desipramine: Plasma drug concentration, cardiovascular effects, plasma and urinary catecholamine levels, and clinical response. *Clinical Pharmacology and Therapeutics, 39,* 72–81.

Ebert, M. H., van Kammen, D. P., & Murphy, D. L. (1976). Plasma levels of amphetamine and behavioral response. In L. A. Gottschalk & S. Merlis (Eds.), *Pharmacokinetics of psychoactive drugs* (pp. 157–169). New York: Spectrum.

Egger, J., Stolla, A., & McEwen, L. M. (1992). Controlled trial of hyposensitisation in children with food-induced hyperkinetic syndrome. *Lancet, 339,* 1150–1153.

Elia, J. (1991). Stimulants and antidepressant pharmacokinetics in hyperactive children. *Psychopharmacology Bulletin, 27,* 411–415.

Elia, J., Borcherding, B. G., Rapoport, J. L., & Keysor, C. S. (1991). Methylphenidate and dextroamphetamine treatments of hyperactivity: Are there true nonresponders? *Psychiatry Research, 36,* 141–155.

Elia, J., Welsh, P. A., Gullotta, C. S., & Rapoport, J. L. (1993). Classroom academic performance: Improvement with both methylphenidate and dextroamphetamine in ADHD boys. *Journal of Child Psychology & Psychiatry & Allied Disciplines, 34,* 785–804.

Evans, R. W., Gualtieri, C. T., & Amara, I. (1986). Methylphenidate and memory: Dissociated effects in hyperactive children. *Psychopharmacology, 90,* 211–216.

Fargason, R. E., & Ford, C. V. (1994). Attention deficit hyperactivity disorder in adults: Diagnosis, treatment, and prognosis. *Southern Medical Journal, 87,* 302–309.

Fine, S., & Johnston, C. (1993). Drug and placebo side effects in methylphenidate-placebo trial for attention deficit hyperactivity disorder. *Child Psychiatry and Human Development, 24,* 25–30.

Firestone, P. (1982). Factors associated with children's adherence to stimulant medication. *American Journal of Orthopsychiatry, 52,* 447–457.

Firestone, P., Davey, J., Goodman, J. T., & Peters, S. (1978). The effects of caffeine and methylphenidate on hyperactive children. *Journal of the American Academy of Child Psychiatry, 17,* 445–456.

Fitzpatrick, P. A., Klorman, R., Brumaghim, J. T., & Borgstedt, A. D. (1992). Effects of sustained-release and standard preparations of methylphenidate on attention deficit disorder. *Journal of the American Academy of Child and Adolescent Psychiatry, 31,* 226–234.

Flintoff, M. M., Barron, R. W., Swanson, J. M., Ledlow, A., & Kinsbourne, M. (1982). Methylphenidate increases selectivity of visual scanning in children referred for hyperactivity. *Journal of Abnormal Child Psychology, 10,* 145–161.

Frick, P. J., Lahey, B. B., Applegate, B., Kerdyck, L., Ollendick, T., Hynd, G. W., Garfinkel, B., Greenhill, L., Biederman, J., Barkley, R. A., McBurnett, K., Newcorn, J., & Waldman, I. (1994). DSM-IV field trials for the disruptive behavior disorders: Symptom utility estimates. *Journal of the American Academy of Child and Adolescent Psychiatry, 33,* 529–539.

Gadow, K. D., Nolan, E. E., & Sverd, J. (1992). Methylphenidate in hyperactive boys with comorbid tic disorder: II. Short-term behavioral effects in school settings. *Journal of the American Academy of Child and Adolescent Psychiatry, 31,* 462–471.

Gadow, K. D., Nolan, E. E., Sverd, J., Sprafkin, J., & Paolicelli, L. M. (1990). Methylphenidate in aggressive-hyperactive boys: I. Effects on peer aggression in public school settings. *Journal of the American Academy of Child and Adolescent Psychiatry, 29,* 710–718.

Gadow, K. D., & Sverd, J. (1990). Stimulants for ADHD in child patients with Tourette's syndrome: The issue of relative risk. *Developmental and Behavioral Pediatrics, 11,* 269–271.

Gammon, G. D., & Brown, T. E. (1993). Fluoxetine and methylphenidate in combination for treatment of attention deficit disorder and comorbid depressive disorder. *Journal of Child and Adolescent Psychopharmacology, 3,* 1–9.

Garfinkel, B. D., Wender, P. H., Sloman, L., & O'Neill, I. (1983). Tricyclic antidepressant and methylphenidate treatment of attention deficit disorder in children. *Journal of the American Academy of Child Psychiatry, 22,* 343–348.

Geller, B. (1991). Commentary on unexplained death of children on Norpramin. *Journal of the American Academy of Child and Adolescent Psychiatry, 30,* 682–684.

Giedd, J. N., Castellanos, F. X., Casey, B. J., Kozuch, P., King, A. C., Hamburger, S. D., & Rapoport, J. L. (1994). Quantitative morphology of the corpus callosum in attention deficit hyperactivity disorder. *American Journal of Psychiatry, 151,* 665–669.

Gittelman, R. (1983). Experimental and clinical studies of stimulant use in hyperactive children with other behavioral disorders. In I. Creese (Ed.), *Stimulants: Neurochemical, behavioral, and clinical perspectives* (pp. 205–225). New York: Raven.

Gittelman, R., Mannuzza, S., Shenker, R., & Bonagura, N. (1985). Hyperactive boys almost grown up. I. Psychiatric status. *Archives of General Psychiatry, 42,* 937–947.

Gittelman-Klein, R., Klein, D. F., Abikoff, H., Katz, S., Gloisten, A. C., & Kates, W. (1976). Relative efficacy of methylphenidate and behavior modification in hyperkinetic children: An interim report. *Journal of Abnormal Child Psychology, 4,* 361–379.

Gittelman-Klein, R., Klein, D. F., Katz, S., Saraf, K., & Pollack, E. (1976). Comparative effects of methylphenidate and thioridazine in hyperkinetic children. I. Clinical results. *Archives of General Psychiatry, 33,* 1217–1231.

Golden, G. S. (1986). Tourette syndrome: Recent advances. *Pediatric Neurology, 2,* 189–192.

Goyer, P. F., Davis, G. C., & Rapoport, J. L. (1979). Abuse of prescribed stimulant medication by a 13-year-old hyperactive boy. *Journal of the American Academy of Child Psychiatry, 18,* 170–175.

Greenhill, L., Puig-Antich, J., Goetz, R., Hanlon, C., & Davies, M. (1983). Sleep architecture and REM sleep measures in prepubertal children with attention deficit disorder with hyperactivity. *Sleep, 6,* 91–101.

Greenhill, L. L., Puig-Antich, J., Novacenko, H., Solomon, M., Anghern, C., Florea, J., Goetz, R., Fiscina, B., & Sachar, E. J. (1984). Prolactin, growth hormone and growth responses in boys with attention deficit disorder and hyperactivity treated with methylphenidate. *Journal of the American Academy of Child Psychiatry, 23,* 58–67.

Gualtieri, C. T., & Hicks, R. E. (1985). Neuropharmacology of methylphenidate and a neural substrate for childhood hyperactivity. *Psychiatric Clinics of North America, 8,* 875–892.

Gualtieri, C. T., Hicks, R. E., Patrick, K., Schroeder, S. R., & Breese, G. R. (1984). Clinical correlates of methylphenidate blood levels. *Therapeutic Drug Monitoring, 6,* 379–392.

Gualtieri, C. T., Quade, D., Hicke, R., Mayo, J., & Schroeder, S. (1984). Tardive dyskinesia and other clinical consequences of neuroleptic treatment in childhood and adolescence. *American Journal of Psychiatry, 141,* 20–23.

Gualtieri, C. T., Wargin, W., Kanoy, R., Patrick, K., Shen, C. D., Youngblood, W., Mueller, R. A., & Breese, G. R. (1982). Clinical studies of methylphenidate serum levels in children and adults. *Journal of the American Academy of Child Psychiatry, 21,* 19–26.

Halperin, J. M., Matier, K., Bedi, G., Sharma, V., & Newcorn, J. H. (1992). Specificity of inattention, impulsivity, and hyperactivity to the diagnosis of attention-deficit hyperactivity disorder. *Journal of the American Academy of Child and Adolescent Psychiatry, 31,* 190–196.

Handen, B. L., Breaux, A. M., Janosky, J., McAuliffe, S., Feldman, H., & Gosling, A. (1992). Effects and noneffects of methylphenidate in children with mental retardation and ADHD. *Journal of the American Academy of Child and Adolescent Psychiatry, 31,* 451–455.

Hart-Santora, D., & Hart, L. L. (1992). Clonidine in attention deficit hyperactivity disorder. *Annals of Pharmacotherapy, 26,* 37–39.

Hechtman, L. (1985). Adolescent outcome of hyperactive children treated with stimulants in childhood: A review. *Psychopharmacology Bulletin, 21,* 178–191.

Hechtman, L., Weiss, G., & Perlman, T. (1984). Hyperactives as young adults: Initial predictors of adult outcome. *Journal of the American Academy of Child and Adolescent Psychiatry, 23,* 250–260.

Hinshaw, S. P., Henker, B., Whalen, C. K., Erhardt, D., & Dunnington, R. E., Jr. (1989). Aggressive, prosocial, and nonsocial behavior in hyperactive boys: Dose effects of methylphenidate in naturalistic settings. *Journal of Consulting and Clinical Psychology, 57,* 636–643.

Hoffman, B. B., & Lefkowitz, R. J. (1990). Catecholamines and sympathomimetic drugs. In L. S. Goodman, A. Gilman, & A. G. Gilman (Eds.), *Goodman and Gilman's The pharmacological basis of therapeutics* (8th ed., pp. 187–220). New York: Pergamon.

Hoge, S. K., & Biederman, J. (1986). A case of Tourette's syndrome with symptoms of attention deficit disorder treated with desipramine. *Journal of Clinical Psychiatry, 47,* 478–479.

Horn, W. F., Ialongo, N. S., Pascoe, J. M., Greenberg, G., Packard, T., Lopez, M., Wagner, A., & Puttler, L. (1991). Additive effects of psychostimulants, parent training, and self-control therapy with ADHD children. *Journal of the American Academy of Child and Adolescent Psychiatry, 30,* 233–240.

Hunt, R. D. (1987). Treatment effects of oral and transdermal clonidine in relation to methylphenidate: An open pilot study in ADD-H. *Psychopharmacology Bulletin, 23,* 111–114.

Hunt, R. D., Lau, S., & Ryu, J. (1991). Alternative therapies for ADHD. In L. L. Greenhill & B. B. Osman (Eds.), *Ritalin: Theory and patient management* (pp. 75–95). New York: Mary Ann Liebert.

Hunt, R. D., Minderaa, R. B., & Cohen, D. J. (1985). Clonidine benefits children with attention deficit disorder and hyperactivity: Report of a double-blind placebo crossover therapeutic trial. *Journal of the American Academy of Child Psychiatry, 24,* 617–629.

Hunt, R. D., Minderaa, R. B., & Cohen, D. J. (1986). The therapeutic effect of clonidine in attention deficit disorder with hyperactivity: A comparison with placebo and methylphenidate. *Psychopharmacology Bulletin, 22,* 229–236.

Hynd, G. W., Hern, K. L., Novey, E. S., Eliopulos, D., Marshall, R., Gonzalez, J. J., & Voeller, K. K. S. (1993). Attention deficit hyperactivity disorder and asymmetry of the caudate nucleus. *Journal of Child Neurology, 8,* 339–347.

Hynd, G. W., Lorys, A. R., Semrud-Clikeman, M., Nieves, N., Huettner, M. I. S., & Lahey, B. B. (1991). Attention deficit disorder without hyperactivity: A distinct behavioral and neurocognitive syndrome. *Journal of Child Neurology, 6,* S37–S43.

Hynd, G. W., Semrud-Clikeman, M., Lorys, A. R., Novey, E. S., & Eliopulos, D. (1990). Brain morphology in developmental dyslexia and attention deficit disorder/hyperactivity. *Archives of Neurology, 47,* 919–926.

Hynd, G. W., Semrud-Clikeman, M., Lorys, A. R., Novey, E. S., Eliopulos, D., & Lyytinen, H. (1991). Corpus callosum morphology in attention-deficit hyperactivity disorder: Morphometric analysis of MRI. *Journal of Learning Disabilities, 24,* 141–146.

Ialongo, N. S., Horn, W. F., Pascoe, J. M., Greenberg, G., Packard, T., Lopez, M., Wagner, A., & Puttler, L. (1993). The effects of a multimodal intervention with attention-deficit hyperactivity disorder children: A 9-month follow-up. *Journal of the American Academy of Child and Adolescent Psychiatry, 32,* 182–189.

Ickowicz, A., Tannock, R., Fulford, P., Purvis, K., & Schachar, R. (1992). Transient tics and compulsive behaviors following methylphenidate: Evidence from a placebo-controlled double-blind clinical trial. *Scientific Proceedings of the American Academy of Child and Adolescent Psychiatry, VII,* 70.

Jaffe, S. L. (1991). Intranasal abuse of prescribed methylphenidate by an alcohol and drug abusing adolescent with ADHD. *Journal of the American Academy of Child and Adolescent Psychiatry, 30,* 773–775.

Jankovic, J. (1993). Deprenyl in attention deficit associated with Tourette's syndrome. *Archives of Neurology, 50,* 286–288.

Keith, R. W., & Engineer, P. (1991). Effects of methylphenidate on the auditory processing abilities of children with attention deficit-hyperactivity disorder. *Journal of Learning Disabilities, 24,* 630–636.

Kelly, D. P., & Aylward, G. P. (1992). Attention deficits in school-aged children and adolescents. Current issues and practice. *Pediatric Clinics of North America, 39,* 487–512.

Kemph, J. P., DeVane, C. L., Levin, G. M., Jarecke, R., & Miller, R. L. (1993). Treatment of aggressive children with clonidine: Results of an open pilot study. *Journal of the American Academy of Child and Adolescent Psychiatry, 32,* 577–581.

Klein, R. G. (1987). Prognosis of attention deficit disorder and its management of adolescence. *Pediatrics in Review, 8,* 216–222.

Klein, R. G. (1991). Effects of high methylphenidate doses on the cognitive performance of hyperactive children. *Bratislavske Lekarske Listy, 92,* 534–539.

Klein, R. G. (1993). Clinical efficacy of methylphenidate in children and adolescents. *Encephale, 19,* 89–93.

Klein, R. G., Landa, B., Mattes, J. A., & Klein, D. F. (1988). Methylphenidate and growth in hyperactive children. A controlled withdrawal study. *Archives of General Psychiatry, 45,* 1127–1130.

Klein, R. G., & Mannuzza, S. (1991). Long-term outcome of hyperactive children: A review. *Journal of the American Academy of Child and Adolescent Psychiatry, 30,* 383–387.

Klorman, R., Brumaghim, J. T., Fitzpatrick, P. A., & Borgstedt, A. D. (1991). Methylphenidate speeds evaluation processes of attention deficit disorder adolescents during a continuous performance test. *Journal of Abnormal Child Psychology, 19,* 263–283.

Kruesi, M. J., & Rapoport, J. L. (1986). Diet and human behavior: How much do they affect each other? *Annual Review of Nutrition, 6,* 113–130.

Kruesi, M. J. P., Rapoport, J. L., Cummings, E. M., Berg, C. J., Ismond, D. R., Flament, M., Yarrow, M., & Zahn-Waxler, C. (1987). Effects of sugar and aspartame on aggression and activity in children. *American Journal of Psychiatry, 144,* 1487–1490.

Kupietz, S. S. (1991). Ritalin blood levels and their correlations with measures of learning. In L. L. Greenhill & B. B. Osman (Eds.), *Ritalin: Theory and patient management* (pp. 247–255). New York: Mary Ann Liebert.

Lahey, B. B., Pelham, W. E., Schaughency, E. A., Atkins, M. S., Murphy, H. A., Hynd, G., Russo, M., Hartdagen, S., & Lorys-Vernon, A. (1988). Dimensions and types of attention deficit disorder. *Journal of the American Academy of Child and Adolescent Psychiatry, 27,* 330–335.

Lahey, B. B., Schaughency, E. A., Hynd, G. W., Calrson, C. L., & Nieves, N. (1987). Attention deficit disorder with and without hyperactivity: Comparison of behavioral characteristics of clinic-referred children. *Journal of the American Academy of Child and Adolescent Psychiatry, 26,* 718–723.

Lahey, B. B., Schaughency, E. A., Strauss, C. C., & Frame, C. L. (1984). Are attention deficit disorders with and without hyperactivity similar or dissimilar disorders? *Journal of the American Academy of Child Psychiatry, 23,* 302–309.

Leckman, J. F., Hardin, M. T., Riddle, M. A., Stevenson, J., Ort, S. I., & Cohen, D. J. (1991). Clonidine treatment of Gilles de la Tourette's syndrome. *Archives of General Psychiatry, 48,* 324–328.

Leckman, J. F., Ort, S., Caruso, K. A., Anderson, G. M., Riddle, M. A., & Cohen, D. J. (1986). Rebound phenomena in Tourette's syndrome after abrupt withdrawal of clonidine. Behavioral, cardiovascular, and neurochemical effects. *Archives of General Psychiatry, 43,* 1168–1176.

Lowe, T. L., Cohen, D. J., Detlor, J., Kremenitzer, M. W., & Shaywitz, B. A. (1982). Stimulant medications precipitate Tourette's syndrome. *Journal of the American Medical Association, 247,* 1729–1731.

Mannuzza, S., Klein, R. G., Bessler, A., Malloy, P., & LaPadula, M. (1993). Adult outcome of hyperactive boys. Educational achievement, occupational rank, and psychiatric status. *Archives of General Psychiatry, 50,* 565–576.

Mannuzza, S., Klein, R. G., Konig, P. H., & Giampino, T. L. (1989). Hyperactive boys almost grown up. IV. Criminality and its relationship to psychiatric status. *Archives of General Psychiatry, 46,* 1073–1079.

Mattes, J. A., & Gittelman, R. (1983). Growth of hyperactive children on maintenance regimen of methylphenidate. *Archives of General Psychiatry, 40,* 317–321.

McBurnett, K., Lahey, B. B., & Swanson, J. M. (1991). Ritalin treatment in attention deficit disorder without hyperactivity. In L. L. Greenhill & B. B. Osman (Eds.), *Ritalin: Theory and patient management* (pp. 257–265). New York: Mary Ann Liebert.

McGee, R., Williams, S., & Feehan, M. (1992). Attention deficit disorder and age of onset of problem behaviors. *Journal of Abnormal Child Psychology, 20,* 487–502.

Medical Economics Data. (1994). *Physicians' desk reference.* Montvale, NJ: Medical Economics Company.

Mefford, I. N., & Potter, W. Z. (1989). A neuroanatomical and biochemical basis for attention deficit disorder with hyperactivity in children: A defect in tonic adrenaline mediated inhibition of locus coeruleus stimulation. *Medical Hypotheses, 29,* 33–42.

Murphy, D. A., Pelham, W. E., & Lang, A. R. (1992). Aggression in boys with attention deficit-hyperactivity disorder: Methylphenidate effects on naturalistically observed aggression, response to provocation, and social information processing. *Journal of Abnormal Child Psychology, 20,* 451–466.

Nehra, A., Mullick, F., Ishak, K. G., & Zimmerman, H. J. (1990). Pemoline associated hepatic injury. *Gastroenterology, 99,* 1517–1519.

Pataki, C. S., Carlson, G. A., Kelly, K. L., Rapport, M. D., & Biancaniello, T. M. (1993). Side effects of methylphenidate and desipramine alone and in combination in children. *Journal of the American Academy of Child and Adolescent Psychiatry, 32,* 1065–1072.

Pelham, W. E., Jr., Carlson, C., Sams, S. E., Vallano, G., Dixon, M. J., & Hoza, B. (1993). Separate and combined effects of methylphenidate and behavior modification on boys with attention deficit-hyperactivity disorder in the classroom. *Journal of Consulting and Clinical Psychology, 61,* 506–515.

Pelham, W. E., Jr., Greenslade, K. E., Vodde-Hamilton, M., Murphy, D. A., Greenstein, J. J., Gnagy, E. M., Guthrie, K. J., Hoover, M. D., & Dahl, R. E. (1990). Relative efficacy of long-acting stimulants on children with attention-deficit-hyperactivity-disorder: A comparison of standard methylphenidate, sustained-release dextroamphetamine, and pemoline. *Pediatrics, 86,* 226–237.

Pliszka, S. R. (1987). Tricyclic antidepressants in the treatment of children with attention deficit disorder. *Journal of the American Academy of Child and Adolescent Psychiatry, 26,* 127–132.

Popper, C. W., & Elliott, G. R. (1990). Sudden death and tricyclic antidepressants: Clinical considerations for children. *Journal of Child and Adolescent Psychopharmacology, 1,* 125–132.

Porrino, L. J., Rapoport, J. L., Behar, D., Ismond, D., & Bunney, W. E. (1983a). A naturalistic assessment of the motor activity of hyperactive boys. *Archives of General Psychiatry, 40,* 688–693.

Porrino, L. J., Rapoport, J. L., Behar, D., Sceery, W., Ismond, D. R., & Bunney, W. E., Jr. (1983b). A naturalistic assessment of the motor activity of hyperactive boys: I. Comparison with normal controls. *Archives of General Psychiatry, 40,* 681–687.

Price, R. A., Leckman, J. F., Pauls, D. L., Cohen, D. J., & Kidd, K. K. (1986). Gilles de la Tourette's syndrome: Tics and central nervous system stimulants in twin and nontwins. *Neurology, 36,* 232–237.

Rapoport, J. L., Buchsbaum, M. S., Weingartner, H., Zahn, T. P., Ludlow, C., & Mikkelsen, E. J. (1980). Dextroamphetamine. Its cognitive and behavioral effects in normal and hyperactive boys and normal men. *Archives of General Psychiatry, 37,* 933–943.

Rapoport, J. L., Buchsbaum, M. S., Zahn, T. P., Weingartner, H., Ludlow, C., & Mikkelsen, E. J. (1978). Dextroamphetamine: Cognitive and behavioral effects in normal prepubertal boys. *Science, 199,* 560–563.

Rapoport, J. L., & Ismond, D. (in press). *DSM-IV training guide for diagnosis of childhood disorders* (3rd ed.). New York: Brunner/Mazel.

Rapoport, J. L., Quinn, P. O., Bradbard, G., Riddle, K. D., & Brooks, E. (1974). Imipramine and methylphenidate treatments of hyperactive boys. A double-blind comparison. *Archives of General Psychiatry, 30,* 789–793.

Rapport, M. D., Carlson, G. A., Kelly, K. L., & Pataki, C. (1993). Methylphenidate and desipramine in hospitalized children: I. Separate and combined effects on cognitive function. *Journal of the American Academy of Child and Adolescent Psychiatry, 32,* 333–342.

Rapport, M. D., Denney, C., DuPaul, G. J., & Gardner, M. J. (1994). Attention deficit disorder and methylphenidate: Normalization rates, clinical effectiveness, and response prediction in 76 children. *Journal of the American Academy of Child and Adolescent Psychiatry, 33,* 882–893.

Rapport, M. D., & Kelly, K. L. (1991). Psychostimulant effects on learning and cognitive function: Findings and implications for children with attention deficit hyperactivity disorder. *Clinical Psychology Review, 11,* 61–92.

Rebec, G. V., & Segal, D. S. (1978). Dose-dependent biphasic alterations in the spontaneous activity of neurons in the rat neostriatum produced by d-amphetamine and methylphenidate. *Brain Research, 150,* 353–366.

Richardson, E., Kupietz, S. S., Winsberg, W. G., Maitinsky, S., & Mendell, N. (1988). Effects of methylphenidate dosage in hyperactive reading-disabled children: II. Reading achievement. *Journal of the American Academy of Child and Adolescent Psychiatry, 27,* 78–87.

Riddle, K. D., & Rapoport, J. L. (1976). A 2-year follow-up of 72 hyperactive boys. Classroom behavior and peer acceptance. *Journal of Nervous and Mental Disease, 162,* 126–134.

Riddle, M. A., Geller, B., & Ryan, N. (1993). Another sudden death in a child treated with desipramine. *Journal of the American Academy of Child and Adolescent Psychiatry, 32,* 792–797.

Riddle, M. A., Geller, B., & Ryan, N. D. (1994). The safety of desipramine [Reply to letter]. *Journal of the American Academy of Child and Adolescent Psychiatry, 33,* 589–590.

Riddle, M. A., Nelson, J. C., Kleinman, C. S., Ramusson, A., Leckman, J. F., King, R. A., & Cohen, D. J. (1991). Sudden death in children receiving Norpramin: A review of three reported cases and commentary. *Journal of the American Academy of Child and Adolescent Psychiatry, 30,* 104–108.

Rubinstein, S., Silver, L. B., & Licamele, W. L. (1994). Clonidine for stimulant-related sleep problems [letter]. *Journal of the American Academy of Child and Adolescent Psychiatry, 33,* 281–282.

Safer, D. J., & Allen, R. P. (1989). Absence of tolerance to the behavioral effects of methylphenidate in hyperactive and inattentive children. *Journal of Pediatrics, 115,* 1003–1008.

Safer, D. J., Allen, R. P., & Barr, E. (1972). Depression of growth in hyperactive children on stimulant drugs. *The New England Journal of Medicine, 287,* 217–220.

Sallee, F. R., Stiller, R. L., & Perel, J. M. (1992). Pharmacodynamics of pemoline in attention deficit disorder with hyperactivity. *Journal of the American Academy of Child and Adolescent Psychiatry, 31,* 244–251.

Sallee, F. R., Stiller, R. L., Perel, J. M., & Bates, T. (1985). Oral pemoline kinetics in hyperactive children. *Clinical Pharmacology and Therapeutics, 37,* 606–609.

Satterfield, J. H., Cantwell, D. P., Schell, A., & Blaschke, T. (1979). Growth of hyperactive children with methylphenidate. *Archives of General Psychiatry, 36,* 212–217.

Saunders, L. (1974). *The absorption and distribution of drugs.* Baltimore: Williams and Wilkins.

Schaughency, E. A., & Rothlind, J. (1991). Assessment and classification of attention deficit hyperactivity disorders. *School Psychology Review, 20,* 187–202.

Schleifer, M., Weiss, G., Cohen, N., Elman, M., Cvejic, H., & Kruger, E. (1975). Hyperactivity in preschoolers and the effect of methylphenidate. *American Journal of Orthopsychiatry, 45,* 38–50.

Schvehla, J. T., Mandoki, M. W., & Sumner, G. S. (1994). Clonidine therapy for comorbid attention deficit hyperactivity disorder and conduct disorder: Preliminary findings in a children's inpatient unit. *Southern Medical Journal, 87,* 692–695.

Semrud-Clikeman, M., Filipek, P. A., Biederman, J., Steingard, R., Kennedy, D., Renshaw, P., & Bekken, K. (1994). Attention-deficit hyperactivity disorder: Magnetic resonance imaging morphometric analysis of the corpus callosum. *Journal of the American Academy of Child and Adolescent Psychiatry, 33,* 875–881.

Sergeant, J., & Van der Meere, J. J. (1991). Ritalin effects and information processing in hyperactivity. In L. L. Greenhill & B. B. Osman (Eds.), *Ritalin: Theory and patient management* (pp. 1–13). New York: Mary Ann Liebert.

Shaffer, D. (1994). Attention deficit hyperactivity disorder in adults. *American Journal of Psychiatry, 151,* 633–638.

Shaywitz, B. A., Shaywitz, S. E., Sebrechts, M. M., Anderson, G. M., Cohen, D. J., Jatlow, P., & Young, G. J. (1990). Growth hormone and prolactin response to methylphenidate in children with attention deficit disorder. *Life Sciences, 46,* 625–633.

Shaywitz, S. E., Hunt, R. D., Jatlow, P., Cohen, D. J., Young, J. G., Pierce, R. N., Anderson, G. M., & Shaywitz, B. A. (1982). Psychopharmacology of attention deficit disorder: Pharmacokinetic, neuroendocrine, and behavioral measures following acute and chronic treatment with methylphenidate. *Pediatrics, 69,* 688–694.

Shaywitz, S. E., Shaywitz, B. A., Jatlow, P. R., Seabrects, M., Anderson, G. M., & Cohen, D. J. (1983). Biological differentiation of attention deficit disorder with and without hyperactivity: A preliminary report. *Annals of Neurology, 14,* 363.

Shekim, W. O., Asarnow, R. F., Hess, E., Zaucha, K., & Wheeler, N. (1990). A clinical and demographic profile of a sample of adults with attention deficit hyperactivity disorder, residual state. *Comprehensive Psychiatry, 31,* 416–425.

Silver, L. B. (1992). Diagnosis of attention-deficit hyperactivity disorder in adult life. *Child and Adolescent Psychiatric Clinics of North America, 1,* 325–334.

Sleator, E. K. (1980). Deleterious effects of drugs used for hyperactivity on patients with Gilles de la Tourette syndrome. *Clinical Pediatrics, 19,* 453–454.

Sleator, E. K., Ullmann, R. K., & von Neumann, A. (1982). How do hyperactive children feel about taking stimulants and will they tell the doctor? *Clinical Pediatrics, 21,* 474–479.

Snyder, S. H., & Meyerhoff, J. L. (1973). How amphetamine acts in minimal brain dysfunction. *Annals of the New York Academy of Sciences, 205,* 310–320.

Sostek, A. J., Buchsbaum, M. S., & Rapoport, J. L. (1980). Effects of amphetamine on vigilance performance in normal and hyperactive children. *Journal of Abnormal Child Psychology, 8,* 491–500.

Spencer, T., Biederman, J., Wilens, T., Steingard, R., & Geist, D. (1993). Nortriptyline treatment of children with attention-deficit hyperactivity disorder and tic disorder or Tourette's syndrome. *Journal of the American Academy of Child and Adolescent Psychiatry, 32,* 205–210.

Spencer, T., Biederman, J., Wright, V., & Danon, M. (1992). Growth deficits in children treated with desipramine: A controlled study. *Journal of the American Academy of Child and Adolescent Psychiatry, 31,* 235–243.

Spencer, T., Wilens, T., Biederman, J., Faraone, S. V., Ablon, J. S., & Lapey, K. (1995). A double-blind, crossover comparison of methylphenidate and placebo in adults with childhood onset attention deficit hyperactivity disorder. *Archives of General Psychiatry, 52,* 434–443.

Sprague, R. L., & Sleator, E. K. (1977). Methylphenidate in hyperkinetic children: Differences in dose effects on learning and social behavior. *Science, 198,* 1274–1276.

Steingard, R., Biederman, J., Spencer, T., Wilens, T., & Gonzalez, A. (1993). Comparison of clonidine response in the treatment of attention-deficit hyperactivity disorder with and without comorbid tic disorders. *Journal of the American Academy of Child and Adolescent Psychiatry, 32,* 350–353.

Stine, J. J. (1994). Psychosocial and psychodynamic issues affecting noncompliance with psychostimulant treatment. *Journal of Child and Adolescent Psychopharmacology, 4,* 75–86.

Sverd, J., Gadow, K. D., & Paolicelli, L. M. (1989). Methylphenidate treatment of attention-deficit hyperactivity disorder in boys with Tourette's syndrome. *Journal of the American Academy of Child and Adolescent Psychiatry, 28,* 574–579.

Swanson, J. M., Cantwell, D., Lerner, M., McBurnett, K., Pfiffner, L., & Kotkin, R. (1993). Treatment of ADHD: Beyond medication. *Beyond Behavior,* 13–22.

Swanson, J. M., Sandman, C. A., Deutsch, C., & Baren, M. (1983). Methylphenidate hydrochloride given with or before breakfast: I. Behavioral, cognitive, and electrophysiologic effects. *Pediatrics, 72,* 49–55.

Sykes, D. H., Douglas, V. I., Weiss, G., & Minde, K. K. (1971). Attention in hyperactive children and the effect of methylphenidate (Ritalin). *Journal of Child Psychology & Psychiatry & Allied Disciplines, 12,* 129–139.

Szatmari, P. (1992). The epidemiology of attention-deficit hyperactivity disorder. *Child and Adolescent Psychiatric Clinics of North America, 1,* 361–371.

Tirosh, E., Sadeh, A., Munvez, R., & Lavie, P. (1993). Effects of methylphenidate on sleep in children with attention-deficient hyperactivity disorder. An activity monitor study. *American Journal of Diseases of Children, 147,* 1313–1315.

Trommer, B. L., Hoeppner, J. B., Rosenberg, R. S., Armstrong, K. J., & Rothstein, J. A. (1988). Sleep disturbance in children with attention deficit disorder. *Annals of Neurology, 24,* 322.

Trott, G. E., Friese, H. J., Menzel, M., & Nissen, G. (1992). Use of moclobemide in children with attention deficit hyperactivity disorder. *Psychopharmacology (Berl),* (Suppl. 106), S134–S136.

Vincent, G. M., Jaiswal, D., & Timothy, K. W. (1991). Effects of exercise on heart rate, QT, QTc and QT/QS2 in the Romano-Ward inherited long QT syndrome. *American Journal of Cardiology, 68,* 498–503.

Waltz, G. (1990). Change in response to pemoline at puberty [letter]. *American Journal of Psychiatry, 147,* 368.

Ward, M. F., Wender, P. H., & Reimherr, F. W. (1993). The WURS: A rating scale to aid in the retrospective diagnosis of attention deficit disorder in childhood. *American Journal of Psychiatry, 150,* 885–890.

Wargin, W., Patrick, K., Kilts, C., Gualtieri, C. T., Ellington, K., Mueller, R. A., Kraemer, G., & Breese, G. R. (1983). Pharmacokinetics of methylphenidate in man, rat, and monkey. *Journal of Pharmacology and Experimental Therapeutics, 226,* 382–386.

Wechsler, D. (1991). *Manual for the Wechsler Intelligence Scale for Children* (3rd ed.). San Antonio, TX: The Psychological Corporation.

Weingartner, H., Langer, D., Grice, J., & Rapoport, J. L. (1982). Acquisition and retrieval of information in amphetamine-treated hyperactive children. *Psychiatry Research, 6,* 21–29.

Weiss, G., (1985). Follow-up studies on outcome of hyperactive children. *Psychopharmacology Bulletin, 21,* 169–177.

Weiss, G., Hechtman, L., Milroy, T., & Perlman, T. (1985). Psychiatric status of hyperactives as adults: A controlled prospective 15-year follow-up of 63 hyperactive children. *Journal of the American Academy of Child Psychiatry, 24,* 211–220.

Weiss, G., Kruger, E., Danielson, U., & Elman, M. (1975). Effect of long-term treatment of hyperactive children with methylphenidate. *Canadian Medical Association Journal, 112,* 159–165.

Weiss, G., Werry, J., Minde, K., Douglas, V. I., & Sykes, D. (1968). Studies on the hyperactive child-V: The effects of dextroamphetamine and chlorpromazine on behavior and intellectual functioning. *Journal of Child Psychology & Psychiatry & Allied Disciplines, 9,* 145–156.

Wender, P. H. (1993). Methamphetamine in child psychiatry. *Journal of Child and Adolescent Psychopharmacology, 3,* iv–vi.

Wender, P. H., Wood, D. R., & Reimherr, F. W. (1984). Studies in attention deficit disorder, residual type (minimal brain dysfunction in adults). *Psychopharmacology Bulletin, 20,* 18–20.

Wender, P. H., Wood, D. R., Reimherr, F. W., & Ward, M. (1983). An open trial of pargyline in the treatment of attention deficit disorder, residual type. *Psychiatry Research, 9,* 329–336.

Werry, J. S. (1994). The safety of desipramine [letter]. *Journal of the American Academy of Child and Adolescent Psychiatry, 33,* 588–591.

Werry, J. S., & Aman, M. G. (1975). Methylphenidate and haloperidol in children. Effects on attention, memory, and activity. *Archives of General Psychiatry, 32,* 790–795.

Werry, J. S., Aman, M. G., & Lampen, E. (1976). Haloperidol and methylphenidate in hyperactive children. *Acta paedopsychiatrica, 42,* 26–40.

Whalen, C. K., & Henker, B. (1991). Social impact of stimulant treatment for hyperactive children. *Journal of Learning Disabilities, 24,* 231–241.

Whalen, C. K., Henker, B., Swanson, J. M., Granger, D., Kliewer, W., & Spencer, J. (1987). Natural social behaviors in hyperactive children: Dose effects of methylphenidate. *Journal of Consulting and Clinical Psychology, 55,* 187–193.

Wilens, T. E., Biederman, J., & Spencer, T. (1994). Clonidine for sleep disturbances associated with attention-deficit hyperactivity disorder. *Journal of the American Academy of Child and Adolescent Psychiatry, 33,* 424–426.

Wolraich, M., Drummond, T., Salomon, M. K., O'Brien, M. L., & Sivage, C. (1978). Effects of methylphenidate alone and in combination with behavior modification procedures on the behavior and academic performance of hyperactive children. *Journal of Abnormal Child Psychology, 6,* 149–161.

Wolraich, M. L., Lindgren, S. D., Stumbo, P. J., Stegink, L. D., Appelbaum, M. I., & Kiritsy, M. C. (1994). Effects of diets high in sucrose or aspartame on the behavior and cognitive performance of children. *The New England Journal of Medicine, 330,* 301–307.

Woodcock, R. W., & Johnson, B. B. (1977). *Woodcock-Johnson Psychoeducational Battery.* Allen, TX: DLM Teaching Resources.

Young, J. G. (1981). Methylphenidate-induced hallucinosis: Case histories and possible mechanisms of action. *Journal of Developmental and Behavioral Pediatrics, 2,* 35–38.

Zametkin, A. J., & Rapoport, J. L. (1987a). Neurobiology of attention-deficit disorder with hyperactivity: Where have we come in 50 years? *Journal of the American Academy of Child and Adolescent Psychiatry, 26,* 676–686.

Zametkin, A. J., & Rapoport, J. L. (1987b). Noradrenergic hypothesis of attention deficit disorder with hyperactivity: A critical review. In H. Y. Meltzer (Ed.), *Psychopharmacology: The third generation of progress* (pp. 837–842). New York: Raven.

Zametkin, A. J., Rapoport, J. L., Murphy, D. L., Linnoila, M., & Ismond, D. (1985). Treatment of hyperactive children with monoamine oxidase inhibitors. *Archives of General Psychiatry, 42,* 962–966.

Zimnitzky, B., & Popper, C. W. (1994). A fifth case of sudden death in a child taking desipramine. *New Research Abstracts, The Sesquicentennial Annual Meeting of the American Psychiatric Association,* 181.

Anxiety Disorders

CHARLES W. POPPER, M.D. and
PETER C. GHERARDI, M.D.

Anxiety symptoms are so common in our culture that clinicians often fail to identify them, especially in children and adolescents. Many adults actually expect children to be shy, anxious, or fearful. Although children can have "age-appropriate anxiety" at certain developmental periods, similar anxiety symptoms are considered pathological when they persist or are unusually severe. For example, an 8-year-old who has difficulty leaving a parent for a weekend trip with friends, or an adolescent who is fearful about speaking up in class, could be suffering from a biopsychiatric disorder which is expressed in part through prominent symptoms of anxiety. In addition, children may experience an abundance of situational stressors, traumatic experiences, and abusive encounters. Children and parents are often surprised to view anxiety, which is commonly attributed to situational and developmental causes, as potentially being an expression of a medical disorder.

EPIDEMIOLOGY

Despite their imprecision, several prevalence studies suggest that anxiety disorders may be the most common of child and adolescent psychiatric disorders. The Epidemiologic Catchment Area (ECA) studies of the 1980s, and more recent community studies, have yielded tentative and limited prevalence estimates across the developmental spectrum (Costello, 1989a, 1989b; Kashani & Orvaschel, 1990; Last, Perrin, Hersen, & Kazdin, 1992; Lewinsohn, Hops, Roberts, Seeley, & Andrews, 1993; Regier et al., 1988). These epidemiological data suggest a 6-month prevalence of anxiety disorders in the general population of child and adolescents of about 9%, approximately as prevalent as in adults (see Table 9.1).

In these studies, preadolescent children appeared to suffer most commonly from separation anxiety disorder and overanxious disorder. Adolescents presented predominantly with overanxious disorder and simple phobias. In contrast, adults reported phobic disorders more frequently than other anxiety disorders.

The 9% prevalence figure in the general population was supported by a more recent study of 1,710 high school students, which estimated the likelihood of developing some form of clinical anxiety disorder before the age of 18 (Lewinsohn et al., 1993). Anxiety disorders were the most prevalent class of psychiatric conditions in this high school population.

Last, Strauss, and Francis (1987) examined the distribution of diagnostic subtypes of anxiety disorders in a clinical population. Among 73 consecutively referred children (ages 5–18 years) in a clinic specializing in anxiety disorders, separation anxiety disorder was reported in 33% of the sample. The next most frequent diagnoses were overanxious disorder, major depression, and social phobia; each of these three disorders

Table 9.1.   Six-Month Prevalence of Anxiety Disorders across the Lifespan in the General Population

Anxiety Disorder	Preadolescents (%)	Adolescents (%)	Adults (%)
Overanxious disorder	4	6	3
Simple phobia	3	4	4.5
Separation anxiety disorder	4	1	NA
Avoidant disorder	2	?	NA
Social phobia	1	?	2.1
Agoraphobia	1	?	2.8
Generalized anxiety disorder	NA	NA	3
Total	8.9	8.7	9.6

Note: Data from various ECA studies.

NA = Diagnostic label is not applied to this age group.

Column sums are greater than column totals because of comorbidity.

Reprinted with permission from Popper, 1993.

were present in 15% of the children. Panic disorder was diagnosed in only 3% of the patients.

Such prevalence estimates are dependent on ascertainment biases, age-related differences in anxiety presentations, variations in reporting agreement between parent and child, use of reliable and validated diagnostic interviews, and use of standardized criteria for impairment in functioning (Bird et al., 1988; Costello, 1989a, 1989b; Kashani & Orvaschel, 1990; McGee et al., 1990). Despite some advances in the development and validation of standardized rating scales for the measurement of anxiety in this population (Clark & Donovan, 1994), there are no reliable anxiety rating scales for children or adolescents.

In view of all these variables as well as the apparent developmental shifting among recognized diagnostic categories, it is surprising that the overall prevalence of anxiety disorders does not appear to change markedly over a lifetime: Prepubertal children, adolescents and adults all have similar 6-month prevalence rates of approximately 9%.

DIAGNOSIS

Concerns about anxiety are often not the initial reason for psychiatric referral of these children. Their anxiety disorders may be comorbid conditions presenting in the context of other concurrent diagnoses, such as depression (Bernstein, 1991; Moreau, Weissman, & Warner, 1989) or ADHD (Biederman, Newcorn, & Sprich, 1991; George, Bouvard, & Dugas, 1993). When an anxiety disorder is identified, it often is just one part of a cluster of concurrent anxiety disorders (Last et al., 1987). Identifying these comorbid anxiety disorders can reduce the severity and especially the chronicity of suffering in many youths.

It is sometimes difficult to distinguish anxiety disorders from anxiety that is caused by situational or developmental factors. Both anxiety and anxiety disorders can involve distractibility, motoric overactivity, transient ego dysfunction, impaired cognition, depersonalization, depression, and angry outbursts. Both might involve a biological predisposition to anxious arousal. Both may be mimicked by or result from primary medical illnesses (hyperthyroidism, diabetes), drug-induced conditions, or other psychiatric disorders. Because anxiety is a final common pathway for various etiological categories, a thorough medical and psychiatric workup is essential to rule out alternative or concurrent causes of anxiety.

The current Diagnostic and Statistical Manual of Mental Disorders (DSM-IV; American Psychiatric Association [APA], 1994) nosology reflects an evolution of thinking on anxiety disorders. In the metamorphosis from DSM-III-R, Overanxious Disorder was subsumed into Generalized Anxiety Disorder, and Avoidant Disorder did not survive (and is now generally coded as Social Phobia). In addition, children may be assigned anxiety diagnoses that are co-opted from the adult nosology, effectively extending the criteria to include children. This change in DSM-IV reflects movement toward recognizing a developmental influence on the nosology of anxiety disorders. The current DSM-IV anxiety disorders are presented in Table 9.2.

This chapter will review the DSM-IV diagnostic categories of anxiety disorders, beginning with the disorders first diagnosed in youth and then proceeding to the adult anxiety disorders. Obsessive-compulsive disorder (OCD) will be discussed in Chapter 10, which covers Tourette's and tic disorders, because of their clinical and genetic interconnections. Each diagnostic category will include a review of clinical presentation, diagnostic evaluation, course and prognosis, established psychopharmacological approaches, and suggestions on clinical use. In the final portion of this review, an overview of the psychopharmacological agents by class will then be presented with particular attention to indications, dosing regimens, and side effects pertinent to the treatment of anxiety disorders.

Currently, the benzodiazepines, beta blockers, tricyclic antidepressants, serotonin reuptake inhibitors, and buspirone are considered the mainstays of treatment of anxiety disorders in children and adolescents. An earlier literature review might have included meprobamate, psychostimulants, neuroleptics, and antihistamines; these agents have fallen out of favor for treating anxiety disorders and are infrequently used at this time. The conventional monoamine oxidase inhibitors (MAOIs), though often quite effective in adults, are rarely selected because it is difficult

Table 9.2. Major Anxiety Disorders in DSM-IV

Anxiety disorders that may be diagnosed in adults or children:
  Panic Disorders (With or Without Agoraphobia)
  Agoraphobia Without a History of Panic Disorder
  Posttraumatic Stress Disorder
  Specific Phobia (formerly Simple Phobia)
  Social Phobia (Social Anxiety Disorder)
  Generalized Anxiety Disorder

   (Includes Overanxious Disorder of Childhood)

  Obsessive-Compulsive Disorder
  Acute Stress Disorder
  Anxiety Disorder due to . . . (Indicate the general medical condition)
  Substance-Induced Anxiety Disorder
  Anxiety Disorder Not Otherwise Specified
  Adjustment Disorder with Anxiety

Disorders usually first diagnosed in infancy, childhood, or adolescence:
  Separation Anxiety Disorder
  Selective Mutism (formerly Elective Mutism)
   [Not classified as an anxiety disorder]

to ensure proper dietary supervision in children and adolescents. No data are yet available on treating childhood anxiety disorders with the new reversible monoamine oxidase inhibitors (RIMAs), such as meclobemide, which do not entail dietary restrictions.

CHILD AND ADOLESCENT ANXIETY DISORDERS

Separation Anxiety Disorder

Although many parents and teachers are familiar with the concept of separation anxiety from reading about child development, relatively few are aware that it may sometimes reflect a significant biomedical disorder. Due to the confounding influence of the developmental phenomenon of separation anxiety, the medical condition called "separation anxiety disorder" is typically not identified as a distinct diagnostic problem before the age of 4 years. Although symptoms may appear during early childhood, the medical disorder is usually first recognized during mid childhood, when it begins to disrupt family or social functioning, or when it includes school absenteeism as one of its manifestations.

DSM-IV continues to subsume school absenteeism under separation anxiety disorder, which is quite misleading and frequently results in some confusion. Not all children with separation anxiety disorder have school absenteeism, and not all children with school absenteeism have separation anxiety (Last, Francis, & Hersen, 1987). In fact, school absenteeism can result not only from separation anxiety disorder, but also from depression, conduct disorder, drug-induced effects, familial influences, sociocultural factors, and a host of additional medical and psychosocial causes (see Table 9.3).

The terms "school phobia," "school avoidance," and "school refusal" are misnomers: most school "phobics" are not actually phobic, and the terms "avoidance" and "refusal" imply psychological mechanisms that do not apply in many cases. The general term "school absenteeism" describes a common child psychiatric problem in a descriptively neutral, mechanism-independent way. This term also alludes to possible similarities with job absenteeism in adults.

School absenteeism is reported in about 75% of children with separation anxiety disorder, and separation anxiety disorder is reported in up to 50% to 80% of school absentees (Klein & Last, 1989).

Clinical Presentation and Diagnostic Evaluation.   Separation anxiety disorder can be understood as essentially a phobic disorder, which differs from other anxiety disorders by its focus on separation. In separation anxiety disorder, cognitive, affective, somatic, and behavioral symptoms appear in response to genuine or fantasied separation from attachment figures. The DSM-IV diagnostic criteria are presented in Table 9.4.

There appear to be some differences in how separation anxiety disorder is expressed at different ages. Francis, Last, and Strauss (1987) reported that younger children (ages 5–8 years) showed the widest range of

Table 9.3.   Sources of School Absenteeism

Truancy (conduct disorder)

Anxiety disorders (especially separation anxiety disorder)

Major depression (and some bipolar disorder)

Overt psychosis

Substance abuse

Medication-induced depression-like reaction (beta blockers, neuroleptics)

Realistic social fear (feeling threatened and unsafe in the face of dangerous school environments)

Pregnancy

Family encouragement (to earn money or to care for family members)

Same-sex attractions

Normative behavior in certain locales ("hanging out")

Reprinted with permission from Popper, 1993.

Table 9.4.   DSM-IV Criteria for Separation Anxiety Disorder

A. Developmentally inappropriate and excessive anxiety concerning separation from home or from those to whom the individual is attached, as evidenced by at least three (or more) of the following:

(1) recurrent excessive distress when separation from home or major attachment figures occurs or is anticipated

(2) persistent and excessive worry about losing, or possible harm befalling, major attachment figures

(3) persistent and excessive worry that an untoward event will lead to separation from a major attachment figure (e.g., getting lost or being kidnapped)

(4) persistent reluctance or refusal to go to school or elsewhere because of fear of separation

(5) persistently and excessively fearful or reluctant to be alone or without major attachment figures at home or without significant adults in other settings

(6) persistent reluctance or refusal to go to sleep without being near a major attachment figure or to sleep away from home

(7) repeated nightmares involving the theme of separation

(8) repeated complaints of physical symptoms (such as headaches, stomachaches, nausea, or vomiting) when separation from major attachment figures occurs or is anticipated

B. The duration of the disturbance is of at least 4 weeks.

C. The onset is before age 18.

D. The disturbance causes clinically significant distress or impairment in social, academic (occupational), or other important areas of functioning.

E. The disturbance does not occur exclusively during the course of a Pervasive Developmental Disorder, Schizophrenia, or other Psychotic Disorder and, in adolescents and adults, is not better accounted for by Panic Disorder with Agoraphobia.

Specify if: Early onset: if onset occurs before age 6 years.

Reprinted with permission from American Psychiatric Association, 1994.

symptoms, including nightmares, worries of harm befalling parents, clinging to caregivers, difficulty staying in school, and somatic symptoms. Older children (ages 9–12) more specifically displayed school absenteeism, distress at separation from attachment figures, and somatizations. Adolescents presented with prominent symptoms of somatic complaints and generally exhibited the fewest symptoms.

Although usually centered around separation from a parent, the characteristic anxiety can also appear at any age as an anticipatory fear of being injured, kidnapped, or killed. Children with separation anxiety disorder commonly experience stomachaches and palpitations, and generally have more somatic complaints than children (Livingston, Taylor, & Crawford, 1988) or adolescents (Francis et al., 1987) with any other psychiatric disorder.

Separation anxiety disorder and school absenteeism have interesting similarities and differences (Last et al., 1987). Both separation anxiety disorder and school absenteeism present, in about 30% of cases, with comorbid major depressive disorder. The conditions differ in age at presentation, gender, and social class. Children with school absenteeism tend to be male and older than 13 years old. Children with separation anxiety disorder tend to be younger than 13 years old, female, and come from lower socioeconomic classes (in comparison with school absenteeism). In both separation anxiety disorder and school absenteeism, the mothers have a high prevalence of anxiety disorders (greater than 50%). Only separation anxiety disorder is associated with a similarly high prevalence of maternal depression.

The etiology of separation anxiety disorder is not clear. Early psychodynamic formulations involve conflicts between aggressive and sexual impulses. Mahlerian developmentalists emphasize the child's uncertainty regarding the location of caretakers after the toddler's initial ambulatory movements. Object relationists and followers of John Bowlby implicate parent-induced anxious attachments. Learning theorists have emphasized the maintenance of symptoms by conditioned fear based on stimulus generalization and reinforcement. Biological psychiatrists focus on heritability, temperament, and the possible relationship between childhood mood and adult anxiety disorders. Interestingly, children with separation anxiety disorder have a high rate of positive findings on the dexamethasone suppression test (Livingston & Martin-Cannici, 1987).

Reliable diagnostic histories may be difficult to obtain because of common misperceptions of "shyness," the broad range of social functioning, family acceptance of the symptoms, parents' beliefs that they themselves had "outgrown" similar problems, and shame (especially among adolescents).

Because separation anxiety disorder and school absenteeism can be a presenting picture for many psychiatric disorders, it is important to consider a broad differential diagnosis, including situational anxiety, major depressive disorder, phobic and panic disorders, posttraumatic stress disorder, psychotic disorders, pervasive developmental disorder, and medical causes. For example, panic disorder has been shown to be misdiagnosed as separation anxiety disorder during childhood until clear-cut panic attacks finally emerge in adolescence (Francis, Robbins, & Grapentine, 1992).

Course of Illness. Once separation anxiety disorder is first recognized in early or mid childhood, it typically has a chronic course with exacerbations at times of stress. Symptoms may worsen during or after even mild medical illnesses, actual separations (family moves, change of schools, or deaths), or periods of danger (threats of separation, unexpected tragedy, natural disasters). Because of the somatic complaints, multiple medical workups with negative results may complicate the course of illness before an accurate diagnosis is made.

Although the symptoms and complications of this disorder are often hard to distinguish, the course often includes absenteeism, academic underachievement and failure, social avoidance and awkwardness, low self-esteem, and depression. In adulthood, manifestations may include pervasive underachievement, chronic sense of failure, repeated job losses, interpersonal isolation, and financial collapse. Alternatively, some individuals find ways to master the behavioral components of the disorder and lead relatively successful lives. However, accumulating evidence suggests that the long-term outcome of children with separation anxiety disorder often involves significant impairment.

A follow-up study of 9 children (ages 2–6 years) with separation anxiety disorder found that 4 children were completely well after 4 years, and did not meet criteria for any DSM-III-R diagnosis (Cantwell & Baker, 1989). Only 1 child continued to meet criteria for separation anxiety disorder, but 3 children fulfilled criteria for another disorder (typically, another anxiety disorder). Although separation anxiety disorder carried the highest rate of recovery of all the psychiatric disorders studied by Cantwell and Baker (1989), its prognosis is decidedly mixed. Various long-term follow-up studies have also suggested an increased risk for the development of additional anxiety disorders (especially panic disorder with agoraphobia) and possibly depressive disorders (Klein & Last, 1989; Kovacs, Gatsonis, Paulauskas, & Richards, 1989).

Standard Pharmacotreatments. Comprehensive treatment for separation anxiety disorder includes individual psychotherapy, behavioral intervention, school consultation, parent guidance, and/or family therapy in conjunction with pharmacotherapy. Tricyclic antidepressants and benzodiazepines have been standard first-line medications for treating separation anxiety disorder, even though the evidence supporting their efficacy is quite thin. The psychosocial treatment of school absenteeism is covered elsewhere (Popper, 1993; Popper & Steingard, 1994).

There have been four double-blind, placebo-controlled studies of tricyclic antidepressants (TCAs) in children with separation anxiety disorder and school absenteeism (Berney et al., 1981; Bernstein, Garfinkel, & Borchardt, 1990; Gittelman-Klein & Klein, 1971; Klein, Koplewicz, & Kanner, 1992). Only one of these studies supports the notion that TCAs can effectively treat separation anxiety disorder: Gittelman-Klein and

Klein (1971) showed a benefit of imipramine (100 to 200 mg daily) over placebo in a sample of 35 children (ages 6–14 years) with school absenteeism, of whom 93% also had separation anxiety disorder. By 6 weeks of treatment, imipramine ($N = 16$) was superior to placebo ($N = 19$) in fostering school attendance (81% vs. 47%) and in diminishing anxiety symptoms and somatic complaints.

Berney et al. (1981), Bernstein (1990), and Klein's subsequent though smaller study (Klein, Koplewicz, & Kanner, 1992) failed to replicate the early positive findings of Gittelman-Klein and Klein (1971). Methodological differences in study design are presumed to account for this difference (Bernstein & Borchardt, 1991). The small sample sizes in the studies by Klein, Koplewicz, and Kanner (1992) and Bernstein, Garfinkel, and Borchardt (1990) might have been insufficient to demonstrate a drug effect, especially in view of the high placebo response rate for separation anxiety disorder in these reports (about 50% in each). The study by Berney et al. (1981) of clomipramine was limited by the use of low dosages (maximum 75 mg daily). In addition, the outcome differences could have been due to confounding variables, such as variations in comorbidity and illness severity. In the study by Klein, Koplewicz, and Kanner (1992), patients were selected for separation anxiety disorder (71% also had school absenteeism), in contrast to her earlier study in which patients were specifically selected for school absenteeism.

It might be expected that the comorbid presence of depression would increase the likelihood of a therapeutic response of separation anxiety disorder to antidepressants, but Ryan et al. (1986) found that the comorbid presence of separation anxiety disorder actually lowered the apparent rate of response to a tricyclic antidepressant in adolescents with major depression. This finding could be viewed in the context of the questionable efficacy of tricyclic antidepressants for treating adolescent depression (Jensen & Elliott, 1992), as evidence of a lack of efficacy of tricyclic antidepressants in treating separation anxiety disorder, or as an example of the relatively treatment-refractory nature of children with comorbid psychopathology.

Although stronger efficacy studies are needed, many clinicians continue to use tricyclic antidepressants in treating separation anxiety disorder. Imipramine in doses up to 5 mg/kg daily is often said to be helpful for certain children with school absenteeism, especially when presenting in combination with separation anxiety disorder, mood disorder, phobic disorder, or panic disorder. However, the usefulness of this treatment remains hypothetical because the recent studies have not shown superiority of tricyclic antidepressants over placebo in treating separation anxiety disorder.

It is even less clear whether these treatments are sensible to use in children with separation anxiety disorder without school absenteeism or, for that matter, in children with school absenteeism who do not have separation anxiety disorder. It is even speculative that the "response" that these children hypothetically show to tricyclic antidepressants is actually due to a direct drug effect on separation anxiety disorder. It could be that these medications affect a different comorbid psychiatric condition, such as panic, phobic or, conceivably, depressive disorders. Perhaps the medication effect is acting instead by way of treating one of these covert conditions.

In short, there is substantive reason to question whether tricyclic antidepressants are effective in treating children with separation anxiety disorder and, even if they are, whether the response is due to a drug effect on separation anxiety disorder or on comorbid psychopathology. In view of the broad spectrum of sources of school absenteeism (see Table 9.3), it is easy to imagine numerous ways that tricyclic antidepressants might alter school absenteeism without affecting separation anxiety disorder.

The current database gives little support for the common practice of using tricyclic antidepressants to treat separation anxiety disorder or school absenteeism. Other categories of antidepressants have not been systematically studied in treating these disorders.

Benzodiazepines also have been used for treating separation anxiety disorder, either for the symptoms of the anxiety disorder or alternatively for the anticipatory anxiety that can develop secondarily around primary anxiety symptoms.

Based on open-label studies, several investigators have suggested that benzodiazepines might be helpful for treating separation anxiety disorder and school absenteeism. In an open-label study of alprazolam (0.75–4.0 mg daily) in 9 children (ages 9–17 years) with school absenteeism (6 of whom met DSM-III criteria for depression as well as either overanxious disorder or separation anxiety disorder), 5 of 9 children had returned to school and 6 showed improvement in anxiety symptoms within 8 weeks (Bernstein et al., 1990). Another open study found that alprazolam (mean dose 2 mg daily, 6 weeks) helped a majority of 18 children, ages 6–17 years, with separation anxiety disorder (Klein, unpublished, discussed in Kutcher, Reiter, Gardner, & Klein, 1992). Two small studies of children with school absenteeism suggest that chlordiazepoxide has some usefulness in facilitating return to school (D'Amato, 1962; Kraft, Ardali, Duffy, Hart, & Pearce, 1965). Clonazepam appeared helpful in uncontrolled trials in two cases of separation anxiety disorder with school absenteeism (Biederman, 1987).

Three well-controlled studies have investigated the potential effects of benzodiazepines in treating these disorders. In contrast to the open trials, these studies have found little encouragement for the use of benzodiazepines.

Simeon et al. (1992) conducted a double-blind, placebo-controlled study with alprazolam in 30 children and adolescents (mean age 12.6 years, range 8–16 years) with separation anxiety, overanxious, and avoidant disorders. All patients received placebo for 1 week, then alprazolam or placebo for 4 weeks, followed by a 1-week taper and a 1-week placebo washout for both groups. Pre- and posttreatment assessment included several clinical rating scales, electroencephalogram (EEG), computerized cognitive testing, and plasma drug levels. The results did not show superiority of drug over placebo in these disorders.

Graae, Milner, Rizzotto, and Klein (1994) conducted a double-blind pilot study of 15 children, ages 7 to 13 years, using a crossover design with 4 weeks of clonazepam (up to 2 mg daily) and 4 weeks of placebo. Again, although 9 of the 12 children who completed the trial appeared to have a moderate to significant clinical improvement, the changes were not statistically significant. This may have been due to the high placebo rate (mean CGI score at week 4 was 15.3 in placebo group and 14.5 in drug group), too rapid drug titration (which may have led to early side effects and high dropout rate), the small number of subjects, comorbidity in the sample, ineffective anxiety rating instruments, the relatively brief treatment, or doses too low for a child and adolescent population.

In a double-blind, placebo-controlled study, Bernstein et al. (1990) found that alprazolam (mean 1.4 mg, range 1–3 mg daily) led to improved school attendance in all 8 drug-treated children, ages 7 to 18 years. However, statistical significance was found only with the clinicians' rating scale of anxiety; other rating instruments produced less convincing data. Also, the results varied depending on which multivariate analysis was used. Although a larger number of subjects might have led to more clear findings in this study, these three double-blind, placebo-controlled studies provide little support for the use of benzodiazepines.

In summary, the evidence for the efficacy of benzodiazepines, as for the tricyclic antidepressants, in treating separation anxiety disorder or school absenteeism remains suggestive at best. Studies of selective serotonin reuptake inhibitors, monoamine oxidase inhibitors, or buspirone in treating separation anxiety disorder and school absenteeism have not been reported. Additional research is needed in view of the high prevalence of these conditions, the significant prognostic findings in long-term studies of children with separation anxiety disorder, the common use of medications to treat separation anxiety disorder and school absenteeism, and the absence of controlled data that support these commonly used treatments.

Selective Mutism (Elective Mutism)

Selective mutism (formerly called elective mutism) is classified in DSM-IV, along with separation anxiety disorder, among the "Other Disorders of Infants, Children, or Adolescents." Although not classified as an anxiety disorder, it is often viewed as a close relative of the anxiety disorders because of its clinical presentation and frequent comorbidity with other anxiety disorders.

Clinical Presentation and Diagnostic Evaluation.   Children with selective mutism do not speak in one or several of the major social contexts in which they live. Partial or total muteness appears selectively in unfamiliar places or particular social situations (see Table 9.5). Typically, speech is normal at home when the child is alone with parents and siblings, and communication is constricted in the presence of teachers, peers, or strangers. When separated from a familiar or comfortable environment, these children might use pantomine, monosyllabic responses, whispers, or written notes but avoid full vocalization. They also show peculiarities or language, interpersonal behavior, and social assertiveness.

Physical and developmental impairments are sometimes associated with selective mutism. Although many of these children have normal language development, about one-third have language disorders and about one-half have a speech disorder or delayed speech development (Hayden, 1980; Kolvin & Fundudis, 1981). In addition, there is an increased prevalence of mental retardation and neurological disorders. A report, based on structured and multi-observer descriptions of 30 children with selective mutism, stated that 97% of children had comorbid social phobia and 30% had specific phobias (Black & Uhde, 1995).

Although controlled studies are beginning to appear, the medical literature on selective mutism still consists mainly of individual case reports. The clinical histories of these children often include early facial injury, mouth trauma (including dental surgery), or oral punishments

---

Table 9.5.   DSM-IV Criteria for Selective Mutism (formerly Elective Mutism)

A. Consistent failure to speak in specific social situations (in which there is an expectation for speaking, e.g., at school) despite speaking in other situations.

B. The disturbance interferes with educational or occupational achievement or with social communication.

C. The duration of the disturbance is at least 1 month (not limited to the first month of school).

D. The failure to speak is not due to a lack of knowledge of, or comfort with, the spoken language required in the social situation.

E. The disturbance is not better accounted for by a Communication Disorder (e.g., Stuttering) and does not occur exclusively during the course of a Pervasive Developmental Disorder, Schizophrenia, or other Psychotic Disorder.

Reprinted with permission from American Psychiatric Association, 1994.

(washing out the mouth or face slapping), especially during the period of speech development.

Because of the associations with speech and language problems, neurodevelopmental delays, and trauma, a proper workup should include an evaluation of the parent and child, neurological examination, speech and language evaluation, possible assessment for learning disabilities, and perhaps a home visit. Special attention should be paid to familial patterns of communication, silence, and anger management. A differential diagnosis should include anxiety disorders (including social phobia), major depressive episode, psychotic depression, schizophrenia, schizoid or schizotypal personality disorder, deafness, aphasia, language-based learning disabilities, and hysteria. A search for comorbid anxiety disorders is warranted.

In the largest available study of selective mutism (Hayden, 1980), four subtypes based on psychodynamic and behavioral observations were described (see Table 9.6). The "symbiotic" form of selective mutism involves a dominant mother who is openly jealous of the child's relationships with other people, a passive or nonverbal father, and a child who appears submissive but can be intensely manipulative. This is the largest subgroup, and closely parallels the usual clinical descriptions. The "passive-aggressive" type uses silence in a defiant and hostile manner, displays antisocial and often aggressive behaviors, and generally has parents with overt antisocial features. The "reactive" type commonly shows depressive features and social withdrawal, has a parent with a mood disorder, and there often is a family history of shyness. The "speech-phobic" children are often afraid to hear their own voices, show autonomic excitation when they hear their own voices, exhibit obvious ritualistic and compulsive behaviors, and show a strong motivation to improve their condition (Hayden, 1980).

Hayden's study suggests that the high prevalence of physical and sexual abuse in the sample is etiologically responsible for the reactive subtype of selective mutism. In this context, muteness could be understood as a defense against realistically based emotional distress, pain, fear of punishment, or disruptive interpersonal relationships. This supposition is questionable, however, because his data on abuse prevalence include higher percentages of both physical and sexual abuse in the speech-phobic than in the reactive subgroups. Although lacking in control groups and validated rating instruments, Hayden's study represents a landmark contribution to the systematic study of selective mutism.

More recent theories on biomedical influences are emerging that may be relevant to selective mutism. The association of selective mutism with a history of early-onset shyness (or a family history of shyness) is consistent with a constitutional or temperamental contribution to childhood shyness (Kagan, Reznick, & Snidman, 1987), anxiety disorder, or mood disorder. Numerous case reports suggest an increased frequency

Table 9.6. *A Classification of Selective Mutism*

	Symbiotic $n = 9$	Passive-Aggressive $n = 16$	Reactive $n = 14$	Speech-Phobic $n = 7$
Dominant mother, plus passive or absent father	97%	0%	7%	0%
School achievement > average	45	0	0	0
Mouthing or whispering	13	0	0	0
Aggressive behavior	0	56	0	0
Antisocial behavior	10	82	14	0
Parental incarceration	3	75	36	0
Onset after age 5 years	6	50	14	0
Depressive features	6	50	100	14
Severe withdrawal, catatonic like	6	37	100	0
Parental depression	3	0	43	0
Familial shyness	10	6	71	29
Shyness	3	0	32	86
Rituals and compulsions	10	6	7	100
Physical abuse (documented)	65	100	71	10
Sexual abuse (documented)	26	50	36	43

Source: Subtyping and data from a study of 68 children (Hayden, 1980).
Reprinted with permission from Popper & Steingard, 1994.

of anxiety, mood, or personality disorders in the parents of children with selective mutism.

The prevalence of selective mutism is about 30 to 80 cases per 100,000; however, broader diagnostic criteria could increase this estimate perhaps tenfold. There is a slight female predominance, with a gender ratio of 1:1–2.

Course of Illness. Developmentally normal children at age 3 to 5 years may still show brief periods of mutism with strangers or in new settings, and a gradual emergence of early "shyness" is often described retrospectively (Kolvin & Fundudis, 1981) in these children. However, selective mutism is typically not diagnosed until the first years at school (ages 5–8 years). If the child's social behavior is compliant, recognition and referral for treatment may be delayed. Once symptoms emerge, their duration may be several weeks to several years. Selective mutism is self-limiting in some children, and about half the children are symptom-free by 10 years of age. If speech does not reappear by this time, the prognosis may be more guarded (Kolvin & Fundudis, 1981). In the rare cases of selective mutism that do not emerge until adolescence, passive-aggressive or antisocial features may predominate, and the prognosis is typically serious (Hayden, 1980).

Complications include academic underachievement, scapegoating, and behavioral regression resulting from the emotional dependency and secondary gains of illness. The disadvantages of inappropriate special classes and school placements are incurred, as teachers become helpless in dealing with the silence. Some children experience teasing and humiliation, though interestingly other children are protected by peers, who may speak on their behalf or who bestow special services and personal attention. Such excessive protection and tolerance by peers or parents may reinforce the mute behavior.

Long-term outcome is unknown. The abnormal social behavior, interpersonal manipulations, shyness and aggressivity appear to persist beyond the period of symptomatic muteness. The relationship of selective mutism to later adult psychopathology needs further study.

Standard Pharmacotreatments. Because of the complex nature and complications of this disorder, pharmacotherapy is just a small part of multimodal treatment. There are many reports on the use of a variety of nonpharmacological interventions (Cline & Baldwin, 1994; Hadley, 1994; Krohn, Weckstein, & Wright, 1992; Labbe & Williamson, 1984; Wright, Miller, Cook, & Littmann, 1985). The treatment of anxiety and fear associated with communication, the promotion of separation and autonomy, and the enhancement of personal assertiveness usually involve treatments of both the child and parents. The return of speech is not considered the hallmark of a successful treatment: Once the mute speech is improving, it may be anticipated that associated psychiatric disorders will continue to require treatment of the child and parents.

Golwyn and Weinstock (1990) described a 7-year-old girl with a 2-year history of selective mutism who was successfully treated with the monoamine oxidase inhibitor, phenelzine (Nardil). Although she spoke at home, she was mute at school and outside the home with nonfamily members. She had failed on a 1-month trial of amantadine (presumably based on a dopaminergic hypothesis of speech activity) at dose of 200 mg daily. Phenelzine was then started and titrated upward gradually. After 6 weeks (at a dose of 37.5 mg daily), the patient began talking outside the home; at 12 weeks (52.5 mg daily), she spoke at day care; and at 16 weeks (60 mg daily), she returned to school. Side effects were minimal. The phenelzine was tapered off by week 24, and she remained free of mutism for at least 5 months after drug discontinuation.

Black and Uhde (1992) reported on a 12-year-old girl with a 6-year history of selective mutism and social phobia, which were not responsive to psychotherapy or behavioral therapy. Desipramine (200 mg for 10 weeks) produced a partial but inadequate response, and was discontinued. One month later, she was started on fluoxetine and her dose was titrated to 20 mg daily. After 4 weeks, she showed marked improvement in the symptoms of both disorders during treatment with fluoxetine. By 7 months of treatment, her social functioning was viewed as within normal limits.

More recently, Black and Uhde (1994) evaluated the effects of fluoxetine in 16 children and adolescents who met criteria for selective mutism in a double-blind, placebo-controlled study. After eliminating placebo responders, 6 subjects (ages 5–16 years) were randomly assigned to 12-week, double-blind treatment with fluoxetine or placebo. The medication was titrated to 0.6 mg/kg (mean maximum dose 21 mg daily) for 10 weeks. Outcome measurement was performed by clinicians, parents, and teachers periodically through the treatment. Results were equivocal, showing significant improvements in parent ratings but insignificant improvements in clinician and teacher ratings.

Although these findings might be viewed as encouraging for a disorder that often requires very difficult and lengthy treatment, additional systematic studies of the pharmacological treatment of selective mutism are needed.

"ADULT" ANXIETY DISORDERS AS THEY PRESENT IN CHILDREN AND ADOLESCENTS

Panic Disorder with and without Agoraphobia

Panic disorder has only recently been recognized in the child and adolescent population, and there remains some debate about whether panic disorder exists in preadolescent children. For example, a community survey of 11-year-olds found no cases of panic disorder among 792 children (Anderson, Williams, McGee, & Silva, 1987). Some clinicians have theorized that immature ego defenses and neurocognitive functioning cannot sustain the necessary mechanisms for a panic episode (Klein, Mannuzza, Chapman, & Fryer, 1992; Nelles & Barlow, 1988), but similar types of theoretical arguments were proposed to disprove the existence of prepubertal depression and have long been discarded.

In fact, Ballenger, Carek, Steele, and Cornish-McTighe (1989) have speculated that one of the factors leading to the underappreciation of anxiety disorders in children is the current overrecognition of their mood disorders.

A factor that needs further investigation is the finding that the prevalence of panic attacks is directly correlated with degree of sexual maturity, as determined by Tanner staging (Hayward et al., 1992).

Clinical Presentation and Diagnostic Evaluation. According to DSM-IV, the clinical criteria for diagnosing panic disorder in children and adolescents are identical to the adult criteria (see Table 9.7). The central feature of the disorder is sudden onset and episodic appearance of anxiety characterized by physical (cardiovascular, gastrointestinal, respiratory, neurological, autonomic) or psychological (depersonalization, fear of dying, fear of going crazy or losing control) symptoms that are (at least partly) unexpected rather than be precipitated by events or discernible triggers (Bernstein, Garfinkel, & Borchardt, 1990).

Using DSM criteria, panic disorder has been described in a total of 78 children and adolescents in case reports and small series (Alessi & Magen,

---

Table 9.7.   DSM-IV Criteria for Panic Disorder (with or without Agoraphobia)

A. Both (1) and (2):

    (1) recurrent unexpected panic attacks

    (2) at least one of the attacks has been followed by 1 month (or more) of one (or more) of the following:

        (a) persistent concern about having additional attacks

        (b) worry about the implications of the attack or its consequences (e.g., losing control, having a heart attack, "going crazy")

        (c) a significant change in behavior related to the attacks

B. Absence or Presence of Agoraphobia, which is defined as:

    (1) Anxiety about being in places or situations from which escape might be difficult (or embarrassing) or in which help may not be available in the event of having an unexpected or situationally predisposed Panic Attack or panic-like symptoms. Agoraphobic fears typically involve characteristic clusters of situations that include being outside the home alone; being in a crowd or standing in a line; being on a bridge; and traveling in a bus, train, or automobile.

    (2) The situations are avoided (e.g., travel is restricted) or else are endured with marked distress or with anxiety about having a Panic Attack or panic-like symptoms, or require the presence of a companion.

C. The Panic Attacks are not due to the direct physiological effects of a substance (e.g., a drug of abuse, a medication) or a general medical condition (e.g., hyperthyroidism).

D. The Panic Attacks are not better accounted for by another mental disorder, such as Social Phobia, Specific Phobia, Obsessive-Compulsive Disorder, Posttraumatic Stress Disorder, or Separation Anxiety Disorder.

1988; Alessi, Robbins, & Dilsaver, 1987; Ballenger et al., 1989; Biederman, 1987; Black & Robbins, 1990; Casat, Ross, Scardina, Sarno, & Smith, 1987; Garland & Smith, 1990, 1991; Hayward, Killen, & Taylor, 1989; Herskowitz, 1986; Kutcher & MacKenzie, 1988; Last & Strauss, 1989; Moreau et al., 1989; van Winter & Stickler, 1984; Vitiello et al., 1990). Moreau et al. (1989) found 7 cases in a sample of 220 preadolescents through structured diagnostic interviewing. In addition, more than 130 children and adolescents have been described with "hyperventilation syndrome" (Enzer & Walker, 1967; Herman, Stickler, & Lucas, 1981; Joorabchi, 1977), a condition that probably constitutes panic disorder in many cases.

In a study of 28 adolescents (mean age 15) with panic disorder, the typical symptoms of panic attacks were (in descending frequency) palpitations (86%), sweating (75%), shortness of breath (71%), nausea (68%), flushing or chills (64%), dizziness (61%), and trembling (54%) (Bradley & Hood, 1993). They reported that almost half of the sample had one or more attacks each week, and that 26 of 28 adolescents identified a precipitating stress before each episode. A history of separation anxiety disorder was noted in half of these adolescents.

Family history data have suggested an increased prevalence of panic disorder among the first- and second-degree relatives of children with panic and overanxious disorder (Last, Hersen, Kazdin, Orvaschel, & Perrin, 1991). Panic disorder has been found to be present on at least one side of the family tree of children and adolescents with panic disorder (Vitiello et al., 1990). Children and adolescents with panic disorder often have psychiatric histories of preexisting separation anxiety disorder (Vitiello et al., 1990; Weissman, Leckman, Merikangas, Gammon, & Prusoff, 1984), and adults with panic disorder and agoraphobia have been found to suffer from separation anxiety disorder as children (Gittelman & Klein, 1984).

Additional findings provide interesting and intriguing leads for a biological understanding of panic disorder. An interesting but still unexplained relationship in adults (Venkatesh, Pauls, Crowe, Noyes, VanValkenburg, Martins, & Kerber, 1980) has been supported by the finding that 2 of 6 children with panic disorder also had mitral valve prolapse (Vitiello et al., 1990). Rosenbaum, Biederman, Hirshfield, Bolduc, and Chaloff (1991) have provided evidence that behavioral inhibition (akin to shyness) may be a precursor to panic disorder (and other anxiety disorders) in later life. The precipitation of panic attacks by lactate infusion, which has been studied extensively in adults, has not been examined in children or adolescents.

Course of Illness.   The peak age for a first panic attack has been reported as 15 to 19 years (von Korff, Eaton, & Keyl, 1985), but the mean interval between an adolescent's first panic attack and a diagnosis of panic disorder may be 3 years or more (Vitiello et al., 1990). Bradley and

Hood (1993), studying panic disorder in a sample of adolescents with a mean age of 15, found a mean age of onset at 12 years of age.

Standard Pharmacotreatments. Pharmacological treatment of panic disorder in adolescents or children has received little study, consisting mainly of uncontrolled reports on benzodiazepines, tricyclic antidepressants, and propranolol.

In a small but ongoing double-blind, placebo-controlled study of adolescents with panic disorder, clonazepam is appearing superior to placebo. Of the 12 adolescents reported so far (Kutcher, 1990), moderate to marked improvement was noted on CGI ratings in about 80% of patients on clonazepam compared with 20% on placebo. The decreases in panic attack frequency and Hamilton Anxiety Score ratings were significantly larger in the clonazepam-treated group than in the placebo group.

In open clinical trials, clonazepam has appeared helpful for four patients with panic disorder (Kutcher & MacKenzie, 1988) and for three patients with paniclike symptoms associated with other anxiety disorders (Biederman, 1987). In addition, alprazolam has been reported to be effective in open trials of four patients with panic disorder and other anxiety disorders (Ballenger et al., 1989; Herskowitz, 1986).

In isolated clinical reports of open-label treatments of panic disorder, imipramine and desipramine were judged to be effective in 13 of a total of 15 patients, ranging in age from 6 to 16 years (Ballenger et al., 1989; Black & Robbins, 1990; Garland & Smith, 1990, 1991; Herskowitz, 1986; Van Winter & Stickler, 1984). Relatively low doses of these tricyclic antidepressants (typically below 125 mg daily) appeared useful, though weight-adjusted (mg/kg) doses were generally not reported. Also, propranolol was reported to be clinically useful in one case (Van Winter & Stickler, 1984) but not in another (Garland & Smith, 1990). Phenelzine was reported effective for a 12-year-old (Casat et al., 1987).

It is impossible to draw conclusions about efficacy without control groups. Except for a single small study that suggests possible efficacy of clonazepam (Kutcher, 1990), there are no controlled studies of any psychotropic medication for treating panic disorder in children and adolescents.

Posttraumatic Stress Disorder

Clinical Presentation and Diagnostic Evaluation. Though there are some notable symptomatic differences, PTSD is generally believed to be phenomenologically quite similar in children, adolescents, and adults (see Table 9.8).

Terr (1981, 1983, 1985) and Pynoos (Pynoos et al., 1987; Pynoos & Nader, 1988) have provided detailed descriptions of children with

Table 9.8. DSM-IV Criteria for Posttraumatic Stress Disorder

A. The person has been exposed to a traumatic event in which both of the following were present:

   (1) the person has experienced, witnessed, or been confronted with an event or events that involve actual or threatened death or serious injury, or a threat to the physical integrity of self or others

   (2) the person's response involved intense fear, helplessness, or horror

   Note: In children, this may be expressed instead by disorganized or agitated behavior.

B. The traumatic event is persistently reexperienced in one (or more) of the following ways:

   (1) recurrent and intrusive distressing recollections of the event, including images, thoughts, or perceptions

   Note: In young children, repetitive play may occur in which themes or aspects of the trauma are expressed.

   (2) recurrent distressing dreams of the event

   Note: In children, there may be frightening dreams without recognizable content.

   (3) acting or feeling as if the traumatic event were recurring (includes a sense of reliving the experience, illusions, hallucinations, and dissociative flashback episodes, including those that occur upon awakening or when intoxicated)

   Note: In young children, trauma-specific reenactment may occur.

   (4) intense psychological distress at exposure to internal or external cues that symbolize or resemble an aspect of the traumatic event

   (5) physiologic reactivity upon exposure to internal or external cues that symbolize or resemble an aspect of the traumatic event

C. Persistent avoidance of stimuli associated with the trauma and numbing of general responsiveness (not present before the trauma), as indicated by three (or more) of the following:

   (1) efforts to avoid thoughts, feelings, or conversations associated with the trauma

   (2) efforts to avoid activities, places, or people that arouse recollections of the trauma

   (3) inability to recall an important aspect of the trauma

   (4) markedly diminished interest or participation in significant activities

   (5) feeling of detachment or estrangement from others

   (6) restricted range of affect (e.g., unable to have loving feelings)

   (7) sense of a foreshortened future (e.g., does not expect to have a career, marriage, children, or a normal life span)

(Continued)

Table 9.8. *(Continued)*

D. Persistent symptoms of increased arousal (not present before the trauma), as indicated by two (or more) of the following:

    (1) difficulty falling or staying asleep

    (2) irritability or outbursts of anger

    (3) difficulty concentrating

    (4) hypervigilance

    (5) exaggerated startle response

E. Duration of the disturbance (symptoms in Criteria B, C, and D) is more than 1 month.

F. The disturbance causes clinically significant distress or impairment in social, occupational, or other important areas of functioning.

Specify if:

    Acute: if duration of symptoms is less than 3 months

    Chronic: if duration of symptoms is 3 months or more

Specify if:

    With Delayed Onset: if onset of symptoms is at least 6 months after the stressor

---

Reprinted with permission from American Psychiatric Association, 1994.

posttraumatic syndromes. In contrast to adults, flashbacks are not prominent in children and adolescents with PTSD. Instead, youths are more likely to show multiple fears, reenactment behavior, posttraumatic play, and fascination with omens.

For children and adolescents with PTSD, the nature and degree of disturbance appears dependent on several factors: (a) the age of the child at the time of the first trauma, (b) whether the trauma was a single event or consisted of repeated exposures, (c) the nature of the trauma (sexual or physical abuse, combined child abuse, murder or rape witness, natural disaster), (d) the extent to which the child perceives receiving support or being in control after the trauma, (e) severity, such as the degree to which the traumatic event is outside the normal range of experience.

The recurrence of traumatic exposure was a critical variable that appeared to determine other aspects of the clinical presentation of PTSD. After single traumatic events, children appeared to have fewer of certain symptoms that are often seen in adults with PTSD, such as denial, amnesia, psychic numbing, and repressive defenses. More typically, such children exhibited play with morbid, aggressive, or traumatic themes. Their language included references to the earlier experiences, often with strikingly inappropriate affect. Some children present with depressed affect. Adolescents tend to become withdrawn, engage in behaviors that repeat the trauma, or develop symptoms of conduct disorder (Van der Kolk, 1985).

Repeated traumatic exposures, especially related to physical or sexual abuse, appear to be a major cause of PTSD in children. The impact of physical or sexual abuse in childhood is difficult to study because the precise nature of the traumatic experience and the personal meaning of the events are often unclear. The episodes may occur over long periods, sometimes without well-defined beginnings and endings. Often, traumatic events tend to occur in families in which there may be confounding influences, such as alcohol abuse, neglect, and abandonment. Nonetheless, Kendall-Tackett, Williams, and Finkelhor (1993) delineated a number of predictors of symptom severity following sexual abuse: high frequency of abuse; long duration of abuse; oral, anal, and vaginal penetration; use of force; lack of maternal support; and close relationship of perpetrator to child.

In a study by McLeer, Deblinger, Atkins, Foa, and Ralphe (1988), the prevalence of PTSD in 31 sexually abused children (ages 3–16 years) was 75% if the child was abused by the biological father, 67% if abused by a stranger, 25% if abused by a trusted adult, and 0% if abused by an older child. It appears that the risk of PTSD in sexually abused youth may depend on the nature of the exposure, including the child's personal relationship with the perpetrator.

Personal "closeness" to the perpetrator can be viewed emotionally or physically. A study of a Los Angeles sniper attack revealed that the number and type of PTSD symptoms, as well as the severity of illness, were proportional to the child's physical distance from the sniper (Pynoos et al., 1987).

The literature delineates between genuine PTSD and PTSD-like behavioral changes that do not meet the full criteria for PTSD. The DSM-IV creation of the acute stress disorder, which is an immediate posttraumatic reaction of less than 4 weeks' duration, begins to address this issue. However, a child may have a large variety of emotional, cognitive, and behavioral reactions to highly stressful events, including some that are quite enduring and which are not adequately described by the criteria for PTSD or acute stress disorder. Although clinicians sometimes use the term PTSD loosely to refer to any posttraumatic behavioral change, this practice undermines the diagnostic concept of PTSD.

The differential diagnosis of posttraumatic stress disorder includes borderline personality disorder (Lonie, 1993), dissociative disorders, panic disorder, and psychosis.

Course of Illness. When a stressor is far outside the normal range of experience, a child is more likely to present with the full range of PTSD symptoms. The duration of illness in these cases usually persists beyond

6 months, and these children are at a higher risk to develop comorbid psychiatric diagnoses, such as other anxiety disorders and depression. Their symptoms may extend into adulthood, often regardless of how comprehensively they are treated.

A short-term follow-up study of symptom change in children with PTSD revealed that improvement over time was seen in children who received maternal support, specialized treatment for PTSD (in addition to supportive counseling), and quick resolution of legal proceedings in a manner that minimized the negative effects of courtroom experiences (Kendall-Tackett et al., 1993). Interestingly, age, gender, race, and socioeconomic status were not consistent predictors of improvement. Symptoms that tended to improve with time were anxiety, fearfulness, and insomnia. Symptoms that tended to worsen were aggression, sexual behaviors, and sexual preoccupations.

Standard Pharmacotreatments.   The use of medication in managing PTSD in children and adolescents has received minimal study. Propranolol, clonidine, and the neuroleptics have received some examination. No studies are yet available with double-blind, placebo-controlled design, so no medication has demonstrated efficacy.

In an open trial of 11 children (mean 8.5 years old), propranolol reduced the aggressivity and anxiety associated with acute PTSD, an effect that reversed on drug discontinuation (Famularo, Kinscherff, & Fenton, 1988). Clonidine, an alpha$_2$ partial agonist which is sometimes used to treat ADHD and reduce hyperarousal states (Hunt, Capper, & O'Connell, 1990), has been reported to reduce startle reactions and avoidant behaviors in children with PTSD (Kinzie & Leung, 1989).

Neuroleptics are sometimes helpful in PTSD patients when they are distressed by frightening flashbacks. Some children and adolescents become so disturbed by flashbacks that they become impulsive, threatening, or aggressive. Small doses of neuroleptics (e.g., chlorpromazine 25 mg four times daily) can clear the sensorium, organize thought processes, and promote calm in these children.

There are no systematic data on tricyclic antidepressants, SRIs, benzodiazepines, or buspirone in children or adolescents with PTSD. In the absence of studies of this common condition, the pharmacological approach to treating children with PTSD is often directed toward treatment of comorbid anxiety or mood disorders or toward management of sympathetic hyperarousal states.

Specific Phobia and Social Phobia (Social Anxiety Disorder)

With the transformation from DSM-III-R to DSM-IV, "simple phobia" was renamed "specific phobia." "Social phobia" remains in the nomenclature, but a new label "social anxiety disorder" has been parenthetically added. In both of these diagnostic categories, additional qualifying criteria have been formulated to assist in classifying disorders of children and adolescents.

Fears are common, normal, and expectable in children and adolescents. About half of otherwise normal preadolescent children have multiple specific fears (LaPouse & Monk, 1964). Typical fears of preadolescents include being hit by a car, being unable to breathe, falling from a height, burglars, fires, earthquakes, death, poor grades, and snakes (Ollendick, King, & Frary, 1989). The expression of specific fears is determined by developmental, environmental, and geographic factors. For example, before the age of 5 years, fears of animals are very frequent; by puberty, social concerns may predominate (Marks & Gelder, 1966).

Fears are considered clinical disorders ("specific phobias") only when they are especially severe, persistent, unreasonable, or disruptive of functioning (see Table 9.9). However, if the anxiety developed in response to an actual and realistic fear-invoking event, it is better not to view it as a biopsychiatrically based phobic disorder, even if the degree of anxiety is unreasonable.

Social phobia is treated here alongside specific phobia only because of the absence of relevant data on social phobia as a distinct disorder in children and adolescents. However, there are substantial reasons not to view social phobia as a type of specific phobia, including differences in epidemiology, natural course, and response to pharmacotherapy.

Clinical Presentation and Diagnostic Evaluation. Clinical features of specific phobias (elicited by specific stimuli) include overt anxiety and distress, seeking and clinging to a safe place or protective person, avoidance, anticipatory anxiety, and (especially if forced to confront the feared object) angry or aggressive outbursts (see Table 9.9). In addition to animal phobias (including insects), children often show nature phobias (storms, water, heights) and injury phobias (including hypodermic needles). Specific phobias in adolescents typically concern specific social settings or activities rather than the pervasive social anxiety seen in individuals with social phobia.

Social phobia (social anxiety disorder) is defined in DSM-IV as a fear of embarrassing or humiliating oneself in front of unfamiliar people (for children, unfamiliar peers) in social or performance situations (see Table 9.10). In children, social phobia may express itself as multiple fears of speaking out in class, talking on the telephone, being observed, eating in the school cafeteria, undressing for gym, attending parties, dancing in public, or using public toilets. Children or adolescents who meet the criteria for social phobia often have concomitant school absenteeism, spend increased time at home with their parents, and may show

Table 9.9.   DSM-IV Criteria for Specific Phobia (Formerly Simple Phobia)

A.   Marked and persistent fear that is excessive or unreasonable, cued by the presence or anticipation of a specific object or situation (e.g., flying, heights, animals, receiving an injection, seeing blood).

B.   Exposure to the phobic stimulus almost invariably provokes an immediate anxiety response, which may take the form of a situationally bound or situationally predisposed Panic Attack.

   Note: In children, the anxiety may be expressed by crying, tantrums, freezing, or clinging.

C.   The person recognizes that the fear is excessive or unreasonable.

   Note: In children, this feature may be absent.

D.   The phobic situation(s) is avoided, or else is endured with intense anxiety or distress.

E.   The avoidance, anxious anticipation, or distress in the feared situation(s) interferes significantly with the person's normal routine, occupational (or academic) functioning, or social activities or relationships, or there is marked distress about having the phobia.

F.   In individuals under age 18 years, the duration is at least 6 months.

G.   The anxiety, Panic Attacks, or phobic avoidance associated with the specific object or situation are not better accounted for by another mental disorder, such as Obsessive-Compulsive Disorder, Posttraumatic Stress Disorder, Separation Anxiety Disorder, Social Phobia, Panic Disorder with Agoraphobia, or Agoraphobia Without a History of Panic Disorder.

Specify type:

   Animal Type
   Natural Environment Type
   Blood-Injection-Injury Type
   Situational Type
   Other Type

Reprinted with permission from American Psychiatric Association, 1994.

comorbid anxiety disorders such as separation anxiety disorder or panic disorder. Exposure to the feared situation may precipitate somatic symptoms (especially dry mouth, blushing, sweating, and tachycardia), crying, tantrums, aggressive behavior, avoidance, or withdrawal. At times, these anxiety episodes appear similar to panic attacks. The level of anxiety may change abruptly as exposure to social stress begins and ends. The adolescent may function quite well when not confronted with social challenge.

The etiology of phobic disorders is not well understood. Freud's "Little Hans" theory of stimulus generalization has been superseded by more biologically based concepts. "Shy," avoidant, or "slow to warm up"

Table 9.10.   DSM-IV Criteria for Social Phobia (Social Anxiety Disorder)

A.   A marked and persistent fear of one or more social or performance situations in which the person is exposed to unfamiliar people or to possible scrutiny by others. The individual fears that he or she will act in a way (or show anxiety symptoms) that will be humiliating or embarrassing.

   Note: In children, there must be evidence of the capacity for age-appropriate social relationships with familiar people and the anxiety must occur in peer settings, not just in interactions with adults.

B.   Exposure to the feared social situation almost invariably provokes anxiety, which may take the form of a situationally bound or situationally predisposed Panic Attack.

   Note: In children, the anxiety may be expressed by crying, tantrums, freezing, or shrinking from social situations with unfamiliar people.

C.   The personal recognizes that fear is excessive or unreasonable.

   Note: In children, this feature may be absent.

D.   The feared social or performance situations are avoided or else endured with intense anxiety or distress.

E.   The avoidance, anxious anticipation, or distress in the feared situation(s) interferes significantly with the person's normal routine, occupational (academic) functioning, or social activities or relationships, or there is marked distress about having the phobia.

F.   In individuals under age 18 years, the duration is at least 6 months.

G.   The fear or avoidance is not due to the direct physiological effects of a substance (e.g., a drug of abuse, a medication) or a general medical condition and is not better accounted for by another mental disorder (e.g., Panic Disorder With or Without Agoraphobia, Separation Anxiety Disorder, Body Dysmorphic Disorder, a Pervasive Developmental Disorder, or Schizoid Personality Disorder).

H.   If a general medical condition or another mental disorder is present, the fear in Criterion A is unrelated to it, e.g., the fear is not of Stuttering, trembling in Parkinson's disease, or exhibiting abnormal eating behavior in Anorexia Nervosa or Bulimia Nervosa.

Specify if: Generalized

Reprinted with permission from American Psychiatric Association, 1994.

children may be predisposed to becoming adults with phobic disorders (Rosenbaum et al., 1991), consistent with familial or genetic theories of transmission.

   Once the clinician has differentiated a phobic disorder from a developmentally normal fear, several additional diagnoses should be considered: major depression, schizophrenia, other psychotic disorders and other anxiety disorders, including PTSD and obsessive-compulsive disorder. If social anxiety is predominant, the clinician should evaluate for possible emerging traits of personality disorder, schizoid or schizotypal personality disorder, or avoidant personality disorder.

Course of Illness.   The mean age of onset for animal phobias in children is 4.4 years (Marks & Gelder, 1966). Specific phobias may be self-limited, especially during childhood, though some may persist into adulthood. In some cases, specific phobias are extinguished by naturalistic exposure or intentional self-exposure over time. If a specific fear resolves spontaneously during childhood, it can be difficult to determine whether it was a developmental fear or a clinically significant specific phobia.

In contrast, social phobia appears to be a chronic disorder. The mean age at onset is 19 years (Amies, Gelder, & Shaw, 1983), either acutely following a specific social humiliation or developing chronically in a gradual manner. Social phobia has not been carefully studied in follow-up studies, especially from early-onset cases.

Standard Pharmacotreatments.   There is no pharmacotherapy for specific phobias in children, adolescents, or adults. Trials of benzodiazepines, beta blockers, tricyclic antidepressants, and even neuroleptics have generally been unsuccessful. Behavioral methods, especially systematic desensitization and relaxation techniques, have demonstrated efficacy in children. If not severe, specific phobias may remit without treatment.

Social phobias are often more treatment-resistant and dysfunctional, perhaps partly because of comorbid conditions. Phenelzine, fluoxetine, and sertraline have been shown to be efficacious in well-controlled studies in adults, though symptomatic improvement is often limited. Performance anxiety, a feature of social phobia, has been successfully treated by beta blockers (mixed but generally positive results in numerous controlled studies) or benzodiazepines (helpful in the two double-blind, placebo-controlled studies) in adults.

Literature is sparse on treating social phobia in children or adolescents. Zwier and Rao (1994) reported a successful treatment with buspirone in a 13-year-old boy for symptoms of social phobia and psychotic features. Buspirone, administered in divided doses up to 20 mg daily, produced marked improvement within 2 weeks. Follow-up after 1 year showed continued resolution of both anxiety and psychotic thought.

Beta blockers, benzodiazepines, tricyclic antidepressants, SRIs, and MAOIs have been used clinically in children and adolescents with social phobia, though systematic studies are unavailable. One of us (CP) has found that a combination of SSRIs and beta blockers can be helpful for certain adolescents with social phobia.

Generalized Anxiety Disorder (Includes Overanxious Disorder of Childhood)

With the advent of DSM-IV, the diagnosis of overanxious disorder of childhood has been semi-eliminated and subsumed into the diagnostic code for generalized anxiety disorder, previously designated as an adult disorder. It survives now only in parenthetical form, formally attached to the new name for the combined adult and child disorder. The new criteria for generalized anxiety disorder include some language that make them easier for children to fulfill (see Table 9.11).

The status of overanxious disorder as a nosological entity had long been challenged, but its journey through diagnostic revisions allowed it to survive into DSM-IV. Its recent semi-elimination was promoted by studies that failed to identify reliable diagnostic variables that distinguish overanxious children from other groups (Beidel, 1991). While it existed as a recognized distinct diagnostic entity, the labeling of overanxious disorder did allow for some research to focus on its characteristics. The research generated about overanxious disorder was limited, and there is not yet any research on children using the criteria for generalized anxiety disorder.

Clinical Presentation and Diagnostic Evaluation. The most prominent feature of overanxious disorder of childhood is worrying. Most of these children worry about future events (Strauss, Lease, Last, & Francis, 1988), but also about personal competence or the appropriateness of past behavior. These children have marked self-consciousness, excessive need for reassurance, and multiple physical complaints, yet have a pseudosophisticated manner and appear developmentally precocious. They often appear shy, overcompliant, and perfectionistic. In contrast to generalized anxiety disorder, children with overanxious disorder may not have the prominent autonomic or cognitive symptoms that are characteristic of adults with generalized anxiety disorder.

The differential diagnosis of overanxious disorder (or generalized anxiety disorder in children) includes various anxiety disorders as well as ADHD and mood disorders. Although not useful for diagnostic purposes, it is intriguing that children with overanxious disorder have a relatively high rate of dexamethasone suppression test (DST) positivity, though not as high as in children with major depression or separation anxiety disorder (Livingston & Martin-Cannici, 1987).

Course of Illness. Children with overanxious disorder have a mean age of onset of 13.5 years and an equal gender prevalence (Last, Strauss, & Francis, 1987). Overanxious disorder (OAD) appears to be associated with age-related shifts in its comorbidity patterns and also with variations

Table 9.11.   DSM-IV Criteria for Generalized Anxiety Disorder (Includes Overanxious Disorder of Childhood)

A. Excessive anxiety and worry (apprehensive expectation), occurring more days than not for at least six months, about a number of events or activities (such as work or school performance).

B. The person finds it difficult to control the worry.

C. The anxiety and worry are associated with three (or more) of the following six symptoms (with at least some symptoms present for more days than not for the past six months).

   Note: Only one item is required in children.

   (1) restlessness or feeling keyed up or on edge

   (2) being easily fatigued

   (3) difficulty concentrating or mind going blank

   (4) irritability

   (5) muscle tension

   (6) sleep disturbance (difficulty falling or staying asleep, or restless unsatisfying sleep)

D. The focus of the anxiety and worry is not confined to features of an Axis I disorder, e.g., the anxiety or worry is not about having a Panic Attack (as in Panic Disorder), being embarrassed in public (as in Social Phobia), being contaminated (as in Obsessive-Compulsive Disorder), being away from home or close relatives (as in Separation Anxiety Disorder), gaining weight (as in Anorexia Nervosa), having multiple physical complaints (as in Somatization Disorder), or having a serious illness (as in Hypochondriasis), and the anxiety or worry do not occur exclusively during Posttraumatic Stress Disorder.

E. The anxiety, worry, or physical symptoms cause clinically significant distress or impairment in social, occupational, or other important areas of functioning.

F. The disturbance is not due to the direct effects of a substance (e.g., drugs of abuse, a medication) or a general medical condition (e.g., hyperthyroidism), and does not occur exclusively during a Mood Disorder, a Psychotic Disorder, or a Pervasive Developmental Disorder.

Reprinted with permission from American Psychiatric Association, 1994.

in the developmental expression of its symptoms (Last, Strauss, & Francis, 1987). Younger children with overanxious disorder presented with more comorbid separation anxiety disorder and ADHD, whereas the adolescents were more likely to have comorbid simple (specific) phobia and major depression. After the age of 12 years, children with overanxious disorder tend to become more concerned with the appropriateness of their past behavior.

The long-term outcome of OAD has not yet been determined. The formerly hypothesized and now formalized developmental connection between overanxious disorder and generalized anxiety disorder has not been empirically demonstrated.

Standard Pharmacotreatments. In the relative absence of treatment studies, the pharmacotherapy of overanxious disorder in children has generally involved antianxiety agents and antidepressants.

Benzodiazepines have been reported to be helpful in two open studies but not in the only controlled study. In an open trial in 12 children, alprazolam (0.5–1.5 mg daily) appeared to improve anxiety, depression, psychomotor excitement, and sleep (Simeon & Ferguson, 1987). Clonazepam was judged helpful in an open clinical trial for an 8-year-old with overanxious disorder and comorbid anxiety disorders (Biederman, 1987).

In a double-blind, placebo-controlled study in 21 children (ages 8–16 years) with overanxious disorder, alprazolam showed a trend (not reaching statistical significance) toward more effectiveness than placebo over a 4-week period. An arbitrary ceiling dose of 0.04 mg/kg/day was not exceeded. The relatively low doses (0.5–3.5 mg daily, mean 1.6 mg daily) might have underestimated the potential medication effects of alprazolam (Simeon et al., 1992).

Buspirone has also received some study, though in open designs only. In a pilot study of buspirone (15 to 30 mg daily) in adolescents with overanxious disorder, symptoms of anxiety were reduced within 6 weeks of treatment (Kutcher et al., 1992). An open trial of a low dose of buspirone (10 mg daily) in a 13-year-old boy with overanxious disorder yielded clinically significant reductions in objective anxiety ratings (Kranzler, 1988).

Apart from the negative study of alprazolam (Simeon et al., 1992), there are no double-blind, placebo-controlled studies of benzodiazepines, buspirone, tricyclic antidepressants, MAOIs, or selective serotonin reuptake inhibitors in the treatment of overanxious disorder of childhood.

PSYCHOPHARMACOLOGY

Apart from obsessive-compulsive disorder, there is no anxiety disorder in children or adolescents for which treatment efficacy of a medication has been established, and so the practice of pharmacotreatment is largely based on general principles, anecdotal evidence, clinical lore, generalizations derived from studies in adults, and "clinical impression" (Popper, 1995a).

Benzodiazepines

Indications. Established uses of benzodiazepines in the pediatric population do not include any anxiety disorders, though the management of children with most of these conditions often includes the use of these agents (Graae, 1990).

Contraindications. Caution should be exercised in the use of benzodiazepines in children or adolescents who have a potential for substance abuse or addictive behavior, and those who have a history of disinhibition or aggressive behavior during prior treatment with benzodiazepines or barbiturates.

Pharmacokinetics. These agents have been extensively studied in adults, and a few pharmacokinetic studies are available in children (Coffey et al., 1983). These studies were typically conducted in children who did not have anxiety disorders, and certain aspects of the kinetics of these agents might speculatively be altered by physiological concomitants of anxiety.

The kinetic characteristics of the different benzodiazepines vary considerably. In adults, peak concentrations are reached in approximately 1 to 3 hours, and their elimination half-lives are roughly 20 to 50 hours. About 80% to 98% of benzodiazepines are bound to plasma proteins. In the liver, these agents are converted to metabolites by hepatic microsomes, are further metabolized by hydroxylation and demethylation, and then are excreted renally as glucuronide or sulfate conjugates.

Relative to adults, children probably metabolize and excrete the benzodiazepines significantly faster because of their more extensive and rapid hepatic drug biotransformation and renal clearance. Primarily due to their fast liver clearance, children often require significantly higher weight-adjusted doses (i.e., expressed as milligram of drug per kilogram of body weight, or mg/kg). Compared with typical adult dosages, the mg/kg doses of benzodiazepines are often up to 50% higher in adolescents and sometimes up to 100% higher in preschool children. The rate of hepatic biotransformation gradually slows from the age of 3 years and typically reaches adult rates by the end of adolescence.

Dosing. Although the final weight-adjusted (mg/kg) dosages may be comparatively large in children and adolescents, medications should be initiated at low doses and titrated upward gradually. A slow rate of dose increase reduces the frequency of untoward reactions and diminishes the surprise associated with side effects. This slow approach can be especially important (and save time) in dealing with an angry, oppositional, or medication-refusing child who might find it difficult to tolerate side effects.

The doses of the shorter half-life benzodiazepines, such as alprazolam or lorazepam, can be increased every 2 to 4 days. Longer half-life agents, such as clonazepam or diazepam, should be titrated somewhat more slowly. Dosing guidelines (see Table 9.12) are only rough estimates, since individual dosing will depend on the appearance of side effects and the resolution of target symptoms in a particular patient. Although Ciraulo et al. (1990) showed that a blood level of alprazolam at 6 ng/ml blocked 100% of panic attacks in adults, there are no indications for benzodiazepine blood-level monitoring in children or adolescents.

Adverse Effects. The side effects of benzodiazepines are usually mild and well tolerated in most children, though the risks of benzodiazepine dependence and withdrawal have not been adequately evaluated in children or adolescents. As in adults, common side effects include sedation, cognitive or performance deficits, behavioral disinhibition and, in adolescents, benzodiazepine abuse. Behavioral disinhibition has been reported in children receiving benzodiazepines, incidence estimates varying from 0% to 30%. Rare but potentially serious side effects include seizures, hallucinations, leuko/thrombocytopenia, or agranulocytosis. Particularly because of their fast clearance, children might speculatively be at greater risk for rebound insomnia, withdrawal syndromes with concomitant autonomic signs, or (with the very short half-life agents) memory loss (Desai, Taylor-Davies, & Barnett, 1983).

Table 9.12. **Suggested Benzodiazepine Dosing Regimen**

	Usual Daily Dose (mg)	Starting Dose (mg qd)	Rate of Increase	Maximum Daily Dose (mg qd)
Adolescents				
Lorazepam	0.5–6	0.5–1	0.5–1 mg q 3–4 days	10
Diazepam	2–20	0.5–1	0.5–1 mg q 5–7 days	20–30
Alprazolam	0.75–4	0.25–0.5	0.25–5 mg q 3–4 days	8–10
Prepubertals				
Lorazepam	0.25–3	0.25–5	0.25–.5 mg q 3–4 days	4
Diazepam	1–10	0.5	0.5 mg q 5–7 days	5–10
Alprazolam	0.25–2	0.25	0.25 mg q 3–4 days	1–4

Reproduced from Coffey (1990) with permission.

Clinical Use.   Benzodiazepines are useful in adults for treating certain psychiatric disorders, emergency situations, and situational reactions in which anxiety is a predominant symptom. In youth, it remains to be seen whether the degree of improvement offered by benzodiazepines is clinically significant, and whether these agents induce a profile of adverse effects in youth that makes them less desirable than in adults. For example, some children seem to experience sedation at dose levels that do not produce much anxiolytic effect. The fast clearance of benzodiazepines in youth might, as noted, make them more vulnerable to memory loss or rebound insomnia. Compliance issues may limit the usefulness of certain benzodiazepines, since most agents require multiple daily dosing and administration during school hours. In adolescents and perhaps some preadolescents, the risk of substance abuse needs to be evaluated. Some patients may make recreational use of their medications, sell the pills to drug-seeking youths, or be "strong-armed" in the schoolyard by peers who demand access to pills.

In a chart review of 25 children and adolescents with various anxiety disorders on high-potency benzodiazepine treatment, 20 patients were found to have Clinical Global Improvement (CGI) scores of "very much improved" or "much improved"; 4 patients were "minimally improved," and one was judged unchanged (Gherardi, Wilens, & Biederman, unpublished manuscript). None of the patients discontinued treatment because of side effects. Although combined pharmacotherapies and patient comorbidity influenced treatment outcome in this descriptive naturalistic study, this study supports common clinical beliefs and prior research findings that suggest benzodiazepines might eventually have a definable role in the treatment of anxiety disorders in youth.

Heterocyclic Antidepressants

Indications.   Based on early findings, the use of tricyclic antidepressants became particularly widespread for treating separation anxiety disorder and school absenteeism; more recent studies have not supported these uses. In addition, the heterocyclic antidepressants are often employed by many clinicians in the treatment of major depressive disorder, panic disorder, agoraphobia, PTSD, generalized anxiety disorder, specific phobia, social phobia, and selective mutism—despite the lack of data supporting their value for any of these indications in the child of adolescent population.

Contraindications.   The heterocyclic antidepressants have the same contraindications in adults and pediatric patients. The use of these medications in a patient with bipolar disorder or schizophrenia may precipitate a psychotic episode. Cardiac conduction abnormalities and arrhythmias, alcohol and cocaine abuse, concomitant use of over-the-counter sympathomimetics, seizure disorders, and thyroid dysfunction pose potential problems. Although not a contraindication, serious suicidality must be considered in making a decision about the use of these agents, which are highly toxic in overdose. A waiting period of at least 14 days should elapse after MAOI discontinuation before beginning treatment with a heterocyclic antidepressant. The combined use of psychostimulants and heterocyclic antidepressants can be quite helpful but requires careful clinical monitoring.

Pharmacokinetics. Due to their fast hepatic clearance of heterocyclic antidepressants, some children experience withdrawal symptoms between doses administered on a once daily regimen; for this reason, some children appear to have fewer adverse drugs effects when their heterocyclic antidepressants are administered in divided doses, given two or even three times daily (Ryan et al., 1987). Also, because of the faster clearance rates, the time required for heterocyclic antidepressants to reach steady-state levels is shorter in children than in adults; presumably (since this has never been directly demonstrated), this would allow measurement of plasma antidepressant levels after 3 or 4 days on a stable dose (in contrast to 5 days in most adults). In both adults and children, the large interindividual variations in steady-state plasma levels are largely determined by differences in drug biotransformation.

Children have a higher free fraction of their plasma drug concentrations than adults: Plasma protein-binding of imipramine is 81% at age 8 and 89% in adults. This difference implies that, when administered concurrently with another medication which might displace the antidepressant from its binding sites, there would be a smaller increase in free antidepressant levels in children than in adults. Further, since the level of protein binding of tricyclic antidepressants is not very high (less than 90%), the clinical significance of such drug interactions is likely to be minimal in most children.

Apart from the faster clearance and slightly lower level of protein binding in youth than in adults, the pharmacokinetics of the heterocyclic antidepressants in adults and youth are similar.

Dosing. A pretreatment electrocardiogram (EKG) is essential for children and adolescents below the age of 17 years. The baseline EKG allows identification of a preexisting heart block or cardiac arrhythmia, which may be a contraindication to treatment.

Taking the example of imipramine, a starting dose of 10–25 mg daily (depending on the size of the child) can be titrated upward slowly by 10–25 mg increments every 3 to 5 days until a dose of 5.0 mg/kg daily is reached, or until adverse effects or EKG changes dictate stopping the dose increases.

The frequency of EKG monitoring during the period of dose elevation is a matter of considerable debate. The purpose of monitoring the EKG during the period of dose elevation is to allow identification of children whose conduction intervals might suggest that a heart block is developing. If the PR interval exceeds 0.21 seconds, QRS interval exceeds 0.12 seconds, or the QTc exceeds 0.45 seconds, then it is reasonable to defer further dose increases until consultation can be obtained (optimally, from a pediatric cardiologist). However, fueled by reports of several sudden deaths in children during treatment with desipramine, certain clinicians have begun to obtain EKGs more frequently during the course of treatment, in the hope that this would provide a warning sign of a risk of sudden death. Thus, some experts have advocated EKG (or rhythm strip) monitoring before each dose increase in a child; in some cases, this could lead to obtaining 10 or more tracings. Other clinicians have been obtaining repeat EKGs prior to each dose increase, but beginning only once the daily dose has reached 3 mg/kg; this could still require numerous EKGs. Another approach is to obtain a second EKG once the dose has reached 3 mg/kg and a third EKG at 5 mg/kg: This latter approach is quite reasonable because there are no data available to indicate whether frequent EKG monitoring reduces the risk of sudden death or, indeed, whether EKGs are able to identify children who are at risk for sudden death. Thus, in the absence of data, it is a purely speculative decision to subject a child to multiple repeated EKGs. A sequence of three EKGs (baseline, 3 mg/kg, and 5 mg/kg) is still justifiable for finding cases of developing heart block. Once a stable dose is reached, it is not necessary to continue frequent EKG monitoring, although it is prudent to repeat this assessment during the annual physical examination for the entire period during which the medication is prescribed.

In addition to monitoring EKG conduction parameters, it is sensible to follow blood pressure and pulse during treatment of youths with heterocyclic antidepressants. There is evidence that some youths may experience an increase in blood pressure during tricyclic antidepressant treatment (Kuekes, Wigg, Bryant, & Meyer, 1992), in contrast to the hypotension that many adults demonstrate. Although the blood pressure and pulse increases observed in youth are typically not of clinical significance, it is reasonable to reevaluate the dosing regimen if the blood pressure changes notably or if the resting heart rate (or pulse while asleep) exceeds 130 beats per minute.

Monitoring of plasma antidepressant levels has been advocated in treating children and adolescents, even though a therapeutic plasma range has not been established for any heterocyclic antidepressant in children. Such monitoring is presumed to be helpful in regulating dosage, although some pitfalls in interpretation can lead to errors in clinical decision making with this approach. It is likely that therapeutic drug monitoring could be helpful in raising a clinician's vigilance in identifying children whose elevated blood levels might be associated with subtle drug-induced cognitive disturbances or other toxic effects. Many clinicians obtain plasma levels of antidepressant levels to provide evidence that a dosage is not in a subtherapeutic or toxic range. However, it is not clear that obtaining repeated blood tests is more effective in identifying toxicity than a careful and thorough examination of adverse effects, including attentive monitoring of cognitive functioning.

Adverse Effects. The heterocyclic antidepressants have common side effects that are similar in children and adults: anticholinergic effects, weight gain, sedation, increases or decreases in blood pressure and/or pulse, and cognitive disruption (especially name-finding and short-term memory). Psychotic episodes might be triggered in patients who have latent or dormant psychotic disorders, and tics might be triggered in patients with a predisposition to tic or Tourette's disorder. Although maprotiline is a particular risk, all heterocyclic antidepressants are capable of lowering seizure threshold, particularly in patients with a neurological vulnerability; drug-induced seizures can typically be managed by concomitant treatment with an anticonvulsant medication. The quinidine-like effects on cardiac conduction can lead to heart block or even arrhythmias, but there is controversy about whether a younger cardiac system is more or less susceptible to the cardiac effects of TCAs and their metabolites (Ryan et al., 1987).

Sudden collapse and death during the course of treatment with desipramine have been described in at least five children and adolescents (Riddle, Geller, & Ryan, 1993; Zimnitzky & Popper, 1994). There have been no published reports of similar deaths with imipramine or other tricyclic antidepressants. These deaths cannot be definitely attributed to desipramine in each case, but the pattern suggests that caution is appropriate. Perhaps more importantly, desipramine is significantly more dangerous following overdose in children and adolescents than other available antidepressants (Popper 1994).

Clinical Use. As with the benzodiazepines, the use of tricyclic antidepressants is quite widespread in youth. In addition to the relatively clear indications for enuresis and ADHD, possible indications include major depressive disorder, Tourette's disorder, and many of the anxiety disorders.

A sensible baseline pretreatment workup would include physical examination, EKG, hematological indices, liver and renal function tests, and thyroid screening.

In view of the concerns raised by the increased risk of lethality following overdose and by the sudden deaths, the safety of desipramine is under some question. It would seem advisable to use one of the many other heterocyclic antidepressants rather than desipramine for routine treatment in children and adolescents.

Specific Serotonergic Reuptake Inhibitors

The specific serotonin reuptake inhibitors (SSRIs) include fluoxetine (Prozac), sertraline (Zoloft), paroxetine (Paxil), and fluvoxamine (Luvox). In addition, clomipramine may be considered a serotonin reuptake inhibitor, but this tricyclic agent also has effects on the neuronal reuptake of catecholamine neurotransmitters; because clomipramine is not as serotonin-selective as the other agents, it is not included in this discussion.

Indications. All the SSRIs appear able to treat obsessive-compulsive disorder and probably panic disorder in adults. Two studies suggest that fluoxetine may also be useful in treating obsessive-compulsive disorder in children (Kurlan, Como, Deeley, McDermott, & McDermott, 1993; Riddle et al., 1992). Although an open study with fluoxetine (Van Ameringen, Mancini, & Streiner, 1993) and a controlled study with sertraline have suggested that these agents can be helpful in treating social phobia in adults, similar data have not been reported with children. Depressed patients with anxious or obsessive traits also might be considered candidates for SSRI treatment, though there are no controlled data suggesting that these agents are effective in treating depression in children or adolescents.

Contraindications. Based on findings in adults, it may be presumed that SSRIs should not be used in conjunction or within two weeks of discontinuing an MAOI antidepressant.

Pharmacokinetics. The four major SSRIs differ in their characteristics regarding disposition and metabolism, as well as their affinities for the various serotonin receptor subtypes. Although not yet examined in children, they are slowly but completely absorbed in adults and reach peak levels between 5 and 8 hours. They are extensively metabolized by the liver in a "first pass" effect (especially sertraline), and so patients of any age may be reasonably advised to take these agents with meals to enhance bioavailability. These agents are cleared by both renal and hepatic mechanisms, though the clearance of the different drugs and metabolites varies widely. Although considerable emphasis has been placed on the long duration of fluoxetine action due to the slow clearance of its active metabolite norfluoxetine, there is considerable variation between adults in hepatic biotransformation (so that rapid clearance of fluoxetine can be observed in some individuals). The more rapid hepatic biotransformation in children would lead to the expectation that fluoxetine may have a relatively short half-life in most children.

Dosing. Early studies in adults, and several in children, have suggested that gradual dose elevation may be critical in reducing the adverse effects of SSRIs. For fluoxetine or paroxetine, a starting dose of 5 mg daily for preadolescents and 10 mg daily for adolescents is reasonable, though some patients may need to begin treatment with one-half of these doses. The doses may be increased by 5–10 mg daily every 5 to 14 days, until a response is attained or disruptive side effects appear. In adults, it appears that doses of 60 mg or higher may be necessary for resolution of obsessional symptoms, doses of 20–40 mg are sufficient for treating major depression, whereas lower doses (5–15 mg daily) may be helpful for low-grade anxiety symptoms. Although subject to ongoing debate, it appears that doses greater than 40 mg do not contribute to the treatment of depression in adults, and that further increases in dosage may contribute mainly to adverse effects. A starting dose of fluoxetine of 20 mg daily in children can lead to marked adverse effects, including prominent behavioral problems (Riddle et al., 1990).

Adverse Effects. The common adverse effects that have been documented in adults appear comparable to the side effects recently reported in children. With fluoxetine, prominent effects include behavioral activation or agitation, anxiety (or "wired feelings"), insomnia, headache, gastrointestinal distress, decreased libido, and anorgasmia. The side effects of sertraline are similar, but with less behavioral agitation and more sweating and gastrointestinal symptoms such as nausea, dyspepsia, and loose stools. Adverse effects to paroxetine are similar to those of fluoxetine and sertraline, except that paroxetine induces more sedation than agitation.

By virtue of their propensity to induce agitation, sleep disturbance, or akathisia, SSRIs might be speculated to decrease the threshold for some patients to act on impulsive or aggressive tendencies. Although some controversy remains about whether the SSRIs increase the risk of suicidal or violent behaviors, there is a formal consensus that these agents do not contribute to such aggressive symptoms in adults. Some incidents of SSRI-induced suicidality and violence have been suggested in children, but formal documentation has remained inconclusive. However, the authors believe that they have seen genuine cases of SSRI-induced suicidality (which could not be merely attributed to the underlying disorder).

A possibly common adverse effect of the SSRIs has received little attention. In children as well as in adults, after several months of treatment with SSRIs, symptoms of apathy or an amotivational syndrome may emerge (Popper, 1995a). For example, in children treated for depression with SSRIs, the mood symptoms may resolve but the school grades might actually worsen. In parents, anxiety symptoms may be reduced but chores may no longer be completed. This lack of motivation is distinct from the anhedonia of depression, since the mood is brightened and interests have returned. Instead, the attitude toward school or chores is one of "I don't care" and "It doesn't bother me." These symptoms are similar to "la belle indifference" and overexcitement/aggressivity associated with frontal lobe syndromes (Hoehn-Saric, Lipsey, & McLeod, 1990). Walkup, who has also observed SSRI-induced apathy in children (Walkup, 1995), speculates that the findings of apathy, as well as the behavioral activation reported in association with SSRI treatment in children (Riddle et al., 1990), may both reflect different aspects of frontal disinhibition. Although the findings of apathy and disinhibition may be quite obvious in some children, our experience suggests that they may be subtly present in the majority of SSRI-treated children. Reducing the dose of the SSRI may help reduce the amotivational syndrome in some patients, but we have observed the apathy reappear on lower doses at a later time in two children.

Another important side effect of SSRIs is the "serotonin syndrome." This presumably rare but potentially life-threatening condition consists of autonomic instability, and in certain ways resembles neuroleptic malignant syndrome in its "hypermetabolic" quality. Symptoms and signs of serotonin syndrome include hyperthermia, rigidity, myoclonus, blood pressure and pulse changes, or mental status alterations (including possible delirium or coma). This side effect is much more common when SSRIs are used in conjunction with other serotonergic treatments; for example, to lessen the risks of this complication, at least 2 drug-free weeks should be allowed to pass when switching between an MAOI and an SSRI. This syndrome is not commonly reported, especially in children. There are no reliable estimates of its incidence in SSRI-treated children, and no estimates of its risk of fatality. Adequate clinical vigilance is important in minimizing the effects of this rare but important adverse effect.

Clinical Use.   In adults, SSRIs have become the drugs of first choice for treatment of major depression (especially for treating depression associated with OCD and/or anxiety) and are often an early selection in the treatment of generalized anxiety disorder and phobic disorders (agoraphobia, social phobia, specific phobia) in adults. The use of SSRIs for treating psychiatric disorders in childhood and adolescence is growing steadily, despite the lack of documentation of their efficacy for these psychiatric disorders in the pediatric population.

Beta Blockers

Indications. Although there are no established uses for beta blockers in children and adolescents, some clinicians have used these agents to treat PTSD, performance anxiety, social phobia, panic disorder, and anxiety symptoms in other anxiety disorders. There is one open-label study in which propranolol was found to be helpful in reducing the anxiety and aggression associated with PTSD in children (Famularo et al., 1988).

Contraindications. As in adults, the major contraindications to the use of beta blockers include major depression, bradycardia and certain cardiovascular conditions, asthma, and diabetes.

Pharmacokinetics. The available data are derived from studies in adults. The agents differ considerably in lipophilicity and receptor selectivity, and so some agents act predominantly outside the central nervous system, and other agents act both centrally and peripherally. In addition, the various beta blockers have markedly different durations of action, rates of hepatic biotransformation, routes of elimination (hepatic vs. renal), and protein binding. These characteristics, observed in adults, would be expected to be qualitatively similar in children and adolescents.

Dosing. It is impossible to provide valid dosing guidelines based on current information in youth. In general, a reasonable starting dose of propranolol would be about 10–25 mg three times daily, with increases of 10–25 mg every 3 days. A therapeutic effect is usually expected before reaching doses of 120 mg daily in preadolescents and 300 mg daily for adolescents. Although not formally investigated in children, it appears that propranolol (Inderal) and atenolol (Tenormin) can be dosed 2 to 3 times daily, and metoprolol (Lopressor) might require 4 daily dosings. Nadolol (Corgard), with its long half-life, has the advantage of requiring only once (or occasionally twice) daily dosing, even in children. It is unknown whether centrally or peripherally acting beta blockers are more advantageous in children or adolescents. However, there are anecdotal suggestions that, for many purposes, the peripheral beta blockers (such as once-a-day nadolol) appear as useful as propranolol.

Adverse Effects. In adults and children, the major side effects of the peripheral and central beta blockers include hypotension, bradycardia, fatigue, weakness, Raynaud's phenomenon (whiteness and numbness in fingers and sometimes toes, due to vasospasm), sexual impotence, bronchoconstriction, and occasional hypoglycemia. With centrally acting beta blockers, side effects may also include depression, dysphoria, and sleep disruption. Because even "peripherally acting" beta blockers gain some degree of entry into the central nervous system, close clinical observation of mood changes is advisable.

Clinical Use. Baseline assessment and regular periodic monitoring of blood pressure and pulse are essential for treatment with any beta blocker. Children with affective symptoms, tremors, other physical manifestations of anxiety, or family histories of depressive or bipolar disorders might do better with peripherally acting agents such as atenolol or nadolol (Corgard). The use of peripherally acting beta blockers may also attenuate the risk of unwanted dysphoric side effects. Asthmatic children should be prescribed beta$_1$ selective agents such as atenolol (Tenormin) and metoprolol (Lopressor).

Buspirone

Indications. This recently marketed agent has received little systematic study in children or adolescents. There are no established uses for buspirone in children and adolescents, but buspirone might be helpful as an alternative for treatment-resistant or medication-intolerant children with overanxious disorder, generalized anxiety disorder, or perhaps other anxiety disorders.

Contraindications. Special caution should be taken when this agent is employed in the setting of the concomitant use of MAOIs, hepatic disorders, or renal dysfunction.

Pharmacokinetics. The distribution and metabolism of this agent in children and adolescents have not yet been examined.

Dosing. In the absence of any scientific data to guide dose selection in children or adolescents, clinicians venturing to use this agent in children are forced to operate from general principles. Although a maximum dose of 60 gm daily for children has been quoted in the literature, an alternative agent might be considered in preadolescents after 4 weeks on buspirone at 40 mg daily.

Adverse Effects. Anxiety, nausea, headache, light-headedness, dizziness, and irritability have been reported in adults. Although buspirone has fewer sedative properties in its standard dose range than benzodiazepines, buspirone appears to require somewhat high doses to achieve antianxiety effects in some cases; at these higher doses, sedation can be problematic. Buspirone is also reputed to have a lower abuse potential than the other anxiolytics, which can be helpful in treating adolescents at risk for substance. There have been two cases reported so far in the literature of psychotic deterioration in children with anxiety disorders treated with buspirone, including paranoia, loose associations, thought-blocking, and delusions (Soni & Weintraub, 1992).

Clinical Use. Because its track record of use in adults is still relatively brief, and it has been minimally studied and used in adolescents and children, buspirone should be reserved for use in youths in whom benzodiazepines have been previously found unsuccessful or are contraindicated. It might also have potential value in children with anxiety disorders who have comorbid ADHD (which is often viewed as a contraindication to the use of benzodiazepines) or substance abuse.

Additional Medications with Antianxiety Properties

Neuroleptics, diphenhydramine, and some other agents have been used in adults and children for management of acute anxiety. Despite their anxiolytic properties, the known adverse effects of the neuroleptics and antihistamines do not make them promising candidates for treating anxiety disorders.

Neuroleptic agents have powerful tranquilizing and sedative effects that can be helpful for reducing the anxiety associated with several anxiety disorders and are commonly employed in managing children in emergency or acute medical situations, situational reactions, and some anxiety disorders. The potential for serious adverse effects, including neuroleptic malignant syndrome and tardive dyskinesia, have led to minimal use for anxiety disorders.

Diphenhydramine and hydroxyzine are two antihistaminic agents that are sometimes used to manage acute anxiety in children, especially preschool children, despite the virtually complete absence of controlled studies of their behavioral effects. Although these antihistaminic agents are reputed to have minimal side effects, they are known to produce cognitive and affective "hangovers" as well as anticholinergic reactions; these adverse effects become particularly problematic during extended treatment.

In addition, clonidine appears able to diminish anxiety, much like the beta blockers, though it is rarely used clinically for this purpose. Speculatively, the "atypical neuroleptic" risperidone might someday be viewed as a valid treatment of anxiety, though its potential for neuroleptic malignant syndrome makes this unlikely. Also speculatively, peripherally acting antihistamines such as terfenadine (Seldane) might exert some beneficial effects on anxiety without the disadvantages associated with the conventional antihistamines. These agents are rarely used for treating anxiety, even in adults, and have not yet been examined in the treatment of anxiety disorders in children.

CHRONICITY AND COMORBIDITY OF ANXIETY DISORDERS IN CHILDREN AND ADOLESCENTS

Based on general considerations, the natural history of the anxiety disorders in children and adolescents may be expected to depend on many factors: the child's age at onset of the disorder, the age at onset of treatment, the diagnosis, the severity and chronicity, preexisting or comorbid psychopathology, family history of anxiety or other psychiatric disorder, family and environmental stressors and supports, economic resources, the adequacy of available treatment (pharmacological, cognitive-behavioral, dynamic, family, parent behavioral counseling), and compliance with treatment by the child and family.

Long-term follow-up studies of children with anxiety disorders are just beginning to be implemented. Initial findings from these investigations have confirmed some expectations. Children with comorbid diagnoses have a greater chance of being referred for treatment (Bird, Gould, & Staghezza, 1993). Among 222 adolescents (ages 9–16 years) who met criteria for any anxiety disorder from a multistage probability sample of 2,036 households distributed across Puerto Rico (Bird et al., 1993), only 7% of the 222 with one comorbid DSM-III-R diagnosis received treatment in comparison to 13% of those with two, 25% of those with three, and 33% of those with four diagnoses (Bird et al., 1993). The degree of symptomatic impairment was measured by the Children's Global Assessment Scale (CGAS). The findings included a clear direct association between impairment as measured by CGAS and (a) the load of diagnosis comorbidity and (b) mental health service utilization. These data suggest that increased comorbidity will increase the chance that a child with an anxiety disorder will present for treatment, and that children who present for treatment with an anxiety disorder will have a high level of psychiatric comorbidity (and probably impairment).

A naturalistic study of outcome in 31 children and adolescents with separation anxiety, overanxious, and avoidant disorders found evidence of persistent morbidity. About 40% to 50% of these patients had persistent impairment from their respective anxiety disorders at follow-up after 4 years (Cantwell & Baker, 1989).

In a similar naturalistic study of the course of illness in 38 children and adolescents with mixed anxiety disorders (85% met DSM-III criteria for overanxious disorder), there were continuing symptoms as assessed by DSM-III criteria over the course of 5 years of treatment. About 65% of those patients still met criteria for anxiety disorders (Keller et al., 1992). The authors postulated that a major reason for the large proportion of patients with persistent illness could be explained by the large proportion (82% of the sample) who received no treatment directly targeting their anxiety disorder. Another factor may have been the high rate of co-morbidity: 37% of the sample also met criteria for a mood disorder, 11% had an additional anxiety disorder, 16% met criteria for ADD, and 16% met criteria for a conduct disorder.

These two studies strongly suggest a high chronicity of anxiety disorders in children, despite routine treatment, and the clinical importance of identifying and targeting treatment to anxiety disorders.

The crucial role of comorbidity is a constant theme in child and adolescent psychiatry, and especially in the anxiety disorders. Multiple investigative groups have shown that the anxiety disorders usually present comorbidly with other anxiety disorders as well as with ADHD, other disruptive behavior disorders, mood disorders, and substance use disorders. For example, Lewinsohn et al., (1993) found that 9% of 1,710 high school students were projected to develop an anxiety disorder before age 18: Among those students, 49% had comorbid depression, 15% had a substance use disorder, and 13% suffered from some type of disruptive behavior disorder.

Specific anxiety disorders may present with different comorbid Axis I diagnoses. In 73 consecutively referred children (ages 5–18) in an anxiety disorder clinic, children with overanxious disorder had the most comorbidity, and children with social phobia or school absenteeism had the least (Last, Hersen, Kazdin, Finkelstein, & Strauss, 1987). These interrelationships are only beginning to be understood.

In addition to comorbid anxiety disorders and other psychiatric disorders, it is always essential to evaluate for possible "medical" comorbidity as well as physical factors that may explain or contribute to the presenting symptoms of anxiety. There is no substitute for a thorough multidimensional evaluation (see Table 9.13).

Because comorbidity often increases treatment resistance, chronicity, and severity, the typical entanglement of the anxiety disorders with other disorders requires vigilant management in clinical practice.

NEW DIRECTIONS

There are, as yet, few definitive findings in child and adolescent psychopharmacology (Popper, 1995b). Across the range of anxiety disorders in children and adolescents, and especially regarding their psychopharmacological treatment, there are few well-controlled studies, and their

Table 9.13.   Assessment of Anxiety Disorders in Children and Adolescents

History/Interview of child and parents.

Reports from school.

Determine severity, accounting for developmental stage.

Medical workup:

> Pediatric exam (especially cardiovascular and respiratory status), pulse and blood pressure (use child cuff).
>
> Consider neurological status (including temporal lobe epilepsy).
>
> In certain cases, rule out hyperthyroidism, hypoglycemia, lupus, pheochromocytosis, cardiac arrhythmia.
>
> Family medical history.
>
> Ask about concurrent medication use, such as psychostimulants.
>
> Check substance abuse, including caffeine and sympathomimetics.

Search for possible physical and sexual abuse.

Evaluate for comorbidity.

Evaluate family, including for anxiety and mood disorders.

In setting treatment goals, look beyond resolution of anxiety symptoms.

Reprinted with permission from Popper, 1993.

findings are mostly suggestive. Clinicians are left to exercise considerable judgment in making even routine treatment decisions. Choices about optimal treatment modalities, medication selection, dosing regimens, treatment duration, and outcome measurement are currently based on judgment and slowly growing knowledge, as we await larger samples and better controls.

A variety of other developments are needed before pharmacological research can give clear guidance to clinicians. While drug studies are proceeding, essential information regarding nosology, development, biology, epidemiology, and natural course of the anxiety disorders of youth will be accumulating.

Confusion still stems from the extensive and at times bewildering comorbidity, blurred boundaries, and crossed diagnostic criteria among the anxiety disorders and other psychiatric disorders of children and adolescents. No amount of highly controlled pharmacological investigations will achieve orderly medication treatments until the nosology becomes better organized. Treatment outcome studies for a variety of medications, along with longitudinal follow-up studies for each of the many anxiety disorders, will be needed to clarify the effects of the drugs and the disorders over time.

Despite these limitations, the current generation of youth with anxiety disorders require treatment. For the time being, many clinicians will use the limited available knowledge (see Table 9.14) and will undoubtedly continue to co-opt methods from adult psychopharmacology while making technical corrections in dosing regimens to respond to children's differences in drug handling.

Some clinicians may question whether there are specific treatments for anxiety disorders that are distinct from the coincidental treatment of the comorbidly appearing conditions. Yet there are studies in which

Table 9.14. **Evidence for the Use of Psychopharmacological Treatment of Anxiety Disorders in Children and Adolescents**

Disorder	Effective in Multiple Well-Controlled Studies	Statistically Significant in a Controlled Study	Successful Open Trials or Trends in Controlled Studies
Separation Anxiety Disorder			Imipramine Alprazolam Clonazepam
School Absenteeism			Imipramine Alprazolam Clonazepam Chlordiazepoxide Buspirone
Selective Mutism		Fluoxetine	
Panic Disorder		Clonazepam	Imipramine Alprazolam
Posttraumatic Stress Disorder			Propranolol
Specific Phobias			None
Social Phobia			(Fluoxetine) (Propranolol)
Generalized Anxiety Disorder			Alprazolam Buspirone
Obsessive-Compulsive Disorder	Clomipramine	Fluoxetine	Buspirone (for augmentation)

Note: These groupings are based on reports in the literature (until Jan 1995) on children and adolescents. Additional treatments may be quite reasonable based on individual circumstances (e.g., comorbidity or family history), psychopharmacological findings in adults, or professional experience.

anxiety symptoms have improved regardless of depressive symptoms, both in school absenteeism (Gittelman-Klein & Klein, 1973) and in OCD (Flament et al., 1985). Also, medication treatment may improve depressive symptoms without helping the symptoms of separation anxiety disorder (Berney et al., 1981). This suggests that anxiety and mood disorders may respond independently, at least in certain children (Gittelman, 1986).

In view of their comorbidity, developmental complexity, and long-term prognosis, we can safely infer that anxiety disorders (like all major psychiatric disorders in children and adolescents) require multimodal treatments. Medications are rarely the sole or even primary treatment of these disorders. As research accumulates on the pharmacotherapies of anxiety disorders, we will in parallel need to evaluate cognitive-behavioral and alternative strategies. Furthermore, the proper treatment of these children often will entail the treatment of anxiety or mood disorders in their parents, just as the proper treatment of parents with anxiety or mood disorders often entails the pharmacological treatment of their children.

It cannot be assumed that drugs effective in adults will be effective in children. In view of the close interrelationships between depressive and anxiety disorders, the surprising finding that depressive youths do not appear responsive to antidepressants should make us leery about drawing inferences from adult psychopharmacology to the treatment of children or even adolescents. The increasing development of anxiety disorder clinics for children and adolescents will be critical to advance research and treatment of anxiety disorders.

As novel pharmacological approaches are developed through a deepening understanding of neurobiology, new mechanisms of action will enhance our understanding of the biology of the anxiety disorders (Dubovsky, 1993). The current use of medications that crudely stabilize noradrenergic and serotonergic neurotransmission, modify limbic benzodiazepine receptors, and act on intracellular messengers and ions can be expected to give way to unforeseen options for clinical treatment.

New drugs are appearing faster than older drugs can be evaluated: Clinicians have substantial reason to be cautious in using both the old and new agents in children. Yet especially for the newly marketed medications whose safety in adults is still under initial postmarketing investigation, there should be no rush to introduce novel "high-tech" agents into the developing bodies and brains of children and adolescents.

The balance of knowledge and judgment (Popper, 1995a) that characterizes clinical thinking in child and adolescent psychopharmacology is essential in view of our current options for the management of anxiety disorders of children and adolescents. We must remain aware that, at present, our firm knowledge of the treatment of the child and adolescent anxiety disorders remains simple: Apart from obsessive-compulsive disorder, no pharmacological treatment of any anxiety disorder has established efficacy in children or adolescents.

REFERENCES

Alessi, N. E., & Magen, J. (1988). Panic disorder in psychiatrically hospitalized children. *American Journal of Psychiatry, 145,* 1450–1452.

Alessi, N. E., Robbins, D. R., & Dilsaver, S. C. (1987). Panic and depressive disorders among psychiatrically hospitalized adolescents. *Psychiatry Research, 20,* 275–283.

American Psychiatric Association (1994). *Diagnostic and statistical manual of mental disorders* (4th ed.). Washington, DC: Author.

Amies, P. L., Gelder, M. G., & Shaw, P. M. (1983). Social phobia: A comparative clinical study. *British Journal of Psychiatry, 142,* 174–179.

Anderson, J. C., Williams, S., McGee, R., & Silva, P. A. (1987). DSM-III disorders in preadolescent children: Prevalence in a large sample from the general population. *Archives of General Psychiatry, 44,* 69–76.

Ballenger, J. C., Carek, D. J., Steele, J. J., & Cornish-McTighe, D. (1989). Three cases of panic disorder with agoraphobia in children. *American Journal of Psychiatry, 146,* 922–924.

Beidel, D. (1991). Social phobia and overanxious disorder in school-age children. *Journal of the American Academy of Child and Adolescent Psychiatry, 30,* 545–552.

Berney, T., Kolvin, I., Bhate, S. R., Garside, R. F., Jeans, J., Kay, B., & Scarth, L. (1981). School phobia: A therapeutic trial with clomipramine and short-term outcome. *British Journal of Psychiatry, 138,* 110–118.

Bernstein, G. A. (1991). Comorbidity and severity of anxiety and depressive disorders in a clinic sample. *Journal of the American Academy of Child and Adolescent Psychiatry, 30,* 43–49.

Bernstein, G. A., & Borchardt, C. M. (1991). Anxiety disorders of childhood and adolescence: A critical review. *Journal of the American Academy of Child and Adolescent Psychiatry, 30,* 519–532.

Bernstein, G. A., Garfinkel, B. D., & Borchardt, C. M. (1990). Comparative studies of pharmacotherapy for school refusal. *Journal of the American Academy of Child and Adolescent Psychiatry, 29,* 773–781.

Biederman, J. (1987). Clonazepam in the treatment of prepubertal children with panic-like symptoms. *Journal of Clinical Psychiatry, 48*(Suppl.), 38–41.

Biederman, J., Newcorn, J., & Sprich, S. (1991). Comorbidity of attention deficit disorder with conduct, depressive, anxiety, and other disorders. *American Journal of Psychiatry, 148,* 564–577.

Bird, H. R., Canino, G., Rubio-Stipec, M., Gould, M., Ribera, J., Sesman, M., Woodbury, M., Huertes-Goldman, S., Pagan, A., Sanchez-Lacay, A., & Moscoso, M. (1988). Estimates of the prevalence of childhood maladjustment in a community survey in Puerto Rico. *Archives of General Psychiatry, 45,* 1120–1126.

Bird, H. R., Gould, M. S., & Staghezza, B. M. (1993). Pattern of diagnostic comorbidity in a community sample of children aged 9–16 years. *Journal of the American Academy of Child and Adolescent Psychiatry, 32,* 361–368.

Black, B., & Robbins, D. R. (1990). Panic disorder in children and adolescents. *Journal of the American Academy of Child and Adolescent Psychiatry, 29,* 36–44.

Black, B., & Uhde, T. W. (1992). Elective mutism as a variant of social phobia. *Journal of the American Academy of Child and Adolescent Psychiatry, 31,* 1090–1094.

Black, B., & Uhde, T. W. (1994). Treatment of elective mutism with fluoxetine: A double-blind, placebo-controlled study. *Journal of the American Academy of Child and Adolescent Psychiatry, 33,* 1000–1006.

Black, B., & Uhde, T. W. (1995). Psychiatric characteristics of children with selective mutism: A pilot study. *Journal of the American Academy of Child and Adolescent Psychiatry, 34,* 847–856.

Bradley, S. J., & Hood, J. (1993). Psychiatrically referred adolescents with panic attacks: Presenting symptoms, stressors and comorbidity. *Journal of the American Academy of Child and Adolescent Psychiatry, 32,* 826–829.

Cantwell, D. P., & Baker, L. (1989). Stability and natural history of DSM-III childhood diagnoses. *Journal of the American Academy of Child and Adolescent Psychiatry, 28,* 691–700.

Casat, C. D., Ross, B. A., Scardina, R., Sarno, C., & Smith, K. (1987). Separation anxiety and mitral valve prolapse in a 12 year old girl. *Journal of the American Academy of Child and Adolescent Psychiatry, 26,* 444–446.

Ciraulo, D. A., Antal, E. J., Smith, R. B., Olson, D. R., Goldberg, D. A., Rand, E. H., Raskin, R. B., Phillips, J. P., Shader, R. I., & Greenblatt, D. J. (1990). The relationship of alprazolam dose to steady-state plasma concentrations. *Journal of Clinical Psychopharmacology, 10,* 27–32.

Clark, D. B., & Donovan, J. E. (1994). Reliability and validity of the Hamilton Anxiety Rating Scale in an adolescent sample. *Journal of the American Academy of Child and Adolescent Psychiatry, 33,* 354–360.

Cline, T., & Baldwin, S. (1994). Selective mutism in children. San Diego, CA: Singular Publishing Group.

Coffey, B. J. (1990). Anxiolytics for children and adolescents: Traditional and new drugs. *Journal of Child and Adolescent Psychopharmacology, 1,* 57–83.

Coffey, B., Shader, R., & Greenblatt, D. (1983). Pharmacokinetics of benzodiazepines and psychostimulants in children. *Journal of Clinical Psychopharmacology, 3,* 217–225.

Costello, E. J. (1989a). Child psychiatric disorders and their correlates: A primary care pediatric sample. *Journal of the American Academy of Child and Adolescent Psychiatry, 28,* 851–855.

Costello, E. J. (1989b). Developments in child psychiatric epidemiology. *Journal of the American Academy of Child and Adolescent Psychiatry, 28,* 836–841.

Crowe, R. R., Noyes, R., Pauls, D. L., & Slymen, D. (1983). A family study of panic disorder. *Archives of General Psychiatry, 40,* 1065–1069.

D'Amato, G. (1962). Chlordiazepoxide in management of school phobia. *Diseases of the Nervous System, 23,* 292–295.

Desai, N., Taylor-Davies, A., & Barnett, D. B. (1983). The effects of diazepam and exprenolol on short-term memory in individuals of high and low state anxiety. *British Journal of Clinical Psychopharmacology, 15,* 197–202.

Dubovsky, S. L. (1993). Approaches to developing new anxiolytics and antidepressants. *Journal of Clinical Psychiatry, 54*(Suppl.), 75–83.

Enzer, N. B., & Walker, P. A. (1967). Hyperventilation syndrome in childhood. *Journal of Pediatrics, 70,* 521–532.

Famularo, R., Kinscherff, R., & Fenton, T. (1988). Propranolol treatment of childhood posttraumatic stress disorder, acute type: A pilot study. *American Journal of Diseases of Children, 142,* 1244–1247.

Flament, M. F., Rapoport, J. L., Berg, C. J., Sceery, W., Kilts, C., Mellstrom, B., & Linnoila, M. (1985). Clomipramine treatment of childhood obsessive-compulsive disorder: A double-blind controlled study. *Archives of General Psychiatry, 42,* 977–983.

Francis, G., Last, C. G., & Strauss, C. C. (1987). Expression of separation anxiety disorder: The roles of age and gender. *Child Psychiatry and Human Development, 18,* 82–89.

Francis, G., Robbins, D. R., & Grapentine, W. L. (1992). Panic disorder in children and adolescents. *Rhode Island Medicine, 75,* 273–276.

Garland, E. J., & Smith, D. H. (1990). Panic disorder on a child psychiatric service. *Journal of the American Academy of Child and Adolescent Psychiatry, 29,* 785–788.

Garland, E. J., Smith, D. H. (1991). Simultaneous prepubertal onset of panic disorder, night terrors and somnambulism. *Journal of the American Academy of Child and Adolescent Psychiatry, 30,* 553–555.

George, G., Bouvard, M. P., & Dugas, M. (1993). Attention-deficit disorder and anxiety disorders: A co-occurrence study. *Annals Pediatrics, 40,* 541–548.

Gherardi, P., Wilens, T., & Biederman, J. (1995). *A chart review of 24 children and adolescents with anxiety disorders on high potency benzodiazepines.* Unpublished manuscript.

Gittelman, R. (Ed.). (1986). *Anxiety disorders of childhood.* New York: Guilford.

Gittelman, R., & Klein, D. F. (1984). Relationship between separation anxiety and panic and agoraphobic disorders. *Psychopathology, 17*(Suppl. 1), 56–65.

Gittelman-Klein, R., & Klein, D. F. (1971). Controlled imipramine treatment of school phobia. *Archives of General Psychiatry, 25,* 204–207.

Gittelman-Klein, R., & Klein, D. F. (1973). School phobia: Diagnostic considerations in the light of imipramine effects. *Journal of Nervous and Mental Diseases, 156,* 199–215.

Golwyn, D. H., & Weinstock, R. C. (1990). Phenelzine treatment of elective mutism. *Journal of Clinical Psychiatry, 51,* 384–385.

Graae, F. (1990). High anxiety in children. *Journal of Clinical Psychiatry, 51,*(Suppl.), 18–19.

Graae, F., Milner, J., Rizzotto, L., & Klein, R. G. (1994). Clonazepam in childhood anxiety disorders. *Journal of the Academy of Child and Adolescent Psychiatry, 33,* 372–376.

Hadley, N. H. (1994). *Elective mutism: A handbook for educators, counselors and health care professionals.* Dordrecht: Kluwer Academic Publishers.

Hayden, T. L. (1980). Classification of elective mutism. *Journal of the American Adademy of Child Psychiatry, 19,* 118–133.

Hayward, C., Killen, J. D., Hammer, L. D., Litt, I., Wilson, D., Simmonds, B., & Taylor, C. (1992). Pubertal stage and panic attack history in sixth and seventh grade girls. *American Journal of Psychiatry, 149,* 1239–1243.

Hayward, C., Killen, J. D., & Taylor, C. B. (1989). Panic attacks in young adolescents. *American Journal of Psychiatry, 146,* 1061–1062.

Herman, S., Stickler, G., & Lucas, A. (1981). Hyperventilation syndrome in children and adolescents: Long-term follow-up. *Pediatrics, 67,* 183–187.

Herskowitz, J. (1986). Neurological presentations of panic disorder in childhood and adolescence. *Developmental Medicine and Child Neurology, 28,* 617–623.

Hoehn-Saric, R., Lipsey, J. R., & McLeod, D. R. (1990). Apathy and indifference in patients on fluvoxamine and fluoxetine. *Journal of Clinical Psychopharmacology, 10,* 343–345.

Hunt, R. D., Capper, L., & O'Connell, P. (1990). Clonidine in child and adolescent psychiatry. *Journal of Child Adolescent Psychopharmacology, 1,* 87–102.

Jensen, P. S., & Elliott, G. R. (Section eds.) (1992). Why don't antidepressants seem to work for depressed adolescents? *Journal of Child Adolescent Psychopharmacology, 2,* 7–45.

Joorabchi, B. (1977). Expressions of the hyperventilation syndrome in childhood: Studies in management, including an evaluation of the effectiveness of propranolol. *Journal of Clinical Pediatrics, 16,* 1110–1115.

Kagan, J., Reznick, J. S., & Snidman, N. (1987). The physiology and psychology of behavioral inhibition in children. *Child Development, 58,* 1459–1473.

Kashani, J. G., & Orvaschel, H. (1990). A community study of anxiety in children and adolescents. *American Journal of Psychiatry, 147,* 313–318.

Keller, M. B., Lavori, P. W., Wunder, J., Beardslee, W. R., Schwartz, L. E., & Roth, J. (1992). Chronic course of anxiety disorders in children and adolescents. *Journal of the American Academy of Child and Adolescent Psychiatry, 31,* 595–599.

Kendall-Tackett, K. A., Williams, L. M., & Finkelhor, D. (1993). Impact of sexual abuse on children: A review and synthesis of recent empirical findings. *Psychological Bulletin, 113,* 164–168.

Kinzie, J. D., & Leung, P. (1989). Clonidine in Cambodian patients with post-traumatic stress disorder. *Journal of Nervous and Mental Diseases, 177,* 546–550.

Klein, R. G., Koplewicz, H. S., & Kanner, A. (1992). Imipramine toxicity in children with separation anxiety disorder. *Journal of the American Academy of Child and Adolescent Psychiatry, 31,* 21–28.

Klein, R. G., & Last, C. G. (1989). *Anxiety disorders in children.* Newbury Park, CA: Sage.

Klein, D. F., Mannuzza, S., Chapman, T., & Fyer, A. (1992). Child panic revisited. *Journal of the American Academy of Child and Adolescent Psychiatry, 31,* 112–116.

Kolvin, I., & Fundudis, T. (1981). Elective mute children: Psychological development and background factors. *Journal of Child Psychological Psychiatry, 22,* 219–232.

Kovacs, M., Gatsonis, C., Paulauskas, S. L., & Richards, C. (1989). Depressive disorders in childhood: IV. A longitudinal study of comorbidity with and risk for anxiety disorders. *Archives of General Psychiatry, 46,* 776–782.

Kraft, I. A., Ardali, C., Duffy, J. H., Hart, J. T., & Pearce, P. (1965). A clinical study of chlordiazepoxide used in psychiatric disorders of children. *International Journal of Neuropsychiatry, 1,* 433–437.

Kranzler, H. (1988). Use of buspirone in an adolescent with overanxious disorder. *Journal of the American Academy of Child and Adolescent Psychiatry, 27,* 789–790.

Krohn, D. D., Weckstein, S. M., & Wright, H. L. (1992). A study of the effectiveness of a specific treatment for elective mutism. *Journal of the American Academy of Child and Adolescent Psychiatry, 31,* 711–718.

Kuekes, E. D., Wigg, C., Bryant, S., & Meyer, W. J. (1992). Hypertension is a risk in adolescents treated with imipramine. *Journal of Child and Adolescent Psychopharmacology, 2,* 241–248.

Kurlan, R., Como, P. G., Deeley, C., McDermott, M., & McDermott, M. P. (1993). A pilot controlled study of fluoxetine for obsessive-compulsive symptoms in children with Tourette's syndrome. *Clinical Neuropharmacology, 16,* 167–172.

Kutcher, S. P. (1990, December). *High potency benzodiazepines in child and adolescent anxiety disorders.* Paper presented at the annual meeting of the American College of Neuropsychopharmacology, Puerto Rico.

Kutcher, S. P., & MacKenzie, S. (1988). Successful clonazepam treatment of adolescents with panic disorder. *Journal of Clinical Psychopharmacology, 145,* 1450–1452.

Kutcher, S. P., Reiter, S., Gardner, D. M., & Klein, R. (1992). The pharmacotherapy of anxiety disorders in children and adolescents. *Psychiatric Clinics of North America, 15,* 41–67.

Labbe, E. E., & Williamson, D. A. (1984). Behavioral treatment of elective mutism: A review of the literature. *Clinical Psychology Review, 4,* 273–294.

LaPouse, R., & Monk, M. (1964). Fears and worries in a representative sample of children. *American Journal of Orthopsychiatry, 29,* 803–818.

Last, C. G., Francis, G., Hersen, M., Kazdin, R. E., & Strauss, C. C. (1987). Separation anxiety and school phobia: A comparison using DSM-III criteria. *American Journal of Psychiatry, 144,* 653–657.

Last, C. G., Hersen, M., Kazdin, A., Finkelstein, R., & Strauss, C. (1987). Comparison of DSM-III separation anxiety and overanxious disorders: Demographic characteristics and patterns of comorbidity. *Journal of the American Academy of Child and Adolescent Psychiatry, 26,* 527–531.

Last, C. G., Hersen, M., Kazdin, A., Orvaschel, H., & Perrin, K. S. (1991). Anxiety disorders in children and their families. *Archives of General Psychiatry, 48,* 928–934.

Last, C. G., Perrin, S., Hersen, M., & Kazdin, A. E. (1992). DSM-III-R anxiety disorders in children: Socioeconomic and clinical characteristics. *Journal of the American Academy of Child and Adolescent Psychiatry, 31,* 1070–1075.

Last, C. G., & Strauss, C. C. (1989). Panic disorder in children and adolescents. *Journal of Anxiety Disorders, 3,* 87–95.

Last, C. G., Strauss, C. C., & Francis, G. (1987). Comorbidity among childhood anxiety disorders. *Journal of Nervous and Mental Diseases, 175,* 726–730.

Lewinsohn, P. M., Hops, H., Roberts, R. E., Seeley, J. R., & Andrews, J. A. (1993). Adolescent psychopathology: I. Prevalence and incidence of depression and other DSM-III-R disorders in high school students. *Journal of Abnormal Psychology, 102,* 133–144.

Livingston, R., & Martin-Cannici, C. (1987). Depression, anxiety, and the dexamethasone suppression test in hospitalized prepubertal children. *Hillside Journal of Clinical Psychiatry, 9,* 55–63.

Livingston, R., Taylor, J. L., & Crawford, S. L. (1988). A study of somatic complaints and psychiatric diagnosis in children. *Journal of the American Academy of Child and Adolescent Psychiatry, 27,* 185–187.

Lonie, I. (1993). Borderline disorder and post-traumatic stress disorder: An equivalence? *Australian and New Zealand Journal of Psychiatry, 27,* 233–245.

Marks, I. M., & Gelder, M. G. (1966). Different ages of onset in varieties of phobia. *American Journal of Psychiatry, 123,* 218–221.

McGee, R., Feehan, M., Williams, S., Partridge, F., Silva, P., & Kelly, J. (1990). DSM-III disorders in a large sample of adolescents. *Journal of the American Academy of Child and Adolescent Psychiatry, 29,* 611–619.

McLeer, S. V., Deblinger, E., Atkins, M. S., Foa, E. B., & Ralphe, D. L. (1988). Post-traumatic stress disorder in sexually abused children. *Journal of the American Academy of Child and Adolescent Psychiatry, 27,* 650–654.

Moreau, D. L., Weissman, M., & Warner, V. (1989). Panic disorder in children at high risk for depression. *American Journal of Psychiatry, 146,* 1059–1060.

Nelles, W. B., & Barlow, D. H. (1988). Do children panic? *Clinical Psychology Review, 8,* 359–372.

Ollendick, T. H., King, N. J., & Frary, R. B. (1989). Fears in children and adolescents: Reliability and generalizability across gender, age and nationality. *Behaviour Research and Therapy, 27,* 19–26.

Popper, C. W. (1993). Psychopharmacologic treatment of anxiety disorders in adolescents and children. *Journal of Clinical Psychiatry, 54* (Suppl.)

Popper, C. W. (1994, May). *Desipramine deaths may be adrenergic* (p. 182). New Research Program and Abstracts, Annual Meeting of the American Psychiatric Association.

Popper, C. W. (1995a, April). Balancing knowledge and judgment: A clinician looks at new developments in child and adolescent psychopharmacology. *Child and Adolescent Psychiatric Clinic of North America, 4,* 483–513.

Popper, C. W. (1995b). Child psychiatry: Pharmacotherapy. In H. Kaplan & B. Sadock (Eds.), *Comprehensive textbook of psychiatry* (6th ed., pp. 2418–2427). Baltimore: Williams & Wilkins.

Popper, C. W., & Steingard, R. (1994). Disorders usually first diagnosed in infancy, childhood, or adolescence. In J. A. Talbott, R. E. Hales, & S. C. Yudofsky (Eds.), *The American psychiatric press textbook of psychiatry* (2nd ed.). Washington, DC: American Psychiatric Press.

Pynoos, R. S., Frederick, C., Nader, K., Arroyo, W., Steinberg, A., Spencer, E., & Nunez, F. (1987). Life threat and posttraumatic stress in school-age children. *Archives of General Psychiatry, 44,* 1057–1063.

Pynoos, R. S., & Nader, K. (1988). Children who witness the sexual assaults of their mothers. *Journal of the American Academy of Child and Adolescent Psychiatry, 27,* 567–572.

Regier, D. A., Boyd, J. H., Burke, J. D. J., Rae, D. S., Myers, J. K., Kramer, M., Robins, L. N., George, L. K., Karno, M., & Locke, B. Z. (1988). One month prevalence of mental disorders in the United States. *Archives of General Psychiatry, 45,* 977–986.

Riddle, M. A., Geller, B., & Ryan, N. (1993). Another sudden death in a child treated with desipramine. *Journal of the American Academy of Child and Adolescent Psychiatry, 32,* 792–797.

Riddle, M. A., King, R. A., Hardin, M. T., Scahill, L., Ort, S. I., Chappell, P., Rasmusson, A., & Leckman, J. F. (1990). Behavioral side effects of fluoxetine in children and adolescents. *Journal of the Child and Adolescent Psychopharmacology, 1,* 193–198.

Riddle, M. A., Scahill, L., King, R. A., Hardin, M. T., Anderson, G. M., Ort, S. I., Smith, J. C., Leckman, J. F., & Cohen, D. J. (1992). Double-blind, crossover trial of fluoxetine and placebo in children and adolescents with obsessive-compulsive disorder. *Journal of the American Academy of Child and Adolescent Psychiatry, 31,* 1062–1069.

Rosenbaum, J. F., Biederman, J., Hirshfeld, D. R., Bolduc, E. A., & Chaloff, J. (1991). Behavioral inhibition in children: A possible precursor to panic disorder or social phobia. *Journal of Clinical Psychiatry, 52,* (Suppl.) 5–9.

Ryan, N. D., Puig-Antich, J., Cooper, T. B., Rabinovich, H., Ambrosini, P., Davies, M., King, J., Torres, D., & Fried, J. (1986). Imipramine in adolescent major depression: Plasma level and clinical response. *Acta Psychiatrica Scandinavia, 73,* 275–288.

Ryan, N. D., Puig-Antich, J., Cooper, T. B., Rabinovich, H., Ambrosini, P., Fried, J., Davies, M., Torres, D., & Suckow, R. F. (1987) Relative safety of single versus divided dose imipramine in adolescent major depression. *Journal of the American Academy of Child and Adolescent Psychiatry, 26,* 400–406.

Simeon, J. G., & Ferguson, H. B. (1987). Alprazolam effects in children with anxiety disorders. *Canadian Journal of Psychiatry, 32,* 570–574.

Simeon, J. G., Ferguson, H. B., Knott, V., Roberts, N., Gauthier, B., DuBois, C., & Wiggins, D. (1992). Clinical, cognitive, and neurophysiological effects of alprazolam in children and adolescents with overanxious and avoidant disorders. *Journal of the American Academy of Child and Adolescent Psychiatry, 31,* 29–33.

Soni, P., & Weintraub, A. I. (1992). Buspirone associated mental status changes. *Journal of the American Academy of Child and Adolescent Psychiatry, 31,* 1098–1099.

Strauss, C., Lease, C. A., Last, C. G., & Francis, G. (1988). Overanxious disorder: An examination of developmental differences. *Journal of Abnormal Child Psychology, 16,* 433–443.

Terr, L. (1981). Psychic trauma in children: Observations following the Chowchilla schoolbus kidnapping. *American Journal of Psychiatry, 138,* 14–19.

Terr, L. (1983). Chowchilla revisited: The effects of psychic trauma four years after a schoolbus kidnapping. *American Journal of Psychiatry, 140,* 1543–1550.

Terr, L. (1985). Children traumatized in small groups. In S. Eth & R. S. Pynoos (Eds.), *Post-traumatic stress disorder in children.* Washington, DC: American Psychiatric Press.

Van Ameringen, M., Mancini, C., & Streiner, D. (1993). Fluoxetine efficacy in social phobia. *Journal of Clinical Psychiatry, 54,* 27–32.

Van der Kolk, B. A. (1985). Adolescent vulnerability to posttraumatic stress disorder. *Psychiatry, 48,* 365–370.

Van Winter, J. T., & Stickler, G. B. (1984). Panic attack syndrome. *Journal of Pediatrics, 105,* 661–665.

Venkatesh, A., Pauls, D. L., Crowe, R., Noyes, R., Van-Valkenburg, C., Martins, J. B., & Kerber, R. E. (1980). Mitral valve prolapse in anxiety neurosis (panic disorder). *American Heart Journal, 100,* 302–305.

Vitiello, B., Behar, D., Wolfson, S., & McLeer, S. (1990). Diagnosis of panic disorder in prepubertal children. *Journal of the American Academy of Child and Adolescent Psychiatry, 29,* 782–784.

von Korff, M. R., Eaton, W. W., & Keyl, P. (1985). Epidemiology of panic attacks and panic disorder: Results from 3 community surveys. *American Journal of Epidemiology, 122,* 970–981.

Walkup, J. T. (1995, May–June). *A differential diagnosis of the adverse behavioral effects of fluoxetine.* Newsletter of the American Academy of Child and Adolescent Psychiatry.

Weissman, M. M., Leckman, J. F., Merikangas, K. R., Gammon, G. D., Prusoff, & B. A. (1984). Depression and anxiety disorders in parents and children: Results from the Yale family study. *Archives of General Psychiatry, 41,* 845–852.

Wright, H. H., Miller, M. D., Cook, M., & Littmann, J. (1985). Early identification and intervention with children who refuse to speak. *Journal of the American Academy of Child Psychiatry, 24,* 739–746.

Zimnitzky, B., & Popper, C. W. (1994, May). *A fifth case of sudden death in a child taking desipramine* (p. 181). New Research Program and Abstracts, Annual Meeting of the American Psychiatric Association.

Zwier, K. J., & Rao, U. (1994). Buspirone use in an adolescent with social phobia and mixed personality disorder (Cluster A type). *Journal of the American Academy of Child and Adolescent Psychiatry, 33,* 1007–1011.

Tic Disorders

**KENNETH E. TOWBIN, M.D. and
DONALD J. COHEN, M.D.**

The authors wish to acknowledge the many contributions of their colleague James F. Leckman, M.D.; his clinical acumen, incisive thinking, and unyielding curiosity have influenced the content of this chapter and benefited a great many patients with Tourette's syndrome.

Gilles de la Tourette's original paper (1885) described nine cases of a syndromic disorder manifesting "twitches," chronic rapid sudden motor contractions associated with phonic productions, echolalia, coprolalia, and preoccupations (Goetz & Klawans, 1982). Between the publication of this report and the 1930s, Gilles de la Tourette's work received only modest recognition. Over the next 40 years, several reviews and case reports expanded our knowledge of treatment, phenomenology, and natural history (Fernando, 1967; Morphew & Sim, 1969). By comparison, however, the past two decades display a tremendous growth of interest and research in these phenomena. Significant discoveries occurred in the phenomenology, genetics, epidemiology, neurophysiology, and treatment of this important neuropsychiatric disorder. Several recent publications review this new information (Chase, Friedhoff, & Cohen, 1992; Kurlan, 1993; Peterson, Leckman, & Cohen, 1995).

The importance of Tourette's syndrome (TS) stems not only from the impact clinical symptoms have on patients and their families, but from its distinctive features as a model child neuropsychiatric disorder (Cohen & Leckman, 1994). Our best understanding of TS suggests that it arises from combinations of genetic vulnerability and life experience mediated by biological and psychological events. The interplay of a variety of factors produces the patient's symptoms. The morphology and timing of symptoms cannot be explained only by genetics or as a result of automatic neuronal discharges alone. Onset and presentation of the disorder have a basis in the emotional life of the patient and are influenced by emotional vicissitudes and intrapsychic events. As a result, TS offers an opportunity to learn about interactions among development, genetic endowment, life events, and intrapsychic experience in the pathogenesis of a childhood disorder (Cohen, 1991; Cohen, Detlor, Shaywitz, & Leckman, 1982). But beyond a quest for clearer understanding of these relationships, an appreciation of this interplay and the vicissitudes of these elements is critical to the clinical care of TS patients and their families.

This overview highlights the pharmacological treatment considerations and interventions for TS. Throughout this discussion, the equivalent term Tourette's syndrome (TS) is used although Tourette's *disorder* is the term designated in the current edition of the *Diagnostic and Statistical Manual of Mental Disorders* (DSM-IV; American Psychiatric Association [APA], 1994).

CLINICAL CRITERIA AND DSM-IV DIAGNOSTIC ISSUES

Clinical Features and Differential Diagnosis

Tics are rapid, recurrent, stereotyped, involuntary movements which may affect any part of the body and imitate any motor act. Specific diagnostic features permit them to be differentiated from other repetitive motor events. Tics are distinctively variable over time and the manner of expression of this variability is observable over at least five properties: frequency, complexity, intensity, location, and duration. Frequency is understood as the number of movements that appear within a period of time and can range widely in persons with tic disorders. At their most severe, tics may be virtually continuous and at the least severe only for minutes in a day.

Complexity is the term used for the variety of movements and muscle groups that are recruited to carry out the tic. Some tics may be described as "simple," meaning they are short-lived and use only a few muscles. In contrast, "complex" tics use many muscle groups and may last for a longer period. Examples of these tics are provided in Table 10.1. Phonic or vocal tics may be categorized in a similar manner. Once again, the general guidelines for characterizing the movements are whether

Table 10.1. Types of Tics

Tic Type	Examples
Simple motor	Blinking, grimacing, raising an eyebrow, puckering, mouth stretching, throwing head to the side, shrugging shoulder, shooting an elbow out, abdominal tensing, kicking leg out, tensing body
Complex motor	Making odd facial expressions, running chin down an arm, combing fingers through hair, stretching neck, shadow punching, picking at body, tapping, hopping, stomping, skipping when trying to walk, hitting self, slamming things, copropraxia (e.g., giving the finger)
Simple vocal	Coughing, "hawwwwk" noises, squeaking, "aaaaaa," "tttttuh," throat clearing, "uh, uh, uh," blowing across upper lip, popping sounds, snorting, gnashing teeth, swishing
Complex vocal	"uh huh," "you bet," "all right," "yeah," palilalia (repeating one's own words, phrases, sentences), echolalia (repeating others' words, phrases, sentences), swearing, obscene language or noises, racial or colloquial insults.

they are brief and use only a few muscles or are more elaborate (Table 10.1). The significance of tic complexity is clinical and social more than prognostic. Even highly complex movements may respond to treatment and individuals with intense complex tics may have virtual disappearance of movements in adulthood. By the same token, simple tics may go on to more complex ones and emerge as a more disabling condition over time. Complex tics ordinarily arise after simple tics have been evident for some time.

Intensity combines concepts of forcefulness and conspicuousness. Tics may erupt frequently yet be virtually unnoticeable to those who see the person day to day. At the other end of the spectrum, tics may arise only three or four times a day but are so prominent that they cannot be ignored. This is a contrast with other movement disorders in which intensity remains relatively constant over time. Intensity also possesses considerable clinical utility because it can be highly correlated with impairment. For some persons, simple but highly quantifiable measures such as frequency may be less satisfactory measures of impairment than intensity (Leckman et al., 1989).

Tics change their location characteristically. It has been shown that TS typically begins with involvement of the mouth, eyes, or forehead and spreads successively to the next most caudal body part. However, even in persons who have involvement restricted to a portion of the body such as face, shoulders, and arms, there are changes over time. The movement itself and the associated muscle groups change location within this region as time passes. As a result, the morphology of the tics is in flux over weeks to months. However, it is not characteristic to have the movements change minute to minute.

Duration is related to frequency, intensity, and complexity but is used to describe how long any particular bout of tics lasts. Ordinarily, any single tic is very short-lived, on the order of a second or less. However it is common for tics to erupt in bouts or clusters that last for many seconds. A series of complex tics may last for as long as a minute. It can be challenging to estimate the duration of tics when the frequency is so great that the patient exhibits an unbroken succession of movements.

Sometimes making the diagnosis is complicated. The most likely disorders to be considered when rapid repetitive movements are seen in children include tics, myoclonus, chorea, psychomotor seizures, dystonia, athetosis, mannerisms, stereotypies, and restless legs (Jankovic, 1992). Historical and physical characteristics of tics usually readily permit the clinician to decide which condition is present. However, unconventional presentations or movements in conjunction with other severe neuropsychiatric conditions may generate more uncertainty. For a great majority of cases, observing the movements, obtaining a detailed history of the symptoms from the patient and those who have witnessed them, and acquiring a careful family history enable the clinician to determine whether a tic disorder or some other condition is present. The previously identified characteristics are helpful in making the diagnosis; taking the patient's sensorium and comorbid findings into account is helpful, too.

Diagnostic Features Found in DSM-IV Criteria

DSM-IV (APA, 1994) criteria for Tourette's Disorder closely resemble the descriptions offered by Gilles de la Tourette (Table 10.2). The current DSM edition reflects efforts to provide a more detailed description of the symptoms and onset for most patients. Comparing the revised third edition (DSM-III-R, APA, 1985) criteria with those from DSM-IV for Tourette's Disorder uncovers only a few changes. Yet those differences are meaningful nevertheless.

The most fundamental change is introduction of an impairment criterion. This puts the tic disorders on the same footing as others in the nosology such as affective, anxiety, and substance abuse disorders and dozens more for which a minimum level of impairment is necessary if the diagnosis is to be ascribed. Although the addition of this criterion is understandable in the light of objectives to create uniformity and establish a minimum standard of severity, it also may have unwanted effects. On the one hand, it seems completely logical that patients would not be assigned a diagnosis when a condition is not creating any social or occupational impairment. This is an important step in placing the diagnosis in a clinical framework and averts the difficulty of creating a class of "patients" who carry diagnoses without any current evidence of signs or symptoms of it. This also means that carrying the diagnosis meets certain criteria of "caseness."

On the other hand, obvious tics that are not a source of impairment may be important nevertheless. Tics that are subthreshold by this criterion alone may be genetically, therapeutically, epidemiologically, and prognostically relevant. Subclinical symptoms may be residual manifestations of a more active phase of the disorder that has passed or is beyond the patient's recall. When ascertained, they should spur the clinician to further inquiry and understanding. The introduction of the impairment standard runs a risk of implying that clinicians can safely ignore these symptoms. Furthermore, subclinical symptoms may expose the presence of a genetic predisposition that imparts risks of developing the disorder to the patient's offspring. If the diagnosis cannot be claimed, assessment and counseling for the individual may be impossible to justify, especially when health-care cost containment requires the provider to defend expenditures on health services. Fortunately, DSM-IV

Table 10.2.   DSM-IV Criteria for Tic Disorders

Tourette's Disorder

A. Both multiple motor and one or more vocal tics have been present at some time during the illness, although not necessarily concurrently. (A *tic* is an involuntary sudden rapid, recurrent, nonrhythmic, sterotyped motor movement or vocalization.)

B. Tics occur many time a day (usually in bouts) nearly every day or intermittently throughout a period of more than 1 year, and during this period there was never a tic-free period more than three months.

C. The disturbance causes marked distress or significant impairment in social, occupational, or other important areas of functioning.

D. Onset before age 18 years.

E. The disturbance is not due to the direct physiological effects of a substance (e.g., stimulants) or a general medical condition (e.g., Huntington's disease or post-viral encephalitis).

Chronic Motor or Vocal Tic Disorder

A. Either vocal or motor tics (i.e., involuntary sudden rapid, recurrent, nonrhythmic, stereotyped motor movement or vocalizations) but not both, have been present at some time during the illness.

B. The tics occur many times a day nearly every day or intermittently throughout a period of more than one year, and during this period there was never a tic-free period more than three months.

C. The disturbance causes marked distress or significant impairment in social, occupational, or other important areas of functioning.

D. Onset before age 18 years.

E. The disturbance is not due to the direct physiological effects of a substance (e.g., stimulants) or a general medical condition (e.g., Huntington's disease or post-viral encephalitis).

F. Has never met the criteria for Tourette's Disorder.

Transient Tic Disorder

A. Single or multiple motor or vocal tics (i.e., involuntary sudden rapid, recurrent, nonrhythmic, stereotyped motor movement or vocalizations).

B. The tics occur many times a day, nearly every day for at least four weeks, for no longer than 12 months.

C. The disturbance causes marked distress or significant impairment in social, occupational, or other important areas of functioning.

D. Onset before age 18 years.

E. The disturbance is not due to the direct physiological effects of a substance (e.g., stimulants) or a general medical condition (e.g., Huntington's disease or post-viral encephalitis).

F. Has never met the criteria for Tourette's Disorder or Chronic Motor or Vocal Tic Disorder.

Specify if: **Single Episode** or **Recurrent**

Reprinted with permission from American Psychiatric Association, 1994.

permits clinical judgment to override strict adherence to criteria when it is in a patient's therapeutic interest:

> *The specific diagnostic criteria included in DSM-IV are meant to serve as guidelines to be informed by clinical judgement and are not meant to be used in a cookbook fashion. For example, the exercise of clinical judgement may justify giving a certain diagnosis to an individual even though the clinical presentation falls just short of meeting the full criteria as long as the symptoms that are present are persistent and severe. (APA, 1994, p. xxiii)*

No system of classification is suitable for every purpose, but under some conditions (e.g., genetic research) use of nonclinical criteria are sometimes necessary. However, there is reason to be concerned about the consequences of unconventional or novel interpretation of diagnostic criteria and impairment rules.

DSM-IV reduced the maximum age of onset from 21 to 18. This resulted from reanalysis of methods used in studies reporting cases commencing in adulthood (Abbuzzahab & Anderson, 1981). Another difference in the new criteria is specification of the duration of active and symptom-free periods. DSM-IV states that symptoms should be present continuously for at least a year and never absent for longer than 3 months. This was added to indicate how one might categorize conditions in which symptoms are episodic throughout their course. It also clarified the diagnostic guidelines for categorizing conditions that first show one or more episodes of transient tics and then months or years later go on to demonstrate typical symptoms of Tourette's Disorder. DSM-IV also has integrated the definition of a tic into the criteria; previously this appeared in the explanation preceding the criteria. As a result, the new edition discarded the DSM-III-R criterion regarding changes over time in location, number, frequency, complexity, and severity although inclusion of the definition sustains the relevance of these features.

Like those for Tourette's Disorder, the DSM-IV criteria for Chronic Motor or Vocal Tic Disorder and for Transient Tic Disorder differ from DSM-III-R in only a few ways. The criterion of impairment has been added for all three. The maximum age of onset for both was decreased to 18, parallel to Tourette's Disorder, and the minimum duration of symptoms to warrant a diagnosis of Transient Tics was increased from 2 to 4 weeks. As a result, the threshold for diagnosing Transient Tic Disorder has been raised. The clinical ramification may be that less severely affected patients who previously were given diagnoses of Transient Tic Disorder will be assigned Tic Disorder Not Otherwise Specified (NOS). Under DSM-IV, the numbers of patients with this NOS diagnosis would be expected to increase. Table 10.3 compares the criteria for the different specific disorders.

Table 10.3. *Parameters Differentiating DSM-IV Tic Disorders*

Tic Disorder	Minimum Duration	Maximum Duration	Longest Period without Tics	Type of Tics Permitted During Active Stage		
				Only Motor Tics	Only Vocal Tics	Concurrent Motor & Vocal Tics
Transient	4 wks	1 year	limitless*	Yes	Yes	Yes
Chronic Motor	12 mos	limitless	3 mos	Yes	No	No
Chronic Vocal	12 mos	limitless	3 mos	No	Yes	No
Tourette's Disorder	12 mos	limitless	3 mos	Yes	Yes	*Required* at some point

*Individuals may undergo single or recurrent episodes.

Source: From Towbin, K., Cohen, D., & Leckmam, J.F., "Assessment and Treatment of Tic Disorders," in Gabbard, Glen (Ed.), *Treatments of Psychiatric Disorder: The DSM-IV Edition.* Washington, DC: American Psychiatric Association. Copyright 1994 American Psychiatric Association Press. Reprinted by permission.

Associated Features That Are Relevant to Treatment

Children who come to treatment for TS frequently exhibit symptoms that are associated with the disorder though they are not tics per se. Obsessions and compulsions may be a symptomatic variant of tics and arise in conjunction with them (Frankel et al., 1986; Grad, Pelcovitz, Olson, Matthews, & Grad, 1987) or as the sole expression of the disorder (Leonard et al., 1992). In any case, it appears that the symptoms of obsessions and compulsions in those with tic disorders cannot be distinguished reliably from those of persons with only obsessive-compulsive disorder (OCD) (George et al., 1993; Grad et al., 1987; Leonard et al., 1992). Family genetic studies (Pauls, Towbin, Leckman, Zahner, & Cohen, 1986) and epidemiological investigations (Apter et al., 1993) offer support for the hypothesis that some OCD may be the symptomatic expression of a TS gene (Pauls & Leckman, 1986). This association produces a clinical picture in as many as 40% of those who have TS in which there is significant impairment as a consequence of obsessions and/or compulsions. For a segment of this group, the impairment resulting from obsessions or compulsions actually exceeds that arising from their tics. Consequently, management of TS often requires the clinician to be competent in care of disabilities emerging from all manner of tics, to understand the spectrum of OCD, and to be able to evaluate and treat obsessions and compulsions.

A more enigmatic diagnostic relationship arises between TS and symptoms of inattention, impulsivity, and hyperactivity. The latter symptoms are frequently seen in children with TS and it can be bewildering trying to decide whether symptoms stem from tics with premonitory urges (Leckman, Walker, & Cohen, 1993), anxiety related to consequences of the tic disorder, or the expression of a separate condition. A similar confusion may follow efforts to decide whether inattention is a cognitive casualty of intrusive urges and obsessions, or the manifestation of comorbid attention deficit/hyperactivity disorder (ADHD). At this point, there are opinions on both sides; some authorities hold that symptoms of inattention, impulsivity, and hyperactivity in persons with TS are separate comorbid conditions (Pauls et al., 1986), whereas others see them as one-and-the-same condition (Comings & Comings, 1987). It is quite possible that there are different varieties of problems with attention and hyperactivity—a mild form arising from the tic disorder itself and a severe type that fully meets criteria for ADHD and genetically appears to segregate independent of TS (Pauls, Leckman, & Cohen, 1993). Whichever is the case, the appearance of both sets of symptoms has major clinical and therapeutic implications. Just as with obsessions and compulsions, the morbidity from symptoms of hyperactivity and impulsivity may exceed that of the tics themselves. In addition, the combination of tics and ADHD challenges teachers and parents. This syndromic complex can pose a serious threat to a child's future development. This combination of disabilities also strongly influences medication treatment decisions as will be discussed further.

Some authorities suggest that a wide variety of other conditions such as conduct, panic, depression, anxiety, and sleep disorders all arise from the same genetic etiology as TS (Comings & Comings, 1987). Critical review of the study designs, especially with regard to possible bias introduced by methods of ascertainment of subjects, diagnostic instruments and ratings, and data analysis, cast doubt on their conclusions (Pauls, Cohen, Kidd, & Leckman, 1988). Subsequent studies employing research architecture geared to avert duplicating these risks suggest that panic, depression, anxiety, and phobias are truly comorbid and not related to TS itself (Pauls, Leckman, & Cohen, 1994).

EPIDEMIOLOGY

Discovering the population prevalence and sex ratio of tic disorders continues to challenge investigators. Although considerable effort has been devoted to learning about the prevalence of TS, there are virtually no general population studies of transient tic disorders or chronic motor or vocal tic disorders. Obstacles to ascertainment and valid reporting plague the research. Development of a credible community survey technique has proved necessary because clinical sources tend to assemble disproportionate numbers of individuals with comorbid features or greater impairment. However, nonclinical community surveys such as the Epidemiologic Catchment Area (ECA) Survey tend to rely on self-reports, and self-perception of tics can be highly inaccurate. Tics are often unrecognized by their possessors, and family members or friends who observe tics may be unwilling to call the possessor's attention to them. Consequently, the available estimates vary widely (Apter et al., 1993; Burd, Kerbeshian, Wikenheiser, & Fisher, 1986; Caine et al., 1988; Comings, Himes, & Comings, 1990). The North Dakota survey asked all physicians in the state to identify patients with TS who were in their care and yielded a prevalence rate of 0.5 per 10,000 for adults and 5.2 per 10,000 for children. Caine and coworkers (1988) relied on referrals from physicians and other health providers through public service announcements, mailings, announcements at local professional meetings, and advertisements. Subjects were evaluated by direct interview and parent interview. Results were estimates of 2.87 per 10,000. In several California public schools, Comings and coworkers (1990) directly observed consecutive referrals to special education evaluation. Using corrected rates for special classes yielded rates of 105 per 10,000 males and 13.2 per 10,000 females. The Israeli investigation (Apter et al., 1993) examined the total population of inductees into the Israeli Defense Forces Center over a period of one year. Roughly 28,000 individuals were screened using interviews and self-reports. Prevalence rates of TS were reported as 4.3 per 10,000 with 4.9 per 10,000 males and 3.1 per 10,000 females.

Many surveys report high male-to-female ratios. The range from these recent surveys is 9:1 (Burd et al., 1986; Comings et al., 1990) to 1:1 (Apter et al., 1993). The peak age of onset is 2 to 15 years with a mean of 7 years.

PSYCHOPHARMACOLOGY OF TICS

There are general guidelines that clinicians should follow whenever prescribing medication for children, but they are particularly important when treating children with tics (Towbin, Riddle, Leckman, Bruun, & Cohen, 1988). These guidelines, listed in Table 10.4, apply to all the medications that will be described in this chapter.

At this point, there are three types of agents used in the treatment of TS and tics. These are listed in Table 10.5.

Dopaminergic Blocking Agents

Effects. The most common, effective, and investigated class of agents in the treatment of TS and chronic motor tic disorders are those that block dopaminergic receptors. Although the pathophysiology of tic

Table 10.4.   Guidelines for the Use of Medication

1. Identify specific symptoms that are targeted for improvement.
2. Start at the smallest possible dose.
3. Increase the dose using the smallest possible increments.
4. Increase the dose only after sufficient time has elapsed to gauge the effects of the current dose.
5. Monitor the effect on specific target symptoms.
6. Look for side effects routinely.
7. Avoid using more than one medication at a time as much as possible.
8. Unless side effects preclude continuing, start a different medication only after a suitable maximum dose of the current medication has been reached.
9. Unless side effects preclude continuing, start a different medication only after a sufficient time has elapsed on the maximum dose of the current medication.
10. Unless delays would engender serious risks to the patient, changes in combinations of medication should be made one medication at a time over intervals that are long enough to permit adequate assessment of the impact of each step.

disorders remains to be fully elucidated, it is apparent that effects on the striatum of the basal ganglia are important. The striatum is richly endowed with D_2 receptor sites; D_2 receptors are characterized by their effect of reducing the frequency of depolarization of dopaminergic neurons and also are correlated with inhibition of adenylate cyclase. Agents which readily bind to D_2 receptors are associated with efficacy in alleviating positive symptoms of psychosis and reducing tics as well. The effectiveness of dopaminergic blocking agents is reliable and consistent. About 80% to 90% of patients will respond to these agents with at least a

Table 10.5.   Agents Useful in the Treatment of Tics

Type of Agent	Class of Agent	Generic Name	Dose Range (mg/d)
Dopaminergic antagonist	Butyrophenone	Haloperidol	0.25–5.0
	Diphenylbutylpiperidine	Pimozide	1.0–8.0
	Phenothiazine	Fluphenazine	0.5–5.0
α_2Adrenergic agonist	Imidazoline	Clonidine	0.1–0.3
	Acetamide	Guanfacine	0.5–3.0
GABA agonist	Benzodiazepine	Clonazepam	0.5–5.0 (max. 0.2 mg/kg/d)

50% reduction of tic symptoms (Shapiro, Shapiro, Young, & Feinberg, 1988). Among all these medications, haloperidol, a butryophenone, is the most studied and commonly used agent for the treatment of tics (Erenberg, 1992). In 1984, pimozide, a diphenylbutylpiperidine with weaker antipsychotic activity than other agents in this class, was introduced in the United States expressly for the treatment of tics and TS. Other dopaminergic blocking agents that traditionally have been prescribed to relieve positive symptoms of psychosis have received less scrutiny for efficacy against tics. There were several open trials of the phenothiazine fluphenazine (Borison et al., 1982; Singer, Gammon, & Quaskey, 1985), and there are anecdotal reports on other agents in this class such as trifluoperazine (Borison et al., 1982).

Dosage and Clinical Use.   All the dopaminergic blocking agents must be prescribed with an understanding that the patient's treatment will be followed closely. Side effects, particularly those that result in physical discomfort, can cause significant morbidity, affect compliance, and/or ruin the patient's relationship with his or her physician. Most side effects are dose dependent; beginning haloperidol at one-quarter (0.25) mg daily will minimize the risks of adverse reactions, though many practitioners initiate treatment with 0.5 mgs per day without complication. The one-half milligram tablets are scored thereby permitting reliable doses as low as 0.25 mgs. There also is a liquid concentrate form containing 2 mgs/ml which can be measured to any dose. The half-life of haloperidol in adults is roughly 24 hours. This means that most patients should take haloperidol before sleep daily. Dose adjustments should be made once the previous dose has reached steady state—after roughly five half-lives or five to seven days.

Side Effects.   The dopaminergic blocking agents commonly produce side effects which can be so intolerable that patients cannot endure remaining on the medication despite its beneficial effects on their tics. Erenberg and coworkers (1987) reported that 84% of their patients experienced "major" side effects on haloperidol; only 45% believed the medication had resulted in good overall improvement.

The most common side effects are sedation, pseudo-parkinsonism, akathisia, tremor, constipation, blunted affect, and anhedonia. The most unpleasant side effects are relatively uncommon and include dystonic reactions, akinesia, akathisia, cognitive blunting, anhedonia, and a particular social phobia reaction (Bruun, 1988; Linet, 1987; Mikkelsen, Detlor, & Cohen, 1981); they are quite troubling to the patient and therefore important. The drug-induced complex of anhedonia, cognitive blunting, and anxiety may be misinterpreted as depression and lead the physician to prescribe additional agents to treat it. There are other effects that arise even less commonly but may be impairing and are especially frightening to children and adolescents. These include endocrine effects (e.g., gynecomastia, impotence, and galactorrhea), and dermatological reactions. One of the most serious effects is tardive dyskinesia, with the potential for confusing the symptoms and care of the patient in whom an additional drug-induced movement disorder becomes superimposed on an existing tic disorder (Riddle, Hardin, Towbin, Leckman, & Cohen, 1987).

Pimozide is a neuroleptic about which concern was raised when a multisite trial resulted in two sudden deaths from cardiac events. As Shapiro and coworkers (1988) have described, these patients were started on pimozide and increased to high doses (80 mgs per day) over a short span of 2 weeks. Further investigation suggested that the effect of pimozide on lengthening the QT_c interval (Fulop et al., 1987) was the probable cause of the cardiac events. Subsequent clinical experience has not resulted in sudden deaths in TS patients on pimozide. However, QT_c changes have been implicated in the deaths of several children with ADHD who were being treated with antidepressants (Riddle et al., 1991). In the light of this potential, it is prudent to routinely monitor ECGs in patients receiving pimozide, in a protocol analogous to those for monitoring tricyclic antidepressants. Current guidelines call for obtaining baseline ECGs, repeating ECG studies with each 2-mg dose increment, and routinely monitoring stable doses on a semiannual schedule for 1 to 2 years.

Alpha₂-Adrenergic Agonists

Effects. Clonidine, a centrally acting α_2-adrenergic agonist, was originally marketed for treatment of hypertension. The hypotensive effect of clonidine is paradoxical because one would predict than an α_2-adrenergic agonist would produce hypertension. The explanation for this paradox stems from clonidine's affinity for presynaptic (autoreceptor) sites. By binding to presynaptic autoreceptors, low doses of clonidine reduce the activity of the α_2-adrenergic system and lower blood pressure. At higher blood levels, postsynaptic sites are occupied and, as predicted, hypertension results. Reduction of α_2-adrenergic activity influences a wide variety of other neurotransmitter systems; downstream effects on serotonin (Leckman et al., 1984) and dopamine (Bunney & DeRiemer, 1982) are hypothesized to occur. The acute and chronic downstream effects of clonidine on dopamine (Martin et al., 1984) are postulated to account for the drug's effect in reducing tics.

Dosage and Clinical Use. Prior to initiating clonidine, it is appropriate to obtain routine blood chemistries including but not limited to liver function studies, LDH, and CPK enzymes, and several baseline blood pressure and pulse readings. Electrocardiographic changes have not been observed.

Clonidine must be started at very low doses, increased gradually, and monitored closely. In general the starting dose is 0.05 mg in the morning. Clonidine is dispensed in 0.1 mg tablets which are scored and may be broken in half. After three days, the dose may be increased to 0.05 mg twice daily. Over the next two weeks, the dose may be increased in 0.05 mg increments, usually by adding doses throughout the day rather than increasing doses at one or two time points. The rationale for this method is that in adults the half-life of clonidine is roughly 12 hours, but the drug may be hypermetabolized in children. More frequent, lower doses appear also to decrease problems with sedation. At 0.2 mg per day most patients will be receiving 0.05 mgs four times a day. Measures of pulse and blood pressure throughout the trial are important.

Benefits of the medication may not been seen as rapidly with clonidine as with dopaminergic blocking agents. It is common that effects may not be observed for at least four weeks on 0.15 to 0.2 mgs per day. The placebo-controlled trials suggested that periods of at least 12 weeks may be needed to judge efficacy (Goetz et al., 1987; Leckman et al., 1991).

Clonidine also is available in a transdermal preparation that can be worn as a patch. Low-dose strategies can be complicated by inconsistent dosing when using a 0.1 mg/d (TTS-1) equivalent path which has been cut in half, and it is sometimes difficult to determine how frequently the patch should be changed. For active children who enjoy sports (and shower often) or watersports, the patch can be an encumbrance and challenging to keep on. For some patients, however, this has been a useful alternative.

It has been suggested that another α_2-adrenergic agonsit, guanfacine, may be at least as effective as clonidine and possess a similar side-effect profile. One open trial has been reported (Hunt, Arnsten, & Asbell, 1995). A possible advantage of guanfacine is that it has a longer half-life and may not require as frequent dosing. There is also some suggestion that guanfacine may possess a greater affinity for frontal lobe α_2-adrenergic sites, which might prove more useful in the treatment of this disorder (Arnsten & Contant, 1992; Arnsten & Goldman-Rakic, 1985).

Side Effects.   The most common side effects of clonidine are sedation, insomnia, dizziness, dry mouth, hypotension, and, in adolescents and adults, problems with impotency. Some patients also may develop depression, lability, or irritability (Goetz et al., 1987). During introduction of clonidine, sedation or insomnia ordinarily are managed by maintaining a constant dose until ill effects decline. Afterward, the dose can be increased again although on a more gradual schedule. If the side effects do not diminish, then dose reduction is indicated. When using the patch system, rashes and pruritis may result from the adhesive. It is necessary to find at least four hairless sites. Using the same site constantly increases the risk of skin reactions and may effect absorption; rotating among three or four sites is usually adequate.

It is most important to remind patients that abrupt cessation of clonidine can be uncomfortable and potentially harmful. Hypertension, diaphoresis, agitation, and behavioral changes have been observed (Leckman et al., 1986; Tollefson, 1981). These symptoms can be avoided by decreasing the medication over 1 to 2 weeks. When using the patch, rebound hypertension and withdrawal symptoms can be seen when the patch spontaneously is sloughed.

Benzodiazepines

Effects.   Clonazepam has received little rigorous investigation for the treatment of TS (Goetz, 1992; Gounce & Barbeau, 1977). It is a benzodiazepine that putatively binds to central benzodiazepine sites and increases the inhibitory effects of gamma-aminobutyric acid (GABA). However, the relationship between these effects and reduction of tics is obscure. Shapiro and coworkers (1988) suspect that the effects are a direct result of sedation alone. Other benzodiazepines have not received attention.

Dosage and Clinical Use.   Routine blood chemistries, including liver function studies, are useful to obtain prior to commencing clonazepam. Doses begin with 0.25 mg/d, usually in the morning. Tablets are available in 0.5, 1.0, and 2.0 mg doses and are scored. Increments should proceed in 0.25 to 0.5 mg steps at 3- to 4-day intervals and by expanding the dose schedule to b.i.d. or even t.i.d. dosing.

Side Effects.   Clonazepam typically is tolerated well at low doses, but effects on tics are not seen until doses in the range of 2.0 to 3.0 mg/day are reached. Sedation often becomes a problem at these doses. Additional problems include memory loss, decreased concentration, lability, and weight loss (Troung, Bressman, Shale, & Fahn, 1988).

PSYCHOPHARMACOLOGY OF INATTENTION-HYPERACTIVITY WITH TICS

Some children who have no previous history of tics develop movements when they are treated for ADHD with stimulants. As a result, there are legitimate concerns about the safety and efficacy of this medication in children in response to three common clinical circumstances:

1. Children with ADHD who have a past history or family history of tics.

2. Children with active tic disorders who have inattention, hyperactivity, and impulsivity.

3. Children who develop tics while on stimulants for ADHD.

Currently, there are several different opinions about treatment approaches to these three groups. Some authorities advocate use of stimulants in any ADHD child whether they have risk factors or not (Sverd, Gadow, Nolan, Sprafkin, & Ezor, 1992). The line of reasoning is that close monitoring will permit the clinician to observe whether there is a decline in the patient's condition after the addition of stimulants and that if the medication is discontinued shortly after tics emerge or become more severe, then there is little risk to the child. In the meantime, the child has the opportunity to receive the agents that are most likely to be helpful to him or her. If tics emerge or worsen, then other strategies can be implemented.

An alternative perspective is that tics should be avoided whenever possible (Golden, 1993). The clinician should first choose other agents over stimulants for those in the two highest risk groups. If nonstimulant agents are unsuccessful, then a trial of stimulants may be inescapable.

The agents that may be useful in the treatment of inattention and hyperactivity symptoms in children with tics are identified in Table 10.6 and discussed in detail in Chapter 8.

Table 10.6. Agents Useful in the Treatment of Inattention and Hyperactivity with Tics

Type of Agent	Generic Name	Dose Range (mg/d)	Max. Dose in mg/kg/d
Stimulants	Methylphenidate	5.0–40.0	1.2
	Dextro-amphetamine	5.0–20.0	0.8
	Magnesium pemoline	18.75–112.5	2.2
α_2Adrenergic agonist	Clonidine	0.1–0.3	—
	Guanfacine	0.5–3.0	—
Cyclic agents	Imipramine	10–250	5.0
	Desipramine	10–250	5.0
	Nortriptyline	10–125	2.5
	Fluoxetine	5–40	—
Monoamine oxidase inhibitors	Deprenyl (selegiline)	5–15	—

Alpha₂-Adrenergic Agonists

The effects, dosing, and side effects for the use of the α_2-agonists were discussed earlier in this chapter.

Stimulants

The effects, dosing, and clinical use, and general side effects of stimulants are discussed in Chapter 8. For those with tics or TS, however, close monitoring for movements is crucial.

Tricyclic Agents

The effects, dosing, and clinical use of tricyclic agents are discussed in Chapter 8. Studies of the effects of these agents in TS patients have included desipramine and nortriptyline (Biederman, Baldessarini, Wright, Knee, & Harmatz, 1989; Riddle, Hardin, Cho, Woolston, & Leckman, 1988; Spencer, Biederman, Wilens, Steingard, & Geist, 1993; Zametkin & Rapoport, 1987a, 1987b).

The dosing strategies for tricyclic agents are given in Table 10.6. The clinical community has grown more cautious about the use of these agents following the reports of sudden death on desipramine (Riddle et al., 1991; Riddle, Geller, & Ryan, 1993). Thorough study is still required, but current recommendations are that clinicians be familiar with the cardiovascular criteria for terminating trials of tricyclic medication and that children with family histories of cardiovascular disease, sudden death, or syncope be carefully evaluated using standard 12-lead ECGs and careful review of QT_c intervals.

Monoamine Oxidase Inhibitors

Effects. Zametkin and coworkers (Zametkin, Rapoport, Murphy, Linnoila, & Ismond, 1985) suggested that monoamine oxidase inhibitors (MAOI) were highly effective in the treatment of inpatients treated for ADHD. Concerns over possible severe adverse reactions to typical MAOIs, such as phenelzine and tranylcypromine, prevented many clinicians from employing them, however. Jankovic (1993), using the MAO-B inhibitor deprenyl (also known as selegiline) in patients with combined TS and ADHD, reported no incidents of hypertension, side effects were minimal, and significant reductions in ADHD-like behaviors were achieved. In this small ($N = 29$) open series, 72% of patients gained some benefit. A small pilot study cannot be promoted as recommendation for widespread clinical application, but deprenyl probably deserves further investigation with traditional double-blind, placebo-controlled or head-to-head comparison trials using stimulants or TCA agents. Without this data, deprenyl should be considered only as a remote alternative.

Other Cyclic Agents

Effects.   There is a single study of use of fluoxetine for treatment of attentional problems in children and adolescents (Barrickman, Noyes, Kuperman, Schumacher, & Verda, 1991). This was an open label trial employing a heterogeneous group of patients ranging from 7 to 15 years of age. No patients specifically suffered from a tic disorder. In this 6-week study, parent-rated Conners ratings decreased an average of 50%. Teacher ratings were only statistically significant demonstrating decrements of 4 points. In view of the sample size, study design, and variables, this might be regarded as pilot data.

Dosage and Clinical Use.   Doses used in this single study were 20 mg to 60 mg/day with an average of 27 mg/d. Recommended preliminary laboratory data is a complete blood count and liver function studies.

Side Effects.   Roughly one-third of patients described side effects (Barrickman et al., 1991). Complaints included sedation, "spacey" feelings, a rash, and a possible case of akathisia.

PSYCHOPHARMACOLOGY OF OBSESSIONS AND COMPULSIONS

The agents and strategies for treating tic-related obsessions and compulsions or frank OCD comorbid with TS are like those for treating OCD itself. This will be discussed in Chapter 11. There are reports of increases in tics with selective serotonin reuptake inhibitors (SSRIs), but it is always difficult to determine whether these case reports reflect the spontaneous waxing of tics or were truly an effect of the medication. In either case, it is crucial to monitor closely patients who have tics when they are treated with these agents.

When treating individuals who possess both TS and OC symptoms, consideration of associated symptoms and concomitant medications may influence the choice of agents. In general, clomipramine generates the greatest frequency, number, and severity of side effects (Pigott et al., 1990) (see Table 10.7). In patients for whom sedation is desirable, this can be an asset, but when combined with other sedating medication such as clonidine or haloperidol, sedation from clomipramine may

Table 10.7. **Agents Useful in the Treatment of Obsessions and Compulsions**

Type of Agent	Generic Name	Dose Range (mg/d)	Max. Dose in mg/kg/d
Tricyclic agents	Clomipramine	25–250	3.0–5.0
Selective serotonin reuptake inhibitors	Fluoxetine	5–40	—
	Sertraline	25–200	—
	Fluvoxamine	25–300	—
	Paroxetine[a]	—[a]	—[a]
Augmentation strategies	Lithium	—[b]	—[b]
	Haloperidol	1–5	—
	Pimozide	2–8	—

[a] Theoretical, no specific studies of OCD.
[b] Blood level of 1.0 meq/dl recommended.

become intolerable and hamper therapeutic efforts. Fluoxetine has been regarded as the current benchmark agent but deserves cautious consideration. Fluoxetine exhibits a moderate half-life of 7 days but the half-life of its active metabolite, norfluoxetine, may be as long as 19 days. Consequently, it is not possible to know the steady-state effects of the active medication and its metabolite in less than 3 or 4 weeks. Fluoxetine has a potent inhibitory effect on P450 microsomal liver enzymes and may cause akathisia. Those prescribing it in combination with dopaminergic blocking or α_2-noradrenergic agents must be mindful of these attributes. Anecdotal experience has led some investigators to question whether the newer, more selective SSRI agents may be less effective than fluoxetine in the treatment of OCD (King, Riddle, & Goodman, 1992), but this hypothesis has not been tested. There is little indication now that any one SSRI agent is superior to others in those with OCD. Sertraline and paroxetine have shorter half-lives and less likelihood of causing akathisia, but they are newer and the clinical community has less experience with their side effects and drug interactions. Some patients experience sedation and weakness on sertraline or paroxetine, and this is potentially burdensome. Their effect on displacing protein-bound compounds can produce dramatic serum-level elevations of other agents when they are added to a stable drug regimen. Fluvoxamine was introduced in 1995. For the treatment of OCD, fluvoxamine has been investigated more extensively than either sertraline or paroxetine, but the design of these studies excluded any subjects with TS or tics (Goodman et al., 1989; Price, Goodman, Charney, Rasmussen, & Heninger, 1987). It is more quickly metabolized than fluoxetine and has no active metabolites. The spectrum of side effects resembles sertraline but it may interfere with metabolism of a variety of other drugs to a greater extent than sertraline and may be more sedating than other SSRIs.

Augmentation strategies have been proposed for patients who do not respond to SSRI agents alone. In patients with tics or family histories of tic disorders, there may be particular value in adding dopaminergic agents (McDougle et al., 1990, 1994). In a double-blind, placebo-controlled trial of haloperidol augmentation of fluvoxamine nonresponders, McDougle and coworkers (1994) reported that in the haloperidol-treated group all 8 OCD patients (100%) with comorbid tic disorder responded to the addition of a neuroleptic, as well as 33% of those without comorbid tics. Overall, when the placebo-treated patients with concomitant tics were offered open-trial neuroleptic, 80% responded yielding a 92% response rate for those with previously refractory OCD and comorbid tics.

There is uncertainty about the value of buspirone, a serotonin agonist, in the adjunctive treatment of OCD symptoms. One study has implied that buspirone offers occasional additional benefit (Markovitz, Stagno, & Calabrese, 1990), but other work suggests that although it is safe it is only rarely beneficial (Grady et al., 1993).

PROGNOSIS

No single morbidity rate or outcome condition can be defined as the prognosis of TS. There are multiple outcome variables one might examine and diverse answers could be submitted depending on which variables are considered. Furthermore, a great deal of the natural history of TS itself remains to be clarified. However, as a generalization, tic symptoms typically worsen during adolescence and become less severe thereafter (Erenberg, Cruse, & Rothner, 1987). Some adults experience episodes of exacerbation or continually escalating severity in later life, but this is uncommon (Bruun & Budman, 1993). Considering only tics, the prognosis is generally very good.

There is greater uncertainty about the course of attentional problems, specific learning disorders, and obsessive-compulsive symptoms. It is unclear whether or in what way the natural history of these associated features changes when they are affiliated with TS. For the majority of patients, the effects of attentional and learning problems are greatest during school years. The influence on late overall academic achievement and occupational success is mediated through family, social, and academic adjustment during primary and secondary school. Research has begun to identify and measure the adverse effects on social adjustment and peer relationships that can emerge from TS (Dykens et al., 1990; Stokes, Bawden, Camafield, Backman, & Dooley,

1991). These studies underscore the crucial role of individual and family psychological treatments to support and educate parents and patients during this developmental period. Detailing and assuaging fears, correcting erroneous attributions, supporting inherent strengths, and cultivating vigorous advocacy improve the chances of an optimal outcome (Towbin, 1995). Psychotherapy has a place in helping the patient cope with and mitigate the conflict within the self that TS can create. Not merely reducing tics but sustaining each child's ability to fulfill his or her greatest psychological, social, and cognitive capacities must remain the primary objective of treatment.

REFERENCES

Abbuzzahab, F. S., & Anderson, F. O. (1981). *Gilles de la Tourette's syndrome, International Registry* (Vol. 1). St. Paul, MN: Mason.

American Psychiatric Association. (1985). *Diagnostic and statistical manual of mental disorders* (DSM-III-R) (3rd ed.-rev.). Washington, DC: Author.

American Psychiatric Association. (1994). *Diagnostic and statistical manual of mental disorders* (DSM-IV) (4th ed.). Washington, DC: Author.

Apter, A., Pauls, D. L., Bleich, A. H., Zohar, A. H., Kron, S., Ratzoni, G., Dycian, A., Kotler, H., Weizman, A., Gadot, H., & Cohen, D. J. (1993). An epidemiologic study of Gilles de la Tourette's syndrome in Israel. *Archives of General Psychiatry, 50,* 734–738.

Arnsten, A. F. T., & Contant, T. A. (1992). Alpha-2 adrenergic agonists decrease distractibility in aged monkeys performing a delay response task. *Psychopharmacology, 108,* 159–169.

Arnsten, A. F. T., & Goldman-Rakic, P. S. (1985). Alpha-2 adrenergic mechanisms in prefrontal cortex associated with cognitive decline in aged non-human primates. *Science 230,* 1273–1276.

Barrickman, L., Noyes, R., Kuperman, S., Schumacher, E., & Verda, M. (1991). Treatment of ADHD with fluoxetine: A preliminary trial. *Journal of the American Academy of Child and Adolescent Psychiatry, 30,* 762–767.

Biederman, J., Baldessarini, R. J., Wright, V., Knee, D., & Harmatz, J. S. (1989). A double-blind placebo controlled study of desipramine in the treatment of ADHD: I. Efficacy. *Journal of the American Academy of Child and Adolescent Psychiatry, 28,* 777–784.

Borison, R. L., Ang, L., Chang, S., Dysken, M., Comaty, J. E., & Davis, J. M. (1982). New pharmacological approaches in the treatment of Tourette syndrome. In A. J. Friedhoff & T. N. Chase (Eds.), *Gilles de la Tourette syndrome. Advances in neurology* (Vol. 35, pp. 377–382). New York: Raven.

Bruun, R. D. (1988). Subtle and underrecognized side effects of neuroleptic treatment in children with Tourette's disorder. *American Journal of Psychiatry, 145,* 621–624.

Bruun, R. D., & Budman, C. L. (1993). The natural history of Gilles de la Tourette's syndrome. In R. Kurlan (Ed.), *Handbook of Tourette's syndrome and related tic and behavioral disorders* (pp. 27–42). New York: Marcel Dekker.

Bunney, B. S., & De Riemer, S. A. (1982). Effects of clonidine on dopaminergic neuron activity in the substantia nigra: Possible mediation by noradrenergic regulation of serotoninergic raphe system. In A. J. Friedhoff & T. N. Chase (Eds.), *Gilles de la Tourette syndrome. Advances in neurology* (Vol. 35, pp. 99–104). New York: Raven.

Burd, L., Kerbeshian, J., Wikenheiser, M., & Fisher, W. (1986). Prevalence of Gilles de la Tourette syndrome in North Dakota adults. *American Journal of Psychiatry, 143,* 787–788.

Caine, E. D., McBride, M. C., Chiverton, P., Bamford, K. A., Redliess, S., & Shiao, J. (1988). Tourette's Syndrome in Monroe County school children. *Neurology, 38,* 472–475.

Chase, T. N., Friedhoff, A. J., & Cohen, D. J. (Eds.). (1992). *Tourette syndrome: Genetics, neurobiology and treatment. Advances in neurology* (Vol. 58). New York: Raven.

Cohen, D. J. (1991). Finding meaning in one's self and others: Clinical studies of children with autism and Tourette's syndrome. In F. Kessel, M. Bornstein, & A. Sameroff (Eds.), *Essays in Honor of William Kessen* (pp. 159–175). Hillsdale, NJ: Erlbaum.

Cohen, D. J., Detlor, J., Shaywitz, B. A., & Leckman, J. F. (1982). Interaction of biological and psychological factors in the natural history of Tourette's syndrome: A paradigm for childhood neuropsychiatric disorders. In T. N. Chase & A. J. Friedhoff (Eds.), *Gilles de la Tourette syndrome. Advances in neurology* (Vol. 35, pp. 31–40). New York: Raven.

Cohen, D. J., & Leckman, J. F. (1994). Developmental psychopathology and neurobiology of Tourette's syndrome. *Journal of the American Academy of Child and Adolescent Psychiatry, 33,* 2–15.

Comings, D. E., & Comings, B. G. (1987). A controlled study of Tourette syndrome: I–VI. *American Journal of Human Genetics, 44,* 701–838.

Comings, D. E., Himes, J. A., & Comings, B. G. (1990). An epidemiologic study of Tourette's syndrome in a single school district. *Journal of Clinical Psychiatry, 51,* 463–469.

Dykens, E., Leckman, J., Riddle, M., Hardin, M., Schwartz, S., & Cohen, D. (1990). Intellectual, academic, and adaptive functioning of Tourette syndrome children with and without attention deficit disorder. *Journal of Abnormal Child Psychology, 18,* 607–615.

Erenberg, G. (1992). Treatment of Tourette's syndrome with neuroleptic drugs. In T. N. Chase, A. J. Friedhoff, & D. J. Cohen (Eds.), *Tourette syndrome: Genetics, neurobiology and treatment. Advances in neurology* (Vol. 58, pp. 241–243). New York: Raven.

Erenberg, G., Cruse, R. P., & Rothner, A. D. (1987). The natural history of Tourette syndrome: A follow-up study. *Annals of Neurology, 22,* 383–385.

Fernando, S. J. M. (1967). Gilles de la Tourette syndrome. *British Journal of Psychiatry, 113,* 607–617.

Frankel, M., Cummings, J. L., Robertson, M. M., Trimble, M. R., Hill, M. A., & Benson, D. F. (1986). Obsessions and compulsions in Gilles de la Tourette's syndrome. *Neurology, 36,* 378–382.

Fulop, G., Philips, R. A., Shapiro, A. K., Gomes, J. A., Shapiro, E., & Nordlie, J. W. (1987). ECG changes during haloperidol and pomozide treatment of Tourette's disorder. *American Journal of Psychiatry, 144,* 673–675.

George, M. S., Trimble, M. R., Ring, H. A., Sallee, F. R., & Robertson, M. M. (1993). Obsessions in obsessive-compulsive disorder with and without Gilles de la Tourette syndrome. *American Journal of Psychiatry, 150,* 93–97.

Goetz, C. G. (1992). Clonidine and clonazepam treatment of Tourette's syndrome. In T. N. Chase, A. J. Friedhoff, & D. J. Cohen (Eds.), *Tourette syndrome: Genetics, neurobiology and treatment. Advances in neurology* (Vol. 58, pp. 245–251). New York: Raven.

Goetz, C. G., & Klawans, H. L. (1982). Gilles de la Tourette on Tourette syndrome. In A. J. Friedhoff & T. N. Chase (Eds.), *Gilles de la Tourette: Vol. 35. Advances in Neurology* (pp. 1–16). New York: Raven.

Goetz, C. G., Tanner, C., Wilson, R., Carroll, V., Como, P., & Shannon, K. (1987). Clonidine and Gilles de la Tourette syndrome: Double blind study using objective rating measures. *Annals of Neurology, 21,* 307–310.

Golden, G. S. (1993). Treatment of attention deficit hyperactivity disorder. In R. Kurlan (Ed.), *Handbook of Tourette's syndrome and related tic and behavioral disorders* (pp. 423–431). New York: Marcel Dekker.

Goodman, W. K., Price, L. H., Rasmussen, S. A., Delgado, P. L., Heninger, G. R., & Charney, D. S. (1989). Efficacy of fluvoxamine in obsessive compulsive disorder. *Archives of General Psychiatry, 46,* 36–44.

Gounce, M., & Barbeau, A. (1977). Seven cases of Gilles de la Tourette's syndrome: Partial relief with clonazepam—a pilot study. *Canadian Journal of Neurological Science, 4,* 279–283.

Grad, L. R., Pelcovitz, D., Olson, M., Matthews, M., & Grad, G. J. (1987). Obsessive compulsive symptomatology in children with Tourette's syndrome. *Journal of the American Academy of Child and Adolescent Psychiatry, 26,* 69–73.

Grady, T. A., Pigott, T. A., L'Heureux, F., Hill, J. L., Bernstein, S. E., & Murphy, D. L. (1993). Double blind study of adjuvant buspirone for fluoxetine treated patients with obsessive compulsive disorder. *American Journal of Psychiatry, 150,* 819–821.

Hunt, R. D., Arnsten, A. F. T., & Asbell, M. D. (1995). An open trial of guanfacine in the treatment of attention-deficit hyperactivity disorder. *Journal of the American Academy of Child and Adolescent Psychiatry, 34,* 50–54.

Jankovic, J. (1992). Diagnosis and classification of tics and Tourette's syndrome. In T. N. Chase, A. J. Friedhoff, & D. J. Cohen (Eds.), *Tourette syndrome: Genetics, neurobiology and treatment. Advances in neurology* (Vol. 58, pp. 7–14). New York: Raven.

Jankovic, J. (1993). Deprenyl in attention deficit associated with Tourette's syndrome. *Archives of Neurology, 50,* 286–288.

King, R. A., Riddle, M. A., & Goodman, W. K. (1992). Psychopharmacology of obsessive compulsive disorder in Tourette syndrome. In T. N. Chase, A. J. Friedhoff, & D. J. Cohen (Eds.), *Tourette syndrome: Genetics, neurobiology and treatment. Advances in neurology* (Vol. 58, pp. 283–291). New York: Raven.

Kurlan, R. (1993). *Handbook of Tourette's syndrome and related tic and behavioral disorders.* New York: Marcel Dekker.

Leckman, J. F., Anderson, G. M., Cohen, D. J., Ort, S., Harcherik, D. F., Hoder, E. L., & Shaywitz, B. A. (1984). Whole blood serotonin and tryptophan levels in Tourette's disorder: Effects of acute and chronic clonidine treatment. *Life Sciences, 35,* 2497–2503.

Leckman, J. F., Hardin, M. T., Riddle, M. A., Stevenson, J., Ort, S. I., & Cohen, D. J. (1991). Clonidine treatment of Gilles de la Tourette's syndrome. *Archives of General Psychiatry, 48,* 324–328.

Leckman, J. F., Ort, S. I., Caruso, K. A., Anderson, G. M., Riddle, M. A., & Cohen, D. J. (1986). Rebound phenomena in Tourette syndrome after abrupt withdrawal of clonidine: Behavioral, cardiovascular and neurochemical effects. *Archives of General Psychiatry, 43,* 1168–1176.

Leckman, J. F., Riddle, M. A., Hardin, M. T., Ort, S. I., Swartz, K. L., Stevenson, J., & Cohen, D. J. (1989). The Yale Global Tic Severity Scale (YGTSS) initial testing of a clinician rated scale of tic severity. *Journal of the American Academy of Child and Adolescent Psychiatry, 28*(4), 566–574.

Leckman, J. F., Walker, D. E., & Cohen, D. J. (1993). Premonitory urges in Tourette's syndrome. *American Journal of Psychiatry, 150,* 98–102.

Leonard, H. L., Lenane, M. C., Swedo, S. E., Rettew, D. C., Gershon, E. S., & Rapoport, J. L. (1992). Tics and Tourette's syndrome: A two to seven year follow-up of 54 obsessive compulsive children. *American Journal of Psychiatry, 149,* 1244–1251.

Linet, L. S. (1987). Tourette syndrome, pimozide, and school phobia: The neuroleptic separation anxiety syndrome. *American Journal of Psychiatry, 142,* 613–615.

Markovitz, P. G., Stagno, S. J., & Calabrese, J. R. (1990). Buspirone augmentation of fluoxetine in obsessive-compulsive disorder. *American Journal of Psychiatry, 147*(6), 798–800.

Martin, R. R., Ebert, M. H., Gordon, E. K., Linnoila, M., & Kopin, I. J. (1984). Effects of clonidine on central and peripheral catecholamine metabolism. *Clinical Pharmacology and Therapeutics, 35,* 322–327.

McDougle, C. J., Goodman, W. K., Leckman, J. F., Lee, N. C., Heninger, G. R., & Price, L. H. (1994). Haloperidol addition in fluvoxamine-refractory obsessive compulsive disorder. *Archives of General Psychiatry, 51,* 302–308.

McDougle, C., Goodman, W. K., Price, L. H., Delgado, P. L., Krystal, J. H., Charney, D. S., & Heninger, G. R. (1990). Neuroleptic addition in fluvoxamine-refractory obsessive compulsive disorder. *American Journal of Psychiatry, 147,* 652–654.

Mikkelsen, E. J., Detlor, J., & Cohen, D. J. (1981). School avoidance and social phobia triggered by haloperidol in patients with Tourette's disorder. *American Journal of Psychiatry, 138,* 1572–1576.

Morphew, J. A., & Sim, M. (1969). Gilles de la Tourette syndrome: A clinical and psychopathological study. *British Journal of Medical Psychology, 42,* 293–301.

Pauls, D. L., Cohen, D. J., Kidd, K. K., & Leckman, J. F. (1988). Tourette syndrome and neuropsychiatric disorders: Is there a genetic relationship? *American Journal of Human Genetics, 42,* 206–209.

Pauls, D. L., & Leckman, J. F. (1986). The inheritance of Gilles de la Tourette syndrome and associated behaviors: Evidence for an autosomal dominant transmission. *New England Journal of Medicine, 315,* 993–997.

Pauls, D. L., Leckman, J. F., & Cohen, D. J. (1993). Familial relationship between Gilles de la Tourette syndrome, attention deficit disorder, learning disabilities, speech disorders, and stuttering. *Journal of the American Academy of Child and Adolescent Psychiatry, 32*(5), 1044–1050.

Pauls, D. L., Leckman, J. F., & Cohen, D. J. (1994). Evidence against a relationship between Tourette's syndrome and anxiety, depression, panic and phobic disorders. *British Journal of Psychiatry, 164,* 215–221.

Pauls, D. L., Towbin, K. E., Leckman, J. F., Zahner, G. E. P., & Cohen, D. J. (1986). Gilles de la Tourette syndrome and obsessive-compulsive disorder. *Archives of General Psychiatry, 43,* 1180–1182.

Peterson, B. S., Leckman, J. F., & Cohen, D. J. (1995). Tourette's syndrome: A genetically predisposed and an environmentally specified developmental psychopathology. In D. Cicchetti & D. J. Cohen (Eds.), *Developmental Psychopathology.* New York: Wiley.

Pigott, T. A., Pato, M. T., Bernstein, S. E., Grover, G. N., Hill, J. L., Tolliver, T. J., & Murphy, D. L. (1990). Controlled comparisons of clomipramine and fluoxetine in the treatment of obsessive-compulsive disorder. *Archives of General Psychiatry, 47,* 926–932.

Price, L. H., Goodman, W. K., Charney, D. S., Rasmussen, S. A., & Heninger, G. R. (1987). Treatment of severe obsessive compulsive disorder with fluvoxamine. *American Journal of Psychiatry, 144,* 159–161.

Riddle, M. A., Geller, B., & Ryan, N. (1993). Another sudden death in a child treated with desipramine. *Journal of the American Academy of Child and Adolescent Psychiatry, 32*(4), 792–797.

Riddle, M. A., Hardin, M., Cho, S. C., Woolston, J. L., & Leckman, J. F. (1988). Desipramine treatment of boys with attention deficit disorder and tics: Preliminary clinical experience. *Journal of the American Academy of Child and Adolescent Psychiatry, 27,* 811–814.

Riddle, M. A., Hardin, M. T., Towbin, K. E., Leckman, J. F., & Cohen, D. J. (1987). Tardive dyskinesia following haloperidol treatment in Tourette's syndrome. *Archives of General Psychiatry, 44,* 98–99.

Riddle, M. A., Nelson, J. C., Kleinman, C. S., Rassmusson, A., Leckman, J. F., King, R. A., & Cohen, D. J. (1991). Sudden death in children receiving norpramine: A review of three reported cases and commentary. *Journal of the American Academy of Child and Adolescent Psychiatry, 30*(1), 104–108.

Shapiro, A. K., Shapiro, E. S., Young, J. G., & Feinberg, T. E. (1988). *Gilles de la Tourette syndrome.* New York: Raven.

Singer, H. S., Gammon, K., & Quaskey, S. (1985). Haloperidol, fluphenazine, and clonidine in Tourette's syndrome: Controversies in treatment. *Pediatric Neurosciences, 12,* 71–74.

Spencer, T., Biederman, J., Wilens, T., Steingard, R., & Geist, D. (1993). Nortriptyline treatment of children with attention deficit disorder and tic disorder or Tourette's syndrome. *Journal of the American Academy of Child and Adolescent Psychiatry, 32,* 205–210.

Stokes, A., Bawden, H. N., Camafield, P. R., Backman, J. E., & Dooley, J. M. (1991). Peer problems in Tourette's disorder. *Pediatrics, 87,* 936–942.

Sverd, J., Gadow, K. D., Nolan, E. E., Sprafkin, J., & Ezor, S. N. (1992). Methylphenidate in hyperactive boys with comorbid tic disorder. In T. N. Chase, A. J. Friedhoff, & D. J. Cohen (Eds.), *Tourette syndrome: Genetics, neurobiology and treatment. Advances in neurology* (Vol. 58, pp. 271–281). New York: Raven.

Tollefson, G. D. (1981). Hyperadrenergic hypomania consequent to the abrupt cessation of clonidine. *Journal of Clinical Psychopharmacology, 1,* 93–95.

Towbin, K. E. (1995). Evaluation, establishing the treatment alliance, and informed consent. *Child and Adolescent Psychiatry Clinics of North America, 4*(1), 1–14.

Towbin, K. E., Riddle, M. A., Leckman, J. F., Bruun, R. D., & Cohen, D. J. (1988). The clinical care of individuals with Tourette's syndrome. In D. J. Cohen, R. D. Bruun, & J. F. Leckman (Eds.), *Tourette's syndrome & tic disorders: Clinical understanding and treatment* (pp. 330–352). New York: Wiley.

Troung, D. D., Bressman, S., Shale, H., & Fahn, S. (1988). Clonazepam, haloperidol, and clonidine in tic disorders. Southern Medical Journal, 81, 1103–1105.

Zametkin, A. J., & Rapoport, J. L. (1987a). Neurobiology of attention deficit disorder with hyperactivity: Where have we come in 50 years? Journal of the American Academy of Child and Adolescent Psychiatry, 26, 676–686.

Zametkin, A. J., & Rapoport, J. L. (1987b). Noradrenergic hypothesis of attention deficit disorder with hyperactivity: A critical review. In H. Y. Meltzer (Ed.), Psychopharmacology: The third generation of progress (pp. 837–842). New York: Raven.

Zametkin, A. J., Rapoport, J. L., Murphy, D. L., Linnoila, M., & Ismond, D. (1985). Treatment of hyperactive children with monoamine oxidase inhibitors, I: Clinical effects. Archives of General Psychiatry, 42(10), 962–968.

Obsessive Compulsive Disorder

KENNETH E. TOWBIN, M.D.

The author wishes to acknowledge the contributions of Mark A. Riddle, M.D., for his valued collaboration and astute methodical approach to this topic. The author is grateful to Donald J. Cohen, M.D., and James F. Leckman, M.D., for their constant support and innumerable lessons on the foundations of the care of very disturbed children.

Child and adolescent psychiatry has witnessed an explosion of information on the phenomenology, epidemiology, genetics, neurophysiology, and treatment of obsessive compulsive disorder (OCD), expanding our knowledge of relationships between brain, mind, and behavior. Writings about OCD in each historical epoch reflect the prevailing paradigms of how the mind operates and the origin of behavior (Towbin & Riddle, in press). Studies over the past 15 years broadened and deepened our knowledge about a disorder that was clearly identified and thoroughly characterized within the *Zeitgeist* of psychoanalytic theory (Freud, 1917/1953). As a result of more contemporary contributions, modern clinicians now blend multiple treatment approaches, among them psychopharmacology, behavioral treatments, adjunctive family treatment, and psychotherapy. These combinations of treatments offer better prognoses and less morbidity from this condition than ever before. Previously debilitated patients have been restored to functional lives; some who labored under serious impairments carry only mild remnants of their symptoms.

Beyond their clinical benefit, the efficacy of these treatments has guided the application of new techniques of neuroimaging, which in turn have fostered a better understanding of the pathophysiology of this disorder. Together, these studies have pointed to involvement of complex central circuits that link frontal lobe, basal ganglia, and thalamic structures and may mediate this complex neuropsychiatric behavior (Baxter et al., 1992; Insel, 1992). This work is relevant to the neurochemistry of obsessional thinking (Insel, 1992; Swedo et al., 1992) and to the neurophysiological effect of behavioral interventions (Baxter et al., 1992).

CLINICAL CRITERIA AND DSM-IV DIAGNOSTIC ISSUES

Clinical Features and Differential Diagnosis

Obsessions are involuntary and unwanted thoughts, images, or impulses that invade the consciousness of the person with OCD. A person with OCD usually realizes that these mental events are senseless or unnecessary, causing functional impairment and distress. The person with OCD does not have control over these mental events. But by contrast to the delusions of thought control in psychotic conditions, patients with OCD still realize that the thoughts or images are generated by their own mental operations. Because they are a product of the mind, obsessions can take an unlimited variety of forms—from simple repetitive words to thoughts, fears, memories, pictures, or elaborate dramatic scenes.

Compulsions are actions arising in response to an internal urge or obligation to follow certain rituals or rules. To be considered a compulsion, the effect of repeatedly carrying out these actions must cause functional impairment. Compulsions may arise as a direct extension of an obsession or in reaction to an obsession in an effort to ward off thoughts, impulses, or fears. Children in particular may report compulsions without the perception of a mental component. Like obsessions, compulsions are forced or involuntary and seen as unnecessary, excessive, or senseless. Compulsive behaviors may display a variety of precise rules for the chronology, rate, order, duration, and number of repetitions of the acts.

The differential diagnosis of OCD includes a variety of conditions. Some of these disorders frequently may arise along with OCD. In earlier versions of the DSM, the relationship between OCD and these other disorders was defined by "hierarchical rules" which forbade the diagnoses of OCD when some conditions (e.g., Tourette's syndrome, anorexia nervosa) were present, or permitted it when certain other diagnoses (e.g., simple phobias) were present. These hierarchical rules implied that in some conditions the symptoms were primarily a product of only one disorder and should be viewed as distinct from "true" OCD. Yet, it became increasingly difficult to sustain this distinction as empirical data pointed to the similarities of manifestation and variety of obsessions and compulsions that these "other" disorders exhibited. Some investigators even argued that schizophrenic patients exhibit OCD. Therefore the revised third edition of the *Diagnostic and Statistical Manual of Mental Disorders* (DSM-III-R; American Psychiatric Association [APA], 1985) eliminated most hierarchical rules. As a result, OCD can be diagnosed in the context of any disorder. As discussed in this chapter, DSM-IV (APA, 1994) makes some amendments to the understanding of these relationships.

Table 11.1 offers a list of conditions in which obsessions or compulsions are commonly seen. Appreciating these comorbid conditions may influence the choice of pharmacological treatment and modify the prognosis. It is useful to remember that OCD can arise from organic conditions including infections, trauma, and vascular events in the central nervous system (McKeon, McGuffin, & Robinson, 1984). In addition, several paraobsessional disorders possess features that are closely related to obsessions or compulsions: Body Dysmorphic Disorder, Trichotillomania, and "Fear of AIDS." In some patients, it can be difficult to distinguish these phenomena for OCD. "Fear of AIDS" may be a contemporary expression of an obsession (Fisman & Walsh, 1994). However, depending on the patient's history and the actual exposure risks for the individual, the clinician may need to consider whether the patient exhibits a Hypochondriacal Disorder or an Anxiety Disorder Due to a Medical Condition.

Diagnostic Features Found in DSM-IV Criteria

The DSM-IV criteria for OCD show several modifications from DSM-III-R. In DSM-IV, greater clarity has been achieved for OCD criteria in two

Table 11.1.   Disorders That May Be Seen in the Context of Obsessive Compulsive Disorder

Anorexia nervosa

Body dysmorphic disorder

Delusional disorder (all types)

Depression

Hypochondriasis

Obsessive-compulsive personality disorder

Organic mental disorder

Panic disorder

Pervasive developmental disorder

Phobias

Posttraumatic stress disorder

Schizophrenia

Schizotypal personality

Somatization disorder

Somatoform disorders

Trichotillomania

Tourette's syndrome

"Fear of AIDS"

Source: From Towbin, K.E., & Riddle, M.A., "Obsessive Compulsive Disorder," in Lewis, M. (Ed.), *Comprehensive Textbook of Child and Adolescent Psychiatry* (2nd ed.), Baltimore: Williams and Wilkins. Copyright Williams and Wilkins. Reprinted by permission.

ways. First, DSM-IV introduced a further caveat into the previous DSM-III-R stance on hierarchical rules. DSM-IV requires that obsessions and compulsions must display a content that is distinct from the earmarks of the other Axis I diagnosis (Table 11.2). DSM-III had hierarchical rules. In DSM-III-R, there were provisions for distinguishing between obsession that actually were part of another Axis I disorder (e.g., continuously intrusive thoughts about ingested calories in an anorexia nervosa patient) versus OCD that was comorbid with another Axis I disorder (e.g., religious preoccupations and excessive religious dietary perfectionism along with typical dieting and exercise in an anorexia nervosa patient). But in DSM-III-R, this was reserved for obsessions only. DSM-IV modifications draw similar guidelines for both obsessions and compulsions. Consequently, the ambiguities that arise in response to compulsive acts in hypochondriacal patients or those with trichotillomania are more readily resolved in DSM-IV. The criteria regarding the relationship of OCD to other disorders has now been established for both obsessions *and* compulsions.

Table 11.2.   *DSM-IV Criteria for Obsessive Compulsive Disorder*

A. Either obsessions or compulsions:
    Obsessions: as defined by (1), (2), (3), and (4):

    (1)   recurrent and persistent ideas, thoughts, impulses, or images that are experienced at some time during the disturbance as intrusive and inappropriate and cause marked anxiety or distress

    (2)   the thoughts, impulses, images are not simply excessive worries about real-life problems

    (3)   the person attempts to ignore or suppress such thoughts or impulses or to neutralize them with some other thought or action

    (4)   the person recognizes that the obsessions are the product of his or her own mind (not imposed from without as in thought insertion)

    Compulsions as defined by (1) and (2):

    (1)   repetitive behaviors or mental acts that the person feels driven to perform in response to an obsession, or according to rules that must be applied rigidly

    (2)   the behaviors or mental acts are aimed at preventing or reducing distress or preventing some dreaded event or situation; however, these behaviors or mental acts either are not connected in a realistic way with what they are designed to neutralize or prevent or are clearly excessive

B. At some point the person has recognized that the obsessions or compulsions are excessive or unreasonable. **Note:** this does not apply to children.

C. The obsessions or compulsions cause marked distress, are time consuming (take more than an hour a day), or significantly interfere with the person's normal routine, occupational functioning, or usual social activities or relationships with others.

D. If another Axis I disorder is present, the content of the obsessions or compulsions is not restricted to it (e.g., preoccupation with food in the presence of an Eating Disorder; hair pulling in Trichotillomania; concern with appearance in the presence of Body Dysmorphic Disorder; preoccupations with having a serious illness in the presence of Hypochondriasis; or guilty ruminations in the presence of a Major Depressive Disorder).

E. Not due to the direct effects of a substance (e.g., drugs of abuse, medication) or a general medical condition.

Second, greater clarity is achieved by formulating a more specific criterion, (B), about insight into the senselessness or excess of the thoughts or acts. This establishes a guideline for an important subgroup of very ill patients. DSM-IV requires "insight" only at *some* point in the disorder, rather than the DSM-III-R implication that it had to be a constant feature. This change stems from work with very disturbed OCD patients who displayed some "insight" or awareness of this excessiveness at one time and at another were virtually delusional about the need to carry out their acts (Insel & Akiskal, 1986; Lelliott, Noshirvani, Basoglu, Mark, & Monteiro, 1988). For children, this criterion for insight is dismissed altogether.

Another essential criterion is functional impairment as a consequence of symptoms. In contemporary practice, it is recognized that many patients may experience symptoms at the threshold of impairment but which are assimilated into day-to-day life and do not cause them trouble. The distinction between OCD and this kind of magical thinking that children (and adults) may entertain is underscored by this criterion and identifying this threshold of functional impairment.

Associated Features That Are Relevant to Treatment

Many clinicians fail to recognize that OCD is not a unitary condition but a heterogeneous collection of symptoms with many potential etiologic and contributing factors. It is critical that clinicians consider the wider context of the symptoms—their onset, morphology, manifestation, family history, course and co-occurring symptoms. Comorbid disorders must be carefully assessed and understood in relation to OCD symptoms. Just as in research protocols, in clinical care it is not sufficient simply to determine that a patient has OCD. As will be seen in this chapter, optimal patient care relies on the clinician to consider what *additional* diagnoses and symptoms are evident, what level of severity they exhibit, how much impairment they produce, and how the treatment plan will address them (Towbin, 1987). In many cases, the choice of behavioral interventions and pharmacological agents will depend on these comorbid features or family history. There is increasing evidence that the success of treatments employing augmentation strategies depends on making choices that account for comorbid features (Goodman, McDougle, Barr, Aronson, & Price, 1993). Consequently, the list in Table 11.1 also can be used as a kind of diagnostic checklist for clinicians to review and decide whether there are other diagnoses in which obsessional or compulsive features are prominent.

EPIDEMIOLOGY

Early reports by Rudin (1953) suggested rates of 0.05% of the population. This was close to clinic rates for children (Berman, 1942), and adults (Hollingsworth, Tanguay, & Grossman, 1980). However, the Epidemiologic Catchment Area (ECA) Survey of 1980 (Robins et al., 1984) reported prevalence rates of 2.0%, or twice that for schizophrenia. The initial response to these rates was skepticism and concerns about the Diagnostic Interview Schedule for Children (DISC) methodology, which made no attempt to determine what impairment if any was a consequence of symptoms. Using the ECA data, several retrospective studies compared clinician and lay interview diagnoses (Karno, Golding, Sorenson, & Burnam, 1988); overall rates produced by each one agreed closely. The investigators concluded that the rates were likely fairly accurate but interrater agreement was poor.

Modern prevalence studies of OCD in children and adolescents were conducted in the late 1980s using new instruments that were designed and modified for this task. Flament and coworkers (1988) employed a modified reduced version of the Leyton Inventory for Children in a suburban New York county high school. They reported a 0.35% point prevalence and lifetime prevalence of 0.4%. Applying weighting techniques similar to ECA methods to account for the period of risk and population, they calculated a point prevalence rate of 1.0% and a lifetime prevalence rate of 1.9%—close to the ECA data.

Zohar and coworkers (1992) looked at inductees into the Israeli Defense Forces, 562 consecutive 16- and 17-year-olds, to determine the prevalence of OCD in a nonclinical population. They reported point prevalences of 3.6%; 50% of cases reported having only obsessions. This was substantially greater than previous reports, but the authors defended their findings as being within statistical chance of the figures reported by Flament and coworkers (Flament et al., 1988).

Altogether, the data support that OCD is much more prevalent than was first proposed in the early 1950s. Explanations include that patients are reluctant to seek treatment or are capable of minimizing their impairment in all but the most severe cases (Berg et al., 1989; Flament et al., 1988). These studies also have instructed the community on the high prevalence of "subthreshold" obsessions and compulsive behaviors that hover at the edge of "caseness" and are not impairing. The follow-up data from the initial Warren County study suggest that individuals with these subthreshold conditions did not blossom into OCD (Berg et al., 1989) but remained stable at this subthreshold level over the 2 years of follow-up without their symptoms transforming into other conditions or declining functionally (Berg et al., 1989).

The *sex distribution* of OCD has been reported throughout clinical trials and epidemiological studies. In adults, several studies have suggested that males and females are affected equally (Black, 1974; Karno, Golding, Sorenson, & Burnam, 1988; Rasmussen & Tsuang, 1986; Robins et al., 1984). However, studies of childhood-onset OCD tend to find a preponderance of males (Flament et al., 1985). One group of investigators concluded that the distribution of early-onset OCD is greater in males but later onset rates show larger numbers of females (Flament et al., 1988). OCD tends to be a chronic condition, which means it remains prevalent in affected individuals; the overall result is that lifetime female prevalence "catches up" in adulthood to that of males. Nevertheless, two nonclinical community surveys of adolescents propose that the sex distribution is equal (Flament et al., 1988; Zohar et al., 1992).

Age distribution has been a source of continuous interest. Early and later studies suggest that 40% of individuals have onset of their OCD by age 18 (Black, 1974; Swedo, Rapoport, Leonard, Lenane, & Cheslow, 1989).

Comorbidity is an important problem in OCD diagnosis and treatment (Towbin, 1987). A majority of patients in clinic surveys possess other Axis I diagnoses. Whether this represents the actual state of the disorder or is a bias that results from relying on clinic samples has not been determined. Affective disorders (depression, dysthymia), anxiety disorders other than OCD, tic disorders, disruptive disorders (ADHD, oppositional defiant disorder), and trichotillomania are reported at higher than expected frequencies in children or adolescents with OCD (Leonard et al., 1993). This compares with the rates and disorders seen in adults, although tics and disruptive disorders are more common among the children, whereas substance abuse is seen more commonly in adults (Rasmussen & Tsuang, 1986).

The prevalence of particular symptoms has received a great deal of attention. Among both children and adults checking, cleaning, and counting rituals are the most common. Most patients possess multiple rituals; the most common presentating symptoms are obsessions with compulsions although some individuals have only one or the other. Typically, the type and number of compulsions change over time. There may be some difference in the frequency of particular symptoms; adults show cleaning, checking, repeating, counting, and ordering (Holtzer et al., 1994) whereas children tend to display cleaning, repeating, checking, and ordering (Swedo, Rapoport, Leonard, Lenane, & Cheslow, 1989). There are suggestions that touching and blinking plus the *absence* of cleaning were more predictive of a history of tic disorder in OCD patients (Holtzer et al., 1994).

PSYCHOPHARMACOLOGY: SELECTIVE SEROTONIN REUPTAKE INHIBITORS (SSRI)

The agents which have been most investigated and appear to be most useful in the treatment of OCD (Table 11.3) share features of inhibiting reuptake of serotonin, but we cannot yet verify that serotonin reuptake inhibition is the characteristic which *uniquely* determines the clinical efficacy of a compound (Goodman et al., 1989). Current lines of evidence suggest that serotonin reuptake inhibition is necessary but not sufficient to produce an effective response (Goodman et al., 1989).

Table 11.3. **Agents Useful in the Treatment of Obsessions and Compulsions**

Type of Agent	Generic Name	Dose Range (mg/d)	Max. Dose in mg/kg/d
Tricyclic agents	Clomipramine	25–250	3.0
Selective serotonin reuptake inhibitors	Fluoxetine	5–40	—
	Sertraline	25–200	—¹
	Fluvoxamine	25–300	—
	Paroxetine[a]	—[a]	—[a]
Augmentation strategies	Lithium	—[b]	—[b]
	Haloperidol	1–5	—
	Pimozide	2–8	—
	Clonazepam	0.5–10	0.2

[a] Theoretical, no specific studies of OCD.

[b] Blood level of 1.0 meq/dl recommended.

For example, it appears that the primary metabolite of clomipramine, desmethylclomipramine, is potent in inhibiting serotonin reuptake yet is not correlated with clinical efficacy (Insel, Mueller, Alterman, Linnoila, & Murphy, 1985). Moreover, there are agents, such as trazodone and perhaps zimelidine, that are inhibitors of serotonin reuptake yet are not effective in ameliorating OCD symptoms (Insel et al., 1985; Pigott et al., 1992). The most effective agents inhibit serotonin reuptake, but some agents that increase serotonin, such as tryptophan, lithium, and fenfluramine, may be effective adjuctively in reducing symptoms of OCD. Further evidence is found in the relative clinical ineffectiveness of monotherapy with agents such as buspirone and fenfluramine, which act to increase serotonin activity but do not influence reuptake. But the picture is even more complicated. Some studies suggest that the agents which are the most selective and potent in their affinity and blockade of serotonin reuptake (e.g., sertraline or paroxetine) may be less effective than less discriminating agents, such as fluoxetine and clomipramine, which affect other transmitter systems as well (Jenike, Baer, et al., 1990; King, Riddle, & Goodman, 1992). These theories are highly speculative at this point and must await direct comparisons under blinded, controlled, randomly assigned conditions.

There are general guidelines which should be followed when prescribing medication for children (Towbin, 1995). These guidelines, listed in Table 11.4, apply to any psychotropic medication use in children. However, they hold particular relevance for treatment of disorders like OCD in which subjective symptoms figure so prominently, there are high levels of anxiety, and patients typically harbor many worries about the effects of medication on their otherwise highly functional lives.

Table 11.4.   Guidelines for the Use of Medication

1. Identify specific symptoms that are targeted for improvement.

2. Start at the smallest possible dose.

3. Increase the dose using the smallest possible increments.

4. Increase the dose only after sufficient time has elapsed to gauge the effects of the current dose.

5. Monitor the effect on specific target symptoms.

6. Look for side effects routinely.

7. Avoid using more than one medication at a time as much as possible.

8. Unless side effects preclude continuing, start a different medication only after a suitable maximum dose of the current medication has been reached.

9. Unless side effects preclude continuing, start a different medication only after a sufficient time at the maximum dose of the current medication has been accomplished.

10. Unless delays would engender serious risks to the patient, changes in combinations of medication should be made one medication at a time over intervals that are long enough to permit adequate assessment of the impact of each step.

Tricyclic Agents: Clomipramine

Effects.   Clomipramine (CI) is the tricyclic compound imipramine with a chlorine molecule substituted at position 3. Clomipramine possesses high avidity for inhibiting presynaptic serotonin (and other monoamine) reuptake, noradrenergic reuptake, and monoamine oxidase type A (Flament, Rapoport, Murphy, Berg, & Lake, 1987). In contrast to other tricyclic agents, CI avidly blocks calcium channels (Flament et al., 1987). It produces an active metabolite, desmethylchlorimipramine, which is highly serotonergic and also noradrenergic (Flament et al., 1987), and possesses acute and chronic effects on serotonin. The chronic effect that has been postulated is "down regulation" of serotonin in the central nervous system. It appears that CI is also significantly bound to dopamine D_2 receptors in vitro assays (Austin et al., 1991).

The double-blind, placebo-controlled trials of children and adolescents at the National Institute of Mental Health (NIMH; Flament et al., 1985) and the multicenter trials (DeVeaugh-Geiss et al., 1992) reported improvement, defined by clinical global impressions and 40% reduction in standardized OCD measures, in 40% to 60% of patients. This parallels the adult experience in which 40% to 60% of patients improved on adequate doses of CI (DeVeaugh-Geiss, Landau, & Katz, 1989).

Dosage and Clinical Use. Dosage of CI is shown in Table 11.4. For children and adolescents, the maximum recommended doses are 3.0 mg/kilo not exceeding 250 mg/day. Medication is generally given before sleep or in divided doses, beginning with 25 mg per day. Pertinent laboratory evaluation should include complete blood counts with differential, liver function studies (ALT, AST), alkaline phosphatase, BUN, creatinine, and an electrocardiogram. It is important to underscore that although there have been no sudden deaths reported on CI, the metabolites and activity of the drug closely resemble imipramine. Cardiac arrhythmias do arise in overdoses, and CI also produces QT_c prolongation. Consequently, it is prudent to obtain ECG recordings prior to initiating CI and subsequent to dose increments.

Side Effects. Clomipramine produces a variety of side effects consistent with those reported for other tricyclic antidepressants such as amitriptyline and imipramine. The most common side effects in children and adolescents are sedation, anticholinergic effects, dizziness, fatigue, tremor, headache, constipation, anorexia, postural hypotension, and tachycardia (DeVeaugh-Geiss et al., 1992). Cardiovascular effects can be a problem so that blood pressure should be monitored. Since CI resembles other tricyclic agents, ECG monitoring is also advised (Riddle et al., 1991). At this point, no data support any curvilinear "window effect" of blood levels and efficacy; in the clinical trials efficacy correlated with higher blood levels. No "therapeutic" CI level has been determined. Currently, therefore, for most child or adolescent patients the merit of CI blood levels is dubious.

Fluoxetine

Effects. Fluoxetine is a two-ringed substituted phenylpropanolamine which potently inhibits serotonin reuptake. It has a long half-life—approximately 4 to 7 days. Its primary metabolite, norfluoxetine, is also a potent serotonin reuptake inhibitor and with a very long half-life of up to 20 days. Fluoxetine and desmethylfluoxetine appear to display little affinity for cholinergic, muscarinic, histaminic, or adrenergic sites. However, there are suggestions that fluoxetine binds to dopamine D_2 receptors in vitro assays (Austin et al., 1992).

Adults with OCD have been treated with fluoxetine under double-blind, placebo-controlled conditions (Montgomery et al., 1993; Pigott et al., 1990; Tollefson et al., 1994). There is only one study of fluoxetine effects on OCD in children and adolescents. Riddle and coworkers (1992) conducted a double-blind, placebo-controlled crossover trial in 14 patients. Of 11 who completed the 8-week trial, pooled improvement in global scores was observed. Reductions in severity scores ranging from 27% to 45% were noted over the 8-week trial. The study was hampered by a relatively high placebo response rate of 12% to 27% and by the small number of the subjects.

Dosage and Clinical Use. The high interindividual variability of its metabolism and long half-life argue strongly for commencing fluoxetine treatment with very low doses. Some clinicians will start with 5 mg *every other* day, but for most children and adolescents 5 mg/day is feasible and reduces side effects. Although maximum doses of 80 mg/day have been employed, doses exceeding 40 mg/day appear to offer little additional benefit for OCD. It is important to remember that fluoxetine exhibits nonlinear kinetics at higher blood levels—as the dose increases, fluoxetine impedes its own metabolism and this increases plasma levels to a greater degree than predicted by linear kinetics (DeVane, 1992). Tablet and liquid forms are available.

Side Effects. Sweating, rash, nausea, dry mouth, and tremor all have been commonly observed in adolescents receiving fluoxetine (Boulos, Kutcher, & Gardner, 1992; Riddle, King, et al., 1991). Emotional side effects including "motor restlessness," silliness, giddiness, and increased suicidal ideation have been reported (King, Riddle, Chappel, et al., 1991; Riddle, King, et al., 1991). Concerns that fluoxetine, when compared with other antidepressant drugs, might carry an increased risk for suicidal ideation have been raised (King et al., 1991; Riddle, King, et al., 1991) but the data to support this contention have not been produced. Sleep difficulties—both insomnia and sedation—may occur and respond to dose reductions (Riddle, King, et al., 1991). Akathisia does arise with fluoxetine, can be quite bothersome, and usually requires dose reduction or cessation of the agent. Fluoxetine also affects the metabolism of other medications. Inhibition of the cytochrome P450 system can elevate blood levels of a variety of medications including anticonvulsants, antipsychotic agents (butryophenones and phenothiazines), calcium channel blockers, benzodiazepines (Callahan, Fava, & Rosenbaum, 1993) and terfenadine (Kivisto, Neuvonen, & Klotz, 1994) with serious or even life-threatening consequences. Extreme caution should be used when combing psychotropic or anticonvulsant agents with fluoxetine. It is dangerous and contraindicated to combine fluoxetine with monoamine oxidase inhibitors. When changing to MAOI agents, fluoxetine's long half-life demands a washout period of at least 5 or 6 weeks before commencing treatment with MAOI agents. In addition, augmentation with L-tryptophan is discouraged strongly when fluoxetine is used (Steiner & Fontaine, 1986). The combination has been especially likely to result in a toxic serotonin syndrome.

Fluvoxamine

Effects. Fluvoxamine was approved for use in the United States in 1995, and there is extensive experience with this agent in Europe. Fluvoxamine is a 2-aminoethyloxime aralkylketone and possesses a unicyclic structure. Purportedly, it is more selective in its effect on serotonin reuptake than fluoxetine or clomipramine but less than either sertraline or paroxetine (Jenike, Hyman, et al., 1990). Like clomipramine and fluoxetine, however, other transmitter systems are influenced, if not initially, then subsequent to chronic administration (Benfield & Ward, 1986; Coleman & Block, 1982). It has no active metabolites and does not affect histaminic or muscarinic receptors to any significant degree (Benfield & Ward, 1986).

The efficacy of fluvoxamine in ameliorating symptoms of OCD has been demonstrated in adults, but to date there have been no child or adolescent cohort studies. Among published reports, over 100 adults have been treated under double-blind conditions, and reports suggest that rates of improvement rival clomipramine or fluoxetine (Goodman et al., 1989; Jenike, Hyman, et al., 1990; Perse, Greist, Jefferson, Rosenfeld, & Dar, 1987; Price, Goodman, Charney, Rasmussen, & Heninger, 1987).

Dosage and Clinical Use. In experimental studies, adult subjects received doses beginning with 25 mg b.i.d. and increased to a maximum of 300 mg per day, divided b.i.d. Fluvoxamine has a somewhat shorter half-life than the other SSRI agents at 13 to 19 hours (DeVane, 1992).

Side Effects. No serious side effects were reported in these early double-blind, placebo-controlled trials. No ECG, blood pressure, or pulse changes were noted. Insomnia, constipation, nausea, dyspepsia, and fatigue were the most common side effects reported and were managed by dose reductions. One case report of onset of tics exists (Fenning, Naisberg-Fenning, Pato, & Weitzman, 1994). Effects in children and adolescents remain to be described. Until wider application is possible and greater experience is gained, one cannot say where fluvoxamine will fall in the hierarchy of agents for treatment of child and adolescent OCD.

Sertraline

Effects. Sertraline is a tetrahydronaphthylamine. Among the antidepressants, it has a novel chemical structure. The half-life of sertraline is reported to be 24 hours, peak levels are reached in 6 to 10 hours, and elimination is primarily through renal excretion (DeVane, 1992). This presents some advantages over the other SSRI agents, especially paroxetine and fluoxetine, which exert a pronounced effect on hepatic metabolism. The primary metabolite of sertraline, *N*-desmethylsertraline, is also active in inhibiting serotonin reuptake and is highly specific. Sertraline and desmethylsertraline possess some affinity for beta-adrenergic receptors but not for dopaminergic, muscarinic, or histaminic receptors (Jenike, Baer, et al., 1990).

Adult studies with sertraline suggest that it too may be effective in diminishing both obsessions and compulsions (Chouinard et al., 1990; Jenike, Baer, et al., 1990). Studies with children and adolescents have yet to be published. Rates of improvement were not as great as has been reported for fluoxetine, clomipramine, or fluvoxamine.

Dosage and Clinical Use.   Without more experience in children, it is difficult to propose guidelines for doses and use. Studies of adults have employed maximum doses of 200 mg/day (Jenike, Baer, et al., 1990). It would be reasonable to conclude that similar doses would be feasible in adolescents, but in the absence of safety and efficacy testing, guidelines for children cannot be proposed now.

Side Effects.   Side effects were virtually absent in the OCD placebo-controlled trials. Minor difficulties with sleep, nausea, and constipation were reported. Sedation and weakness can be a problem. No patient stopped medication as a result of side effects. It should be kept in mind that significant toxic side effects can emerge with combinations of monoamine oxidase inhibitors and sertraline. If added to a previously stable drug regimen, sertraline tends to displace protein-bound compounds creating major serum elevations.

Paroxetine

Effects.   Paroxetine is a drug in the class of phenylpiperidine agents. It is a new agent, and where it will fit into the armamentarium of medications to treat depression or obsessive compulsive disorder has yet to be determined.

Dosage and Clinical Use.   There are no published large-scale trials reporting use of paroxetine in children or adolescents for any disorder and no reliable data about the use or efficacy of paroxetine in treatment of OCD. Consequently, it is difficult to propose appropriate doses for children and adolescents.

Augmentation Strategies

As many as 40% to 60% of patients who are treated with SSRI agents as their sole medication are unimproved despite use of adequate doses for a sufficient duration to demonstrate efficacy (McDougle et al., 1994). As a result, there is keen interest in whether one can boost the effect of SSRI agents using pharmacological augmentation techniques. The agents which have been studied are listed in Table 11.3.

Lithium. The evidence in support of lithium augmentation stems from case reports (Feder, 1988; Golden, Morris, & Sack, 1988; Rasmussen, 1984) and small cohorts given double-blind, placebo-controlled augmentation trials (McDougle, Price, Goodman, Charney, & Heninger, 1991). Despite proposed mechanisms of boosting serotonergic activity, the results have been equivocal in the controlled larger trials; none reached statistical or clinically relevant significance (McDougle et al., 1991). McDougle and coworkers (1991) suggest that augmentation with lithium may be reasonable for patients in whom depression is prominent. Doses used in this study were sufficient to attain lithium levels in the range of 0.8 to 1.0 meq/l. Recent reports suggest that lithium augmentation of fluoxetine may produce high rates of adverse reactions (Gelenberg, 1994). Employing low serum levels of lithium and smaller doses of fluoxetine are recommended for this application (Gelenberg, 1994).

Dopaminergic Antagonists: Haloperidol and Pimozide. The belief that a single neurotransmitter system exclusively governs complex behaviors does not conform to the biological intricacy of the central nervous system (DeSimoni, Daltoso, Fodritto, Sokola, & Algeri, 1987). Relying on the efficacy of SSRIs to advance the theory also ignores the actual affinities of these agents, which are relatively, not *purely*, selective for serotonin.

In this vein, there has been a dedicated effort to understand how the SSRI agents ameliorate symptoms of OCD. The hypothesis that clinical efficacy was derived from antidepressant effects was not supported. Effective antidepressants like desipramine were no more effective than placebo when compared with clomipramine or fluvoxamine (Goodman et al., 1990; Leonard, Swedo, Rapoport, Coffey, & Cheslow, 1989). Further evidence against an exclusive role for serotonin is suggested by the impact of tryptophan depletion in patients with OCD (Barr et al., 1994). Fifteen SSRI responsive patients with OCD were maintained on medication and given diets low in tryptophan. In contrast to depressed patients, patients with OCD who were treated with SSRI sustained their symptomatic relief under conditions of tryptophan depletion. Depressed patients displayed a resurgence of symptoms suggesting that serotonin is not a powerful mediator of continued symptom relief in OCD but is important in sustaining recovery from depression.

Observations that persons with disorders which affect basal ganglia, such as Parkinson's disease, Sydenham's chorea, and Tourette's syndrome, frequently exhibit obsessions and or compulsions suggested a link between dopaminergic function and OCD (McDougle, Goodman, Leckman, & Price, 1993; Swedo et al., 1993). Discrete reports of inflammatory or toxic disorders that displayed damage to basal ganglia and symptoms of OCD also were suggestive (Laplane et al., 1989; McDougle, Goodman, Leckman, & Price, 1993). In addition, connections between frontal lobes, basal ganglia, and the thalamus, termed cortico-striatal-thalamo-cortical (CSTC) tracts were observed to be involved in OCD (Alexander, Crutcher, & DeLong, 1990). PET scan data following treatment with SSRIs or behavioral treatment suggested that changes in frontal lobes and basal ganglia correlated with clinical improvement (Baxter et al., 1992; Swedo et al., 1992).

These observations led investigators to consider augmentation strategies employing dopaminergic blocking agents like haloperidol and pimozide (McDougle et al., 1990, 1994). In a double-blind, placebo-controlled trial, haloperidol in doses of 2 to 10 mg/day was given to adults with OCD who were unresponsive to adequate doses of fluvoxamine (McDougle et al., 1994). Augmentation resulted in improvement in 11 of 17 (65%) subjects on haloperidol and none on placebo. Those who received placebo were given an open trial of haloperidol, and 8 of 14 (57%) responded. Side effects of augmentation were mild; 9 of 31 (75%) developed akathisia, and anticholinergic effects were observed. It is significant that every subject with OCD and comorbid tic disorder ($N = 8$) responded to addition of haloperidol. In an earlier open label trial, subjects with comorbid schizotypal personality features and OCD also responded to neuroleptic augmentation (McDougle et al., 1990).

Although there have been no comparable trials in children or adolescents, it may be possible to generalize from these adult studies. In SSRI-refractory child or adolescent patients, comorbid features of tic disorder, family history of tic disorder, or features of schizotypal personality disorder should suggest consideration of augmentation with haloperidol.

Combining SSRI Agents.   Simeon and coworkers (Simeon, Thatte, & Wiggins, 1990) reported on 6 cases of relatively CI-refractory patients who received an open trial of CI plus fluoxetine for 4 to 28 weeks. Using the combination, moderately positive results were observed in 5 of 6 subjects. It is difficult to evaluate the generalizability of open drug trials in small samples; controlled trials have not been published. As reported earlier, the inhibition of cytochrome P450 micorenzymes by fluoxetine may cause accumulation to reach toxic levels of tricyclic antidepressants like CI. For this reason, very low doses (25 to 50 mg/day) of CI were used in combination with 20 to 40 mg/day of fluoxetine. Until results of further trials are made available, it would be premature to resort to this combination. It may be that paroxetine carries the same risk but sertraline does not appear to inhibit cytochrome P450IID6. Although this might favor use of sertraline, doubts about its efficacy for OCD must first be resolved.

Clonazepam. Clonazepam in a benzodiazepine with unique properties. Clonazepam may possess serotonergic as well as GABA-ergic activity (Goodman et al., 1993). The possibility that the effect is simply anxiolytic has been proposed, but without further testing, this is speculative also (Goodman et al., 1993). With growing success in the use of such agents in children who display anxiety disorders, there may be a role for clonazepam. On the positive side, it is attractive for its relatively minor side effects and reversibility. However, concerns over memory impairment and difficulties with learning new information while on shorter acting benzodiazepine agents should be considered when prescribing clonazepam. The efficacy of augmentation with this agent in children and adolescents has not been established but warrants further attention.

Beginning with doses in the range of 0.5 mg/day is desirable. Incrementing at doses of 0.5 every week with maximum doses of no more than 10 mg total is suggested. Sedation, Lethargy, and dizziness, may be seen initially. Rare late side effects of disinhibition have been observed. The combination of fluoxetine with clonazepam may lead to clonazepam accumulation and toxicity as a result of cytochrome P450IID6 inhibition. Blood levels should be monitored closely or an alternative SSRI should be considered. Clonazepam may be a desirable consideration in the context of comorbid anxiety disorders (Goodman et al., 1993).

Buspirone. Buspirone, a serotonin agonist, may warrant consideration as an augmentation agent, but the general clinical experience is that it is not especially useful. Under carefully controlled conditions, one study reported that buspirone offered occasional additional benefit (Markovitz, Stagno, & Calabrese, 1990) yet other work found it only rarely beneficial though safe (Grady et al., 1993). In general, there may be a role in considering buspirone augmentation in anxious children or adolescents though controlled trials selecting subjects based on comorbid features have not been conducted.

Other Agents: Fenfluramine and L-Tryptophan. There are case reports of responses to L-tryptophan, the amino acid precursor to serotonin. Currently, this agent is not available in the United States as a result of an allergic reaction—eosinophilia myalgia syndrome (Hertzman et al., 1990). Furthermore, the combination of L-tryptophan with fluoxetine produces a toxic reaction and is contraindicated. Consequently, the safety of this augmentation strategy requires further testing employing other SSRIs.

Fenfluramine reduces whole blood serotonin by facilitating release from intracellular storage and inhibiting reuptake at presynaptic sites (Aman & Kern, 1989). It possesses amphetamine-like activity and consequently has some abuse potential, which led to its classification as a class IV agent. Augmentation of fluoxetine- or CI-refractory adults treated in an open trial of fenfluramine 20 to 60 mg/day reported moderate improvement in 6 of 7 subjects (Hollander, DiCaria, Schneier, Liebowitz, & Klein, 1990). Animal investigations have suggested a high risk for neurotoxicity but this was not observed in drug trials with adults. Side effects of weight loss, lethargy, and sleep difficulties were the most common, consonant with amphetamine-like activity of this drug. Despite the absence of neurotoxicity in patients treated in many trials, when using fenfluramine as an augmenting agent, it should be kept in mind that its safety has not been clearly established (Aman & Kern, 1989).

TREATMENT OF INDIVIDUALS WITH TICS AND OCD

Clinicians treating patients with OCD, especially children and adolescents, should remember that a large minority of these individuals may possess personal or family histories of tic disorders. Rates of tic disorders are elevated among individuals with OCD whether the sample under consideration is a nonclinical cohort from the community (Zohar et al, 1992) or patients from the clinic (Leonard et al., 1992); the prevalence of tic disorders among persons with OCD has been estimated to be as high as 50% (Leonard et al., 1992; Zohar et al., 1992). By the same token, individuals with tic disorders, especially Tourette's syndrome, display increased frequency of obsessive-compulsive symptoms and OCD (Frankel et al., 1986; Grad, Pelcovitz, Olson, Matthews, & Grad, 1987; Pauls & Leckman, 1986; Pauls, Towbin, Leckman, Zahner, & Cohen, 1986). The distinctions and evaluation of OCD with tics or in individuals with a family history of tics is beyond the scope of this chapter. If medication for OCD is used, care should be taken to introduce agents cautiously, as exacerbation of tics can result. In addition, drug interactions may affect the success of an antiobsessional agent if medications for tics must be introduced. For further information, the reader should review the relevant section of Chapter 10.

PROGNOSIS

The prognosis for OCD has improved considerably since 1980. The typical waxing and waning course of the disorder makes it difficult to determine the prognosis for children and adolescents. Some individuals will experience a "spontaneous" remission, whereas others will go on to have exacerbation and remission of symptoms with periods without symptoms interepisodically. Others yet will have continuous symptoms that worsen and improve but never disappear. The largest and most thorough prognostic studies of children and adolescents have been conducted by the NIMH group, which follows community cohorts and clinical cohorts over 2 to 5 years (Berg et al., 1989; Leonard et al., 1993).

In the community study, 12 students from a public high school were identified with clinical OCD in the initial phase of the study (Berg et al., 1989). Two years later, the pooled data of these 12 subjects revealed a decrease to total interference scores by 7.6 to a level beneath the cutoff for caseness. Five of 12 (42%) continued to meet criteria, 57% reported persistent symptoms but without impairment, and 12% were asymptomatic; 58% did not meet criteria for OCD. This would support the "spontaneous remission" rate of 65% proposed by Rachman and Hodgson (1980). Results of the community survey suggested that patients with clinical OCD were at high risk for persistent symptoms at 2-year follow-up.

The outcome of adolescents who exhibited subclinical obsessions and compulsions was also noteworthy. Initially there was a belief that these individuals were "on the way" to impairment and would exhibit OCD on follow-up. This hypothesis was not borne out, however. Of the 10 subjects who reported obsessions or compulsions at a subclinical level in the first phase of the study, only one was diagnosed with OCD 2 years later (Berg et al., 1989).

Longitudinal study of the clinical cohort also was informative (Leonard et al., 1993). During the follow-up study, patients reported waxing and waning of symptoms. The prevalence of the diagnosis changed, and at one point during the follow-up period, 37% met criteria for OCD and 63% did not. It is important to recall that all the patients were receiving treatment throughout this period. The response to treatment was also monitored; half the patients sustained the diagnosis of OCD regardless of the modalities used and duration of treatments (Leonard et al., 1993).

Features predictive of outcome were explored in the clinical cohort. The results suggested that outcome was best predicted by the level of impairment after 5 weeks of CI treatment, presence of parental psychopathology on Axis I, and lifetime history of tics. Severity at baseline (prior to initiating treatment) and amount of improvement at 5 weeks were not predictive of outcome. Severely impaired children who made modest gains were more likely to have a poor outcome than mildly impaired children who made mild gains. The emergence of high levels of expressed emotion as a risk factor for outcome in OCD is also interesting. It should be underscored that the only comorbid condition that predicted a poor outcome for OCD symptoms was presence of a tic disorder.

Altogether, an overview supports considerable optimism for the treatment of OCD in children and adolescents. Significant symptom relief can be achieved in 50% to 60% of patients who might otherwise suffer a chronic course. Additional treatments with family and behavioral interventions (March, Mulle, & Herbel, 1994) may hold particular value. Clinicians are increasingly familiar with the nature of OCD and are capable of employing sophisticated pharmacological interventions to benefit their patients. A comprehensive evaluation of the patient including consideration of comorbid diagnoses, family and peer functioning, and past medical and psychiatric history continues to be indispensable (Towbin, 1987, 1995). OCD is obviously a chronic illness. Consequently, especially for children and adolescents, it is critical that the physicians take time to establish and cultivate a relationship that will withstand the changing severity and course of the patient's illness (Towbin, 1995). As we learn more about the etiology and natural history of OCD and discover new agents and treatments that may be helpful, we are increasingly able to tailor our interventions to the needs of the patient. Consequently, our patients are able to receive better care and achieve better results than ever before.

REFERENCES

Alexander, G. E., Crutcher, M. D., & DeLong, M. R. (1990). Basal ganglia-thalamocortical circuits: Parallel substrates for motor, oculomotor, "prefrontal" and "limbic" functions. *Progress in Brain Research, 85*, 119–146.

Aman, M. G., & Kern, R. A. (1989). Review of fenfluramine in the treatment of the developmental disabilities. *Journal of the American Academy of Child and Adolescent Psychiatry, 28*, 549–565.

American Psychiatric Association. (1985). *Diagnostic and statistical manual of mental disorders* (DSM-III-R) (3rd ed-rev.). Washington, DC: Author.

American Psychiatric Association. (1994). *Diagnostic and statistical manual of mental disorders* (DSM-IV) (4th ed.). Washington, DC: Author.

Austin, L. S., Lydiard, R. B., Ballenger, J. C., Cohen, B. M., Laraia, M. T., Zealberg, J. J., Fossey, M. D., & Ellinwood, E. H. (1991). Dopamine blocking activity of clomipramine in patients with obsessive compulsive disorder. *Biological Psychiatry, 30*, 225–232.

Barr, L. C., Goodman, W. K., McDougle, C. J., Delgado, P. L., Heninger, G. R., Charney, D. S., & Price, L. H. (1994). Tryptophan depletion in patients with obsessive compulsive disorder who respond to serotonin reuptake inhibitors. *Archives of General Psychiatry, 51*, 309–317.

Baxter, L. R., Schwartz, J. M., Bergman, K. S., Szuba, M. P., Guze, B. H., Mazziota, J. C., Alazraki, A., Selin, C. E., Ferng, H. K., Munford, P., & Phelps, M. E. (1992). Caudate glucose metabolic rate changes with both drug and behavioral therapy for obsessive compulsive disorder. *Archives of General Psychiatry, 49*, 681–689.

Benfield, P., & Ward, A. (1986). Fluvoxamine, a review of its pharmacodynamic and pharmacokinetic properties and therapeutic efficacy in depressive illness. *Drugs, 32,* 313–334.

Berg, C. A., Rapoport, J. L., Whitaker, A., Davies, M., Leonard, H. L., Swedo, S. E., Braiman, S., & Lenane, M. (1989). Childhood obsessive-compulsive disorder: Two year prospective follow-up of a community sample. *Journal of the American Academy of Child and Adolescent Psychiatry, 28,* 528–533.

Berman, L. (1942). Obsessive compulsive neurosis in children. *Journal of Nervous and Mental Disease, 95,* 26–39.

Black, A. (1974). The natural history of obsessional neurosis. In H. R. Beech (Ed.), *Obsessional states* (pp. 19–55). London: Methuen.

Boulos, C., Kutcher, S., & Gardner, D. (1992). An open naturalistic study of fluoxetine in adolescents and young adults with treatment resistant major depression. *Journal of Child and Adolescent Psychopharmacology, 2,* 103–111.

Callahan, A., Fava, M., & Rosenbaum, J. F. (1993). Drug interactions in psychopharmacology. *The Psychiatric Clinics of North America, 16,* 647–671.

Chouinard, G., Goodman, W. K., Greist, J., Jenike, M., Rasmussen, S., White, K., Hackett, E., Gaffney, M., & Bick, P. A. (1990). Results of a double blind placebo controlled trial of a new serotonin uptake inhibitor, sertraline, in the treatment of obsessive compulsive disorder. *Psychopharmacology Bulletin, 26,* 279–284.

Coleman, B. S., & Block, B. A. (1982). Fluvoxamine maleate, a serotonergic antidepressant: A comparison with cholorimipramine. *Progress in Neuropsychopharmacology and Biological Psychiatry, 6,* 475–478.

DeSimoni, M. G., Daltoso, G., Fodritto, F., Sokola, A., & Algeri, S. (1987). Modulation of striatal dopamine metabolism by the activity of dorsal raphe serotonergic afferents. *Brain Research, 411,* 81–88.

DeVane, C. L. (1992). Pharmacokinetics of selective serotonin uptake inhibitors. *Journal of Clinical Psychiatry, 53*(Suppl.), 13–20.

DeVeaugh-Geiss, J., Landau, P., & Katz, R. (1989). Preliminary results from a multicenter trial of clomipramine obsessive compulsive disorder. *Psychopharmacology Bulletin, 25,* 36–40.

DeVeaugh-Geiss, J., Moroz, G., Biederman, J., Cantwell, D., Fontaine, R., Greist, J. H., Reichler, R., Katz, R., & Landau, P. (1992). Clomipramine hydrochloride in childhood and adolescent obsessive compulsive disorder—A multicenter trial. *Journal of the American Academy of Child and Adolescent Psychiatry, 31,* 45–49.

Feder, R. (1988). Lithium augmentation of clomipramine. *Journal of Clinical Psychiatry, 49,* 458.

Fenning, S., Naisberg-Fenning, S., Pato, M., & Weitzman, A. (1994). Emergence of Tourette's syndrome during fluvoxamine treatment of obsessive compulsive disorder. *Psychological Medicine, 164,* 839–840.

Fisman, S. N., & Walsh, L. (1994). Obsessive compulsive disorder and fear of AIDS contamination in childhood. *Journal of the American Academy of Child and Adolescent Psychiatry, 33*(3), 349–353.

Flament, M. F., Rapoport, J. L., Berg, C. Z., Sceery, W., Kilts, C., Mellstrom, B., & Linnoila, M. (1985). Clomipramine treatment of childhood obsessive compulsive disorder: A double blind controlled study. *Archives of General Psychiatry, 42,* 977–983.

Flament, M. F., Rapoport, J. L., Murphy, D. L., Berg, C. Z., & Lake, C. R. (1987). Biochemical changes during clomipramine treatment of childhood obsessive compulsive disorder. *Archives of General Psychiatry, 44,* 219–225.

Flament, M. F., Whitaker, A., Rapoport, J. L., Davies, M., Berg, C. Z., Kalikow, K., Sceery, W., & Shaffer, D. (1988). Obsessive compulsive disorder in adolescence: An epidemiologic study. *Journal of the American Academy of Child and Adolescent Psychiatry, 27,* 764–772.

Frankel, M., Cummings, J. L., Robertson, M. M., Trimble, M. R., Hill, M. A., & Benson, D. F. (1986). Obsessions and compulsions in Gilles de la Tourette syndrome. *Neurology, 36,* 378–382.

Freud, S. (1953). Introductory lectures on psychoanalysis. In J. Strachey (Ed.), *The standard edition of the complete psychological works of Sigmund Freud* (Vol. 15). London: Hogarth. (Original work published 1917)

Gelenberg, A. J. (1994). Fluoxetine plus lithium. *Biological Therapies in Psychiatry, 17,* 26–27.

Golden, R. N., Morris, J. E., & Sack, D. A. (1988). Combined lithium-tricyclic treatment of obsessive compulsive disorder. *Biological Psychiatry, 23,* 181–185.

Goodman, W. K., McDougle, C. J., Barr, L. C., Aronoson, S. C., & Price, L. H. (1993). Biological approaches to treatment resistant obsessive-compulsive disorder. *Journal of Clinical Psychiatry, 54*(Suppl. 6), 16–26.

Goodman, W. K., Price, L. H., Delgado, P. L., Palumbo, J., Krystal, J. H., Nagy, L. M., Rasmussen, S. A., Heninger, G. R., & Charney, D. S. (1990). Specificity of serotonin reuptake inhibitors in the treatment of obsessive compulsive disorder: Comparison of fluvoxamine and desipramine. *Archives of General Psychiatry, 47,* 577–585.

Goodman, W. K., Price, L. H., Rasmussen, S. A., Delgado, P. L., Heninger, G. R., & Charney, D. S. (1989). Efficacy of fluvoxamine in obsessive compulsive disorder. *Archives of General Psychiatry, 46,* 36–44.

Grad, L. R., Pelcovitz, D., Olson, M., Matthews, M., & Grad, G. J. (1987). Obsessive compulsive symptomatology in children with Tourette's syndrome. *Journal of the American Academy of Child and Adolescent Psychiatry, 26,* 69–73.

Grady, T. A., Pigott, T. A., L'Heureux, F., Hill, J. L., Bernstein, S. E., & Murphy, D. L. (1993). Double blind study of adjuvant buspirone for fluoxetine treated patients with obsessive compulsive disorder. *American Journal of Psychiatry, 150,* 819–821.

Hertzman, P. A., Blevins, W. L., Mayer, J., Greenfield, B., Ting, M., & Gleich, G. J. (1990). Association of the eosinophilia myalgia syndrome with the ingestion of L-tryptophan. *New England Journal of Medicine, 322,* 869–873.

Hollander, E., DiCaria, C. M., Schneier, H. A., Liebowitz, M. R., & Klein, D. F. (1990). Fenfluramine augmentation of serotonin uptake blockage antiobsessional treatment. *Journal of Clinical Psychiatry, 51,* 119–123.

Hollingsworth, C., Tanguay, P., & Grossman, L. (1980). Long-term outcome of obsessive-compulsive disorder in childhood. *Journal of the American Academy of Child Psychiatry, 19,* 134–144.

Holzer, J. C., Goodman, W. K., McDougle, C. J., Baer, L., Boyarsky, B. K., Leckman, J. F., & Price, L. H. (1994). Obsessive compulsive disorder with and without a chronic tic disorder. *British Journal of Psychiatry, 164,* 469–473.

Insel, T. R. (1992). Toward a neuroanatomy of obsessive compulsive disorder. *Archives of General Psychiatry, 49,* 739–745.

Insel, T. R., & Akiskal, H. (1986). Obsessive-compulsive disorder with psychotic features: Phenomenologic analysis. *American Journal of Psychiatry, 143,* 1527–1533.

Insel, T. R., Mueller, E. A., Alterman, I., Linnoila, M., & Murphy, D. L. (1985). Obsessive-compulsive disorder and serotonin: Is there a connection? *Biological Psychiatry, 20,* 1174–1188.

Jenike, M., Baer, L., Summergrad, P., Minichiello, W. E., Holland, A., & Seymour, R. (1990). Sertraline in obsessive-compulsive disorder: A double blind comparison with placebo. *American Journal of Psychiatry, 147,* 923–928.

Jenike, M., Hyman, S., Baer, L., Holland, A., Minichiello, W. E., Buttolph, L., Summergrad, P., Seymour, R., & Ricciardi, J. (1990). A controlled trial of fluvoxamine in obsessive compulsive disorder: Implications for a serotonergic theory. *American Journal of Psychiatry, 147,* 1209–1215.

Karno, M., Golding, J., Sorenson, S. B., & Burnam, M. A. (1988). The epidemiology of obsessive-compulsive disorder in five U.S. communities. *Archives of General Psychiatry, 45,* 1094–1099.

King, R. A., Riddle, M. A., Chappell, P. B., Hardin, M. T., Anderson, G. M., Lombroso, P., & Scahill, L. (1991). Emergence of self-destructive phenomena in children and adolescents during fluoxetine treatment. *Journal of the American Academy of Child and Adolescent Psychiatry, 30,* 179–186.

King, R. A., Riddle, M. A., & Goodman, W. K. (1992). Psychopharmacology of obsessive compulsive disorder in Tourette syndrome. In T. N. Chase, A. J. Friedhoff, & D. J. Cohen (Eds.), *Tourette syndrome: Genetics, neurobiology and treatment. Advances in neurology* (Vol. 58, pp. 283–291). New York: Raven.

Kivisto, D. T., Neuvonen, P. J., & Klotz, U. (1994). Inhibition of terfanadine metabolism: Pharmacokinetic and pharmacodynamic consequences. *Clinical Pharmacokinetics, 27,* 1–5.

Laplane, D., Levasseur, M., Pillon, B., Dubois, B., Baulac, M., Mazoyer, B., Trandinh, S., Sette, G., Danza, F., & Baron, J. C. (1989). Obsessive compulsive and other behavioral changes with bilateral basal ganglia lesions: A neuropsychological, magnetic resonance imaging, and positron tomographic study. *Brain, 112,* 699–725.

Lelliott, P. T., Noshirvani, H. F., Basoglu, M., Marks, I. M., & Monteiro, W. O. (1988). Obsessive compulsive beliefs and treatment outcome. *Psychological Medicine, 18,* 697–702.

Leonard, H. L., Lenane, M. C., Swedo, S. E., Rettew, D. C., Gershon, E. S., & Rapoport, J. L. (1992). Tics and Tourette's syndrome: A two to seven year follow-up of 54 obsessive compulsive children. *American Journal of Psychiatry, 149,* 1244–1251.

Leonard, H. L., Swedo, S. E., Lenane, M. C., Rettew, D. C., Hamburger, S. D., Bartko, J. J., & Rapoport, J. L. (1993). A two to seven year follow-up study of 54 obsessive compulsive children and adolescents. *Archives of General Psychiatry, 50,* 429–439.

Leonard, H. L., Swedo, S. E., Rapoport, J. L., Coffey, M., & Cheslow, D. (1989). Treatment of obsessive compulsive disorder with clomipramine and desipramine in children and adolescents: A double blind crossover comparison. *Archives of General Psychiatry, 46,* 1088–1092.

March, J. S., Mulle, K., & Herbel, B. (1994). Behavioral psychotherapy for children and adolescents with obsessive compulsive disorder: An open trial of a new protocol driven treatment package. *Journal of the American Academy of Child and Adolescent Psychiatry, 33,* 333–341.

Markovitz, P. G., Stagno, S. J., & Calabrese, J. R. (1990). Buspirone augmentation of fluoxetine in obsessive-compulsive disorder. *American Journal of Psychiatry, 147,* 798–800.

McDougle, C. J., Goodman, W. K., Leckman, J. F., Lee, N. C., Heninger, G. R., & Price, L. H. (1994). Haloperidol addition in fluvoxamine-refractory obsessive compulsive disorder. *Archives of General Psychiatry, 51,* 302–308.

McDougle, C. J., Goodman, W. K., Leckman, J. F., & Price, L. C. (1993). The pharmacology of obsessive-compulsive disorder: Implications for treatment and pathogenesis. *Psychiatric Clinics of North America, 16*(4), 749–766.

McDougle, C. J., Goodman, W. K., Price. L. H., Delgado, P. L., Krystal, J. H., Charney, D. S., & Heninger, G. R. (1990). Neuroleptic addition in fluvoxamine refractory obsessive compulsive disorder. *American Journal of Psychiatry, 147,* 652–654.

McDougle, C. J., Price, L. H., Goodman, W. K., Charney, D. S., & Heninger, G. R. (1991). A controlled trial of lithium augmentation in fluvoxamine refractory obsessive compulsive disorder. *Journal of Clinical Psychopharmacology, 11,* 175–184.

McKeon, I., McGuffin, P., & Robinson, P. (1984). Obsessive-compulsive neurosis follow head injury: A report of four cases. *British Journal of Psychiatry, 144,* 190–192.

Montgomery, S. A., McIntyre, A., Osterheider, M., Sarteschi, P., Zitterl, W., Zohar, J., Birkett, M., & Wood, A. J. (1993). A double blind placebo controlled study of fluoxetine in patients with DSM-III-R obsessive compulsive disorder: The Eli Lilly European OCD Study Group. *European Neuropsychopharmacology, 3,* 143–152.

Pauls, D. L., & Leckman, J. F. (1986). The inheritance of Gilles de la Tourette syndrome and associated behaviors: Evidence for an autosomal dominant transmission. *New England Journal of Medicine, 315,* 993–997.

Pauls, D. L., Towbin, K. E., Leckman, J. F., Zahner, G. E. P., & Cohen, D. J. (1986). Gilles de la Tourette syndrome and obsessive-compulsive disorder. *Archives of General Psychiatry 43,* 1180–1182.

Perse, T. L., Greist, J. H., Jefferson, J. W., Rosenfeld, R., & Dar, R. (1987). Fluvoxamine treatment of obsessive compulsive disorder. *American Journal of Psychiatry, 144,* 1543–1548.

Pigott, T. A., L'Heureux, F., Rubenstein, C. S., Bernstein, S. E., Hill, J. L., & Murphy, D. L. (1992). A double blind, placebo controlled study of trazodone in patients with obsessive-compulsive disorder. *Journal of Clinical Psychopharmacology, 12,* 156–162.

Pigott, T. A., Pato, M. T., Bernstein, S. E., Grover, G. N., Hill, J. L., Tolliver, T. J., & Murphy, D. L. (1990). Controlled comparisons of clomipramine and fluoxetine in the treatment of obsessive-compulsive disorder. *Archives of General Psychiatry, 47,* 926–932.

Price, L. H., Goodman, W. K., Charney, D. S., Rasmussen, S. A., & Heninger, G. R. (1987). Treatment of severe obsessive compulsive disorder with fluvoxamine. *American Journal of Psychiatry, 144,* 159–161.

Rachman, S., & Hodgson, R. (1980). *Obsessions and compulsions.* Englewood Cliffs, NJ: Prentice-Hall.

Rasmussen, S. A. (1984). Lithium and tryptophan augmentation in clomipramine-resistant obsessive-compulsive disorder. *American Journal of Psychiatry, 141,* 1283–1285.

Rasmussen, S. A., & Tsuang, M. T. (1986). Clinical characteristic and family history in DSM-III obsessive-compulsive disorder. *American Journal of Psychiatry, 143,* 317–322.

Riddle, M. A., King, R. A., Hardin, M. T., Scahill, L., Ort, S. S., Chappell, P., Rasmusson, A., & Leckman, J. F. (1991). Behavioral side effects of fluoxetine in children and adolescents. *Journal of Child and Adolescent Psychopharmacology, 1,* 193–198.

Riddle, M. A., Nelson, J. C., Kleinman, C. S., Rassmusson, A., Leckman, J. F., King, R. A., & Cohen, D. J. (1991). Sudden death in children receiving norpramine: A review of three reported cases and commentary. *Journal of the American Academy of Child and Adolescent Psychiatry, 30*(1), 104–108.

Riddle, M. A., Scahill, L., King, R., Hardin, M. T., Anderson, G. M., Ort, S. S., Smith, J. C., Leckman, J. F., & Cohen, D. J. (1992). Double-blind, crossover trial of fluoxetine and placebo in children and adolescents with obsessive-compulsive disorder. *Journal of the American Academy of Child and Adolescent Psychiatry, 30,* 1062–1069.

Robins, L., Helzer, J. E., Weissman, M. M., Orvaschel, H., Gruenberg, E., Burke, J. D., & Regier, D. A. (1984). Lifetime prevalence of specific psychiatric disorders in three sites. *Archives of General Psychiatry, 41,* 949–958.

Rudin, E. (1953). Ein Beitrag zur Frage der Zwangskrankheit, insobesondere ihrere hereditaren Beziehungen. *Archiv Psychiatrie und Nervenkrankheit, 191,* 14–54.

Simeon, J. G., Thatte, W., & Wiggins, D. (1990). Treatment of adolescent obsessive compulsive disorder with clomipramine-fluoxetine combination. *Psychopharmacology Bulletin, 26,* 285–290.

Steiner, W., & Fontaine, R. (1986). Toxic reaction following the combined administration of fluoxetine and L-tryptophan: Five case reports. *Biological Psychiatry, 21,* 1067–1071.

Swedo, S. E., Leonard, H. L., Schapiro, M. B., Casey, B. J., Mannheim, G. B., Lenane, M. C., & Rettew, D. C. (1993). Sydenham's chorea: Physical and psychological symptoms of St. Vitus Dance. *Pediatrics, 91,* 706–713.

Swedo, S. E., Pietrini, P., Leonard, H. L., Schapiro, M. B., Rettew, D. C., Goldberger, E. L., Rapoport, S. I., Rapoport, J. L., & Grady, C. L. (1992). Cerebral glucose metabolism in childhood onset obsessive compulsive disorder: Revisualization during pharmacotherapy. *Archives of General Psychiatry, 49,* 690–695.

Swedo, S. E., Rapoport, J. L., Leonard, H. L., Lenane, M. C., & Cheslow, D. (1989). Obsessive compulsive disorder in children and adolescents: Clinical phenomenology of 70 consecutive cases. *Archives of General Psychiatry, 46,* 335–341.

Tollefson, G. D., Rampey, A. H., Potvin, J. H., Jenike, M. A., Rush, A. J., Dominguez, R. A., Koran, L. M., Shear, M. K., Goodman, W. K., & Genduso, L. A. (1994). A multicenter investigation of fixed-dose fluoxetine in the treatment of obsessive-compulsive disorder. *Archives of General Psychiatry, 51,* 559–567.

Towbin, K. E. (1987). Drug treatment of obsessive compulsive disorder: A review in the light of diagnostic and metric limitations. *Psychiatric Developments, 1,* 25–50.

Towbin, K. E. (1995). Evaluation, establishing the treatment alliance, and informed consent. *Child and Adolescent Psychiatry Clinics of North America, 4*(1), 1–15.

Towbin, K. E., & Riddle, M. A. (in press). Obsessive-compulsive disorder. In M. Lewis (Ed.), *Child and adolescent psychiatry: A comprehensive textbook* (2nd ed.). Baltimore, MD: Williams and Wilkins.

Zohar, A., Ratzoni, G., Pauls, D. L., Apter, A., Bleich, A., Kron, S., Rappaport, M., Weizman, A., & Cohen, D. (1992). An epidemiologic study of obsessive compulsive disorder and related disorders in Israeli adolescents. *Journal of the American Academy of Child and Adolescent Psychiatry, 31,* 1057–1061.

Disorders of Conduct and Behavior

MARKUS J. P. KRUESI, M.D. and DAVID F. LELIO, M.D.

Disruptive behavior disorders constitute the most frequent referral to psychiatric treatment for the pediatric age group. This category includes attention deficit/hyperactivity disorder (ADHD), oppositional defiant disorder (ODD), and conduct disorder (CD). Children and adolescents who exhibit symptoms within this category frequently demand a considerable amount of attention and time from teachers, parents, relatives, pastors, police, and others in the community. Mental health professionals search for effective treatments to control associated behaviors (threats, fighting, stealing, lying, truancy, temper outbursts, irritability, anger, defiance, etc.) and negative attitudes of these children.

This chapter will cover diagnostic criteria, epidemiology, and pharmacological interventions for oppositional defiant and conduct disorders from the recent literature (ADHD is covered in Chapter 8). The goals of the authors are to (a) introduce the reader to diagnostic criteria, including changes in the *Diagnostic and Statistical Manual of Mental Disorders,* Fourth Edition (DSM-IV; American Psychiatric Association [APA], 1994), (b) discuss the epidemiology and comorbidity of the disorders, (c) describe the most recent studies regarding pharmacological treatments, and (d) use the available data for guidance in pharmacological treatment.

DIAGNOSTIC CRITERIA

In DSM-IV, Conduct Disorder (CD), Oppositional Defiant Disorder (ODD), Disruptive Behavior Disorder Not Otherwise Specified, and Attention Deficit/Hyperactivity Disorder (ADHD) are grouped under the heading of Disruptive Behavior and Attention Deficit Disorders. The DSM-IV criteria for CD and ODD are outlined in Table 12.1.

Several forces have affected the evolution of diagnostic categories for disruptive behavior disorders. Some argue that the categories of CD and ODD overlap considerably and thus are not separate entities. Some studies, utilizing DSM-III (American Psychiatric Association [APA], 1980) or DSM-III-R (American Psychiatric Association [APA], 1987) criteria, examined associated noncriterion features (familial discord, social agency contacts, familial psychiatric or physical illness, familial social status, etc.) to distinguish oppositional disorder (OD is the DSM-III diagnosis that evolved into ODD in later iterations) from CD and found that ODD and CD can be considered a single disorder on a continuum of severity in the DSM-IV.

A study by Rey et al. (1988) compared subjects who fit the criteria for CD, ODD, ADD with and without hyperactivity, adjustment disorder, affective disorder, anxiety disorder, and other Axis I diagnoses. They examined the validity of ODD as a separate diagnostic category utilizing

Table 12.1.   DSM-IV Criteria for Conduct Disorder and Oppositional Defiant Disorder

Diagnostic criteria for Conduct Disorder (312.8)

A. A repetitive and persistent pattern of behavior in which the basic rights of others or major-age-appropriate societal norms or rules are violated, as manifested by the presence of three (or more) of the following criteria in the past 12 months, with at least one criterion present in the past 6 months.

Aggression to people and animals

(1)   often bullies, threatens, or intimidates others

(2)   often initiates physical fights

(3)   has used a weapon that can cause serious physical harm to others (e.g., a bat, brick, broken bottle, knife, gun)

(4)   has been physically cruel to people

(5)   has been physically cruel to animals

(6)   has stolen while confronting a victim (e.g., mugging, purse snatching, extortion, armed robbery)

(7)   has forced someone into sexual activity

Destruction of property

(8)   has deliberately engaged in fire-setting with the intention of causing serious damage

(9)   has deliberately destroyed others' property (other than by fire-setting)

Deceitfulness or theft

(10)   has broken into someone else's house, building, or car

(11)   often lies to obtain goods or favors or to avoid obligations (i.e., "cons" others)

(12)   has stolen items of nontrivial value without confronting a victim (e.g., shoplifting, but without breaking and entering; forgery)

Serious violations of rules

(13)   often stays out at night despite parental prohibitions, beginning before age 13 years

(14)   has run away from home overnight at least twice while living in parental or parental surrogate home (or once without returning for a lengthy period)

(15)   is often truant from school, beginning before age 13 years

B. The disturbance in behavior causes clinically significant impairment in social, academic, or occupational functioning

C. If the individual is age 18 years or older, criteria are not met for Antosocial Personality Disorder.

(Continued)

Table 12.1.   *(Continued)*

Specify type based on age at onset:

> **Childhood-Onset Type:** onset of at least one criterion characteristic of Conduct Disorder prior to age 10 years

> **Adolescent-Onset Type:** absence of any criteria characteristics of Conduct Disorder prior to age 10 years

Specific severity:

> **Mild:** few if any conduct problems in excess of those required to make the diagnosis **and** conduct problems cause only minor harm to others

> **Moderate:** number of conduct problems and effect on others intermediate between "mild" and "severe"

> **Severe:** many conduct problems in excess of those required to make the diagnosis or conduct problems cause considerable harm to others

Diagnostic criteria for Oppositional Defiant Disorder (313.81)

A. A pattern of negativistic, hostile, and defiant behavior lasting at least 6 months, during which four (or more) of the following are present:

> (1)   often loses temper
>
> (2)   often argues with adults
>
> (3)   often actively defies or refuses to comply with adults' requests or rules
>
> (4)   often deliberately annoys people
>
> (5)   often blames others for his or her mistakes or misbehavior
>
> (6)   is often touchy or easily annoyed by others
>
> (7)   is often angry and resentful
>
> (8)   is often spiteful or vindictive

Note: Consider a criterion met only if the behavior occurs more frequently than is typically observed in individuals of comparable age and developmental level.

B. The disturbance in behavior causes clinically significant impairment in social, academic, or occupational functioning.

C. The behaviors do not occur exclusively during the course of a Psychotic or Mood Disorder.

D. Criteria are not met for Conduct Disorder, and, if the individual is age 18 years or older, criteria are not met for Antisocial Personality Disorder.

---

four instruments: DSM-III diagnoses on Axes I, IV, and V, Child Behavior Checklist (CBCL), Psychosocial Adversity Index (PSAI), and social class. They found considerable overlap among the OD, CD, and adjustment disorder groups and determined that the OD group functioned better and had fewer problems than the adolescents in the CD group.

They concluded that although some differences exist between OD and CD, ODD may be only a milder form of CD.

Another study that sought to determine the validity of a separate diagnostic category for ODD compared six groups of children who were admitted to an inpatient child psychiatric unit: ADDH; CD; ODD; ADDH plus CD; ADDH plus ODD, and a control group with no evidence of a disruptive behavior disorder (Soltys, Kashani, Dandoy, Vaidya, & Reid, 1992). Groups were compared using the Diagnostic Interview for Children and Adolescents (DICA), the Piers-Harris Children's Self-Concept Scale, the Revised Children's Manifest Anxiety Scale (RCMAS), the Dimensions of Temperament Survey (DOTS), the Life Events Checklist (LEC), and the Personality Inventory for Children (PIC). Subjects in the ODD group had lower threshold scores on the DOTS than subjects in the CD group. CD and ODD groups were similar on all other measures, supporting the view that ODD may be a milder form of CD.

Other evidence supporting the similarity of ODD and CD comes from a study by Schachar and Wachsmuth (1990) that compared subjects with DSM-III diagnoses of ODD, CD, or normal controls in terms of demographic characteristics, other forms of psychopathology, academic attainment, quality of social relationships, family dysfunction, and parental psychopathology. Seventeen of the 22 CD subjects (77%) also met the criteria for ODD; however, CD subjects displayed more serious social failure, exhibited by a lack of affectional bonds, than ODD subjects. In addition, ODD subjects were from families that reported more marital dissatisfaction than the CD group.

In contrast, Loeber, Lahey, and Thomas (1991) examined the distinctions between ODD and CD by investigating the evidence on patterns of behavioral covariation, age of onset, the developmental course, correlates and risk factors, stability and predictability, seriousness ratings (the seriousness of oppositional and conduct problems as rated by teachers and mental health professionals), and treatment implications. They point to a variety of features which argue that CD and ODD should be considered separately.

Age of onset has been found to be helpful in distinguishing ODD from CD. Loeber, Green, Lahey, Christ, and Frick (1990) interviewed the mothers of 87 clinic-referred boys, 10 to 13 years old, and asked at which age the mothers first noticed various problem behaviors in their sons. It was found that ODD symptoms peaked at age 8, and CD symptoms (more serious problem behaviors) emerged at older ages. In another study by Loeber et al. (1991), parental reports from over five hundred 13-year-old boys yielded similar results: Older boys demonstrated more serious behavior problems such as breaking and entering, running away from home, and raping. LeBlanc and Frechette (1989) sampled an older group of boys and found that more serious delinquent behaviors continued to emerge after age 13. Thus, mean age of onset was found to be useful in distinguishing ODD from CD.

ODD symptoms appear to be less serious than CD symptoms. Two studies examined the perceptions of teachers and mental health professionals regarding oppositional and conduct problems. Although these studies were conducted 50 years apart, each found that ODD symptoms were judged less serious than most CD symptoms (Vidoni, Fleming, & Mintz, 1983; Wickman, 1928).

Utility of treatment is another parameter suggesting differentiation of ODD and CD. A study conducted by Patterson (1982) found some children diagnosed with ODD improved with treatment. However, Loeber and LeBlanc (1990) and Kazdin (1987) found that treatment was often unsuccessful with adolescents diagnosed with CD. It has been speculated that as children grow older, their personalities become more defined and their behaviors more entrenched and stable. Other studies have supported the finding that as problem behaviors become more fixed and intransigent, more intense effort will be needed to produce change (Wolf, Braukmann, & Ramp, 1987). The authors concluded that treatment is likely to be more effective in children with ODD symptoms rather than CD symptoms.

Distinguishing ODD from CD has been gaining favor. In a 1993 review, Rey, who had earlier viewed ODD and CD as part of a continuum, found the evidence more compelling to view ODD as a separate diagnostic category. The studies that were reviewed examined the developmental patterns of ODD symptoms, differences between ODD symptoms and normal conduct, reliability of the diagnosis of ODD, epidemiology (sex, age, socioeconomic status), comorbidity of ODD with other disorders, validity of the diagnosis of ODD, etiology of ODD, and treatment response of children diagnosed with ODD.

ODD symptoms appear to be relatively stable over time but differ from CD symptoms in developmental profile and gender distribution. The developmental patterns of behavior with ODD (arguing, screaming, disobedience, and defiance) appear to follow a different course from those of CD, with ODD symptoms peaking between the ages of 8 and 11 years and then declining in frequency. However, CD symptoms (truancy, stealing, etc.) increase during late childhood and adolescence (Rey, 1993). Rey also noted that ODD was diagnosed more often in boys than in girls who were 12 years old or younger. However, there was a higher prevalence of ODD in adolescent girls. In contrast, CD was diagnosed more often in boys of all age groups.

Frick, Lahey, Applegate, Kerdyck, et al. (1994) conducted field trials to generate data regarding possible revisions of DSM-III-R criteria for ODD and CD. The sample consisted of 440 clinic-referred youths, 336 boys and 104 girls between the ages of 4 and 17 years with childhood disruptive behavior disorder diagnoses. Structured diagnostic interviews, standardized clinicians' validation diagnoses, and several measures of impairment were used to generate diagnoses, validate presence and clinical significance of disorders, and obtain global ratings of impairment. Utilizing symptom analyses, factor analysis of symptoms, and multiple regression, the authors found that with some exceptions the symptom lists in DSM-IV for ODD and CD were similar to the DSM-III-R symptoms and ODD and CD inclusion criteria have been modified.

Diagnostic criteria for ODD have been shortened from nine to eight and the minimal number of criteria for diagnosis has been decreased. The DSM-III-R ODD symptom, "often swears or uses obscene language" as well as the three subcategories of severity have been eliminated. A minimum of four criteria need to be present for the diagnosis of ODD instead of five. The severity of ODD is now defined as "the disturbance in behavior causes significant impairment in social, academic, or occupational functioning," rather than "mild, moderate, or severe" (APA, 1987, 1994).

For a diagnosis of CD, inclusion criteria have been expanded to include "often bullies, threatens, or intimidates others," and "often stays out at night despite parental prohibitions, beginning before 13 years of age" (APA, 1994). Also, the DSM-III-R symptom of "often lies" was dropped and replaced by a more specific symptom of "often lies or breaks promises to obtain goods or favors from others (i.e., "cons" others)."

As a result of the DSM-IV field trials for ODD and CD, internal consistency and test-retest agreement for these diagnoses and the validity of the diagnosis for ODD have been improved.

The DSM-IV has addressed the suggestions made by clinicians and researchers to further distinguish diagnostic criteria for CD and ODD. However, Rey (1993) suggested that "if it could be shown that children with oppositional defiant disorder respond to specific treatments more consistently than those with conduct disorder," this consistency could further support the validity of the diagnosis of ODD. Although some studies have attempted to investigate the efficacy of medications in the treatment of ODD and CD, results are limited.

EPIDEMIOLOGY

Prevalence rates reported for oppositional defiant disorder and conduct disorder vary. Differences have been attributed to methodological differences in criteria employed, populations studied, and informant utilized. Assessment techniques have included rating scales such as the Child Behavior Checklist (CBCL) and Rutter Scales. Interviews have included the Diagnostic Interview Schedule for Children (DISC), the Child Assessment Schedule (CAS), the Children's Global Assessment

Scale (CGAS), and the Diagnostic Interview for Children and Adolescents (DICA). Bird et al. (1988) utilized the parent and teacher rating scales of the CBCL and the Rutter Scales, followed by the DISC and the CGAS instruments in their community survey in Puerto Rico. Cohen et al. (1987) utilized the DISC to collect data on their population in their New York study. Instrument variability has been reported across several studies (Kashani, Carlson, Beck, & Hoeper, 1987; Offord et al., 1987), complicating assessment of prevalence of ODD and CD.

Criteria have also varied between studies. The *International Classification of Diseases* (ICD; World Health Organization [WHO], 1978) and the *Diagnostic and Statistical Manual of Mental Disorders* (DSM) have both been used to diagnose ODD and CD. The most recent DSM versions have also undergone criteria changes, further complicating the picture.

Study populations have differed in terms of cultural, religious, ethical, and legal systems. Bird et al. (1988) studied a Puerto Rican population; Anderson, Williams, McGee, and Silva (1987) studied a Dunedin, New Zealand, population; and Esser, Schmidt, and Woerner (1990) studied children from Mannheim, Germany. Prevalence rates also may vary across studies because of sample diversity.

Varied sources of information also add to prevalence rate variability. Parent, teacher, and child reports about a child's behavior vary, as well as the clinician's bias for one diagnosis over another. Source or method variance in ratings of conduct disorder was documented by Fergusson and Horwood (1989). In their study of 776 children, the correlation between maternal and teacher ratings of conduct disorder ranged from +.33 to +.40. In comparison, the correlations across a 3-year span for teachers ranged from +.56 to +.65 and the across-time correlation of maternal ratings ranged from .66 to .74. Although evaluated at a single point in time, child ratings increased only in the between-rater category.

Similar results were found in measures of aggression in a group of 43 patients with disruptive behavior disorders in another study (Kruesi, Hibbs, et al., 1994). Parents' account of aggression on the CBCL correlated significantly with their account of the child's aggression toward people on a structured interview, the DICA-P, but there was no correlation between the parent-rated CBCL and their child's report of aggression on the parallel structured DICA interview. Analyses of conditional agreements between parents and children (p [parent|child]; p [child|parent]) on conduct disorder behaviors suggests it is important for the assessment of conduct problems to include both informants (Loeber, Green, Lahey, & Stouthamer-Loeber, 1989).

Other forms of child psychopathology suffer similar difficulties in defining the prevalence of specific disorders because of the variability of data collection sources. Prevalence rates for ODD and CD vary according to age, sex, geographic location, socioeconomic status, and familial structure and attributes. Conduct disorder was reported in 4.2% of the general population of 10- to 11-year-olds in the Isle of Wight study by Rutter, Tizard, and Whitmore (1970). The rate was 6.2% for boys versus 1.6% for girls in their sample. Similarly, Offord and colleagues (1987) reported an overall prevalence rate of 5.5%, with boys at 8.2% versus 2.8% for girls of their 4- to 16-year-old Canadian population. Cohen et al. (1987) reported CD prevalence rates of 0% and 3% in their sample of preadolescent and adolescent girls, respectively, compared with 8% and 9% for preadolescent and adolescent boys, respectively.

Prevalence rates for ODD have also been compared by gender. For example, the rate for ODD was 3% and 8% for preadolescent and adolescent girls, respectively, and 7% in both age categories for boys in the study of the 775 upstate New York individuals (Cohen et al., 1987). Kashani et al. (1987) reported an overall ODD prevalence rate of 6%, with girls at 8% versus boys as 4% for their 14- to 16-year-old population from Missouri. Kashani, Beck, et al. (1987) identified ODD only if a diagnosis of CD had not coexisted, thus reducing the overall rate. In summary, consistent sex and age differences are evident in the prevalence rates of ODD and CD in several preadolescent and adolescent populations.

The prevalence rate for CD varied little by geographic location in the Isle of Wight population (Rutter, Tizard, & Whitmore, 1970). A rate of 5.6% was reported in the urban sample versus 5.2% in the rural group. However, low socioeconomic status was reported to have doubled the rates of CD when Rutter and colleagues (Rutter, Cox, Tupling, Berger, & Yule, 1975) studied a poor population in London, England.

Several longitudinal studies have identified other factors that affect the prevalence rates for ODD and CD. In addition to low SES, Velez, Johnson, and Cohen (1989) reported family structure (unwed mothers and divorce) and parental attributes (e.g., level of sociopathy) as risk factors for development of disruptive behavioral disorder in their New York population. Similarly, Stanger, McConaughy, and Achenbach (1992) identified SES and marital status (unwed, divorced, or separated) as predictors of delinquent behaviors. Esser et al. (1990) also identified problematic family relations (parental discord, divorce, etc.) as a risk factor for the development of disruptive behaviors in their German population. In summary, low SES, disrupted family structure, and familial sociopathy are identified risk factors associated with increased prevalence rates of ODD and CD.

Comparison of prevalence rates in other common child- and adolescent-onset disorders is helpful in putting the frequency of ODD and CD in perspective. Attention deficit/hyperactivity disorder (ADHD) has been reported to have a prevalence rate between 0.09% and 14.3% in various populations of children (Szatmari, Offord,

& Boyle, 1989). Higher rates for ADHD have been consistent with younger age (Bird et al., 1988), with Szatmari et al. (1989) reporting a peak prevalence of 8% between 6 and 9 years.

Childhood depression has been reported by Kashani and Sherman (1988) to have an incidence rate among a nonreferred sample of 0.9% in preschoolers, 1.9% in school-age children, and 4.7% in adolescents. Bipolar disorder occurs in approximately 1% of the general population. It has not been frequently diagnosed in adolescents and even less often in younger children. Carlson and Kashani (1988) reported 0.6% of their nonreferred population of 150 adolescents (14 to 16 years old) met diagnostic criteria for mania. Anxiety disorders in children and adolescents have been reported to have prevalence rates varying from 5% to 50% (Links, Boyer, & Offord, 1989). Rutter et al. (1970) found diagnosable anxiety disorders in approximately 1% of over 2,000 children (aged 10–11 years) studied in his sample.

To summarize, oppositional defiant and conduct disorders have been reported to have similar prevalence rates to ADHD, but consistently higher rates than depression, bipolar disorder, and anxiety disorders in studies of child and adolescent populations.

Other disorders are often diagnosed concurrently with ODD and CD. Comorbidity becomes an important factor when treatment options are considered (Stoewe, Kruesi, & Lelio, 1994). ADHD is probably the most common comorbidity for ODD or CD. In community studies, Anderson et al. (1987) and Bird et al. (1988) have reported that approximately 45% of children diagnosed with either ODD or CD have a comorbid diagnosis of ADHD, consistent with the range of 30% to 50% reported by Biederman, Newcorn, and Sprich (1991) in their review of the literature. In a clinical sample, an estimate of up to 90% of children referred for conduct disorders (CD and/or ODD) were reported to have ADHD (Abikoff & Klein, 1992).

In comparison, in samples of child and adolescent populations, comorbidity of depression and conduct disorders has been reported to range from 23% to 37% (Carlson & Cantwell, 1980; Kashani, Carlson, et al., 1987; Kovacs, Paulaukas, Gatsonis, & Richards, 1988; Marriage, Fine, Moretti, & Haley, 1986; Puig-Antich, 1982). Anxiety disorders are reported to have a high rate of comorbidity with disruptive disorders. If mood and/or anxiety disorders are considered together, the range of comorbidity (30% to 50%) equals that of ADHD (Zoccolillo, 1992).

MEDICATIONS

Treatment approaches for children and adolescents with disruptive behaviors include behavioral, psychosocial, and pharmacological therapies.

This chapter focuses on psychopharmacological treatments of conduct and oppositional defiant disorders. We will discuss indications for medication in the treatment of conduct/oppositional disorders, evidence for medications most commonly utilized, side effects, and dosage.

When are medication trials indicated? Not all patients with disruptive behavior are appropriate for medication trials (Campbell, Gonzalez, & Silva, 1992). We focus on problematic behavior that has failed to decrease during nonmedication interventions. Medication is likely to be considered when other treatments have failed, when significant aggression is present, or when there are comorbid diagnoses that seem likely to respond to medication (Kruesi & Tolan, in press). Evidence does not generally support medication as a first-line treatment for noncomorbid conduct or oppositional defiant disorder (Campbell, Gonzalez, & Silva, 1992; Stoewe et al., 1994; Werry, 1994). As a framework for understanding medication intervention, we use the following stepwise conception of pharmacological treatment in children and adolescents (Rapoport & Kruesi, 1985):

1. Diagnostic evaluation.
2. Symptom measurement.
3. Risk-benefit ratio analysis.
4. Establishment of a contract of therapy.
5. Periodic reevaluation.
6. Termination or tapered drug withdrawal.

A number of caveats need to be heeded. Interpretation of existing medication trials is complicated by heterogeneous populations, comorbid diagnoses, and the wide range of presenting symptoms, such as aggressive dyscontrol, oppositionality, explosive affect, impaired school performance, anger, irritability, truancy, poor social skills, and impulsivity. Variability of measurement techniques for symptoms adds to the complexity. For example, the definition of aggression is poorly and inconsistently operationalized (Kruesi, Hibbs, et al., 1994).

Defining "aggression" can be pertinent in medication trials. Pharmacological treatment can benefit patients with more severe but relatively less frequent episodes of aggression without significant benefit for patients with less severe but more frequent aggression (Gardner & Cowdry, 1985). Similarly, in the Campbell et al. (1984) study, both haloperidol and lithium were rated as significantly decreasing aggression on the Children's Psychiatric Rating Scale but causing nonsignificant decreases on the conduct factor on Conner's Rating scale. This may be because items on the conduct factor do not explicitly frame physical aggression and most items making up the factor describe other behaviors, thus according physical aggression relatively less weight. In addition, severity, frequency, and chronicity of symptoms differ significantly within populations, suggesting caution in generalizing.

In reviewing evidence from recent psychopharmacological studies on populations of children and adolescents with disruptive disorders, study design also will be taken into account. This chapter will place emphasis on double-blind, placebo-controlled studies for the class of medications described. Case reports and open trials will be used to illustrate certain points or when no controlled and/or blinded trials are available. Case reports and open trials are more likely to be published when the results are positive, thus caution in interpreting results is indicated. Each class of medication will be discussed in terms of effects, clinical usage, dosage, and potential side effects. We have delineated the degree of benefit, the time-course of response, and the dose range.

Antipsychotics (Neuroleptics)

The heading antipsychotics draws attention to issues surrounding use of this class of medications in subjects with nonpsychotic disorders. Campbell, Gonzalez, Ernst, Silva, and Werry (1993) point out that children and adolescents are given neuroleptics for a wide variety of symptoms and diagnoses, frequently differing from those identified in adults. Neuroleptics are most often prescribed in adults demonstrating psychotic symptoms, whereas in children, there is more variability in the targeted symptoms (aggression, dyscontrol, etc.). Table 12.2 outlines "classical" neuroleptics (meaning newer medications such as clozapine or risperidone are excluded), comparing the relative potencies, severity of side effects, approved age of use, and recommended doses (for child and adolescent populations).

Clozapine has been studied in pediatric populations; however, reports focus on psychosis and no study of effects on aggression are available (Frazier et al., 1994; Jacobsen, Walker, Edwards, Chappel, & Woolston, 1994; Towbin, Dykens, & Pugliese, 1994). Reports from adults with schizophrenia (Ratey, Leveroni, Kilmer, Gutheil, & Swartz, 1993; Volavka, Zito, Vitrai, & Czobar, 1993) as well as animals (Garmendia et al., 1992) suggest that the antiaggressive properties of clozapine or other nonclassical neuroleptics may deserve more systematic investigation in individuals with severe aggression who have not responded to other interventions.

Several neuroleptics have demonstrated effectiveness when administered chronically in controlling symptoms of aggression in child and adolescent populations. For instance, haloperidol was reported to be clinically beneficial to a sample of children hospitalized for aggression

Table 12.2. **Neuroleptics**

Category	Name (Generic/Trade)	Relative Potency (equiv. oral dose mg)	Approved Age	Effects* S/A/E	Daily Dose (mg) (Child/Adolescent)
Phenothiazine	Chlorpromazine/ Thorazine	100	>6 mos	3/3/2	10–200/50–600
	Thioridazine/ Mellaril	100	2 yrs	3/3/2	10–200/50–600
	Trifluoperazine/ Stelazine	3–5	6 yrs	2/1/3	2–15/2–40
Butyrophenones	Haloperidol/ Haldol	2	3 yrs	1/1/3	0.5–6/1.5–15
Thioxanthene	Thiothixene/ Navane	5	12 yrs	1/1/3	1–5/5–45
Diphenylbutyl- piperidine	Pimozide/ Orap	10	>12 yrs	1/1/3	—/1–10
Dinydroindolone	Molindone/ Moban	6–10	12 yrs	2/1/1	1–100/75–225
Dibenzoxazepine	Loxapine/ Loxitane	15	16 yrs	2/2/3	—/25–200
Dibenzodiazepine	Clozapine/ Clozaril	75	16 yrs	3/3/—	—/100–800

*Effects: S = Sedation, A = Autonomic (Antiadrenergic, Anticholinergic), E = Extrapyramidal Rxn.
Ratings: 3–High, 2–Moderate, 1–Mild.

(Campbell et al., 1984). The 61 children studied ranged in age from 5 to 12 years, were given the DSM-III diagnosis of conduct disorder, and were of average intelligence. Symptoms of fighting, bullying, and explosiveness improved both clinically and statistically in double-blind, placebo-controlled conditions. Campbell and associates (1984) reported that the group receiving haloperidol were less hyperactive ($t = 3.99$, $p = .001$), less aggressive ($t = 6.50$, $p < .0001$), and less hostile ($t = 3.03$, $p = .007$), than the placebo group; haloperidol was shown to be as effective as lithium.

In another study, an inpatient population of 31 children, aged 6 to 11, with conduct disorder, undersocialized, aggressive type, were treated with molindone hydrochloride and thioridazine, in an 8-week, double-blind, placebo-controlled study (Greenhill, Solomon, Pleak, & Ambrosini, 1985). Symptoms of aggression, hyperactivity, hostility, and social responsiveness improved with the use of molindone hydrochloride or thioridazine when compared with placebo administration. The two medications were similar in their benefits. Another study used pimozide (Orap) with a group of 87 aggressive children (34 were autistic), ranging in age from 3 to 16 years, using a double-blind, placebo-controlled design. Naruse et al. (1982) reported that pimozide and haloperidol had similar benefits in terms of reducing aggression.

Whether neuroleptics have antiaggressive properties or whether the clinical benefit is a result of their sedative properties has long been questioned (Miczek & Barry, 1976). Zametkin and colleagues were interested in the efficacy of a sedating phenothiazine (commonly used for sedation of young children at that time) that lacked significant antipsychotic efficacy for disruptive behavior symptoms in their treatment of ADHD children (without CD). Promethazine hydrochloride and methylphenidate were studied in eight 4- to 12-year-old, clinically referred outpatient children (7 boys/1 girl) in a 2-week open crossover study (Zametkin, Reeves, Webster, & Werry, 1986). Four of the children showed behavioral deterioration (increased aggression, hypermotility, impulsivity, agitation, etc.), while the other children showed no clinical improvement with promethazine administration. Despite the previously reported benefits of phenothiazines in childhood psychopathology (Winsberg & Yepes, 1978), promethazine was behaviorally ineffective in the individuals studied. Thus, this more chronic (2 weeks) use of sedatives corresponds to the acute sedative (diphenhydramine) trial of Vitiello et al. (1991) in suggesting sedative properties alone are insufficient for aggression reduction.

Neuroleptics also are known to be used clinically on a p.r.n. (*pro re nata* "as needed") basis for acute aggressive, disruptive, or self-injurious behavior, particularly when the behavior is not responsive to nonpharmacological intervention (Ahsanuddin et al., 1983; Vitiello, Ricciuti, &

Behar, 1987). But no controlled trial documenting the benefit of neuroleptics over placebo in p.r.n. usage has been conducted in pediatric patients.

Side Effects. Despite evidence for the benefits of neuroleptics in children and adolescents with disruptive behaviors, potential adverse effects have made clinicians wary of prescribing them. Tardive dyskinesia (TD) and cognitive impairment have been reported in individuals treated with neuroleptics, as well as extrapyramidal effects, akathisia, and hypotension.

A recent trial by Klein (1991) challenged the view that cognitive impairment is likely with neuroleptic treatment. Thirty-seven ADHD children, aged 6 to 12 years, receiving thioridazine (mean dose, 193 mg at 4 weeks, 160 mg at the end of 12 weeks), were compared with 40 ADHD children on placebo. The impact of thioridazine on cognitive performance was minimal. Complete review of medication effects on learning and cognition in pediatric patients can be found elsewhere (Werry, 1988).

Tardive dyskinesia may be severely disabling and irreversible, and may develop within only a few days following the initiation of the medication. Campbell, Grega, Green, and Bennett (1983) reported the prevalence of tardive and withdrawal dyskinesias in children receiving neuroleptics to range from 8% to 51%. Unfortunately, they did not differentiate TD and withdrawal dyskinesias. Difficulties in differentiating tardive dyskinesia from stereotypies have been reported (Shay et al., 1993). In a study of autistic children, blind raters of videotapes could only differentiate dyskinesias from stereotypies 59% of the time (Shay et al., 1993).

Neuroleptic malignant syndrome (NMS) has been reported in persons receiving neuroleptics regardless of the age of the individual or the specific category of neuroleptic. This is a life-threatening condition with symptoms of severe muscular rigidity, stupor, autonomic lability, altered consciousness, hyperpyrexia, and raised creatinine phosphokinase. Onset usually follows the initiation or a change in dose of neuroleptic therapy. Steingard, Khan, Gonzalez, and Herzog (1992) discovered 35 reported cases of NMS, while Latz and McCracken (1992) discovered 49 cases; both groups performed literature searches of the previous 20 years. They concur that NMS is a rarely reported occurrence in this population, but that the mortality rate of 14% (Steingard et al., 1992) to 16% (Latz & McCracken, 1992) warrants close monitoring, early evaluation, and rapid treatment.

Dosing. Anderson et al. (1984) reported an optimal dose of 0.5–3.0 mg of haloperidol per day and Campbell and colleagues (1984) reported an optimal dose range of 1.0–6.0 mg per day in their population of children with CD. Greenhill and colleagues (1985) reported initiating molindone hydrochloride at 25 mg and thioridazine at 125 mg per day; the overall mean molindone dose was 26.8 mg per day (1.3 mg/kg/day; chlorpromazine equivalents: 270 mg/day) and the overall mean thioridazine dose was 169.9 mg per day (4.64 mg/kg/day; chlorpromazine equivalents: 169.9 mg). Clinical evaluation of the efficacy of a particular medication takes precedence over blood levels and suggested dosing because of the variability of the individual response. To summarize, studies reporting neuroleptics to be beneficial for aggression/conduct disorder use a range of 25–300 mg of chlorpromazine equivalents per day, which is consistent with other recommendations for doses of less than 5 mg/kg/day of chlorpromazine equivalents in pediatric behavior disorders (Campbell et al., 1993; Whitaker & Rao, 1992).

In clinical practice, when neuroleptics are used for aggression on a recurrent basis as opposed to imminent dangerousness, dose is started at 25–50 mg of chlorpromazine equivalents and increased by a similar increment every three days until aggression lessens. In the case of imminent dangerousness in an adolescent where oral medication is not possible, 1–2 cc of droperidol IM or 25–50 mg chlorpromazine IM may be used as an initial dose depending on clinical necessity.

Antidepressants

Antidepressants have been studied in a variety of diagnoses in children and adolescents including recent studies of the newer serotonin reuptake inhibitors in populations of depressed, hyperactive, and/or obsessional children and adolescents. However, limited research has been done on response to antidepressants of CD and/or ODD in child and adolescent populations. Table 12.3 outlines this class of medications by comparing sedative potential, anticholinergic property, starting doses, and common side effects.

Depression is frequently comorbid with conduct disorder. An early clinical recognition by Cytryn and McKnew (1972) referred to "masked" depression wherein conduct disorder was obvious but "cloaked" a depression. The exciting possibility that antidepressant treatment would benefit this group of patients with "mixed" conduct and depression was raised by a report from Puig-Antich (1982). Thirteen such comorbid boys received imipramine treatment and had symptomatic improvement in their depression. In this mixed disorder group, subjects experienced onset of depression before their conduct disorder. With remission of depression, 11 of 13 (85%) had improvement of their conduct disorder.

Unfortunately, tricyclics have not proved significantly more efficacious than placebo in pediatric patients with depression (for reviews see Ambrosini, Bianchi, Rabinovich, & Elia, 1993; Jensen, Ryan, & Prien, 1992). A decade later, Puig-Antich's statement (1982) that antidepres-

Table 12.3. **Antidepressants**

Category	Name (Generic/Trade)	Neurotransmitters	Effects[a] S/A	Common Starting Dose (mg) (Child/Adolescent)
Tricyclic				
3 Amines	Imipramine/Tofranil	Acetylcholine (1); NE & 5-HT (2)	3 4	25–50/50–75
	Amitriptyline/Elavil	Acetylcholine (1); 5-HT (2)	5 5	—/50
2 Amines	Desipramine/Norpramine	Norepinephrine	1 1	—/25–50
	Nortriptyline/Pamelor	ACH & NE (1) 5-HT (2)	2 3	25/25
Tetracyclic	Maprotiline/Ludiomil	Norepinephrine	4 2	—/75
Triazolopyridine	Trazodonel/Desyrel	Serotonin	5 2	—/150
Benzenepropanamine	Fluoxetine/Prozac	Serotonin	1 1	5–10/20
Propiophenone	Buproprion/Wellbutrin	Dopamine	1 1	—/200

[a] Effects: S = Sedation, A = Anticholinergic.
Ratings: 5–High, 4–Low-High, 3–Moderate, 2–Mild, 1–Low-Mild.

sant treatment is not a panacea for conduct disorder still holds, as does his call for well-designed, double-blind, placebo-controlled studies in a carefully selected sample of prepubertal children who simultaneously meet criteria for major depression and conduct disorder. Because tricyclics are efficacious for the broad band of disruptive behavior disorders (Biederman, Baldessarini, Wright, Keenan, & Faraone, 1993), this understudied question deserves more scrutiny. Sixty-two 6- to 17-year-old children with ADD and comorbid conduct and oppositional symptoms were treated with desipramine in a randomized, double-blind, placebo-controlled study (Biederman et al., 1993). Comorbidity of depression, anxiety, or conduct disorder with ADHD or a family history of ADHD did not alter response to desipramine or placebo.

Yepes and colleagues (Yepes, Balka, Winsberg, & Bialer, 1977) studied 24 children, aged 7 to 13 years, who showed evidence of hyperactivity and/or aggressivity, in a double-blind, placebo-controlled, crossover trial with methylphenidate and amitriptyline in a 2-week treatment duration. Of these subjects, 8% responded only to amitriptyline, 33% only to methylphenidate, and 21% to both drugs; 33% showed no benefit from either medication.

A possible biochemical rationale for use of newer antidepressants which have prominent serotonergic effects comes from adult and pediatric studies finding associations between aggressive and/or disruptive behavior and altered serotonergic function (Brown et al., 1986; Coccaro, Kavoussi, & Lesser, 1992; Kruesi, 1989; Kruesi, Linnoila, Rapoport, Brown, & Peterson, 1985; Kruesi, Rapoport, et al., 1990; Kruesi, Swedo, Leonard, Rubinow, & Rapoport, 1990; Kruesi et al., 1992; Linnoila & Virkkunen, 1992; Stoff et al., 1992). A recent study of children and adolescents with disruptive behavior disorders has found significant inverse correlations between the cerebrospinal fluid concentration of the serotonin metabolite, 5-hydroxyindoleacetic acid (5-HIAA), and aggression measures both historically, and on prospective follow-up (Kruesi, Rapoport, et al., 1990; Kruesi et al., 1992).

Trazodone alone or in combination with the amino acid precursor of serotonin, tryptophan, has serotonergic effects. Open trials in adults suggest benefit (O'Neill, Page, & Adkins, 1986; Pinner & Rich, 1988). More recently, two open trials in pediatric age groups found similarly encouraging results. In an open trial of 3 children (aged 7–9) with diagnoses of disruptive disorder, all of them showed a significant decrease of aggression using 75 mg of trazodone (Ghazziudin & Alessi, 1992). From the ODD diagnostic group, the item "often argues with adults" improved by 67% and "often loses temper" improved 60% in 22 hospitalized children (aged 5–12) described as behaviorally disturbed and treatment-resistant (Zubieta & Alessi, 1992). Diagnoses included disruptive behavior disorders, anxiety disorders, mood disorders, psychotic disorders, developmental delays, learning disability, and speech and language disorders. The most frequent improvement in the conduct-disordered group was in "cruelty to people" and "frequency of fights" (63% and 57% of cases respectively). Improvement of outward aggression was found most frequently in 70% of patients (14 of 20) as evaluated by the Iowa-Conners (Loney & Milich, 1985).

Fluoxetine was the first specific serotonergic reuptake inhibitor (SSRI) marketed in the United States. Markowitz (1992) studied 21 severely to profoundly mentally retarded individuals, ranging in age from 17 to 56 years, who demonstrated self-injurious, emotionally labile, and aggressive behaviors and were treated in an open study with fluoxetine (Prozac). Nineteen subjects (86%) were reported to be responders to fluoxetine (13—marked; 4—moderate; 2—mild) by global ratings of behavior. Although retarded patients had reductions in aggression with fluoxetine, generalizing these results to nonretarded children is ill advised. As discussed later, considerable differences were seen in the responses of retarded and nonretarded individuals to fenfluramine.

Side Effects. Because of reports of three deaths possibly related to the administration of desipramine (Norpramin) in two 8-year-old boys and one 9-year-old boy, concern about side effects with tricyclic antidepressants has focused on cardiac arrhythmias (Riddle et al., 1991). Each boy had received desipramine for at least 6 months prior to death.

Riddle, Geller, and Ryan (1993) reported a fourth case of sudden death also possibly related to the administration of desipramine. A 12-year-old girl had received desipramine for 6 months for symptoms of ADHD, with the cause of death related to cardiac arrhythmia.

Other less severe, but still bothersome side effects also have been described with the administration of antidepressants, including drowsiness (96% of study population, Yepes et al., 1977), seizures, anxiety, insomnia, confusion, psychosis, nausea, vomiting, dry mouth, blurred vision, constipation, impotence, headaches, tremor, skin rash, dizziness, hypomania, and changes in sex drive.

In the trial involving 22 children on trazodone, side effects noted were orthostatic hypotension (50%), drowsiness (27%), increased nervousness (9%) and miscellaneous other complaints occurring in individual children (Zubieta & Alessi, 1992). One child experienced painful erections. Painful priapism occurs in adults at a rate of about 1:15,000 (Carson & Mino, 1988) and can occur in pediatric patients. Trazodone (Desyrel) has been implicated in cases of priapism in both adolescent and adult males. Warner and colleagues (Warner, Peabody, Whiteford, & Hollister, 1987) reported 57 cases ranging in age from 14 to 64 years of trazodone-related priapism from a review of data from a reporting system of the Food and Drug Administration. Most of the cases occurred within the first 28 days of treatment and with daily doses of 150 mg/day or less (Warner et al., 1987). The treatment is a surgical emergency and although rare, the possibility must be considered when trazodone is prescribed.

Dosing. Due to the limited studies on symptoms related to the diagnosis of either ODD or CD, optimal dosing is less than certain. Most clinicians use doses of tricyclics comparable to those tried for other diagnoses. Antidepressants for the treatment of symptoms related to depression, obsessive thoughts, enuresis, and anxiety in child and adolescent populations are outlined in other chapters of this book, and describe this information in detail.

The dosage of trazodone started at 50 mg/day and increased to a maximum dose of 4.8 mg/kg/day plus or minus 1.7 mg/kg/day in divided doses in the Zubieta and Alessi study.

Lithium

Lithium carbonate has been used in child and adolescent populations for control of severe aggression and symptoms of mania. Campbell and colleagues (1984, 1995) have repeatedly demonstrated the efficacy of lithium for aggression in conduct disorder in double-blind, placebo-controlled trials. The earlier study demonstrated clinical and statistical superiority of lithium carbonate (and haloperidol) over placebo. The recent replication (Campbell et al., 1995) examined an additional 50 inpatient children with conduct disorder and treatment-refractory explosive aggressiveness. The pattern of behavioral benefit from lithium was very similar in both studies: Global ratings improved but scores on Conners Teacher rating scales did not. Additional support that more physically aggressive symptoms respond to lithium comes from a study of 66 institutionalized adolescents and young adults, who probably met conduct disorder criteria, which found that the number of major infractions decreased with lithium treatment (Sheard, Marini, Bridges, & Wagner, 1976). Not all aggressive and/or conduct-disordered individuals respond to lithium. Open studies report response rates for lithium in children and adolescents ranging from a low of 15% (Delong & Aldershof, 1987) to as high as 76% (Vetro, Szentistvanyi, Pallag, Vargha, & Szilard, 1985). In both the Campbell et al. studies noted previously, there were subjects who improved significantly on placebo.

Reports of no significant benefit or behavioral worsening with lithium treatment of conduct disorder or aggression exist. Rifkin and colleagues (Rifkin, Karajgi, Boppana, & Pearl, 1989; Rifkin, 1992) performed a 2-week study comparing lithium to placebo on a group of hospitalized adolescents diagnosed with CD (without ADHD) and reported no evidence of improvement with lithium versus placebo. Similarly, in a review of pharmacological treatments for CD children, Abikoff and Klein (1992) note their negative trial of lithium in a group of 80 children and adolescents with conduct disorder (Klein, Abikoff, Klass, Shah, & Seese, 1994). Outpatients, aged 6 to 15, were assigned to a double-blind trial of lithium, methylphenidate, or placebo. Methylphenidate produced improvement over placebo but lithium did not. A possible distinction between this sample and those of Campbell et al. (1984, 1995) is that the outpatient sample (Klein et al., 1994) lacked explosiveness. Others have reported cases of worsening of aggression with lithium (Dale, 1980; Worrall, Moody, & Naylor, 1975).

Integrating results from the preceding positive and negative studies leads to a few conclusions. Lithium is obviously not a panacea for conduct disorder but is likely to be beneficial for at least some. The benefit is more apt to be seen on larger, more severe aggressive behaviors. When trials are carried out, they must be longer than 2 weeks. Based on the results of the preceding studies, 8 weeks appears a reasonable duration for a trial. Data from the lithium trials adds to the growing literature suggesting subtyping aggression is likely to be useful in pharmacological trials.

Side Effects. Potential side effects of lithium administration have been described in several studies of adult and child and adolescent populations. Most of these untoward effects diminish or disappear within the first 2 weeks of administration. Fine tremor, polydipsia, polyuria, nausea, malaise, diarrhea, headache, sedation, weight gain, anorexia, exacerbation of acne, hypothyroidism, hair loss, and leukocytosis are some of the side effects associated with lithium usage. An analysis of the data collected by Campbell and colleagues (1984) contrasted side effects associated with lithium administration to those reported with placebo in the sample of hospitalized, aggressive children (Silva et al., 1992). Forty of the 46 children (87%) who received lithium and 21 of the 45 (47%) receiving placebo experienced side effects; the most commonly experienced side effects shared between the groups were vomiting, headache, and stomachache; enuresis, fatigue, and ataxia were seen only in the lithium group. Tremor was also noted in 26% of the individuals who received lithium (12 of 46).

Campbell and associates (Campbell et al., 1991) reported an inverse correlation between the development of side effects and the age of the individual receiving lithium in a group of 5- to 12-year-olds. The potential untoward effects associated with lithium should alert the prescribing physician to investigate baseline symptoms, along with laboratory indicators of underlying abnormalities prior to initiating medication.

Dosing. Baseline electrolytes, creatinine, thyroid function, urinalysis, and behavior measures are gathered prior to initiating lithium treatment. A pretreatment EKG is useful for comparison, but is not considered mandatory for all pediatric lithium candidates (Green, 1991). When initiated for conduct disorder, our preference is to start the dose low (e.g., 150 mg per dose) using a b.i.d. and later if needed a t.i.d. schedule. After 2 days, titrate upward every 2 to 3 days as tolerated and as determined by serum concentration to reach a serum concentration of 0.6–1.2 mEq/L. Studies documenting benefit have reported serum levels from 0.32 to 1.51 mEq/L (Campbell et al., 1984; Vetro et al., 1985). Vitiello et al. (1988) studied the pharmacokinetics of lithium carbonate in a group of children ranging in age from 9 to 12 years and reported a shorter half-life and a higher total renal clearance compared with adults. This becomes important clinically as steady-state and therapeutic blood levels can be reached more rapidly in children.

To summarize, at least some children and adolescents with aggressive symptoms and/or CD diagnoses may benefit from lithium administration, and side effects can be minimized with baseline laboratory tests and monitoring of serum lithium levels. As discussed earlier, an 8-week trial is likely to be sufficient to clarify therapeutic response.

Anticonvulsants

Few studies are available that have looked at the efficacy of anticonvulsants for the population of children and adolescents with CD or ODD. Table 12.4 lists the most common anticonvulsants and compares half-life, therapeutic dose range, and common side effects.

In an open study, Kafantaris et al. (1992) studied 10 hospitalized children (aged 5–11 years), with aggressiveness and explosiveness, and diagnosed as having CD, who received carbamazepine (Tegretol) treatment. They reported clinical and statistical improvements in targeted symptoms (i.e., fighting with peers, bullying, temper outbursts, impulsivity, inattention, frustration, and mood changes) according to symptom instruments and clinician ratings in 9 of the 10 (90%) subjects (4—markedly improved; 4—moderately improved; 1—slightly improved). In support of their findings of efficacy with carbamazepine, 4 of the 10 children (40%) who responded had been previous nonresponders to lithium. Of this group, 3 children markedly improved and 1 moderately improved with carbamazepine (1 child did not respond to either medication).

Carbamazepine (CBZ) also was studied by Groh (1975) in a population of 20 nonepileptic children and adolescents with symptoms correlating with the diagnosis of CD, utilizing a double-blind, placebo-controlled crossover design, reporting significant improvements in behavior problems, drive, mood, anxiety, and aggression with carbamazepine administration. Another controlled trial of CBZ in children with conduct disorder demonstrated significant improvement (Puente, 1976). Both studies provide only limited methodological information, and neither is

Table 12.4. Anticonvulsants

Name (Generic/Trade)	Half-Life (hours)	Common Dose (mg/kg/day)	Therapeutic Range (μg/ml)	Side Effects
Carbamazepine/ Tegretol	10–25	10–40	5–14	Drowsiness, headache, hepatotoxicity, blood dyscrasia
Phenytoin Dilantin	5–27	4–8	10–20	Drowsiness, gingival hyperplasia, anemia, ataxia, tremor, nystagmus
Valproic Acid/ Depakene or Depakote	5–18	50–100	50–100	GI upset, drowsiness, hepatitis, ataxia, tremors
Clonazepam/ Klonopin	24–40	0.05–0.10	N/A	Drowsiness, ataxia, behavioral problems

in a peer-reviewed journal. Nonetheless, until subsequent blinded and controlled trials are available, these remain landmarks.

Additional open studies (Mattes, 1990; Vincent, Unis, & Hardy, 1990) also support the efficacy of carbamazepine in populations of aggressive children and adolescents. Vincent et al. (1990) reported a 70% responder rate in terms of individual improvement in aggressive, hyperactive, and delinquent symptoms with their population. Mattes (1990) reported improvements in mean severity ratings for assaultiveness in a group of 80 inpatients (16 years of age or more) treated with either carbamazepine or propranolol (adolescent vs. adult responses were not analyzed separately).

As evident in the previously mentioned studies, carbamazepine has been shown to be an effective agent in adult, child, and adolescent populations with a diagnosis of CD and/or symptoms of aggression, impulsivity, and temper outbursts. However, worsening of aggression with carbamazepine has also been reported (Meyers & Carrerra, 1989; Pleak et al., 1988; Silverstein, Parrish, & Johnston, 1982). Some of the cases of worsening of aggression can be explained on the basis of a "switch" into mania precipitated or exacerbated by carbamazepine.

Other anticonvulsants are less studied in child and adolescent populations with conduct or oppositional defiant disorders but have been used in adult populations with various presentations. Valproic acid (Depakene; Depakote) has become increasingly popular in the treatment of bipolar disorder in adults (Bowden et al., 1994), and phenytoin (Dilantin) was reported to significantly reduce the frequency of aggressive acts in an adult male, inmate population (Barratt, Kent, Bryant, & Felthous, 1991). Phenytoin was also used in blinded controlled studies of pediatric populations; however, benefit was not reported in terms of symptoms of severe aggressivity and disruptiveness (Conners et al., 1971; Lefkowitz, 1969).

Side Effects. Kafantaris and colleagues (1992) reported that the side effects experienced by their population did not warrant discontinuation of carbamazepine in any of the children studied. They reported worsening of behavioral symptoms, loosening of associations, and transient decreases in white blood cell counts. Additional side effects include drowsiness, light-headedness, clumsiness, nausea, blurred vision, nystagmus, skin rashes (acne, folliculitis, xerosis cutis, psoriasis, cutaneous ulcers, etc.), liver toxicity, psychosis, and induction of liver enzymes (leading to decreased levels of carbamazepine).

Hyponatremia has been described in adults, ranging from 6% to 31% (Lahr, 1985; Yassa et al., 1987), but thus far not reported in children or adolescents receiving carbamazepine. Side effects have been more commonly reported with rapid dose increases and when exceeding the therapeutic serum range of 4–12 µg/ml. A baseline physical exam and laboratory tests are recommended prior to the initiation of carbamazepine; these tests should include complete blood count with differential, liver function tests, renal function tests, and an electrocardiogram. Follow-up lab tests are also recommended to assess bone marrow, liver, and kidney functions.

Dosing. Following baseline evaluations and assessments, carbamazepine (Tegretol) was administered by Kafantaris and colleagues (1992) in the range of 200–800 mgs per day; serum concentrations did not exceed 12 µg/ml. The most effective dose range for carbamazepine has been reported to be between 10 and 50 mg/kg of body weight per day, with a starting dose of 100 mg per day and weekly dose increments of 100 mg (Trimble, 1990). A divided dosing regime of 2 to 3 times per day is also recommended. Barratt and colleagues (1991) administered phenytoin to their population of inmates at 100 mg or 300 mg per day. Conners et al. (1971) gave 200 mg/day of phenytoin to the 9- to 14-year-old boys in their study. Thus, dose is unlikely to explain the discrepancy in results.

After baseline laboratory studies, carbamazepine is started at 50 to 100 mg b.i.d. and increased by 100 mg weekly to a t.i.d. schedule using serum concentrations and clinical response as indicators.

Stimulants

This class of medications consists of methylphenidate (Ritalin), magnesium pemoline (Cylert), and dextroamphetamine (Dexedrine). What follows is a selective review of stimulant studies focusing on conduct, oppositional, and/or aggressive behavior. Table 12.5 outlines this class of medications and compares serum half-life, peak serum levels, age of approval, starting dose, and maximum recommended daily dosing of each medication.

As noted earlier, CD and ODD have a high rate of comorbidity with ADHD; consequently, many studies of child and adolescent populations with ADHD actually include a larger variety of symptom presentations. Several studies have found that conduct-disordered children have a poorer prognosis when they have comorbid ADHD than when CD is diagnosed alone (Magnusson & Bergman, 1988; Walker, Lahey, Hynd, & Frame, 1987).

In reviewing studies of methylphenidate's effects on aggression in pediatric patients Campbell and colleagues (Campbell, Gonzalez, & Silva, 1992) postulated that severity of aggression may be a significant factor in the clinical effectiveness of methylphenidate (milder symptoms respond better to methylphenidate). Yepes and colleagues (1977) reported that methylphenidate was effective (according to improved scores

Table 12.5. Stimulants

Name (Generic/Trade)	Half-Life (hours)	Peak Serum Time (range in hours)	Approved Age (years)	Maximal Dose (mg/day)	Side Effects
Methylphenidate/ Ritalin	2–3 (reg.)[a] 3–5 (SR)[b]	0.5–3 (Reg.)	>6	60	Insomnia, appetite, moodiness, anxiousness, HR
Magnesium Pemoline/ Cylert	8–10	2–4	>6	112.5	Insomnia, appetite, elevated liver, enzymes
D-Amphetamine Sulfate/ Dexedrine[c]	3–5	1–2	>3	40	Insomnia, appetite, irritability, HR

[a] Reg. = Regular form of methylphenidate.
[b] SR = Slow Release form.
[c] Sustained release form also available.

utilizing behavioral rating scales and performance tasks) in reducing symptoms of hyperactivity and aggressivity in 33% of the 22 children with diagnoses of hyperkinetic reaction of childhood (DSM-II) studied in a double-blind, placebo-controlled, crossover study design.

Kaplan, Busner, Kupietz, Wasserman, and Segal (1990) were interested in the effects of stimulants on symptoms of aggression in a population of nine 13- to 16-year-old boys with both ADHD plus CD or ODD diagnoses. Three subjects were studied in an open design and six were studied in a double-blind, placebo-controlled, crossover design utilizing methylphenidate. In the open study, total score ratings focusing on aggression and hyperactivity scales were lower with the use of methylphenidate when compared with the drug-free baseline. Similarly, the double-blind trials produced significant improvements in four out of the six subscales (physical threats, verbal harm, responsibility difficulties, and violations of rules; but not for physical harm or damage to property).

Improvement in verbal aggression but not physical aggression is consistent with the interpretation of Campbell et al. (1992). Hinshaw, Heller, and McHale (1992) compared a control group with 22 boys (aged 6–12 years) diagnosed with ADHD on covert antisocial behaviors such as stealing, property destruction, and cheating in a laboratory situation. A video-camera recorded boys' behavior in sessions where they believed they were unobserved. The frequency of covert conduct disorder behaviors was assessed in the ADHD group in a methylphenidate/placebo crossover study. At the start, 38% of the comparison group and 64% of the ADHD participants stole at least one object; 18% and 43% of each group stole money, respectively; whereas 14% of the comparison group sessions and 36% of the sessions with ADHD subjects showed property destruction; 25% and 52% of the comparison and ADHD participant sessions involved cheating. The authors (Hinshaw et al., 1992) reported that stealing and property destruction behaviors improved with methylphenidate administration; however, cheating was increased with methylphenidate in their ADHD population (explained as improved on-task involvement and motivation). This gives evidence that methylphenidate does improve some CD symptoms in a population of ADHD males.

Dextroamphetamine was reported to have a significant effect ($p < 0.05$) on aggressive behavior (amount of time spent hitting a bop bag) in a group of 10 boys diagnosed with ADHD plus prevalent conduct problems, under double-blind, placebo-controlled conditions (Amery, Minichiello, & Brown, 1984). Pemoline has long been recognized as ameliorating ADHD symptoms as measured by the Conners Teacher Questionnaire including items such as defiance similar to the other two stimulants (Conners et al., 1972) but no studies have been published that specifically address conduct disorder symptoms such as physical aggression or theft.

Side Effects.   Side effects are relatively consistent across this class of medications. The most common adverse effects are anorexia, insomnia, headaches, stomachaches, tearfulness, dizziness, emotional lability, and paradoxical worsening of symptoms. Less commonly experienced effects are social withdrawal, psychosis, growth reduction, weight loss, and development of abnormal movements. The frequency and severity of reported side effects vary and may or may not result in the discontinuation of the medication. Yepes and colleagues (Yepes et al., 1977) reported the most frequently experienced side effects of methylphenidate were anorexia (33%), insomnia (16%), and headaches (12%); less common were abdominal cramps, nightmares, tremor, listlessness, irritability, and bad taste in the mouth. Caution with stimulant use in patients with a history of tics or a family history of Tourette's disorder is warranted. Stimulants prescribed with MAOI antidepressants may potentially lead to a hypertensive emergency.

Dosing.   Optimal dosing of stimulants depends on the targeted symptoms and the side effects. A dose range of methylphenidate for symptoms of aggression has been reported as 0.3–2.0 mg/kg/day; dose range of dextroamphetamine reported as 0.25–1.5 mg/kg/day for aggression. Single doses of methylphenidate or amphetamine rarely exceed 1.0 or 0.5 mg/kg respectively. For example, the Kaplan and colleagues (1990) study that found a beneficial effect on aggression used a maximum of 30 mg per dose of methylphenidate. The actual dose received ranged from 0.36–0.56 mg/kg of body weight.

Campbell and colleagues (1992) note that side effects were reported more frequently with daily doses of methylphenidate in excess of 1.0 mg/kg (weight loss, tics, self-injurious behavior). Amery and colleagues (1984) treated their group of boys with dextroamphetamine ranging from 15–30 mg/day (0.75 mg/kg/day in 2 doses) over a 2-week period.

Green (1991) recommends starting with 5 mg of methylphenidate once or twice daily, raising the dose gradually by 5–10 mg per week, with the optimal dose range of 0.3–0.7 mg/kg/dose or 0.9–2.1 mg/kg/day. He also recommends starting with 2.5–5 mg of dextroamphetamine daily, increasing the dose by 5 mg one to two times per week, with the optimal dose falling between 0.15 and 0.5 mg/kg/dose or 0.3–1.5 mg/kg/day. Additionally, a starting dose of 37.5 mg of magnesium pemoline, increasing weekly by 18.75 mg, with the maximum daily dose of 112.5 mg, was also outlined by Green (1991).

Clonidine

Clonidine is an alpha-adrenergic agonist that acts by inhibiting the release of noradrenaline and lowering serotonin. In adults, clonidine has been used for the treatment of opiate withdrawal, aggression, mania, anxiety, and neuroleptic-induced movement disorders. There are no FDA-approved uses of clonidine in the treatment of children and adolescents; however, it has been used in the treatment of ADHD and tic disorders, such as Tourette's syndrome (Hunt, Capper, & O'Connell, 1990). Hunt and colleagues (1985) studied ADHD children treated with clonidine in a double-blind, placebo-controlled, crossover study, and reported a 70% response rate, with improvements noted as decreased motor activity, increased frustration tolerance, increased compliance and cooperation. Double-blind data in pediatric populations focusing specifically on aggressive behavior or children with CD or ODD diagnoses are not yet available.

Another open pilot study utilizing clonidine was performed on 17 aggressive children and adolescent outpatients (aged 5–15 years) who met DSM-III-R diagnostic criteria for CD or ODD (Kemph, DeVane, Levin, Jarecke, & Miller, 1993). Fifteen patients treated with clonidine for 1 to 18 months showed at least a decrease on the global impression of aggressiveness from a level of 5 (intolerable behavior; frequently physically attacks others and destroys property) to 3 (moderately severe; either fights or is destructive). Three of the individuals with a pretreatment score of 5 were scored 1 (no aggressiveness reported) on their follow-up; and seven were scored 2 (mild; verbally abusive and resistive) on their follow-up.

Additional impetus for controlled trials on aggression and/or oppositional behavior are data that suggest clinical usage of clonidine is increasing for these problems (Stoewe et al., 1994).

Side Effects.   Drowsiness or sedation has been the most commonly reported untoward effect (Hunt et al., 1990; Kemph et al., 1993). Other common side effects include hypotension, decreased pulse rate, headache, dizziness, nausea, and stomachache. Drowsiness usually appears in the first 2 to 3 weeks of clonidine use and is quickly tolerated; occurring at a peak of 1 hour after ingestion and a duration of 30 to 60 minutes (Green, 1991). Regular checks of cardiovascular parameters (pulse and blood pressure) are recommended. Dermatologic reactions to the transdermal form are common. Comings, Comings, Tacket, and Li (1990) reported that 30% of their total population experienced a localized skin reaction to the clonidine patch.

Less common side effects are rebound hypertension, anticholinergic effects, and depression. Precocious pubertal development was attributed to oral clonidine use in two children (Levin, Burton-Teston, & Murphy, 1993).

Dosing.   Based on a review of the relevant literature (Hunt et al., 1990; Kemph et al., 1993), the following practice is recommended: a starting dose of 0.05 mg at bedtime, with a dosing increase of 0.05 mg every 3 days in 3–4 divided daily doses; reaching a total daily dose of 0.15–0.4 mg (or 3–6 μg/kg per day). The transdermal patch may enhance compliance with a final dosing between one-quarter and two 0.1 mg patches (Comings et al., 1990); however, localized dermatologic reactions can limit use. The duration of effectiveness for the transdermal route is between 5 and 7 days. Clonidine should be tapered for discontinuation to avoid rebound hypertension.

Beta-Adrenergic Blockers

This class of medications includes propranolol (Inderal), atenolol (Tenormin), metoprolol (Lopressor), nadolol (Corgard), and pindolol (Visken), which were initially used for control of hypertension, angina pectoris, and other cardiovascular problems. More recently, beta blockers have been used in psychiatry. For instance, because beta blockers reduce peripheral autonomic tone, they have been reported effective in decreasing the symptoms of anxiety, related to autonomic activation. Beta blockers also may reduce symptoms of posttraumatic stress disorder (Famularo, Kenscherff, & Fenton, 1988), episodic dyscontrol (Grizenko & Vida, 1988), and aggression (Greendyke, Kanter, Schuster, Verstreate, & Wooton, 1986; Kuperman & Stewart, 1987) in some populations of adults, children, and adolescents. Problematic symptoms of aggression have been mostly studied with beta blockers in populations of organically brain-damaged individuals (Greendyke & Kanter, 1986; Ratey, Morill, & Oxenkrug, 1983; Yudofsky, Williams, & Gorman, 1981); there have been very few studies which address efficacy of beta blockers in children and adolescents diagnosed with CD or ODD. Table 12.6 outlines this class of medications and compares them in terms of specific receptor sites of action, half-life, and dosing guidelines (if available).

Table 12.6.   Beta-Adrenergic Blockers

Name (Generic/Trade)	Half-Life (hours)	B-Receptor Affinity	Starting Dose in Children/Adolescent (mg/kg/day)
Propanolol/ Inderal	2–9	Nonselective	1–2
Metoprolol/ Lopressor	3–7	Beta-1	1–2
Nadolol/Corgard	20–24	Nonselective	0.5–2.0
Atenolol/Tenormin	6–7	Beta-1	Unknown
Pindolol/	8	Nonselective	Unknown

Samples of children and adolescents diagnosed with CD and/or ODD, have not yet been reported in double-blind, placebo-controlled studies utilizing beta-adrenergic blocking medications. One group (Sims & Galvin, 1990) reported on two child cases treated with propranolol in open conditions who were diagnosed with CD and no identified organic cause of their symptoms. Sims reviewed the chart on a 5-year-old boy diagnosed with CD, undersocialized, aggressive type, previously treated with a psychostimulant and a neuroleptic (with limited results), and hospitalized for disruptive and aggressive behaviors toward peers and adults. They reported a decrease in the total number of hours of seclusion and improvement in his aggressiveness and agitation (minimal improvement), according to the CTRS and a global assessment.

Sims and Galvin (1990) also reviewed the chart on a 14-year-old boy previously treated with methylphenidate, who had been diagnosed with CD, solitary, aggressive type, and hospitalized due to assaultive and aggressive behavior. Some decrease in his aggressive behavior (minimal improvement) was noted but dosing was limited by side effects. These reports were limited by their retrospective nature and should be supported by further studies of this select population.

An open-design study using propranolol was reported by Kuperman and Stewart (1987), who were interested in the treatment of physically aggressive behavior in 16 subjects, 12 of whom were between 4 and 17 years. Seven subjects were diagnosed with CD, undersocialized, aggressive type (5 were autistic, 2 were moderately retarded, 1 had borderline intellectual functioning, and 1 had ADHD), and all demonstrated physically aggressive behavior as the main problem. Ten of the 16 subjects (62.5%) were rated moderately or much improved according to the ratings by parents, teachers, and clinicians following at least a 3-month trial of propranolol. Two of the nonresponders had shown an initial, marked decrease in their aggressive behaviors, but became noncompliant when discharged from the unit. This study suggests a role for propranolol in the treatment of aggression in CD and other diagnosed individuals, but adequate studies utilizing atenolol, nadolol, or pindolol have not been conducted. Matthews-Ferrari and Karroum (1992) reported on using metoprolol in an 11-year-old boy for control of severe aggressive outbursts that had been previously treated unsuccessfully with methylphenidate and carbamazepine. Further research is still needed to determine the most effective treatment of aggression and dyscontrol with beta-adrenergic agents. Side effects, however, may be limiting use in child and adolescent populations.

Side Effects. Two types of receptors are affected by this class of medications: beta-1 receptors and beta-2 receptors. Most of the medications in this class (propranolol, pindolol, nadolol, and metoprolol) are nonselective and may demonstrate a combination of both beta-1 and beta-2 receptor side effects. Beta-1 receptors are found mainly in the heart and brain; beta-2 receptors are located in vascular, gastrointestinal, and bronchial tissues. Beta-1-specific blocking agents (atenolol) decrease heart rate, cardiac output, and blood pressure; beta-2 blocking agents lead to increased airway resistance by blocking bronchodilation, may increase symptoms of nausea, vomiting, epigastric distress, abdominal cramping, diarrhea, and also may lead to arterial insufficiency (Raynaud type) and limb parathesias. In pediatric psychiatric use, bradycardia, fatigue, and hypotension are the most common side effects (Grizenko & Vida, 1988; Kuperman & Stewart, 1987; Sims & Galvin, 1990). Less commonly reported side effects are mental depression, male impotence, bronchoconstriction, Raynaud's phenomenon, diarrhea, insomnia, and hypoglycemia (due to alteration in carbohydrate metabolism and masking of symptoms associated with low serum glucose).

Dosing.   Beta blockers are not apt to be used as a first-line treatment of aggressive behavior because there are other treatments that have double-blind efficacy data supporting their use. However, the presence of organic brain damage may suggest a trial of beta blockers. Start the initial dose at 10 mg and work upward while monitoring vital signs and symptom improvement. Generally, a t.i.d. dose schedule will suffice but long-acting preparations are available for maintenance dosing on a less frequent schedule. Dose can be raised by 30 mg every 3 days.

Metoprolol was prescribed by Matthews-Ferrari and Karroum (1992) at 25 mg, 3 times a day (dose adjustments were not reported). Ratey and colleagues (1992) treated their adult population with between 40 and 120 mg of nadolol per day while monitoring vital signs.

In summary, beta blockers appear beneficial to control aggressive behaviors in child and adolescent populations; however, many of the subjects had a history of organic brain symptoms. In addition to a more homogeneous, nonorganically brain-damaged study population, double-blind, placebo-controlled studies and the use of other beta-blocking agents should take place.

Benzodiazepines

The efficacy of "contemporary" benzodiazepines has not been shown in child and adolescent populations for disorders of conduct and behavior. A review of the literature revealed the use of chlordiazepoxide (Librium) in studies of male children and adolescents targeting symptoms of impulsivity, anxiety, fear, and hostility (Gleser, Gottschaek, Fox, & Lippert, 1965; Petti, Fish, Shapiro, Cohen, & Campbell, 1982). Neither study reported clinically significant improvement in aggression or conduct. Some concerns with benzodiazepines have been the potential for abuse/dependency and for overdose, especially in ODD or CD individuals where problems of substance use and risk-taking practices are more frequently encountered, limiting their use. Side effects also add to the risk of benzodiazepine administration. A report of midazolam use for aggressivity in mentally retarded individuals suggests it may be premature to dismiss this category of drugs (Bond, Mandos, & Kurtz, 1989). However, due to studies showing little benefit on CD or aggression (Gleser et al., 1965; Petti et al., 1982) and due to the side effect/abuse potential, routine benzodiazepine use for treatment of CD or ODD is not encouraged.

Side Effects. The most commonly reported side effects associated with benzodiazepines are sedation, psychomotor slowing, dizziness, weakness, and unsteadiness. Other side effects have included disorientation, depression, nausea, change in appetite, headache, and insomnia. Petti and colleagues (1982) reported the occurrence of excessive sedation in 5 of the 9 (56%) children in their study; they also reported behavior toxicity and neurological side effects (slurred speech, dizziness, and ataxia) with chlordiazepoxide administration. Behavior toxicity has been described as paradoxical aggression (DiMascio, 1973), aggressive dyscontrol (Dietch & Jennings, 1988), and behavioral disinhibition (Gardner & Cowdry, 1985). This side effect includes a spectrum of complaints ranging from excitability to verbal and physical assaultiveness. One review (Dietch & Jennings, 1988) reported an occurrence rate of this phenomena of less than 1% in patients (mixed age groups) treated with benzodiazepines. Percentages of side effects are less clear in children and adolescents receiving benzodiazepines. Clinicians should be aware of the array of side effects with benzodiazepine administration and prescribe only when close monitoring and assessment of behavioral and cognitive changes can be expected.

Other Medications

Buspirone (Buspar) is an antianxiety agent that is neither chemically nor pharmacologically related to benzodiazepines or barbituates. Its mechanism of action is unknown, but is has been associated with an increased affinity to the serotonin (5-HT1A) and dopamine (D_2) receptors of the brain, while not affecting GABA binding. Buspirone has been reported to decrease aggression in open trials (Ratey, Sovner, Mikkelsen, & Chmielinski, 1989). An additional study by Realmuto, August, and Garfinkel (1989), reported the effects of buspirone in autistic children, utilizing an open, 4-week design, comparing buspirone with either methylphenidate or fenfluramine. The targeted symptoms were hyperactivity, aggression, stereotypy, and rumination in their population of 4 autistic children (3 males, 1 female; aged 9–10½ years). Two of the children showed at least mild improvement in hyperactivity and aggression when receiving buspirone (5 mg, 3 times per day); 2 children also showed improvement in stereotypic behaviors on buspirone. Methylphenidate and fenfluramine had not been beneficial to the patients studied. These two studies suggest some benefit in buspirone use for hyperactive and aggressive symptoms, but no studies are available that address use in populations of CD or ODD children and adolescents.

Opiate antagonists have been shown to be of benefit in populations of mentally retarded and developmentally handicapped individuals (both adult and child/adolescent) for the control of self-injurious behaviors (SIB), but have not been studied in CD/ODD child and adolescent populations (Sandman, 1990/1991).

Campbell et al. (1989) studied 10 autistic children (8 were aggressive), aged 3 to 6½ years, treated with naltrexone (dose: 0.5, 1.0, and 2.0 mg/kg/day) in an open study. Eight of the subjects (80%) were reported as responders with improvement in autistic signs (withdrawal, underproductive speech, and stereotypies (only at higher doses)) and with restlessness, disturbing others, demanding behaviors, and temper outbursts (total score improved; $p < 0.005$). Campbell and colleagues also studied 41 autistic children (aged 2–7 years) treated with naltrexone (dose: 0.5 to 1.0 mg/kg/day) under double-blind, placebo-controlled conditions and reported a reduction in hyperactivity and SIB (not superior to placebo), but reported no improvement in core autistic symptoms or discriminative learning. Both studies reported that excessive sedation and decreased appetite (with weight loss) were the most commonly experienced side effects.

Fenluramine (Pondimin), a sympathomimetic amine with antiserotonergic properties that has been approved for the treatment of exogenous obesity in the children 12 and older has been studied in the treatment of ADHD and autism. Donnelly and colleagues (Donnelly et al., 1989) reported no clinical benefits on behavioral parameters including aggression or hyperactivity in their study of children with ADHD. However, two studies have found decreases in aggression and/or conduct problems in controlled trials with mentally retarded subjects (Aman, Kern, McGhee, & Arnold, 1993; Seilkowitz et al., 1990).

Antihistamines have long been recognized to have sedating effects. In a small ($N = 21$) double-blind, placebo-controlled study of p.r.n. sedative antihistamine (diphenhydramine) in child psychiatric inpatients aged 5 to 13 (Vitiello et al., 1991), 18 of the 21 patients had a disruptive behavior disorder and the remaining 3 had major depression. Patients in acute dyscontrol blindly received either oral or intramuscular placebo or diphenhydramine (25–50 mg). No difference was attributable to drug but intramuscular injection tended to be more effective than oral ingestion, regardless of whether placebo or active drug was given. Thus, the available data indicate p.r.n. antihistamines are not efficacious for acute dyscontrol.

SUMMARY AND CONCLUSIONS

Individual disruptive behavioral disorders (DBD) are often comorbid with another DBD and/or other psychiatric disorders and pharmacological studies of CD or ODD alone are infrequent. DSM-IV provides refined criteria to delineate oppositional defiant and conduct disorders. The present iteration may help increase our understanding of pharmacological treatment in these disorders because evidence supporting differential pharmacological responsiveness by aggression subtype is growing. The frequent comorbidity of ODD and CD with anxiety, attention deficit, and depressive disorders must be factored into the clinician's diagnosis, treatment planning, and treatment implementation. Nonetheless, the impact of these individuals on their communities compels researchers to investigate new forms of behavioral, psychosocial, and pharmacotherapies.

Epidemiologic studies show that ODD and CD are frequent in clinically referred and general populations of children and adolescents; ODD and CD occur as often as ADHD. In addition, reported rates are influenced by cultural, economic, and familial issues that must be considered in treatment decisions.

Treatments have included outpatient therapy (behavioral modification, group, family, etc.), inpatient interventions, residential placement, correctional facility placement, and pharmacotherapy. Pharmacotherapy is not a first-line intervention for either ODD or CD, but it can be a beneficial adjunct in some cases.

Figure 12.1 provides a flowchart for pharmacological treatment in conduct disorder and/or aggression in pediatric patients. A thorough evaluation is used to identify any diagnostic entity that can be ameliorated with diagnosis-specific treatments. These diagnostic entities should be treated first. For example, where ADHD comorbidity exists, stimulants remain the first-line medication to try because of their demonstrated efficacy and comparative safety (Campbell et al., 1992; Stoewe et al., 1994). Specific nonpsychopharmacological treatments (e.g., individual, group, milieu, family therapies, special education intervention, behavior modification, environmental manipulation, substance abuse programs) must be utilized as part of a multimodal approach. In the absence of comorbidity, pharmacological treatment is more of an empirical trial.

Choice of the pharmacological agent depends on several factors such as level of dangerousness, immediacy of need, history of medication failure, age of the child, physical status (e.g., beta blockers should not be used in patients with asthma), the risk-benefit ratio, subjective

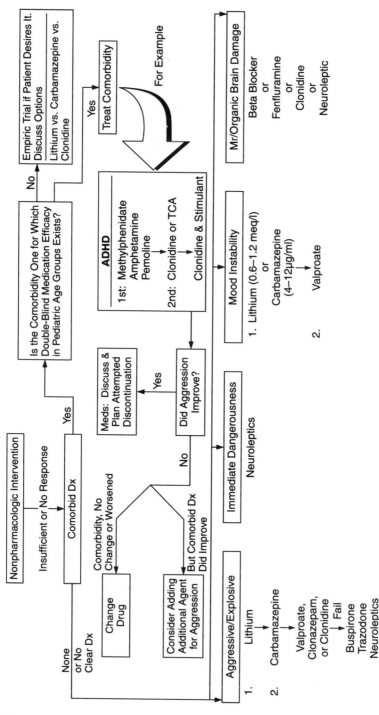

Figure 12.1. Treatment for conduct disorder and/or aggression.

distress of the child, level of patient and family cooperation and compliance and known drug-drug interactions. Finally, polypharmacy is not generally recommended, but additive or complementary actions may be beneficial (e.g., methylphenidate and clonidine). Neuroleptics remain a benchmark against which other agents with proposed benefit for aggressive symptoms are likely to be measured. This is only partially due to their historical use—the evidence supporting effectiveness without any negative trials in the literature is comparatively better than that available for other compounds. Nonetheless, side effects, potential side effects, and suboptimal responses urge research for better answers.

Prevalence data hints at an increase in clonidine usage for conduct and/or oppositional symptoms (Stoewe et al., 1994). Controlled and blinded trials assessing efficacy would help clarify whether this reflects real-world effectiveness or not.

Subtyping aggression appears promising in the further refinement of our understanding of pharmacotherapy for conduct and oppositional symptoms. Dimensions of intent and affect (instrumental vs. hostile or predatory vs. affective) along with separating physical from nonphysical aggression are likely to be useful (Atkins, Stoff, Osborne, & Brown, 1993; Vitiello, Behar, Hunt, Staff, & Ricciuti, 1990).

The bottom line remains that medications are at best adjunctive treatment for conduct and oppositional disorders. Medications are not curative and there is no data to justify their use as sole treatment for ODD or CD. Psychopharmacology should be used judiciously for treatable conditions, aggressive dangerousness to self or others, when other treatments have failed or can be enhanced by medication, or when the child or adolescent's subjective distress dictates the need. Conversely, to deny a controlled trial may also do harm; physicians are often faced with diagnoses that have only suboptimal treatment. Severity of the presenting symptoms, previous treatment modalities, and the patient's attitude toward receiving help for his or her difficulties are areas that should be explored prior to a medication trial.

REFERENCES

Abikoff, H., & Klein, R. G. (1992). Attention-deficit hyperactivity and conduct disorder: Comorbidity and implications for treatment. *Journal of Consulting and Clinical Psychology, 60*(6), 881–892.

Ahsanuddin, K. M., Ivey, J. A., Schotzhaurer, D., et al. (1983). Psychotropic medication prescription pattern in 100 hospitalized children and adolescents. *Journal of the American Academy of Child Psychiatry, 4*, 361–364.

Aman, M. G., Kern, R. A., McGhee, D. E., & Arnold, L. E. (1993). Fenfluramine and methylphenidate in children with mental retardation and ADHD: Clinical and side effects. *Journal of the American Academy of Child and Adolescent Psychiatry, 32*(4), 851–859.

Ambrosini, P. J., Bianchi, M. D., Rabinovich, H., & Elia, J. (1993). Antidepressant treatments in children and adolescents, I. Affective disorders. *Journal of the American Academy of Child and Adolescent Psychiatry, 32*(1), 1–6.

American Psychiatric Association. (1980). *Diagnostic and statistical manual of mental disorders* (3rd ed.). Washington, DC: Author.

American Psychiatric Association. (1987). *Diagnostic and statistical manual of mental disorders* (3rd ed. rev.). Washington, DC: Author.

American Psychiatric Association. (1994). *Diagnostic and statistical manual of mental disorders* (4th ed.). Washington, DC: Author.

Amery, B., Minichiello, M. D., & Brown, G. L. (1984). Aggression in hyperactive boys: Response to d-amphetamine. *Journal of the American Academy of Child and Adolescent Psychiatry, 23*(3), 291–294.

Anderson, L. T., Campbell, M., Grega, D. M., Perry, R., Small, A. M., & Green, W. H. (1984). Haloperidol in the treatment of infantile autism: Effects on learning and behavioral symptoms. *American Journal of Psychiatry, 141,* 1195–1202.

Anderson, J. C., Williams, S., McGee, R., & Silva, P. A. (1987). DSM-II disorders in preadolescent children: Prevalence in a large sample from the general population. *Archives of General Psychiatry, 44,* 69–76.

Atkins, M. S., Stoff, D. M., Osborne, M. L., & Brown, K. (1993). Distinguishing instrumental and hostile aggression: Does it make a difference? *Journal of Abnormal Child Psychology, 21*(4), 355–365.

Barratt, E. S., Kent, T. A., Bryant, S. G., & Felthous, A. R. (1991). A controlled trial of phenytoin in impulsive aggression [Letter to the editor]. *Journal of Clinical Psychopharmacology, 11*(6), 388–389.

Biederman, J., Baldessarini, R. J., Wright, V., Keenan, K., & Faraone, S. (1993). A double-blind placebo-controlled study of desipramine in the treatment of ADD: III. Lack of impact of comorbidity and family history factors on clinical response. *Journal of the American Academy of Child and Adolescent Psychiatry, 32,* 199–204.

Biederman, J., Newcorn, J., & Sprich, S. (1991). Comorbidity of attention deficit hyperactivity disorder with conduct, depressive, anxiety, and other disorders. *American Journal of Psychiatry, 148,* 564–577.

Bird, H. R., Canino, G., Rubio-Stipec, M., Gould, M. S., Ribera, J., Sesman, M., Woodbury, M., Huertas-Goldman, S., Pagan, A., Sanchez-Lacay, A., & Moscoso, M. (1988). Estimates of the prevalence of childhood maladjustment in a community survey in Puerto Rico: The use of combined measures. *Archives of General Psychiatry, 45,* 1120–1126.

Bond, W. S., Mandos, L. A., & Kurtz, M. B. (1989). Midazolam for aggressivity and violence in three mentally retarded patients. *American Journal of Psychiatry, 146,* 925–926.

Bowden, C. L., Brugger, A. M., Swann, A. C., Calabrese, J. R., Janicak, P. G., Petty, F., Dilsaver, S. C., Davis, J. M., Rush, A. J., Smail, J. G., Garza-Trevino, E. S., Risch, S. C., Goodnick, P. J., & Morris, D. D. (1994). Efficacy of divalproex vs. lithium and placebo in the treatment of mania. *Journal of the American Medical Association, 271*(12), 918–924.

Brown, G. L., Kline, W., Goyer, P., Minichello, M., Kruesi, M., & Goodwin, F. K. (1986). Relationship of childhood characteristics to cerebrospinal fluid 5-hydroxyindoleacetic acid in aggressive adults. In C. Shagass, R. C. Josiassen, W. H. Bridger, K. J. Weiss, D. Stoff, & G. M. Simpson (Eds.), *Biological psychiatry* (pp. 177–179). New York: Elsevier.

Campbell, M., Adams, P., Small, A. M., Kafantaris, V., Shell, J., Perry, R., & Overall, J. E. (1995). Lithium in hospitalized aggressive children with conduct disorder: A double-blind and placebo controlled study. *Journal of the American Academy of Child and Adolescent Psychiatry, 34*(4), 445–453.

Campbell, M., Gonzalez, N. M., Ernst, M., Silva, R. R., & Werry, J. (1993). Antipsychotics (neuroleptics). In J. Werry & M. Aman (Eds.), *Practitioners guide to psychoactive drugs for children and adolescents* (pp. 269–296). New York: Plenum.

Campbell, M., Gonzalez, N. M., & Silva, R. R. (1992). The pharmacologic treatment of conduct disorders and rage outbursts. *Psychiatric Clinics of North America, 15*(1), 69–85.

Campbell, M., Grega, D. M., Green, W. H., & Bennett, W. G. (1983). Neuroleptic-induced dyskinesias in children. *Clinical Neuropharmacology, 6,* 207–222.

Campbell, M., Overall, J. E., Small, A. M., Sokol, M. S., Spencer, E. K., Adams, P., Foltz, R. L., Monti, K. M., Perry, R., Nobler, M., & Roberts, E. (1989). Naltrexone in autistic children: An acute open dose range tolerance trial. *Journal of the American Academy of Child and Adolescent Psychiatry, 28*(2), 200–206.

Campbell, M., Silva, R., Kafantaris, V., Locascio, J., Gonzalez, N., Lee, D., & Lynch, N. (1991). Predictors of side effects associated with lithium administration in children. *Psychopharmacology Bulletin, 27,* 373–380.

Campbell, M., Small, A. M., Green, W. H., Jennings, S. J., Perry, R., Bennett, W. G., & Anderson, L. (1984). Behavioral efficacy of haloperidol and lithium carbonate: A comparison in hospitalized aggressive children with conduct disorder. *Archives of General Psychiatry, 41,* 650–656.

Carlson, G. A., & Cantwell, D. P. (1980). Unmasking masked depression in children and adolescents. *American Journal of Psychiatry, 137,* 445–449.

Carlson, G. A., & Kashani, J. H. (1988). Manic symptoms in a non-referred adolescent population. *Journal of Affective Disorder, 15,* 219–226.

Carson, C., & Mino, R. (1988). Priapism associated with trazodone therapy. *Journal of Urology, 139,* 369–370.

Coccaro, E. F., Kavoussi, R. J., & Lesser, J. C. (1992). Self- and other-directed human aggression: The role of the central serotonergic system. *International Clinical Psychopharmacology, 6*(Suppl. 6), 70–83.

Cohen, P., Velez, N., Kohn, M., Schwab-Stone, M., & Johnson, J. (1987). Child psychiatric diagnosis by computer algorithm: Theoretical issues and empirical tests. *Journal of the American Academy of Child and Adolescent Psychiatry, 26*(5), 631–638.

Comings, D. E., Comings, B. G., Tacket, T., & Li, S. (1990). The clonidine patch and behavior problems [Letter to the editor]. *Journal of the American Academy of Child and Adolescent Psychiatry, 29*(4), 667–668.

Conners, C. K., Kramer, R., Rothschild, G. H., et al. (1971). Treatment of young delinquent boys with diphenylhydantoin sodium and methylphenidate. *Archives of General Psychiatry, 24,* 156–160.

Conners, C. K., Taylor, E., Meo, G., et al. (1972). Magnesium pemoline and dextroamphetamine: A controlled study in minimal brain dysfunction. *Psychopharmacologia, 26,* 321–336.

Cytryn, L., & McKnew, D. (1972). Proposed classification of childhood depression. *American Journal of Psychiatry, 129,* 149–155.

Dale, P. G. (1980). Lithium therapy in aggressive mentally subnormal patients. *British Journal of Psychiatry, 137,* 469–474.

Delong, G. R., & Aldershof, A. L. (1987). Long-term experience with lithium treatment in childhood: Correlation with clinical diagnosis. *Journal of the American Academy of Child and Adolescent Psychiatry, 26*(3), 389–394.

Dietch, J. T., & Jennings, R. K. (1988). Aggressive dyscontrol in patients treated with benzodiazepines. *Journal of Clinical Psychiatry, 49*(5), 184–188.

DiMascio, A. (1973). The effects of benzodiazepines on aggression: Reduced or increased? *Psychopharmacologia, 30,* 95–102.

Donnelly, M., Rapoport, J. L., Potter, W. Z., Oliver, J., Keysor, C. S., & Murphy, D. L. (1989). Fenfluramine and dextroamphetamine treatment of childhood hyperactivity. *Archives of General Psychiatry, 46,* 205–212.

Esser, G., Schmidt, M. H., & Woerner, W. (1990). Epidemiology and course of psychiatric disorders in school-age children: Results of a longitudinal study. *Journal of Child Psychology and Psychiatry, 31*(2), 243–263.

Famularo, R., Kenscherff, R., & Fenton, T. (1988). Propranolol treatment for childhood post-traumatic stress disorder, acute type. *American Journal of Diseases of Children, 142,* 1244–1247.

Fergusson, D. M., & Horwood, L. J. (1989). Estimation of method and trait variance in ratings of conduct disorder. *Journal of Child Psychology and Psychiatry, 30,* 365–378.

Frazier, J. A., Gordon, C. T., McKenna, K., Lenane, M., Kaysen, D., Fahey, K., & Rapoport, J. L. (1994). An open trial of clozapine in 11 adolescents with childhood onset schizophrenia. *Journal of the American Academy of Child and Adolescent Psychiatry, 33,* 658–665.

Frick, P. J., Lahey, B. B., Applegate, B., Kerdyck, L., Ollendick, T., Hynd, G. W., Garfinkel, B., Greenhill, L., Biederman, J., Barkley, R. A., McBurnett, K., Newcorn, J., & Walderman, I. (1994). DSM-IV field trials for the disruptive behavior disorders: Symptom utility estimates. *Journal of the American Academy of Child and Adolescent Psychiatry, 33*(4), 529–539.

Gardner, D., & Cowdry, R. (1985). Alprazolam-induced dyscontrol in borderline personality disorder. *American Journal of Psychiatry, 142,* 98–100.

Garmendia, L., Sanchez, J. R., Azpiroz, A., Brain, P. F., & Simon, V. M. (1992). Clozapine: Strong antiaggressive effects with minimal motor impairment. *Physiology and Behavior, 51*(1), 51–54.

Ghaziuddin, N., & Alessi, N. (1992). An open clinical trial of trazodone in aggressive children. *Journal of Child and Adolescent Psychopharmacology, 2,* 291–298.

Gleser, G. C., Gottschalk, L. A., Fox, R., & Lippert, W. (1965). Immediate changes in affect with chlordiazepoxide—Chlordiazepoxide administration in juvenile delinquent boys. *Archives of General Psychiatry, 13,* 291–295.

Green, W. (1991). *Child and adolescent clinical psychopharmacology.* Baltimore, MD: Williams and Wilkins.

Greendyke, R. M., & Kanter, D. (1986). Therapeutic effects of pindolol on behavioral disturbances associated with organic brain disease: A double blind study. *Journal of Clinical Psychiatry, 47*(8), 423–426.

Greendyke, R. M., Kanter, D. R., Schuster, D. B., Verstreate, S., & Wooton, J. A. (1986). Propranolol treatment of assaultive patients with organic brain disease. *Journal of Nervous and Mental Disease, 174*(5), 290–294.

Greenhill, L. L., Solomon, M., Pleak, R., & Ambrosini, P. (1985). Molindone hydrochloride treatment of hospitalized children with conduct disorder. *Journal of Clinical Psychiatry, 46*(8), 20–25.

Grizenko, N., & Vida, S. (1988). Propranolol treatment of episodic dyscontrol and aggressive behavior in children [Letter to the editor]. *Canada Journal of Psychiatry, 33*, 776–778.

Groh, C. (1975). The psychotropic effect of tegretol in nonepileptic children. In W. Birkmayer (Ed.), *Epileptic seizures behavior pain* (pp. 259–263). Vienna: Hans Huber.

Hinshaw, S. P., Heller, T., & McHale, J. P. (1992). Covert antisocial behavior in boys with attention-deficit hyperactivity disorder: External validation and effects of methylphenidate. *Journal of Consulting and Clinical Psychology, 60*(2), 274–281.

Hunt, R. D., Capper, L., & O'Connell, P. (1990). Clonidine in child and adolescent psychiatry. *Journal of Child and Adolescent Psychopharmacology, 1*(1), 87–102.

Hunt, R. D., Minderaa, R. B., & Cohen, D. J. (1985). Clonidine benefits children with attention deficit disorder and hyperactivity: Report of a double-blind placebo crossover therapeutic trial. *Journal of the American Academy of Child and Adolescent Psychiatry, 24*, 617–629.

Jacobsen, L. K., Walker, M. C., Edwards, J. E., Chappel, P. B., & Woolston, J. L. (1994). Clozapine in the treatment of a young adolescent with schizophrenia. *Journal of the American Academy of Child and Adolescent Psychiatry, 33*, 645–650.

Jensen, P. S., Ryan, N. D., & Prien, R. (1992). Psychopharmacology of child and adolescent major depression: Present status and future directions. *Journal of Child and Adolescent Psychopharmacology, 2*(1), 31–45.

Kafantaris, V., Campbell, M., Padron-Gayol, M. V., Small, A. M., Locascio, J. J., & Rosenberg, C. R. (1992). Carbamazepine in hospitalized aggressive conduct disorder children: An open pilot study. *Psychopharmacology Bulletin, 28*(2), 193–199.

Kaplan, S. L., Busner, J., Kupietz, S., Wassermann, E., & Segal, B. (1990). Effects of methylphenidate on adolescents with aggressive conduct disorder and ADHD: A preliminary report. *Journal of the American Academy of Child and Adolescent Psychiatry, 29*(5), 719–723.

Kashani, J. H., Beck, N. C., Hoeper, E. W., Fallahi, C., Corcoran, C. M., McAllister, J. A., Rosenberg, T. K., & Reid, J. C. (1987). Psychiatric disorders in a community sample of adolescents. *American Journal of Psychiatry, 144*, 584–589.

Kashani, J. H., Carlson, G. A., Beck, N. C., & Hoeper, E. W. (1987). Depression, depressive symptoms, and depressed mood among a community sample of adolescents. *American Journal of Psychiatry, 144*, 931–934.

Kashani, J. H., & Sherman, D. D. (1988). Childhood depression: Epidemiology, etiological models, and treatment implications. *Integrative Psychiatry, 6*, 1–8.

Kazdin, A. E. (1987). Treatment of antisocial behavior in children: Current status and future directions. *Psychology Bulletin, 102*, 187–203.

Kemph, J. P., DeVane, C. L., Levin, G. M., Jarecke, R., & Miller, R. L. (1993). Treatment of aggressive children with clonidine: Results of an open pilot study. *Journal of the American Academy of Child and Adolescent Psychiatry, 32*(3), 577–581.

Klein, R. (1991). Thioridazine effects on the cognitive performance of children with attention-deficit hyperactivity disorder. *Journal of Child and Adolescent Psychopharmacology, 1*(4), 263–270.

Klein, R., Abikoff, H., Klass, E., Shah, M., & Seese, L. (1994, June). Controlled trial of methylphenidate, lithium, and placebo in children and adolescents with conduct disorders. In L. Hechtman, *Controlled trials of new treatment approaches in childhood disorders.* Paper presented at the annual meeting of the Society for Research in Child and Adolescent Psychopathology, London, England.

Kovacs, M., Paulauskas, S., Gatsonis, C., & Richards, C. (1988). Depressive disorders in childhood: III. A longitudinal study of comorbidity with a risk for conduct disorders. *Journal of Affective Disorders, 15,* 205–217.

Kruesi, M. J. P. (1989). Cruelty to animals and CSF 5-HIA. *Psychiatry Research, 28,* 115–116.

Kruesi, M. J. P., Hibbs, E. D., Hamburger, S. D., Rapoport, J. L., Keysor, C. S., & Elia, J. (1994). Measurement of aggression in children with disruptive behavior disorders. *Journal of Offender Rehabilitation, 21,* 159–172.

Kruesi, M. J. P., Hibbs, E. D., Zahn, T. P., Keysor, C. S., Hamburger, S. D., Bartko, J. J., & Rapoport, J. L. (1992). A two year prospective followup study of children and adolescents with disruptive behavior disorders: Prediction from CSF 5-HIAA, HVA and autonomic measures? *Archives of General Psychiatry, 49,* 429–435.

Kruesi, M. J. P., Leonard, H. L., Swedo, S. E., Nadi, S. N., Hamburger, S. D., Liu, J. C. S., & Rapoport, J. L. (1994). *Endogenous Opioids and Quay's interpretation of Jeffrey Gray.* In D. K. Routh (Ed.), Disruptive behavior disorders in childhood: Essays honoring Herbert C. Quay. New York: Plenum.

Kruesi, M. J. P., Linnoila, M., Rapoport, J. L., Brown, G. C., & Petersen, R. (1985). Carbohydrate craving, conduct disorder and low CSF 5-HIAA. *Psychiatry Research, 16,* 83–86.

Kruesi, M. J. P., Rapoport, J. L., Hamburger, S., Hibbs, E., Potter, W. Z., Lenane, M., & Brown, G. L. (1990). CSF monoamine metabolites, aggression and impulsivity in disruptive behavior disorders of children and adolescents. *Archives of General Psychiatry, 47,* 419–426.

Kruesi, M. J. P., Swedo, S. E., Leonard, H. L., Rubinow, D. R., & Rapoport, J. L. (1990). CSF somatostatin in childhood psychiatric disorders: A preliminary investigation. *Psychiatry Research, 33,* 277–284.

Kruesi, M. J. P., & Tolan, P. H. (in press). Disruptive behavior. In J. Noshpitz (Ed.), *Basic handbook of child psychiatry* (2nd ed.). New York: Basic Books.

Kuperman, S., & Stewart, M. A. (1987). Use of propranolol to decrease aggressive outbursts in younger patients. *Psychosomatics, 28*(6), 315–319.

Lahr, M. (1985). Hyponatremia during carbamazepine therapy. *Clinical Pharmacology and Therapeutics, 37,* 693–696.

Latz, J. R., & McCracken, J. T. (1992). Neuroleptic malignant syndrome in children and adolescents: Two case reports and a warning. *Journal of Child Adolescent Psychopharmacology, 2,* 123–129.

LeBlanc, M., & Frechette, M. (1989). *Male criminal activity from childhood through youth: Multilevel and developmental perspectives.* New York: Springer-Verlag.

Lefkowitz, M. M. (1969). Effects of diphenylhydantoin on disruptive behavior. Study of male delinquents. *Archives of General Psychiatry, 20*(6), 643–651.

Levin, G. M., Burton-Teston, K., & Murphy, T. (1993). Development of precocious puberty in two children treated with clonidine for aggressive behavior. *Journal of Child and Adolescent Psychopharmacology, 3*(2), 127–130.

Links, P. S., Boyer, M. H., & Offord, D. B. (1989). The prevalence of emotional disorder in children. *Journal of Nervous and Mental Disease, 177*, 85–91.

Linnoila, V. M., & Virkkunen, M. (1992). Aggression, suicidality, and serotonin. *Journal of Clinical Psychiatry, 53*(Suppl.), 36–51.

Loeber, R., Green, S. B., Lahey, B. B., Christ, M. A., & Frick, P. J. (1990). *Developmental sequences in the age of onset of disruptive child behaviors.* Unpublished manuscript, Western Psychiatric Institute and Clinic, University of Pittsburgh, Pittsburgh, PA.

Loeber, R., Green, S. B., Lahey, B. B., & Stouthamer-Loeber, M. (1989). Optimal informants on childhood disruptive behaviors. *Development and Psychopathology, 1*, 317–337.

Loeber, R., Lahey, B. B., & Thomas, C. (1991). Diagnostic conundrum of oppositional defiant disorder and conduct disorder. *Journal of Abnormal Psychology, 100*(3), 379–390.

Loeber, R., & LeBlanc, M. (1990). Toward a developmental criminology. In M. Tonry & N. Morris (Eds.), *Crime and justice: An annual review of research, 12* (pp. 375–473). Chicago: University of Chicago Press.

Loney, J., & Milich, R. (1985). Hyperactivity, aggression and inattention in clinical practice. In M. Wolraich & D. Routh (Eds.), *Advances in developmental and behavioral pediatrics* (pp. 113–147). Greenwich, CT: JAI Press.

Magnusson, D., & Bergman, L. R. (1988). Individual and variable-based approaches to longitudinal research on early risk factors. In M. Rutler (Ed.), *Studies of Psychosocial Risk* (pp. 117–124). New York: Cambridge University Press.

Markowitz, P. (1992). Effect of fluoxetine on self-injurious behavior in the developmentally disabled: A preliminary study. *Journal of Clinical Psychopharmacology, 12*(1), 27–31.

Marriage, K., Fine, S., Moretti, M., & Haley, G. (1986). Relationship between depression and conduct disorder in children and adolescents. *Journal of the American Academy of Child and Adolescent Psychiatry, 25*, 687–691.

Mattes, J. A. (1990). Comparative effectiveness of carbamazepine and propranolol for rage outbursts. *Journal of Neuropsychiatry Clinical Neurosciences, 2*(2), 159–164.

Matthews-Ferrari, K., & Karroum, N. (1992). Metoprolol for aggression [Letter to the editor]. *Journal of the American Academy of Child and Adolescent Psychiatry, 31*(5), 994.

Meyers, W. C., & Carrera, F. (1989). Carbamazepine induced mania with hypersexuality in a 9 year old boy. *American Journal of Psychiatry, 146*, 400.

Miczek, K. A., & Barry, H. (1976). Pharmacology of sex and aggression. In S. D. Glick & J. Goldfarb (Eds.), *Behavioral pharmacology* (pp. 176–257). St. Louis: Mosby.

Naruse, H., Nagahata, M., Nakane, Y., Shirahashi, K., Takesada, M., & Yamazaki, K. (1982). A multicenter double-blind trial of pimozide (Orap), haloperidol and placebo in children with behavioral disorders, using crossover design. *Acta Paedopsychiatrica, 48*(1), 73–184.

Offord, D. R., Boyle, M. H., Szatmari, P., Rae-Grant, N., Links, P. S., Cadman, D. T., Byles, J. A., Crawford, J. W., Blum, H. M., Byrne, C., Thomas, H., & Woodward, C. A. (1987). Ontario child health study II. Six-month prevalence of disorder and rates of service utilization. *Archives of General Psychiatry, 44*, 832–836.

O'Neill, M., Page, N., & Adkins, W. N. (1986). Tryptophan-trazodone treatment of aggressive behavior. *Lancet, 10*(11), 859–860.

Patterson, G. R. (1982). *Coercive family process.* Eugene, OR: Castalia.

Petti, T. A., Fish, B., Shapiro, T., Cohen, I. L., & Campbell, M. (1982). Effects of chlordiazepoxide in disturbed children: A pilot study. *Journal of Clinical Psychopharmacology, 2,* 270–273.

Pinner, E., & Rich, C. (1988). Effects of trazodone on aggressive behavior in seven patients with organic mental disorders. *American Journal of Psychiatry, 145,* 1295–1296.

Pleak, R. R., Birmaher, B., Gavrilescu, A., et al. (1988). Mania and neuropsychiatric excitation following carbamazepine. *Journal of the American Academy of Child and Adolescent Psychiatry, 27,* 500–503.

Puente, R. (1976). The use of carbamazepine in the treatment of behavioral disorders in children. In W. Birkmayer (Ed.), *Epileptic seizures-behavior-pain* (pp. 243–247). Bern: Hans Huber.

Puig-Antich, J. (1982). Major depression and conduct disorder in prepuberty. *Journal of the American Academy of Child and Adolescent Psychiatry, 21,* 118–128.

Rapoport, J. L., & Kruesi, M. J. P. (1985). Organic therapy. In H. I. Kaplan & B. J. Sadock (Eds.), *Comprehensive textbook of psychiatry IV,* Baltimore, MD: Williams and Wilkins.

Ratey, J. J., Leveroni, C., Kilmer, D., Gutheil, C., & Swartz, B. (1993). The effects of clozapine on severely aggressive psychiatric inpatients in a state hospital. *Journal of Clinical Psychiatry, 54*(6), 219–223.

Ratey, J. J., Morill, R., & Oxenkrug, G. (1983). Use of propranolol for provoked and unprovoked episodes of rage. *American Journal of Psychiatry, 140*(10), 1356–1357.

Ratey, J. J., Sorgi, P., O'Driscoll, G. A., Sands, S., Daehler, M. L., Fletcher, J. R., Kadish, W., Spruiell, G., Polakoff, S., Lindem, K. J., Bemporad, J. R., Richardson, L., & Rosenfeld, B. (1992). Nadolol to treat aggression and psychiatric symptomatology in chronic psychiatric inpatients: A double-blind, placebo-controlled study. *Journal of Clinical Psychiatry, 53*(2), 41–46.

Ratey, J. J., Sovner, R., Mikkelsen, E., & Chmielinski, H. E. (1989). Buspirone therapy for maladaptive behavior and anxiety in developmentally disabled persons. *Journal of Clinical Psychiatry, 50*(10), 382–384.

Realmuto, G. M., August, G. J., & Garfinkel, B. D. (1989). Clinical effect of buspirone in autistic children. *Journal of Clinical Psychopharmacology, 9,* 122–125.

Rey, J. M. (1993). Oppositional defiant disorder. *American Journal of Psychiatry, 150*(12), 1769–1778.

Rey, J. M., Bashir, M. R., Schwarz, M., Richards, I. N., Plapp, J. M., & Stewart, G. W. (1988). Oppositional disorder: Fact or fiction? *Journal of the American Academy of Child and Adolescent Psychiatry, 27*(2), 157–162.

Riddle, M. A., Geller, B., & Ryan, N. (1993). A case study: Another sudden death in a child treated with desipramine. *Journal of the American Academy of Child and Adolescent Psychiatry, 32*(4), 792–797.

Riddle, M. A., Nelson, J. C., Kleinman, C. S., Rasmusson, A., Leckman, J. F., King, R. A., & Cohen, D. J. (1991). A case study: Sudden death in children receiving norpramin: A review of three reported cases and commentary. *Journal of the American Academy of Child and Adolescent Psychiatry, 30*(1), 104–108.

Rifkin, A. (1992). Pharmacological treatment of conduct disorder. *New Directions for Mental Health Services, 54,* 59–63.

Rifkin, A., Karajgi, B., Boppana, V., & Pearl, E. (1989, May). *Lithium treatment in hospitalized adolescents with conduct disorder.* Paper presented at the 29th annual meeting of the New Drug Clinical Evaluation Units, National Institute of Mental Health, Key Biscayne, FL.

Rutter, M., Cox, A., Tupling, C., Berger, M., & Yule, W. (1975). Attainment and adjustment in two geographical areas: I. Prevalence of psychiatric disorder. *British Journal of Psychiatry, 126,* 493–509.

Rutter, M., Tizard, J., & Whitmore, K. (1970). *Education health and behavior.* London: Longmans.

Sandman, C. (1990/1991). The opiate hypothesis in autism and self-injury. *Journal of Child and Adolescent Psychopharmacology, 1*(3), 237–245.

Schachar, R., & Wachsmuth, R. (1990). Oppositional disorder in children: A validation study comparing conduct disorder, oppositional disorder and normal control children. *Journal of Child Psychology and Psychiatry, 31*(7), 1089–1102.

Seilkowitz, M., Sunman, J., Pendergast, A., et al. (1990). Fenfluramine in prader-willi syndrome: A double blind, placebo controlled trial. *Archives of Diseases of Childhood, 65,* 112–114.

Shay, J., Sanchez, L. E., Cueva, J. E., et al. (1993). Neuroleptic related dyskinesias and stereotypies in autistic children: Videotaped ratings. *Psychopharmacology Bulletin, 29,* 359–363.

Sheard, M. H., Marini, J. L., Bridges, C. I., & Wagner, E. (1976). The effect of lithium on impulsive aggressive behavior in man. *American Journal of Psychiatry, 133*(12), 1409–1413.

Silva, R. R., Campbell, M., Golden, R., Small, A. M., Pataki, C. S., & Rosenberg, C. R. (1992). Side effects associated with lithium and placebo administration in aggressive children. *Psychopharmacology Bulletin, 28,* 319–326.

Silverstein, F. S., Parrish, M. A., & Johnston, M. V. (1982). Adverse behavioral reactions in children treated with carbamazepine. *Journal of Pediatrics, 101,* 785–787.

Sims, J., & Galvin, M. R. (1990). Pediatric psychopharmacologic uses of propranolol: Review and case illustrations. *Journal of Child and Adolescent Psychiatric and Mental Health Nursing, 3*(1), 18–24.

Soltys, S. M., Kashani, J. H., Dandoy, A. C., Vaidya, A. F., & Reid, J. C. (1992). Comorbidity for disruptive behavior disorders in psychiatrically hospitalized children. *Child Psychiatry and Human Development, 23*(2), 87–98.

Steingard, R., Khan, A., Gonzalez, A., & Herzog, D. B. (1992). Neuroleptic malignant syndrome: Review of experience with children and adolescents. *Journal of Child and Adolescent Psychopharmacology, 2,* 183–198.

Stoewe, J., Kruesi, M. J. P., & Lelio, D. F. (1994). *Psychopharmacology of conduct disorder and aggressive states.* Manuscript submitted for publication.

Stoff, D. M., Pasatiempo, A. P., Yeung, J., Cooper, T. B., et al. (1992). Neuroendocrine responses to challenge with dl-fenfluramine and aggression in disruptive behavior disorders of children and adolescents. *Psychiatry Research, 43*(3), 263–267.

Stanger, C., McConaughy, S. H., & Achenbach, T. M. (1992). Three-year course of behavioral/emotional problems in a national sample of 4- to 16-year olds: II. Predictors of syndromes. *Journal of the American Academy of Child and Adolescent Psychiatry, 31*(5), 941–950.

Szatmari, P., Offord, D. R., & Boyle, M. H. (1989). Ontario child health study: Prevalence of attention deficit disorder with hyperactivity. *Journal of Child Psychology and Psychiatry, 30*(2), 219–230.

Towbin, K., Dykens, E. M., & Pugliese, R. G. (1994). Clozapine for early developmental delays with childhood onset schizophrenia: Protocol and 15 month outcome. *Journal of the American Academy of Child and Adolescent Psychiatry, 33,* 651–657.

Trimble, M. R. (1990). Anticonvulsants in children and adolescents. *Journal of Child and Adolescent Psychopharmacology, 1*(2), 107–124.

Velez, C. N., Johnson, J., & Cohen, P. (1989). A longitudinal analysis of selected risk factors for childhood psychopathology. *Journal of the American Academy of Child and Adolescent Psychiatry, 28*(6), 861–864.

Vetro, A., Szentistvanyi, I., Pallag, L., Vargha, M., & Szilard, J. (1985). Therapeutic experience with lithium in childhood aggressivity. *Pharmacopsychiatry, 14,* 121–127.

Vidoni, D. O., Fleming, N. J., & Mintz, S. (1983). Behavior problems of children as perceived by teachers, mental health professionals, and children. *Psychology in the Schools, 20,* 93–98.

Vincent, J., Unis, A., & Hardy, J. (1990). Pharmacotherapy of aggression. *Journal of the American Academy of Child and Adolescent Psychiatry, 29*(5), 839–840.

Vitiello, B., Behar, D., Malone, R., Delaney, M. A., Ryan, P. J., & Simpson, G. M. (1988). Pharmacokinetics of lithium carbonate in children. *Journal of Clinical Psychopharmacology, 8,* 355–359.

Vitiello, B., Behar, D., Hunt, J., Staff, D., & Ricciuti, A. (1990). Subtyping aggression in children and adolescents. *Journal of Neuropsychiatry, 2,* 189–192.

Vitiello, B., Hill, J. L., Elia, J., Cunningham, E., McLeer, S. V., & Behar, D. (1991). P. R. N. medications in child psychiatric patients: A pilot placebo-controlled study. *Journal of Clinical Psychiatry, 52,* 499–501.

Vitiello, B., Ricciuti, A. J., & Behar, D. (1987). P. R. N. medications in child state hospital patients. *Journal of Clinical Psychiatry, 48,* 351–354.

Volavka, J., Zito, J. M., Vitrai, J., & Czobar, P. (1993). Clozapine effects on hostility and aggression in schizophrenia. *Journal of Clinical Psychopharmacology, 13*(4), 287–289.

Walker, J. L., Lahey, B. B., Hynd, G. W., & Frame, C. L. (1987). Comparison of specific patterns of antisocial behavior in children with conduct disorder with or without coexisting hyperactivity. *Journal of Consulting Clinical Psychology, 55*(6), 910–913.

Warner, M. D., Peabody, C. A., Whiteford, H. A., & Hollister, L. E. (1987). Trazodone and priapism. *Journal of Clinical Psychiatry, 48*(6), 244–245.

Werry, J. (1988). Annotation: Drugs, learning and cognitive function in children—An update. *Journal of Child Psychology and Psychiatry, 29,* 129–141.

Werry, J. (1994). Pharmacotherapy of disruptive behavior disorders. *Child Adolescent Psychiatric Clinics of North America, 3*(2), 321–341.

Whitaker, A., & Rao, U. (1992). Neuroleptics in pediatric psychiatry. *Psychiatric Clinics of North America, 15,* 243–276.

Wickman, E. K. (1928). *Children's behavior and teacher's attitudes.* New York: Commonwealth Fund.

Winsberg, B. G., & Yepes, L. E. (1978). Antipsychotics. In J. S. Werry (Ed.), *Pediatric psychopharmacology* (pp. 234–274). New York: Brunner/Mazel.

Wolf, M. M., Braukmann, C. J., & Ramp, K. A. (1987). Serious delinquent behavior as a part of a significantly handicapping condition: Cures and supportive environments. *Journal of Applied Behavioral Analysis, 20,* 347–359.

World Health Organization. (1978). *International classification of diseases* (9th ed.). Geneva.

Worrall, E. P., Moody, J. P., & Naylor, G. J. (1975). Lithium in non-manic-depressives: Anti-aggressive effect and red blood cell lithium values. *British Journal of Psychiatry, 126,* 464–468.

Yassa, R., Nastase, C., Camille, Y., Henderson, M., Belzile, L., & Beland, F. (1987). Carbamazepine, diuretics, and hyponatremia: A possible interaction. *Journal of Clinical Psychiatry, 48,* 281–283.

Yepes, L. E., Balka, E. B., Winsberg, B. G., & Bialer, I. (1977). Amitriptyline and methylphenidate treatment of behaviorally disordered children. *Journal of Child Psychology and Psychiatry, 18,* 39–52.

Yudofsky, S., Williams, D., & Gorman, J. (1981). Propranolol in the treatment of rage and violent behavior in patients with chronic brain syndromes. *American Journal of Psychiatry, 138*(2), 218–220.

Zametkin, A. J., Reeves, J. C., Webster, L., & Werry, J. S. (1986). Promethazine treatment of children with attention deficit disorder with hyperactivity—Ineffective and unpleasant. *Journal of the American Academy of Child and Adolescent Psychiatry, 25*(6), 854–856.

Zoccolillo, M. (1992). Co-occurrence of conduct disorder and its adult outcomes with depressive and anxiety disorders: A review. *Journal of the American Academy of Child Adolescent Psychiatry, 31,* 547–556.

Zubieta, J., & Alessi, N. (1992). Acute and chronic administration of trazodone in the treatment of disruptive behavior disorders in children. *Journal of Clinical Psychopharmacology, 12,* 346–351.

Eating Disorders

ROBERT L. HENDREN, D.O. and
CLAUDIA K. BERENSON, M.D.

Anorexia nervosa is characterized by the refusal to maintain a minimal normal body weight. Once considered a rare disorder, it is now thought to be relatively common, occurring as a diagnosable disorder in 0.5% to 1.0% of young females in developed countries (American Psychiatric Association [APA], 1994). Its incidence is believed by many to have increased in recent years, but Lucas, Beard, O'Fallon, and Kurland (1988) report a stable prevalence in one midwestern community. Females account for more than 90% of all individuals with anorexia nervosa. Bulimia nervosa is characterized by consumption of large quantities of food in a discrete period of time accompanied by inappropriate methods of preventing weight gain. Bulimia nervosa was first recognized as a discrete diagnostic entity in 1980 by DSM-III and the number of studies of the disorder has grown rapidly since. It occurs in 1% to 3% of young females in the general population with less than 10% of all identified cases occurring in males. Both disorders occur in milder forms in 20% or more of high-risk populations (Hendren, Barber, & Sigafoos, 1986; Maloney & Ruedisueli, 1993).

In this chapter, the diagnostic categories of anorexia nervosa and bulimia nervosa are reviewed and etiologic factors are described as they relate to the treatment of these disorders. The rationale for medications proposed for usage, their adverse effects in eating-disordered patients, and the use of complementary treatment modalities are presented. Finally, studies of prognosis are reviewed.

CLINICAL CRITERIA AND DIAGNOSTIC ISSUES

The hallmarks of anorexia nervosa include a refusal to attain or maintain minimal body weight (85% of normal weight), an intense fear of gaining weight, a distorted body image, and amenorrhea in postmenarchal females (APA, 1994). Two subtypes are described—a restricting type where weight loss is the result of starvation without purging; and a binge-eating/purging type where the low-weight person also engages in binging and weight loss methods such as self-induced vomiting or the abuse of laxatives, diuretics, or enemas. Criteria to make the diagnosis of anorexia nervosa according to the *Diagnostic and Statistical Manual of Mental Disorders,* Fourth Edition (DSM-IV; APA, 1994) along with the specific type are listed in Table 13.1.

Individuals with anorexia nervosa often lack insight into the nature of their disorder and frequently deny its existence. Depressive symptoms such as dysphoria, social withdrawal, irritability, and sleep disturbance occur in some individuals with anorexia nervosa and often are secondary to starvation. Obsessive-compulsive and controlling features are

Table 13.1. *Diagnostic Criteria for Anorexia Nervosa*

A. Refusal to attain or maintain minimal body weight (85% of normal weight).

B. Intense fear of gaining weight.

C. Distorted body image.

D. Amenorrhea in postmenarchal females.

Specific type:

Restricting type: Weight loss is the result of starvation without purging.

Binge-eating/Purging type: The person with anorexia nervosa also engages in bingeing and weight loss methods such as self-induced vomiting or the abuse of laxatives, diuretics, or enemas.

Source: Adapted from (DSM-IV, 1994).

associated with the restricting subtype, whereas impulse-control problems are associated with the binge-eating purging type.

Medical conditions that may be confused with anorexia nervosa include pituitary or hypothalamic disorders, hyperthyroidism, gastrointestinal disorders such as ulcerative colitis, regional enteritis, and parasites, malignancy, tuberculosis, and chronic drug use. The psychiatric differential diagnosis should include Major Depressive Disorder, and schizophrenia. Most individuals with these latter disorders do not exhibit the relentless pursuit of thinness and the distorted body image found among individuals with anorexia nervosa.

The other principal eating disorder, bulimia nervosa, is characterized by the eating of excessive quantities of food in a discrete period of time followed by inappropriate compensatory methods to prevent weight gain, which occurs at least twice a week for 3 months. This is accompanied by a feeling of a loss of control over eating during the episode and an excessive importance given to body shape and weight in the establishment and maintenance of self-esteem. The diagnosis of bulimia nervosa rather than anorexia nervosa is made when the individual with eating disorder symptoms is able to maintain at least a minimal body weight. Two subtypes are described—a purging type; and a nonpurging type where compensation for binging does not regularly involve purging but may include such behaviors as fasting or excessive exercise. Criteria for the diagnosis of bulimia nervosa and the specific types based on DSM-IV (APA, 1994) are listed on Table 13.2.

Individuals with bulimia nervosa often have associated symptoms of depression and anxiety. Additional impulse control problems such as substance abuse also are common. Comorbid cluster B personality disorders (borderline, antisocial, histrionic, and narcissistic) are reported in up to one-half of patients with bulimia nervosa (Rossiter, Agras, Telch, &

Table 13.2. Diagnostic Criteria for Bulimia Nervosa

A. Eating of excessive quantities of food in a discrete period of time accompanied by a feeling of a loss of control over eating during the episode.

B. Inappropriate compensating methods to prevent weight gain such as self-induced vomiting or the abuse of laxatives, diuretics, or enemas which occur at least twice a week for 3 months.

C. Excessive importance given to body shape and weight in the establishment and maintenance of self-esteem.

D. Binge/purging behavior does not occur exclusively during episodes of anorexia nervosa.

Specific type:

Purging type: Compensation for bingeing involves regular purging.

Nonpurging type: Compensation for bingeing does not regularly involve purging but may include such behaviors as fasting or excessive exercise.

Schneider, 1993). However, the rate of these disorders decreases as the eating disorder improves (Ames-Frankel et al., 1992). When binge eating and purging occur with the symptoms of anorexia nervosa, the diagnosis of anorexia nervosa, binge-eating/purging type, rather than bulimia nervosa is appropriate. Medical disorders or atypical Major Depressive Disorder can usually be ruled out by the presence of compensatory weight-loss behavior as a result of the binge in bulimia nervosa. Eating-disordered behavior resembling anorexia nervosa or bulimia nervosa, but not satisfying the criteria for diagnosis, may be diagnosed as Eating Disorder Not Otherwise Specified.

The diagnosis of anorexia nervosa and/or bulimia does not exclude the possibility of additional psychiatric or physical disorders. The nature of the diagnostic symptoms and the influence of other psychiatric disorders are important considerations in the evaluation of successful treatment approaches in the heterogeneous populations of eating-disordered patients.

PHYSICAL SIGNS AND SYMPTOMS

The physical complications from anorexia nervosa and bulimia nervosa are listed in Table 13.3. When considering pharmacological treatment options, it is important to remember that cardiac complications are the most frequent cause of death in patients with eating disorders (Practice Guidelines, 1993).

Table 13.3. Physical Complications in Eating Disorders

	Anorexia Nervosa	Bulimia Nervosa
Cardiovascular	Bradycardia Hypotension Cardiomyopathy	Arrhythmias

Gastrointestinal	Mobility disturbance
	Delayed emptying
		Gastric & esophageal
		  irritation, bleeding
		Delayed emptying
		Erosion of dental enamel
		Salivary gland enlargement
		  & hyperamylasemia

Dermatologic	Dry skin Hair thinning Lanugo hair Carotinemia	Callus on hands
Musculoskeletal	Osteoporosis Reduced stature Delayed bone maturation	

Hematologic	Neutropenia anemia WBC,
	  ESR
		Electrolyte, mineral & fluid
		  imbalance

Endocrine	Hypercortisolemia T_3, T_4,
	  TSH
	Amenorrhea
	Low gonadotropins, estrogen,
	  testosterone	

Neurological	Cortical atrophy Seizure Peripheral neuritis	Seizure
Metabolic	Elevated cholesterol Elevated BUN Peripheral edema Hypothermia Electrolyte disturbance	Hypokalemia Hyponatremia Peripheral edema

Renal	Acute and chronic renal
	  failure
	Partial diabetes
	  insipidus	

ETIOLOGY

The etiology of eating disorders involves an interplay between biological, psychological, and social factors with vulnerabilities and stress in each area leading to the eventual outcome (Yates, 1989).

BIOLOGICAL INFLUENCES

First-degree biological relatives of individuals with anorexia nervosa exhibit an increased incidence of eating disorder and affective disorder (Yates, 1989). Twin studies of anorexia nervosa (Crisp, Hall, & Holland, 1985) and bulimia nervosa (Fichter & Noegel, 1990) demonstrate higher concordance rates for monozygotic twins compared with dizygotic twins. There appears to be an increased incidence of affective disorders (Hudson & Pope, 1987) and substance abuse disorders (Mitchell et al., 1988) in the first-degree biological relatives of individuals with bulimia nervosa.

Nutrient intake, endocrine response, and sympathetic nervous system activity act on the hypothalamic-pituitary axis to control energy balance and food intake (Martin, White, & Hulsey, 1991). Central Nervous System (CNS) neurotransmitters demonstrate abnormalities related to the eating behavior and emotional state in anorexia nervosa and bulimia nervosa (Fava, Copeland, Schweiger, & Herzog, 1989).

The noradrenergic and adrenergic neurotransmitter systems stimulate or inhibit feeding depending on the area of the brain. Lower than normal norepinephrine activity is found in both anorexia nervosa and bulimia nervosa. Serotonin inhibits feeding and exhibits low or normal turnover in anorexia nervosa and low turnover in bulimia nervosa. A plasma insulin and amino acid-mediated mechanism is thought to modulate brain serotonin concentration, thereby regulating carbohydrate consumption (Pijl et al., 1993). The dopaminergic system stimulates or inhibits feeding depending on the amount of neurotransmitter and is found to be normal or low in anorexia nervosa. Most of the available appetite-suppressant drugs act on noradrenergic and possibly dopaminergic receptors to produce satiety and a few increase neuronal serotonin (Bray, 1993). The opioid system stimulates feeding and is found to be lower in extremely underweight patients with anorexia nervosa (Kaye et al., 1987).

These neurochemical abnormalities are relevant to the mechanism of action of the psychotropic drugs used to treat eating disorders. They also underlie such physical consequences of eating disorders as osteoporosis, infertility, and amenorrhea (Fava et al., 1989).

These neurotransmitter systems are implicated in the pathogenesis of several of the psychiatric symptoms associated with eating disorders, most especially depression, anxiety, obsessive-compulsive behavior, and impulse control disorders. Recent studies suggest a link between anorexia nervosa, bulimia, and affective disorder. This association arises from four major sources:

1. Reports that a high percentage of eating-disordered patients demonstrate signs of depression during the illness and at follow-up.
2. Family history studies that identify a high incidence of affective disorders in relatives of eating disordered patients.
3. Similarities in some neuroendocrine abnormalities between eating-disordered patients and affective disordered patients.
4. Reports of response to antidepressant medication.

This linkage is not, however, a simple or direct one. It is likely that similar brain areas and similar neurotransmitter systems are involved, but with varying degrees of overlap (Yates, 1989).

PSYCHOLOGICAL INFLUENCES

Psychological characteristics of anorexia nervosa include a pervasive sense of ineffectiveness and difficulty identifying and expressing feelings. Dieting and weight loss are attempts to gain control of oneself and of one's feelings.

Both anorexia nervosa and bulimia nervosa tend to have their onset near developmentally stressful periods such as puberty, going away to school, or starting a first job. Preoccupation with eating and weight, and equating thinness with success, become a way to simplify complex emotions.

Patients with anorexia nervosa often have obsessive personality traits and conflicts about dependency and autonomy; whereas patients with bulimia nervosa are more likely to have problems with impulse control, sensitivity to rejection, and family conflicts (Yates, 1989). Cognitive assumptions and distortions are common in both disorders.

SOCIAL INFLUENCES

Eating disorders appear to be much more common in developed countries where there is an abundance of food and where thinness is linked to attractiveness. Participating in activities such as ballet, wrestling, or certain sports where thinness is valued also has been shown to increase the prevalence of eating disorders (Yates, 1989).

Evidence of family dysfunction often is present. In bulimia nervosa, the prevalence of substance abuse in the family has been reported at 37% and 32% prevalence for affective disorders in families with a bulimic member (Practice Guidelines, 1993). The eating disorder often exacerbates family stress, causing increased dysfunction.

Poor peer and family relationships may precede the onset of the eating disorder, but the presence of the eating disorder further impairs social relationships. Preoccupation with dieting and losing weight can lead to social withdrawal and isolation as the young woman with anorexia nervosa centers her life around eating and not eating. The young woman with bulimia nervosa may appear more socially involved than the person with anorexia nervosa, but she often needs several hours a day and a private place to binge and purge, and she often avoids situations that involve eating. She also frequently feels a great deal of shame and secrecy about her disorder.

TREATMENT

Treatment of eating disorders should be multimodal, individualized, and flexible. Treatment interventions should be directed at correcting the biological, psychological, and social deficits that have resulted in or from the eating disorder. The first step is correcting or ameliorating the malnutrition and its medical consequences. Initially, this is done through behavioral techniques including support and clear expectations. Improved nutrition often leads to an alleviation of depression, personality disturbance, and obsessional thinking (Yates, 1990).

For patients with anorexia nervosa, hospitalization on a unit skilled in working with eating disorders may be necessary in the presence of the following:

1. Weight loss greater than 25% to 30% in the past 3 months or significant metabolic disturbance.

2. Marked depression or suicidality.

3. Family demoralization or interference with treatment.

4. Failure to respond to outpatient treatment.

Hospitalization is less likely to be needed for the management of bulimia nervosa.

Outpatient management includes medical monitoring, nutritional education and behavioral interventions, family guidance and therapy, and group and individual cognitive or interpersonal psychotherapy. Day hospital programs may provide the structure necessary for the eating-disordered patient who does not require hospitalization but needs more than outpatient psychotherapy.

Treatment should be directed to the eating disorder itself and to concurrent disorders such as depression, substance abuse, or anxiety disorders. A combination of individual, family, and group treatment should be tailored to the individual needs and abilities of the patient and family.

Psychotherapy should be aimed at cognitive and attitudinal distortions, dysfunctional family systems, social skills, developmental conflict, and maladaptive behaviors (Practice Guidelines, 1993). The goal of therapy is enhanced autonomy, healthy identity formation, and increased self-esteem in addition to healthy eating behaviors.

Cognitive-behavioral therapy for bulimia nervosa has proven superior to nondirective support group (Kirkley, Schneider, Agras, & Bachman, 1985), to interpersonal psychotherapy on psychological variables (Fairburn, Kirk, O'Connor, & Cooper, 1986), and marginally superior to psychodynamic psychotherapy (Garner et al., 1993). Cognitive-behavioral therapy is most effective when administered more than once a week (Mitchell, Raymond, & Specker, 1993). Cognitive-behavioral therapy has been found superior to antidepressant treatment, and the combination does not seem to improve short-term outcome (Abbott & Mitchell, 1993; Mitchell et al., 1993) although it may help prevent relapse (Agras et al., 1992).

Family therapy has been shown to be more effective with younger patients with a recent onset of eating disorder, whereas individual psychotherapy was more effective with older patients with anorexia nervosa (Russell, Szmukler, Dare, & Eisler, 1987).

Group psychotherapy generally makes use of a combination of approaches including cognitive-behavioral, educational, supportive, and psychodynamic therapies, nutritional counseling, and social-skills training. Although group psychotherapy is more frequently recommended for individuals with bulimia nervosa, patients with anorexia nervosa have also shown benefit when they are in a group of similar aged females with a mixture of anorexia nervosa and bulimia nervosa (Hendren, Atkins, Bailey, & Barber, 1987).

Education about nutrition, appetite regulation, and the biopsychosocial etiology of eating disorders can help correct misinformation and distortions although this may be more difficult to do in younger, sicker, and anorexic patients. Discussion of the culturally mediated distortions regarding eating and weight is also valuable in identifying these distortions and modifying them.

GENERAL PRINCIPLES OF MEDICATION MANAGEMENT

When considering the use of medication in the treatment of eating disorders, it is crucial to keep in mind that there are no controlled trials of medications specifically directed to the child and adolescent population. Recommendations for psychopharmacological interventions are either extrapolated from the adult population or gathered from case reports and clinician judgment.

Developmental factors, including more rapid metabolism, differences in gastrointestinal absorption, the amount of body adipose tissue and the rate of drug biotransformation, all differentially influence drug dosage in children and adolescents as compared with adults (Paxton & Dragunow, 1993). Because of higher hepatic drug biotransformation in children and adolescents, all liver-metabolized psychotropic agents should be administered in higher mg/kg doses than would be expected in adults and may necessitate divided doses (Popper, 1993).

Also, the disordered eating and resultant metabolic abnormalities in both bulimic and anorectic patients increase the frequency of side effects and complicate prediction and evaluation of medication response.

Finally, the psychopathology of young eating-disordered patients results in frequent noncompliance with medication.

ANTIDEPRESSANTS

The possibility of an association between anorexia nervosa and bulimia with affective disorder led several investigators to treat these illnesses with antidepressant medication. In addition to evaluating general improvement in depressive symptomatology, the use of antidepressants has been targeted to weight gain, binge eating/purging and obsessionality in either anorexia or bulimia. Initially, tricyclic antidepressants (TCAs) were studied in open trials on a limited number of cases (Mills, 1976; Needleman & Waber, 1977; White & Schnaulty, 1977). Despite claims of success, meaningful conclusions could not be drawn because of insufficient cases or controls.

The tricyclic antidepressants have been studied most extensively in eating disorders with substantial benefit in bulimia and questionable benefit in anorexia. Though both imipramine and amitriptyline received favorable reports in case studies of anorectic patients, only amitriptyline has been studied in controlled double-blind studies (Biederman et al., 1985; Halmi, Eckert, LaDu, & Cohen, 1986) with only marginal improvement. Significant adverse side effects were noted from both medications in anorectic patients.

In contrast, tricyclic antidepressants have resulted in positive responses as measured by reduction in binge/vomiting behavior in a number of double-blind, placebo-controlled studies in bulimic patients (Agras, Dorian, Kirkely, Arnow, & Backman, 1987; Barlow, Blouin, Blouin, & Perez, 1988; Blouin, Blouin, Perez, Bushnik, Zuro, & Mulder, 1988; Hughes, Wells, Cunningham, & Ilstrup, 1986; Mitchell & Groat, 1984; Pope, Hudson, Jonas, & Yurgelun-Todd, 1983). Several limitations were noted however by Mitchell and colleagues (Mitchell, Raymond, & Specker, 1993) when reviewing these studies including (a) brevity (6–8 weeks) of drug trials, (b) poor compliance in extended time trials, and (c) lack of complete abstinence in bulimic behaviors, which may be a predictor of long-term outcome. In an attempt to measure long-term effects of desipramine versus placebo in bulimia nervosa, Walsh and colleagues (Walsh, Hadigan, Devlin, Gladis, & Roose, 1991) found that poor compliance precluded statistical analysis of their study group. Lower serum levels of TCA than is recommended for treating depression have resulted in improvement. Additionally, the combination of TCA with other nonmedication therapeutic strategies has resulted in increased improvement (Agras, et al., 1992; Walsh, 1991; Walsh, et al., 1991).

Among the SSRIs (fluoxetine, fenfluramine, fluvoxamine, sertraline, paroxetine), fluoxetine has been most extensively studied for treatment of eating disorders and was recently approved by the Federal Drug Administration for the treatment of bulimia nervosa. These drugs, because of their favorable side-effect profile and low potential for toxicity on overdose, are rapidly becoming favored antidepressants.

Clomipramine, a TCA and potent SSRI specifically efficacious in obsessive-compulsive disorder, has been used with some success in anorexia and warrants further study in view of the obsessionality often seen in anorectic patients (Crisp, Lacey, & Crutchfield, 1987; Rothenberg, 1986). Lacey and Crisp (1980) reported a double-blind, placebo-controlled study of clomipramine in the treatment of 16 patients with anorexia nervosa. Both placebo and treatment groups reached their goal weights. Clomipramine was significantly associated with increased hunger, appetite, and energy levels. The authors suggest that clomipramine, acting at the level of the hypothalamus, alters hunger and eating behaviors according to the body weight of the patient.

Fluoxetine has been reported to improve mood and weight gain in an open trial of refractory anorexia (Gwirtzman, Guze, Yager, & Gainsley, 1990). Also, there is some evidence that fluoxetine may prevent relapse and reduce obsessional symptoms in anorectic patients who have achieved their goal weight, though this has not been substantiated in controlled drug trials (Kaye, Weltzin, Hsu, & Bulik, 1991).

Substantial improvement in the symptoms of bulimia has been uniformly reported with fluoxetine (Goldbloom & Olmsted, 1993; Solyom, Solyom, & Ledwidge, 1990; Wood, 1993). Studies have underscored the optimal dose of fluoxetine for both behavioral and attitudinal change in bulimia may be up to 60 mg/day (Wood, 1993).

In open studies on nonvomiting bingers (Ayuso-Gutierrez, Palazon, & Ayuso-Mateos, 1994; Gardiner, Freeman, Jesinger, & Collins, 1993), fluvoxamine resulted in improvement in depression and reduction in hunger.

Though specific use of antidepressants in the eating disorders has not been conclusively supported by clinical trials, they have widespread use in clinical practice. The majority of youth with either anorexia or bulimia present with associated depressive symptoms, and it is these symptoms that are most frequently targeted in pharmacotherapeutic treatment. Many youth qualify for both dysthymia and major affective disorders in addition to the lead diagnosis of eating disorder. The use of antidepressants in the treatment of anorexia is frequently less helpful. Also, it is well-known that depression is one result of altered brain metabolism secondary to starvation. Because of this, it is recommended that the degree of depressive symptomatology be assessed after weight restoration in anorectics or low-weight bulimics before instituting a trial of antidepressants.

Additionally, side effects of the tricyclics, particularly orthostatic blood pressure changes and tachycardia, seem to be more prominent in low-weight anorectics. No specific guidelines have been established for the dose of TCAs in the eating disorders. Because of this, the premedication workup, safe dose levels, and the EKG monitoring standard for treatment of depressive disorders is recommended.

The efficacy of antidepressants for treatment of depressive symptoms and binge/purge behavior in bulimia is more robust. The prescribing physician should be alert, however, to the noncompliance and the difficulty of judging medication levels and effects due to purging in the bulimic patient. Fluoxetine, both because of its favorable side-effect profile and recent studies that endorse improvement in weight, attitude, and obsessionality, is endorsed for bulimia nervosa and may prove to be of benefit for anorexia nervosa.

Isocarboxazid, Phenylzine, Tranylcypromine

Monoamine oxidase inhibitors (MAOIs) are reported to be effective in the treatment of bulimia, especially when associated with an atypical depression with reactive mood and increased appetite, hypersomnia, fatigue, or sensitivity to personal rejection (Walsh, Stewart, Wright, Harrison, Roose, & Glassman, 1982). An initial report by Walsh describes the dramatic response of 6 patients with bulimia and atypical depression to phenelzine (up to 90 mg/day) or tranylcypromine (40 mg/day). This was expanded (Walsh, Stewart, Wright, Roose, & Glassman, 1983) to the successful treatment of 7 out of 10 bulimic patients. Binge frequency and depressive symptoms were both reduced in the responding group in this open study.

In 6 to 8 weeks of controlled trials, both phenelzine and isocarbox-azid (Kennedy et al., 1988; Walsh, Stewart, Roose, Gladis, & Glassman, 1984) have been demonstrated to reduce binge-eating frequency. However, the tyramine-restrictive diet and resultant potential of hypertensive crises with noncompliant patients limit the safe use of this drug in bulimic patients who are secretive and impulsive in binging behavior.

Atypical Antidepressants

Among atypical antidepressants, mianserin (Sabine, Yonaco, Farrington, Barratt, & Wakeling, 1983) and trazadone (Pope, Keck, McElroy, & Hudson, 1989) have been demonstrated to improve bulimic symptoms. The use of buproprion, though showing improvement, is currently contraindicated because of the association of a 6% prevalence of grand mal seizures during experimental studies (Horne et al., 1988).

Lithium

One placebo-controlled study of lithium in anorexia nervosa (Gross, Ebert, Faden, Goldberg, Nee, & Kaye, 1981) and in bulimia (Hsu, Clement, Santhouse, & Ju, 1991) demonstrated some improvement in symptoms of both disorders. More research is needed. Clinically, lithium should be used with caution in the eating-disordered patient because of the narrow range of therapeutic efficacy and the potential for toxicity.

Neuroleptics

The hypothesis that central dopaminergic activity is related to weight gain led to an interest in the use of neuroleptics in anorexia nervosa several decades ago (Kennedy & Goldblum, 1991). Low-dose chlorpromazine continues to be used for anorectic patients who demonstrate significant obsessionality or agitation. No controlled studies have been conducted to attest to its usefulness in improving weight (Hoffman & Halmi, 1993). Pimozide and sulperide (a neuroleptic not available in the United States) have been studied in placebo-controlled trials with no substantial benefit for anorectic patients in weight gain, attitude, or behavior (Walsh & Devlin, 1992).

Anticonvulsants

Because of their mood-altering properties, anticonvulsants have been considered in the treatment of eating disorders. The striking compulsivity and the disordered eating of bulimic patients and the clinical description of a state resembling an aura (Hoffman & Halmi, 1993) have been additional considerations in the use of anticonvulsants. Finally, some bulimic or compulsive eating-disordered patients exhibit nonspecific EEG abnormalities (Greenway, Dahms, & Bray, 1977). Trials of diphenyl hydantoin and phenytoin did not result in replicable improvement in those patients with abnormal EEGs (Wermuth, Davis, Hollister, & Strunkard, 1977; Greenway et al., 1977).

The symptom of affective instability demonstrated by many bulimic patients has led to several studies and case reports with carbamazepine and sodium valproate (Herridge & Pope, 1985; Kaplan, Garfinkel, Darby, & Garner, 1983). Those few patients who improved had a co-occurring diagnostic picture of bipolar illness.

No dosage levels of either carbamazepine or valproate have been established for the eating-disordered child and adolescent. Accepted guidelines are those recommended for the treatment of siezure disorders.

Other Medications

Cyproheptadine, an antiserotonin agent that stimulates appetite has been used in high doses of 32 mg/day (Halmi, Eckert, & Falk, 1983) with more rapid weight gain than placebo. Additionally, cyproheptadine decreased depressive symptomatology. The improvement was limited to those anorectics who did not gorge. Metaclopramide (Saleh & Lebwohl, 1980) and domperidone (Russell, Freidman, Feiglen, Jeejeebhoy, Swinson, & Garfinkel, 1983), medications that increase gastric emptying, are reported to be helpful adjuncts during refeeding in those patients who complain of bloating and rapid satiety. Naloxone, an opioid antagonist was used successfully to promote weight gain (Luby, Marrazzi, & Kinzie, 1987) in anorectic patients. A double-blind, placebo-controlled study of bulimic patients on naltrexone did not result in therapeutic benefit (Mitchell et al., 1989).

Anxiolytic medication administered prior to meals and used for a brief period of time to allay the anxiety associated with eating may be a useful treatment adjunct in the hospitalized anorectic patient (Wachsmuth & Garfinkel, 1993). The advantage of a specific anxiolytic in the treatment of anxiety associated with eating in anorectic patients has not been established. Aprazolam and clonazepam are the most widely studied among the benzodiazepines recommended for the treatment of specific anxiety disorders in children and adolescents (Kutcher, Reiter, Gardner, & Klein, 1992). Although a specific dose range has not been established for the child and adolescent population, Werry and Aman (1993) recommend a daily dose of 0.01–0.05 mg/kg of clonazepam and 0.014–0.08 mg/kg of aprazolam.

The risk of osteoporosis is reduced by estrogen replacement in amenorrheic patients, but pediatric gynecologists have recommended waiting for one year with active efforts to restore weight, which may result in normal menses before beginning estrogens (Practice Guidelines, 1993).

PROGNOSIS

Studies of outcome among individuals with eating disorders are difficult to evaluate and compare for the following reasons:

1. Differences and deficiencies in research design and assessment methods.

2. The heterogeneity of the disorders, especially bulimia nervosa.

3. Differences in defining such terms as recovery and relapse.

4. The duration of follow-up (Herzog, Keller, Lavori, & Sacks, 1991).

For anorexia nervosa, a review of outcome studies reveals that 44% of patients have a "good" outcome (weight restored to within 15% of normal and regular menses); 28% had an intermediate outcome; 24% had a poor outcome; and 5% were dead (Hsu, 1990). A recent controlled study of 51 cases evaluated 6.7 years after the reported onset and 4.9 years after the first diagnostic study found 47% reported themselves as recovered on several outcome measures (Gillberg, Rastam, & Gillberg, 1994). Deficit in empathy was found to be an important predictor of poor outcome.

For bulimia nervosa, a review of outcome studies reveals a recovery rate of 30% to 70% for outpatient-based studies of at least one year's duration and 13% to 40% for inpatient studies (Herzog et al., 1991). A follow-up study of women who had been hospitalized 2 to 9 years previously found 39% had fully recovered, 20% had partially recovered, and 41% were currently bulimic (Fallon, Walsh, Sadik, Saoud, & Lukasik, 1991). Typically, the illness has an up-and-down course with a relapse rate found to be 31% during a 2-year period, the majority of which occurred in the first 6 months (Olmsted, Kaplan, & Rockert, 1994). Predictors of relapse include younger age, higher vomiting frequency, and a higher score on the bulimia subscale of the Eating Attitudes Test before treatment and a higher score of the interpersonal distrust subscale of the Eating Disorder Inventory at the end of treatment (Olmsted et al., 1994). Measures of depressive symptomatology are variably related to relapse (Olmsted et al., 1994; Wozniak & Herzog, 1993).

Cluster B personality disorders in conjunction with bulimia nervosa are associated with a less positive treatment outcome (Rossiter et al., 1993). In addition, stressful life events are often but inconsistently associated with outcome for patients with either anorexia nervosa or bulimia nervosa (Sohlberg & Norring, 1992). The prognostic importance of having both anorexia nervosa and bulimia nervosa is unclear at this point, but it appears that personality disorders are more likely to be associated with both together rather than either alone (Yager, 1987).

SUMMARY AND CONCLUSIONS

The role of psychotropic medications in the treatment of anorexia nervosa is limited to the medical management of starvation side-effects and to psychological symptoms remaining after the effects of malnutrition are corrected. There is an as yet unsubstantiated possibility that fluoxetine may lead to symptom improvement.

In spite of the clear effectiveness of antidepressants in the treatment of bulimia nervosa, their role is still unclear because cognitive-behavioral therapy is reported to be at least as effective. Should antidepressants be used to help prevent relapse? Should they be used with treatment-resistant patients or when several-times-a-week treatment is not available? Further long-term studies of the treatment of eating disorders are necessary to determine the lasting benefits of psychotropic medications, their role alongside psychological treatments, and the match between psychotropic medication and symptom constellation (Walsh & Devlin, 1992).

REFERENCES

Abbott, D. W., & Mitchell, J. E. (1993). Antidepressants vs. psychotherapy in the treatment of bulimia nervosa. *Psychopharmacology Bulletin, 29,* 115–119.

Agras, W. S., Dorian, B., Kirkely, B. G., Arnow, B., & Backman, J. (1987). Imipramine in the treatment of bulimia: A double-blind controlled study. *International Journal of Eating Disorders, 6,* 29–38.

Agras, W. S., Rossiter, E. M., Arnow, B., Schneider, J. A., Telch, C. F., Raeburn, S. D., Bruce, B., Perl, M., & Koran, L. M. (1992). Pharmacologic and cognitive-behavioral treatment for bulimia nervosa: A controlled comparison. *American Journal of Psychiatry, 149,* 82–87.

American Psychiatric Association. (1994). *Diagnostic and statistical manual of mental disorders (DSM-IV)* (4th ed.). Classification: Eating disorders (pp. 539–550). Washington, DC: Author.

Ames-Frankel, J., Devlin, M. J., Walsh, B. T., Strasser, T. J., Sadik, C., Oldham, J. M., & Roose, S. P. (1992). Personality disorder diagnoses in patients with bulimia nervosa: Clinical correlates and changes with treatment. *Journal of Clinical Psychiatry, 53,* 90–96.

Ayuso-Gutierrez, J., Palazon, M., & Ayuso-Mateos, J. (1994). Open trial of fluvoxamine in the treatment of bulimia nervosa. *International Journal of Eating Disorders, 15,* 245–249.

Barlow, J., Blouin, J., Blouin, A., & Perez, E. (1988). Treatment of bulimia with desipramine: A double-blind crossover study. *Canadian Journal of Psychiatry, 33,* 129–133.

Biederman, J., Herzog, D. B., Rivinus, T. M., Harper, G. P., Ferber, R. A., Rosenbaum, J. F., Harnatz, J. S., Tondorf, R., Orsulak, P. J., & Schildkraut, J. J. (1985). Amitriptyline in the treatment of anorexia nervosa: A double-blind, placebo-controlled study. *Journal of Clinical Psychopharmacology, 5,* 10–15.

Blouin, A. G., Blouin, J. H., Perez, E. L., Bushnik, T., Zuro, C., & Mulder, E. (1988). Treatment of bulimia with fenfluramine and desipramine. *Journal of Clinical Psychopharmacology, 8,* 261–269.

Bray, G. A. (1993). Use and abuse of appetite-suppressant drugs in the treatment of obesity. *Annals of International Medicine, 119,* 707–713.

Crisp, A. H., Hall, A., & Holland, A. J. (1985). Nature and nurture in anorexia nervosa: A study of 34 pairs of twins, one pair of triplets and an adoptive family. *International Journal of Eating Disorders, 4,* 5–29.

Crisp, A. H., Lacey, J. H., & Crutchfield, M. (1987). Clomipramine and "drive" in people with anorexia nervosa. An in-patient study. *British Journal of Psychiatry, 150,* 355–358.

Fairburn, C. G., Kirk, J., O'Connor, M., & Cooper, P. J. (1986). A comparison of two psychological treatments for bulimia nervosa. *Behavior Research and Therapy, 24,* 629–643.

Fallon, B. A., Walsh, B. T., Sadik, C., Saoud, J. B., & Lukasik, V. (1991). Outcome and clinical course in inpatient bulimic women: A 2- to 9-year follow-up study. *Journal of Clinical Psychiatry, 52,* 272–278.

Fava, M., Copeland, P. M., Schweiger, U., & Herzog, D. B. (1989). Neurochemical abnormalities of anorexia nervosa and bulimia nervosa. *American Journal of Psychiatry, 146,* 963–971.

Fichter, M. M., & Noegel, R. (1990). Concordance for bulimia nervosa in twins. *International Journal of Eating Disorders, 9,* 255–264.

Gardiner, H. M., Freeman, C. P., Jesinger, D. K., & Collins, S. A. (1993). Fluvoxamine: An open pilot study in moderately obese female patients suffering from atypical eating disorders and episodes of binging. *International Journal of Obesity & Related Metabolic Disorders, 17,* 301–305.

Garner, D. M., Rockert, W., Davis, R., Garner, M. V., Olmsted, M. P., & Eagle, M. (1993). Comparison of cognitive-behavioral and supportive expressive therapy for bulimia nervosa. *American Journal of Psychiatry, 150,* 37–46.

Gillberg, C., Rastam, M., & Gillberg, C. (1994). Anorexia nervosa outcome: Six-year controlled longitudinal study of 51 cases including a population cohort. *Journal of the American Academy of Child and Adolescent Psychiatry, 33,* 729–739.

Goldbloom, D. S., & Olmsted, M. P. (1993). Pharmacotherapy of bulimia nervosa with fluoxetine: Assessment of clinically significant attitudinal change. *American Journal of Psychiatry, 150,* 770–774.

Greenway, F. L., Dahms, W. T., & Bray, G. A. (1977). Phenytoin as a treatment of obesity associated with compulsive eating. *Current Therapeutic Research, 21,* 338–342.

Gross, H. A., Ebert, M. H., Faden, V. B., Goldberg, S. C., Nee, L. E., & Kaye, W. H. (1981). A double-blind controlled trial of lithium carbonate in primary anorexia nervosa. *Journal of Clinical Psychopharmacology, 1,* 376–381.

Gwirtsman, H. E., Guze, B. H., Yager, J., & Gainsley, B. (1990). Fluoxetine treatment of anorexia nervosa: An open clinical trial. *Journal of Clinical Psychiatry, 51,* 378–382.

Halmi, K. A., Eckert, E., & Falk, J. (1983). Cyproheptadine an antidepressant and weight inducing drug for anorexia nervosa. *Psychopharmocology Bulletin, 19,* 103–105.

Halmi, K. A., Eckert, E. D., LaDu, T., & Cohen, J. (1986). Anorexia nervosa: Treatment efficacy of cyproheptadine and amitriptyline. *Archives of General Psychiatry, 43,* 177–181.

Hendren, R. L., Atkins, D., Bailey, G., & Barber, J. (1987). A model for the group treatment of eating disorders. *International Journal of Group Psychotherapy, 37,* 589–602.

Hendren, R. L., Barber, J. K., & Sigafoos, A. (1986). Eating-disordered symptoms in a nonclinical population: A study of female adolescents in two private schools. *Journal of the American Academy of Child Psychiatry, 25,* 836–840.

Herridge, P. L., & Pope, H. G. (1985). Treatment of bulimia and rapid-cycling bipolar disorder with sodium valproate: A case report. *Journal of Clinical Psychopharmacology, 5,* 229–230.

Herzog, D. B., Keller, M. B., Lavori, P. W., & Sacks, N. R. (1991). The course and outcome of bulimia nervosa. *Journal of Clinical Psychiatry, 52,* 4–8.

Hoffman, L., & Halmi, K. (1993). Psychopharmacology in the treatment of anorexia nervosa and bulimia nervosa. *Psychiatric Clinics of North America, 16,* 767–777.

Horne, R. L., Ferguson, J. M., Pope, H. G., Hudson, J. I., Lineberry, C. G., Ascher, J., & Cato, A. (1988). Treatment of bulimia with bupropion: A multicenter controlled trail. *Journal of Clinical Psychiatry, 49,* 262–266.

Hsu, L. K. G. (1990). *Eating disorders.* New York: Guilford.

Hsu, L. K. G., Clement, L., Santhouse, R., & Ju, E. S. Y. (1991). Treatment of bulimia nervosa with lithium carbonate. A controlled study. *Journal of Nervous and Mental Disease, 179,* 351–355.

Hudson, J. I., & Pope, H. G., Jr. (1987). *The psychobiology of bulimia.* Washington, DC: American Psychiatric Press.

Hughes, P. L., Wells, L. A., Cunningham, C. J., & Ilstrup, D. M. (1986). Treating bulimia with desipramine. *Archives of General Psychiatry, 43,* 182–186.

Kaplan, A. S., Garfinkel, P. E., Darby, P. L., & Garner, D. M. (1983). Carbamazepine in the treatment of bulimia. *American Journal of Psychiatry, 140,* 1225–1226.

Kaye, W. H., Berrettini, W. H., Gwirtsman, H. E., Chretien, M., Gold, P. W., George, D. T., Jimerson, D. C., & Ebert, M. H. (1987). Reduced cerebrospinal fluid levels of immunoreactive pro-opiomelanocortin related peptides (including beta-endorphin) in anorexia nervosa. *Life Science, 41,* 2147–2155.

Kaye, W. H., Weltzin, T. E., Hsu, L. K., & Bulik, C. M. (1991). An open trial of fluoxetine in patients with anorexia nervosa. *Journal of Clinical Psychiatry, 52,* 464–471.

Kennedy, S. H., & Goldblum, D. S. (1991). Current perspectives on drug therapies for anorexia nervosa and bulimia nervosa. *Drugs, 41,* 367–377.

Kennedy, S. H., Piran, N., Walsh, J. J., Prendergast, P., Mainprize, E., Whynot, C., & Garfinkel, P. E. (1988). A trial of isocarboxazid in the treatment of bulimia nervosa. *Journal of Clinical Psychopharmacology, 8,* 391–396.

Kirkley, G. B., Schneider, J. A., Agras, W. S., & Bachman, J. (1985). Comparison of two group treatments for bulimia. *Journal of Consulting and Clinical Psychology, 5,* 43–48.

Kutcher, S. P., Reiter, S., Gardner, D. M., & Klein, R. G. (1992). The pharmacotherapy of anxiety disorders in children and adolescents. *Psychiatric Clinics of North America, 15*(1), 41–67.

Lacey, J. H., & Crisp, A. H. (1980). Hunger, food intake, and weight: The impact of clomipramine on a refeeding anorexia nervosa population. *Postgraduate Medical Journal, 56*(Suppl. 1), 79–85.

Luby, E. D., Marrazzi, M. A., & Kinzie, J. (1987). Treatment of chronic anorexia nervosa with opiate blockade. *Journal of Clinical Pharmacology, 7*(1), 52–53.

Lucas, A. R., Beard, C. M., O'Fallon, W. M., & Kurland, L. T. (1988). Anorexia nervosa in Rochester, Minnesota: A 45-year study. *Mayo Clinic Proceedings, 63,* 433–442.

Maloney, M. J., & Ruedisueli, G. (1993). The epidemiology of eating problems in nonreferred children and adolescents. *Child and Adolescent Psychiatric Clinics of North America, 2,* 1–13.

Martin, R. J., White, B. D., & Hulsey, M. G. (1991). The regulation of body weight. *American Scientist, 79,* 528–541.

Mills, I. H. (1976). Amitriptyline therapy in anorexia nervosa [Letter to the editor]. *Lancet, 2,* 687.

Mitchell, J. E., Christenson, G., Jennings, J., Huber, M., Thomas, B., Pomeroy, C., & Morley, J. E. (1989). A placebo-controlled double-blind crossover study of naltrexone hydrochloride in out patients with normal weight bulimia. *Journal of Clinical Psychopharmocology, 9,* 94–97.

Mitchell, J. E., & Groat, R. (1984). A placebo-controlled, double-blind trial of amitriptyline in bulimia. *Journal of Clinical Psychopharmacology, 4,* 186–193.

Mitchell, J. E., Hatsukami, D., Pyle, R., & Eckert, E. (1988). Bulimia with and without a family history of drug abuse. *Addictive Behaviors, 13,* 245–251.

Mitchell, J. E., Raymond, N., & Specker, S. (1993). A review of the controlled trials of pharmacotherapy and psychotherapy in the treatment of bulimia nervosa. *International Journal of Eating Disorders, 14,* 229–247.

Needleman, H. L., & Waber, D. (1977). The use of amitriptyline in anorexia nervosa. In R. Vigersky (Ed.), *Anorexia Nervosa* (pp. 341–348). New York: Raven Press.

Olmsted, M. P., Kaplan, A. S., & Rockert, W. (1994). Rate and prediction of relapse in bulimia nervosa. *American Journal of Psychiatry, 151,* 738–743.

Paxton, J., & Dragunow, M. (1993). Pharmacology. In J. Werry and M. Aman (Ed.), *Practitioners Guide to Psychoactive Drugs for Children and Adolescents* (pp. 23–55). New York: Plenum Publishing Corp.

Pijl, H., Koppeschaar, H. P., Cohen, A. F., Iestra, J. A., Schoemaker, H. C., Frolich, M., Onkenhout, W., & Meinders, A. E. (1993). Evidence for brain serotonin-mediated control of carbohydrate consumption in normal weight and obese humans. *International Journal of Obesity & Related Metabolic Disorders, 17,* 513–520.

Pope, H. G., Hudson, J. I., Jonas, J. M., & Yurgelun-Todd, D. (1983). Bulimia treated with imipramine: A placebo-controlled, double-blind study. *American Journal of Psychiatry, 140,* 554–558.

Pope, H. G., Keck, P. E., McElroy, S. L., & Hudson, J. I. (1989). A placebo controlled study of trazodone in bulimia nervosa. *Journal of Clinical Psychopharmocology, 9,* 254–259.

Popper, C. (1993). Psychopharmacologic treatment of anxiety disorder in adolescents and children. *Journal of Clinical Psychiatry, 54*(Suppl.), 52–63.

Practice Guideline for Eating Disorders (1993). *American Journal of Psychiatry, 150*(2), 208–228.

Rossiter, E. M., Agras, W. S., Telch, C. F., & Schneider, J. A. (1993). Cluster B personality disorder characteristics predict outcome in the treatment of bulimia nervosa. *International Journal of Eating Disorders, 13,* 349–357.

Rothenberg, A. (1986). Eating disorders as a modern obsessive-compulsive syndrome. *Psychiatry, 49,* 45–53.

Russell, D. M., Freidman, M. L., Feiglen, D. H., Jeejeebhoy, K. N., Swinson, R. P., & Garfinkel, P. E. (1983). Delayed gastric emptying and improvement with doperimide in a patient with anorexia nervosa. *American Journal of Psychiatry, 140*(9), 1235–1236.

Russell, G. F. M., Szmukler, G. I., Dare, C., & Eisler, I. (1987). An evaluation of family therapy in anorexia nervosa and bulimia nervosa. *Archives of General Psychiatry, 44,* 1047–1056.

Sabine, E. J., Yonaco, A., Farrington, A. J., Barratt, K. H., & Wakeling, A. (1983). Bulimia nervosa placebo controlled double-blind therapeutic trial of mianserin. *British Journal of Clinical Pharmacology, 15,* 195S–202S.

Saleh, J. W., & Lebwohl, P. (1980). Metaclopramide-induced gastric emptying in patients with anorexia nervosa. *American Journal of Gastroenterology, 74,* 127–132.

Sohlberg, S., & Norring, C. (1992). A three-year prospective study of life events and course for adults with anorexia nervosa/bulimia nervosa. *Psychosomatic Medicine, 54,* 59–70.

Solyom, L., Solyom, C., & Ledwidge, B. (1990). The fluoxetine treatment of low-weight, chronic bulimia nervosa. *Journal of Clinical Psychopharmacology, 10,* 421–425.

Wachsmuth, J. R., & Garfinkel, P. E. (1993). *Child and Adolescent Clinics of North America, 2A*(1), 145–160.

Walsh, B. T. (1991). Psychopharmacologic treatment of bulimia nervosa. *Journal of Clinical Psychiatry, 52*(Suppl), 34–38.

Walsh, B. T., & Devlin, M. J. (1992). The pharmacologic treatment of eating disorders. *Psychiatric Clinics of North America, 15,* 149–160.

Walsh, B. T., Hadigan, C. M., Devlin, M. J., Gladis, M., & Roose, S. P. (1991). Long-term outcome of antidepressant treatment for bulimia nervosa. *American Journal of Psychiatry, 148,* 1206–1212.

Walsh, B. T., Stewart, J. W., Roose, S. P., Gladis, M., & Glassman, A. H. (1984). Treatment of bulimia with phenelzine: A double blind, placebo-controlled study. *Archives General Psychiatry, 41,* 1105–1109.

Walsh, B. T., Stewart, J. W., Wright, L., Harrison, W., Roose, S. P., & Glassman, A. H. (1982). Treatment of bulimia with monoamine oxidase inhibitors. *American Journal of Psychiatry, 139,* 1629–1630.

Walsh, B. T., Stewart, J. W., Wright, L., Roose, S. P., & Glassman, A. H. (1983). Treatment of bulimia with monoamine oxidase inhibitors. Presented at the annual meeting of the *American Psychiatric Association,* May, 1983, New York City.

Wermuth, B. M., Davis, K. L., Hollister, L. E., & Strunkard, A. J. (1977). Phenytoin treatment of the binge-eating syndrome. *American Journal of Psychiatry, 134,* 1249–1253.

Werry, J. S., & Aman, M. G. (1993). Anxiolytics, Sedatives and Miscellaneous Drugs. In J. Werry and M. Aman (Ed.), *Practitioners Guide to Psychoactive Drugs for Children and Adolescents* (pp. 391–415). New York: Plenum Publishing Corp.

White, J. H., & Schnaulty, N. L. (1977). Successful treatment of anorexia nervosa with imipramine. *Diseases of the Nervous System, 38,* 567–568.

Wood, A. (1993). Pharmacotherapy of bulimia nervosa—experience with fluoxetine. *International Clinical Psychopharmacology, 8,* 295–299.

Wozniak, J., & Herzog, D. B. (1993). The course and outcome of bulimia nervosa. In J. L. Woolston, (Ed.), *Child and Adolescent Psychiatric Clinics of North America, 2,* 109–128.

Yager, J. (1987). Eating disorders. *American Psychiatric Association Guidelines.*

Yates, A. (1989). Special Article: Current perspectives on the eating disorders: I. History, psychological and biological aspects. *American Academy of Child and Adolescent Psychiatry, 28,* 813–828.

Yates, A. (1990). Special Article: Current perspectives on the eating disorders: II. Treatment, outcome, and research directions. *American Academy of Child and Adolescent Psychiatry, 29,* 1–9.

Elimination and Sleep Disorders

DAVID SHAFFER, M.D. and BRUCE D. WASLICK, M.D.

ENURESIS

Clinical Criteria and Diagnostic Issues

By the criteria in the Diagnostic and Statistical Manual of Mental Disorders, Fourth Edition (DSM-IV; American Pychiatric Association [APA], 1994) enuresis is the repeated voiding of urine into the bed or clothes in the day or night by a child who would normally be expected to be able to remain continent based on developmental achievement. Usually the diagnosis is not given until the child has achieved a chronological age of 5, or a mental age of 5 in a developmentally delayed child. DSM-IV also distinguishes between subtypes, including (a) *Nocturnal Only*, where the child voids only at night; (b) *Diurnal Only*, where the child voids only during the day; and (c) *Nocturnal and Diurnal*, where the child voids both in the night and day. Repeated voiding is defined in DSM-IV as twice a week for at least 3 consecutive months, but also considers the clinical significance of less frequent voiding, such that the diagnosis may be made if the frequency criteria are not met but the child suffers significant impairment in social, academic, or other areas of functioning.

Epidemiology

The prevalence of enuresis increases in children between the ages of 4 and 7 because of the onset of secondary enuresis in some children. After age 7, the prevalence declines. Of 7-year-old boys, 7% wet at least weekly, while 15% have significant wetting but at a frequency of less than one time per week (Dejonge, 1973). Children who wet on a nightly basis are the most likely to be referred for treatment, but they make up only 15% of all enuretics (Foxman, Valdez, & Brook, 1986). Enuresis is equally common in girls and boys at age 5, but the male : female ratio by age 11 is 2:1 (Essen & Peckham, 1976; Oppel, Harper, & Rider, 1968; Rutter, Yule, & Graham, 1973). This may be because (a) boys are more likely to develop secondary enuresis and (b) boys may be less likely to have spontaneous remission of their symptoms than do girls (Essen & Peckham, 1976). The prevalence of enuresis in adults is not known, but one study found that 3% of 1,129 patients who were enuretic in childhood were still wetting after age 20 (Forsythe & Butler, 1989).

Daytime wetting occurs in up to 2% to 4% of children on a weekly basis between the ages of 5 and 7, but may occur monthly in up to 8% (Dejonge, 1973). The prevalence falls to 1% who wet monthly at age 12 (Oppel et al., 1968). Daytime wetting, unlike nighttime wetting, occurs more frequently in girls. Of children who wet in daytime, 50% also wet at night, while only a minority of nighttime wetters wet during the day as well (Blomfield & Douglas, 1956; Hallgren, 1956; Jarvelin et al., 1988).

Medication Treatments

Desmopressin Acetate (DDAVP).

EFFECTS.   DDAVP is a synthetic analog of the natural hormone vasopressin. Normally, the human body secretes vasopressin in increased amounts during the night, which in turn reduces urine production during the normal hours of sleep. There is some evidence to suggest that, in at least some patients, there is a reduced capacity to secrete vasopressin in the nighttime to decrease urine production (Norgaard, Pedersen, & Djurhuus, 1985; Rittig et al., 1989), thus leading to nighttime polyuria, volume overload of the bladder, and nocturnal enuresis (this would not explain the child's failure to awaken and voluntarily urinate). DDAVP may decrease urine production at night by providing an exogenous source of a vasopressin-like substance that has similar biological effects, preventing volume overload of the bladder and inappropriate urine discharge.

CLINICAL USAGE.   DDAVP is available in oral preparations, as well as a form that can be sprayed intranasally. Most children respond to a dose of 20–40 μg intranasally (or 200–400 μg orally), and these doses generally are well tolerated. Usually the medication is administered shortly before bedtime. In general, it can be expected that 80% of children will have a significant or complete reduction of their symptoms almost immediately (Miller, Goldberg, & Atkin, 1989), although only 25% will become completely dry during treatment (Moffatt et al., 1993). The treatment appears to be mostly symptomatic, in that the majority of children relapse shortly after discontinuation of the medication (Moffatt et al., 1993).

SIDE EFFECTS.   Side effects associated with treatment with DDAVP are relatively minor. Their may be some nasal mucosal irritation if the medication is administered intranasally, and children may experience rhinitis. Because of the medication's tendency to induce water retention, rare cases of hyponatremia have been reported, but if water intake is closely monitored, then the development of this condition is unlikely. Suppression of endogenous Anti-Diuretic Hormone (ADH) secretion does not appear to be a complication of treatment (Rew & Rundle, 1989).

Tricyclic Antidepressants.

EFFECTS.   Tricyclics have been used in the treatment of enuresis since the early 1960s (Maclean, 1960). Although demonstrated to be effective in suppressing the symptoms of nocturnal enuresis in a number of studies, the mechanism of action is unknown. The therapeutic activity may be associated with the ability of tricyclics (such as imipramine) to block reuptake in central nervous system noradrenergic neurons (Rapoport et al., 1980). Imipramine also has been demonstrated to increase functional bladder volume during waking hours and during sleep (Shaffer, Stephenson, & Thomas, 1979).

CLINICAL USAGE. Imipramine is effective in reduction of symptoms in doses between 1.0 mg/kg and 2.5 mg/kg, usually given in a single dose at bedtime (Jorgenson et al., 1980). Exceeding a combined desipramine-imipramine (DMI-IMI) serum level above 60 ng/ml usually is not necessary therapeutically (Degatta et al., 1984, 1990; Rapoport et al., 1980), and would only increase the child's risk of experiencing side effects. Similar to DDAVP, short-term suppression of wetting episodes (both in terms of severity and frequency) has been demonstrated in multiple studies. However, also similar to DDAVP, most children relapse after treatment is discontinued (Rapoport et al. 1980; Shaffer, Costello, & Hill, 1968), so that "cure" is achieved in only a small number of cases.

SIDE EFFECTS. Typical side effects associated with the use of tricyclics can be anticipated. These include anticholinergic effects, such as dry mouth, blurred vision, and constipation. Orthostatic hypotension is possible, although the doses used in the treatment of enuresis are fairly low. Accidental poisonings have been noted to occur with the treatment with tricyclics (Goel & Shanks, 1974), and these can be potentially fatal due to the cardiovascular system effects associated with high serum levels. The less favorable side-effect profile of the tricyclics, in combination with a fairly similar rate of effectiveness and relapse rates when discontinued, probably makes this treatment inferior overall to the use of DDAVP.

Other Medications

Several other types of medications also have been investigated in the treatment of enuresis. Anticholinergic medications, such as belladonna, propantheline, oxybutinin chloride, and terodiline, have significant effects on micturition but do not appear to reduce nighttime wetting (Baigrie et al., 1988; Elmer et al., 1988; Lovering, Tallett, & McKendry, 1988; Rapoport et al., 1980; Wallace & Forsythe, 1969). These medications do have more efficacy in the treatment of daytime wetting (Baigrie et al., 1988; Elmer et al., 1988). Their physiological effects include increasing functional bladder capacity and reducing neurogenic bladder contractions. Sympathomimetic stimulants also have been tried in the treatment of enuresis, and although they do reduce the depth of sleep, they are not thought to be effective in decreasing bed-wetting (McConaghy, 1969).

The prostaglandin synthesis inhibitor—diclofenac sodium—has recently been shown, in uncontrolled studies, to reduce nighttime wetting (Metin & Aykol, 1992).

Nonmedical Treatments

Nonmedication interventions, such as nighttime urinary alarm systems, in combination with behavioral conditioning techniques, are the most effective treatments available to the clinician. Short-term remission of symptoms occurs equivalent to or exceeding results obtained with currently available medication treatments (Forsythe & Butler, 1989), but often can be maintained for longer periods of time, and are less frequently associated with relapse once the treatment is discontinued. Nonmedical treatments may take longer to produce initial symptom reduction than do medication treatments (Kolvin et al., 1972). There is evidence to suggest that combining medication and behavioral treatments may produce results exceeding either treatment used alone (Sukhai & Harris, 1989).

Prognosis

Children with enuresis tend to get better with time, but the exact time when patients will spontaneously remit is not easily predictable on an individual basis. Generally, preceding remission, children will go through a phase where they will only wet intermittently or sporadically, and then follows a period where they will wet only when ill or during cold weather (Miller et al., 1960). With medication treatment, most children will show a symptomatic improvement, where their wetting will decrease or even stop. However, as previously stated, these children are generally not cured, since the majority relapse once medication is withdrawn. Night waking methods offer the best currently available treatment, with a substantial cure rate being achieved and only one-third of children relapsing over the ensuing year after treatment is terminated (Doleys, 1977).

ENCOPRESIS

Clinical Criteria and Diagnostic Issues

Encopresis is the repeated passage of stool into inappropriate places, usually of an involuntary nature, in children who would normally be expected to have achieved fecal continence based on developmental level (APA, 1994). Soiling of clothes or, less frequently, the inappropriate depositing of feces in unusual places must occur monthly for at least 3 months, and DSM-IV states that the child must have achieved the developmental age equal to a normal 4-year-old to make the diagnosis. Two subtypes are identified by DSM-IV. *Encopresis with Constipation and Overflow Incontinence* is by far the most common subtype and is identified by the presence of constipation on physical exam or by history. *Encopresis without Constipation and Overflow Incontinence* usually is accompanied by stools of normal form and consistency and may result in the feces being deposited in unusual locations besides the child's pants.

Epidemiology

Bellman (1966) assessed the prevalence of fecal soiling in a population of school children by parental questionnaire and found that 1.5% of children between the ages of 7 and 8 were soiling with a male to female ration of 3.4:1. Rutter et al. (1973) studied an older sample and found that in children aged 10 to 12, 1.3% of boys were encopretic compared with 0.3% of girls (a male-to-female ratio of 4.3:1). The prevalence of encopresis decreases in older age groups, and it is rare to find an encopretic child aged 16 or older.

Medication Treatments

Classes. Medication treatment of this disorder is not true "psychopharmacology" in that the drugs used are not thought to exert their influence in the central nervous system as much as affect the consistency of the stool or the motility of the gastrointestinal tract. Medications used in the treatment of this disorder are targeted at improving the ability of the bowel to pass stools, either by altering the form or consistency of the stool or by promoting bowel motility and functioning.

Laxatives. Laxatives are commonly used in the initial stages to bring about a disimpaction of fecal constipation in those children whose encopresis occurs as the result of stool seepage around an impacted constipation mass in the rectal vault. Mineral oil, senna derivatives and milk of magnesia may be of benefit in the initial stages of treatment. Occasionally, enema therapy is needed.

Bowel motility-enhancing medications, such as Cisapride (Murray et al., 1990), may act by a different mechanism than laxatives, as they directly increase peristalsis of the gastrointestinal tract, and may help children who fail laxative therapy.

Effects. The effect of laxative therapy is to allow for continued passage of stool in children who may have a physiological predisposition to accumulate feces in their lower gastrointestinal tract. Many investigations of bowel physiology in children with encopresis due to constipation have identified a number of abnormalities (Loening-Baucke, 1992). Failure to adequately sense rectal fullness and the need for evacuation, or abnormal ability to expel feces from the rectal vault, leads to the accumulation of feces and impaction. Once impacted, liquefied stool proximal to the impaction seeps around the impacted mass and leaks involuntarily into the child's underclothes. Laxatives help make the stool of a softer consistency and easier to pass than the child's natural stools. Stool frequency is noted so that any suspicion of accumulation of feces is identified early and appropriate intervention is achieved. Bowel motility-enhancing medications also help prevent accumulation of feces by maintaining and enhancing gastrointestinal tract peristalsis.

CLINICAL USAGE.   There is evidence that combining medical management with behavioral techniques gives significantly better results than behavioral interventions by themselves (Nolan et al., 1991). Medical treatment of constipated, soiling children usually is divided into phases (Levine, 1982). The goal of the first phase of treatment is to disimpact or "clean out" the fecal vault through a regimen of oral or suppository laxatives, alone or used in combination with enemas (Howe & Walker, 1992). Once removal of the impacted fecal mass is accomplished, increased dietary fiber, stool softeners and/or laxatives are then used to maintain soft stool consistency and allow for continued passage of feces with the prevention of recurring constipation. Maintenance treatment of the encopretic child continues until adequate stooling and prevention of constipation is achieved. After a period of prolonged recovery, the child is then permitted to attempt a slow taper of the medical regimen and is closely observed to see if the gastrointestinal tract continues to function adequately. Occasionally, children will require long-term maintenance therapy, as a subgroup of children appear to begin to reaccumulate fecal impaction when cessation of laxative therapy is attempted.

SIDE EFFECTS.   Side effects associated with laxative therapy are few. Overmedication can result in diarrhea with mineral, electrolyte and possibly vitamin loss. Few systemic complications should occur in this treatment.

Nonmedical Treatment

Medical therapy in the treatment of this disorder is usually accompanied by other interventions aimed at encouraging behavioral change in the child's stooling habits. Education of the parents and, as much as is possible, the child, about the condition is important. Baseline assessment of the child's history of toilet training and symptom development is obtained. The child and parent are educated about the need for regular toiletting to promote the passage of available stool and the prevention of constipation. Often children are encouraged to establish a regular "sitting" routine, where they go to sit on the toilet at regular times to promote rectal evacuation (Boon & Singh, 1991). Most authors promote sitting shortly after regular mealtimes to take advantage of the "gastrocolic reflex." A system of rewards for stooling and adequate toileting behavior is advocated by most, and some suggest administering mild punishments for inappropriate stooling (e.g., taking responsibility for cleaning one's clothes) or failure to adhere to the toileting routine (Doleys et al., 1977).

Prognosis

There have been reports of good outcomes with a variety of treatment approaches, but most of these have been uncontrolled clinical investigations. For example, Levine and Bakow (1976), using a combination of medical and behavioral techniques, found that after one to two years of follow-up, 70% to 80% had a substantial reduction or complete remission of symptoms. It would appear that about 20% of children respond inadequately to standard treatment (Levine, 1982), and others relapse after initial remission of symptoms. Some children show a recurrence of symptoms whenever attempts at withdrawing medical treatment is attempted, and they will generally require long-term maintenance laxative therapy.

SLEEP DISORDERS

DSM-IV (APA, 1994) distinguishes between primary sleep disorders, sleep disorders due to another mental disorder (e.g., depression), and sleep disorders due to other factors, such as a general medical condition or substance abuse. This section will focus on diagnosis and treatment of primary sleep disorders in children and adolescents.

Diagnosis

Primary sleep disorders in DSM-IV are divided into two broad categories: the *Dyssomnias,* which characteristically are abnormalities in the amount, quality, or timing of sleep, and the *Parasomnias,* which represent abnormal behavior or unusual physiological events occurring during sleep. Dyssomnias include inability to initiate or maintain sleep (insomnias), excessive sleepiness (hypersomnias), intrusion of sleep and sleep phenomena into normal wakefulness (narcolepsy), breathing-related sleep problems (sleep apnea), and alterations in the normal sleep-wake cycle (circadian rhythm sleep disorders). Parasomnias include nightmare disorder, sleep terrors, sleepwalking, and sleep paralysis. Often the parasomnias are associated with specific phases of sleep. For example, nightmares generally occur in the rapid eye movement (REM) phase of sleep, whereas night terrors and sleepwalking appear when the child moves from a deep stage of non-REM sleep to a lighter stage. Cataplexy is the intrusion of the abrupt decrease or loss of muscle tone, normally associated with REM sleep, in an awake individual, often as a component of narcolepsy. The paralysis can be precipitated by strong emotions, and may lead to REM sleep episodes.

Epidemiology

Some sleep-related problems are quite common in childhood, with as many as a third of all children showing evidence of frequent night wakings between the ages of 2 and 4 (Adair & Bauchner, 1993; Sheldon, Spire, & Levy, 1992). Others, such as narcolepsy, are quite rare, with an estimated prevalence in the general population being 0.04% to 0.09% (Guilleminault, 1987). The incidence, prevalence, and natural history of these disorders in childhood has not been studied as well as in adult populations.

Medication Treatments

Sedatives and Hypnotics.

INDICATIONS. As reviewed by several authors (Coffey, 1990; Dahl, 1992; Richman, 1985), the dearth of controlled studies of the use of these medications in childhood, as well as the fairly frequent clinical use in children, is remarkable. Perhaps as many as 25% of young children are medicated for sleep disturbance despite there being little evidence for the short-term or long-term benefit of this type of treatment. Commonly used medications include antihistamines, chloral hydrate, short-acting benzodiazepines and sedating antidepressants. Available controlled studies demonstrate minimal benefit to the use of diphenhydramine and trimeprazine.

EFFECTS. The use of medication in insomnia attempts to produce drowsiness in children who have difficulty falling asleep, and to reduce nighttime arousals in children who have trouble maintaining sleep. Any of a variety of medications that produce consistent drowsiness may be helpful in allowing children to initially achieve sleep onset.

CLINICAL USAGE.   Coffey (1990) offers guidelines for use of antihistamines and benzodiazepines in sleep induction in children and adolescents. She notes that these guidelines are based on clinical experience as opposed to controlled studies. For antihistamines, a low dose of diphenhydramine or hydroxyzine (10–25 mg) before bedtime may be a reasonable starting dose, with a gradual increase in dosage every few days until a desired clinical response is achieved. Dosages higher than 5 mg/kg are not recommended. For benzodiazepines, the use of short-acting preparations such as triazolam and flurazepam may be reasonable in older adolescents for the short-term treatment of sleep induction.

SIDE EFFECTS.   Rebound insomnia may occur as the result of discontinuation of treatment with any medication for sleep problems. During treatment with benzodiazepines, daytime sedation, cognitive decline, and behavioral disinhibition are particularly concerning side effects in children and adolescents. Anticholinergic side effects are not uncommon during treatment with antihistamines. These include dry mouth, blurred vision, constipation, and possible urinary retention at high doses. Other side effects during treatment with antihistamines include daytime sedation, reduction of seizure threshold and gastrointestinal side effects.

Stimulants.

INDICATIONS.   Psychostimulants have been a mainstay of treatment for certain disorders of excessive somnolence, as occurs in narcolepsy, idiopathic hypersomnolence, and Kleine-Levin syndrome (a disorder featuring intermittent episodes of daytime sleepiness, hypersexuality, and compulsive overeating) (Sheldon et al., 1992). In narcolepsy, Dahl (1992) recommends that stimulant treatment be a part of a comprehensive treatment plan that also includes education and counseling about the disorder; the individual patient should maintain good behavioral sleep hygiene, such as regular sleeping hours and scheduled daytime naps. Dahl also notes the paucity of scientific data to guide medication treatment of this disorder in children in terms of recommendations to parents, dosing, and efficacy.

EFFECTS.   The goal of medication treatment is to decrease daytime sleepiness and improve the child's functioning. Expected effects would include improved daytime alertness and reduced daytime sleep periods. Case reports on children who benefited from a combination of stimulant medication and behavioral management techniques are available, but controlled trials are lacking. The associated symptoms of cataplexy may improve if the excessive sleepiness improves, or may require additional medication treatment with REM sleep suppressant medications, such as a tricyclic antidepressant.

CLINICAL USAGE. Short-acting psychostimulants such as methylphenidate or amphetamines are the preferred medication treatment recommended by most authors. Different regimens are recommended, but generally there are no hard-and-fast rules for selection of appropriate dosage. Dahl (1992) recommends beginning at 5–10 mg twice a day of methylphenidate and titrating the dosage to clinical response. Longer acting stimulants such as pemoline and sustained-release methylphenidate may be used, but this may interfere with the concurrent intervention of scheduled daytime naps that some clinicians recommend.

SIDE EFFECTS. The side effects of psychostimulants are well known based on their extensive use in children with ADHD. These include appetite suppression, irritability, occasional depression, insomnia, and possible association with motor and vocal tics.

REM Sleep Suppressants.

INDICATIONS. This group of medications is effective in suppressing REM-sleep associated disorders, such as the cataplexy of narcolepsy. This class mainly consists of the tricyclic antidepressants, and of these medications, the most experience is with imipramine and protryptaline in the treatment of sleep disorders. By suppressing the time spent in REM sleep at night, and decreasing the onset of sudden attacks of motor paralysis by the intrusion of REM-sleep associated states in daytime, the clinician could reasonably expect a reduction in these problems with adequate treatment. However, there are no controlled trials of these medications in REM-associated sleep disorders in children, and therefore meaningful statements about the advisability of using these treatments in this age group are difficult to make.

EFFECTS. The effect of treatment is to prevent the onset of unwanted REM sleep-associated symptoms by the physiological actions of these medications on the sleep cycle of children and adults. The precise mechanism of action is unknown, but the therapeutic effects of tricyclics in the treatment of cataplexy are recognized (Linnoila, Simpson, & Skinner, 1980; Schmidt, Clark, & Hyman, 1977).

CLINICAL USAGE. For symptoms of cataplexy, Dahl (1992) recommends protryptaline because of its effectiveness and relative decreased frequency of inducing sedation compared with other tricyclics. Doses in the range of 15–25 mg/day may be effective. Low doses should be tried first and titrated with clinical effectiveness.

SIDE EFFECTS.   The side effects of the use of tricyclics in children are not insignificant. Included in these are sedation, anticholinergic effects, postural hypotension, and concerns about altering the electrophysiological status of the cardiac conduction system. Caution about accidental poisonings and overdose is warranted due to the dangerousness of overdose in children.

Sleep Arousal Suppressants.

INDICATIONS.   This class of medications generally is used in the treatment of symptoms associated with partial arousals from sleep such as occur in sleep terrors and sleepwalking disorder. These symptoms generally occur when the child moves from a deep stage of sleep to a lighter stage, and usually in the first part of the night's sleep when deep sleep stages predominate. By suppressing these partial arousals, the likelihood decreases of symptoms emerging. Longer-acting benzodiazepines, such as diazepam, have been found to be most effective in this form of medication treatment (Sheldon et al., 1992) but are usually reserved for particularly severe cases.

EFFECTS.   The mechanism by which these medicines are effective is not known, but physiologically, the presumed effect is to prevent the partial arousal associated with moving from a stage of deep sleep to a lighter stage during the course of a night's sleep.

CLINICAL USAGE.   Long-acting benzodiazepines are generally recommended for this form of treatment. Diazepam may be particularly effective and it is approved for use in children as young as 6 months of age. It is used in low dosages initially and titrated based on clinical results, with a maximum dose in the order of 0.8 mg/kg (Coffey, 1990).

SIDE EFFECTS.   As previously stated, the use of benzodiazepines in children is a poorly studied area. Paradoxical effects of hyperarousal have been noted, as have increased daytime sedation and diminished cognitive performance.

Nonmedication Treatments

A comprehensive description of behavioral interventions in the treatment of childhood sleep problems is beyond the scope of this chapter. However, it is necessary to state that with the paucity of data available to the clinician documenting the effectiveness of medications in the treatment of these conditions, most authors (Dahl, 1992; Mindell, 1993; Sheldon et al., 1992; Skuse, 1994) feel that behavioral interventions should be adequately tried for most children's problems prior to the use of medication treatments. Parents' behavior can subtly reinforce settling and waking problems at night. Encouraging parents to regard bedtime and bedtime routines as a time for helping children quiet themselves and separate for sleep is an important intervention. Excessive somnolence may be best treated by attention to regular sleep schedules, planned naps, and improved "sleep hygiene." For adolescents whose sleep cycle has been disrupted by meeting the demands of late-night social schedules in combination with the early morning requirements of attending school, resetting the circadian rhythm clock by gradual "sleep phase delay" (asking the child to stay awake to later hours little by little until he or she moves back into the appropriate sleeping hours) is a common strategy. Referral to a sleep specialist for comprehensive assessment, diagnosis, and treatment planning is indicated in particularly severe or complicated problems and may be beneficial prior to attempts at medication intervention by inexperienced clinicians.

Prognosis

Longitudinal follow-up studies of psychopharmacological treatment of sleep disorders in children are not currently available. Although some sleep problems of children may be situationally related or transient, others are persistent. Evidence indicates that at least a portion of children with settling or waking problems in early childhood continue to experience difficulties as they get older (Bax, 1980). One of the few available controlled medication treatment studies in settling and waking problems of childhood suggests that medication is of marginal short-term benefit and has no lasting positive effects 6 months later (Richman, 1985). The natural history of narcolepsy and other disorders of excessive somnolence in children has not been adequately described. Parasomnias persist in a minority of children and may be severe enough to interfere with functioning or safety in a small subgroup, but the long-term effects of medication intervention are not known. Caution is indicated because there is evidence that medications can exacerbate the symptoms of some sleep disorders, and also because the side effects and toxicity of medications used in sleep disorders of childhood are not inconsequential.

REFERENCES

Adair, R. H., & Bauchner, H. (1993). Sleep problems in childhood. *Current Problems in Pediatrics, 23*(4) 147–170.

American Psychiatric Association. (1994). *Diagnostic and statistical manual of mental disorders* (4th ed.). Washington, DC: Author.

Baigrie, R. J., Kelleher, J. P., Fawcett, D. P., & Pengelly, A. (1988). Oxybutinin: Is it safe? *British Journal of Urology, 62,* 319–322.

Bax, M. C. O. (1980). Sleep disturbance in the young child. *British Medical Journal, 280,* 1177–1179.

Blomfield, J. M., & Douglas, J. W. B. (1956). Bedwetting-prevalence among children aged 4–7 years. *Lancet, 1,* 850–852.

Boon, F. F. L., & Singh, N. N. (1991). A model for the treatment of encopresis. *Behavior Modification, 15,* 355–371.

Coffey, B. J. (1990). Anxiolytics for children and adolescents: Traditional and new drugs. *Journal of Child and Adolescent Psychopharmacology, 1,* 57–83.

Dahl, R. E. (1992). The pharmacologic treatment of sleep disorders. *Psychiatric Clinics of North America, 15,* 161–178.

Degatta, M. M., Galindo, P., Rey, F., Gutierrez, J. R., Tamayo, M., Garcia, M. J., & Dominguez-Gil, A. (1990). The influence of clinical and pharmacological factors on enuresis treatment with imipramine. *British Journal of Clinical Pharmacology, 30,* 693–698.

Degatta, M. M., Garcia, M. J., Acosta, A., Rey, F., Gutierrez, J. R., & Dominguez-Gil, A. (1984). Monitoring of serum levels of imipramine and desipramine and individualization of dose in enuretic children. *Therapeutic Drug Monitoring, 6,* 438–443.

Dejonge, G. A. (1973). A survey of the literature. In I. Kolvin, R. MacKeith, & S. R. Meadow (Eds.), *Bladder control and enuresis.* London: Heinemann/Spastics International Medical Publications.

Doleys, D. M. (1977). Behavioral treatments for nocturnal enuresis in children: A review of the recent literature. *Psychological Bulletin, 84,* 30–54.

Doleys, D. M., McWhorter, M. S., Williams, S. C., & Gentry, R. (1977). Encopresis: Its treatment and relation to nocturnal enuresis. *Behavior Therapy, 8,* 77–82.

Elmer, M., Norgaard, J. P., Djurhuus, J. C., & Adolfsson, T. (1988). Terodiline in the treatment of diurnal enuresis in children. *Scandinavian Journal of Primary Health Care, 6,* 119–124.

Essen, J., & Peckham, C. (1976). Nocturnal enuresis in childhood. *Developmental Medicine and Child Neurology, 18,* 577–589.

Forsythe, W. I., & Butler, R. J. (1989). Fifty years of enuretic alarms. *Archives of Disease in Childhood, 64,* 879–885.

Foxman, B., Valdez, R. B., & Brook, R. H. (1986). Childhood enuresis: Prevelance, perceived impact, and prescribed treatments. *Pediatrics, 77,* 482–487.

Goel, K. M., & Shanks, R. A. (1974). Amytryptyline and imipramine poisoning in children. *British Medical Journal, 1,* 261–263.

Guilleminault, C. (1987). Narcolepsy and its differential diagnosis. In C. Guilleminault (Eds.), *Sleep and its disorders in children* (pp. 181–193). New York: Raven.

Hallgren, B. (1956). Enuresis: A study with reference to certain physical, mental and social factors possibly associated with enuresis. *Acta Psychiatrica et Neurologica Scandinavica, 31,* 405–436.

Howe, A. C., & Walker, C. E. (1992). Behavioral management of toilet training, enuresis, and encopresis. *Pediatric Clinics of North America, 39,* 413–432.

Jarvelin, M. R., Vikevainen-Tervonen, L., Moilanen, I., & Huttunen, N. P. (1988). Enuresis in seven year old children. *Acta Paediatrica Scandinavia, 77,* 148–153.

Jorgenson, O. S., Lober, M., Christiansen, J., & Gram, L. F. (1980). Plasma concentration and clinical effect in imipramine treatment of childhood enuresis. *Clinical Pharmacokinetics, 5,* 386–393.

Kolvin, I., Taunch, J., Currah, J., Garside, M. F., Nolan, J., & Shaw, W. B. (1972). Enuresis: A descriptive analysis and a controlled trial. *Developmental Medicine and Child Neurology, 14,* 715–726.

Levine, M. D. (1982). Encopresis: Its potentiation, evaluation and alleviation. *Pediatric Clinics of North America, 29,* 315–330.

Linnoila, M., Simpson, D., & Skinner, T. (1980). Characteristics of therapeutic response to imipramine in cataplectic men. *American Journal of Psychiatry, 137*(2), 237–238.

Loening-Baucke, V. A. (1992). Elimination disorders. In D. E. Greydanus & M. Wolraich (Eds.), *Behavioral pediatrics* (pp. 280–297). New York: Springer-Verlag.

Lovering, J. S., Tallett, S. E., & McKendry, J. B. J. (1988) Osybutynin: Efficacy in the treatment of primary enuresis. *Pediatrics, 82,* 104–106.

Maclean, R. E. G. (1960). Imipramine hydrochloride and enuresis. *American Journal of Psychiatry, 117,* 551.

McConaghy, N. (1969). A controlled trial of imipramine, amphetamine, pad and bell, conditioning and random awakening in the treatment of enuresis. *Medical Journal of Australia, 2,* 237–239.

Metin, A., & Aykol, N. (1992). Diclofenac sodium suppository in the treatment of primary nocturnal enuresis. *International Urology and Nephrology, 24,* 113–117.

Miller, F. J. W., Court, S. D. M., Walton, W. S., & Knox, E. G. (1960). *Growing up in Newcastle-Upon-Tyne.* London: Oxford University Press.

Miller, K., Goldberg, S., & Atkin, B. (1989). Nocturnal enuresis: Experience with long-term use of intranasally administered desmopressin. *Journal of Pediatrics, 14,* 723–726.

Mindell, J. A. (1993). Sleep disorders in children. *Health Psychology, 12,* 151–162.

Moffatt, M. E. K., Harlos, S., Kirshen, A. J., & Burd, L. (1993). Desmopressin acetate and octurnal enuresis: How much do we know? *Pediatrics, 92,* 420–425.

Murray, R. D., Li, B. U. K., McClung, H. J., Heitlinger, L., & Rehm, D. (1990). Cisapride for intractable constipation in children: Observations from an open trial. *Journal of Pediatric Gasteroenterology and Nutrition, 11,* 503–508.

Nolan, T., Debelle, G., Oberflaid, F., & Coffey, C. (1991). Randomised trial of laxatives in treatment of childhood encopresis. *Lancet, 338,* 523–527.

Norgaard, J. P., Pedersen, E. B., & Djurhuus, C. (1985). Diurnal anti-diuretic hormone levels in enuretics. *Journal of Urology, 134,* 1029–1031.

Oppel, W. C., Harper, P. A., & Rider, R. V. (1968). Social, psychological and neurological factors associated with enuresis. *Pediatrics, 42,* 627–641.

Rapoport, J. L., Mikkelsen, E. J., Zavardil, A., Nee, L., Gruenau, C., Mendelson, W., & Gillin, C. (1980). Childhood enuresis II: Psychopathology, tricyclic concentration in plasma and antienuretic effect. *Archives of General Psychiatry, 37,* 1146–1152.

Rew, D. A., & Rundle, J. S. H. (1989). Assessment of the safety of regular DDAVP therapy in primary nocturnal enuresis. *British Journal of Urology, 63,* 352–353.

Richman, N. (1985). A double-blind drug trial of treatment in young children with waking problems. *Journal of Child Psychology and Psychiatry, 26,* 591–598.

Rittig, S., Knudsen, U., Norgaard, J., et al. (1989). Abnormal diurnal rhythm of plasma vasopressin and urinary output in patients with enuresis. *American Journal of Physiology, 256,* 664.

Rutter, M. L., Yule, W., & Graham, P. J. (1973). Enuresis and behavioural deviance: Some epidemiological considerations. In I. Kolvin, R. MacKeith, & S. R. Meadow (Eds.), *Bladder control and enuresis.* London: Heinemann/Spastics International Medical Publications.

Schmidt, H., Clark, R., & Hyman, P. (1977). Protriptyline: An effective agent in the treatment of the narcolepsy-cataplexy syndrome and hypersomnia. *American Journal of Psychiatry, 134*(2), 183–185.

Shaffer, D., Costello, A. J., & Hill, J. D. (1968). Control of enuresis with imipramine. *Archives of Diseases of Childhood, 43,* 666–671.

Shaffer, D., Stephenson, J. D., & Thomas, D. V. (1979). Some effects of imipramine on micturition and their relevance to their antienuretic activity. *Neuropharmacology, 18,* 33–37.

Sheldon, S. H., Spire, J. P., & Levy, H. B. (1992). *Pediatric sleep medicine.* Philadelphia: W. B. Saunders.

Skuse, D. (1994). Feeding and sleep disorders. In M. R. Rutter, E. Taylor, & L. Hersov (Eds.), *Child and adolescent psychiatry: Modern approaches* (pp. 467–489). Oxford: Blackwell Scientific Publications.

Sukhai, R. N., Mol, J., & Harris, A. S. (1989). Combined therapy of enuresis alarm and desmopressin in the treatment of nocturnal enuresis. *European Journal of Pediatrics, 148,* 465–467.

Wallace, I. R., & Forsythe, W. I. (1969). The treatment of enuresis: A controlled clinical trial of propantheline, propantheline and phenobarbitone, and placebo. *British Journal of Clinical Practice, 23,* 207–210.

Author Index

Subject Index

511